The Many Sides of History

Readings in the Western Heritage

VOLUME II
The Seventeenth Century to the Present

EDITED BY
Steven Ozment
HARVARD UNIVERSITY

Frank M. Turner
YALE UNIVERSITY

MACMILLAN PUBLISHING COMPANY
NEW YORK

Copyright © 1987, Macmillan Publishing Company,
a division of Macmillan, Inc.

PRINTED IN THE UNITED STATES OF AMERICA

All rights reserved. No part of this book may be reproduced or transmitted in any form or by any means, electronic or mechanical, including photocopying, recording, or any information storage and retrieval system, without permission in writing from the Publisher.

Macmillan Publishing Company
866 Third Avenue, New York, New York 10022

LIBRARY OF CONGRESS CATALOGING-IN-PUBLICATION DATA

The many sides of history.

Contents: v. 1. The ancient world to early modern Europe—v. 2. The seventeenth century to the present.
1. Europe—History. I. Ozment, Steven E. II. Turner, Frank M. (Frank Miller), 1944-
D20.M316   1987   940   86-16379
ISBN 0-02-390300-7 (v. 1)
ISBN 0-02-390310-4 (v. 2)

Printing: 1 2 3 4 5 6 7   Year: 7 8 9 0 1 2 3

Preface

In recent years many new dimensions have been added to our understanding of the European past. Historians have begun to probe one novel area of research after another. Groups of people previously virtually neglected have now found a place in the historical record. Areas of human activity once ignored or spurned by historians now find themselves the subject of intense investigation. At the same time many of the more traditional fields of historical writing have continued to attract distinguished researchers and to arouse ongoing curiosity.

This collection of essays in recent European historical writing presents a selection of excellent work across the spectrum of contemporary research. No existing anthology has attempted to represent the pluralism and variety of such writing. It is that pluralism—the many sides of contemporary historical research—that this reader seeks to make available to teachers and students. However it may be used—whether as supplementary reading in introductory European survey courses or in courses on historical method—its editors hope that both students and instructors will come to admire the sheer variety of contemporary historical writing and to realize that the complexity of the past necessarily invites investigation along numerous different paths of interest and methodology.

The editors would like to thank Eric Carlson and Eva Milofsky for their assistance in preparing the selections.

S. O.
F. M. T.

Contents

INTRODUCTION   *1*

PART ONE
The Seventeenth Century   *11*

ANTHONY FLETCHER
    The Outbreak of the English Civil War   *13*
RICHARD BONNEY
    The Personal Rule of Louis XIV   *26*
MARGARET JACOB
    The Social Meaning of Newtonianism   *40*

PART TWO
The Eighteenth Century   *55*

ISABEL DE MADARIAGA
    The Revolt of the Cossacks and the Peasant War in Russia   *57*
JOHN MCMANNERS
    Death as an Instrument: The Public Execution in France   *77*
JENNIFER TANN
    Marketing Methods in the International Steam Engine Market: The Case of Boulton and Watt   *94*
ROBERT DARNTON
    The Encyclopédie Wars of Prerevolutionary France   *112*
MICHAEL L. KENNEDY
    The Civil Constitution of the Clergy in the French Revolution   *133*
KLAUS EPSTEIN
    The Genesis of German Conservatism   *150*

PART THREE
The Nineteenth Century   *167*

FRANKLIN L. BAUMER
    The Romantic World   *169*
JOAN W. SCOTT AND LOUISE A. TILLY
    Women's Work and the Family in Nineteenth-Century Europe   *184*

ANTHONY S. WOHL
    Fever! Fever!   204
EUGEN WEBER
    Civilizing in Earnest: Schools and Schooling   226
GORDON CRAIG
    The Constitution of the German Empire   241

PART FOUR
Imperialism, War, and Revolution   257

DANIEL R. HEADRICK
    The Tools of Imperialism: Technology and the Expansion of
    European Colonial Empires in the Nineteenth Century   259
MICHAEL HOWARD
    Men Against Fire: Expectations of War in 1914   280
TSUYOSHI HASEGAWA
    Petrograd Worker Unrest in World War I   295
ROBERT WOHL
    Lost Legions of English Youth   312

PART FIVE
Authoritarianism and Diplomatic Confrontation
in the Mid-Twentieth Century   331

SALLY MARKS
    The Myths of Reparations   333
RICHARD F. HAMILTON
    The Recruitment and Training of Early Nazi Militants   347
ROBERT C. TUCKER
    The Rise of Stalin's Personality Cult   367
RONALD M. SMELZER
    Nazi Dynamics, German Foreign Policy and Appeasement   388
WILLIAMSON MURRAY
    Munich, 1938: The Military Confrontation   403
MICHAEL MANDELBAUM
    NATO: The Nuclear Alliance   419

Introduction

To enter the present world of historical scholarship is to encounter a remarkably complex intellectual landscape, much of which has been opened to exploration for little more than three decades. Today, as never before, only the curiosity of the historian and the scope of human activities stand as limits to historical research and writing. The areas of human experience now being investigated by historians for the first time have always been there, just as the phenomena of physical nature being studied by scientists for the first time have been. However, in both cases new contemporary concerns, new technology, and unleashed imaginations have led to discoveries and interpretations that have required much reconsideration of past understanding. And in history, as in science, the new knowledge and methods have generated still further novel research.

One may compare the recent changes in historical scholarship to the planning and construction of a highway system. Newly perceived economic needs, the desire for better opportunity, and sometimes new machinery make the building of the highway possible. Once the highway has been constructed, the requirements of transport, the possibility of establishing new businesses or new communities, and the curiosity of travellers assure the road will find use. Travellers with their various goals and the entrepreneurs who provide services for their travel interact with each other and with the people in the territory into which the highway has penetrated as they could not have done prior to its construction. As workers and tourists follow the new highway, they confront landscapes and sometimes cultures they have not previously encountered. They may also establish new communities. Eventually they find that they must integrate those new experiences, communities, and ideas with the world they knew before the highway existed. In turn, those persons who have not travelled the road must integrate their experiences with the news and knowledge provided by returning travellers. Those who remain in the original community will also find that their social and economic lives are now almost inevitably interrelated with those of the communities recently built along the highway and those that lie at its other end. With the opening of new highways of research, the community of professional historians now constitutes a large gathering of scholars attempting to integrate old and new knowledge.

Until approximately the 1950s the primary concerns of European historians were issues surrounding state-building, diplomatic relations, religious institutions, and the role of great *men* in the past. Certainly there were some exceptions to this general pattern of historical writing. Some quite notable books and articles did appear on economic life, workers, children, and women, but their number was relatively small. Diplomacy, public policy, ecclesiastical disputes, and political controversy commanded most of the attention. Geographically, the setting for most of the activity described and analyzed by historians was the capital city of the particular country under consideration, and historians narrated the projects of the political and intellectual elites within that capital. Furthermore, historians wrote within a very European-centered context or world-view. Non-European peoples received at best marginal attention. Historians generally regarded other cultures as less interesting, less important, and less worthy than European culture.

This historical outlook and these specific concerns were themselves the product of a particular era of European history. Betweeen 1850 and 1945 European nations exercised more dominance throughout the world than during any previous age. The major European powers exerted vast military, political, and economic influence around the globe. What allowed this European predominance had been the development of industrial economies and strong central political states possessing powerful armies and navies. Indeed, it must be recognized that the nation-state supported by an industrial economy and strong armed forces has been for better or worse the most powerful organization ever created by human beings. The power and actions of these nation-states long fascinated historians and necessarily commanded their attention. The beginning of the decline of the dominance of political history can actually be traced to the disillusionment of historians, especially those in France during the 1920s, with the character of their respective nation-states.

But the relationship between historical scholarship and the emergence of nation-states had another fundamental dimension. In the nineteenth century the writing of history and the forging of historical consciousness went hand in hand. History served to undergird faith in national civic life. A major factor in nineteenth- and twentieth-century state-building was the institutionalization of education programs that emphasized the historical development of nations and that stressed the role of great national figures (usually male—Joan of Arc and Queen Elizabeth I of England being the major exceptions) with whom people living in a variety of disparate local settings could identify. Throughout the nineteenth century, numerous historians such as Macaulay in England, Guizot in France, and Treitschke in Germany wrote multivolume histories intended to foster pride in a national past and faith in the particular kinds of national political traditions and institutions that these historians believed benefited their respective nations. This tradition of historical writing continued into the twentieth century, as European nationalism and nation-state rivalries flourished both before and after the First World War.

The events of the nineteenth and first half of the twentieth centuries also directed the attention of historians to politics and the nation-state. From the time of the French Revolution through the Second World War, considerable political turmoil occurred in all European nations. The French Revolution itself was followed by Napolean, the revolutions of 1830, the revolutions of 1848, the unifications of Italy and Germany, unrest among the subject nationalities throughout the Austro-Hungarian Empire, the emergence of large socialist parties, revolution in Russia, the establishment of new nation-states in eastern Europe, the Fascist movement in Italy, and the Nazi movement in Germany. Those political disturbances and revolutions were among the most interesting and significant events of the day. They touched the lives of virtually tens of millions of Europeans. It was no wonder that historians wrote about them and about their antecedent causes. Even relatively stable nations, such as Great Britain, commanded the attention of political historians who sought to account for their political stability.

The wars of the late nineteenth and first half of the twentieth centuries similarly brought political and diplomatic issues to the fore of historical research. Between the Crimean War that began in 1854 and World War II, the states of Europe engaged in numerous conflicts to sort out their relative power relationships on the European continent. They also engaged in various colonial conflicts throughout the world as they transferred their rivalries overseas and established their colonial empires. War and the possibility of war dominated much public life and debate. The wars that occurred, especially the two great wars of the twentieth century, caused the loss of a staggering number of lives and the destruction of much property. Again it was little wonder that the relations of great powers dominated so much historical writing.

Since the end of World War II several factors have allowed and even compelled historians to break through the boundaries of what by then had come to be considered traditional historical writing. Europe has enjoyed over forty years of peace. During that era European statesmen have been determined to prevent repetition of the conditions of domestic political and social unrest that gave rise to interwar authoritarian political movements and eventually to war. Consequently, social and economic factors have loomed much larger in public debate and discussion than distinctly political ones. This postwar stability, the shift to domestic concerns, and the furnishing of social services by the state have led to greater historical interest in factors that foster social and economic stability. Society has come to rival the state as an object for historical analysis.

Almost fifty years of European peace have also made the issues of inter-European diplomatic relations seem somewhat less immediately pressing. The continent now lies between the two great superpowers of the United States and the Soviet Union. The end of the European overseas empires and the process of decolonization greatly reduced the size of the arena in which the European nations could pursue their rivalries. The result for historical writing of these shifts in the relative power status of the European states has not been the end of diplomatic history, but rather the possibility of its being pursued with more scholarly detachment and less inclination to regard it as an extension of particular national foreign policies.

The older, more traditionally investigated historical issues generally have not vanished, nor have all of the major intellectual problems and puzzles posed by them been solved—although some present-day historians may choose to dismiss them as if that were the case. Rather the past several decades have brought to the fore new interests among historians and new tools with which they may pursue those interests. The result has been a burgeoning in the variety of historical subjects now under investigation. The social sciences have contributed most of these new methods—quantitative analysis, econometric models, the sociology of knowledge, psychology, psychoanalysis, and various anthropological theories. These investigative and analytic methods allow the historian to put to meaningful use documents that long lay neglected and unconsulted, including records of baptisms and burials, the financial accounts of landed estates, police reports, writings of physicians and public health officers, and tax records. Furthermore, the theories of the social sciences have allowed historians to attempt to give meaningful interpretations to modes of social behavior that once seemed simply curious to observers living many centuries later. In particular, this approach has opened the world of peasant life and popular culture to historical examination and analysis. Consequently, as the tools of historical analysis have increased in number, they have allowed the historian to move into new areas of research. Yet it should be emphasized that the power of these tools and methods is never greater than the imagination of the persons using them. More important than the new methods has been the curiosity driving historians to ask new questions and to probe modes of human experience previously neglected.

The single most notable change occurring within recent modern European historical scholarship has been the emergence of social history. This somewhat diffuse term covers a wide variety of historical interests and subjects. First and foremost it has focused historical attention on those kinds of people previously given little or no attention by historians. Groups of human beings who rarely or never entered the political or social power structure, especially peasants, industrial laborers, women, and children, are now receiving their historical due. No longer are they regarded merely as the passive materials upon which more powerful political and social forces worked their wills. Rather they are now recognized as having actively participated in the making of history. Second, social historians, often drawing upon anthropology, have become particularly concerned with the social patterns and economic experiences of the daily lives of such people. Marriages, sexual relations, gender-determined social roles, family life and child rearing, rituals of death, the securing of food and shelter, the procurement and uses of natural resources, and local economic structures loom large on the pages of social history. Finally, whereas in the past the winners of political and social struggles received primary treatment from historians, social historians have tended to be interested in those historical experiences and phenomena that Edward Thompson, one of the most eloquent spokesmen for social history, has described as "the blind alleys, the lost causes, and the losers themselves."[1] In this regard social historians have repeatedly attempted to give historical voice to the previously voiceless and nameless figures of the past and historical strength to those who in a previous age found themselves overpowered by social and political change. This moral quality of social history has accounted for much of its attraction.

Like the earlier history that emphasized politics, diplomacy, and male elites, social history is itself perhaps the inevitable result of present historical conditions. Since 1945, throughout the Western world, enrollments in universities have burgeoned with millions of students who are themselves democratically drawn from just those social groups previously excluded from the world of elite politics and culture. In the course of time these students have come to ask about the historical experience of persons like themselves and their forebears in the past. Before working-class men and women were admitted in considerable numbers to universities, there were few people who wanted to know the history of the working class. People who by the 1960s had come to understand that they need not accommodate

---

[1] E. P. Thompson, *The Making of the English Working Class* (New York, 1963), p. 12.

themselves to the politics or culture of past elites in a truly democratic age began to pursue the study of the nonelite history. Upon their graduation they have themselves in many cases helped to constitute a new generation of scholars interested in questions quite different from those of their predecessors.

The recent important explorations into the history of women similarly reflect the changes in the social and political environment of the past three decades. Not only are more women receiving higher education, but perhaps more important, the advance of the feminist movement has spurred new concern for reclaiming and understanding the past experience of women. Research into that experience has necessarily required extensive investigation into issues of marriage, family life, childrearing, the family economy, and the work experience of women, as well as earlier examples of political participation by women.

Yet it would be a mistake to overemphasize the discontinuity between past and present historical scholarship. Many historians, though by no means all, are today attempting to provide an historical social consciousness to people who are perceived as living in a class society, whereas in the nineteenth and early twentieth centuries historians attempted to provide a sense of national political consciousness to people who were perceived as living in nationalist states. In both the past and present the work of historians reflects the contemporary social and political milieu. No less now than in the past are historians of all areas of specialization concerned with issues of power, whether they arise in the context of the nation-state, the labor union, the village, or the family. Furthermore, just as political and diplomatic history came to the fore in a period dominated by such questions, so social history has come to the fore in an age dominated by social conflict and the welfare state.

Do all of these changes, and the emergence of social history, mean that one way of approaching the past has been eclipsed and that another now looms permanently on the horizon? The answer to that question is a cautious, but emphatic, no. To return to the highway metaphor: The enrichment of curiosity, the appropriation of new methods, and the perception of new problems in the last several decades of historical scholarship have opened new roads, but they have not closed others. Thus far many travellers and laborers on the new highway have returned with reports about the previously unexplored landscape and of the great intellectual opportunities that lie just around the bend. Some have even established early pioneering communities. Their excitement reflects the novelty of that experience and their personal commitment to the enterprise. But in time the old and the new will become integrated. Often when a new highway is opened, traffic deserts the previously established road. But eventually traffic reappears on the older road because the new has become overcrowded or the features in the old landscape become unfamiliar and attract new spectators.

Four dynamic factors at work in the historical community assure the continuation of pluralism. First, some major problems of traditional historical concern, such as the rise of the absolutist state, the outbreak of the English Civil War, or the onset of World War II, by their very significance and complexity spur ongoing research. In each of these, as well as in many other areas of traditional inquiry, important and lively work is being done. Second, the new understanding of social forces, local history, and material life themselves become driving forces for the reconsideration of long-recognized historical problems such as imperialism, the coming of the Russian Revolution, or the rise of Nazism. Third, within the historical profession as elsewhere in human life, there exists a pendulum effect. The concern for new issues in history today may lead to less research in once-active fields. In time the new areas will become over-researched and the issues investigated trivial, as was previously the case in diplomatic history. The older areas of investigation will come to be recognized as neglected fields and their still-unsolved problems, of which there are many, will arouse the curiosity of future historians. Furthermore, the controversy and debate aroused by new varieties of historical investigation will lead to new kinds of probes into the past. Finally, historians seem in their investigations of the past to respond to contemporary concerns. As those contemporary concerns shift, as they inevitably do, new arenas for historical research will command our attention. One thing seems certain: Just as past and present historical studies have not been locked in an iron-tight mold, neither will those of the future.

Several of the following essays will lead the reader directly into the new area of social history and illustrate the wide variety of research carried out by social historians. In some cases the historian examines classes or groups long ignored or regarded as acted upon rather than acting for themselves in history. For example, Isabel de Madariaga recounts the events of the greatest peasant revolt in Russian history and relates that discontent to changes in traditional peasant rights. Joan Scott and Louise Tilly trace the manner in which young women from the country who moved into nineteenth-century cities attempted to retain rural customs in the new urban environment. Tsuyoshi Hasegawa examines changes in the economic and social structures of the wartime Petrograd labor force that made it ripe for revolutionary change during World War I.

In other essays, the social historian discerns a social dimension previously unnoticed or perhaps underestimated. Margaret Jacob points to the social lessons that certain early eighteenth-century

English theologians drew from Newton's science. Michael Kennedy portrays the interaction between the French revolutionary government in Paris and the local Jacobin clubs in regard to the shifts in the religious policy of the revolution. Richard Hamilton relates the recruitment of the early members of the Nazi party to the social experiences of the defeated German soldiers from World War I. In each of these essays, an appreciation of social factors furthers our understanding of the reception of scientific ideas, the development of a governmental policy, or the growth of a political movement.

Sometimes the approach of the social historian allows us to understand behavior that has previously seemed odd, curious, or simply barbarously cruel. In this regard, John McManners analyzes the social function of the brutality of the public execution in eighteenth-century France. Other social historians help us to have some sense of what life at the time was like. Anthony Wohl presents the dangers and fears that all classes confronted in the nineteenth century from diseases for which cures had not yet been devised.

The new emphasis on society has not lessened the need to understand what ideas influenced people at given moments in European history. Indeed, the two are often closely related. The essays of Franklin Baumer and Klaus Epstein explore the rise of ideas that opposed the French Revolution and that questioned the Enlightenment. These essays help us to understand the actions of early nineteenth-century conservatives and romantics. Robert Darnton's discussion of the business side of the publication of the *Encylopédie* explores the manner in which ideas are diffused throughout a society when the government may be hostile to many of them. Eugen Weber's portrayal of the impact of the new school systems in nineteenth-century France demonstrates how ideas propagated through public education established a new sense of nationhood in France. He also portrays the clash between priests and secular schoolmasters for influence in the French provinces. Michael Howard analyzes the ideas of offensive warfare that directly led to the deaths of hundreds of thousands of soldiers in World War I. Robert Wohl underscores the manner in which a great event such as the First World War can generate within a decade sets of myths that confuse both understanding of the past and expectations for the present.

Historians have also discovered that they cannot ignore economics and technology. Robert Darnton again brings to the fore the sheer technical difficulties involved in the vast publishing project of the *Encyclopédie*. Jennifer Tann explores the difficulties that the early manufacturers of steam engines encountered in marketing their epoch-making invention. Daniel Headrick relates the remarkable establishment of European dominance over much of the globe in the late nineteenth century to the technological advancement of Europe. Michael Mandelbaum traces the impact of changes in nuclear weapons development and delivery systems on the character of the NATO alliance.

Politics and questions of great-power diplomacy still retain a central role in historical research. Anthony Fletcher traces the series of often unlikely events that fueled the outbreak of the English Civil War. Richard Bonney describes Louis XIV drawing virtually all political power into his own hands to establish the classic model of monarchical absolutism, and Robert Tucker looks at the manner in which, over two centuries later, Stalin established a modern twentieth-century version of personal political rule. Sally Marks's analysis of reparations suggests that quite often what people think about a political or economic situation may be more important than its real character. Ronald Smelser and Williamson Murray open new dimensions of understanding on the whole question of the policy of appeasement and the Munich Pact.

Yet few of these selections can or should be seen as illustrating only one of the many sides of history. Those dealing with politics necessarily take into account social structures and personal social expectations. Social historians must take into account ideas, and no intellectual historian can write without a knowledge of the society and political structures of the time under investigation. Indeed, what is perhaps now one of the most important but not always thoroughly appreciated aspects of historical research and writing is the very interdependence of the various methods of approaching the past. Although it is convenient to speak or write of compartments of human activity, life itself is not experienced in a compartmentalized fashion and history cannot properly be written in that fashion.

The selections in this reader illustrate the lively and richly pluralistic character of recent writing in European history, and are intended to help students and other readers appreciate the rich variety of its intellectual outlooks. Having completed the reading of these essays, the student may come to realize that a description applied more than a century ago by a Victorian writer to a Renaissance humanist is today no less appropriate for the historical profession:

> For the essence of humanism is that belief which he seems never to have doubted, that nothing which has ever interested living men and women can wholly lose its vitality—no language they have spoken, no oracle beside which they have hushed their voices, no dream which has once been entertained by actual human minds, nothing about which they have ever been passionate, or expended time and zeal.[2]

That vast realm of past human experience in all its multiplicity is the world that historians seek to uncover, to describe, and to explain.

[2] Walter Pater, *The Renaissance: Studies in Art and Poetry* (1873, rep. Berkeley, 1980), p. 38.

King Louis XIV (1643-1715).   *Giraudon/Art Resource, NY*

PART ONE

The Seventeenth Century

During the seventeenth century, new institutions of political authority began to organize themselves in Europe. At the heart of the process lay the character of the relationship between central monarchies and centers of local political power, in particular the nobility and other large landowners. Two very different political models eventually came to the fore—one in England and the other in France. As might be expected, the lingering religious turmoil of the Reformation cast a very dark shadow over this process.

In England in 1640 a civil war broke out between forces loyal to the monarchy and those loyal to a Parliament dominated by large landowners. Major religious conflicts stirred up by Calvinists who were called Puritans sharpened the original constitutional differences. Anthony Fletcher explains how Puritan parliamentary leaders exploited popular religious fears of a Roman Catholic plot against English liberties in their assault on the policies of Charles I. The civil war that resulted brought twenty years of upheaval to England, but this period of turmoil, followed later in the century by the Revolution of 1688, established the English political model within which the rule of monarchy stood limited by the role of an elected Parliament and also within which religious tolerance prevailed.

In France, Louis XIV assumed personal rule in 1661. During his childhood Louis had witnessed the last revolt of the French nobility, known as the *Fronde*. As an adult he was determined never to have his authority so challenged. Richard Bonney traces the manner in which the Sun King acted to bring one center of political power after another, including the nobility and the towns, under the direct influence and control of the monarchy. Furthermore, in 1685 he revoked the Edict of Nantes, ending toleration of French Protestants and thus establishing a unitary Roman Catholic state. The resulting political model was that which is normally termed *absolutism* and which various monarchs on the continent attempted to imitate in the next century.

But politics alone did not dominate the seventeenth century. It also saw the culmination of the movement in scientific thought that had commenced with Copernicus. The *scientific revolution* is the term used to denote this new human understanding of the physical universe and especially of astronomy. In less than a century and a half European scientific thinkers had moved from an earth-centered universe to a universe in which the earth moved around the sun. The great names in this achievement were Copernicus, Kepler, Galileo, and Newton. Margaret Jacob explains how Christian writers in England used the new understanding of the orderliness of the physical universe to advocate political and social stability, and how revolutionary scientific thought thus came to be used for conservative social ends.

The Outbreak of the English Civil War

ANTHONY FLETCHER

The English Civil War was among the most tumultuous events of seventeenth-century Europe. It began in 1642, and by 1649 the Church of England had been subjected to radical reformation, the House of Lords abolished, and the monarch executed. Eleven more years of turmoil lay ahead before the Restoration of 1660. Before 1642 no one would have predicted such events; then a civil war between forces loyal to the monarch and forces loyal to Parliament would have seemed virtually unthinkable. So vast was the upheaval that in its aftermath the outbreak of conflict came to be ascribed to clashes over great constitutional principles and religious ideas. Few people asked exactly what immediate events and what immediate shifts in political climate had led to the breakdown of political order and the choosing of sides.

To be sure, there had been areas of conflict between Charles I and Parliament from the mid-twenties onward. The king had raised revenues and governed without calling a Parliament from 1629 to 1639; during those same years Puritanism, with its stress on Calvinist theology, Bible reading, a preaching ministry, and personal piety, had spread throughout the land. It had met strong opposition from the bishops of the Church of England, who adopted an Arminian theology and a sacramental liturgy and whom Charles had consistently supported. Charles was also married to a French princess who was a practicing Roman Catholic. These factors provided the basis for conflict of a serious nature, but not necessarily for civil war.

In 1639 Charles at long last summoned a Parliament to request funds to pursue war against Scotland for the purpose of imposing the English Book of Common Prayer and ecclesiastical government by bishops on the strongly Calvinist Scottish Church. Parliament refused to vote the taxes, and Charles dismissed it. Thus it became known as the "Short Parliament." In 1640 he summoned another Parliament,

---

Reprinted with adaptations by permission of New York University Press and Edward Arnold (Publishers) Ltd. from *The Outbreak of the English Civil War* by Anthony Fletcher. Copyright © 1981 by Anthony Fletcher.

which became known as the "Long Parliament." Among its leaders was John Pym, an outspoken critic of the king and a strong Puritan. As Parliament and the king confronted a series of sharp disagreements and after Charles attempted to arrest members of Parliament, Pym and his followers began to claim that there existed a papist plot to impose Roman Catholicism on England and thus to subvert liberty and true religion. Pym and his parliamentary supporters presented this view of Charles in the Great Remonstrance of 1641. The years of distrust, the recent clashes between the king and Parliament, and the debate about who should have authority over the army now engaged in putting down an Irish rebellion allowed many people to believe these accusations. In a matter of months Charles became associated in the public mind with the evil intentions of the alleged papist plot, and Parliament with the defense of liberty and true religion. It was under these confused and confusing circumstances that the civil war began, with the king and Parliament symbolizing great constitutional and religious principles now in conflict.

Great events do not necessarily have great causes, though it is natural for historians to seek them. Until recently early seventeenth-century parliamentary history has suffered from the straightjacket of the whig tradition, with its overriding but anachronistic concepts of 'government' and 'opposition'. Now it is plain there was no high road to civil war. There was not bound to be a struggle between king and parliament in order that the balanced constitution of the eighteenth century could be its outcome. Nor, it has been established, can the war be explained in terms of social revolution: the ultimate split was quite clearly a split within the governing class. A new interpretation based on the notions of 'court' and 'country' is also unsatisfactory. Most of those involved in the story told here did not think of themselves as belonging exclusively to either entity. No one who knows the Puritan world of lectures, fasts and exercises and who has also raised their eyes to Rubens's apotheosis of Stuart monarchy on the ceiling of Inigo Jones's Banqueting House in Whitehall can possibly doubt that there was a clash of cultures in the 1630s. Yet it takes more than a clash of cultures for a king and his subjects to go to war.

What then is the meaning of these events? A detailed step-by-step account of an occurrence as important as the outbreak of civil war certainly reveals the complexity of any such political process, the concatenation of circumstances necessary to produce something so completely at odds with all men's assumptions about social and political relationships. But there is no need for political narrative to drain the story of all deep-seated meaning. The English civil war was in no sense merely accidental. Chance and coincidence played their part: things might have been very different, for example, if the Irish rebellion had not happened at the precise time it did. But the story is also full...of personal idealism, collective emotion and ideological passion.

Studies of parliaments and administration in the period 1603 to 1640 have shown that there was a functional breakdown in early Stuart government. It became most obvious under the stress of war in the 1620s and again in 1640. But it is important to note that, superficially at least, the administrative problems brought into focus by the Scottish war were solved during 1641 by Pym's reform of the subsidy, the imposition of a poll tax, the peace treaty with Scotland and the disbandment of the armies. If there was a crisis of the constitution in 1640 and 1641, in other words, it was a crisis that was surmounted without recourse to civil war.

Some have seen the central interest of the period from 1640 to 1642 as residing in the need to explain the defection from the parliamentary cause of many of those who opposed Arminianism and ship money, wished Strafford removed from the scene and desired regular parliaments. But this view begs the question of defining the 'parliamentary cause' at the opening of the Long Parliament. Most of those who rode up to Westminster in November 1640 had no concept of a parliamentary cause in their minds. Reconciliation and settlement were seen as the purposes of parliaments and the reforms that most MPs envisaged seemed perfectly compatible with such an end. Only Pym and a few close friends saw the matter in totally different terms: for them the parliamentary cause was the extirpation of a conspiracy that struck at the core of the nation's life. Their fundamental misconception of the political situation, relentlessly propagated and pursued over the next months, must surely be the starting point for an explanation of how war came about. The central problem is not so much why did some defect as why did so many, both at Westminster and beyond, hold fast to Pym and his associates despite their deluded and over-dramatized view of the nation's troubles?

The brilliance of Pym's leadership and the skill with which he mastered the devoted support of a core of sympathizers in both Houses has been emphasized.... But one cannot fail to note the contrast between the shrewdness and practicality of Pym's tactics and the emotional basis of his policies. The policies themselves suggest the abnegation of reason. The parliamentary leaders were men who were in no position to distinguish between truth and rumour and had no desire to do so. From the start rhetoric was their trade. Distrust festered, faith was gradually broken and step by step the chances of restoring confidence in the king and those around him disappeared. External events and contingencies contributed to this process, bringing home to MPs the apparent substance of Pym's story and turning it into a self-fulfilling prophecy. The army plots, the Incident [a plot in Scotland against critics of the king], the Irish Rebellion and the king's attempt to arrest the five members all played into Pym's hands. Each time something happened to make the plot more real, it also brought it closer to the person of the king himself. The skirmishes at Westminster and in Whitehall in December 1641 and the presence of the king in the chamber of the Commons a few days later appeared to be the logical culmination of everything that Pym and his associates had been saying since 7 November 1640. Richard Baxter, a man who later expounded Pym's interpretation of the war, must surely have been thinking of those days when he wrote that 'the war was begun in our streets before king or parliament had any armies'.

Despite the wave of hostility he then suffered, Pym had acquired a powerful London following by the autumn of 1641. Secretary Nicholas reflected on the main obstacle to reassertion of royal authority: 'the noise of an intention to introduce popery was that which first brought into dislike with the people the government both of the Church and commonwealth.' An indication of the mood of the capital is provided by a letter from Teige O'Brien, a Catholic resident of Covent Garden, to Sir Philip Percival. 'Though I am both their Majesties' sworn servant', he wrote, 'yet I dare not go out of doors, the persecution is so fearfully cruel and hot.'

It naturally took the provinces rather longer to grasp Pym's message but the Grand Remonstrance... finally did the trick. An alert observer like Thomas Stockdale in Yorkshire was then quite ready to slot the accusation of the five members into place as a Jesuit plot. Parliament's propaganda related every royal action between January and November 1642 to the papist conspiracy. The king's purging of the commissions of the peace, to take but one example, was alleged on 11 July to be a preparation to ease the 'great change in religion and government' intended. The impact of this propaganda, evident in the spring petitions, remained massive throughout the summer. New petitions renewed the parrot cries of February and March. The outburst of anti-Catholicism in the Stour valley exemplified popular receptivity. So far from bringing reassurance, searches of recusants' homes in many counties revealed stores of money and arms, which, because they were well publicized, merely increased tension.

Pym's triumph was that by imposing his own fears of popery so sweepingly on a susceptible populace he had many really believe that the papists were kindling a civil war. It was widely rumoured, not without foundation of course, that the papists were providing Charles with the money he needed. According to one report going the rounds in July he had already received £80,000 from the papists and clergy. Time and again people attributed royalist aggression to the king's Catholic subjects. 'The papists are upon Lancashire and threaten some heavy doom to befall the Protestants in those parts', John Osborne informed Henry Oxinden on 27 July.

'All the papists and Jesuits in England did conspire together to ruin him and his house', the earl of Stamford told MPs on 8 July, reporting events in Leicestershire. 'Thou hast a rotten stinking heart within thee, for if thou wilt be for the king thou must be for the papists', an apothecary of Grantham had told a neighbour who confessed his royalism a few days earlier. There was much gossip about papists who swarmed to the court at York. In a letter of 31 July a Monmouthshire gentleman confessed his fears that parliament's order for disarming separatists would be used locally to 'disarm the best Protestants and then leave them naked to the papists, who were not yet disarmed, to cut their throats.' Goring held Portsmouth in early August, it was alleged, with the help of four or five hundred 'cavaliers and papists'. Sir Bevil Grenville, so that story went, visited most of the papist gentry of Cornwall and Devon in disguise during August to raise men and money for the king. Sir John Biron took control of Oxford with 'sundry papists and other desperate persons.' The Kentish JPs reported to Speaker Lenthall on 23 November that the trained bands were troubled about papists finding favour after one had been released by the Lords from Maidstone goal: 'seeing all the declarations name them with the prelatical party the only causes of all miseries and distractions.'

Pym's circle had never been so naive as to suppose that the papists could overturn English religion and government singlehanded. The potency of the Catholic design, the Grand Remonstrance stressed, rested on its enjoyment of the support of a band of fellow travellers consisting of the bishops, 'the corrupt part of the clergy' and councillors or courtiers working for private ends, which might include their own advancement through furthering the interests of foreign states. The swift reaction to the bishops' protestation on 30 December 1641 reflected firmly held assumptions about their treasonable predilections. Once Strafford was removed many thought them 'the most suspected party of the kingdom.' Rooting out dissolute clergy ... was treated equally seriously, for as D'Ewes remarked on 21 July 1642, the House's investigations had proved that clergy who had brought in 'wicked tenets' such as Arminianism were 'for the most part men of most scandalous lives.' Writing to the Committee of Safety on 12 October, the parliamentary command at Worcester recommended that the Michaelmas rents of all the bishops, deans and chapters should be sequestered, 'they being that generation of men who have showed themselves most active instruments in procuring of our present miseries.'

The notion of a broadly constituted malignant party bent on the destruction of the nation was expounded increasingly persuasively as the events of late 1641 and 1642 unfolded. Individuals like Digby and Goring were easily drawn into the net. The latter was a 'loose and profane man', D'Ewes believed, working with the papists to make Portsmouth a royalist garrison. It was impossible to miss the simple fact that the army officers who fought with the London citizens at Westminster and in Whitehall at the end of December 1641, attended Charles on 4 January and then caroused at

Kingston, henceforward called the cavaliers, quickly became as important in their influence on the king as his well established counsellors. Sir John Hotham noted that many of those with the king at the gates of Hull on 24 April were men 'that were at the parliament door.'

Thus the conspiracy made more sense than ever as its boldest protagonists revealed themselves: no one who was in the grip of Pym's propaganda doubted that papists lurked behind bishops, clergy and cavaliers. In a letter to Sir John Bankes on 31 May, the earl of Essex summarized the nation's enemies as 'delinquents, papists and men that desire to make their fortunes by the troubles of the land'. Five months later, in his letters announcing a 'happy victory' at Edgehill, he dismissed the royalist army more succinctly as 'desperate persons ill affected to the state.' There were a few like Henry Marten who scorned the fiction that the king was the innocent captive of his advisers, but most of the leading parliamentarians probably at least half believed their own propaganda. 'I am persuaded that His Majesty would be graciously pleased to come to his parliament if those delinquents and cavaliers which are with him might be saved harmless, which he much desires', wrote Thomas Toll to his Norwich constituents on 10 September. This is probably the note that most MPs would have struck. There is no reason to doubt the sincerity of Denzil Holles's letter to Bankes, hastily scribbled in the Commons chamber on 21 May. He was confident parliament would 'most readily cast itself at the king's feet with all faithful and loyal submission upon the first appearance of change in His Majesty, that he will forsake those counsels which carry him on to so high a dislike and opposition to their proceedings by mispossessing himself of them.'

The strength of the parliamentary cause, both at Westminster and beyond, was its immediacy and indisputability. The nation's enemies appeared unquestionably evil and obviously implacable. Thus a sense of identification with and trust in parliament was a necessary defensive reaction.... [T]his sense emerged in the petitions of early 1642 and ... it was expressed in some of the summer musters under the militia ordinance. How much more powerfully must it have affected those who had actually toiled in the Commons for months on end. In a speech on 27 January 1642, Denzil Holles expressed his conviction that parliament preserved standards of probity and public duty which singled it out as the instrument called upon for the salvation of the state: 'whosoever shall for favour or affection or for hatred or by ends shall not freely deliver his mind here is not fit to sit within these walls and I am sure will never enter the kingdom of heaven.' Sir Simonds D'Ewes spoke on 16 May of how he felt his own pride and dignity was bound up with the Long Parliament's achievement. 'For mine own part', he declared, 'I think they must have a wisdom beyond the moon that dream of any happiness to themselves after the ruin of this parliament, which I shall never desire to overlive.'

All this though is only one side of the picture. Charles I and his most intimate advisers lived in an equally closed mental world. His experience in the 1620s had given Charles a jaundiced view of parliaments and a strong sense of distrust of certain individuals who he believed were ready to challenge his monarchy for private and selfish ends. His troubles with the Scots had strengthened his belief that Puritans were inherently seditious, a view strongly pressed on him by Con in their conversations during 1638 and 1639 about the possibility of the pope coming to his aid. Con portrayed the Scottish rebellion as the product of greed and ambition cloaked by religion. The king plainly saw the English one in the same terms. Parliament would put him and his children, he told the Yorkshire gentry on 4 August, 'into the hands of a few malignant persons who have entered into a combination to destroy us.' 'You shall meet with no enemies', he declared to his army on 19 September, 'but traitors, most of them Brownists, Anabaptists and atheists, such who desire to destroy both Church and state.' At Wrexham, in his speech to the inhabitants of Denbighshire on 27 September he summarized his case as follows: 'I have been dealt with by a powerful malignant party in this kingdom, whose designs are no less than to destroy my person and crown, the laws of the land and the present government both of Church and state.'

Charles's strength of character was based on his enduring sense that he was answerable only to God. At the head of his army two days before the battle of Edgehill, he spoke of the 'inhuman and impious misbelief' of those who would not accept his word that he had no end but the kingdom's happiness and the defence of the Church, the law and the liberty of his subjects. 'Ambition which fills the veins of great ones to be greater', he insisted, 'must needs be free from us since we are greatest; envy and malice are as far since we have no competitor.' The king's misunderstanding of his opponents' aims and motives would have been less serious if his character had been different. He was a man who magnified distrust even in the most loyal hearts. What men saw was the king's aloofness, his rigidity, his immersion in a cosmopolitan court culture they did not understand, his deep affection for his French wife who meant nothing to them. What they suspected, quite correctly, was his deviousness and taste for intrigue. During a debate about execution of the recusancy laws in the 1625 parliament, an MP could say without fear of contradiction that the king's heart was 'as right towards religion as we would desire it.' No one would have dared to make such a statement in 1641.

Charles's wavering and indecisive policy during the first half of 1641 jolted men's confidence in him. His hard line thereafter seemed like proof that the papists had captured his mind. The king's blunders—above all the five-members débâcle—did much to make the political crisis insoluble. So did the general weakness of the Stuart monarchy at this particular moment. The specific grievances of the 1630s could be answered by new laws, but the disastrous loss of confidence brought about by the reversal of James I's foreign and religious policies and the introduction of an alien court culture could not quickly be restored. Because the prestige of the monarchy was so low it was unusually vulnerable to a conspiracy story of the kind that Pym had to tell.

'Our sickness', the earl of Bristol observed in a speech to the Lords on 20 May 1642, 'is rather continued out of fancy and conceit (I mean fears and jealousies) than out of any real distemper or defect'. His analysis was perceptive: 'it is much easier to compose differences arising from reason, yea even from wrongs, than it is to satisfy jealousies, which arising out of diffidence and distrust, grow and are varied upon each occasion.' The earl of Northumberland had offered an equally cool analysis in a letter to Sir John Bankes only the day before. 'It is too apparent that neither king nor parliament are without fears and jealousies', he wrote, 'the one of having his authority and just rights invaded, the other of losing that liberty which freeborn subjects ought to enjoy and the laws of the land do allow us.' 'The alteration of government', declared Northumberland harking back to the phrase first used in 1628, 'is apprehended on both sides.' Some parliamentarians were quite explicit that their concern was to preserve their liberties. 'Peace and our liberties are the only things we aim at', wrote Sir Ralph Verney in June 1642, 'till we have peace I am sure we can enjoy no liberties and without liberties I shall not heartily desire peace.' John Hutchinson, according to his wife, was satisfied that a conspiracy existed to introduce popery 'yet he did not think that so clear a ground of the war as the defence of the just English liberties.' What Verney and Hutchinson seem to have been saying was that they could not trust the king to rule according to the law.

It is vitally important to distinguish between the issues raised by the political crisis of 1641 and 1642, such as the militia or appointment of counsellors, and what it was actually about. The earls of Bristol and Northumberland surely saw the matter correctly. The civil war was based on mutual distrust. As early as 1626 two growing fears, of 'parity' on the one hand and 'popery' on the other, have been identified in English public life, fears which 'present a mirror image to each other and came to enjoy a curious interdependence, each being necessary to validate the other.' What happened in 1641 and 1642 was that two groups of men became the prisoners of competing myths that fed on one another, so that events seemed to confirm two opposing interpretations of the political crisis that were both originally misconceived and erroneous. This may seem a frail foundation for civil war. But the war must be seen in the context of the imaginative poverty of the seventeenth century. This was a society in which people were made scapegoats for processes, which lacked the capacity to conceive of and weigh in the balance alternative political systems, which took a highly traditional view of the world as a place of 'limited good' where no one can prosper save at someone else's expense.

For all this, any account of the origins of the civil war which fails to give due weight to its ideological content must be incomplete. If fear and distrust at the centre of the nation's affairs finally made war unavoidable, there was surely in addition something more positive which drove men to take up arms against their own countrymen. There were many on both sides in 1642 who believed they were fighting for a cause, not just to defend the state against a faction or a conspiracy. The civil war came about because of the coincidence of hopeless misunderstanding and irreconcilable distrust with fierce ideological conflict.

The royalists' ideology is the harder to define at the outbreak of the war because it was slow to crystallize. Generalized and amorphous conservative sentiment gave the king a good deal of his initial support. But it has been suggested here that royalism had its foundation in a critical attitude to the aims and tactics of the dominant clique at Westminster. The positive idealism which informed and sustained those royalists who were Protestants became apparent during 1642: its essence was attachment to a traditional and moderate concept of the role of the Church in society, emphasizing the importance of order both in worship and Church government.

The heart of parliamentarian ideology was the connection in men's minds between the struggle against popery and the preservation of true religion. The essence of the conflict with the king, as one historian has put it, was seen as a 'collision between true religion and popery.' We can only understand the zeal of the parliamentarians at the start of the war if we appreciate the frustration many of them felt at the bizarre appearance of a Church half reformed, the inspiration afforded by the vision of a new Jerusalem and the shock created by the king's assault in the previous decade on the mainstream of moderate Puritan evangelicalism. Protestants, as Holles put it in a speech on 22 June 1642, had seen the 'truth and substance' of religion 'eaten up with formality, vain pomp and unnecessary ceremonies; the gross errors of popery and Arminianism imposed upon us as the doctrine of our Church; a way opened to all licentiousness.' Essex petitioners ... spoke of religion as more precious than their lives and liberties. 'Our chief aim is to preserve religion', declared an MP in the debate about the king's reply to the propositions sent to Beverley on 25 July, 'now before the parliament the main design was to destroy religion.'

What was really at stake at the deepest level of this crisis was not the issue of the militia or appointment of councillors, the immediate expressions of political distrust, but the future of the Church. The legislative priorities of the Commons in the summer of 1642 were the bills for summoning the assembly of divines, abolishing pluralities, extirpating Arminian innovations and removing scandalous ministers. These were the bills that MPs were trying to hasten in the Lords, that they insisted upon in the Nineteen Propositions, that they kept in the forefront of the Treaty of Oxford negotiations in the first months of 1643. In a speech on 6 July, D'Ewes argued that, whereas 'the liberty and propriety' of the subject had been clearly asserted, 'the main matter which yet remains to be secured to us is the reformation of religion.' He was one of those who believed parliament could simply not run the risk of a repetition of the Arminian attack on true religion: 'seeing those ceremonies which do give offence are no ways necessary, they are to be utterly abolished... and so we shall have no further trouble how to satisfy weak consciences in the use of them, which can scarcely stand without the abuse of them.' D'Ewes had emphasized a few days earlier that parliament did not wish to alter 'any fundamental or essential part of our religion established, but only to alter some things in the outward frame or government of the Church.' It was ironic that, while royalists vilified parliament for condoning sectarianism, it was in fact taking repressive action: in September 1642, for instance, a feltmaker was imprisoned by order of the Commons for preaching publicly in Holborn.

The Puritan core of the parliamentarian party could not abandon their belief in the supremacy of truth and that belief had become incompatible with the Foxeian tradition of obedience to the godly prince. Thus anti-Catholicism was turned against the court and even the monarch and the force of it carried men into rebellion. It was the king therefore who had opened the way for the call to apocalyptic warfare that thundered from the London pulpits in 1642 and who had forced a section of the gentry into an unnatural alliance with radical Puritans from further down the social scale. In this sense it is correct to state that the connection between Puritanism and the civil war was largely of Charles I's own making.

At the start of the war popular support was crucial to the parliamentarians' strength. In a county like Sussex the entrenched Puritan oligarchy could surely not have fought parliament's battles without the spontaneous enthusiasm of the yeoman families of the weald and the eastern rapes, an enthusiasm that was nourished by decades of household piety and yearning for a godly commonwealth. If men like Sir William Brereton, Herbert Morley and John Pyne offered the necessary leadership, men like the tradesman Nehemiah Wallington of London, the Yorkshire clothier Samuel Priestley and fervent townsman John Coulton of Rye sustained the parliamentarian cause in the field. Wharton's descriptions of the parliamentarian march to Worcester exemplify militant Puritanism in action. 'Though I and many thousands more may be cut off', he wrote after the reverse at Powick Bridge, 'yet I am confident the Lord of Hosts will in the end triumph gloriously.' Priestley's brother left an account of how he went to war, against the entreaties of his family, insisting that he would rather die in the field in a good cause than see the same tragedy as had occurred in Ireland enacted in England. Samuel Turner's letter to his brother in London about a cavalier raid on Henley in January 1643 radiates the same spirit: 'Certainly he was more than blind that could not see God manifestly in every particular of this fight, working deliverance for us and confusion to our enemies.' Ralph Josselin, who defined his motives for contributing on the Propositions as 'my affection to God and his gospel', heard the news of Edgehill three days after the battle, as he was on his way to deliver a fast day sermon. He noted that the time it had been fought coincided with his prayers the previous Sunday, 'when I was earnest with God for mercy upon us against our enemies.' There is a real sense in which the English civil war was a war of religion.

So war and bloodshed came to England, as no one could have foreseen or predicted they would two years previously. This was an unnatural war, as men recognized at the time. Englishmen's sense of security in this period rested on ideas of balance, harmony and degree in civil society. Even their architecture and church monuments tell us how they clung to these notions. Men were not equipped to harmonize political change or upheaval with the fixed points of their mental world. Civil war made precedent irrelevant and forced a painful emancipation from the past. If it was not inevitable... then it was all the more tragic. A curious mixture of folly and idealism lies behind the events that have been described. At the outbreak of hostilities there was also a macabre element of farce: the royalists slew eight of their own men when a cannon split before Warwick Castle in August 1642, four soldiers in the earl of Bedford's regiment were blown up by 'careless looking to their powder' on the march to Sherborne a few weeks later.

The final impression one is left with is of the pathos of the individual's dilemma, as men and women were caught up in a conflict that was not of their making yet in a sense was made by them all. For many in England's governing class it seemed that civilized life was at the brink of destruction. The sorrow men felt about the coming of war reaches out to us from their letters. In those euphoric early days of the Long Parliament, Thomas Knyvett had dreamed of a country cottage: 'I do fancy a little house by ourselves extremely well', he told his wife, 'where we may spend the remainder of our days in religious tranquil, for this parliament surely will settle all peace and quiet amongst us.' In the summer of 1642 he reflected sadly on the state of the nation: both sides strove for the maintenance of the laws 'and the question is not so much how to be governed by them as who shall be master and judge of them; a lamentable condition to consume the wealth and treasure of such a kingdom, perhaps the blood too, upon a few nice wilful quibbles.'

The pain was worst for the genuine moderates, those who could not see the quarrel in black and white yet could not avoid joining one party or the other. The strain on deeply held friendships was acute. In his letters to Lady Temple in the autumn of 1642, Lord Saville expressed his bitterness at the way his reputation was being traduced at Westminster, but comforted himself with the thought that his friend Viscount Saye was probably as 'falsely represented' at court. 'Do your friend right against scandalous tongues which I hear blast me', wrote Sir John Potts to D'Ewes on 2 September, 'Sir, I assure you my conscience leads me to uphold the commonwealth to which I will prove no changeling.'

So many of the gentry who were activists in the civil war could not envisage an outright victory for either side. 'I would not have the king trample on the parliament', declared Saville, 'nor the parliament lessen him so much as to make a way for the people to rule us all.... For as much as I love the king, I should not be glad to beat the parliament though they were in the wrong.' Sir William Waller... confessed afterwards that he abhorred the war though he acted in it, but it 'was ever with a wish... that the one party might not have the worse nor the other the better.' John Hotham wrote as follows to the earl of Newcastle on 9 January 1643: 'I honour the king as much as any and love the parliament but do not desire to see either absolute conquerors; it is too great a temptation to courses of will and violence.'

Civil war led the English gentry into the dark and they tried to maintain the courtesies of life as they knew it while the country was becoming consumed by strife. 'My Lord, I take it as a great favour that these differences that I hope God in his good time will make up again cause you not to forget ancient friendship', wrote John Hotham to Newcastle in a letter of 18 December 1642 about an exchange of prisoners. There is perhaps no letter which expresses so well the poignancy of civil war as that written by Lady Brilliana Harley to Viscount Scudamore on 27 December 1642, about the treatment she was receiving from the Herefordshire royalists:

> My thoughts are in a labyrinth to find out the reason why they should be thus to me. When I look upon myself I can see nothing but love and respect arising out of my heart to them and when I look upon the many bonds by which most of the gentlemen in this country are tied to Sir Robert Harley, that of blood and some with alliance, and all with his long professed and real friendship and for myself that of common courtesy as to a stranger brought into their country, I know not how these who I believe to be so good should break all these obligations.

The gentry could not know at this point that there would be no English revolution.

Bibliography

R. ASHTON, *The English Civil War, 1603–1649* (1978).
W. HALLER, *Liberty and Reformation in the English Revolution* (1938).
C. HIBBARD, *Charles I and the Popish Plot* (1983).
C. HILL, *The Century of Revolution, 1603–1714*, 2nd ed. (1980).
D. HIRST, *The Representative of the People?* (1975).
J. P. KENYON, *Stuart England* (1978).
J. MORRILL, ed., *Reactions to the English Civil War, 1642–1649* (1982).
J. MORRILL, *The Revolt of the Provinces: Conservatives and Radicals in the English Civil War, 1630–1656* (1980).

J. G. A. Pocock, ed., *Three British Revolutions: 1641, 1688, 1776* (1980).
C. Russell, *Parliaments and English Politics, 1621–1629* (1979).
L. Stone, *The Causes of the English Revolution, 1529–1642* (1972).
L. Stone, *The Crisis of the Aristocracy, 1558–1641* (1965).
D. E. Underdown, *Revel, Riot, and Rebellion: Popular Politics and Culture in England, 1603–1660* (1985).

The Personal Rule of Louis XIV

RICHARD BONNEY

The years of personal rule by Louis XIV of France (1661–1715), following the death of Cardinal Mazarin, established monarchical absolutism in France and a political model that other European monarchs aspired to imitate. More than any previous French or European ruler, Louis drew virtually all political power into his hands. The monarch himself, rather than a chief minister, was in charge of the government. No other person, group of persons, or corporate body was to be as powerful as the monarchy nor capable of challenging the will and policy of the monarch.

Louis first brought all of his ministers under his direct control. He made clear the kind of loyalty and service he expected by arresting Foucquet, the former superintendent of finance, who had enriched himself from his office. Later, Louis even oversaw the work of his most esteemed minister, Colbert. Louis then moved to curb the independence of towns so that their wealth could be taxed by the central monarchy. He set about limiting the civil rights of French Protestants, a policy that culminated in the formal revocation of the Edict of Nantes in 1685. Having as a child lived through the aristocratic revolt known as the *Fronde*, Louis devoted much energy to circumscribing the powers of the nobles whether they held their title by virtue of birth or of office. He strictly limited the authority of the local *Parlements*, which were courts dominated by nobles. The monarch intended each of these policies to limit the power of any group who might attempt to assert independent authority or to take actions independent of his will.

Ultimately much tragic irony surrounded the policies of the personal rule of Louis XIV. He sought to exalt the monarchy and its domestic power so that he might pursue an aggressive foreign policy, and his foreign ventures required France to be on a wartime footing from 1667 through 1712, but by the latter date the wars that he had

---

* Copyright © Richard Bonney 1978. Reprinted from *Political Change in France under Richelieu and Mazarin 1624–1661* by Richard Bonney (1978) by permission of Oxford University Press.

undertaken had left his kingdom drained of human and material resources and had sharply reduced the powers and prestige of the monarchy itself.

Louis XIV was already experienced in government when he declared his intention, on the day following the death of Mazarin (9 March 1661) of ruling without a chief minister. The young king had first presided over the council of state on 7 September 1649, at the age of eleven. The first political decision taken on his own authority was the arrest of Cardinal de Retz (19 December 1652). By 1653–5, Mazarin and Louis were going over government business for at least an hour every day. Morosini the Venetian ambassador, noted that when Louis considered that the decisions taken in the council 'ne conviennent pas vraiment à son service, quoiqu'elles soient approuvées par les autres il les casse, en les désapprouvant résolument...'[1] Mazarin had thus introduced Louis slowly, but progressively, to the process of government. The *Frondeurs* had feared that Mazarin would use his position as *surintendant de l'éducation du roi* [Superintendent of the King's Education] to indoctrinate the young king into Mazarin's 'fausse et pernicieuse politique' [false and pernicious politics]. Their fears proved well-founded, but it was the position of chief minister rather than *surintendant de l'éducation* which had given Mazarin his opportunity to teach Louis his political principles. Louis not only liked Mazarin: he greatly admired his political achievement. The guiding principles of Louis's first years of personal rule were thus in most respects a consolidation of the policies pursued by Mazarin before his death. Indeed, Louis implemented the principles formulated by Mazarin on his death-bed and dictated by Louis to one of his secretaries on 9 March 1661. Louis XIV was thus the political disciple of Mazarin.

Mazarin advised Louis to respect the sovereign courts but to 'les obliger de se tenir dans les bornes de leur devoir'—the direct result of this advice was the decree of 8 July 1661 confirming the supremacy of the king's council over the sovereign courts. The *Parlement* of Paris considered this decree 'un coup fatal à la dignité des compagnies souveraines...' but Louis reassured them that 'il n'avoit point entendu diminuer l'authorité de la compagnie mais seulement régler ses fonctions comme celles du conseil'. Louis followed up this measure in October 1665 by renaming the sovereign courts *cours supérieures*. 'Les compagnies... se regardaient comme autant de souverainetés séparées et indépendantes', Louis commented in his memoirs. 'Je fis

---

[1] ["do not really suit his service, although approved by others, he breaks them, resolutely disapproving of them..."]

connaître que je ne souffrirais plus leurs entreprises.'[2] In 1673 the right of remonstrance was restricted, so that remonstrances could be issued only after registration of the relevant legislation. Louis may not have intended the measure to be permanent, but merely a temporary response to a wartime situation. However, France remained at war or on a war footing from 1673 until Louis's death in 1715 and the edict remained in force during his lifetime. As the political role of the courts declined, so too did their economic privileges. Up to 1665, offices had retained their investment value reasonably well. It is true that the *gages* [salary] had been cut after 1639 and suspended altogether in 1648, and that in the 1640s the *parlementaires* of Aix and Rouen had seen the value of their offices fall dramatically with the establishment of *semestres* which had virtually doubled the membership of their courts. Yet they had resisted such measures by armed force in 1649 and obtained their revocation. However, after 1652 no *Parlement* resorted to armed force against the French monarchy, while after 1661 very few remonstrances were issued. This political decline was not permanent—the *parlements* were active in politics once more after 1715—but it was of crucial significance in the short term. It coincided with a government victory in the area of political theory: with the exception of Protestant theorists such as Jurieu after 1685, ideas of resistance, and especially of resistance manifested by institutional means, virtually disappeared in France. There was no theorist of the office-holders to follow the path of Charles Loyseau, and argue the rights of the sovereign courts against the government of Louis XIV. Independent political thought by the office-holders was thus in abeyance, and this decline was symptomatic of the general position of the sovereign courts—they were in no position to defend themselves in December 1665, when Colbert arbitrarily reduced the value of offices. Colbert argued that the capital value of offices was too high and deprived other sectors of the economy of productive investment. This measure attempted to reduce the value of certain existing offices by one-third. Moreover, the courts saw their burden of cases being reduced as a result of several extraordinary royal commissions during the 1660s and 1670s (the *chambre de justice* [Chamber of Justice]; the *réformation de la noblesse* [Reform of the Nobility]; the verification of the debts; the *réformation des eaux et forêts* [Reform of Lakes and Forests], and so on). Members of the courts thus lost

---

[2] ["Marzarin advised Louis to respect the sovereign courts but to "oblige them to remain within the bounds of their duty"—the direct result of this advice was the decree of 8 July 1661 confirming the supremacy of the king's council over the sovereign courts. The *Parlement* of Paris considered this decree "a fatal blow against the dignity of the sovereign courts ..." but Louis reassured them that "it was not intended to diminish the authority of the court but only to regulate its functions as those of the council." Louis followed up this measure in October 1665 by renaming the sovereign courts superior courts. "The courts...regarded themselves as separate and independent sovereignties," Louis commented in his memoirs. "I made them understand that I would not endure their encroachments."]

much of their income from cases (*épices*) which in turn confirmed the fact that office was a depreciating captial asset. Louis XIV created innumerable new offices—including offices in the *parlements*, particularly in the 1690s —and reduced the salaries of existing office-holders, without meeting any resistance from the courts comparable to the 1640s.

Mazarin may well have warned Louis to beware of Foucquet's ambition; he certainly told him that 'un roi qui ne pouvait gouverner n'était pas digne de régner...'[3] The decision to rule without a chief minister, proclaimed by Louis on 10 March 1661, was thus the implementation of one of Mazarin's death-bed wishes. Mazarin also recommended Louis to employ Colbert as Foucquet's assistant. While Colbert had served Mazarin faithfully since 1651 and thus appeared to personify continuity in government, his criticisms of Foucquet since 1659 implied a determination to break with some aspects of the past, notably the system of war finance and the excessive power enjoyed by the *surintendant*. Colbert, moreover, needed to destroy Foucquet: the immense fortune left by Mazarin on his death, amounting to about 37 million *livres*, required that Colbert eliminate all traces of a somewhat compromising political past as Mazarin's financial agent, and transfer all blame to Foucquet. The arrest of Foucquet on 5 September 1661 was followed ten days later by the abolition of the *surintendance* and the establishment in its place of a *conseil royal des finances* [Council of Royal Finance]. This new council—which was below the council of state but superior to the lesser councils (the *conseil privé* and the *conseil d'état et des finances* [Privy Council and Council of Finance]) was created with the purpose of providing more effective direction than that of the *surintendant*, without any corresponding threat to the crown. Louis XIV presided over this council, and thus unlike his father—and himself in the 1650s—was really informed about the detailed state of the finances and the routine working of government. Louis jealously guarded his powers over this council. He struck off items of expenditure which he considered unwarranted. When Louis left for the war front in 1672, the Queen was left to preside over the council in his absence. Two years later, Louis was even more cautious. Colbert was to inform him each week of the important business of the council, but Louis reserved to himself, on his return, the power of verifying the accounts of the royal finances.

The council of finance (*conseil d'état et des finances*) under the presidency of Chancellor Séguier between 1635 and 1661 had failed to provide a firm check on the authority of the *surintendant*, and was thus relegated to overseeing the details of financial administration and removed from the area of political initiative. As a result of the ruling of 15 September 1661, the Chancellor was no longer automatically a minister with entry to the council of state or the new *conseil royal des finances*. Le Tellier, who was appointed in 1677, and Pontchartrain, who was appointed in 1699, were Chancellors who

---

[3] ["a king who could not govern certainly did not deserve to reign."]

enjoyed these rights. Séguier from 1661 until his death in 1672, Étienne III d'Aligre, who was appointed in 1672, and Boucherat, who was appointed in 1685, did not. This decline of the Chancellorship had been foreshadowed under Richelieu and Mazarin by its subordination to the requirements of a system of government based upon a chief minister. The new *conseil royal des finances* allowed freedom of action to a small inner group of the most able councillors—in the first instance, Colbert, Aligre, Sève, Marin, Le Tonnelier de Breteuil, and Hervart (all of whom had served as royal commissioners in the provinces, and three of whom had served as provincial intendants under Richelieu and Mazarin)—without the debilitating influence of an ageing Chancellor and a large council membership. In the *conseil d'état et des finances*, Colbert as an *intendant des finances* [Intendent of Finance]—and, after 1665, as *contrôleur-général* [Controller General] as well—could merely act as *rapporteur* [Reporter] of decrees: by contrast in the new council he kept the registers of receipts and expenses and proposed measures of the greatest political and fiscal importance. Colbert exercised a real responsibility without enjoying independent political power: on the rare occasions that he overstepped the mark, he received a sharp rebuke from the king.

Colbert regarded the *conseil royal des finances* as the instrument by which a systematic reform of the finances of the French monarchy might be undertaken. The chief aspect of this reform was economy. Colbert managed to reduce total expenditure to 42 million *livres* in 1663. Such restraint could not be maintained, but when Colbert complained to Louis XIV in 1670 that increased expenditure was undermining his reforms, the figure he was criticizing—75 million—was lower than that of any year between 1636 and 1662 for which evidence is available. Colbert's reforms earned both political and financial advantages for the government in the short term. They were politically advantageous in that to Louis XIV and Colbert accrued the prestige of having achieved some of the more constructive aims of the *Chambre Saint-Louis*. They were financially advantageous in that the reduction of government expenditure and the fines levied on the financiers by the extraordinary financial tribunal (*chambre de justice*) of 1661 facilitated the balancing of the budget and further reductions in government expenditure. At the same time as he was eliminating wasteful expenditure, Colbert set about reorganizing the income of the French monarchy. He appreciated that the *taille* could not be relied upon as the major revenue of the French crown. Accordingly, he remitted the arrears from the last years of Mazarin's ministry, and reduced the amount of the *taille* [head tax] progressively. Even during the Dutch war of 1672–8, it was kept to 40 million *livres*, well below the level of 1658, and by 1680 it had been reduced again to 32 million. Unfortunately, the effects of these cuts were largely nullified by the agricultural depression after 1670. Moreover, the corollary of Colbert's policy of reducing the *taille* was the expansion of the indirect revenues. In 1662, Colbert negotiated leases totalling 44 million. On his death in 1683, the figure was 65.8 million. The indirect taxes, therefore, brought in about

50 per cent of the total revenues of the crown, whereas the *taille* had fallen to about 30 per cent of the total. The lease negotiated with Fauconnet in 1680 marked the beginning of that most successful of financial institutions in eighteenth-century France, the *ferme-générale* [Tax farmer], which brought together a number of indirect taxes into a single tax farm. Linked to these measures were changes in the methods of tax collection. In 1661 Colbert substituted the *receveurs-généraux* [Receivers-General] and the *voies ordinaires* [ordinary process] for the financiers and coercion by the troops. The government may well have been feeling its way towards this decision in the last months of Foucquet's ministry, but Colbert greatly accelerated the process. With relatively few exceptions, coercion of payment by the intendants and the special brigades was a thing of the past by the 1660s. After 1661, Colbert was much more scrupulous than his predecessors about the recourse to troops for the purposes of tax-collection. It was above all as a result of his financial reforms and this new moderation on the part of the government that the prestige of the intendants rose after 1661. Colbert's financial reforms were only part of his overall economic measures which aimed at assisting French manufactures, commerce and agriculture in a period of economic depression. At a national level, this policy was marked by Colbert's 'tariff war' against the Dutch and his attempts to establish French trading companies. At a local level, Colbert encouraged the intendants to establish new manufacturing industries with government subsidies. The intendants also sought local investment for Colbert's commercial enterprises and came to play an important part in poor relief and in distributing grain, notably during the subsistence crises of 1693–4 and 1709–10.

Colbert's attitude to the intendants has been a subject of some controversy among historians, and his instructions to the *maîtres des requêtes* [Master of Requests] in September 1663 have frequently been misunderstood. It has been argued that Colbert regarded the intendants as no more than temporary investigators and that he envisaged the possibility of doing without them altogether. This view rests on one equivocal passage in the instructions and on the fact that they were issued to the *maîtres des requêtes* and not the intendants as such. In reality, the terms *maître des requêtes* and intendant had become virtually synonymous by this date. Although there was a rapid turnover of intendants in the 1660s, this does not necessarily imply that the intendants were regarded as no more than temporary investigators: the need to appoint former intendants to serve as judges at the trial of Foucquet, the patronage conflict between Colbert and Le Tellier, and the military reviews of Louvois in 1666 were all factors in this situation. It is inconceivable that Colbert envisaged the abolition of the intendants. As early as 1658 he had appreciated the advantages of resident intendants, while in a memorandum of 1 October 1659 to Mazarin he had considered the intendants the essential instruments of fiscal reform: 'toutes ces choses', he wrote, 'ne peuvent estre exécutées dans les provinces que par le ministère des intendants.'[4] Moreover, the government was unlikely to abolish the intendants for the very fact that in 1660–1 the *trésoriers* and *élus* [Treasury officials who collected the *taille*] held illegal meetings to press this issue: the government rejected the claims of the financial officials, left the intendants with their fiscal powers intact, and indeed ordered the intendants to ensure an end to the meetings of the *trésoriers* and the *élus*. Thus Colbert confirmed the fiscal responsibilities of the intendants on 16 November 1661, 12 February, 25 August and 6 September 1663. Any authority retained by the *trésoriers* was essentially as a result of commissions received from the council: not without reason might the *trésoriers* lament that 'nos charges sont tombés dans la dernière décadence' and that the intendants 'retiennent ce qui est de plus honnorable et plus effectif et ne laissent dans les bureaux que le fardeau du grand nombre d'expéditions pour le Roy'.[5] The *élus* retained most of their civil and criminal jurisdiction, but a number of cases of corruption involving the *élus* came before the king's council in the 1660s which confirmed the need for close supervision by the intendants. All the intendants could hope to do was to prosecute those officials who committed serious offences when there was clear evidence against them....

After 1669, the intendants began to stay longer in the provinces than had previously been the case. In the fifty years between 1666 and 1716, the 'average' intendant stayed five years in his province, two years longer than his predecessor after the Fronde. It thus appears that the 'three-year rule', after which an intendant appointed by Richelieu and Mazarin had to be re-appointed, sent to a new province, or recalled, was abandoned during the years of Louis XIV's personal rule. Each province might have expected to experience the administration of nine or more intendants in the fifty years between 1666 and 1716. There was much less mobility in the *pays d'états* than in the *pays d'élections*. The *généralité* [District] of Montauban saw eleven intendants; Alençon, Moulins, Poitiers, and Rouen experienced even more. In contrast, Bouchu served as intendant in Burgundy for 27 years (1656–83) while Basville served in Languedoc for 33 years (1685–1718). Why was it that the intendants tended to stay longer in their provinces? One reason was Colbert's investigation into the debts of the towns. Bouchu had observed in 1666 that it was not enough to liquidate existing debts: it was essential to prevent the communities from incurring new ones. Colbert appreciated the point. In a memorandum to the intendants of 29 February 1680, he asked for suggestions on how this should be achieved. The reports of the intendants were enacted in the decree of 18 November 1681 and the

---

[4] ["all of these things cannot be carried out in the provinces except by the ministrations of the intendants."]

[5] ["not without reason might the *trésoriers* lament that 'our offices have fallen into their final decline' and that the intendants 'retain that which is more honorable and more effective and allow to the personnel of this office only the burden of the large number of expeditions for the King'."]

edict of April 1683. The edict transferred the control of municipal finance from the towns to the intendants, and with the exception of the years between 1764 and 1771, provided the framework of the relationship between the government and the towns until the French Revolution. The edict did not prescribe the audit of municipal accounts by the intendants and Colbert did not favour this procedure. He considered it 'un travail immense qui ne produiroit aucun avantage aux peuples'. However, this was the logical outcome of Colbert's legislation and it was this, more than any single factor, which led to the *tutelle administrative* [protective administration] over the towns. The amount of work carried out by the intendants was greatly increased as a result of this measure and its implications. The intendants had to rely on subordinate officials during the verification and liquidation of the debts 'pour avancer un travail si nécessaire'. By 1718 business concerning the towns had become the '[travail] ordinaire' of the intendant who relied on a network of local *subdélégués* [subdelegates] to establish whether projected expenditure by the towns was worthwhile. The towns were deprived of political and financial independence, and as a result the crown was able to exploit them even more ruthlessly and systematically than had hitherto been possible. After 1683, abuse and exploitation by local notables was replaced by the ruthless exploitation of the towns by the state. The fiscal demands of the Nine Years War and the War of the Spanish Succession began a process which was consummated during the Wars of the Polish and Austrian Successions [in the eighteenth century].

A second factor in prolonging the periods of residence of the intendants was the stricter control over the Protestants imposed by Louis XIV. By 1657, the Protestants of the Midi had feared imminent persecution. Events in the following years, and particularly after 1661, demonstrated that their fears were not ill-founded. A discussion between representatives of the clergy and Chancellor Séguier on 23 February 1661 resulted in agreement that the *commissaires pour l'exécution de l'édit de Nantes* [Commissioners for the Execution of the Edict of Nantes] envisaged in 1656 should be sent out. No action was taken before Mazarin's death on 9 March. Within a month or so of the death of the chief minister, however, the first commissions were drawn up. On 15 June 1661, Louis XIV gave the clergy a further assurance that the declaration of 1656 would be implemented in full. Ironically, at a time when the political influence of the *dévots* [a movement of Roman Catholic Devouts] was on the wane their policy triumphed: Louis XIV was able to destroy the *dévot* movement by making the anti-Protestant crusade government policy. The king recalled in his memoirs that in 1661 he had sought to restrict the concessions accorded by the edict of Nantes. The way in which he did this was through the work of commissioners in not less than thirteen provinces throughout France. In Languedoc, the work of Bazin de Bezons and De Peyremales constituted a systematic assault on the rights of the Protestants to participate in municipal government through the *consulats mi-partis* [Bipartite Chambers]. In 1663, Catholic control was reimposed at

Sommières Bédarieux, Montpellier, and Mazamet. The Protestants sometimes retained their rights, but the ground work had been laid: the new theory, as expressed in 1666, was that 'la communauté ne peut être divisée ni partagée. Elle est toute catholique.'[6] The rights to hold Protestant services, as defined in articles 10 and 11 of the edict of Nantes were severely restricted. Generally, the Protestant commissioner was anxious to retain royal favour and followed the view of the Catholic intendant. The intendants sometimes summoned additional Huguenots to assist in the work — men who were their clients and whom, they hoped, would weaken the resolve of the Protestant commissioners. Thus Bazin de Bezons summoned Anoul, the *juge royal* [Royal Judge] of Uzès, to assist in the investigation in 1661. Even if the Protestant commissioner did not follow the Catholic intendant, a commission of the council of state heard the appeals. This commission of the council was, of course, composed exclusively of Catholics including two prominent members of the *dévot* party (Ormesson and Boucherat) and the son of an acting intendant (Bazin de Bezons). Thus the procedure was from the start weighted heavily against the Protestants. It resulted in the declaration of 2 April 1666, which severely limited the edict of Nantes.

The judicial persecution of the Huguenots had begun. On 21 January 1669, the *chambres de l'édit* [Edict Chambers] of Paris and Rouen were suppressed; that of Castres was transferred to the Catholic town of Castelnaudary. Ten years later, the remaining *chambres de l'édit* were abolished and incorporated into the local *parlements*. A flood of restrictive legislation was passed after 1679 in a sense rendering the edict of Fontainebleau (18 October 1685) — which revoked the edict of Nantes — unnecessary. The forced conversions of the Protestants in Poitou and elsewhere after 1681 had of course created a new situation; so too had Louis XIV's deepening conflict with the Papacy. The revocation of the edict of Nantes was thus produced by a particular set of circumstances, foreign and domestic. However, it could not have been implemented effectively without the elimination of Protestant civil rights in the years before 1685. After that date, the work of the intendants concerning the *nouveaux convertis* [new converts] — as the Protestants were now called — was greatly increased. The intendants were ordered to prosecute Protestants captured trying to flee abroad. They were ordered by a decree of the council of state, dated 13 May 1686, to supervise the drawing up of inventories of the possessions left behind by Protestant exiles, as a preliminary measure to the confiscation of such property. The intendants prosecuted those *nouveaux convertis* who remained in France in the hope of practising their old religion and who were captured by the troops at illegal Protestant prayer meetings. The intendants even carried out posthumous prosecutions of *nouveaux convertis* who refused to receive the Catholic sacraments on their death-bed. The influence of certain

---

[6] ["The community cannot be divided or shared. It is all Catholic."]

intendants in the formation of government policy towards the Protestants was great. Basville engaged in a long controversy with Bossuet, the greatest Catholic mind of the age, on whether or not the *nouveaux convertis* should be forced by the intendants and the troops to attend Mass—significantly, the intendant thought that the converts should be forced to attend. Basville came to have doubts about the policy of coercing Protestants—but this was later, during the long struggle with the *Camisard* rebellion in the Cévennes after 1702.

It has been suggested that while Louis XIV was the political disciple of Mazarin, he adopted certain new policies in the 1660s: a new council was established; an attempt was made to reform the finances of the French monarchy; the verification and redemption of municipal debts was carried out; the Protestants lost all civil rights, and later were coerced to abjure their faith. As a result of this combination of factors, the intendants came to stay longer in the provinces than had been the case before 1661. Had Louis XIV opted to maintain peace, he would have enjoyed much greater freedom of action, and—if he had so wished—might have renounced the legacy of Richelieu and Mazarin. Colbert's financial reforms were geared essentially to the exceptional conditions of twelve years of peace between 1660 and 1671. So too were his plans to strengthen French manufactures, commerce, and agriculture in a period of economic depression. Colbert was probably not an advocate of war, which was in flat contradiction to his policy of retrenchment and reform. Yet Louis had no intention of maintaining peace for its own sake. He had designs on the Spanish Succession; he wanted to reinterpret the Westphalian settlement of 1648 in the interest of France; above all, in 1672 he wanted to punish the Dutch for having formed the Triple Alliance against him four years earlier. The Dutch war rapidly escalated into a German war as well. By 1674, total expenditure reached 113 million *livres*, approximately the level in 1653. The debt left by the war accounted for expenditure of over 130 million in 1679 and 1681. After Colbert's death in 1683, his reforms were completely undermined. In 1689, Louis XIV began the first of two major struggles with the formidable financial resources of England. The council established in 1661—the *conseil royal des finances*—now rarely met. When it met at all, it merely ratified decisions taken by the *contrôleur-général des finances*, acting as a latter-day *surintendant*. Colbert had hoped that the indirect revenues would provide the basis of a more equitable distribution of taxation: but the successful levy of indirect taxes depended on the maintenance of peace. With the outbreak of war in 1689, the income from the indirect revenues quickly fell and the government had once more to fall back on the *taille* and creations of offices as the means of financing the war. There was once more a widening gap between expenditure and revenue. The crown thus had no choice but to rely on the service of financiers such as Samuel Bernard and Antoine Crozat—and to pay the high rates of interest the financiers demanded for their services. Louis XIV set his course along the path of war rather than of continued retrenchment and reform. Louis thus believed that the demands of French foreign policy had to take precedence over all domestic considerations, and in this respect the later years of his reign form a direct link with the ministries of Richelieu and Mazarin.

It meant that the chief concerns of government in the years after 1672 were essentially similar to the concerns of government in the years 1653–61: how could the war be financed without provoking a major insurrection of the French taxpayers? Concern for the welfare of the peasant taxpayers of France had been an aspect of government emphasized by Mazarin on his death-bed, and the remission of the arrears of the *taille* in the early 1660s suggest that the idea had some influence on Louis XIV. Yet prolonged war meant higher taxes and the lot of the peasant could only worsen in a period of economic depression. Even in the years of peace there had been major revolts, such as those of the Bénauge in 1661–2, of the *Lustucru* in the Boulonnais in 1662, of Audijos in the Chalosse in 1663–5, and of Roure in the Vivarais in 1670. There were further riots and revolts following the outbreak of war in 1672, most notably at Agen in 1673 and Bordeaux and le Mans two years later. The revolt of the *Bonnets-Rouges* [Red Caps] or *Torrében* of Brittany in 1675 witnessed perhaps the greatest degree of social antagonism in any peasant rebellion in seventeenth-century France. The later wars brought major rebellions in their wake, too, notably the Protestant *Camisard* rising of 1702 (which was in part a rebellion against taxation) and the revolt of the *Tard-Avisés* of Quercy in 1707. While 'tax rebellion' took place on a significant scale during the personal rule of Louis XIV, and on occasion involved the intendants, the scale was much less than under Richelieu and Mazarin. There is no simple explanation why this was the case, because in part it was the result of a change in peasant attitudes. By forcing the peasants to concentrate above all on scratching a livelihood, the agricultural depression may actually have hindered rather than encouraged active protest: the peasants at the time of Richelieu and Mazarin were somewhat more prosperous and thus in a sense had more to lose from increased taxation paid to the state. The greater strength of government, especially in terms of the availability of troops in most years, the more certain status of the intendants after 1661, and the more savage punishment meted out to rioters were other contributory factors.

The relative quiescence of the nobles certainly assisted the government in its task of isolating and suppressing rural rebellions. Mazarin on his death-bed had counselled Louis XIV to preserve the privileges of the nobles, and Louis certainly did so with regard to their social and economic privileges. Yet Louis did not allow nobles from the older and more established families to enter government except on an occasional, individual basis—the most notable example being the duc de Beauvillier after 1691. The remarkable fact about Louis XIV's personal rule, and the great contrast with the situation in his minority, is that the magnates did not rebel at their exclusion. The conspiracies of the chevalier de Rohan in 1674 and of Schomberg in 1692 were abortive although they produced the usual manifestos proclaiming the need to restore the privileges of the nobility, the *Parlements*, the provinces, and to reduce the burden of taxation. Louis XIV's foreign policy and his domestic religious policy combined to prevent all but a tiny minority of the population from active subversion. The *dévot* argument of the 1620s that the war was unjust because it divided Catholic Europe at a time when there was a significant Protestant minority at home was scarcely applicable after 1666 and incorrect after 1685: Louis XIV fought the Protestant English and Dutch and forced the abjuration of his Huguenot community. The willingness of the Emperor to partition the Spanish inheritance with France after 1668 removed the possibility of a strong 'Catholic' alliance of Habsburg Spain and Austria against France.

Within the provinces, the lesser nobility was gradually transformed in the 1660s and 1670s as a result of conscious royal policy. A highly seditious and ill-defined social group at the time of Richelieu and Mazarin, they became during the personal rule of Louis XIV a highly independent but nevertheless legally-defined, and increasingly law-abiding, group of privileged persons. The *réformations* of the nobility undertaken by the intendants on the orders of Colbert were extremely important, not least because they were desperately unpopular with the nobles themselves. There were clear precedents for the investigation into titles of nobility: in 1598, 1634, 1640, and 1655 recent letters of *anoblissement* [ennoblement] had been revoked and investigations of claims to nobility had been undertaken. In the *généralité* of Caen, for example, this had resulted in two armorials of nobility being drawn up—respectively by Mesmes de Roissy in 1598-9 and by Étienne III d'Aligre in 1634-5. In other provinces, however, the investigation was probably less thorough or else the records of the enquiry were subsequently lost. Colbert's survey was much more complete, extending at various times throughout most of France. One aspect of the enquiry had a fiscal purpose, to ensure that all false titles were annulled so that 'le fardeau de la taille soit porté avec égalité par tous ceux que la naissance y assujetit'. [The burden of the taille may be carried equally by all to whom birth assigns it.][7] Yet there was also a political aspect to the enquiry. However uneven the results of the investigation into noble titles, there were three important consequences. The first was that throughout France—the chief exceptions were Brittany and Provence—the intendant, in close contact with the king's council (but without reference to the governor), became the arbiter of what was, and what was not, a legal title to nobility. In every province there were 'false nobles' whose claims were dismissed (*déboutés*) and who were required to pay a fine of not less than 100 *livres*. Many illustrious noble families (*nobles d'ancienne extraction*), on the assumption that their lineage was beyond dispute, had not bothered to keep archives. Accordingly, they found themselves in great difficulty when faced with the intendant's desire for the *preuves nobiliaires* [proof of nobility]. The search for relevant documents at the local law-courts, among the church records, and the records of notaries was both an expensive and an uncertain procedure. By contrast, the *noblesse de robe* had little difficulty in proving a claim to nobility that did not often reach back beyond 1550: the dates of provisions to offices conveying nobility were known, and the recent *anobli* was likely to have been more methodical in conserving his documents. A second consequence of the investigation was a new definition of nobility: the nobleman was no longer he who claimed to be a noble, he who was thought of as a noble, or he who enjoyed exemption from direct taxation. The nobleman became the person who had obtained an *ordonnance de maintenu de noblesse* from the intendant, a legally binding document after an enquiry into written evidence. A third consequence of the investigation, and other associated government measures, was a closing of the ranks of the nobles after the 1660s. Increasingly, the distinction between *nobles de robe* and *nobles d'epée* began to disappear. In part, this was because of the decline in the profitability of office during the reign of Louis XIV: the majority of the *noblesse de robe* had to rely on their lands for the major part of their income to offset the loss of revenues from law practice and the depreciating capital asset represented by the ownership of most of the expensive offices. At the same time, the investigation into noble titles made it much more difficult to gain new exemptions from taxation. The 'usurpation' of nobility—or gaining nobility through prescription without a clear title—was always possible in the *ancien régime:* but the intendants' control of the *taille* was meant to reduce false claims to fiscal exemption as much as possible. Noble independence was never completely undermined by the Bourbon monarchy: but through the *recherches de noblesse* [research into nobility] undertaken by the intendants, and through other associated forms of judicial and political control, the threat posed by the nobles to the body politic between 1624 and 1661 was removed. At the same time, the peasants lost their champions in 'tax rebellion' against the crown, and the potentially rebellious governor lost his power base.

The extent of Louis XIV's innovations after 1661 should not be exaggerated. In most respects, his changes did little more than consolidate the political achievement of Richelieu and Mazarin. The threads of continuity were strengthened by the fact that substantially the same families dominated government and the intendancies before and after 1661. Louis XIV's ministers before 1700 were drawn predominantly from families which had risen to prominence under Richelieu and Mazarin. Colbert, his brother Colbert de Croissy, Colbert's son Seignelay, and Croissy's son Colbert de Torcy formed one group of ministers. Michel Le Tellier, his son Louvois, and Louvois's son Barbezieux formed a second group. There were few ministers—such as Pontchartrain and Chamillart—who were not allied with one or other group. Lionne, Louis XIV's foreign minister from 1663 until 1671 was the nephew of Servien and had been a member of the government since at least 1651. Pomponne, who succeeded Lionne, had been a *protégé* of Foucquet and had served as an intendant of the army in the 1650s. Similarly, several intendants appointed by Mazarin served during Louis XIV's personal rule. Bazin de Bezons did so in Languedoc until 1673, Bouchu did so in Burgundy until 1683, Hotman de Fontenay did so at Paris until 1681, and Pellot did so at Bordeaux and Montauban until 1669. Pommereu de la Bretesche, the first intendant in Brittany when the intendants were re-established in that province in 1689, had served as intendant of Moulins in 1660. In addition to intendants appointed by Mazarin who continued to serve during Louis XIV's personal rule, there were also sons and grandsons of intendants appointed by Richelieu and Mazarin: over twenty intendants came into this category. For such reasons alone, it would have been difficult for Louis XIV to have formulated and implemented radically different policies from those pursued by Richelieu and Mazarin.

Bibliography

P. GOUBERT, *Louis XIV and Twenty Million Frenchmen* (1966).
R. HATTON, ed., *Louis XIV and Europe* (1976).
W. H. LEWIS, *The Splendid Century* (1953).
A. L. MOOTE, *Revolt of the Judges: The Parliament of Paris and the Fronde* (1971).
D. OGG, *Europe in the Seventeenth Century* (1925).
L. ROTHKRUG, *Opposition to Louis XIV: The Political and Social Origins of the French Enlightenment* (1965).
J. C. RULE, ed., *Louis XIV and the Craft of Kingship* (1970).
W. J. STANKIEWICZ, *Politics and Religion in Seventeenth-Century France* (1960).
G. R. R. TREASURE, *Seventeenth-Century France* (1966).
J. B. WOLF, *Louis XIV* (1968).

The Social Meaning of Newtonianism

MARGARET JACOB

The publication of *Principia Mathematica* (1687) by Isaac Newton marked the culminating point of the scientific revolution. Thereafter, Newton's theory of universal gravitation and his general understanding of the rational, mechanistic operation of physical nature became popularized throughout the learned circles of Europe and influenced many areas of intellectual life not directly related to physical nature. Important among these were religious life in an age when religious considerations were intimately related to thought about society.

In England another scientist, Robert Boyle, endowed a series of lectures in which the learning of science was to be employed to support natural religion, that is, the belief that truths of religion and by implication truths of morality may be learned from observing and investigating nature. A number of prominent English Newtonians, including Richard Bentley, Samuel Clarke, William Derham, John Harris, and William Whiston, delivered Boyle lectures during the late seventeenth and early eighteenth centuries. Their writings illustrate both the religious and social uses to which Newtonian physics were put in the years after the Glorious Revolution of 1688.

These particular Boyle lecturers were latitudinarians, or theological moderates, in the Church of England. On the one hand, they wished to fend off the atheistic materialism associated with Thomas Hobbes; on the other hand, they sought to resist any resurgence of religious enthusiasm associated with the unrest of the English Civil War. They contended that the proper understanding of the rational, orderly, machine-like world of Newton's physics should lead to the belief that God was also rational and should be worshiped in a reasonable manner. They also believed that Newtonian physics implied that society should be orderly, like physical nature. They urged wealthy persons to curb their pursuit of self-interest so that reckless selfishness might not lead to social and political turmoil. They also contended that contemplation of the orderliness of physical nature

Reprinted with the permission of Cornell University Press from *The Newtonians and the English Revolution, 1689–1720* by Margaret C. Jacob. Copyright © 1976 by Cornell University.

would lead one to see society as being naturally ordered into a clear social heirarchy against which it was wrong or sinful for human beings to protest. In this fashion, the Boyle lecturers felt they combined support for the virtue of a moderate pursuit of self-interest with strong support for the social and political status quo. Both lessons—the one directed to the rich, the other to the poor—found confirmation in their interpretation of the Newtonian world-view.

The lecture series endowed by Robert Boyle and administered in its early years by his close friends Evelyn and Tenison set the content and tone of English natural religion during the eighteenth century. By 1711 the reading of the Boyle lectures formed a part of an educated man's knowledge, and of all the lectures those by [Richard] Bentley (1692) and to a larger extent by [Samuel] Clarke (1704-05) and [William] Derham (1711-12) exercised the greatest influence throughout Europe. When d'Holbach attacked theism in 1770 he focused on the natural philosophy of the Boyle lectures, and when Rousseau expressed his sense of God's presence in nature he enlisted Clarke as his primary defense. Samuel Johnson learned much of what he knew about science from his reading of the Boyle lecturers.

The considerable reputation of these lectures in the eighteenth century is an indication of the moderate faction's service to the church. The lecturers were carefully chosen by the trustees, and they marshaled their arguments in defense of natural and revealed religion with the conviction that their efforts were critically important to the maintenance of the church's moral leadership and political influence in a society threatened at every turn by atheism. Both in retrospect and at the time, the most significant intellectual achievement of the Boyle lecturers in the period 1692-1714 was the integration of Newtonian natural philosophy as the new underpinning of liberal Protestant social ideology. This integration was mainly the work of Bentley and Clarke and to a lesser extent of John Harris, William Derham, and William Whiston....

Almost without exception the Newtonianism of this early period has been analyzed solely as an intellectual phenomenon, devoid of social and political content, transcendent of ideology. Within very recent historiography only Newton himself has fared slightly better as a social and political creature, subject to the concerns of his day and prepared to adjust his natural philosophy accordingly. The "ism" of his followers (with which he substantially concurred) and the sources of their opposition to the freethinkers emerge in recent writings, however, as solely religious or philosophical. These churchmen adopted Newton's natural philosophy, it is argued, because they feared the mechanical philosophy of Descartes and the support it would afford to atheists and materialists. But why did they fear atheism and more particularly materialism if based on Cartesianism? Was it only simple Christian piety that was at stake? Was Newtonianism simply another weapon in the war between orthodoxy and heterodoxy? That view renders religion as solely a matter of emotional conviction and spiritual experience devoid of social reality. Or we are told that Newtonianism reasserted the nominalist and voluntarist strain of Christian theology developed in the late thirteenth century and that consequently "it is unnecessary, and, indeed misleading to postulate the influence of social and political analogies—for the influence was, if anything, exerted in the opposite direction." It is extremely useful and important to recognize that the Newtonian natural philosophy belongs to a tradition of Christian thought, but it is a highly mechanical notion of intellectual change to assert that ideas are adopted simply because they are there to be adopted. Such an approach rests on the methodological assumption that the ideas of the Newtonians could and did exist independent of, or isolated from, a prevailing social, political, and economic environment....

The churchmen who forged Newtonianism spoke not only for themselves and the trustees of the Boyle lectureship, but also for the latitudinarian faction within the church. Since the early Restoration they had concerned themselves with finding a comprehensive and liberal Protestantism that could address the moral issues of their time. The threat to the church's political and religious power coming from the radicals had been checked at the Restoration, and gradually their political influence all but disappeared. Yet churchmen were not content. In the era prior to 1688–1689 they bemoaned the immorality of their age and sought to win their congregations to the pursuit of enlightened self-interest as sanctioned by providence and confirmed by the laws of nature.

Latitudinarian natural religion was a well-developed creed by the time of James II. Suddenly the church's interests were once again threatened —now by monarchy itself. Some low-churchmen turned to the prophecies for guidance and solace; most sat on the sidelines as a revolution engineered by gentlemen and princes salvaged the church's hegemony.

As a result of the Revolution, an event of dubious morality in the eyes of churchmen, the latitudinarians obtained control over the church, but their position within the political establishment was ambiguous. The church had gained security, but its political power and teaching authority rested on a precarious alliance with secular authority. At the Revolution government devised by contract and the necessities of self-interest had triumphed and the latitudinarians were caught in a dilemma. The Boyle lectures of the Newtonians accurately reflect their plight. The natural religion of their Restoration predecessors appeared to be the only solution. A liberal Christianity resting on the achievements of science, as obvious and unassailable as they seemed, would secure allegiance to religion against the claims made by the Hobbists and freethinkers. Loyalty to natural religion meant in the minds of low-churchmen loyalty to the church, and from that allegiance would emerge social and economic behavior governed by providence. Stability and prosperity would abound, and the millenarian dreams of the church would be accomplished.

For some of the Newtonians, such as Whiston, this meant the arrival of the literal "new heaven and new earth" proclaimed by Scripture. For others such as Clarke, the dream came to mean a stable and harmonious order governed by providence where the necessities of the marketplace presented no contradictions to the dictates of natural religion. The Newtonians used the science of their master to support their aims. Newton's natural philosophy served as an underpinning for the social ideology developed by the church after the Revolution....

After 1688–1689 the formulation of the moderate church's social ideology rested on a new conception of the role of religion within the civil polity. Religion now exists in order to ensure the smooth running of the well-ordered society. The virtues instilled by religion, [John] Harris claims, "do naturally and essentially conduce to the Well-being and Happiness of Mankind, to the mutual Support of Society and Commerce, and to the Ease, Peace, and Quiet of all Governments and Communities." Religion supplies the appropriate means to the ends of self-interest, and the ends are questionable only when the means employed in their attainment violate the norms of Christian ethics.

Bentley expresses this new conception of the place of religion in the state when, in the course of his attack on Hobbes, he asks his opponent: "Why, then, dost thou endeavour to undermine this foundation, to undo this *cement of society*, and to reduce all once again to thy imaginary state of nature and original confusion? No community ever was or can be maintained, but upon the basis of religion." As the social cement, religion binds in mutual attraction the various disparate forces that threaten the stability of society.

Resulting from the role now openly assigned to religion, the necessity arose to reorient church teachings toward the public sphere of human activity and away from the private matters of individual piety and worship of the creator. The practice of social virtue offers great reward to the individual, but more particularly, to society in general. Samuel Clarke admits to his listeners that this social reward is so obvious "that even the greatest enemies of all religion, who suppose it to be nothing more than a worldly or state-policy, do yet by that very supposition confess thus much concerning it."

In order to reorient the aims of religion away from "other-worldiness," private devotion, or communication with the creator, and toward the formulation of a "state-policy," or the exercise of public and social virtue, religious thinkers had to place the highest possible value on the result obtained by such a reorientation. At the beginning of his lectures, Bentley presents the values promised by the social function of religion: "Religion itself gives us the greatest delights and advantages even in this life also, though there should prove in the event to be no resurrection to another. *Her ways are ways of pleasantness and all her paths are peace."*

Churchmen offered peace as the goal obtained by society when religion served as its support. To make credible their offer they enlisted Christ as the final authority for their attitudes. They claimed that he "hath enjoined us a *reasonable service,* accommodated to the rational part of our nature. All his laws are in themselves, abstracted from any consideration of recompense, conducing to the temporal interest of them that observe them. For what can be more availing to a man's health, or his credit, or estate, or security in this world, than charity and meekness, than honesty and diligence in his calling." The sense of Bentley's statement is extremely important: Christ out of his own selflessness brought Christianity to men so they may ensure their temporal welfare by the pursuit of self-interest.

Religion condones and encourages a social and economic order based on the rights of private property and self-aggrandizement. It asks in return that men pursue their interests reasonably, that they observe the social virtues of justice and honesty. As Evelyn remarked in 1688, religious men do not abhor riches, they condemn only the *"vanity* of riches." Clarke agreed that only the ruiners and spoilers "suffer themselves to be swayed by unaccountable arbitrary humours, and rash passions, by lusts, vanity and pride, by private interest, or present sensual pleasure, these, setting up their own unreasonable self-will in opposition to the nature and reason of things." The worldly men are "attempting to destroy that order, by which the universe subsists."

Since churchmen were never very specific when they described the worldly minded, the historian can only be equally general in identifying those bugbears of the religious sensibility. The protest that began in the early 1690s against the moneyed classes became a flood of social criticism and satire in Augustan England. Much of this social criticism, especially by Tory wits such as Swift, Bolingbroke, and Gay, aimed at exposing the crude display of wealth and the vulgarity of manners typical of the new moneyed class. Its existence depended not on birth and often not even on the "laudable" acquisition accepted by Evelyn as a criterion for aristocratic stature. Rather, this new class assumed the social status of the lesser gentry and even the aristocracy largely because the great commercial and financial expansion of England after 1688 created a new social group based solely on its ability to invest wisely and to profit steadily. Their social mobility, coupled with a concomitant weakening of Restoration religious teachings and church influence, produced a new social order. Social and political power no longer followed necessarily from one's high status in church circles, and religious sentiment that justified worldly success no longer ensured it.

The crafty, ill-principled men threatened the order of society and the place of religion within that order. Often they benefited at the expense of virtuous men, and as Clarke lamented, they created a situation which would "not only hinder [the virtuous] from enjoying those public benefits, which would naturally and regularly be the consequence of their virtue, but oft-times bring upon them the greatest temporal calamities, even for the sake of that very virtue." Thus the delicate social order conceived by the Newtonians was continually jeopardized by the actions of irrational men bent on the ruthless pursuit of economic self-interest.

To ensure the order of society, religious men sought to create a model for its workings. They believed it necessary to expound this model publicly because the

> corruptness of the present estate which human nature is in, the generality of men must not by any means be left wholly to the workings of their own minds, to the use of their natural faculties, and to the bare convictions of their own reason; but must be particularly taught and instructed in their duty, must have the motives of it frequently and strongly pressed and inculcated upon them with great weight and authority, and must have many extraordinary assistances afforded them; to keep them effectually in the practice of the great and plainest duties of religion.

In an effort to correct the corruptness of men, to exhort them frequently and strongly "with great weight and authority," churchmen turned to the study of physical nature. Before discussing the important lessons they drew from nature and the application made of those lessons to society we must pause to consider the question of why so many churchmen in the late seventeenth and early eighteenth centuries turned to scientific study, an endeavor that contributed so decisively to the respectable development of modern science and technology.

A partial answer is provided for us by Samuel Clarke, probably one of the few churchmen in England who genuinely understood Newtonian physics and who, in turn, based his entire philosophical and ethical thinking on the physical concepts underlying Newton's scientific achievements. As has been argued, English religious thinkers in the late seventeenth century came to assign meaning to religion insofar as it served a social function. Religion performed the task of contributing order to society, of checking greed and avarice, or ensuring stability within the society it served to cement. Concomitant with the new emphasis placed on the social role of religion was the importance awarded to God's providence in the universe and in the affairs of men. God directs the operations of both realms; it is his "wisdom and justice and goodness in the disposition and government of the moral world, which necessarily depends on the connexion and issue of the whole scheme." Confidently, Clarke asserts that God's providence operates in both the world natural and the "world politick."

Yet Clarke reveals his concern, and a vexing and troubling one it must have been, that God's providential action in the "world politick" is hidden from us, that we see only dimly the effects of his providence in our affairs.

But in the natural order God is clear and distinct; he is as clear as the logic with which Clarke explicates his attributes and effects.

> It may here at first sight [Clarke writes] seem to be a very strange thing that through the system of nature in the material, in the inanimate, in the irrational part of the creation, every single thing should have in itself so many and so obvious, so evident and undeniable marks of the infinitely accurate skill and wisdom of their almighty creator, that from the brightest star in the firmament of heaven, to the meanest pebble upon the face of the earth, there is no one piece of matter which does not afford such instances of admirable artifice and exact proportion and contrivance, as exceeds all the wit of man (I do not say to imitate, but even) ever to be able fully to search out and comprehend; and yet, that in the management of the rational and moral world, for the sake of which all the rest was created, and is preserved only to be subservient to it, there should not in many ages be plain evidences enough, either of the wisdom, or of the justice and goodness of God, or of so much as the interposition of his divine Providence at all, to convince mankind clearly and generally of the world's being under his immediate care, inspection and government.

The evidence of God's efficacy in the moral and political order would be present only after "the period and accomplishment of certain great revolutions." That is, man's complete dependence upon God will become fully evident even to the most uninhibited atheist when the divine plan in history is fulfilled and the new heaven and the new earth are accomplished. Until such time, men must simply believe in God's providential action in the "world politick." But when men are searching to interpret the implications of the providential design for the nature of society, faith is simply not enough. If God's plan in the natural world can be understood, and nature does serve as a guide or model for the processes of the moral world, then in the study of physical nature may be found an alternative to the corruptness and wickedness of "this vicious age." By the late seventeenth century, science provided clearer evidence than did society for the efficacy of providence, and churchmen were drawn to the study of natural philosophy in increasingly large numbers.

As an alternative to "this vicious age," Clarke presents in the Boyle lectures the conclusions drawn from his study of nature. The physical principles and laws of motion that express that fiat of God and comprise the structure of the Newtonian natural philosophy served for Clarke to explicate the nature of the social order.

On the surface it might appear that concepts such as the void, absolute space and time, matter and motion, bear little relevance to a model of society desired by churchmen. Yet the very philosophy of nature that lay beneath Newton's mathematical and experimental endeavors, and was in turn adopted by his commentators, arose from an intellectual and social milieu that gave even notions about physical nature an ideological significance. The notion that matter is dead or lifeless received its most rigorous explication by the Cambridge Platonists, Henry More and Ralph Cudworth. They argued their case in the face of mid-[seventeenth] century materialists and atheists who asserted a life-principle in matter and thereby proposed the mortality of the soul. These ostensibly philosophical notions were integral to the radical social and political aims of certain sects such as the Levellers. Newton, of course, drew much of his natural philosophy from the Cambridge Platonists. I do not wish at this time to discuss the complexities of these political and ideological controversies of mid-century. It is necessary only to point out that even in its mid-century origin the natural philosophy of Newton and his commentators was never divorced from its social context.

The notion that matter is dead or lifeless, extended and impenetrable, is fundamental to the Newtonian natural philosophy. Whether in the form of a planet or in its elemental atomic state, matter is moved only by an outside, immaterial force. The source of motion is God. He is the origin and constant source of the motion present in the universe. Newton expresses his concept of matter most clearly in the thirty-first query to the *Opticks* (1717–1718): "The *Vis inertiae* is a passive Principle by which Bodies persist in their Motion or Rest, receive Motion in proportion to the Force impressing it, and resist as much as they are resisted. By this Principle alone there never could have been any Motion in the World."

The laws of motion, such as universal attraction, operate on matter at a distance. The void is essential to this operation. The space within which matter is attracted and moved is an entity unto itself; within that entity God's power in the universe operates. In effect, the law of universal attraction is the will of God expressed in the universe, and its "admirable order" manifests the providential will of an intelligent and all-powerful being.

After the Revolution, it supporters argued that this same providential will had brought about the events of 1688–1689. In keeping with this providentialist theology the Newtonian commentators emphasized God's role in the universe. At creation, God put the atoms of the universe into order; out of the primeval chaos God constituted the "present frame of things." This frame is maintained only because of God's constant intervention. "Consequently [Clarke tells us] there is no such thing as what men commonly call the course of nature, or the power of nature. The course of nature, truly and properly speaking, is nothing else but the will of God producing certain effects in a continued, regular, constant, and uniform manner; which course or manner of acting, being in every moment perfectly arbitrary, is as easy to be altered at any time as to be preserved." God as a pure, spiritual being, immense, omnipresent, full, and all-powerful, exercises complete authority over matter. He is the final source of all motion in the universe; and he may delegate this power to man.

In the Newtonian system, the power given to man to regulate, to move, or to change matter and ultimately the course of nature vindicates latitudinarian social teachings. Matter is "brute and stupid," and man has ultimate control, by virtue of his reason, over the things of the world, Bentley finds it absurd to imagine "that atoms can invent arts and sciences, can institute society and government, can make leagues, and confederacies, can devise methods of peace and stratagems of war" or could "transact all public and private affairs, by sea and by land, in houses of parliament, and closets of princes." The Newtonian definition of the relationship between man and matter gives a philosophical sanction to the pursuit of material ends, to using the things of this world to one's advantage, in effect, to bargain, to sell, to engage in worldly affairs with the knowledge that this activity is a God-given right. Man's power to acquire material possessions is an extension of his right to change the very course of nature, to control "brute and stupid" matter. But in his material dealings, man must instill an order similar to that imposed on nature by God. Just as God is continually promoting the universal benefit of the whole, men must also engage in universal benevolence. Man is "obliged to obey and submit to his superiors in all just and right things, for the preservation of society."

In the process of controlling matter, men are assigned certain stations. It is essential for the preservation of social order that the individual "attend the duties of that particular station or condition of life, whatsoever it be, wherein providence has at present placed him; with diligence, and contentment; without being either uneasy and discontented, that others are placed by providence in different and superior stations in the world; or so extremely and unreasonably solicitous to change his state for the future, as thereby to neglect his present duty." The social structure is sanctioned by God; it is singularly perverse to attempt its alteration.

Such an attempt was made during the Interregnum when "men of ambitious and turbulent spirits, that were dissatisfied and uneasy with privacy and retirement, were allowed by his [Epicurus'] own principles to engage in matters of state." Bentley refers to the divisive sectaries who, by their inroads into the power of the aristocracy, men of "privacy and retirement," and the court, undermined the political and social order. Bentley describes their actions as Epicurean and atheistical, attitudes that he discerns in post-1688 society.

Likewise, Samuel Clarke makes constant mention of the corruption and disorder infecting the world around him: "The condition of men in this present state is such, that the natural order of things in this world is in event manifestly perverted, and virtue and goodness are visibly prevented in great measure from obtaining their proper and due effects in establishing men's happiness proportionable to their behavior and practice." The pessimism produced by this insight into the worldly conduct of men who ignore God's providence and government of affairs leads Clarke, as it led other contemporary churchmen, to associate the perversion of social values with the decay of nature. The analogy is ever-present in his sermons:

> The sun's forsaking that equal course, which now by diffusing gentle warmth and light cherishes and invigorates everything in a due proportion through the whole system; and on the contrary, his burning up, by an irregular and disorderly motion, some of the orbs with insupportable heat, and leaving others to perish in extreme cold and darkness: what this, I say would be to the natural world; that very same thing, injustice and tyranny, iniquity and all wickedness, is to the moral and rational part of the creation.

Clarke believed that the decay of moral values and consequently of social stability prefigured the physical decay of nature. If the destruction of nature is to be prevented, then the decay of moral values must cease. The principles of order and reason demand assertion, and to do this, the order inherent in nature must be affirmed and applied to the moral and social order. Thus churchmen turned to the Newtonian system as the model inherent in nature and applied its principles to the society within which they lived.

Gravity, the universal and mutual attraction of all bodies in the universe, is the ordering principle of nature. It is the fiat of God operating as the laws of gravitation which instills order and harmony in the universe. Gravity acts on matter in a void, and because of this vacuum it is possible for the atoms to be moved into place, to be formed by gravity, into the matter and form of the universe. The power of mutual attraction is "a new and invincible argument for the being of God." It is the evidence of mutual attraction in the universe which gives final affirmation to God's providential activity in nature. Clarke bases his assertion of God's providence on this argument:

> that most universal principle of gravitation itself, the spring of almost all the great and regular inanimate motions in the world, answering... not at all to the surfaces of bodies (by which alone they can act one upon another), but entirely to their solid content, cannot possibly be the result of any motion originally impressed on matter, but must of necessity be caused (either immediately or mediately) by something which penetrates the very solid substances of all bodies, and continually puts forth in them a force or power entirely different from that by which matter acts on matter. Which is, by the way, an evident demonstration, not only of the world's being made originally by a supreme intelligent cause; but moreover that it depends every moment on some superior being, for the preservation of its frame.... Which preserving and governing power, whether it be immediately the power and action of the same supreme cause that created the world, of him "without whom not a sparrow falls to the ground, and with whom the very hairs of our head are all numbered"; or whether it be the action of some subordinate instruments

appointed by him to direct and preside respectively over certain parts thereof; does either way equally give us a very noble idea of providence.

The physical principles explained mathematically by Newton in the *Principia* offered to churchmen what appeared to them as undeniable proof of God's providence. The principle of universal gravitation presented a means whereby the decay of nature might be avoided; it became the basis of a system "for keeping the several Globes of the universe from shattering to Pieces." An alternative could be offered to Evelyn's fears that this world would go up "like a bomb" unless we accomplish the reformation. The Newtonian commentators were never simply intent on explicating a principle that would ensure the stability of the natural order. Their system only began with the physical principles explained in the *Principia*. They knew that ultimately events in the natural realm hinged directly upon events in the "world politick." Their aim was to construct both a physical and moral model, a social ideology grounded upon Newton's science, that would bring about the reformation.

Clarke makes manifestly clear the purpose of the system he constructs on the basis of the universal and mutual attraction of all bodies: "All inanimate and all irrational beings, by the necessity of their nature, constantly obey the laws of their creation; and tend regularly to the ends for which they were appointed. How monstrous then is it, that reasonable creatures, merely because they are not necessitated should abuse that glorious privilege of liberty, by which they are exalted in dignity above the rest of God's creation, to make themselves the alone unreasonable and disorderly part of the universe!"

The disobedience of rational creatures, endowed by God with the power of moving matter and thereby defining their freedom through action, has worked against God's will and thereby blurred our vision of God's providential action in the moral order. But with the pattern of God's providence and benevolence in the world natural revealed by a study of Newtonian physics, Clarke returns to the "world politick" and argues for the insertion of a comparable order based on the obedience of rational creatures to the providential will of God. The reasonableness of the natural world must be effected in the civil polity: "And the practice of universal justice, equity, and benevolence, is manifestly... as direct and adequate a means to promote the general welfare and happiness of men in society, as any physical motion or geometrical operation is to produce its natural effect."

With a puritanism common to moderate churchmen, the explicators of Newton catalogued the impiety and profanity of their age. The considered "what vast Loads of Filth, of all Kinds, are to be seen up and down in Heaps amongst us. Atheism and Deism, Scepticism and Infidelity, Immorality and Profaneness, often Contempt of God and all Religion; and prostituting of all things to private Profit and Advantage." This bleak characterization by

Harris aptly expresses sentiments common in church circles after the Revolution of 1688. The "possessive individualism" seen by modern historians in the writings of Locke and Hobbes had become a dominant aspect of social behavior in Augustan England. Yet in their criticism of this behavior, moderate churchmen did not simply condemn the pursuit of self-interest. In contrast to their high-church peers, the Newtonians offered justification for a certain style to be used in the pursuit of one's self-interest. They condemned only those who separate private interest from public interest, those who "find fault with each other's management, and, through self-conceit, bring in continual innovations and distractions." The disorderly pursuit of self-interest disturbed Newton's followers. In society men must assume a power and direction over matter similar to the power exercised by the divine fiat in nature. As the only other beings endowed with the power of moving matter, they must impose an order and pattern in the exercise of their prerogative.

Man must acquire in his conduct of worldly affairs the same overriding reason evident in God's operation of the physical universe. Just as God's absolute power is never arbitrary because of his eminent reason, the power of men over matter, their power to mold the inanimate to suit their needs, must be controlled by the cultivation of reason. The harmonious effects of God's reason are natural to the universe; the efficacy of reasonable men, "Truth Justice, and Benevolence, do naturally and essentially conduce to the Well-being and Happiness of Mankind, to the mutual Support of Society and Commerce, and to the Ease, Peace, and Quiet of all Governments and Communities."

In the arguments used by Newtonian commentators, a new definition of social virtue emerges. The right of the individual to pursue his self-interest is affirmed; the preservation of one's interests is analogous to the process of self-preservation inherent in the natural order. This process always works for the benefit of the whole; nature is integral and harmonious. Likewise, private interest must bend to public necessity. The obedience found in the inanimate order is a model upon which the dictates of self-interest must be tempered by the needs of society. The desire for power is natural, but its misuse is unnatural. Thus social virtue becomes "natural" to man, and antisocial behavior renders him aberrant or "unnatural." The Newtonian social ideology primarily deemed man's social sinfulness unnatural.

Man's power over matter places him in a relationship with society analogous to God's relationship with the universe. Just as the divine goodness regulates the course of nature and promotes the universal benefit of the whole, man must also engage in universal social benevolence. His power to regulate the course of things enables him to structure society such that its workings produce a universal harmony.

The desire for social harmony common to all the early commentators on Newton, and indeed to the entire moderate faction of the church, led them to subdue even religious emotion to the needs of the ordered society. Out of zeal for social harmony, Clarke argued that social virtue must arise from "a frequent and habitual contemplating [of] the infinitely excellent perfections of the all-mighty creator and the all-wise governor of the world." The study of the physical order leads to social virtue, and "a due subjecting [of] all our appetites and passions to the government of sober and modest reason [is] the directest means to obtain such settled peace and solid satisfaction of mind as is the first foundation and the principal and most necessary ingredient of all true happiness." Religious feeling finds its most socially useful expression through the systematic study or contemplation of nature. All other human emotion must similarly be controlled by reason. In the sober world of the Newtonian commentators, science and natural philosophy flourish along with piety and moderation, and the irrational in man is repressed to fit the needs of the harmonious society.

This system, wherein individual endeavor is socially directed and arises from an essentially religious motivation, and wherein human needs are met only when their satisfaction suits the needs of society, receives, its final sanction from a providential God. He presides over the modern world. His subjects do his work because it suits their self-interest; they subdue their power to the needs of the whole. Their reward consists in social harmony and in the knowledge that their behavior is "natural." Its significance is cosmic; when acting reasonably man complements the natural order. The resulting complacency is in turn augmented by a study of nature, or science, for it reassures men that the natural model remains intact....

Yet churchmen saw moral disorder and political confusion rife in their society. And because they believed in the analogy between the "world politick" and the world natural, they often feared that should disorder triumph in their world, then destruction became imminent in the natural order. The Newtonians primarily sought to present a vision of society that would nurture stability and harmony and would also guarantee a Christianized pursuit of the individual's power and duty in the social order. But to secure that vision the secular-minded who ruthlessly pursued power and preferment, and who would undermine the foundation of all government and authority, had to be stopped. By their denial of God's providence and their advocacy of Hobbist or Epicurean notions, the libertine and atheistical would constitute society on terms that excluded religion as a political or social force. They would undermine the position of the church. In so doing, they would set society on a course that could only lead to its destruction. The Newtonians never ceased to fear the designs of worldly men who, they imagined, would constitute society and government along purely secular lines.

What the moderate churchmen never realized was that their social teachings, based on the formidable order of the Newtonian universe, offered a powerful justification for the very order that disturbed them. For in the market society that flourished in eighteenth-century England under the sanction of God's providential design, even the "crafty, ill-principled" men eventually found a place, albeit unwittingly, in the new and grand design.

Bibliography

M. Boas, *The Scientific Renaissance, 1450–1630* (1962).
I. B. Cohen, *Revolution in Science* (1985).
E. J. Dijksterhuis, *The Mechanization of the World Picture* (1961).
C. C. Gillispie, *The Edge of Objectivity: An Essay in the History of Scientific Ideas* (1960).
A. R. Hall, *The Revolution in Science, 1500–1750* (1983).
M. Hunter, *Science and Society in Restoration England* (1981).
A. Koyré, *From the Closed World to the Infinite Universe* (1957).
B. J. Shapiro, *Probability and Certainty in Seventeenth-Century England: A Study of the Relationships between Natural Science, Religion, History, Law and Literature* (1983).
R. E. Schofield, *Mechanism and Materialism: British Natural Philosophy in an Age of Reason* (1970).
R. E. Sullivan, *John Toland and the Deist Controversy: A Study in Adaptations* (1982).
R. S. Westfall, *Never at Rest: A Biography of Isaac Newton* (1980).
R. S. Westfall, *Science and Religion in Seventeenth-Century England* (1958).

Denis Diderot (1713-1784), above, Jean d'Alembert (1717–1783), below, surrounded by the principal contributors to the Encyclopedia. *Giraudon/Art Resource, NY*

PART TWO

The Eighteenth Century

Life in Europe during the century or so prior to the outbreak of the French Revolution in 1789 is usually termed the Old Regime or the *ancien régime*. It seemed to some people who lived afterwards a time of calm before the tempestuous years of the revolution. However, during the eighteenth century European society was very lively indeed, and all was by no means stagnant or uneventful. The seeds of a new kind of society, intellectual life, and economy were being sown.

All European governments had to face very real problems relating to law and order. The vast majority of the population were peasants and lived on the land, where there were numerous peasants' riots and rebellions over disputes relating to traditional land rights, rents, and enclosures. Isabel de Madariaga describes the largest and most momentous of such uprisings, Pugachev's rebellion of peasants and Cossacks in the Russia of Catherine the Great. In the expanding cities, different problems of law and order arose. There the governing classes often resorted to very harsh penalties for criminal behavior. John McManners discusses the public execution in France as a ritual intended to deter crime and to achieve community assent to the governance of the existing elites.

The eighteenth-century European economy saw the foundation of the industrial revolution and the expansion of commerce. Jennifer Tann explores the difficulties confronted by the early manufacturers of steam engines in developing markets for their products. Robert Darnton looks at the economic side of the Enlightenment and the manner in which the great *Encyclopédie* was published and how its volumes, which were filled with ideas for religious, economic, and political reform, came to be sold throughout France.

One of the key features of the thought of the Enlightenment, as embodied in the *Encyclopédie* and in the writings of other *philosophes*, was harsh criticism of Christianity and of the established churches in Europe. Once the French Revolution began, few of its policies proved more controversial or divisive than its attack on the Church. Michael Kennedy discusses the impact of the *Civil Constitution of the Clergy* of 1790 and the resulting debates and divisions that laid the foundation for the attempt to dechristianize France during the reign of terror. Klaus Epstein, in turn, explores how the Enlightenment and the revolutionary attack on religion generated the emergence of conservative political and social outlooks in Germany. Indeed, the emergence of conservatism in Europe can be seen as the result of a whole century of new transforming social and political pressures that made the governing classes eventually realize that theirs was a position that required fresh arguments of self-justification.

The Revolt of the Cossacks and the Peasant War in Russia

ISABEL DE MADARIAGA

Prior to the Revolution of 1917, the most serious challenge to the Russian state was the eighteenth-century revolt of the Cossacks and peasants led by Emelyan Pugachev between 1773 and 1775. Like so many revolts, riots, and local disturbances throughout eighteenth-century Europe, this one involved attempts to restore traditional privileges and social customs that were being lost through the modernizing and rationalizing policies of a strong central monarchy. Pugachev gathered around himself a variety of discontented people. Militarily the most important were Cossacks, generally horse-mounted soldiers outside the regular army who, in exchange for certain privileges, defended certain frontiers of the Russian Empire. They wished to return to a less disciplined way of life and to regain easier access to land. Peasants also rallied in large numbers to Pugachev in search of wider personal freedom, more land, and relief from the burdens of their landlords. In addition there were "Old Believers" who resented the changes made over a century earlier in the practices of the Russian Church, and serfs who worked in the metal foundries established during and after the reign of Peter the Great.

All of these groups looked for the appearance of a "true tzar" whom they believed would generously address their particular grievances. They became easily convinced that the German-born Empress Catherine, who had come to the Russian throne in 1762 after the murder of her husband Peter III, was not such a ruler. Pugachev proclaimed himself to be the "true tzar" for whom so many illiterate Cossacks and peasants yearned. But why did so many of them follow this most unlikely of would-be rulers? That question cannot be fully answered. Certainly in part people accepted him as the "true tzar" because in his own crude manner he fulfilled their expectations. He adopted what he believed to be the appearance of a tzar, established a court, and issued proclamations directed toward their concerns. In

---

Reprinted with the permisson of Yale University Press from *Russia in the Age of Catherine the Great* by Isabel de Madariaga. Copyright © 1981 by Isabel de Madariaga.

this manner the leader of the revolt and his chief supporters adopted the outward appearances of legitimate political authority. They acted the role they were expected to play. Moreover, Pugachev enjoyed initial military success that further confirmed his claims.

During the early stages of the revolt, Catherine could not use her regular army because she was still involved in war against the Porte or Turkish Empire. After victoriously concluding that conflict, she loosed the army against the Cossacks and peasants. Pugachev was eventually defeated, but not until after several weeks of intense, vicious social war. For Catherine and the government, it was important not only to defeat Pugachev, but also to demonstrate that the forces of official authority were stronger than those of the illicit counter-authority raised by a false Cossack tzar.

The great revolt of 1773–5 must be seen against the background of the increasing tension in the Cossack Hosts, as the 'regulating' power of the Russian state was inexorably extended over them. It was triggered off by the emergence of a potential leader, the Don Cossack deserter, Emelyan Pugachev, after five years of war, plague, rising prices and increasingly heavy service burdens and recruit levies. The substance of much Cossack discontent had already emerged from the instructions and the speeches of their deputies in the Legislative Commission, as well as from the constant unrest of the late 1760s and the 1770s. All the Hosts suffered from friction between the upper ranks in the hierarchy and the rank and file, between rich and poor, between those who could buy themselves out of service and those who had to serve, and from the exactions of the Russian government and the individual ambitions of Cossack leaders. In 1768, as a result of a mutiny among the Zaporozhian Cossacks, their leader, Peter Kalnyshevsky, called on Russian troops to defend the starshina [chief Cossack officers]. Soon he was himself threatening to seek the protection of the Porte [Turkish government] if the grievances of the Host were not remedied by the Russian government.

On the Don, the ambitions of ataman [Cossack headman] Yefremov kept the Host in a turmoil. He had participated in Catherine's *coup d' état* and been amply rewarded. But since the outbreak of war he had been intriguing with the Kubán Tartars in the Ottoman Empire, and seeking to increase his own authority in the Host at the expense of that of the government. When the authorities attempted to arrest him in November 1772, the Cossacks rioted and killed several regular officers. Yefremov was eventually arrested and tried for treasonable relations with the Kubán Tartars. He was sentenced to exile in Livonia, while peace was restored in the Host.

More serious ultimately were the disturbances in the Yaik Host, where the tensions between the starshina and the rank and file split the community into two factions, the 'obedient' and the 'disobedient'. In 1769 several hundred of the latter mutinied, refusing to serve in a distant outpost. Government troops under General Traubenberg crushed the mutiny, handing down the usual harsh sentences. When a deputation to St Petersburg got nowhere with an appeal against the sentences, fresh disturbances broke out in January 1773, in which Traubenberg was killed. More troops were sent under General Freyman to restore order. Arriving in June 1773, Freyman reorganized the administration of the Host, strengthening government control over appointments, and set up a special commission to try the ringleaders of the 1773 revolt. Again there were many condemnations to the knut [a form of whipping], hard labour, etc., and the 2,461 ordinary Cossacks implicated in the revolt were ordered to pay a collective fine of 20,000 rubles. The sentences were carried out in Yaitsk itself, in July 1773. As a result, the Host was like a powder keg, needing only a spark to set it ablaze.

In such a situation rumours that another tsar was alive who might give legitimacy to the claims of the discontented were bound to fall on fertile soil. Throughout the seventeenth and eighteenth centuries Russians had pinned their hopes of escape from oppression on the existence somewhere of a true tsar deprived of his throne by the machinations of the boyars [nobles]. The instability of the succession in the eighteenth century led to the emergence of a number of pretenders claiming to be Peter II (1727–30), or the young Ivan VI, or even Aleksey Petrovich, the son of Peter the Great. How far did these pretenders believe that they were who they claimed to be? How far did their followers believe in them? It seems probable that they all lived in a world of simultaneous belief and disbelief—believing in order to justify themselves, in order not to sin against the divinely appointed tsar from whom alone an improvement in their lot could be expected; and disbelieving the moment they came up against the harsh reality of arrest and brutal punishment. Rarely did the common people ask for any proof of the identity of a pretender, beyond inspecting him to see if his body bore the 'marks of tsardom'. The fact that rumours always centred around those who had never reigned or reigned only briefly, or who had died young, who were thus unknown and mysterious and full of promise of better times, places the whole phenomenon of 'pretenderism' in the world of folklore, myth, ballad and heroic poetry, in which the imagination of the humiliated and oppressed has ever found refuge. It is worth noting that no one ever claimed to be Peter the Great, or that he was not dead.

Peter III's short reign made him an obvious candidate for 'pretenderism' and rumours that he was still alive had spread in St Petersburg almost immediately after his death. In 1763 a soldier was denounced for declaring that he was alive; when asked how he knew, he replied: 'Don't you know that the Bishop of Rostov [Arseniy Matseyevich] has been defrocked because he falsely buried Peter III?'—a classical example of the way political events are turned into myths. In the same year a rumour was current in Orenburg that Peter III had taken refuge with the Yaik Cossack Host. Other pretenders came and went (ten all told between 1764 and 1772) of whom F. I. Bogomolov, a fugitive serf, was probably the most important in crystallizing Cossack hopes. With Cossack support he had put himself forward in March 1772 as 'Peter III'. He was arrested in December, and died on the way to Siberia. But rumours about him spread so widely that the government ordered special publicity to be given in the Don Cossack Host and on the Volga to the arrest and punishment of a so-called tsar. As a result belief in the survival of Peter III became even more widespread among the Cossacks.

Only a few weeks after the carrying out of the sentences on the Yaik Cossacks in July 1773, a new and more formidable 'Peter III' appeared on the scene. Emelyan Pugachev was born around 1742 in a rank and file Don Cossack family. He served in the Seven Years' War, and again in the war against the Porte in 1768, in which he earned promotion to the rank of *khorunzhiy*, the lowest Cossack officer rank. In 1771 he deserted, wandering south to Taganrog, where he had relatives, then to the Cossack community on the Terek river. After further peregrinations from Old Believer settlement to Old Believer settlement, he took advantage of one of the many amnesties proclaimed by the Russian government for returning fugitives and reappeared in the Don Host, ostensibly as a native of Poland. Given a passport in August 1772, he started again on his wanderings, staying with Old Believers, and frequently posing as a wealthy merchant. In November he turned up in Yaitsk, and was again lodged by an Old Believer. It was only five months since the mutiny in the Host; the sentences were still to come.

At this stage, Pugachev put himself forward as a wealthy merchant, 'with more than 200,000 rubles abroad, let alone merchandise to the tune of 70,000 rubles'. He offered to lead the discontented Cossacks out of Russia to the Kubán in the Crimean khanate [area of the Tartars]; he would give twelve rubles to any Cossack who would follow him, and assured his hearers that the 'Turkish pasha' would welcome them. For the first time here, in Yaitsk, Pugachev claimed to be Peter III. The circumstances in which he did so remained mysterious in view of the conflicting evidence given later by Pugachev himself and his partisans, anxious to disculpate themselves. According to Pugachev's account he told his host that he was the Emperor Peter III, who had been miraculously saved from death and had afterwards wandered in Egypt, Constantinople and Poland.

There is no doubt that Pugachev found the mood among the Yaik Cossacks encouraging. What remains uncertain is what he himself was planning at that stage to do. Undoubtedly he had long lived in a world of fantasy. While still in the army, he had bragged that his 'trusty' sword had been given to him by his 'godfather Peter the Great'. The report of the claim of Bogomolov to be Peter III and of his arrest may have given him precisely the stimulus he needed to pretend that he himself was the tsar. On the other hand the idea may have emerged first among the Yaik Cossacks and been suggested to him. The assumption that Pugachev invented the idea himself is popular in Soviet historiography, since it strengthens one of its fundamental assumptions, namely that Pugachev was consciously planning a nation-wide revolt against serfdom, and decided to assume the character of Peter III as a vital strategic move in his campaign. The evidence for such a far-reaching plan is however somewhat slender. The accounts of his followers speak of Pugachev as planning to lead them over the border into Turkey. They too may have been falsifying their evidence in order to minimize their guilt in the eyes of the Russian government. Yet departure into other lands was more consonant with Cossack tradition than a frontal assault on the Russian state. Pugachev's words show him to be essentially concerned with the crisis in the Cossack way of life caused by the pressure of the Russian state, not with the woes of the peasantry as a whole.

Pugachev stayed only a week on this, his first visit to the Yaik Host, and returning to the Don, he was soon afterwards arrested as a deserter. He was taken to Kazán early in January 1773, and admitted under interrogation that he had urged the Yaik Cossacks to flight, but made no mention of his claim to be Peter III. He succeeded in escaping in May 1773, and was on the run again until August 1773, when he reappeared once more in Yaitsk. Here, in the bath, Pugachev showed his hosts the 'marks of tsardom', in this case the scars of scrofula on his chest—a curious inversion of the traditional attributes of the divinely appointed king. From now on, the report that the merchant Pugachev was in reality Peter III began to be widely believed in the Host, which, it will be remembered, was still smarting under the sentences inflicted on the mutineers in July 1773. Visiting Cossacks explained their grievances to 'Peter III'; Russian officials wanted to introduce new 'establishments', new formations, while the Cossacks wanted to serve as of old, as 'in the days of Peter I and according to their charters'. Together with a small group of bold spirits among the Cossacks, and a few Tartars, Pugachev now devised the programme by means of which he would secure recognition as Peter III by the Yaik Host. He promised to guarantee the old, free way of life, which could be summed up as free access to the fisheries of the Yaik, free use of land and appurtenances, tax-free access to pasturage, free salt, and to each Cossack twelve rubles per annum, and twelve 'chetverti' of corn.

These particular Cossacks were fully aware that Peter III was in fact the runaway Don Cossack, Pugachev. They must be regarded as leading spirits in planning the revolt, aware of the necessity, if it was to spread, of assuming the mantle of legitimacy. Indeed, in the existing state of seething discontent they clearly welcomed the arrival of a resolute man, prepared to take over the role. The circle in the secret of Pugachev's true identity grew larger, comprising both Cossacks with simple Cossack aims, and such figures as the fugitive ex-leader of the Yaik 'disobedient' faction, I. Ul'yanov, who hoped that Pugachev would 'seize the state' and that he, Ul'yanov, 'would become a great man'. It may also be true that Pugachev's claim to be tsar was the more easily accepted precisely because he was a simple Cossack—an easily identifiable father of his people, not a man separated from his followers by an unbridgeable cultural gulf. Hence the mixture of familiarity and respect with which he was treated may not have been part of a plot, but a genuine effort to live in the real and the false worlds at one and the same time.

The actual rising was planned for the opening of the winter fishing season. Meanwhile Pugachev's supporters found him suitable raiment—a crimson kaftan and a velvet cap—and a secretary, Ivan Pochitalin, since he was illiterate. But outside events precipitated matters. The commandant of Yaitsk heard rumours of the presence of a pretender, and sent out patrols to arrest him. The conspirators decided to act at once. Pugachev's first manifesto was hastily drafted, and on the morning of 17 September 1773 it was read out at the *khutor* [farmstead] of a wealthy Cossack family a hundred versts (1 verst = .66 mile] from Yaitsk, to some 60–100 assembled Cossacks who were joined by a number of Kalmucks and Tartars. In the name of 'amparator Petr Fadaravich', Pugachev's subjects were forgiven all previous crimes towards him, and the Cossack programme was put before them, namely 'the freedom of the rivers from their sources to their mouths, and the land and the growth thereon and payment in money, and lead and powder and supplies of corn'.

Pugachev moved at once on Yaitsk, [see Figure 1] and by the next day, when he stopped before the fort, his forces numbered 300. They carried the Cossack standards of the revolt of 1772 aloft on pikes, with the Old Believer Cross sewn on to them. The commandant in Yaitsk had over a thousand troops but he knew that he could not rely on the Cossacks, many of whom went over at once to Pugachev. Others were seized and hanged by the rebels as an example. But a rebel assault on the fort was beaten off on 19 September, and Pugachev realized that he could not stand up to the gunfire of regular troops. He moved away along the river Yaik, mopping up the smaller forts as he went. Everywhere the Cossacks and the soldiers went over to the rebels or were shot. Cossack and army officers as well as some priests were hanged. One Cossack officer who went over to Pugachev was the ex-deputy to the Legislative Commission, T. Padurov.

The choice of the next target reflects the essentially Cossack priorities of the rebel movement at this stage. Pugachev could have turned towards the Samara line and the interior. He chose instead to advance on Orenburg, the military administrative centre which had dominated the Yaik since its foundation in 1735. He arrived before the city on 5 October 1773 with over 3,000 men and 20–30 guns but was not strong enough to take it by storm. He settled down therefore to besiege Orenburg, making his headquarters in Berda, some 5 versts away.

Meanwhile news of the appearance of a new 'Peter III' on the Yaik at last reached St Petersburg on 15 October 1773. It seemed from a distance to

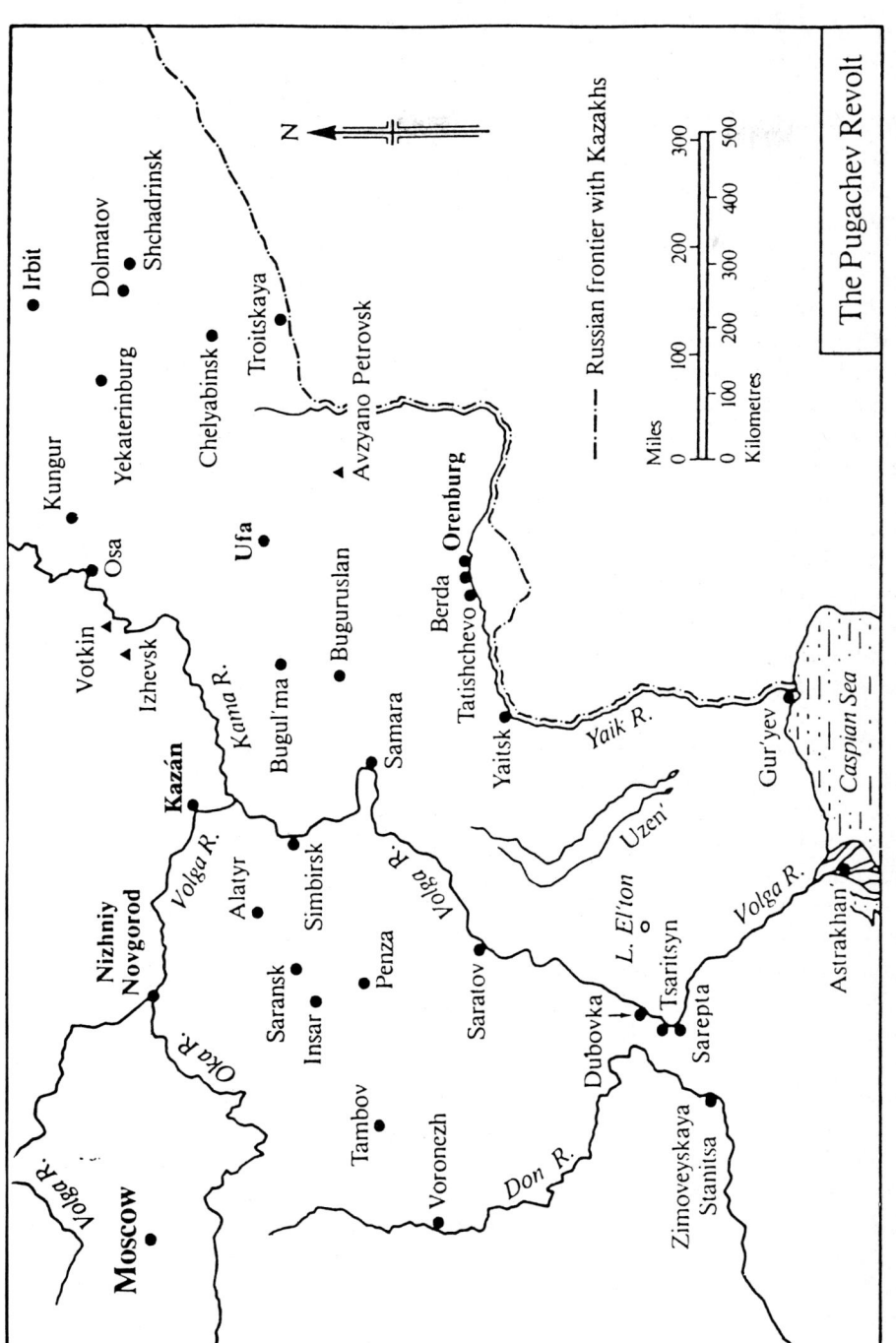

Figure 1. The Pugachev Revolt.

be but a minor, local affray, a continuation of the rebellion of 1772. The government was well aware that the guberniya of Orenburg, which comprised most of Bashkiria, was thinly settled and lightly garrisoned. In the vast neighbouring guberniya of Kazán, there were only eighty permanent officials for two and a half million inhabitants. But Catherine was straining every nerve to mount a fresh offensive against the Turks, and seasoned troops could not be spared. Hence a small punitive expedition was dispatched under General Kar, from Kazán, together with two other detachments from Simbirsk and Siberia. But Kar's force was defeated early in November, and he himself departed for the capital to report. A week later Pugachev's forces defeated the government detachment coming from Simbirsk (and hanged the colonel). Flushed with victory, indeed, drunk with it in the strict sense of the word, Pugachev allowed the third column with 2,400 men and 22 guns to slip into Orenburg, thus enabling its resolute governor, Reinsdorp, to concentrate on sitting out a siege which was to last six months. In Yaitsk too the commandant shut himself up in the citadel and prepared to defend it, leaving the rest of the town to the rebels.

The defeat of the imperial punitive expeditions opened the way for the extension of the revolt into Bashkiria, where Zarubin Chika, one of Pugachev's ablest lieutenants, laid siege to Ufa at the end of November, while another of his followers, Ilya Arapov, briefly occupied Samara (where he was greeted with church bells and prayers were said for Peter III) at the end of December 1773.

Meanwhile the very success of the initial revolt gave rise to problems of organization and supply which could no longer be dealt with by the small group of intimates who had provided the leadership in the first phase of the rising. Hence, on 6 November 1773, in Pugachev's headquarters in Berda, the main governmental organ of the rebels was founded: the 'College of War'. Its name was borrowed from the existing central governmental institution because the College of War was the body most familiar to the Cossacks. Moreover the establishment of such a body strengthened the illusion of a revolt led by the tsar, who was at the same time able to erect a barrier between himself and his followers—necessary for the effective organization of the revolt, but tending to reduce the element of egalitarianism which had characterized its earlier stages.

The principal official or *sud*, 'judge', of the College in accordance with normal Russian terminology, was a prosperous member of the Yaik starshina, Andrey Vitoshnov. Ivan Pochitalin, who had drafted Pugachev's manifestos, was appointed *dumnyy d'yak* (*duma* clerk or clerk of the council), reviving a Muscovite title which had lapsed since the reforms of Peter the Great. The rebel College of War also recruited a number of literate clerks and one of the few hereditary nobles to go over to the rebels, M. A. Shvanvich, conducted its correspondence in German and French. Two leading Tartars, Idyr Baymekov, and his son Baltay, conducted the correspondence and wrote manifestos in 'Arabic, Persian, Turkic and

Tartar'. The functions of the College were both civil and military: it dealt with the reception of the volunteers who flocked to join Pugachev, usually armed only with farming tools or pikes, and with their organization into military formations based on the Cossack model. Once a volunteer was accepted into the force he was recognized as a Cossack to distinguish him from the 'soldiers' who fought for Catherine. From the moment that Pugachev settled down in his headquarters at Berda, outside Orenburg, the rebel movement was faced with the problem of recruitment. Sizable bodies of rebels came to operate at some distance from Berda, around Ufa, and as far as Yekaterinburg and Chelyabinsk. The need to extend the area of operations, or to prepare for defence against government troops, soon led the rebel leaders to borrow a weapon from the tsarist armoury, namely conscription. Orders were issued to the local population to produce recruits at the rate of 'one man for three households' or even 'one man per household'. In January 1774 a rebel ukaz ordered 'to take people into the service of the Lord Peter Fyodorovich against their will, and destroy those who refuse and take away their property'. Taking the oath to 'Peter III' served as a formal declaration of allegiance, and all who came before the pretender or were captured were thus forced to declare themselves. There was scant choice, since the penalty was immediate and usually painful death for those who refused.

The rebel College of War also had to cope with the problems of supply of munitions, food and forage. This brought it into relationship with the civil population in areas controlled by Pugachev's forces, or where his adherents had killed their previous officials and elected new ones. In the first flush of the revolt some local landowners, their wives, children and household serfs, as well as local officials, church servants, etc., had been killed, often with terrifying barbarity. The rebel College of War attempted to exercise some control in this field by 'ukazy' which reserved judgment to headquarters. It was also the final instance in the quarrels which inevitably broke out between Cossacks and Bashkirs on the one hand, and the civil population on the other.

'Tsarist illusions' were maintained in the rebel camp by a device which illustrates the psychological tensions within the leadership. Pugachev set up his own court, also modelled on that of Catherine. A number of his closest collaborators adopted the names and titles of magnates at Catherine's court. M. Shigayev, one of the original group, who acted as treasurer for the copper money (Pugachev kept the silver himself) and *de facto* as Pugachev's deputy, called himself Count Vorontsov. Ovchinikov, one of the most outstanding and faithful military leaders, called himself Count Panin, another leader became Count Orlov, and Zarubin Chika, the boldest of them all, called himself Field-Marshal Count Chernyshev, after the vice-president of the College of War in St Petersburg. In February 1774 Pugachev, who had abandoned his wife and children on the Don, 'married' the daughter of a Yaik Cossack, Yustina Kuznetsova. She was treated as

'Her Imperial Majesty' and Cossack women were appointed her Maids of Honour (*freyliny*). However, Pugachev's marriage weakened his position. All knew that 'Peter III' had a wife, Catherine, who had seized his throne. It was to win this throne from his usurping wife that the common people had joined his force. Moreover a real tsar would not marry the daughter of a common Cossack. Selfish personal motives tore through the veil of illusion.

Again in the interests of authenticity, but reflecting the only conception of the legitimate source of power which the Cossack world could grasp, 'Peter III' issued 'ukazy' [proclamations], drafted as far as possible in Russian eighteenth-century officialese. Some were even printed, since only printed ukazy were legal in Russia, and sealed with a variety of seals. Among the most picturesque is one Pugachev used in August 1774, which bears the inscription 'Peter III by the grace of God emperor of the "corown" (*karuna*)', surrounding the portrait of a man in a wig, with a moustache, and dressed in armour, with the broad ribbon of an order across his breast—resembling if anything an imaginary portrait of Peter the Great Other leaders used seals with the arms of noble families, of factories, even of a distillery.

It is very difficult to assess what degree of authority Pugachev himself exercised in the inner circle of those who knew his real identity. In public he was treated with deference. In private the leaders sat and feasted together. Those who had risen to the top at first tried to prevent others from approaching Pugachev and acquiring influence with him. 'My street is but narrow,' he exclaimed one day to a boon companion. He was not always able to save those he wished to save, and frequently found himself faced with *faits accomplis*. Though the leaders may have hoped to introduce some discipline in the rebel camp, it remained, according to contemporaries, a dissolute rabble. Prayers were said daily for the emperor, 'Peter III' and for his wife, Catherine, until Pugachev married Yustina. But the camp was full of the wives and daughters of officers, who had been captured and distributed as booty among the rebels; executions took place at any moment, the surrounding ravines were full of unburied corpses, drunken feasting was common.

From the very beginning of the rising, in September 1773, Pugachev had directed his appeals to the non-Russian peoples of the vast area between the Volga, the Yaik, and Western Siberia. Among his very first supporters in September 1773, there were 20 Tartars and 20 Kalmucks out of a total of 80 men, and his first manifesto was specifically directed also to them. It included an amnesty for all those who had fought long and hard against the Russian state in the Bashkir wars of the 1740s. A number of manifestos were issued in October 1773, promising the Bashkirs their traditional way of life: the freedom of lands, water and woods, their faith and their laws, food, clothing, salaries, powder and shot, and also their 'bodies', presumably a promise not to enslave them, and the right to 'be like wild animals of the steppe', or to a free nomadic life. But in contrast with the appeals directed to his Russian followers, Pugachev's manifestos were addressed not to the underdogs of Bashkiria, urging them to rise against their chiefs, but to the Bashkir tribal leaders, urging them to throw off the oppression of the Russian state.

By October 1773, Pugachev had been joined by at least a thousand Bashkirs under the leadership of Kinzya Arslanov who was to be with him to the very end. Almost at once the Bashkirs turned on one of the most hated signs of the Russian presence in their land: the foundries. By the end of the year some 44 foundries and mines were in rebel hands, providing Pugachev with substantial supplies of guns, ammunition and the possibility of making more. The industrial enterprises did not however always go over at once to the rebels. Pugachev's manifestos had not specifically referred to the problems of the assigned peasants or the factory serfs. The assigned peasants were sometimes used by the rebels to keep the industries working. The industrial serfs, who had become more closely identified with factory life, sometimes defended their enterprise against Bashkir efforts to destroy it.

By the beginning of January 1774, a mixed force of some 2,000 Tartars, factory-serfs, farmer soldiers, and assigned peasants, commanded by the young Bashkir leader, Salavat Yulyayev, and I. Kuznetsov, launched an attack on the copper foundries of the Urals. Kungur and Yekaterinburg defended themselves, but Chelyabinsk was briefly occupied. The rebels then moved on the great Dalmatov monastery, which had had a very bad reputation in the days when the Church owned serfs. The monastery was surrounded by high walls, and possessed sixteen guns of various calibres; the defence consisted of monks and church officials and unreliable peasants. But the monastery was relieved on 14 March by government forces which defeated the rebel army in the neighbourhood.

Government forces were indeed at last on the move. The news of the defeat of Kar's detachment in October 1773, coupled with the reports from the governor of Orenburg, aroused Catherine in November to the seriousness of the situation. On 29 November 1773, General A. I. Bibikov, the ex-marshal of the Legislative Commission, was appointed to put down the rising, with full powers over military, civil and ecclesiastical authorities, 'on the basis of existing military and civil laws'. Bibikov was also to set up a commission of inquiry into the origins and the course of the revolt, which eventually became known as the Kazán Secret Commission.

Making Kazán his headquarters, Bibikov, who arrived on 26 December, took immediate steps to re-assert the government's authority and to restore morale. The nobles were persuaded to form a number of volunteer corps, arming their own peasants. The empress followed suit, and as a 'landowner of Kazán', she ordered a levy to be made among court peasants and sent officers to command them. The Church hierarchy took an active part in distributing government manifestos and exposing the imposture of Pugachev. By the end of January the major part of the troops which had been placed at Bibikov's disposal had arrived, and various detachments were sent out to clear the rebel bands operating between Kazán and Ufa.

Meanwhile Ufa had been loosely under siege since mid-November 1773. Almost the whole of the non-Russian population of the province took part in the rising, but the voyevoda and the civil population as well as the commander of the regular forces kept their nerve and proceeded to organize an effective defence. On 24 January 1774 a strong attack was mounted by Zarubin Chika with 12,000 men, but it was beaten off. The rebels now settled down to a blockade, and during February and March 1774 military operations languished, while Zarubin Chika conducted frequent negotiations for a surrender with the defenders of Ufa. Meanwhile government troops were advancing under Lieutenant-Colonel Mikhel'son, a veteran of the Seven Years' War, and quarrels broke out within the rebel leadership. On 23–4 March Zarubin Chika, with between seven and ten thousand men, was defeated in a fierce battle with Mikhel'son's professional soldiers. The siege of Ufa was lifted; Zarubin and Ul'yanov were seized by Cossacks and handed over to Mikhel'son.

There still remained Orenburg, under siege for nearly six months, and the commandant of Yaitsk was still shut up in its citadel. In both places the shortage of food, fodder and fuel was acute throughout the winter months. To relieve them both, large forces were being concentrated in the area of Buguruslan and Bugulma, under the overall command of General P. M. Golitsyn, for a drive against Pugachev himself. The rebel leader decided to make a stand at Tatishchevo, which commanded the junction of the roads to Orenburg and to Yaitsk, and brought up some 9,000 men and 36 guns. Golitsyn had 6,500 soliders and 22–25 guns. The decisive battle took place on 22 March, and after a fierce artillery duel Golitsyn's regulars broke the rebels' resistance. Once again, rebel forces had proved unable to stand up to smaller units of trained soldiers, but there were heavy casualties on both sides: Golitsyn lost 140 killed and over 500 wounded; the rebels 1,315 killed, a further 1,180 cut down in the pursuit, and nearly 4,000 prisoners. Pugachev and a few other leaders galloped off to Berda.

The defeat at Tatishchevo precipitated a crisis among the rebels. The hard core of the Yaik Cossacks—the force closest to Pugachev—replaced the peasants and soldiers on guard duty at Berda. At the same time some of them began to load up their belongings on transports, arousing the suspicions of the non-Cossack masses. With government forces approaching, it was clear that only those owning horses would be able to get away. The peasants would have to be left to look after themselves. But in abandoning the poorly armed *muzhiki* [peasants] to their fate, the Cossacks were consciously or unconsciously revealing the fundamental contempt of the warrior for the tillers of the soil: 'for the common people are not fighters, the common people are just sheep.' At the same time many of the Cossacks began to think of saving their own skins. A plot to seize Pugachev and surrender him was foiled just in time. Tension within Berda grew worse, and on 23 March Pugachev abandoned his headquarters with 2,000 men and 10 guns. On the same day Golitsyn's advance guard entered Berda, which broke up in an orgy of looting, drunkenness and panic. Remnants of Pugachev's escaping force were hunted down and captured, including most of the leaders of the 'College of War', and the secretary, Pochitalin. The siege of Orenburg was over. On 16 April, the garrison of Yaitsk, almost starving by now, was relieved, and a fortnight later, the fort of Gur'yev, at the mouth of the Yaik on the Caspian Sea, was cleared of rebels. The architect of victory did not live to consolidate it. Bibikov, who had directed the troop movements, fell ill of a fever, and died on 7 April, to Catherine's great distress. His military command devolved upon Lieutenant-General Prince F. F. Shcherbatov.

The Secret Commission set up by Bibikov in Kazán had meanwhile been pursuing its investigation into the origins of the revolt: how Pugachev came to call himself 'Peter III'. Was there any foreign influence at work, French or Turkish? What was the extent of participation by disgruntled nobles and Old Believers? The Secret Commission, or Bibikov alone, was empowered to pass and execute death sentences, though in the case of nobles and officials it was normal to refer them to the empress for confirmation. In the first weeks of its activities, the Kazán Secret Commission was sparing in its use of the death penalty. One serf was hanged for murdering his mistress, and a few Tartar soldiers were hanged for taking part in the revolt. Others were sentenced to the usual variety of corporal punishments, many of those only marginally involved were released after renewing their oath of allegiance to the empress. The Secret Commission undoubtedly used the classic method of extorting confessions, namely the knut, in spite of Catherine's efforts to reduce the use of torture. 'I don't doubt you will keep to my rules,' wrote Catherine to Bibikov, on 15 January 1774, 'though at times severity will be necessary.' 'Please order the Secret Commission to be cautious in deciding what punishments to inflict: in my opinion soldiers X and Y were flogged though innocent. Also what need is there to flog during investigations? For twelve years the Secret Expedition under my own eyes has not flogged a single person under interrogation, and every single affair has been properly sorted out, and even more came out than we needed to know,' she wrote again on 15 March. But Catherine confirmed the death sentences, particularly on officers who had failed in their duty, though she left the actual execution to Bibikov's discretion, and some of them got off with running the gauntlet (usually up to six times, in Catherine's reign), and garrison service as a private.

As the government forces defeated the various rebel bands the number of prisoners increased so much that Kazán could no longer hold them. In many cases officers commanding the relieving forces meted out punishment on the spot, sending only the ringleaders to Kazán, and granting certificates of pardon to the rest. With the death of Bibikov, the Secret Commission found itself without a master, with 169 prisoners in Kazán, over 4,000 in

Orenburg, and many others in different centres. In the belief that the back of the revolt was broken, Catherine on 16 April 1774 appointed General F. F. Shcherbatov to take over from Bibikov, but without his wide powers, and confirmed the arrangment the latter had already made to set up a branch of the Secret Commission in Orenburg. Both Secret Commissions were placed for the time being under the authority of the respective local governors.

But the government had rested too quickly on its laurels: Pugachev was still at large. Abandoning all hope of making for the Kubán, or even Persia, Pugachev, with a following of some 5,000 poorly armed Bashkirs, and a leavening of factory serfs and Cossacks, advanced from foundry to foundry in a wide arc through Bashkiria. Some of the Bashkir leaders were already beginning to make their peace with the government and assist the patrols of regular soldiers. But others, like Salavat Yulyayev, continued the struggle, whether in the interests of Pugachev or their own remains uncertain. Lieutenant-Colonel Mikhel'son, in overall command of the government detachments in the area, chased Pugachev from foundry to foundry, but the thaw which had set in in earnest rendered operations difficult for both sides. After forty days of almost continuous pursuit, Mikhel'son's forces were so exhausted that he withdrew to Ufa to rest and recoup. The whole of Bashkiria was in an uproar, and even the town of Ufa trembled again for its safety. No one knew where Pugachev was, and where he would strike next. Bypassing Ufa, he had in fact gone north, and appeared before the fort of Osa on 18 June 1774. After a three-day siege, the fort surrendered to 'Peter III' who was greeted with military and imperial honours. The next step was to cross the Kama and make for Kazán. Factory serfs and peasants flocked from Perm' guberniya to join the rebels, together with many more Bashkirs. Pausing to burn down the Izhevsk and Votkin foundries where, in spite of the efforts of the defenders, Pugachev was welcomed by the peasants and factory serfs with bells and icons, the rebel army, with nothing behind it, and nothing in front, advanced on defenceless Kazán.

Kazán was a city of some 11,000 inhabitants, many of whom were Tartars. It was mainly built of wood; even the kremlin, or fort, was wooden. General von Brandt, the ailing governor, had already been aware of his danger, and on 24 June he wrote urgently to the commander-in-chief in the whole area, Prince F. F. Shcherbatov, demanding reinforcements, and sent couriers in all directions, notably to Mikhel'son. Shcherbatov stayed where he was—in Orenburg—until 5 July. But Mikhel'son pressed forward in an effort to cross the Kama, and intercept Pugachev. He hoped to reach Kazán by 8 or 9 July but was delayed by the need to ford a number of rivers, and had only just crossed the Kama on 3 July—well behind Pugachev, who on 11 July appeared with some 20,000 men before the city. On 12 July a three-pronged rebel attack overwhelmed the improvised defence of the city, and the government forces fled back to the citadel, and barricaded themselves in. An orgy of looting and destruction followed, lasting from

6 a.m. to midnight; according to a contemporary, 'those in German dress and without a beard were killed', women in 'German dress' were seized and taken to Pugachev's camp. All government prisoners were freed, among them Pugachev's first and only real wife and his children, who were taken to his camp, where their presence caused the pretender a certain embarrassment. They were introduced as the wife and children of his old friend the Don Cossack, Emelyan Pugachev, and lodged together with the women who formed his harem. The city was set on fire at nine different points, and the rabble roamed the streets, looting, drinking, raping, until the smoke drove them off. Of 2,873 houses in the city, 2,063 were destroyed by fire.

On the evening of 11 July, Mikhel'son was only 65 versts from Kazán. Having rested his horses for three hours, he started at 1 a.m. on 12 July on a forced march to the city, from which rising columns of smoke could soon be discerned. At the village of Tsaitsyn, Mikhel'son heard that Pugachev awaited him with some 12,000 men. With his exhausted force of only 800, Mikhel'son launched a fierce attack against the rebel centre, which broke in disorder after a five-hour battle. But Mikhel'son's forces were too worn out to pursue the rebels.

On 13 July 1774, Mikhel'son entered Kazán and began at once to mop up the parties of rebel looters. But he was not yet done with Pugachev. With a smaller force the rebel leader returned to the charge the next day, and was again beaten by the government forces. Undaunted, Pugachev moved some twenty versts away, regrouped and refilled his ranks, and returned with what was no longer an army, but a mob of some 15,000. Mikhel'son went out to meet him on the same field where they had first met outside the city. Pugachev's forces now fought with the courage of despair, but after a four-hour battle they were completely routed, with the loss of 2,000 killed and wounded and 5,000 prisoners. Some 10,000 captives of both sexes held in Pugachev's camp were now freed.

Where would Pugachev go next? An advance on Nizhniy Novgorod would carry the revolt into the heartland of serf-owning Russia. The governor-general of Moscow, now Prince N. M. Volkonsky, began to plan the defence of the city and the surrounding countryside. In a number of smaller towns the local gentry and townspeople met and decided to raise troops locally to meet the challenge. But it never came; Pugachev had turned south. Did he ever really plan to march on Moscow? It was frequently spoken of among his closest intimates. Pugachev was reported to have said: 'If I can take Orenburg and Yaitsk, then I will go with just the cavalry to Kazán and after taking it I will march on Moscow and Petersburg, send the empress to a convent, and pay the boyars back in kind.' This does not have the ring of a well-thought out plan of campaign. But 'marching on Moscow' was a necessary psychological element in the process of legitimizing Pugachev's role as 'Peter III' who had been forced by wicked dvoryane to wander in strange lands for years and was now returning to recover his throne. However, when faced with probable defeat,

Pugachev did what one might expect: he made for home, to the ground he knew well, the land of the Don Cossacks.

The decision to march south led to a change of emphasis in Pugachev's manifestos, related to the nature of the area in which he was now operating. He was cut off from Bashkiria (though the revolt continued to rumble there) and to a great extent he was also cut off from the support of the factory workers. He was now entering an area very largely peopled by small landowners with under twenty serfs, though there were also some very large estates. By contemporary standards the peasants were relatively prosperous, but it was mainly a subsistence economy, with very little cultivation for sale or for local marketing. It was however overwhelmingly an area of barshchina [compulsory labor] cultivation though some of the larger estates were on obrok [annual money tax]. The towns too were mainly overgrown agricultural settlements providing no market for the countryside, since the town-dwellers grew their own food. Thinly settled, the whole region was the refuge of many bold spirits, runaway peasants, Old Believers, and there was also a population of some 1–2 per cent of Little Russians and non-Christian native tribes.

The manifestos issued by Pugachev, and carried from village to village by his emissaries, now specifically called on the serfs to rise against their masters, to overthrow the whole system of serfdom and to take over the land. The new Peter III appealed to Old Believers by granting 'the old cross and prayers, heads and beards'; he granted them liberty, 'and to be forever Cossacks', free from the poll-tax and the recruit levy, and from the taxes and money dues imposed by evil landowners and corrupt judges. He urged the peasants to seize those who had previously been nobles and oppressors of the peasants, and to execute and hang them and treat them in the same unchristian fashion as they had treated the peasants. With or without benefit of Pugachev's manifestos, or Pugachev's presence, serf risings now spread from village to village. Sometimes small groups of Cossacks appeared in a village and encouraged the peasants to rise against their landowners; elsewhere peasants rose on their own initiative, stimulated by rumour and the bush telegraph. Larger groups of peasants sometimes roamed far afield, recruiting and destroying as they went, sufficiently strong even to give a good account of themselves in pitched battles with government troops. If the rising took place within measurable distance of Pugachev's main forces, the peasants brought the gentry and officials with them to his headquarters, to be 'sentenced' by the 'emperor' himself. Elsewhere vengeance was immediately wreaked on the landowners—men, women and children—and on officials, stewards, priests, contractors. Significantly, it was mainly the owners of small estates who were murdered, where personal contact was close, and barshchina common.

Meanwhile Pugachev's own forces were advancing from town to town, leaving a trail of destruction. On 23 July he arrived in Alatyr and was met with solemn oaths of loyalty, church services and processions. Here he filled up his ranks, both with volunteers, and with conscripts 'among those fit for service'. The same performance was repeated on 26 July in Saransk, where Pugachev dined in the house of the voyevoda's widow and then hanged her. The primitiveness of the area, and of the people taking part on both sides in this social war, led to increasing ruthlessness. Before the revolt, armed conflicts between rival dvoryane leading their serf followers had not been unknown, and the authority of the civil administration over the 'gentry' was but slender. Major Mellin, in charge of one of the government detachments, was horrified to hear reports 'which I refuse to believe', that, profiting from the general disorder, some nobles were fighting each other and destroying each other's estates and hanging their enemies. On the other hand the spectacle of nobles hanged in droves, with heads, hands and feet cut off, roused the forces of order to equally savage repressions.

On 1 August a group of Cossacks proclaimed in the marketplace in Penza that 'Peter III' was on his way, and if he were not welcomed with bread and salt, all in the city down to the last baby would be put to the sword. Pugachev was duly welcomed, the treasury was looted and 200 men were forcibly recruited. Knowing that government forces were hard on his heels, Pugachev and his motley force made for Saratov on the Volga. The numbers in his 'army' cannot be estimated exactly; contemporary accounts range from eight hundred to several thousand. But it was no longer a fighting force. Volga boatmen and fugitive serfs provided a core of tough fighters, but they were untrained. The peasants who flocked to volunteer as often faded away. The hard core of some 300–400 Yaik Cossacks was also much reduced, and not all were now loyal to 'Peter III.'

On the other hand the 'towns' which Pugachev had so far seized with such ease were towns only in name. Saratov was another matter. It was one of the most important urban centres on the Lower Volga, the administrative capital of the foreign colonists. There were a few small factories in the neighbourhood (hats, stockings and rope). The population numbered some 7,000 including about 1,000 kuptsy. But the town had suffered a serious fire in May 1774, which had laid it waste and its fortifications were negligible, though the garrison numbered 780 men.

Divided counsels among the defenders (in which the poet Derzhavin played a somewhat inglorious part) contributed directly to the fall of the town on 6 August. Pugachev camped outside Saratov for three days. Solemn oaths of loyalty to 'Peter III' were sworn, and church services were held in honour of the emperor, his heir, 'Paul', and his 'wife' Yustinya. Twenty-four landowners and twenty-one chancery clerks were hanged and the massacre of men and women of all ranks continued. Half-drunk priests administered oaths of loyalty to those fit for service. The state depots of corn, liquor and money were broken open and the contents looted. Even after Pugachev's main host had moved away, some twenty-nine armed bands roamed the neighbourhood, looting, killing and destroying.

As Pugachev raced southwards towards Tsaritsyn, he made constant efforts to win the Don Cossacks to his cause. But from the beginning of the revolt the government had been aware of this particular danger and had taken steps to ward it off. In October 1773, orders were issued to watch out for any sign of dissaffection in the Host, and to seize and burn all Pugachev's manifestos. Countermanifestos were issued by the War Chancery of the Don Cossacks, warning them against the pretender Pugachev. It was only, however, when Pugachev was actually in the area between the Volga and the Don that the danger became acute. He issued a manifesto on 13 August 1774, specially directed to the Don Cossacks, stressing that Peter III had been acknowledged by nearly the whole of Russia and that he had promised the Cossacks 'freedom, the cross, prayers, heads and beards of our ancestors, and that now the Cossacks were blinded and misled by the wiles of the cursed race of nobles, who not content with Russia want to turn the native Cossack Host into peasants, and destroy the Cossack people'. Thus once again Pugachev proclaimed the utopia of the Cossack Old Believers. But it was in vain. A reward of 20,000 rubles had been promised for the capture of Pugachev, and the Don Cossacks mostly remained loyal. In all likelihood they were held back from joining the rebels by two factors: the signature of the treaty of Kuchuk Kainardzhi on 14 July 1774 and the end of the war with the Porte would release troops which could be used to repress the revolt: and reluctance to join an evidently losing side. Thus, though a few wavered at times, and joined Pugachev, elsewhere Don Cossacks were used against the rebel forces. The Cossacks of the Lower Don were in any case well aware that Pugachev was Pugachev and not Peter III.

Still in the hope of arousing his fellow-Cossacks, Pugachev issued a further manifesto, one of the most revealing of the general objects of the movement: 'the Christian law of the old tradition of our holy fathers has been completely destroyed, and instead of it, a new law, of evil intent, and German habits have been introduced into Russia, and the most disgusting shaving of the beard, and the other outrages against the Christian faith and cross.' Here again Pugachev declared that he had been deprived of his throne because he wanted to bring about freedom in Russia (*uchinit' vo vsey Rossii vol'nost'*) and that he had already been accepted as ruler in Kazán, Orenburg and among the Kalmucks and the Bashkirs.

Finally, on 21 August, Pugachev appeared before Tsaritsyn. The commandant had already taken steps to defend the town, by summoning Don Cossack regiments, and he was expecting reinforcements from the Second Army in the South. Encamped before Tsaritsyn, Pugachev went forward to parley with a group of Don Cossacks who came forward to meet him, and was publicly recognized. From that moment, disbelief spread among the Don Cossacks, and also among Pugachev's close followers. Cracks began to appear in their faith in the pretender; the world of suspended belief in which so many lived began to collapse about their ears, and thoughts for their own safety came to the fore.

After a five-hour artillery duel with the garrison of Tsaritsyn, Pugachev withdrew down the river, pausing to ravage the German Herrenhut colony at Sarepta. The next day, his convoy of barges loaded with treasure and noble and other prisoners was seized by the commandant of Tsaritsyn. On the same day, Colonel Mikhel'son, who had been pursuing Pugachev as fast as he could, arrived in the city. Stopping only to leave his sick and rest his horses, and taking with him the Don Cossacks in the garrison, he started off again on 23 August, and two days later the final encounter took place. Pugachev had some 10,000 men, though more than half were unarmed peasants. Dividing his force into three, and taking command of the centre, Mikhel'son broke the centre of Pugachev's army, in spite of heavy gunfire. The defeat became a rout. Pugachev, with some thirty followers, managed to cross the Volga, taking his wife—the real one—with him.

Where was Pugachev to go now? Reinforced by some 200 Yaik Cossacks who had managed to rejoin him, and accompanied by Kinzya Arslanov and a few more intimates, Pugachev now abandoned the idea he had put forward before the final battle, of going to Persia through Turkestan, 'where there were khans friendly to him'. He proposed instead to go either to the Zaporozhian Sech, or to Siberia, or beyond the Caspian to arouse the 'Hordes' (Tartars). The Yaik Cossacks refused to go to all these 'foreign lands' (counting the Zaporozhians as foreign), and insisted on returning to the Yaik, where after all they had left their homes and families. According to the evidence given to the investigating Secret Commission by Ivan Tvorogov, who had joined the revolt at the very beginning, in October 1773, he had, just before the attack on Saratov, discovered that Pugachev was an impostor. He and a Yaik Cossack, also one of the original conspirators, now acted as the moving spirits in a plot to save themselves by seizing Pugachev and delivering him to the authorities. A number of other Cossacks were won over to the plot, and persuaded Pugachev to agree to march into the Kalmuck steppe, towards Uzen', and Lake El'ton. On the way, the Cossacks seized the horses of the non-Cossacks in the company, thus forcing them to drop behind. Kinzya Arslanov was allowed to continue with them since otherwise Pugachev's suspicions would be aroused. His wife and son Trofimov also continued with the fugitives. Beyond Uzen', the conspirators seized and disarmed Pugachev; he made one desperate bid for freedom, but was finally bound. 'How dare you raise your hands on your emperor? You will not achieve anything. If I do not punish you, I have still an heir, Paul Petrovich,' exclaimed 'Peter III', but the imposture was over. Hearing that 'a just judge' was now in charge in Yaitsk, the Cossacks determined to deliver their prisoner to him. So, on 15 September 1774, the revolt ended where it had begun, on the Yaik.

Bibliography

J. ALEXANDER, *Autocratic Politics in a National Crisis: The Imperial Russian Government and Pugachev's Revolt, 1773–5* (1969).

J. ALEXANDER, *Emperor of the Cossacks: Pugachev and the Frontier Jacquerie of 1773–1775* (1973).

P. ANDERSON, *Lineages of the Absolutist State* (1974).

P. Avrich, *Russian Rebels, 1600–1800* (1973).
R. P. Bartlett, *Human Capital: The Settlement of Foreigners in Russia, 1762–1864* (1979).
P. Dukes, *The Making of Russian Absolutism, 1613–1801* (1982).
P. Dukes, *Russia under Catherine the Great: Volume One: Select Documents on Government and Society* (1978).
J. G. Garrard, ed., *The Eighteenth Century in Russia* (1973).
L. Gordon, *Cossack Rebellions: Social Turmoil in the Sixteenth-Century Ukraine* (1983).
J. M. Hittle, *The Service City: State and Townsmen in Russia, 1600–1800* (1979).
W. M. Pinter and D. K. Rowney, eds., *Russian Officialdom: The Bureaucratization of Russian Society from the Seventeenth to the Twentieth Century* (1980).
D. L. Ransel, *The Politics of Catherinian Russia: The Panin Party* (1975).

Death as an Instrument: The Public Execution in France

JOHN McMANNERS

Few aspects of society under the Old Regime so shock modern readers as the penalties for criminal behavior. In all countries scores and in some hundreds of offenses were subject to capital punishment. Torture was not uncommon. To understand the prevalence of these practices, historians must probe the legal, social, political, and religious attitudes that both approved and fostered these criminal policies.

Research has begun to clarify several points. There was a certain degree of real system and genuine regulation of both torture and execution. Moreover, in particular with executions, from the pronouncement of sentence through the moment of death and even disposal of the body elaborate public rituals were involved. These rituals served to demonstrate the frightful consequence of criminal behavior and served as a vehicle to reassert the importance and sanctity of public order. The very prominent role of priests in the rituals of execution served to indicate approval by the Church and the close connection between the public and the divine orders. By inviting broad viewing of the event on the part of the general nonelite public, the authorities elicited evidence of a widespread community approval of the legal decision.

By the middle of the eighteenth century, writers associated with the Enlightenment program of reform began to raise questions and protests about both torture and execution. Yet even the reformers generally refrained from demanding an end to capital punishment. Rather they tended to adopt a utilitarian stance that sharply limited the types of offenses for which execution might be considered appropriate. Ironically, their view that capital punishment should be restricted to matters such as treason later provided one justification for

© John McManners 1981. Reprinted from *Death and the Enlightenment: Changing Attitudes to Death among Christians and Unbelievers in Eighteenth-Century France* by John McManners (1981) by permission of Oxford University Press.

the thousands of political executions carried out during the French Revolution.

'Malheur à la société renfermant les hommes qui en voient mourir d'autres sans frémir,' ["Woe to the society containing men who see others die without quivering."] said Pierre Pastoret, a reforming lawyer, reflecting on the multitude of crimes for which the death penalty could be exacted. This was in 1790, in the magic days before revolutionary enthusiasm had run into disillusionment, and when the Terror was still just a cloud no bigger than a man's hand upon the horizon of the future. According to Pastoret, the jurisprudence of the *ancien régime* had accumulated no less than 115 capital crimes, though some melancholy satisfaction of a patriotic kind could be derived from the consideration that the French total was half the English one, the sturdy and barbarous islanders being contemptuous of death, even their own. In eighteenth-century France treason, murder, attempted murder, infanticide, robbery and smuggling under arms, were offences liable to the death penalty—so too were duelling, coining, false witness, forgery of legal documents, theft of property worth more than 3,000 *livres*, breaking and entering, more especially at night, fraudulent bankruptcy, the forcible abduction of an heiress, rape, bigamy if forgery was involved, sexual relations with a nun or of a manservant with his mistress and certain other flagrant kinds of adultery, breaches of the press censorship, sacrilege, sodomy, incest, and the exercise of the Protestant ministry. Executions were public and the painfulness of the manner of dying was adjusted to fit the crime. For an attack on the king's person there was a lurid ritual of savageries laid down by the Parlement of Paris, which was revived in all its gruesome details to provide a lingering end for Damiens in 1757 for the crime of lifting his hand against Louis XV; in addition, the close relatives of the traitor were deprived of their family name and banished, and the family house was razed to the ground. For most capital offences, the penalty was hanging; for crimes of violence it was breaking on the wheel; for poisoning, sodomy, and bestiality and some cases of sacrilege it was burning. Sometimes the punishments were cumulative: in 1787 a parricide had his hand cut off, was broken on the wheel, then consigned to the flames. There was a ritual of torture too, which might be made a preliminary to execution—*la question préparatoire* [the preparatory question] to extract an avowal of guilt, and *la question préalable* [the preliminary question] to obtain the names of accomplices, and these grim methods of persuasion were divided into two grades of intensity, *ordinaire* and *extraordinaire*. According to Diderot's guess, there were something like 300 executions annually in France at the end of the *ancien régime*. Comparatively speaking, this is not a great number: as

Diderot himself crudely put it, as many were killed by carriages, a high wind, a diseased whore, or a bad—indeed a good—doctor. Even so, it represents a harsh, imaginable total of human agony, a rough edge of reality to nag and fray the complacency of our pattern-weaving in the history of ideas.

The French legal system was cruel, but it did not make light of men's lives. In theory, the death sentence could be passed only if the evidence was conclusive. If it amounted to certainty but fell short of complete demonstration, the magistrates ought to impose a lighter penalty. According to Serpillon's commentary, published in 1767, for criminal cases a 'moral certainty' was not enough, a 'physical certainty' was required, 'celle qui dépend des témoins qui ont vu commettre le crime' [testimony by those who saw the crime committed]. His examples of the sort of evidence required are demanding. In practice, however, high-flown language about conclusive evidence must be set in the context of the standard methods of procedure, which were devised to supplement the inefficient police methods rather than to protect the accused. The investigation was conducted in secret; the accused was ignorant of the charge until he was confronted by the witnesses, and as these had already made their depositions, he could not hope to persuade them to risk the penalties they would incur if they changed their testimony. The defence advocate moved in an unreal world of written submissions in which it was impossible to unpick the web of the prosecution argument. Too much has been made (on the basis of Voltaire's savage ironies) of the fractional 'proofs' that could be added together to make a whole one; this was legal jargon rather than a fair description of the way the magistrates operated, though it is indicative of the way in which, in the last resort, the 'instinct' of the judges fed by prejudices of class or *milieu*, could take over the decision without conscious dishonesty....

The parlements and other sovereign courts exercising final jurisdiction in cases involving the death sentence had a wide discretion concerning the degree of pain and ignominy with which a criminal had to die. Hanging (or, for nobles, decapitation) was the most merciful. Wretches who were condemned to the wheel or the fire might be spared the full agony (more especially if they revealed their accomplices), since the judges, by a *retentum* [proviso] at the foot of the *arrêt* [judgment] of execution (revealed only to the executioner), might order strangulation beforehand, or after a certain number of minutes or hours, or a specified number of blows. These gruesome calculations were regarded as a serious part of the duties of the magistrate: insofar as there was a science of criminology in the eighteenth century, it consisted in making the punishment fit the crime. Judicial torture was far from being an arbitrary proceeding, let alone a sadistic one. The lawyers had built up a code of rules to regulate its application. The charge must concern a crime for which death was the penalty, the documentation must be complete, so that the admissions extracted were an addition to the structure of proof, not part of it, the resort to the *question* had to be confirmed by the court of final jurisdiction, even if the suspect had not made an appeal to it. Evidence of guilt must be compelling—'des preuves presque complètes et de violentes présomptions' [virtually absolute proof with violent presumptions]. For example, a dying man's accusation was not enough; if the suspect was of good reputation one witness was insufficient; if he was of doubtful reputation one might do, but in this case it must be an actual eyewitness and a person of good moral standing (eyewitness being tightly defined—two people seeing the accused leaving the scene of a murder waving a blood-stained sword were not proof enough unless evidence of previous threats or feuding was forthcoming). Youths under fourteen years of age were not subject to torture and men over seventy were allowed some relaxation of its rigours. Doctors had to be in attendance, perhaps to certify the point at which the grim ritual began to defeat its object, but also to offer the solace of bleeding. The amount of pain to be inflicted was prescribed; four wedges between the planks that compressed the legs for the *question ordinaire* and another four for the *extraordinaire*; or if it was the water torture, six measures of water exactly, down the funnel. There was discussion, though no formal regulation was made, about precautions to avoid crippling the victim permanently; every detail of iron rings, tightness of ropes, and height of trestles was specified and, astonishingly, by a regulation of the Parlement of Paris dating from 1697, the water torture was to be applied only with warm water and in a comparatively warm dungeon.

By the rules of legal procedure, extenuating circumstances were taken into account only after the death sentence had been actually pronounced. An offender who was very young or very old, or who was certified as mad, or who could claim to have acted in self-defence or under extreme pressure, might be pardoned by *lettres de grâce* [letters of grace] issued from the Chancellery attached to the sovereign court which had passed sentence; those who had committed their crime under the influence of passion might be pardoned too, though their *lettres de grâce* had to come from the Grande Chancellerie because this was an exercise 'of the full plenitude of the power of the Sovereign, being the result, not so much of his justice, as of his clemency'. When grave and violent crimes were being judged, pleas of mitigation arising from the disabilities of the criminal, whether youth, age, or mental deficiency, were only grudgingly considered by the courts. The *bailliage* court of Alençon in 1718 allowed a youth of fifteen to escape the gallows for homicide because of his 'extreme youth and drunkenness at the time'; but the sentence was to the galleys for life. The Châtelet [Law Court] of Paris in 1788 condemned two octogenarians to breaking on the wheel for murder. The Parlement in its latter days condemned two boys, one fifteen and one sixteen years of age, to the same punishment, and burned a sixteen-year-old girl who had poisoned her mother. Youth, indeed, in the sense of 'imbecility' and irresponsibility was narrowly defined, ending at the age of seven; from seven to fourteen a minor was sentenced at the court's discretion, which did not exclude the galleys for crimes of violence. As for madness, it was not until the last decade before the Revolution that it became a serious medical concept. The Châtelet rarely took account of the mental state of the people it sentenced, unless, indeed, some startling character emerged, like Pierre Charenton, who murdered his mistress because she distracted him from his religious duties, 'preferring to sacrifice [her] life rather than lose his soul before God'. In 214 cases of arson before the Parlement of Paris from 1750 to 1789, an *information de démence* [insanity inquiry] was asked for in only 27 cases; true, in five of these the culprit escaped death as a result of the medical verdict and was locked up for life in the Salpêtrière or Bicêtre. For treason and parricide, madness was not taken into any sort of account, the necessity of making a fearful example being regarded as paramount over all other considerations....

This priority of the issue of public tranquillity is probably the best clue to the interpretation of the sentencing policy of the various parlements, whose magistrates would act with hysterical ferocity, or with a mildness which undermined the force of royal edicts. A murder by a servant, an ambush on the highway, an affair of black magic with undertones of a conspiracy against morals could lead to breakings and burnings. Yet, in spite of the strictness of royal edicts, of the 44 duellists brought before the Parlement of Paris between 1700 and 1725, 12 were acquitted, 26 released under the *plus amplement informé* [ample proceeding] formula, and 6 were sentenced—one to pay expenses, one hanged in effigy, one banished for nine years, one to the galleys for nine years—none was executed. Fraudulent bankruptcy, since 1673 a capital crime, was not treated as such in practice; writers and publishers who evaded the censorship went in fear of their freedom, but hardly of their lives (though one of the panic measures taken after Damiens's attempt was a renewed ordinance prescribing death for printing and selling books against religion and the tranquillity of the State). In cases of homicide, letters of remission would normally be forthcoming if a proprietor had been repelling nocturnal thieves, a woman resisting rape, or a young man had been forced into a duel or a soldier insulted, or if a husband had killed his wife caught in bed with her lover (though this must be in the family home, and not elsewhere). Yet even if it was obviously a case where letters of remission would be forthcoming, the death sentence had to be passed—for no one was entitled to disturb the peace of society, France being a kingdom 'where all acts of violence are absolutely forbidden'....

The central argument of the lawyers was the necessity of maintaining order. They also had a secondary argument—or, rather, it was a nuance, an extension of the first. Muyart de Vouglans spoke of the need to 'purge' society, to 'avenge' society for the scandal and damage caused to it. Another legal writer in 1773 tells of the 'vengeance' which is forbidden to men, but which the king and his officers can exact by virtue of a delegation of authority from God. Another, four years later, speaks of the necessity 'to punish and avenge the crime by the public satisfaction imposed on the criminal'. It was not enough for the magistrate to preside intelligently over the operation of a calculus of deterrence: he must also feel that he is an agent of divine vengeance, the vindicator of an outraged social order. It was not enough for the malefactor to appear as a horrifying example of the fate of transgressors: he must also make, and be seen to make, a public reparation, a recognition of the majesty of the law and of the sovereign he has flouted. There is a revealing sentence in Jousse when he speaks of the importance of fair and open procedures—'il faut encore que les accusés se jugent et se condamnent eux-mêmes en quelque sorté—the accused must condemn themselves. The *question préparatoire* was not, in theory, torture applied to complete the proof of guilt, for this proof was supposed to amount to a moral certainty already; rather, it was to extract the formal avowal which the process of reparation demanded. Immediately before his execution, a condemned man was encouraged to make a *testament de mort* [death testament]. This was distinct from any record of admissions under the *question* and was not a last will and testament of the ordinary kind, for having incurred civil death (*la mort civile*), he was no longer capable of disposing of his property; it was, simply, a formal avowal of guilt 'par acquit de conscience'. A magistrate of the court accompanied by a clerk and the executioner would interview the prisoner just before he was taken out to the scaffold, or at some staging point on the way; they would interrogate him on oath, and if he volunteered a confession it would be formally recorded, ending with a formula recognizing the justice of the sentence and asking pardon of God. If he refused to make such a testament, there was still a chance on the scaffold itself, and the clerk in attendance was authorized to take the record without the presence of a magistrate. Often, the death sentence would include an injunction for the criminal to make the *amende honorable* [full apology] on the way to the place of execution. Before the portals of the cathedral or other principal church of the town, on a cart, facing backwards, dressed only in a shirt, rope round neck and candle in hand, and bearing placards declaring the nature of his offence, the condemned man would kneel and ask pardon 'of God, the King and of Justice'. Any outrageous crime, even if it had not warranted the death sentence, might be the subject of such an act of reparation. Sometimes, the ceremony would be supplemented by the inauguration of some more permanent memorial, paid for from the estate of the criminal—the foundation of a mass for the soul of the man he had murdered, or the engraving of an epitaph to commemorate the victim and the sentence of the court.

In the *amende honorable* the condemned man was asking pardon, in the first place, from God. Thus, he was not only making an act of public reparation, he was also completing the act of reconciliation towards his Maker which—presumably—he had begun by making his confession to a priest in his cell. If he persisted in denying his guilt and refused to make the *amende honorable*, it was for his confessor, there with him on the cart, to exhort him. Reformers publicized the courageous reply of the baker of Saint-Omer wrongly convicted of murdering his drunken mother (in 1770): 'Are you prepared to take onto your conscience before God the lie which you wish me to utter at the door of this church?' Religion, of course, was not only concerned with the *amende honorable*, but with the whole execution, which was a lurid prefiguration of the death that comes equally to us all and makes us all equal when it comes, a reminder of the end of the sinner, of the necessity for confession, restitution, and reparation, and of the hope and assurance of forgiveness to the truly penitent. From the religious point of view, the central figure of the drama was not the executioner, but the confessor. In France, it was the custom to offer no other sacrament to the condemned but that of penitence, the confessor limiting himself to instructing and exhorting to the spiritual reception of the benefit of Communion and extreme unction. Absolution was to be withheld if the names of accomplices were not forthcoming, though the Capuchins were said to err on the side of mercy in this respect. The confessor (there were two for Damiens and for Calas, but one was usual) accompanied the victim to the scaffold and stayed with him to the end, offering the crucifix to kiss as the torments intensified. The handbooks of the confessional always emphasized the infinite extent of God's mercy: a sincere repentance, even at the very last breath, could reconcile the most depraved of sinners. Some of the clergy, however, wondered if, in practice, in the bitterness of an agony officially imposed, it was possible for a man to turn his mind towards his Maker, and their voice was joined to those who wanted an end to the wheel and the faggots. Other clergy wished to have practice conform to the strict logic of the Christian doctrine of mercy: the repentant sinner, however odious his offence had been, should be given, not only absolution, but also the viaticum [communion served to someone dying]. The eighteenth-century editions of the *Rituels* of various dioceses made it clear why communion was refused — it was solely because of the legal rule by which the death penalty was normally put into effect on the very day of the sentence, so that 'le corps adorable de Jésus Christ' would be united with a body soon to be exposed to the utmost indignities. The case for withholding the sacrament was weak, and from the Edict of 1788 was non-existent, for a delay of a month was then prescribed to allow time for royal review and, possibly, pardon. But the rule remained unchanged: at least three of the *cahiers* [lists of grievances brought to the Estates General] of the clergy in 1789 complained of this unchristian severity.

Lay society, whether represented by critics of the Church or critics of the penal code, did not seek to deny the clergy their melancholy right to monopolize the last moments of the criminal on the scaffold — with the exception of Boucher d'Argis, who in 1781, on grounds of religion alone, wanted priests to absent themselves from such scenes of cruelty. The spectators, he said, curse them as if they are in league with the judges, while the dying criminal blasphemes against the God who has abandoned him. In fact a more usual reaction was to admire the confessors who performed these sickening duties. Restif de la Bretonne tells of a priest escorting a livid figure, half-dead already from the tortures of the preliminary *question*, to the scaffold: 'I saw him embrace the wretch, devoured with fever, as infected as the dungeons from which he was taken, covered with vermin. And I said to myself—'Oh religion, here is your triumph!' In some towns, this 'triumph of religion' was emphasized by the presence at the execution of one of the *Confréries des Agonisants*; there were those like the Pénitents de la Croix, of Autun, the Pénitents de la Miséricorde of Lyon and the Pénitents Pourpres of Limoges who undertook the special obligation to attend funerals and bury the dead. The Pourpres of Limoges held an auction among themselves the night before an execution for the grim honour of collecting the corpse from the gibbet or wheel and wrapping it in its shroud. Then on the morrow, in their blood-red robes, and cowls, with black girdles and rosaries of black beads encircled with a crown of thorns, they processed with candles to the place of execution, their two ecclesiastical members, arrayed in black stoles, supporting the prisoner. They sang a *De profundis* and litanies to Christ and the saints, and when all was over, bore the shrouded body back to the Church of St. Cessateur. There, they kept their vigil over it all night, then buried it in the cemetery of that church—a cemetery which had been used only for criminals since the great plague of 1632. These sombre proceedings were a testimony to the Christian hope and to the solidarity of all believers in the great drama of sin and redemption; to complete the demonstration, a pious *confrère* would sometimes instruct his heirs to have him buried alongside the outcasts he had accompanied on their last journey of pain....

The famous manifesto of the Enlightenment against the cruelties and illogicalities of the penal code was Beccaria's *Trattato dei delitti e delle pene* [*Treatise on Crimes and Punishments*] (1764). In France, it had enormous influence, through the translation of 1766, through essays by Servan and Voltaire popularizing its ideas, and, as is the way with refutations, through the writings of the jurists who attacked it. Yet the Italian reformer and the French lawyers accepted the same basic utilitarian principle. To Beccaria, the argument from deterrence was everything. He accepted death as the appropriate fate for those who threatened the internal or external security of the State, but for other crimes, he argued that perpetual slavery would be a more effective deterrent. A cruel execution arouses sympathy for the victim and thereafter is forgotten: a slave in fetters is an ever-present object-lesson. Beccaria, in fact, carried the utilitarian principle to its logical extreme. The *amende honorable* and all the ideas of 'vengeance' and 'reparation' played no part in his scheme; all that mattered was the damage to society. He took no account of the dignity of the person injured or of the status of the criminal or of the offence to the majesty of God; by ignoring these considerations he was, by implication, defining society as essentially egalitarian and secular. He abolished the sombre *mystique* that had been woven around the concept of the official execution. Rousseau had just demonstrated how this mystique could be transferred from the law books of the parlements to the new egalitarian city of the General Will, where the power of life and death comes, not from delegation by God, but from delegation from every man who enjoys the benefits of the social order. So that I will not fall victim to an assassin, I agree to my own death if I become one.' More than this, criminal conduct carries the stigma of rebellion and treachery (and there is a further, more sinister extension of this idea in the chapter on the Civil Religion). Beccaria rejects all this. No one ever gave another power over his own life. Death is just one evil more. Executing a man may be a utilitarian necessity, but it is not derived from any sort of consent: it is an act of war. Beccaria is not defending the Christian principle of the sacredness of human life; he is asking those who propose to destroy a life not to deceive themselves about what they are doing. There is a simple test of honesty in this matter: do you, in fact, accept the public executioner as a 'good citizen who is contributing to the general welfare' or do you shrink from him?

Beccaria's famous principles of punishment—public, prompt, the least possible in the circumstances, proportionate to the crime, and fixed by the law—were accepted already by the French lawyers. The difference lay in the enormous discrepancy in their definition of what was 'necessary', 'least', 'proportionate', and 'fixed'. Montesquieu had already proposed to draw a line: the death penalty should not be exacted in matters of religion and morals or (in favoured states where fortunes were not too unequal) for offences against property. Rousseau had taken a different criterion: it was wrong to execute a man who could be left alive without danger. The application of these limitations would have transformed the jurisprudence of the *ancien régime*. Voltaire had denounced useless cruelties and wanted to force a reconsideration of all death sentences by having the warrant signed by the sovereign in person. And in 1762 he had begun his campaign against the injustices of French criminal procedure, his first victory coming in March 1765 with the rehabilitation of the memory of Calas....

'The least possible in the circumstances': it was easy to insist that there were circumstances where the death penalty was necessary, but difficult to defend specific obscenities like breaking on the wheel or burning. Aided by the upsurge of *sensibilité* [sensibility] in literature, which at the least provided the humanitarian *clichés* of discourse, protests against cruel punishments became insistent. In 1770 Voltaire was willing to retain painful methods of execution for parricides, traitors, and incendiaries: seven years later, he wanted 'simple death' alone. Nothing should be added to the sentence of death, said Boucher d'Argis in 1781, ridiculing the idea that there ought to be 'nuances entre les suppliciés when captial punishment was in question. Brissot compares the civilized executions of ancient Egypt, when the criminal was drugged with a grain of incense, to the barbarous penalty of the wheel, an invention of northern Europe artificially introduced into the more civilized south. If possible, he held, we ought to make it easy for the condemned man to die, yet at the same time make the execution appear terrible to the spectators—'rendez affreux l' appareil du supplice, mais que la mort soit douce,' said Marat, adopting the same formula. This humanitarian propaganda began to have its effect. Before the Revolution torture was abolished—the *question préparatoire* in 1781 and the *question préalable* in 1788 (typically of the age, the magistrates had been abandoning the *question préparatoire* before authorized by the Edict of 1781, but did not entirely give it up afterwards)....

One practical way of applying Beccaria's principle of utility was to look at each capital crime individually—on its demerits, as it were—to see if the death penalty really constituted an efficient deterrent. This was done for desertion from the army by Merlet, an old professional officer, in an essay published in 1770. He was cashing in on a growing public interest: Sedaine's opera *Le Déserteur* had some success in 1769, and Mercier was at work on a prose drama on the same theme. Merlet describes how the army enforced its punishments—deserters to the enemy were hanged; ordinary deserters were clubbed to death by an execution squad of fellow soldiers. Yet the crime was common. Some who fled had grievances about the way they had been enlisted—impressed, or bribed into signing on; most were peasants who did not regard loyalty to the colours as a virtue. It was always the young soldiers who ran away, those who had not had time to get over their grievances or to become inured to discipline—and who would be most useful to their country if their lives were spared. In future, Merlet suggests, deserters should continue to serve the State: they should be sent to the galleys, and on release take a new oath of fidelity and begin a new term of military service. Six years later, his argument of social utility was put forward by the abbé Jaubert in support of a plea to spare the lives of girls convicted of infanticide; they deserved to die, but executing them meant the destruction of fully grown individuals, reared at the expense of society and capable of serving it, to avenge the death of undeveloped infants. It was equally wasteful and harsh, said Jaubert, to put smugglers to death, for men are more valuable than manufacturers. The splendid principle of utility had its dangers, however—there would not always be a humanitarian outcome. Venereal disease, said the Swiss writer of a 'code of happiness', causes more damage to the State in a single year than the capital crimes of a whole century; this being so, he recommended the scaffold for the immoral characters who propagated it.

Another way of applying the principle of utility—and allying it with the rising force of *sensibilité*—was to examine the impact of the rituals of the scaffold on society generally; even if individuals with criminal tendencies were restrained by fear, there might be others whose minds were corrupted and drawn to an unhealthy interest in violence by the savage repressive measures society itself employed. This is Landreau de Maine-au-Picq's contention. A sinister vortex of brutal instincts swirls around public executioners, their affairs, and their families: anatomy students are depraved by working on the corpses of criminals whose faces show evil and terror rather than the repose of death, the multitude is hardened by the sights and sounds of the scaffold. That is why, says Landreau, our police receive no co-operation from the public; if the criminal law was made clear and simple and its penalties moderate, the whole population would collaborate to enforce it... When the first massacres of the Revolution came, a legal pamphleteer took up Landreau's theme—we have seen the people bathing in human blood: 'where did it get the idea of this so-called right to massacre unless it is the same right that society is said to have?'

This pamphleteer, Perreau, wanted the total abolition of capital punishment on the ground that it is wrong to kill a fellow human being under any circumstances; no writer before him, he complained and boasted, had had the courage to go to this logical extreme. With the possible exception of Landreau de Maine-au-Picq, he seems to be right in his contention. For even the most humane theorists, like Servan and Lacretelle, there are crimes so heinous that the criminal who commits them thereby proves he is no longer a human being—he is a 'monster', his 'soul is dead within him', he can be exterminated. The main theme of reforming thought ran very much on the line of Beccaria: the death penalty would remain, but would rarely be exacted; it would be replaced generally, by perpetual slavery. The idea of repriving sturdy rogues from the gallows and setting them to work for economic reasons had occurred to Frenchmen before Beccaria published. Faignet de Villeneuve had advocated the establishment of barracks for 'des galériens de terre', felons spared from execution, branded on the face to prevent them ever regaining normal society, and spending their lives repairing roads or working in the mines. Beccaria made this thrifty scheme more respectable by adding humanitarian enthusiasm and a lawyer's calculation about its deterrent effect. Voltaire took up the idea with enthusiasm and for all the reasons, particularly the economical one—'un homme pendu n'est bon à rien' ['a hanged man is good for nothing']. From 1777 he was asking for the ending of the death penalty for murderers; they could become useful, as England had proved by sending gallows-birds to the colonies and Russia by sending convicts to Siberia. Diderot, a realistic supporter of the death penalty, proposed to spare all but the most desperate murderers for employment of public works: 'because one man has been killed is no reason for killing another'. And he put the calculation of the value of a human being in those days of high morality with harsh precision. 'When we put to death a man of thirty years of age, we do not know what we are doing. We have not made the calculation that this man is the sole survivor of twenty men. Our criminal legislation does not know the value of the life of a man of thirty.' The idea of replacing the death penalty with perpetual penal servitude became generally accepted by the French reformers; Boucher d'Argis, Mirabeau, Pastoret, Brissot, and 'Moheau' all urge the acceptance ('Moheau' adding the sinister utilitarian variant of surgical experiments on criminals who might opt for vivisection, with a marginal chance of release, rather than life imprisonment). Landreau de Maine-au-Picq recommended imprisonment instead of execution, and in his overflowing Christian charity, stipulated kind treatment and release at the age of seventy, naïvely observing that these patriarchs of the prison out on parole would give good advice to young people. In 1970, the *avocat* Vasselin drew the attention of the National Assembly to the pool of well-motivated labour which could be made available by rescinding the death penalty: 'Thus, the most crying abuse of despotism can become the most splendid institution of our new legislation.' It seems odd than the thinkers of the eighteenth century should so easily have persuaded themselves of the potential value of a prison labour force; but colonial slavery was profitable, the doctrine of work was developing as against the Christian practice of alms-giving, populationists were making the multitude of toiling hands in a State the test of successful government, the more effective disciplinary methods being tried in military camps, schools, factories, and workhouses seemed to offer hope of an effective penal regime, and there was an undue confidence in the possibilities of a rational reorganization of society....

Death penalty or no, there was agreement that the fate of a criminal was to be made into a public spectacle: this followed from the view, common to both reactionaries and reformers, of punishment as a deterrent. If men are regarded as free agents, the deterrent view must be qualified by moral considerations, for motive will be the blameable element in criminal conduct, rather than its effects. Since the structure of order was so fragile, there was good reason to give priority to the effects—to the suppression of dangerous consequences—and this tendency was encouraged among reformers by a fashionable current of thought which cast doubt on human freedom. There was Diderot, thinking chiefly of hereditary factors and inextricably entangled in all the problems concerning the freedom of the will; there was Helvétius, preoccupied with the conditioning force of education and *milieu*; and La Mettrie reducing men to predetermined products of seed and soil like vegetables, so that to him the notorious robber and murderer Cartouche was 'made to be Cartouche' and could be no other. There were writers on the fringe of determinism but clinging to moral responsibility like Voltaire, and others, like d'Holbach, who coolly accepted the end of moral responsibility altogether. In so far as these thinkers accepted any kind of determinism, their ideas of punishment were bound to be affected: d'Alembert put the case clearly—if men are free, punishment is both necessary and just; if they are not free, it is necessary only. In the last resort and, maybe, without any moral condemnation, there will have to be some amputation, some maladjusted individual will have to be removed from society. If men are what they are because of some mysterious predestination, then we say to them, when we are dissatisfied with their conduct, that they are also predestined to punishment. If, as is more likely, they are the product of conditioning factors subject to manipulation, the levers of punishment must be adjusted to produce the social type most useful to our common life. So we come back, albeit with a more humane and enlightened imagination, to the calculus of pain as operated by the lawyers of the *ancien régime*, who had believed that they were dealing with free agents. Whether man was free or psychologically determined, there were arguments to justify the crowds in the place de Grève, the weekly prison peepshow in Le Peletier's abolitionist utopia, and the *tricoteuses* at the foot of the guillotine....

Biographers point the contrast between Robespierre's opposition to the death penalty before the Revolution, and his advocacy of the Terror. But there is no inconsistency. Beccaria had accepted death as the appropriate punishment for those who threaten the security of the State, and virtually all the French abolitionists follow him. Like the jurists of the *ancien régime*, they thought of punishment as primarily deterrent, and thus it seemed axiomatic that rebels should be deprived of all hope of rescue by fellow conspirators. Treason would never prosper, not only for semantic reasons, but because the traitors would not be there to see it. The scaffold, said Servan, is our final weapon 'to rid us of those rare criminals whom we cannot keep in our midst without danger'. Voltaire would use it if there was no other way of saving the lives of the greatest number; it would be like killing a mad dog. Brissot and Pastoret make death the punishment for treason—for 'secret conspiracies...tumultuous uprisings', said Pastoret, 'which menace the fatherland so long as the agitators are not executed'. He was writing at the dawn of a new era, and the earlier abolitionists had been looking forward to some great reform. When they wrote of treason they had in mind, not just the *salus populi suprema lex* of the Roman history which had been the staple of their studies in the *collèges*, still less of Diderot's cynical version of it: 'the supreme law is the...safety of those who govern the people'. It was not just their country as it was, but as it would be, that they were protecting, and this gives a new edge to their hatred of conspiracy. On behalf of his utopia, his dream of a free and egalitarian nation, Marat goes to the verge of asking for the retention of the cruelties of the scaffold which had darkened the legal system of the *ancien régime*. For the man who would set fire to ships, arsenals, archives, or public edifices, he wanted death, and 'que l'appareil de son supplice soit effrayant, et qu'il en soit témoin lui-même. This sombre eloquence—though no one could have foreseen it—was one day to find an application to the monarch himself. The idea of the sacredness of the person of kings, which had justified the torments of Damiens, went on into the Revolution in the constitutional concept of 'inviolability', and Marat was to lead in demanding its redefinition by a trial and a sentence of death. 'How should the former monarch be judged? With pomp and with severity. Far from us those false ideas of clemency and generosity by which the national vanity is flattered!' 'And it is sad to see how, in the debate on Louis's 'treason', the darker side of Beccaria and Brissot's theme of exemplary slavery in place of the death penalty was appropriated by the lunatic fringe of hatred in sansculotte rhetoric about tyrants exhibited in cages as object-lessons to the people of Europe.

More and more, the writers of the Enlightenment showed an awareness of the need for social reform to remove the causes of crime. Beccaria had blamed excessive taxation, the paternalistic family, and the bias of the laws as the source of violence in society. A government which made its people happy and prosperous, said d'Holbach, would not need to devise cruel punishments for murderers. The rich who made the laws, said Voltaire, should study what to do to help the poor before calling in the executioner: if they set up discreet institutions for fallen girls, for example, there would be no infanticide. Boucher d'Argis pointed out the injustice of making domestic theft by a servant a capital crime, such offences being most often the result of the contrast between the luxury of the master and the poor wages he pays to his employees. Marat wanted an egalitarian, puritanical reform of society—the land shared out, education available to all, old people well cared for—thereafter the legislator would be able to return to the best traditions of classical antiquity, and to use the laws to reward virtue rather than to suppress vice. 'Man is not born an enemy of society,' wrote Brissot, 'it is circumstances that make him such—poverty and misfortune.' Equalize fortunes, moderate taxation, give moral education to all, simplify the laws so they can all be put in a slim volume as cheap to buy as a catechism, and the vast majority of citizens will become worthy and law-abiding. Some pages of Brissot came near to making criminology a social science, more especially when he sees that many criminals need re-education or medical assistance. Some atrocious crimes, said La Mettrie (he was speaking of a woman who had killed and eaten her children), can only be the result of mental derangement; in these cases, the judges should not be lawyers, but experienced medical practitioners—such indeed, as La Mettrie was himself. In this respect as in others, Landreau de Maine-au-Picq is the most generous of the humanitarian reformers, since he regards all criminals as mentally disturbed people: 'all criminals are really mad, and ought to be treated as such by those that are sane.' Even so, to all these writers deterrence is the primary object of punishment, and to all except Landreau, the death penalty remains as the indispensable weapon to deal with conspiracies against the State.

To what extent was the sentencing policy of the magistrates of the parlements and the other great lawcourts influenced by the ideas of legal reformers? According to Roederer, an informed observer, the courts became more merciful during the last decade before 1789. He was probably right, though it is difficult to confirm this impression with entirely convincing statistics. The policies of the magistrates cannot be analysed in isolation, for criminal conduct was evolving, presenting new problems and dangers. In the latter years of the *ancien régime*, more offenders were being brought to trial; there were twice the number of entries in the prison registers of Aix for an average year in the early seventies as there had been in 1750. In

Normandy, Languedoc, and within the jurisdiction of the parlements of
Lille, Valenciennes, and Flanders, there is clear evidence of a switch from
the predominant crimes of violence of the early century to crimes against
property later on, and there is also evidence of theft becoming more
professionally organized. Society was becoming more civilized, better
policed, more property-conscious, while on their side; the criminal classes
were developing their own brands of efficiency. Maybe there was a greater
pressure towards dishonesty as the increasing population outran the
resources of certain areas. Certainly, there was an increase of vagabondage,
and a growing unease among the propertied classes. In face of a rising
criminality of a new kind, the Parlement of Toulouse seems to have inclined
towards severity, and the parlements of northern France towards leniency.
The Parlement of Flanders condemned 39 to death out of the 160 people
convicted between 1721 and 1730, but between 1781 and 1790, out of 500
criminals, only 26 received capital sentences. The Parlement of Paris
increased its death sentences in 1760–2, but thereafter—perhaps because of
a developing social awareness—greatly reduced them (there were 7 only in
1787). On the other hand, it sent many more convicted felons to the galleys.
Here, it might be supposed, is an intention to try the reforming schemes of
exemplary penal servitude instead of capital punishment, though so grim
was the existence of a *galérien* [galley slave] that it was more like an
alternative way of giving effect to the death penalty than anything else.
Unless he was of an unusually strong constitution, a man sentenced for life
to the galleys did not last long. Of the 4,000 convicts at the base of Marseille
in 1748, barely 200 had been sentenced before 1720, and over 2,500 had
been locked into their fetters within the last eight years (not all were serving
life sentences of course, but most were serving long terms, and the end of a
term was no guarantee of release). The spectacle of the *galériens* being
dragged on their 'chain' through the countryside and the stories of the living
death that awaited them under the Mediterranean sunshine constituted, no
doubt, a deterrent, but it would not be fair to Beccaria and his followers to
suggest that they had anything so grim in mind. The truth was that the
ancien régime had not reached the point of mental conviction at which there
was a willingness to pay for, or a capacity to organize, penal establishments
which would be both humane and effective. Things might have been
different if Australia had fallen to the French and Brissot and Lafayette had
been called in to organize a transportation system. There were prisons
galore in France. Some of them were spectacles of Piranesian horror—the
underground dungeons of the Citadel of Caen where, ankle deep in water,
the fettered legs of the inmates grew gangrenous; the iron cages of the
Parlement of Paris in which a man could not stand upright and could stay
for years without seeing sunshine, a fire, or a confessor; *maisons de force*
[workhouses] where delinquent women and children and dubious characters saved from a worse fate by family influence and a *lettre de cachet*
[arbitrary arrest warrant] rotted away among incorrigible vagabonds and

debauchees. Other prisons were symbolic ruins, furnished with doors with broken hinges and windows without bars, and run by incompetent and venal gaolers. But, apart from the galleys, where a technical necessity called for slave labour, the *ancien régime* had no prison system directed to any other purpose than temporary incarceration, no concept of an institution which could be used as an alternative to the scaffold.

We have seen what life was worth to the reformers of the French Enlightenment. To what extent did the legislation of the Revolution put their ideas into effect? The *cahiers* of 1789 give an impression of the extent to which these ideas had permeated society—at least, among the literate classes. Some *cahiers* demand the end of cruel punishments 'which revolt humanity', the reduction of the number of capital crimes, and the equality of nobles and commoners on the scaffold. But only one asks for the abolition of the death penalty, and that with the rider 'as far as may be possible'. The Code of 1791 went beyond the *cahiers* and was a fair reflection of the lowest common denominator of reforming enthusiasm. A new method of execution, the same for all classes was prescribed; it was the least cruel method known to science (the good Doctor Guillotin did not invent the fatal machine, but he conducted laborious experiments to refute the proposition that severed heads feel pain). Fairer procedures gave more guarantees to the innocent —though, by contrast, there was no hope of pardon. Punishment no longer extended to the family of a condemned man, whether by confiscation, or through the concept of legal disgrace. Death was no longer the penalty for offences against property, morals, or religion. But for murder and violence, capital punishment remained, and executions were still to be public spectacles. And above all, the new *régime* was as insistent as the old on the paramount necessity of preserving the State, now made doubly sacred by the presumed consent of the people. The death penalty was retained for treason, for any attempt on the life of the prince, and also for attempts against the legislative assembly, the publication by a minister of a law which had not been voted, the illegal collection of taxation, and trafficking in parliamentary votes. The legal highway to the Terror was being kept wide open.

Bibliography

D. Bien, *The Calas Affair: Persecution, Toleration, and Heresy in Eighteenth-Century Toulouse* (1960).
J. A. Cary, *Judicial Reform in France before the Revolution of 1789* (1981).
D. D. Cooper, *The Lesson of the Scaffold: The Public Execution Controversy in Victorian England* (1974).
W. R. Cornish, et al., *Crime and Law in Nineteenth-Century Britain* (1978).
R. Forster and O. Ranum, eds., *Deviants and the Abandoned in French Society* (1978).
D. Hay, ed., *Albion's Fatal Tree: Crime and Society in Eighteenth-Century England* (1975).
M. Ignatieff, *A Just Measure of Pain: The Penitentiary in the Industrial Revolution, 1750–1850* (1978).

J. H. LANGBIEN, *Torture and the Law of Proof: Europe and England in the Ancien Regime* (1977).
P. B. MUNSCHE, *Gentlemen and Poachers: The English Game Laws, 1671–1831* (1981).
P. O'BRIEN, *The Promise of Punishment: Prisons in Nineteenth-Century France* (1982).
L. RADZINOWICZ, *A History of English Criminal Law and Its Administration from 1750*, 4 vols. (1948–1968).
R. SMITH, *Trial by Medicine: Insanity and Responsibility in Victorian Trials* (1981).
E. P. THOMPSON, *Whigs and Hunters: The Origin of the Black Act* (1976).
G. WRIGHT, *Between the Guillotine and Liberty: Two Centuries of the Crime Problem in France* (1983).
H. ZEHR, *Crime and the Development of Modern Society: Patterns of Criminality in Nineteenth-Century Germany and France* (1976).

Marketing Methods in the International Steam Engine Market: The Case of Boulton and Watt

JENNIFER TANN

The steam engine constituted probably the single most important invention of the early phase of the industrial revolution. It produced a source of transportable energy that allowed factories to be built near available supplies of resources or labor rather than along country streams. The steam engine could also be employed to do a wide variety of heavy work.

But the invention and manufacture of the steam engine represented only part of the process we have come to call industrialization. A market had to be found or created for this new invention. Buyers had to be discovered, and the engines sold under conditions that would protect the economic interests of the inventor and manufacturer. When the steam-engine partnership of James Watt and Matthew Boulton attempted to market their product overseas as well as in Britain, the chief danger was that foreign engineers would attempt to copy the machines and produce them on their own. For this reason the firm sought to secure patent rights throughout Europe. While seeking thus to protect themselves, Watt and Boulton also had to seek out famous or well-placed customers whose purchase of the machine might persuade other people to do likewise.

Watt and Boulton, like many firms dealing with heavy capital goods two centuries later, discovered that the steam engine would not simply sell itself. As a sales incentive, they sent out their own expert mechanics to build and service engines purchased abroad. Still another technique was an attempt to "package" their engines. This device involved selling the machine, its construction, and an

---

Reprinted with the permission of the author and the Economic History Association from "Marketing Methods in the International Steam Engine Market: The Case of Boulton and Watt" by Jennifer Tann, in *Journal of Economic History*, vol. 38 (1978), pp. 363–389. Copyright © *Journal of Economic History*.

agreement to operate and service it for a particular period of time. They also sought to sell whole factories abroad, most particularly mills to grind grain and mints to strike coins and medals.

Their various techniques did create an overseas market that Watt and Boulton regarded as significant. But the reader will be struck by the relatively limited size of that market and by the very considerable scarcity of trained engineers who were essential to the construction and operation of the steam engines. Both factors should be kept in mind in order to understand how small in expanse and how relatively slow in time was the advance of the early industrial revolution.

James Watt patented his improved steam engine in 1769 but, as is well known, lacked the capital and other facilities to exploit the patent. It was not until the commencement of his partnership with Matthew Boulton in 1775, after Boulton had successfully obtained an Act of Parliament extending the patent to 1800, that the technical development and commercial exploitation of his engine could be effected. The first engines were all reciprocating ones operating pumping and, later, blowing machinery. But, partly in response to Boulton's insistence that demand for factory engines would escalate, Watt developed and in 1782 patented his rotative engine.

For the first twenty years of their partnership certain smaller engine parts were manufactured at Boulton's Soho factory, built in the early 1760s for the production of steel toys and other hardware articles. The larger castings and forgings were subcontracted out to iron works in the Midlands and farther afield. Only with the opening of their own engine foundry in 1795–96 did Boulton and Watt manufacture complete engines. The subcontracting system, though advantageous in permitting the partners to operate on a small capital, nevertheless severely restricted output. Few iron founders and forgers could meet the high standards of production required by Boulton and Watt, and those who could had other, more lucrative work than engine parts. Thus a small upswing in demand could lead to a long waiting list and delays of up to eighteen months. In the first ten years of the firm's existence 108 engines, twenty-one of them for Cornwall and four for overseas, were erected, and 187 between 1786 and 1795, of which twelve were for overseas customers. Demand by overseas customers increased from the last decade of the eighteenth century and a total of 110 engines was ordered by 1825, eight being countermanded.

Before 1800 Boulton and Watt's domestic profit derived from the sale of a premium to work their engine, from supplying drawings, from the sale of parts made by them, and from the small surcharge they sometimes imposed on articles manufactured by subcontractors. In the overseas market a surcharge was added to the sum of materials cost and services, plus British premium, and in the majority of cases a London guarantor was required. From about 1810, most of the overseas orders for Boulton and Watt engines were placed and paid for through London, Liverpool, or Bristol merchants. When Watt's patent expired (by which time the engines were manufactured wholly by Boulton and Watt), prices in the domestic market did not fall as expected; and the price differentials between their engines and others' remained. Increasingly, their domestic customers, other than the government, were exceptionally large firms or firms that had purchased Watt engines before 1800 and sought to replace or augment them. Prices in the overseas market also remained high, at a similar level to the years before 1800. By 1825 both Watt and high pressure engines were being manufactured at more competitive prices in France, Belgium, Russia, Germany, and the U.S.A. From this date overseas demand for the Watt engine fell sharply.

When Boulton and Watt formed their partnership, Boulton had already been firmly established in the Birmingham toy trade for over ten years. During this time he had created a marketing network consisting of both full-time salaried agents and independent ones, paid on a commission basis. His wares were sold throughout Europe and agents supplied him with detailed market information as to lines that were likely to be favored, changes in fashion, and the competition that his goods were facing both from other British firms and from overseas toy manufacturers. Boulton, like Wedgwood, was keenly aware of the importance of advertisement, and of setting a trend by captivating royalty and the nobility, believing that the rest of society would follow. In the consumer goods industries of the eighteenth century, as earlier, firms could prosper, survive, or fail by their marketing methods. As McKendrick and Robinson have shown, both Wedgwood and Boulton had largely perceived the complexities of marketing fashion goods and had developed some sophisticated selling methods as a result. Watt, on the other hand, had no experience in marketing either at home or abroad. But while Boulton had made important contributions to the technology of toy manufacture, had demonstrated his skill as a production engineer in the planning of Soho Manufactory, and had even shown interest in the steam engine before he and Watt discussed partnership, he had no experience in the manufacture and sale of industrial goods.

The early overseas marketing strategies of Boulton and Watt were Boulton-inspired. Some, adopted from the toy trade, proved inappropriate. There was less opportunity to create a demand for steam power than for fashion goods. Nevertheless, the considerable sprinkling of loyal, noble, and government purchasers among Boulton and Watt's overseas customers suggests that they successfully appealed to a section of the potential market for whom cost-effectiveness was a low-priority consideration. This category of customers could, moreover, be more receptive to, and able to act on, requests for protection.

I

The Boulton and Watt partnership was created to exploit a British patent and Watt's rights were jealously guarded, infringers being pursued through the British courts. Protection was thus a central issue in the formulation of their domestic business policy—and no arguments were advanced for modifying this policy in overseas markets. The question of some form of patent coverage was the firm's almost invariable response to inquiries from potential overseas engine customers during the 1770s and 1780s.

The earliest serious negotiations for the sale of engines abroad were undertaken with customers from France, and the partners insisted on obtaining an *arrêt de conseil* before confirming their acceptance of the orders. Boulton employed his well-tried British parliamentary lobbying techniques, approaching, among others, members of the government, a French count, and a Paris banker. The cause was assisted by the nature of the French orders: one customer was a member of the aristocracy, another an inspector of mines, and the third was a newly-launched public works company formed to supply Paris with water. An *arrêt de conseil* was awarded in April 1778, but for the terms to be operative a trial of Boulton and Watt's engine had to be made alongside an atmospheric engine, either at Paris or on the count's land in Normandy. When the Comte d'Heronville's tentative order was cancelled the Inspector of Mines, Jary, obtained permission for the location of the trial to be changed to the Mine du Nord in Brittany. The *arrêt* was confirmed in October 1778. In return for his services towards obtaining protection for the Watt engine in France, Jary was granted the sole rights for selling and erecting Boulton and Watt engines there, with the agreement not to erect any other engines without the partners' consent. Almost immediately Boulton and Watt violated their agreement with Jary by accepting an order for two large engines from the Paris Waterworks, an action that was rationalized by arguing that this public work was an exception and would serve to advertise their engine.

Response to the *arrêt* was minimal. During the following three years some interest was demonstrated but Boulton and Watt received no further orders from France. Fearing that French engineers might obtain subsequent steam engine orders, the partners solicited Genet's support for further confirmation of their *arrêt* by letters patent. A "Memorial to Genet" was sent to Versailles in which Boulton and Watt justified their claim by their experience as engineers, for "they conceive themselves to be more capable to further the views of the Court of France in the extension of Manufacturers and Public Works." Genet was encouraging; in July 1783 he confirmed that, "Je crois être autorisé à vous assurer que vous trouverez la protection la plus signalée dans notre Ministère lorsque vous en aurez besoin."[1] But when,

---

[1] "I am authorized to assure you that you will find the most definite protection in our Ministry when you will need it."

after Boulton and Watt's visit to France in 1786, orders again failed to materialize, the matter was dropped.

The poor market response in France did not inhibit Boulton and Watt in their attempts to obtain patents in other overseas markets. So firmly planted was the idea of the necessity for protection that employees at Soho came to regard it as unshakable policy, and in so doing nearly lost a prestigious Russian customer. When Van Liender of Rotterdam made a tentative approach to Boulton and Watt in 1783 Boulton counselled Watt against any feelings for a fellow scientist: "I believe the best answer that can be given ... is to tell him that we are not anxious about the honour of acquiring gold medals nor of making an eclat in philosophical societies. We will not merely talk about a thing but we will actually do it *provided an exclusive priviledge could be obtained for us* in the United Provinces." Negotiations began in 1785 with Van Liender petitioning for a patent in the names of the Batavian Society and himself, on behalf of Boulton and Watt. A fifteen-year patent was granted in January 1786.

In seeking patent protection overseas the partners were aided by Boulton's international connections—hardware agents, merchants, and social contacts made during visits to the Continent. Also supportive were Watt's admirers among the international scientific community, scientists and philosophers whose vision was not blinkered by territorial boundaries. J. H. de Magellan, for instance, besides acting as intermediary between Boulton and Watt and both Heronville and Genet in the French negotiations, also promoted their interests in the Austrian Netherlands. He attempted to obtain a government engine order, asking the partners "if you still require to have an exclusive priviledge in that country." Nothing came of the order or patent, but four years later negotiations for a Spanish patent commenced. As in France with Jary the patent promoter and first customer, Don Pasquale Mensa y March, was rewarded with sole selling rights of the Boulton and Watt engine. But while there had been much interest in Watt's engine at government level in France, Mensa feared indifference in Spain, for "at present the importance and utility of your Engines as well as the applications ... is entirely unknown." Boulton thereupon sent a "Memorial to the King of Spain" setting out his case, and a twenty-year patent was granted in 1790.

The terms of the Spanish engine agency agreement committed Boulton and Watt to supply engines at agreed prices, to advise on the applications of steam power, to furnish drawings of millwork, to find mechanics, and to ship the goods. The agent agreed not to manufacture engines nor to purchase them from any other manufacturer. The agent could charge what the Spanish market would bear, with "Boulton and Watt confining their profits only to the prices of the materials as contained in the said tariff." Before the agreement was finalized, however, Boulton and Watt received an independent order for a large saw mill engine from Spain. Arguing both that the size demanded far exceeded the sizes set out in the Spanish tariff and that the sole agency agreement had not been ratified, Boulton and Watt agreed, as in the case of the Paris Waterworks, to supply this engine.

Negotiations were also undertaken with W. von Kempelin, holder of an exclusive privilege for the erection of steam engines in the Austrian Empire. Boulton and Watt suggested that the privilege remain in von Kempelin's name but that they, in return for a fixed tariff, supply him with engines. Although there might have been certain advantages for Boulton and Watt—which is by no means certain—von Kempelin's gains would have been few. As with the privileges proposed earlier in Prussia and, possibly, in Italy, no agreement was reached.

Several early pioneers of steam power in the United States attempted to obtain some form of state or national protection of their interests. In 1788 James Rumsey had talks with Boulton and Watt prior to his application for a United States patent. Central to the terms under discussion was a clause by which Rumsey would be supplied with engines solely by Boulton and Watt and would prevent the manufacture of Watt engines in the United States by any other person. A patent was to be sought in the United States in the joint names of Boulton and Watt and Rumsey, the former paying two thirds of the cost. The profits were to be divided: Boulton and Watt would receive two thirds of the profits accruing from land engines and Rumsey one third, besides all those from marine engines. Rumsey, however, considered the proposed terms too restrictive and Boulton and Watt's prices excessive; no agreement was reached.

None of the patents nor agreements was enforceable in practice, and the terms of the proposed American agreement were unworkable. Protection such as Boulton and Watt sought was, it could be argued, highly unrealistic, and could only operate in an atmosphere of absolute mutual trust. This was difficult enough in the domestic market, let alone overseas. As Boulton remarked in connection with the proposed Austrian agreement, "when a man takes a partner he puts it into his power to ruin him, and therefore he should consider it as the next serious thing to the taking of a wife."

Underlying the demands for protection in foreign markets was the assumption that one-off foreign sales could not be profitable; Boulton, in connection with the Spanish engine business, commented that he would require a patent or a reward of £1,000 over and above the cost of one engine. The partners must have hoped more orders would result from a patent, yet this was seen to be unfounded optimism. Boulton and Watt received few orders after the French *arrêt* and their engine was rapidly pirated by local engine manufacturers. Nevertheless, they actively sought protection in other foreign markets until 1790. Thereafter the apparent futility of attempting to protect their engine abroad was effectively emphasized by the difficulties encountered in protecting it even at home. Thus, their interest in foreign patents rapidly waned.

Boulton and Watt has obtained some form of patent coverage in three overseas countries—France, Spain, and the Netherlands—and terms were discussed in four or five more (Prussia, the Austrian Netherlands, the U.S.A. and, possibly, Italy). The protection, where secured, was anything but watertight, and "pirate" engine manufacturers commenced production in France unmolested. And if the prime aim was to secure overseas markets, the policy was a failure, for few orders materialized during the terms of the patents. Boulton's acceptance of a large order from both France and Spain, by-passing the Soho-appointed sole selling agencies in those countries, produced profits in the short term but was a disincentive to the agents to seek further orders. This action was tantamount to an admission that sole selling rights were not expected to further Boulton and Watt's business interests overseas and were only offered as a reward for patents. But Boulton and Watt incurred no expense in securing their overseas protection, and therefore lost nothing in attempting to obtain monopolies. Certainly their patent activities publicized the Watt engine; viewed in these terms, the patent negotiations can be considered an inspired form of advertising.

II

For the first ten years or so of the Boulton and Watt partnership much of their active overseas market research and sales promotion, besides being Boulton-impelled, was also carried out by representatives of Boulton's other business interests. Clerks and travelers from his hardware partnership and merchant house were directed to carry out specific engine marketing tasks at no charge to the engine partnership. An agent visiting Russia in 1777, for instance, circulated papers about the Boulton and Watt engine at court. He was told, however, "that they would not do in this country... [for] as one great object of your Engine is a saving of labour... [and] the workmen are all Slaves the advantage is of no moment." Another agent about to depart for Germany and the Low Countries in 1787 was given similar directions. Other contacts in the mercantile and political world offered their services to Boulton from patriotic motives; Lord Macartney, for example, engaged to promote Boulton's engine interests in China in 1792.

In 1786, however, Boulton and Watt undertook their first overseas sales drive, directing their energies to France as the market with the greatest potential. On this occasion, too, Boulton's other business interests played an important role for he had been commissioned by the French government to make recommendations on the improvement of the toy factory at La Charité, and thus had access to important ministers. The French ministry seemed "much disposed to employ us in the line of our business there," according to Watt. Shortly afterwards Boulton began veiled negotiations with William Wilkinson on the creation of an engine factory in France, probably through the development of an established ironworks. John L.

Baumgartner, a merchant acquaintance of Boulton, suggested that the partners might, with profit, establish an engine agency in Marseilles—but the Revolution intervened. Some years later Boulton turned his attention once more to Russia, employing, as before, one of the representatives of his merchant house. The impetus to this second Russian sales drive was probably the encouraging signs of a major Russian government order for mint engines; besides which, "when they hear of a novel and pretty thing [they] cry after it and must have it." Here, it seemed, elements of a capital goods market might behave in a similar way to the consumer goods markets in which Boulton had so much experience.

Walker, Boulton's agent responsible for seeking commissions in Russia, felt confident that, "without possessing mechanical knowledge, I might be inabled in any part of the world to state to an enquirer the exact price and size of a steam engine adequate to the performance of such a quantity of work as may be demanded." He perceived his task as "the fixing of a permanent and invariable general basis on which for you to act in future, independent of any accidental commissions that may fall in my way here; & which... will also leave you a safe and unerring Road open by which at all times to proceed in the acquisition of such Comm^s as are worth acceptance, without incurring superfluous expenses in their attainment."

Rather than establish a Soho-staffed agency, Walker suggested that an agreement be made with an Englishman already resident in St. Petersburg. Dismissing the English mercantile community, which he considered "altogether unqualified for the task," he proposed a connection "amongst those who were originally mechanical Adventurers and Speculators.... [who] have in consequence, advanced rapidly on the road to favour and fortune." Such a man was Charles Baird, a Scottish founder and engineer resident in St. Petersburg and "pretty intimately acquainted with the Mechanical Professors in general, both Russian and foreigners—also with many of the principal Nobility; and with the proper mode of applying the Key to the private Doors of the Chief Officers in most of the Government Departments." Interest was expressed on both sides but no agreement was concluded. Rather than becoming an ally, Baird predictably became "the most troublesome opponent."

Evaluated in terms of market response, active overseas sales promotion at government level was a failure. No further orders were obtained in Russia and not even the presence of the partners themselves succeeded in eliciting new orders in France. Nevertheless, since the promotion was undertaken at no cost to Boulton and Watt—even the French tour was charged as a specific piece of independent consultancy—the engine partnership could only stand to gain by these activities. As with patents, their value in advertising should not be underestimated, although the majority of overseas sales were clearly the result of the pull rather than the push mechanism in the market.

III

A more successful approach to foreign marketing was achieved by the firm's making available certain engineering services, which influenced the operation of the pull mechanism. For both the foreign and British customer a crucial factor in the innovation decision was access to a skilled mechanic, preferably one trained at Soho, to erect the engine, to train men to operate it, and perhaps even to remain in charge of it.

The shortage of skilled mechanics was a fact of life in the late eighteenth and early nineteenth centuries. The high reputation of a select few firms, such as Boulton and Watt, John Rennie, Jukes Coulson, and Carron Company, enabled them to attract a disproportionately large number of skilled men from the labor market. In the early years of the exploitation of the overseas engine market Boulton and Watt generally agreed to supply a mechanic. Recognizing the advertisement potential of a successful royal, noble, or government-owned steam-powered enterprise, they endeavored to send some of their most able men to these customers. Watt suggested, for instance, that his son might travel from France to superintend the erection of the first Spanish engine. A trusted and respected London agent oversaw the erection of the Nantes corn mill engine, and another able Soho mechanic accompanied the King of Naples' engine to Italy. Boulton, concerned for the successful outcome of the first Russian order, the St. Petersburg Mint, placed social acceptability above engineering capability and sent his nephew, a merchant. Once dressed in a velvet suit on Boulton's instructions and armed with gifts to the secretary of finance, the architect to the court, and others, he was able to move in the appropriate circles including the not inconsiderable British community at St. Petersburg.

> It seems a rule to contrast the extreme affability and urbanity of the master's manner when once introduced to him with the brutal ignorance and insolence of an endless list of shabby secretaries and servants who obstruct every advance and render it next to an impossibility to proceed beyond the first ante-chamber for anyone not wearing half a dozen stars, crosses and Ribands nor scarcely to gain admittance into the courtyard without a carriage and four; as the only criterion of human merit in this capital of misery and magnificance seems to consist in the number of horses a person is entitled to drive, his nominal Rank in Society and the quantity of money he can get at by whatever means and squander foolishly away.

The social position of the British mechanic abroad was mutually recognized by Boulton and Watt and their foreign customers to surpass that he could claim at home. He seemed, moreover, to be peculiarly immune to the upheavals and dangers of the French Revolution and the Napoleonic Wars. "Men who are able to erect [engines] are so scarce that we are become their servants rather than their masters and must put up with their humours however disagreeable it may prove." When Boulton and Watt inquired whether the man they intended sending to Spain in 1791 would run the risk of ill treatment on his journey, they were assured that "he will on the contrary be protected with distinction." One mechanic, described by Watt as "a very honest servant...," once in Italy was "looked upon as a very great man and they increase his pay daily to induce him to remain here."

In an attempt to prevent both British and foreign engine customers from making offers to their mechanics, Boulton and Watt introduced a three-year contract system for most engine erectors. The overseas market, however, presented particular problems: it was almost impossible to trace mechanics who absconded, let alone bring them back. And the erection of distant engines could take a mechanic abroad for more than three years anyway. The wages offered to mechanics accompanying engines abroad were generally higher than in Britain. Additionally, it was customary to expect a "handsome present" on the successful completion of the job. For some millwrights and mechanics, the higher wage was the sole inducement to go abroad. Others recognized that the period of guaranteed paid employment under contract would enable them to make a sufficient number of foreign contacts, either to become established as independent millwrights or to find the right permanent employment with prospects. One Soho mechanic remained in Italy and built several mills and other works there before dying in indifferent circumstances shortly after the French invasion of the country. Another erected an engine in the Netherlands in 1793 and then disappeared. When efforts to trace him had failed, Watt postulated that he might have gone to Spain: "what confirms this opinion in his having always expressed a desire to be employed from home, probably that he might be at a proper distance from his wife whose excess of affection for him sometimes carried her to violent lengths." He was subsequently reported to have been seen in Amsterdam in the company of an American; by the later 1790s he was in the U.S.A., employed at Nicholas I. Roosevelt's Soho engineering works. By 1800 Roosevelt could claim that he did not lack "artists to erect engines upon the most improved plans of Messrs. Boulton and Watt for we are indebted to you not only for the free use of your Patents but for the engineers who execute, we think even improve, them."

After several mechanics had failed to return to Soho, Boulton and Watt began to question the desirability of accepting orders from overseas customers who required a mechanic to accompany the engine, unless it seemed likely that further business would be forthcoming. In 1793, for instance, a tentative foreign order was declined "on account of the difficulties attending the sending of a workman to erect it and other inconveniences attending so small a concern." And it was doubtless for this reason that three engine orders from Austria and Hungary were only undertaken on condition that mechanics would not be required to be sent out with the engines. As Boulton explained to a Viennese customer: "We should be happy to furnish you with engines... but as to our undertaking to send Men to instruct others in the erection of one engine only at so great a distance it would on our part be the most egrarious Folly."

Thereafter, whenever possible Boulton and Watt recruited a millwright or mechanic for the specific foreign customer upon receipt of a firm order, with every expectation that the man would remain abroad. When an overseas customer ordered a British "package" which, besides engine, included millwork from another manufacturer, Boulton and Watt were sometimes able to pass the responsibility for finding a suitable mechanic to the millwrighting firm. Samuel Gray, for example, a millwright formerly employed by Rennie, went to Brazil to superintend the erection of the mint engine and machinery there.

The equivocal nature of the legislation prohibiting the export of artisans, tools, and machinery could, in principle, affect the position of engine mechanics intending to go abroad. Although the legislation did not specifically prohibit the export of steam engines, the ambiguities made engine manufacturers unsure of their position. Benjamin Huntsman, for example, sought Boulton's advice in 1789: "Pray would you chuse or is it right to export steam engines. Pray inform me as I am apply'd to for one." In 1792 Boulton and Watt sought counsel's opinion, pointing out that in their view sending a mechanic abroad to erect an engine made in Britain was different from sending a mechanic to manufacture British products abroad. And, they argued, the importance of the mechanic was such that if engine erectors were to be prohibited from leaving Britain, it would be tantamount to prohibiting the export of the Boulton and Watt engine. The essence of counsel's opinion was that Boulton and Watt should act as they thought best, assessing the merits of each case. Within the same year, therefore, Boulton and Watt declined to send a mechanic to Spain to erect a saw mill engine (instead persuading a former employee, then in Italy, to erect it), and were involved in exporting a complete corn mill package of engine, millwork, and machinery to Nantes, as well as the mechanics to erect it. Three engines were ordered by French customers at the height of the American War of Independence, but by numerous petitions to and personal lobbying of members of the Privy Council, Boulton obtained passports to export the goods as well as the lifting of a shipping embargo on the vessels concerned. John Wilkinson, the ironmaster, noted: "Mr. Boulton will do more in such business than any two knights of the Shire." Nevertheless, an engine was stopped by customs searchers until "by a proper dose of the golden powder the eye sight had been cleared." In their discussions during these transactions, an almost transparent layer of patriotism veiled the self-interest. It happened that the Paris Waterworks Co., instead of purchasing the two complete engines originally ordered, purchased one engine only together with parts of a second and certain steel fitting tools. The fact that Boulton and Watt were aware of the illegality of this is seen in their decision to describe the tools as "engine parts." During his negotiations for the St. Petersburg Mint contract, Boulton exported a model of the mint to St. Petersburg. Aware that he was sailing near the wind, he requested Ivan Smirnove to ensure that no obstacles prevented shipment, and warned him not to go to the customs house in person in case suspicions were aroused. When the orders were finally received, Private Acts were obtained for the export of the Russian and Danish mints and their engines, in spite of considerable opposition. Certainly in this aspect of their marketing policy Boulton and Watt can hardly be described as consistent, except insofar as they never allowed legislation to prevent them from exporting models, engines, artisans to erect them and, on occasion, millwork, machinery, and tools as well.

The paradox was most obvious in Boulton and Watt's attitude to overseas visitors to Soho. Their ambivalence was due, on the one hand, to a recognition of the value of entertainment as a sales technique and, on the other, of being hyper-sensitive to suspected industrial espionage. Some visitors probably never intended purchasing a Boulton and Watt engine. While the exploits of industrial spies in the home market were occasionally ridiculous, the colorful intrigues of overseas industrial spies—the assumption of obviously fake titles and pseudonyms—verged on farce. George and Ernst Wolfe warned Boulton and Watt in 1787 of a Dane "of a sallow complexion, rather a down cast look and waddles pretty much in his manner of walking" who was in company with a Pole, "who passes by the title of Baron Richagenius." Even if the Soho engine workshops were closed, it was well nigh impossible to prevent overseas visitors from seeing Boulton and Watt engines at work elsewhere—indeed, this had to be encouraged. Baron Stein obtained the information he required at Barclay and Perkins' London brewery by bribing a mechanic. After the event, the partners sought the advice of Sir Joseph Banks who moralized "never to countenance a foreigner who I do not think incapable of attempting to steel inventions."

How effective industrial espionage was to the countries promoting it is debatable. The German, Buckling, managed to construct an engine on Boulton and Watt's principle, but its working left much to be desired and he had to return to England for further enlightenment. This incident supports Boulton's insistence that British mechanics were essential for putting an exported engine into order, the technological gap between exporting and adopting country otherwise being too great. But where espionage was conducted by mechanics or engineers, the results could usually be more fruitful. Although they were less likely to be admitted to the partners' homes, lacking unguent speech and titles real or assumed, their observations could be more penetrating and effective. Boulton and Watt's first two foreign customers had both attempted to obtain "pirate" Watt engines, and both finally purchased engines from Soho on far more favorable terms than later customers. Mechanics were not sent to erect these engines, though not because Britain and France were at war: both customers insisted they did not require mechanics. When there remained a possibility that some would go with the Paris Waterworks engines, the waterworks engineer, Perier, countered with the plea that he would lose face in France. Blueprints and tools accompanied the engines instead, thereby expediting the manufacture of Watt engines in France which was, without doubt, Perier's object.

IV

A further important influence on the operation of the pull mechanism in the overseas market was the availability of production engineering advice. With some notable exceptions, such as Van Liender of the Netherlands and Robert Fulton of the U.S.A., Boulton and Watt's overseas customers were less well versed in matters mechanical than their British counterparts. Even in an enterprise such as the Nantes flour mill, where an able French engineer was closely involved, Boulton and Watt were required to supply a production engineering service and were frequently consulted at the design stage. Moreover, liaison between Boulton and Watt and John Rennie, a former employee, as well as with the M. Boulton Mint Co. enabled the partners to provide a complete package for overseas clients who required a custom-designed system and engine, together with millwork and, occasionally, machinery.

Boulton and Watt's production engineering consultancy was in greatest demand in the application of steam power to two industries, grain milling and minting, in both of which one of the partners had practical experience. The experience gained at their experimental corn mill at Soho Manufactory and later as partners in the Albion Steam Corn Mill, London, made Boulton and Watt seeming authorities on milling technology and management, although in fact Albion Mill posed both technical and managerial problems not met with on the much smaller scale at Soho. Approximately two thirds of the prospective customers for steam engines in the milling industry requested detailed information on the productivity of milling machinery, on millwork design, and on the plan of the building, and in no case did the entrepreneur appear to be already engaged in corn milling on a smaller scale—Albion Mill was indeed a powerful advertisement. In five out of seven overseas steam corn mill projects Boulton and Watt acted as consulting production engineers, and in two cases (Nantes and Cadiz mills) the "package" included the complete millwork and machinery from Rennie. When a Danish steam corn mill was contemplated in 1794 Boulton and Watt were requested to undertake everything for the mill except responsibility for erecting the building. After the destruction of Albion Mill by fire Watt advised the Nantes concern on simple methods of fireproofing.

During Boulton and Watt's period of euphoria over Albion Mill, prospective engine customers, besides obtaining advice on the production and mechanical engineering aspects of milling by steam power, also sought and obtained data on the costs of innovation in corn milling. Before their disenchantment Boulton and Watt's fixed costs appear modest and the profits persuasive. In 1785 Watt was involved in discussions concerning the establishment of a steam milling concern in Lyons. He drafted a detailed statement of the fixed and annual costs of a mill containing six pairs of stones working continuously (probably eight pairs in all) to grind 720 bushels (17 loads) of wheat per day. This costing was not sent, being considered too detailed, and the shortened version subsequently provided was amended to reduce the estimated coal costs to £999, thereby lowering the annual expenses to £3,870. 3s. 4d. and increasing the apparent advantages of milling by steam to 5/5d. per load.

Another detailed costing exercise was carried out in about 1789 for "a Fire Engine with its corresponding Mill to grind Wheat, the plantification, Conclusion and Establishment in the Province of Andalusia in Spain," the capacity to be 1210 bushels per day. To emphasize the advantages of a steam mill to their Spanish customers Boulton and Watt compared it with the requisite number of *ataonas* or mule corn mills to produce an equivalent quantity. But as the unprofitability of Boulton and Watt's own milling venture in London became increasingly apparent, their enthusiasm for proferring financial advice to prospective customers in the milling industry cooled.

Matthew Boulton's fine coins and commemorative medals reached the hands of monarchs and influential members of the aristocracy, besides members of governments and merchants in many foreign countries, within a few years of Soho mint's becoming operational. Their value as advertisements was recognized and with Boulton's high reputation as an inventor of mint machinery, together with his innovative design of a flow production system in minting, they led to his mechanical and production engineering advice being frequently sought by prospective mint engine customers. Towards the end of his life Boulton increasingly devoted his time and attention to his mint business. Thus this engineering consultancy was, on the whole, more realistic than Boulton and Watt's milling advice. He avoided being drawn into a discussion of the financial aspects of minting, which to many of his foreign customers was not a high priority consideration anyway. The distinguished potential and actual foreign mint customers—governments, monarchs, and noblemen—generally inquired for or ordered mint engines directly from Boulton during the course of negotiations for a complete mint system. Matthew Boulton, and later his son, was responsible for the production engineering and mint machinery as well as, in partnership with Watt, the engine.

Boulton's ability to design and take responsibility for the erection of a complete mint was a crucial element in the successful negotiations for mint engines in Russia, Denmark, Brazil, and India.

> I do not profess myself architect but my experience has enabled me to arrange and systematise a great Imperial Mint...[It is necessary] to arrange the rooms in such order that the money shall go forward progressively from one

room to another until it is compleatly packed and ready to deliver for circulation and never go backward and forward.... I must beg that no alteration may be made in any of the rooms which are destined to hold and work the machinery... as the buildings are in some degree combined with my machinery.

Perhaps doubting some customers' priorities, he added, "I should prefer a simple, clean, orderly, convenient, modest building with good machinery to that which is magnificently bad."

The apparent readiness of Boulton and Watt to advise overseas customers on broader engineering and financial issues led to their being regarded as a potential source of capital for export. Several entrepreneurs sought the partners' financial involvement in overseas industrial concerns through offers of shares and partnerships. Boulton's capital was solicited for an iron rolling and slitting works in Russia, as well as a mine in Germany, a corn mill in Paris, a copper rolling and coining project in Paris, a copper mine in the U.S.A., and various projects in Nova Scotia. And both partners were involved in separate negotiations towards financial involvement in a foreign manufacturing concern—Boulton in the Monnerons brothers' Paris copper rolling and coining project, and Watt in the Lyons steam corn mill—but neither project came to fruition. As partners they became shareholders in the Paris Waterworks, although only when it became increasingly clear that they were unlikely to receive full payment in cash for their engines. Boulton and Watt's acceptance of shares in the Paris Waterworks Company did not appear to them to be unpatriotic, or inconsistent witth Boulton's antagonistic attitude to British interests in foreign hardware and toy firms. Nor, having railed at expatriate toymakers, did Boulton concern himself with the seeming inconsistency of his engineering consultancy for and intended financial involvement in the Paris mint: "I considered that I was giving to France my Invention... besides which I shall assist with what ever can be done in this country [France] for the benefit of the concern." Matthew Boulton was a businessman first, an Englishman second.

V

Boulton and Watt engine prices in the domestic market remained remarkably stable between the mid-1780s and the 1820s, fluctuations in factor prices being absorbed in large measure by the manufacturers. While lists were never published, the figures quoted to their prospective British customers kept fairly close to the firm's agreed domestic prices. There were no general price lists for the foreign market, and Spain was the only country for which a tariff was drawn. This list represented a mark-up on British prices which allowed the manufacturers an additional 20–30 percent profit, despite their disclaimer to be charging no premium. The list was not strictly adhered to, even in Spain, but the majority of prices quoted or paid in overseas markets between 1790 and 1810 were marked up by similar proportions to the Spanish tariff. This surcharging did not affect engine sales, however, for engine price was never the reason given either for failure to proceed with an order, or for the cancellation of an order.

The high proportion of public works projects which, along with noble customers and the early adopters in private enterprise, comprised 42.7 percent of Boulton and Watt's foreign customers, may partly explain the purchasers' acquiescence over price; and where the sellers observed room for maneuver, engine prices were more a matter of what the market would bear. The King of Naples, for example, paid £1,000 for his engine materials and an additional £1,000 for services, drawings, and profit, when the cost price was £778. Watt considered this an unduly large profit and cautioned Boulton, who was then concerned in negotiations with a French count, to "make the best bargain you can but consider you are not now selling an invention to a King but making an Engine for a merchant." The Danish government mint engines of 1804 were about 50 percent dearer than prices in Boulton and Watt's British list, and senior clerks at Soho seem to have had some degree of freedom in quoting prices for foreign customers. Watt, Jr., commented that he considered one clerk's estimate for the Hudson's Bay Company in 1811 too high, but he let the matter rest and they obtained the order. When an order for two 70 h.p. marine engines was placed by the Dutch government in 1825 Watt, Jr., quoted £9,000, noting that "For this price [they] appeared perfectly prepared . . . [although] it much exceeds that for which we have contracted for the Post Office 70s." He added that Fawcett of Liverpool had contracted with a customer for two 75 h.p. marine engines at £8,800. . . . Boulton and Watt expected to make a profit of between 71 percent and 111 percent on the sale of engines abroad compared with 52 percent to 87 percent on domestic sales. Attempts were made to standardize the surcharging for overseas customers in 1821 when Watt's son proposed that 2½ percent be added to British prices, but by 1825 the suggestion had not been fully implemented. The Dutch market was the price exception, the negotiating merchant house being charged sums that closely approximated British engine prices. But this house was treated as an exception in another respect, in that Boulton and Watt waived their normal requirement of a London guarantor upon receipt of orders.

The only general circumstance in which the partners considered waiving their larger profit on overseas engines was with the first customer from a country in which subsequent sales could be expected. Jary, Boulton and Watt's first French customer, negotiated for a fixed payment in lieu of premiums which "he thinks ought to be put on a better footing than others as being the first." In short, as was remarked by Wilkinson, "he is a knowing hand and as such a very proper person for to make a beginning." The first Netherlands engine was supplied at cost price to the Batavian Society, but when a Dutch enquiry for a 3 h.p. engine followed in 1791

Boulton and Watt quoted 300 guineas. They justified that "we have already made one engine without profit for the Conviction of the people of Holland, but cannot go on in that way. What we have asked of you is the lowest price we can execute such an engine for." On the other hand, a prospective Canadian customer was quoted £1,100 in 1789 for a 16 h.p. engine, a figure which was well above the Spanish tariff of the same date, and allowed a profit of 139 percent in spite of the makers' claim to "have charged our premium very low as being the first in the country."

It is not possible to cost the time and effort expended by Boulton and Watt in the prosecution of their foreign business. Nor is it possible, save in a very few cases, to estimate the sums involved in entertaining and the presentation of gifts to foreign customers. Expenses totalling nearly £2,000 were incurred during Z. Walker's stay in St. Petersburg, for instance, a figure which excludes not only his salary but also those of the four mechanics who erected the mint engines. While Boulton and Watt's admitted responsibility ended with the delivery or completion of the engine at Soho—and the customer was required to pay the first installment on the purchase price at this point—the firm often, in practice, assisted with the arrangements for insurance and shipping although the cost of these, as well as the wages of the engine mechanic sent to erect the engine, was borne by the customer. The actual price paid by a foreign customer is not always known, but an estimate of the turnover in foreign sales can be made if it is assumed that the Spanish tariff was fairly closely adhered to. Although some foreign customers were charged less, the majority were charged more than the tariff; thus the final figure will be an underestimate. On this basis, the 102 foreign sales (excluding West Indies) made between 1775 and 1825 produced a total turnover of £136,467.

There were considerable annual fluctuations in the anticipated profits from overseas sales, the £4,044 for 1779 not being exceeded until ten years later and not again until 1822. By December 1800 foreign sales had produced an estimated profit of £18,509. This figure had almost doubled by the end of 1815 and, with the accelerating overseas demand for marine engines from 1816 (orders worth an estimated profit of £24,748), over half the total profits on overseas sales (£33,998) were obtained in the years 1816–1825, culminating in an estimated total of £65,638 by 1825.

Overseas demand was uncertain. High initial expectations resulting from the two French orders of 1779 were not confirmed. Despite some interest in France, Germany, Italy, Hungary, and Russia in the following five years, no further overseas orders were obtained until 1785 and no valuable ones until the French and Spanish orders of 1789. The French wars of 1793–1815 undoubtedly affected European sales. Only two inquiries and no orders were received from France, an Austrian order was cancelled, and there was no communication from Italy between Naples' peace with the French in 1801 and the end of the wars. A similar pattern can be observed in Spain and Portugal. Overseas orders were far more consistent from 1816 onwards, the level never falling below two and rising on four occasions to nine or more per year.

The failure of the push mechanism in the overseas market has already been observed. It was no doubt with this in mind that M. R. Boulton commented, in the context of the Russian market, that the expenditure of any more time and effort would have been imprudent while Boulton and Watt could "obtain more orders from their wealthy neighbours than can be executed." This may have been a pertinent observation in the short term but, through the provision of expert ancillary services which influenced the pull mechanism, the long-term profits accruing to Boulton and Watt from the overseas market justified the sales efforts and vindicate Matthew Boulton's statement of intent, made seven years before he commenced engine production with Watt, to "serve all the world with engines of all sizes."

Bibliography

I. T. BEREND and G. RANKI, *The European Periphery and Industrialization, 1780–1914* (1982).
F. BRAUDEL, *Capitalism and Material Life, 1400–1800* (1974).
F. BRAUDEL, *The Structures of Everyday Life: The Limits of the Possible* (1982).
P. DEANE, *The First Industrial Revolution*, 2nd ed. (1979).
E. L. JONES, *Agriculture and Economic Growth in England, 1650–1815* (1968).
D. LANDES, *The Unbound Prometheus: Technological Change and Industrial Development in Western Europe from 1750 to the Present* (1969).
J. LORD, *Capital and Steam Power, 1750–1800*, 2nd ed. (1966).
N. MCKENDRICK, et al., *The Birth of a Consumer Society: The Commercialization of Eighteenth-Century England* (1982).
P. MATHIAS, *The First Industrial Nation: An Economic History of Britain 1700–1914* (1969).
A. E. MUSSON, and E. ROBINSON, *James Watt and the Steam Engine* (1969).
S. POLLARD, and C. HOLMES, *Documents of European Economic History: The Process of Industrialization, 1750–1870* (1968).
S. POLLARD, *The Genesis of Modern Management: A Study of the Industrial Revolution in Great Britain* (1965).
S. POLLARD, *Peaceful Conquest: The Industrialization of Europe, 1760–1970* (1981).
R. E. SCHOFIELD, *The Lunar Society of Birmingham: A Social History of Provincial Science and Industry in Eighteenth-Century England* (1963).

The Encyclopédie Wars of Prerevolutionary France

ROBERT DARNTON

Books that made history may also have an important history themselves. Such is the case of *L'Encyclopédie* (*The Enclyclopedia*), the most famous publication of the Enlightenment. When Diderot first undertook the project in the 1750s, he confronted much opposition from the political and religious authorities under Louis XV of France, but he succeeded in bringing the great multivolume set to a conclusion by 1772. The work contained articles on literature, philosophy, and religion by virtually all the major enlightened writers, as well as essays and prints of contemporary economic life that remain a major source of our knowledge of mid-eighteenth-century farming and manufacturing methods.

This part of the story is relatively familiar. But once written and printed, how did the volumes become distributed? What happened to the *Encyclopedia* after its first edition? Who profited from the venture? Who bought the sets and where did the purchasers live? The answers to these questions about the business of enlightenment lead the historian deep into the social history of the Old Regime. They reveal dealings in large-scale finance, attempts at swindling, the smuggling of books across national borders, the overcoming of shortages of paper, ink, and printing presses, and a world of tough and unrelenting competition. Both intellectual daring and shady business practices lay behind the dispersion of the light of reason via the *Encyclopedia*. But in pursuing the history of its publication, the historian comes to discover significant changing attitudes on the part of the French government toward the enterprise and also establishes a remarkably clear picture of the kinds of people who acquired, and some of whom no doubt read, the *Encyclopedia*.

Reprinted with the permission of the author from "The *Encyclopédie* Wars of Prerevolutionary France" by Robert Darnton, in *American Historical Review*, vol. 78 (1973), pp. 1331–1352. Copyright © 1973 by Robert Darnton.

The publication of the *Encyclopédie* has long been recognized as a turning point of the Enlightenment. In permitting Diderot's text to appear in print the state, however reluctantly and imperfectly, gave the philosophes an opportunity to try their wares in the market place of ideas. But what was the result of this break-through in the traditional restraints on the printed word in France? By concentrating on the duel between the *encyclopédistes* and the French authorities, scholars have told only half the story. The other half concerns some basic questions in the social history of ideas: how did publishers plan and execute editions in the eighteenth century? How well did works like the *Encyclopédie* sell? And who bought them? This essay is addressed to those questions. By recounting the life cycle of one book, it is intended to suggest some of the possibilities in the history of publishing, a field that has lain fallow too long despite its attractive location at the crossroads of intellectual, social, economic, and political history.

When Diderot and his publishers brought out the last volume of the *Encyclopédie* in 1772, they had won more than a moral victory over the system for controlling French publishing. The first edition probably produced about 2,500,000 livres in gross profits. But the government refused to let the book sell openly, and most of the 4,225 sets went to customers outside France. The second edition also seems to have been primarily a non-French affair. It was a folio[1] reprint of the original text, produced in Geneva by a consortium of publishers allied with Charles Joseph Panckoucke of Paris. Its sales records have not survived, but its publishers originally hoped to market half of their 2,200 sets in France; and they had sold 1,330 sets throughout Europe when they settled their accounts in June 1775. So by that date only 3,000 copies of the first two editions, at the very most, existed in France. The country had not been inundated with *Encyclopédies*, despite the semi-legal status granted to the book.

But the publishing of the next editions—the three quarto and the two octavo printings of the original text—is a very different story; and unlike the publishing history of the first two editions, it can be told in detail, thanks to the papers of the Société Typographique de Neuchâtel in Neuchâtel, Switzerland. The story begins with Panckoucke, the extraordinary entrepreneur known as "the Atlas of the book trade," and his system of alliances and alignments within the world of publishing and politics.

In December 1768 Panckoucke bought from the original publishers the plates of the *Encyclopédie* and the rights to future editions of it. Precisely what these rights were is difficult to say. Panckoucke used the terms "droits" and

---

[1] [The terms *folio*, *quarto*, and *octavo* refer to the size of a book, which is the result of the number of pages printed on a standard sheet of printing paper. A folio has two pages printed on each side for a total of four pages; a quarto has four pages printed on each side for a total of eight pages; an octavo has eight pages printed on each side for a total of sixteen pages. The printed sheet is folded so as to constitute a normal portion of a book or pamphlet. The more printed pages on the sheet, the smaller the size of the type and of the printed page.]

"privilège" throughout his correspondence, but the government had revoked the formal privilege of the *Encyclopédie* in 1759, and the registers of privileges in the Bibliothèque Nationale give no indication that it was ever restored. They do reveal that Panckoucke received a twelve-year *privilège général* on March 29, 1776, for a "Recueil des planches sur les sciences, arts et métiers," which may have been enough to substantiate his claim to possess a kind of copyright. In any case, he asserted that claim in the most absolute manner, citing not only the contract by which he bought out the original publishers but also the sanction of the French government; and he sold portions of his "privilege" to a whole series of partners, periodically buying them back and reselling them again to new associates for new editions.

Panckoucke's first *Encyclopédie* was the second edition, the folio reprint of 1771–76. Those were hard years in the book trade, owing to the repressive measures of the "triumvirate" ministry of Maupeou, Terray, and d'Aiguillon, so Panckoucke had the edition printed in Geneva by his partners, who included Voltaire's publisher, "the angel Gabriel" Cramer. It was a stormy affair, involving quarrels among the associates, conflict with a rival, a "Protestant" *Encyclopédie* being produced by Barthélemy de Félice in Yverdon, and a losing battle with the French government, which had confiscated six thousand volumes that Panckoucke had originally printed in Paris. Whether Panckoucke ever had much success in cracking the French market with this edition cannot be known, but his difficulties did not discourage him. By the accession of Louis XVI he remained convinced that there was still a fortune to be made in *Encyclopédies*, and the liberal character of the new ministry swelled his hopes. He found doors opening for him everywhere within the government. His coach carried him into Versailles "like an official with a portfolio." And his letters burgeoned with assurances of "protections" from lieutenants of police, directors of the book trade, and ministers.

On July 3, 1776, Panckoucke sold an interest of fifty per cent in his newly consolidated "rights and privileges" in the *Encyclopédie* for 143,000 livres to the Société Typographique de Neuchâtel, one of the most important publishers of French books during the twenty years before the Revolution. After toying with a plan to publish another folio reprint, this new association decided to produce a completely revised edition. The text was to be rewritten by a whole stable of philosophes—including Marmontel, Morellet, La Harpe, D'Arnaud, St. Lambert, and Thomas—under the direction of Suard, with D'Alembert and Condorcet as associates. Panckoucke did not enlist Diderot, "*une mauvaise tête,* who demanded 100,000 écus and would have driven us to despair." But he counted heavily on D'Alembert, who was to solicit the protection of Frederick II and perhaps even to persuade him to accept the dedication of the new work. D'Alembert also considered writing a history of the *Encyclopédie* for the new edition, but that essay died stillborn, like other potential classics of the Enlightenment—a history of French Protestantism by Raynal, a history of Turgot's ministry by Voltaire—that never got beyond the stage of projects knocked about in negotiations between authors and publishers. In the end this new *Encyclopédie* itself miscarried, despite the grandiose plans of its backers, because it was undercut by a quarto edition of the original text, which was launched in 1776 by Joseph Duplain of Lyons, the antihero of this story and one of the most intrepid buccaneers in the era of "booty capitalism."

Like many provincial bookdealers Duplain built his business on the demand for cheap, pirated works, often of a racy or philosophical character, which were produced in the printing houses flourishing beyond the fringes of France's borders, thanks to the system of privileges and thought control that stifled innovative publishing within the kingdom. Duplain smelled a fortune in cut-rate *Encyclopédies*. He announced the opening of a subscription for a cheap quarto edition, which would incorporate the five-volume supplement in the original text. He protected himself by attributing the edition to Jean Léonard Pellet, a Genevan printer who received three thousand livres for acting as straw man. And when the flow of subscriptions proved strong enough, Duplain contracted the printing to several Genevan shops, keeping the financial and administrative work to himself. He counted on getting the books into France either by smuggling—he had great influence in the booksellers' gild of Lyons, although he had powerful enemies in the Parisian gild—or by winning the benevolent neutrality of the French authorities. But he had not reckoned with Panckoucke.

Panckoucke could choose either to beat Duplain or to join him. The first alternative appealed to Panckoucke because he was convinced that he could use his protections effectively enough to block the channels of the underground book trade. But the success of the subscription created a greater temptation. Panckoucke knew "every step that Duplain takes," thanks to secret reports from an allied Lyonnais bookseller called Gabriel Regnault. Regnault learned that the subscription was selling spectacularly, and corroborative information "from everywhere" made it look as though the quarto *Encyclopédie* could turn into the most profitable publication of the century. So Panckoucke shelved the project for the revised edition and entered into negotiations, bartering his monopoly on legality against a cut of the subscriptions. On January 14, 1777, he and Duplain signed what later became known as the "Treaty of Dijon." Each took a half interest in the quarto enterprise, which they subsequently divided among their own associates (the Société Typographique de Neuchâtel eventually came to own five twenty-fourths of the entire enterprise). Duplain committed himself to administer the production, distribution, and financing of the edition according to conditions specified in great detail by the contract. And Panckoucke promised to supply half the capital, the three volumes of plates, and the covering protection of his privilege. The last item was no small advantage. In August 1777 Panckoucke wrote that Le Camus de Neville, the director of the Librairie, "will protect our great affair" and had even given permission for Panckoucke to import the books directly to his warehouses in Paris, bypassing the customs, the booksellers' gild, and the censorship. At the same time, writing as if he were himself a minister, Panckoucke directed the inspector of books in Lyons to give clear passage to the crates being shipped from Switzerland. In fact Panckoucke pulled strings so effectively that the Swiss printers began to stuff their shipments of *Encyclopédies* with prohibited books. Far from drawing the fire of the established authorities, as it had done in the 1750s, the *Encyclopédie* circulated under the protective covering of their patronage; and that protection served as camouflage for the diffusion of works that the state wanted to suppress.

Panckoucke and Duplain had no idea that a small smuggling operation had grafted itself onto their enterprise. They gave all their attention to the maximization of profits, and the quarto proved to be extraordinarily profitable: orders poured in from everywhere, traveling salesmen reaped unheard-of harvests, and booksellers marveled at a hunger for the *Encyclopédie* that had remained dormant among clients who had not been able to buy the folio editions. "There is no other work so universally widespread," wrote Dufour of Maestricht. "Our streets are paved with it," said Resplandy of Toulouse, echoing exactly the observation of a Lyonnais salesman: "Our town is paved with it." And Panckoucke exulted, "The success of this quarto edition passes all belief." In opening the subscription Duplain had set his sights high: he hoped to sell 4,000 copies. The subscription filled to overflowing with astonishing speed; so Duplain opened another, for 2,000 more copies. It, too, filled rapidly, and Duplain opened a third, making a total of 8,000 sets of thirty-nine quarto volumes each—an extraordinary amount for an era when printings of single-volume works normally ran to 1,000 copies or so.

This succession of subscriptions explains the mystery of the missing second quarto edition, which has plagued bibliographers who have been able to locate only the first, or "Pellet," edition and the third, or "Neuchâtel," edition of the quarto *Encyclopédie*. Duplain committed himself to print the second subscription when the printers had reached sheet "T" of volume 6, working at a press run of 4,000 copies. He directed them to reprint 2,000 copies of everything they had completed and then to continue at a run of 6,000. So there was no distinct second edition. The third subscription coincided with a separate "third edition," because each sheet was reset and run off at 2,000 copies, and the title page of each volume proclaimed it to be "troisième édition, à Neuchâtel, chez la Société typographique." In fact this imprint was a ruse devised by Duplain to inveigle subscriptions from persons who had been put off by the slipshod quality of the Pellet editions. The Société Typographique actually printed only one volume of "its" edition and four of the volumes that appeared under Pellet's name. In every case Duplain subcontracted the printing and remained hidden behind his typographical false fronts.

Duplain used printers in Neuchâtel, Geneva, Lyons, Trévoux, and Grenoble, putting more than forty presses at work to turn out about 300,000 volumes. To produce and distribute books on such a scale required assembling one of the largest operations in premodern printing and strained resources throughout the publishing industry. For two and a half years the *Encyclopédie* dominated printing in the region around Lyons. "Except for a few liturgical works, nothing else is being printed here, in all the shops, only the *Encyclopédie*," an agent reported in 1778. The Société Typographique took five months, using about half the capacity of its twelve presses and its work force of about thirty-five men, to print a press run of 6,000 copies of one of the huge, double-column tomes. Financing 8,000 copies of thirty-six such volumes required so much capital that Panckoucke and Duplain fell back on consortia of French and Swiss bankers, and the same agent in Lyons observed, "Whoever had a little money to put into books every month or every year has placed it on the *Encyclopédie* quarto." The *Encyclopédie* consumed so much paper that in December 1777 a buyer for the Société Typographique could not find a single sheet of the requisite kind in Lyons. The Société managed to continue printing only by sending paper scouts throughout France and western Switzerland in search of every last ream of *fin*, twenty-pound (Lyonnais measure) *carré* or *raisin*. Founders could not supply type rapidly enough to satisfy the demand (the quarto was printed, appropriately, in a type called "Philosophie"), and so some Genevan printers failed to begin work on schedule in 1777. The Neuchâtelois had to suspend printing at a crucial moment because they received a barrel of bad ink, and the inkmaker, a Parisian called Langlois who had a strangle hold on the quality-ink trade, kept inching up his prices, while lamenting about his own increased costs, which he attributed to poor olive harvests in the Midi. Wagoners also took advantage of increased orders to force up their rates. And the *Encyclopédie* produced chaos in the labor market of printing. Not only did the printers have to send hundreds of miles for workers, but the supply was so scarce that they took to raiding each other's shops through the use of industrial spies like Louis Marcinhes, a down-and-out watchmaker in Geneva, who wrote to the Société Typographique in July 1777,

> Pellet and Bassompierre have by inflated promises seduced many workers and drained off the printing shops of the surrounding area. But they only want to pay them 15 florins 9 sols of our money per sheet. So a good number want to leave, because they are asking for 17 florins per sheet. The man leaving this week [for Neuchâtel] is one of those. He is called Caisle. Two pressmen, who have promised to come talk with me, also should leave.... I won't lose sight of any occasion to send to you the discontented from the shops of Pellet, Bassompierre, and Nouffer.

In short, the quarto *Encyclopédie* sent repercussions into the remotest sectors of the economy. For it to come into being a whole world had to be set in motion: ragpickers, olive growers, financiers, and philosophers collaborated to create a work whose corporeal existence corresponded to its intellectual message. As a physical object and as a vehicle of thought, the *Encyclopédie* synthesized a thousand sciences, arts, and crafts; it represented the Enlightenment, body and soul.

Its publishers probably spent too much time calculating costs and profits to entertain such lofty thoughts. The Société Typographique estimated the total revenue of the enterprise at 2,454,092 livres, the total cost at 1,117,354 livres, and the gross profit at 1,336,738 livres: a return of one hundred twenty per cent on expenditures. No wonder they considered this affair "the most beautiful ever to be done in publishing," or that it touched off a series of fierce commercial wars.

Duplain, who had originally floated the quarto as a privateering venture, had no way, once he turned legitimate, of burying his treasure. Other pirates got wind of it and raced to the attack. First came announcements of rival counterfeit editions from Geneva and Avignon. Panckoucke read them as bluffs and counseled his associates to ride them out, since "I have arranged everything here in such a manner that none of those editions can enter France, and without France no success." He was right: the announcements were a way of holding the quarto publishers up for ransom by threatening to undersell them unless they paid a certain sum in protection money. The danger in this game was that one could not distinguish between a fake and a real attack until he saw the whites of his assailant's eyes. After the quartos of Geneva and Avignon had disappeared over the horizon, J. S. Grabit and J. M. Barret of Lyons announced plans to publish another quarto *Encyclopédie*, and they proved that they meant business by actually printing a few volumes. In this case Duplain and Panckoucke agreed that it would be wiser to capitulate. They bought out Grabit and Barret for 27,000 livres—the rough equivalent of a lifetime's wages for one of their printers—and received in return only a legalized promise to abstain from further counterfeiting. Then they learned that a consortium of publishers in Lausanne and Bern planned to produce an even smaller, even cheaper *Encyclopédie*, an octavo edition that would sell for approximately 200 livres. This time Duplain and Panckoucke decided to stand and fight.

At first the quarto publishers hoped that the octavo venture would simply collapse. They joked that the small type of "cette miniature" would blind its readers, and Panckoucke proclaimed "that octavo edition may cause some alarm, but it won't hurt us.... It is folly to print the *Encyclopédie* in such a small text. Moreover, we will be defended here. I am waiting for the magistrate [Le Camus de Neville] to return so that I can reveal everything to him. I promise you firmly that that *Encyclopédie* will never enter France." The Société Typographique replied, "You hold the keys to the kingdom." But reports from provincial booksellers indicated that the octavo subscriptions were selling as spectacularly as the quarto had done. So the quarto group began pourparlers—not with any serious intention of making peace but rather to delay the execution of the octavo until the quarto could be completed and the new, revised edition announced, thereby stealing the octavo market. The publishers of Lausanne and Bern, who were veterans of pirate publishing, detected this strategy after a few rounds of negotiation and resolved to proceed with their printing. Duplain then attempted to overwhelm them with a frontal assault: he published an announcement that the quarto group would produce its own octavo edition at an even cheaper price than the octavo of Lausanne and Bern. On November 1, 1777, Lausanne and Bern retaliated with an ultimatum: withdraw your announcement within fifteen days, or we will drop the price of our octavo to the level of yours, and we will undermine your quarto by producing a still cheaper quarto of our own.

> You will have to give in to us or lower your own price. In this way we will cut each other's throats, but you have set the example and are forcing this necessity upon us. And don't think that this is an idle threat. The prospectuses are ready, and we have the same type, the necessary presses etc. at our disposition in Yverdon.

This maneuver forced Duplain to retreat, but it also resulted in open war; for although negotiations continued intermittently—the usual style in eighteenth-century warfare—each side campaigned fiercely, attempting to destroy the other's market.

The octavo group relied on a strategy of smuggling. They filled their subscription and counted on reaching their clients through the underground circuits of the clandestine book trade. The quarto group calculated on blocking those circuits. Panckoucke promised his partners, "I guarantee that they will not penetrate France. The magistrate promised me so.... You understand, Messieurs, that being armed with a privilege, you should not concede your rights any more than I. Because of our contracts, our privilege, Duplain had to come make terms with us. The Lausannois will have to do the same." The system of privilege and protection that had nearly destroyed the first edition of the *Encyclopédie* was being used as the main line of defense in the effort to save its successor. So much had conditions changed from the reign of Louis XV to that of Louis XVI that the government treated *encyclopédisme* more as a commercial than an ideological matter. This new attitude suggests that enlightened ideas permeated the government itself, but it does not necessarily imply weakness; in fact the contest between the strategy of smuggling and the strategy of policing provides a test case of the government's ability to control the printed word.

In mid-1778 the Société Typographique de Neuchâtel sent an agent, Jean-François Favarger, on a tour of southern and central France. Favarger's first assignment was to check the society's supply lines along the French-Swiss border. In Saint Sulpice, the last town on the Swiss side of the border, he learned that the smuggling outfit of Meuron Frères had recently taken care of five 500-pound crates containing volume 1 of the octavo *Encyclopédie*. The Meuron brothers told him so themselves, with more than a hint of professional pride, because they handled the society's own smuggling but only as occasional substitutes for Pion of Pontarlier, the society's first-string smuggler, whom they wanted to replace. On the other side of the border, in Pontarlier, Pion told Favarger that he had seen five *acquits à caution*—a customs permit used by the French state to control imports of foreign books—that had been fraudulently discharged by Capel, syndic of the booksellers' gild in Dijon. Since Capel was officially required to confiscate the books that he forwarded, Dijon now promised to surpass Besançon as the main entrepôt of this underground route, as Favarger announced triumphantly in notifying his employers that the octavo had passed from Bern to Saint Sulpice to Dijon and was now headed toward Paris. The Société Typographique hid Capel's name in the hope that "for money he will provide us with the same service" and relayed the rest of the information to Panckoucke, who alerted the French authorities, who eventually captured the crates. The authorities engineered other confiscations on their own—in Toulouse, for example, where a big bust inflicted huge casualties on the octavo group. By August Favarger's field reports showed that subscribers were deserting the octavo in droves throughout the Midi. And in early 1779 the octavo publishers sued for peace.

The negotiations dragged on for a year, while the quarto group finished a mopping-up operation in France and the octavo group tried to repair its losses through sales in Central and Eastern Europe. Finally in February 1780 Panckoucke sold the entry into France to the Lausanne-Bern consortium for 24,000 livres. That was a steep price—roughly eight per cent of the octavo's current manufacturing cost—and it shows how strong the demand for *Encyclopédies* remained, at least in the calculations of publishers who had discovered a new, undernourished public. Thinking they were safe at last, the octavo group increased their printing to 6,000 copies—hence the explanation of another "missing" edition—and promptly fell into another of Panckoucke's traps. Because they had not been able to pay off Panckoucke in cash, they had persuaded him to accept his ransom in kind—that is, in 24,000-livres' worth of octavo *Encyclopédies*. Panckoucke dumped his octavos on the French market at a reduced price and then compounded the damage to the octavo group's future sales by spreading the word that he would soon produce an *Encyclopédie* to end all *Encyclopédies*—not the revised edition that he had originally planned with the Société Typographique de Neuchâtel, but the *Encyclopédie méthodique*, which he was then organizing with the support of a consortium from Liège. That was not the last low blow in this battle, because four years later the old members of the octavo group joined by none other than Panckoucke's former ally, the Société Typographique, announced a plan to pirate the *Encyclopédie méthodique*. It did not get far beyond the drawing board, however; so the quarto-octavo war may be said to have ended in the defeat of Lausanne and Bern.

The publishing wars did not cut off the supply of relatively inexpensive *Encyclopédies* to France. On the contrary they show how fiercely publishers struggled to satisfy the French market and how important that market must have been. They also illustrate the aggressive, entrepreneurial character of Enlightenment publishing in contrast to the conservative publishing industry that was dominated by the gild structure within France. And finally they expose the inadequacy of the common view that the Enlightenment and the regime were locked into a fight to the death; for the quarto group captured the market by enlisting the state on its side—a strategy of protection and privilege that typifies the ways of the Old Regime and that also suggests a shift in the tone of government in the mid-1770s. The book that had barely survived persecution under Louis XV became a best seller under Louis XVI—with the blessing of the government.

The last episode in the *Encyclopédie* wars was purely domestic, a civil war between Duplain and his associates. In February 1779 they met in Lyons to assess their affairs. Contrary to all expectations, Duplain gave a pessimistic account of the sales. The first two subscriptions had done splendidly, he explained, but that very success had tempted the associates to overextend themselves, and the third edition now looked like a disaster. They might rescue it, however, if they divided up one thousand unsold sets so that each associate could market them in areas where his sales were normally strongest. Panckoucke accepted this proposal, because the Parisian territory was reserved for him and, anyway, he would allot almost half of his five hundred sets to the Société Typographique. Six months later, in a still gloomier report, Duplain warned that this maneuver had not sufficed to save the third edition. Hundreds of volumes would rot in their warehouses unless they took drastic measures. Fortunately Duplain had found a merchant, a certain Perrin, who had caught the *Encyclopédie* fever, and they could dump their unsold copies on him. To be sure, Perrin demanded extraordinary terms—a fifty-per-cent reduction—but they would be lucky to get rid of their excess stock at any price, and Perrin would take a huge number: 422 sets, as well as 160 from Panckoucke's share of the thousand that had been split between him and Duplain in February. Panckoucke accepted the proposal, but soon after signing the Perrin contract he began to harbor suspicions. He learned that Duplain had tried to involve a mutual friend in a secret conspiracy to raid his reserved quarto market in Paris, and he found that Duplain's letters sounded disturbingly vague about Perrin, whom they described as "a commercial agent in Strasbourg, who has a business in Lyons, or rather, I believe, in Paris, anyhow an extremely rich man for whom I can reply." By September 1779 Panckoucke confided to the Société Typographique, "I am quite persuaded that this Perrin is only an imaginary being or, at most, a straw man. Duplain is avaricious and makes no pretense about being delicate." He had become convinced that Duplain was "a vile soul," "a voracious man, who loves money with a fury"; "his rapacity has no limits." And he advised the Société Typographique to slip a spy into Duplain's shop. They needed no prompting, for they had done so long ago. In fact all the associates spied on each other. Panckoucke had his own man watching Duplain; the Neuchâtelois received secret reports on Panckoucke; they kept an agent in Geneva; and their man in Lyons spun such a web of industrial espionage that they finally trapped Duplain in February 1780.

The Lyonnais network managed to track down the elusive Perrin, who indeed turned out to be a straw man in Duplain's pay, and then it made an even bigger catch: it got hold of a copy of a secret subscription list, Duplain's record of the actual number of *Encyclopédie* sales. The list made no reference to the Perrin sale; instead it contained 978 more subscriptions than Duplain was later to report at the final settling of accounts in February 1780. The Société Typographique suspected the fraud before this meeting and verified it, once Duplain made his report, by writing to the booksellers whose subscriptions had been falsified, according to a comparison of the reported subscriptions and the secret list. So it discovered that the flow of orders never had dried up, as Duplain had claimed. On the contrary, the entire third edition had been sold at the normal price, except for the five hundred sets that Duplain had dumped on Panckoucke. Duplain had hidden the sales in order to collect the full amount from them, while paying nothing for five hundred of the *Encyclopédies* that he sold and paying for the rest at half price through the phony intermediary of Perrin.

Instead of contenting himself with this spectacular double swindle, a matter of more than 200,000 livres, Duplain piled fraud on fraud in combinations too complex to be fully explained here. His role as general administrator of the enterprise offered enormous opportunity for peculation, because the quarto association allotted him set amounts for all his expenses. He therefore contracted the printing to the lowest bidder, pocketing the difference between what he was allotted and what he paid. He also cheated on the costs of paper and transport and even collaborated in a technique of fraudulent spacing and paragraphing worked out by a Genevan printer— an item that might have seemed trivial to a lesser embezzler but that expanded volume 19 by 96 unnecessary pages, worth 744 livres. Panckoucke and the Société Typographique calculated that Duplain's kickbacks and rake-offs came to 127,000 livres, but that was only an estimate, one that probably did not do justice to his genius. His intentionally unintelligible accounts could have concealed far more peculation, because they scrambled more than three million livres of expenses and revenues, and Duplain seems to have cheated at every possible point. For example, he attributed 494 subscriptions to the Lyons firm of Audambron and Jossinet at the usual reduced price for booksellers of 294 livres plus one free set for every twelve subscribed, which brought their total up to 535 subscriptions. The anti-Duplain network discovered that Audambron and Jossinet operated as a false front to hide the fact that Duplain had sold all 535 sets at the full subscription price of 384 livres, thereby robbing the association of 60,204 livres.

Since the quarto enterprise had been conducted like a conspiracy from the beginning, it exploded in the end like the denouement of a *drame bourgeois*—or an "English cockfight," as the Société Typographique put it. The anti-Duplain forces had concealed their suspicions while they accumulated enough ammunition to destroy Duplain at the final meeting for the settling of accounts at Lyons in February 1780. This strategy of counterdissimulation had not been easy, as the Société Typographique confessed to Panckoucke: "You have wisely counseled us to dissimulate with him until the very end and not to reveal our just discontent, but by devil it gets more and more difficult every day." When the showdown came, therefore, Duplain's associates surprised him with a barrage of accusations that they had been preparing for almost a year. They produced a correct version of the accounts, exposing a spectacular string of embezzlements. They unveiled the Perrin affair; they stripped the camouflage from Audambron and Jossinet; and they produced the secret subscription list with letters from booksellers testifying to the enormity of the swindles in sales. Even then Duplain refused to break down and confess. So they raided his office with a police commissioner, an attorney, and a bailiff, demanding confiscation of his papers; and they turned his family and friends against him, threatening to ruin the family's name by revealing the entire affair to the public. Finally Duplain surrendered. He agreed to compensate his partners with 200,000 livres, if they would sweep everything under the rug, where it has remained until today.

What sort of a man was this Duplain? The question has a certain fascination, both for economic history and for the history of the human soul. Duplain was a robber baron of the book trade, a gambler who played off high risks against high profits and who made a business of Enlightenment. He decided to stake everything on the quarto *Encyclopédie*. He sold his shop, his stock of books, his house, and his furniture and moved into a furnished room in order to concentrate exclusively on the great affair. Then he hit the jack pot; for this supreme gamble made him a rich man, even after the settlement of 200,000 livres. And once he knew he was wealthy, Duplain began to buy. First he acquired a wife, a beautiful young Lyonnaise who dazzled Panckoucke; then an estate in the provinces; finally the office of *maître d'hôtel du Roi*—that is, nobility. He began signing his letters "de St. Albine." He served the king for the requisite time in Versailles and lived with his bride in offensive luxury in Paris before carrying her off to his château.

What is the moral of this story? It is a Balzacian drama: the tale of a bourgeois entrepreneur who clawed his way to the top and then consumed his fortune conspicuously, in aristocratic abandon. It is a saga of fortunes made and *illusions perdues* in publishing. In a way it is the story of French capitalism. And its supreme irony is that the vehicle for Duplain's rise into

France's archaic hierarchy, only a few years away from destruction, was Diderot's *Encyclopédie*. Perhaps Duplain's story may also serve as a warning against placing too much confidence in sociological analysis of the sort that follows; for even if you can put a man perfectly in some socioeconomic category, his heart may be elsewhere. Duplain, the perfect bourgeois capitalist, turns out to be a pseudonoble—or was pseudonobility the essence of the French bourgeoisie?

The inside story of the warfare among the men who produced the *Encyclopédie* may reveal something of the spirit of entrepreneurial capitalism in early modern France, but it does not answer the larger question of what the battles were all about. Of course "booty capitalism" was waged for booty. Panckoucke and the pirates, Duplain and the Swiss, and their supporting cast of financiers, smugglers, and traveling salesmen all realized that they could make a fortune by satisfying the vast market in France for a "popular" edition of the supreme work of the Enlightenment. The ferocity of the competition to supply that demand suggests that the interest in enlightened ideas had spread very widely throughout France—to a *grand public* if not a mass audience. But what was the character of that public? That question, like so many problems in the sociology of literature, is difficult to resolve, but one can measure the outside boundaries of the readership of the *Encyclopédie*. First it is necessary to review the basic facts about all the editions of Diderot's text; then it should be possible to calculate the economic limits to their different consumption patterns; and finally one can attempt to chart the geographical and social distribution of the quarto editions, which were by far the most numerous in prerevolutionary France.

Aside from the Italian editions published (in French) in Lucca and Leghorn, the expurgated Protestant *Encyclopédie* published in Yverdon by Barthélemy de Félice, and the *Encyclopédie méthodique*—a completely reorganized work that ran to 202 volumes and was not completed until 1832—Diderot's text went through four main metamorphoses.

1. The first edition (1751–52): this was a folio edition consisting of 17 volumes of text and 11 plates, followed by a five-volume *Supplément* and a two-volume *Table Analytique*. There were 4,225 sets printed, but only half, or perhaps merely a quarter, of them were sold in France. The subscription price was 980 livres, and the market price in the 1770s varied from 1,200 to 1,500 livres.
2. The Genevan reprint (1771–76): it had the same number of folio volumes in a printing of 2,200 sets. The subscription price was 794 livres, but by June 1777 it was selling at 700 livres, owing to competition from the quarto editions.
3. The three quarto "editions" (1771–81): these correspond to Duplain's three subscriptions and appeared under the names of Pellet and the Société Typographique de Neuchâtel, as explained above. The quartos

contained 36 volumes of text and three volumes of plates. They included 8,011 sets in all and were almost entirely sold out at the subscription price of 384 livres—the price paid by individual subscribers; booksellers subscribed at a reduced price of 294 livres and received one free copy for every dozen they ordered.
4. The two octavo "editions" (1778–82): these were really one expanded edition representing two subscriptions, published at Lausanne and Bern. The octavos consisted of 36 volumes of text and three of plates. They included 6,000 sets in all, and each sold at a subscription price of 231 livres.

This enumeration of facts and figures suggests a surprising conclusion: there were far more *Encyclopédies* in prerevolutionary France than anyone—except eighteenth-century publishers—has ever suspected. Although the subscription figures in the publishers' papers make it difficult to calculate precisely how many copies remained in the kingdom, they permit a safe estimate: between 14,000 and 16,000 *Encyclopédies* existed in France before 1789, and half of them can be traced. So without pretending to know how many of those *Encyclopédies* were read, or in what way the readers responded to them, it seems legitimate to hypothesize that *encyclopédisme* could have spread far more widely through French society than is generally believed.

As the *Encyclopédie* progressed from edition to edition its format decreased in size, it contained fewer plates, its paper declined in quality, and its price went down. And as the publishing consortia succeeded one another, they cast their nets more and more widely, reaching out with each new edition toward remoter sections of the reading public. The price differential set some rough limits to this ever-broadening sales pattern: the quarto edition cost a little more than one-fourth and the octavo edition about one-fifth of the market price of the first folio in the 1770s. But what were the social boundaries of *Encyclopédie* "consumption"? The question may seem impertinent, since economics offers no explanation of what it is to "consume" a book and since book buying and book reading are quite different activities. Nonetheless, the purchase of a book is a significant act when considered culturally as well as economically. It provides some indication of the diffusion of ideas beyond the intellectual milieu within which cultural history is usually circumscribed. And as there has never been a study of the sales of any eighteenth-century book, a sales analysis of the most important work of the Enlightenment ought to be worthwhile.

One can estimate how closely the *Encyclopédie* came into contact with the lower classes by translating its price into bread, the key commodity of the Old Regime and the basic element in the diet of most Frenchmen. A first folio *Encyclopédie* was worth about 3,500 loaves of bread and a quarto 960 loaves, the standard of measurement being the "normal" price of 8 sous for a four-pound loaf of rye bread in prerevolutionary Paris. An unskilled laborer with a wife and three children would have to buy at least 18 loaves a week to keep his family alive. In good times he would spend half his income on bread. A "cheap" quarto *Encyclopédie* therefore represented more than a year of his family's precarious nutriment. It would have been as inconceivable for him to buy it—even if he could read it—as for him to purchase a palace. Skilled laborers—locksmiths, carpenters, and printers—made 15 livres in a good week. The first folio would have cost them 93 weeks' wages, the quarto 26 weeks' wages, and the octavo $15\frac{1}{2}$ weeks' wages. So even the upper strata of the working classes, artisans like the men who printed the book, could never have afforded to buy it.

But the men who wrote it, the "Gens de Lettres" invoked on its title page, could have purchased the cheaper editions. Diderot himself made an average of 2,600 livres a year for his thirty years of labor on the *Encyclopédie*. A quarto would have cost him $7\frac{1}{2}$ weeks of his wages and an octavo $4\frac{1}{2}$—not an extravagant sum, considering that he had other sources of income. Many writers were wealthier than Diderot, thanks to patrons and pensions. B. J. Saurin, a typical figure from the upper ranks of the Republic of Letters, now deservedly forgotten, made 8,600 livres a year in pensions and "gratifications." He could have treated himself to a quarto, the equivalent of $2\frac{1}{3}$ weeks' income. The octavo was for hack writers like Durey de Morsan, a literary adventurer who lived off the crumbs from Voltaire's table and who wrote as one of the octavo's "zealous subscribers" to the Société Typographique de Neuchâtel:

> The number of poor literary men far surpasses that of rich readers. I myself am delighted that this work, too expensive until now, does not exceed the means of the semi-indigent such as myself. I would like the door of the sciences, of the arts, and of useful truths to be open, day and night, to every human who can read.

It is impossible to produce typical figures for the wide variety of incomes among the middling classes of the provinces, but the following calculations should give some idea of the expensiveness of the *Encyclopédie* for persons located well below the great noblemen and financiers and well above the common people. Although curés received only 500 livres as their *portion congrue* after 1768, their annual income often amounted to 1,000–2,000 livres. So a quarto *Encyclopédie* represented ten weeks' income for a prosperous curé. Magistrates of the baillage courts stood at the top of the legal profession among provincial bourgeois and often earned 2,000–3,000 livres a year: a quarto *Encyclopédie* was worth six or seven weeks of their income. To live "noblement" a bourgeois had to count on at least 3,000–4,000 livres a year in *rentes:* the purchase of a quarto *Encyclopédie* would have taken five weeks of his revenue.

In strictly economic terms, therefore, the first two editions were so expensive that they cannot have penetrated far beyond the restricted circle of courtiers, salon lions, and progressive *parlementaires* who made up the cultural avant-garde. The cheaper editions were luxury items, but with some squeezing they could have been made to fit into many middle-class budgets, rather as encyclopedias do today. The cost, like the content, of the quarto and octavo *Encyclopédies* appealed to a wide variety of small-town notables and country gentlemen but not to anyone below the bourgeoisie. As the publishers remarked—and they knew their clientele—"The in-folio format will be for grands seigneurs and libraries, while the in-quarto will be within the reach of men of letters and interested readers [*amateurs*] whose fortune is less considerable." The *Encyclopédie* entrepreneurs realized that they could widen their profit margin as they broadened their market. They had discovered a gold mine of untapped literary demand, and their scramble to exploit it shows how advanced culture reached the general reading public. But where were those readers located, and who were they?

The map (see Figure 1), drawn up from Duplain's secret subscription list, shows the geographical distribution of almost all the quarto copies, that is approximateely half the *Encyclopédies* that existed in prerevolutionary France. It demonstrates that the *Encyclopédie* reached every corner of the country and that its distribution coincided fairly well, as far as one can tell, with the distribution of population. Subscriptions in the Parisian area and the northwest were few, perhaps because those markets were sated by other editions. Beyond Rennes, Brittany looks like an intellectual desert, which might have been the case, but a surprising fertile crescent of *Encyclopédies* curves through the Midi, from Lyons to Nimes, Montpellier, Toulouse, and Bordeaux. Even the Massif Central shows a fairly high density of subscriptions. So there is little evidence here for the hypothesis that France was divided into a backward south and a progressive north by the "Maggiolo line" of literacy, running from Mont St. Michel to Geneva. The *Encyclopédies* seem to have sold best in towns where there were parlements and academies, but it sold very well everywhere: that is probably the main conclusion to be drawn from the map. Once reincarnated in a comparatively cheap edition, Diderot's text traveled farther and wider than has been appreciated (see Table 1).

Duplain's secret subscription list does not identify all of the subscribers; it contains only the names of booksellers, who generally bought lots of a dozen or more sets, which they retailed among their local clients. But there is one list of individual purchasers of the quarto edition in the Franche Comté. It has been translated into the bar graph (see Figure 2), which covers Besançon, a judicial, administrative, ecclesiastical, and military center, where sales were unusually strong. The graph shows a high percentage of purchasers in the legal profession, both lawyers and members of the parlement of Besançon. The *Encyclopédie* sold well in the first two estates, and especially among noblemen in the army, as might be expected in a garrison town. Royal administrators, almost all of them nonnoble, also bought the book in large number, and so did bourgeois professional men, particularly doctors, though to a lesser extent. Fourteen of the 137 sets went

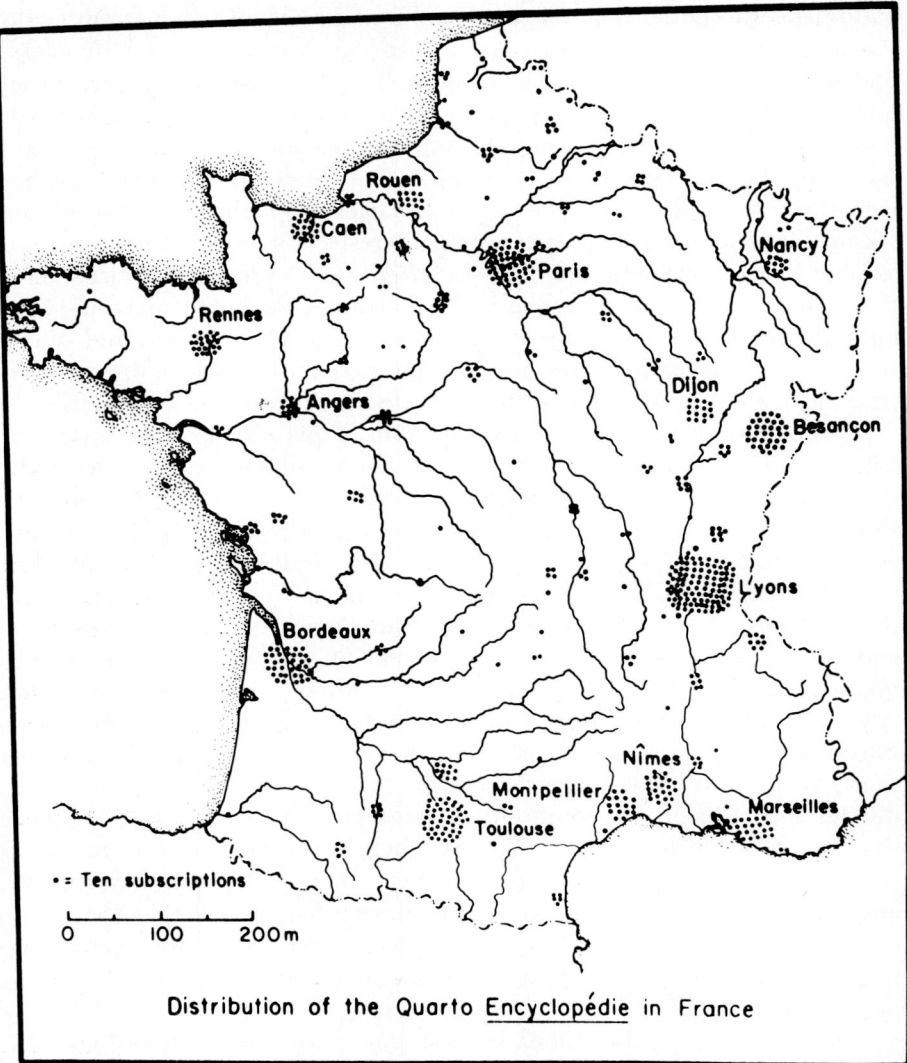

Distribution of the Quarto Encyclopédie in France

Figure 1. This map is drawn up from Duplain's secret subscription list, MS 1220 in the Bibliothèque de la Ville de Neuchâtel. The list covers all but one of the 8,011 sets printed. Of these 828 were foreign and so do not figure on the map. The map also excludes 76 sets that were sold to unidentified individuals and 25 sets that were given away—either as compensation for employees and associates or to procure protections; at least 10 of these went to Lyons, and Panckoucke dispensed 4 in Paris. The unidentified sales all involved single sets, except in four cases, which appear on the list simply as "Ollier 6," "Vasselier 4," La Flèche 39," and "Berage 8." "La Flèche" could have been a

to merchants and manufacturers—a large proportion in comparison with Daniel Roche's statistics on provincial academicians and Jacques Proust's analysis of the contributors to the *Encyclopédie*. Approximately one-half of one per cent of the people in Besançon bought the quarto *Encyclopédie*—a high percentage, but one that seems credible, given the above economic analysis of cost and clientele. The town's two main booksellers, Lépagnez and Charmet, had not expected to sell more than a dozen or so sets and were astounded at the book's success, especially as their trade had fallen into a slump since 1777. "Please don't believe that I enjoy any great consumption of books here," Lépagnez wrote to the Société Typographique. "I swear to you that after *L'Histoire universelle*, *L'Histoire ecclésiastique*, that of the Gallican Church, the Bible of Vance, the *Encyclopédie*, and the Rousseau, everything else has given me no business at all for the last two years."

The sales pattern of Besançon may not have been typical of France as a whole, but nonstatistical information shows a similar enthusiasm for the *Encyclopédie* in other provincial centers. In Toulouse, at the other extremity of the kingdom, a bookbinder called Gaston sold 182 quartos in three weeks and expected to place 400 octavos. And in general, when French booksellers mentioned their quarto clients in their correspondence they named lawyers, royal officials, and local noblemen—unlike their counterparts in Northern, Central, and Eastern Europe, who referred only to courtiers. So all the evidence points in the same direction: the prerevolutionary France the *Encyclopédie* worked its way into the world of the provincial notables who assumed the leadership of the Revolution and who continued to dominate the countryside throughout the nineteenth century.

No one can pretend to know what message "took" in the minds of those readers. Many of them must have bought the *Encyclopédie* for what it claimed to be: a compendium of all knowledge, rather than philosophic propaganda. As Panckoucke put it, "The *Encyclopédie* will always be the first book of any library or cabinet"—but it could have been a book to display on shelves, not to read. In fact Panckoucke reported that some subscribers in Lyons could not read at all. But it is difficult to believe that a high proportion of its owners never got through even its Preliminary Discourse, which is a manifesto of the Enlightenment. And far more people must have read the

---

person but probably represents La Flèche, Maine, where there was a famous school, originally founded for the Jesuits by Henry IV. The large number of copies sold in Lyons as compared with Paris resulted in part from the way the business was handled: Duplain directed the marketing operations from Lyons, while Panckoucke's many affairs kept him too busy to be much of a salesman in Paris. Also, the Parisian market was probably pretty well supplied by earlier editions. This map therefore should not be taken to prove that the capital of the Enlightenment absorbed relatively few *Encyclopédies*. What it provides is a fairly accurate picture of *Encyclopédie* diffusion in the provinces.

TABLE 1
Subscriptions to the Quarto Encyclopédie in France

City	#	City	#	City	#
Abbéville	26	Dôle	52	Paris	487
Aire	8	Embrun	3	Perigueux	36
Aix	6	Evreux	65	Peronne	15
Alençon	34	Falasie	45	Perpignan	52
Amiens	59	Douai	14	Poitiers	65
Angers	109	Grenoble	80	Reims	24
Argentin	3	Gueret	19	Rennes	218
Arras	26	La Fère	15	Riom	46
Auch	65	Langres	26	Roanne	26
Aurillac	13	Laon	17	Rochefort	27
Autun	39	La Rochelle	56	Rethel	40
Auxerre	10	Le Havre	52	Roquemaure	7
Auxonne	1	Le Mans	40	Rouen	125
Avignon	55	Le Puy	39	St. Chamond	2
Bayonne	16	Lille	28	St. Didier	1
Beaune	26	Limoges	3	St. Etienne	13
Beauvias	8	Lisieux	27	St. Flour	24
Bergerac	13	Lunéville	1	St. Lô	7
Bergues	1	Laigle	3	St. Omer	5
Besançon	338	Lyons	1078	St. Quentin	16
Billom	2	Macon	17	Saintes	26
Bordeaux	356	Mantes	8	Saumur	1
Boulogne-sur-Mer	34	Marseilles	228	Sedan	2
Bourg	91	Meaux	30	Sète	13
Bourg-Saint-Andéol	4	Metz	22	Soissons	52
Bourges	20	Montargis	26	Strasbourg	2
Brest	20	Montauban	105	Tarbes	52
Caen	221	Millau	8	Thiers	39
Cambray	57	Montbrisson	6	Toulon	21
Carpentras	2	Montpellier	169	Toulouse	451
Castelnaudary	27	Morlaix	1	Tours	65
Castres	28	Mortagne	22	Troyes	53
Chalon-sur-Saône	67	Moulins	52	Tulle	4
Châlons-sur-Marne	1	Nancy	120	Valence	65
Champagne	2	Nantes	38	Valenciennes	13
Chartres	75	Nîmes	212	Verdun	12
Chatillon	39	Niort	58	Versailles	4
Clermont	13	Noyon	26	Vichy	2
Colmar	1	Orléans	52	Villefranche	37
Dijon	152				

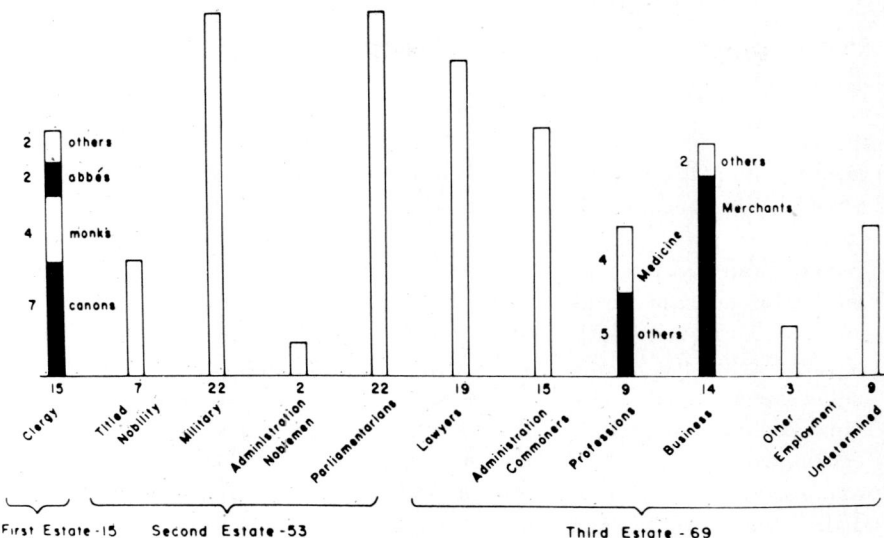

Figure 2. Subscribers to the Quarto *Encyclopédie* in Besancon. This bar graph is drawn from the list of individual purchasers of the quarto edition in Lough, *Essays on the Encyclopédie*, 466–73. It contains the names and *qualités* of 253 subscribers from the Franche Comté, of whom 137 were from Besançon. Duplain's secret list shows there were 390 subscriptions sold in the province, a figure that is confirmed by letters from the two booksellers who collected them. Therefore the representativeness of the Comtois list, which was drawn up according to the order in which the subscriptions arrived, is far from being complete—it amounts to two-thirds of the subscriptions sold. But the last third of the subscribers probably tended to come from outlying areas of the large, mountainous province, and so the bar graph probably gives a fairly accurate picture of the subscription pattern within Besançon. The military category seems to have been made up entirely of noblemen—most had titles but are not entered under "titled nobility"—but the "parlementaires" probably included an undetermined number of commoners, so the second estate appears somewhat larger on the graph than it was in reality. The same may be true of the third estate, because some of the "undetermined" category could have been noblemen. The three men represented by "other employment" were identified on the list as "intendant du Prince de Bauffremont," "Conseil de Mgr. le Duc du Châtelet," and "gardemagasin," presumably an army position.

Encyclopédie than owned it, as would be common in an era when books were liberally loaned and when *cabinets littéraires* were booming. It therefore seems legitimate to conclude that the biography of this book—the protection accorded it by French authorities, the struggle to exploit it among bookdealers, and its diffusion among a clientele of middle-range notables everywhere in the country—that this extraordinary success story reveals an Enlightenment that had spread far beyond the elite of court and capital and had penetrated throughout the upper echelons of the Old Regime. As the Société Typographique wrote to a customer in August 1779:

> Never has an enterprise of this kind and this scope had a greater success, nor has one been conducted with such speed. In less than two and a half years, and after having renewed the subscription twice, we have printed 8,000 copies of this *Encyclopédie*, of which we have only a small number yet to sell. The public seems to have waited impatiently to be served by publishers less rapacious than the producers of the first edition [a dubious statement]. We and our associates pride ourselves in having satisfied it in this respect; and you will observe, Sir, that if Enlightenment [*lumières philosophiques*] lacks in this best of all possible worlds, it will not be our fault.

Bibliography

T. BESTERMAN, *Voltaire* (1969).
E. CASSIRER, *The Philosophy of the Enlightenment* (1951).
H. CHISICK, *The Limits of Reform in the Enlightenment: Attitudes toward the Education of the Lower Classes in Eighteenth-Century France* (1981).
R. DARNTON, *The Business of Enlightenment: A Publishing History of the Encyclopedia, 1775–1800* (1979).
R. DARNTON, *The Literary Underground of the Old Regime* (1982).
P. GAY, *The Enlightenment: An Interpretation*, 2 vols. (1966, 1969).
N. HAMPSON, *A Cultural History of the Enlightenment* (1969).
M. C. JACOB, *The Radical Enlightenment: Pantheists, Freemasons, and Republicans* (1981).
J. LOUGH, *The Contributors to the Encyclopédie* (1973).
F. MANUEL, *The Eighteenth Century Confronts the Gods* (1959).
A. M. WILSON, *Diderot* (1972).

The Civil Constitution of the Clergy in the French Revolution

MICHAEL L. KENNEDY

Beginning in the late spring of 1789, France underwent almost a decade of revolutionary social and political upheaval that overthrew the monarchy and established a republic. Although the revolutionary government reconstructed virtually all French institutions, it carried out its most radical changes in the area of religion.

The religious policy of the revolutionary government went through several stages. Although priests had supported many of the earliest actions of the National Assembly, that body confiscated church lands in the autumn of 1789 and soon also suppressed monasteries. Thereafter, various clergy and conservative laymen began to voice religious opposition to the revolution. There were numerous local clashes between supporters of the church and the government. In June, 1790, the Constituent Assembly passed the most momentous religious legislation of the revolution—the Civil Constitution of the Clergy. This law in effect transformed the church into an arm of the state. Bishops and priests were henceforth to hold their positions through popular elections. All clergy were required to take an oath of allegiance to the Civil Constitution of the Clergy. Many bishops and priests refused to take the oath and became known as "refractory" clergy; those who did take the oath were known as "constitutional" clergy. As the clergy divided, French laymen also took sides. The king worshiped with refractory priests.

While the Paris government passed legislation on these matters, the Jacobin clubs were active in the provinces. These clubs, which corresponded with each other and with a central club in Paris, represented the cutting edge of the revolution. Initially, the Jacobins (like other revolutionary groups) were not overly hostile to the church, but their stance changed as clerical resistance, contested ecclesiastical

From Michael L. Kennedy, *The Jacobin Clubs in the French Revolution: The First Years*. Copyright © 1982 by Princeton University Press. Chapter VIII reprinted by permission of Princeton University Press.

elections, and accompanying local violence developed. By late 1791, on the eve of the reign of terror, the Jacobins who had two years earlier been moderate on matters of religion stood in the forefront of the demands to dechristianize the nation.

This selection provides an excellent analysis of the interaction between the authorities in Paris and the Jacobin revolutionaries in the provinces, and of the manner in which the revolution became increasingly radical as time passed.

Disbelief was hardly fashionable in the Jacobin clubs of the Constituent. The register of Colmar begins with the Latin phrase: *In nomine redemptoris Jesu Christi*. And biblical metaphors and tributes to religion leap out at the reader from the minutes and correspondence of other societies. The provincial clubbists might decry the worldliness of the church hierarchy, but all concurred that religion contributed to good citizenship and that it should be exploited in molding the new France. Quite early, they formed the habit of printing patriotic sermons at their own expense and commemorating revolutionary triumphs and tragedies with Christian rites. Catholic clergymen were fixtures in the societies, and, in parts of France, Protestant pastors enrolled as well. The respect in which Jacobin ecclesiastics were held caused them to be elected as officers with far greater regularity than their numbers warranted.

And yet, within the clubs, seeds were sown which yielded the savage harvest of dechristianization during the Terror. A new era of religious turmoil had commenced in France on November 2, 1789, when ecclesiastical lands were confiscated to pay the debt. In conjunction with this decision, the National Assembly declared that it would provide for the expenses of public worship, the salaries of the clergy, and poor relief. The prospect of reductions in their incomes estranged the hierarchy. A decree of December 19, prescribing the sale of 400,000,000 livres of confiscated property, added to the disaffection, as did the law of February 13, 1790 suppressing monastic orders. Soon cries began to be heard from the Right that the Assembly intended to destroy the Church.

Nettled by this criticism, one of the members of the Ecclesiastical Committee, the pious monk Dom Gerle mounted to the tribune on April 12 to defend the Assembly's policies. In the naïve hope of easing tensions, he invited his colleagues to declare "that the Catholic, apostolic and Roman religion was and would remain always the religion of the nation, and that its worship alone would be authorized." Conservatives immediately demanded acceptance of the motion, but the Left, seeing it as a threat to religious liberty which had been guaranteed by article ten of the Declaration of the Rights of Man, succeeded in getting it deferred. That night a tumultuous meeting took place at the Paris Jacobins, in which Gerle, who was a member, abjectly apologized for his impetuosity. The next day, following an acrimonious debate, the Assembly sidestepped the issue by expressing its attachment to Catholicism but refusing, out of regard for freedom of conscience, to adopt Gerle's motion. In protest, a minority of 297 royalist and Catholic deputies (called henceforth "noirs") assembled at the Convent des Capushins and drew up a manifesto declaring religion to be in peril.

The six weeks following the publication of the Capuchin's protest are pivotal ones in Jacobin history. A rapid proliferation of provincial societies had just commenced, and for the first time they acted in unison on an issue of national import. The correspondence committee of the Paris Jacobins circulated a pamphlet on the Dom Gerle incident written by the Baron de Menou, but the emotional recoil of the clubs was not triggered by directives from the mother society. Rather, it was a testament to the powerful passions aroused by the issue of religious intolerance. Never again, Jacobins fervently hoped, would France experience the horrors of the reign of "the tyrant, Louis XIV." Protestants were entitled to liberty of worship, admission to schools and colleges, and full participation in civic life. Jews also deserved toleration.

When the audience at the Club National of Bordeaux heard the reading of the minority protest on May 9, shouts of "à la lanterne et au feu" welled up spontaneously. Those in attendance voted to print the offending tract together with "infamous notes directed against the deputies who had signed it." On May 10 the original was burned in front of the principal entrance of the café, and mannequins representing the five guilty deputies from Bordeaux were hung from lanterns on the rue du Chapeau-rouge. The words "Traitors to the Fatherland" were stitched to their backs.

The Club National published an account of these incidents, thereby encouraging sister societies to strike blows against intolerance. On May 11 the Society of Friends of the Constitution of Bordeaux indignantly rejected the protest of the "bad citizens." Then, May 25, it composed an address on the maxim "The Church in the State and not the State in the Church." At its inaugural session, May 15, the club of Bergerac assailed the opposition deputies for 'attempting to disturb the peace"; by the next day it had convinced municipal officers to send a letter of censure to the National Assembly. At their first-known meeting, May 20, the friends of the constitution of Tulle adhered solemnly to all the laws. In a transcript forwarded to Paris, they accused the "noirs" of wanting to "plunge the Empire into anarchy" and opined that "too marked a preference for one religion leads inevitably to intolerance." At Foix, on May 28, the President convoked a special session to denounce a corresponding member named Font. "You have learned," he told those present, "of the grave crime of this deputy. You have seen his signature at the bottom of this declaration that fanaticism and private interest have engendered." In spite of the evidence, however, the clubbists found it inconceivable that Font had committed this "outrage." They voted to ask him by letter if his signature had been forged or if he had merely been duped into joining the "abettors of aristocracy" who wished France to strangle in her own blood.

Throughout June the clubs heaped maledictions on the "noirs." To commemorate the infamy of the 297, Montpellier inscribed their names "in red letters on a black panel." Then, like the club of Marvejols, it cajoled the departmental electoral assembly into taking a vow of eternal enmity against rebels to the laws. Charolles pontificated that "the names and persons of those who signed or adhered to this contumacious libel, would be covered with opprobium and ignominy, until they had purified themselves of this infamous stain by an authentic retraction." In a letter to the *Révolutions de Paris*, Arras also upbraided the "hypocrites and perjurors," declaring the decree of April 13 to be "completely worthy of a free and religious people." Ambert postulated that the law, far from blackening religion, represented "the most beautiful hommage that our legislators could render to it." St.-Omer and Châlons-sur-Marne expressed analogous sentiments in letters to the National Assembly. And Lille asked its affiliates to work through the "mother society" to procure a law forcing the protestors to apologize or face the loss of their rights as active citizens.

What added to the alarm of the clubs were the religious disturbances that the "noirs" incited in the provinces. A particularly serious incident took place at Montauban. In this city of 25,000, old rancours divided the Catholic majority and Protestants, who represented one-sixth of the population. Catholics dominated the municipality, and, despite pressure from the patriotic National Guard, had impeded the application of the decrees on Church property and monastic orders. On May 10, the day finally set for the inventory and expropriation of monasteries and convents, armed conflict erupted. Several patriots were murdered, and others incarcerated. Apprized of these developments, the two societies of Bordeaux urged all "persons of goodwill" to volunteer for a military expedition to Montauban. Shortly thereafter, 1,500 National Guardsmen set off on a rescue mission. Further bloodshed was averted only when this rag-tag army learned at Moissac of the release of the Montauban patriots, and triumphantly returned home.

Nîmes, a city of 40,000 Catholics and 13,000 Protestants, also smouldered with religious hatreds. At one pole stood a clerical-aristocratic clique buttressed by its own armed force, functioning independently of the National Guard; on the other extreme was a patriotic, anti-clerical faction led by the Society of Friends of the Constitution founded on April 11. On April 20 militant Catholics, feeling religion and monarchy to be menaced, drew up a petition to the National Assembly signed by 3,127 citizens. It demanded that Catholicism be recognized as the religion of state, that no alteration be made in the hierarchy, and that the King be permitted to review the decrees enacted by the National Assembly since September 19.

This petition outraged the clubs of the *Midi*. The 162 members of the society of Nîmes composed a counter-manifesto straightway. Vienne, Crest, Grenoble, Valence, Pontoise, Marvejols, and Montpellier also issued statements reproving the blasphemies of the "fanatics." Was it possible, the latter queried, that the spirit of intolerance "which brought shame and misfortune on our fathers" still lived "in the eighteenth century, in the age of the renaissance of liberty"?

The club of Nîmes sought to ally itself in the event of trouble with its sisters in Marseille and Montpellier. Marseille published an address vowing to defend the Nîmois to the death, dispatched two commissioners on May 10 to pledge armed assistance if needed, and secured authorization from its municipality to organize a confederation of the National Guards of Provence. But these preparations could not prevent violence. On June 13 aristocrats made an armed attack on patriots. After two days' fighting, the latter defeated their enemies with the aid of volunteers from neighboring towns, but then abused their victory by executing several "counter-revolutionaries." The tragic events at Nîmes sent a tremor of horror through the network. Montpellier convoked an extraordinary session on June 14, sent a deputation to the commanders of the National Guard, and began a monetary subscription to help finance an expedition. Marseille sent fifty wagon loads of wheat to Nîmes to feed the families of suffering patriots. Valence held a memorial service on July 2. And on July 10 Strasbourg printed 4,000 copies of an account of the troubles (in German) as a warning to those who might kindle fanaticism in Alsace.

Just one day before the upheaval at Nîmes, June 12, the National Assembly approved the Civil Constitution of the Clergy. This celebrated measure annulled the Concordat of 1516 with the Papacy and reorganized the French Church. Henceforth, bishops and priests were to be elected. Their salaries were to be paid by the state and set at levels ending the huge disparities of the Old Regime. Bishops were forbidden to be absent from their dioceses more than fifteen days a year. All collegial and cathedral chapters were suppressed. The number of bishoprics was reduced from 139 to 83. And countless small parishes were eliminated.

French Catholicism had a tradition of national independence. And the deputies scrupulously avoided any adulteration of Church doctrine. But opposition developed instantaneously. Several ecclesiastical deputies refused to vote on June 12. Battle lines hardened after October 30, when thirty bishops in the National Assembly issued the famous *Exposition des principes sur la constitution civile du clergé* [*Exposition of the Principles of the Civil Constitution of the Clergy*]. It challenged the right of the state acting alone to alter Church structure, disapproved the participation of Protestants in the choice of bishops, rejected the election of priests altogether, and questioned why the Pope, who had invested bishops for two centuries, had not been asked for his opinion. Louis XVI did appeal for Pius VI's approval when he reluctantly gave his sanction to the decree on August 24, but the latter had already repudiated the religious policies of the Revolution in a speech before a secret consistory in Rome on March 29. Although he refrained from making a public pronouncement until the spring of 1791 a negative decision on his part was assured.

The provincial Jacobins gave the Civil Constitution of the Clergy their unwavering support. Indeed, as the minutes of society after society clearly show, no other issue stirred them to such a state of white-hot intensity. Club involvement in the dispute commenced in September–October 1790, when the law was published in the departments, and certain bishops and chapters drew up complaints. At Strasbourg, where economics and politics had previously been the principal topics of debate, religion suddenly began to agitate all spirits. On October 5 a member denounced a Capuchin who had "preached sedition" in the Church of St.-Pierre-le-Vieux. In the session of October 9, the curé of St.-Pierre-le-Vieux was called to account for failing to read the decrees of the National Assembly, and the society heard the report that a canon of St.-Léonard, near Obernai, had given an incendiary discourse. On October 15, 1790, the club took up the question of the organization of the Protestant clergy; the next day it discussed ecclesiastical salaries.

Everywhere, the admittance of patriotic priests to membership abruptly assumed a special significance, and tongue-lashings of refractory clergy became commonplace. The number of complaints reaching the *comité des recherches* [Committee of Research] of the National Assembly swelled dramatically. Amiens and Béziers censured pastoral letters of their bishops (October 22, November 12); Toulouse and Verdun condemned the insubordination of the hierarchy in general (November 10, 30); during the same period, Tours transmitted to Paris sixteen documents relating to the sedition of its cathedral clergy.

On November 3, Aix published a significant address, demanding that the National Assembly fix a date by which ecclesiastics had to take an oath to the Constitution or be deprived of all their religious functions, salaries, and pensions. Toulouse and Beauvais received copies and adhered ecstatically. Rennes also joined in, composing a fiery petition which Guingamp and Quimper adopted, blandishing the National Assembly to proscribe clerical troublemakers: "A dangerous conspiracy has formed.... Fanaticism, that insatiable and bloodthirsty monster, that deformed child of religion, stirs in their hands the torch of discord. The language of heaven is on their lips, rage and despair lurks at the bottom of their hearts."

These outcries strengthened the hand of patriotic deputies in the Constituent. Irritated by the clerical opposition, they enacted an ordinance on November 27 which widened the breach between Church and State. It required all bishops, priests, vicars, and clergy exercising public functions to pledge allegiance to the Constitution in the presence of the faithful and officials of their communes. Whoever refused automatically renounced his office. Non-oathtakers who attempted to carry on past functions in violation of the law could be deprived of their rights to active citizenship, or in cases of open sedition made liable to criminal prosecution.

On December 27, the day after Louis XVI signed this decree, Grégoire appeared at the rostrum of the National Assembly, delivered a defense of the Civil Constitution of the Clergy, and swore allegiance to the constitution.

One hundred and eight ecclesiastical deputies followed his example in the next week. Despite threats on their lives from crowds in the galleries, however, forty-two of the forty-four bishops and the remainder of the lower clergy in the Constituent refused. During the implementation of the decree in Paris on January 9, riots broke out at St.-Sulpice. According to a compilation of doubtful authenticity prepared by the Commune, only sixty percent of the clergy of the capital adhered.

Amiens spoke for the majority of the clubs of province when it expressed rejoicing over the decree of November 27. Tours won support from a part of the network for its petition of early December insisting on Louis XVI's immediate sanction. Before the King had given his stamp of approval, Charolles voted on December 12 to send commissioners into every parish of its district to verify that ecclesiastics had taken the prescribed vows. Rodez, in January, required its members to attend the oath-taking ceremonies "en sabre et baudrier." And, like other societies, it alternately praised and damned local administrators for measures taken to implement the rites and safeguard the peace.

Denunciations of episcopal intrigues to sabotage the oaths crackled across the network in December and early January. Autun even accused its cathedral chapter of bribing clergymen to refuse. The societies countered episcopal propaganda with patriotic flyers directed at clerics and fellow-citizens. Autun and Valence printed a missive of Talleyrand to the clergy of his diocese. Metz disseminated 1,000 copies of a rebuttal by the deputy, François-Xavier Laurent, of the "false insinuations" of the Bishop of Treves. Caen printed 500 copies of an apologia pronounced, December 3, by a certain, M. Colombier, at St.-Marcellin. An adroit eulogy of the religious laws by Dufraisse, curé de Vernines (Puy-de-Dôme), passed from club to club in central France. Grenoble brought out Joseph-Vincent Dumolard's *Réfutation des principes contenus dans les dernières protestations de plusieurs membres du clergé* [*Refutation of the Last Protests of Many Members of the Clergy*]; and Beaune and Besançon reprinted it. Limoges assigned a professor of theology at the College of Sainte-Marie the job of composing a dissertation on the Civil Constitution. And Auch, Bordeaux, and Castres so esteemed the sermonettes prepared by the Abbé Paul-Benoit Barthe of the club of Toulouse that they ordered 2,000, 500, and 200 copies respectively.

Club publications of the time harped upon the dismal plight of the lower clergy and the unequal distribution of wealth under the old regime. Good priests were beatified. Recalcitrant members of the hierarchy, rather than being sincere defenders of the faith, were portrayed as self-seekers, regretting only the loss of their vast revenues to which they had no more right than "the last of the priests." Great stress was placed on the supposition that the dogma, morality, and the spiritual authority of the Church had in no wise been impaired. As one clubbist declaimed: "The National Assembly has religiously circumscribed itself to the properties of Caesar and has scrupulously rendered to God everything which belongs to God."

Oath-taking commenced in the departments on January 9–16 and dragged on for several weeks. Only seven of the 139 bishops complied. The best estimates place the initial figure for the entire clergy at fifty to sixty percent. Some clubs tabulated the results and notified the Paris Jacobins or National Assembly. La Mothe-Chalencon, Sezanne, Brignoles, and Aigues-Vives boasted that nearly all the clerics of their districts had complied. Auch, Nancy, Gimont, Hesdin and Port-Louis moaned that only small fractions had adhered. Resistance was normally strongest in capitals of the old dioceses. Bourges indicated that only two of fourteen ecclesiastics inside the city had obeyed the law. That a majority had conformed in rural areas of the Cher, it attributed to an address that it had circulated.

Many priests submitted with reservations. Desiring peace, municipal authorities were often willing to accept qualified oaths; but the clubs demanded strict orthodoxy. Tulle grumbled to Paris when local authorities did nothing about two priests who prefaced their vows with the words: "The National Assembly having assured by its decrees to respect the faith and maintain the Christian religion, I swear...." Retractions likewise caused consternation. When the curé of Loperhet recanted on February 2, explaining that the Civil Constitution endangered the spiritual authority of the Church, the society of Quimper replied scornfully: "You wish to edify us!... There is only one means; it is to obey a law to which the apostles and Jesus Christ himself would have submitted."

Jacobin priests commonly delivered patriotic homilies at the time of their oaths. Doubtless most were inspired by noble principles. The clubbist St.-Sardes, the only one of seventeen priests at Montauban to take the oath, had long been renowned for his humility and for giving the greater part of his income to the poor. The Abbé Quéré of the society of Fougères claimed that what he was doing was a "sacred duty... not inspired by ambition, interest, or fear, but undertaken voluntarily and dictated by reason." But the cynic is tempted to hypothesize that many clerics were attention-seekers who hoped to put themselves in line for positions vacated by superiors. As one authority, Timothy Tackett, has pointed out: "Invariably, economic gain was a factor in the curés' evaluation of the new ecclesiastical constitution."

The clubs published and distributed the sermons of oath-takers in profusion, making them instant celebrities. A discourse of Le Verdier, parish priest and president of the society of Choisy-le-Roi, was printed by both Rouen and Caen, and read avidly in distant Toulouse. Grenoble imprinted a speech of the curé of Congis, near Meaux. Bergerac informed all the municipalities of its district of the patriotism of a priest of Ste.-Foy. And the future bishop of the Aveyron, Claude Debertier, enhanced his reputation by sending his comments on the oath to the Society of Friends of the Constitution of Rodez.

The most acclaimed exhortation, however, came from the lips of the Abbé Jacques Thommeret, curé of Noisy-le-Sec. It was published in Paris,

Charleville, Montpellier, Aire, and Metz. Citing Samuel, Jeremiah, Gregory the Great, St. Augustine, and Fénelon as authorities, Thommeret contended: "If there is a Catholic verity universally recognized by the Church and consigned in holybooks, if there is a maxim adopted by all schools and repeated from all Christian chairs, it is that ministers of altars cannot withdraw themselves from the authority of the legislative powers of the earth, without being guilty of sedition." Having sanctified his own oath, he revived arguments which proponents of the legislation in the National Assembly had employed the previous June. The new administrative division represented merely a return to the early days of Christianity when dioceses had been co-extensive with provinces of the Roman Empire. During this pristine era the faithful had elected bishops and priests. Restrictions on the power of Popes were mandatory because of their blasphemies and greed in past epochs. Could anyone in a "century of light" wish to resuscitate "the ultramontain delirium"?

From the month of January 1791 a state of quasi-religious warfare existed in the French provinces. In Provence, Languedoc, and Alsace violent confrontations took place between partisans of the new Church and the old. For the first time, sizeable elements of the lower clergy turned against the Revolution. Bishops who did not flee France issued inflammatory statements and forbade jurors to administer the sacraments. Those who emigrated left instructions to refractory curés to remain in their parishes if at all possible, minister to their flocks openly or secretly, and treat constitutional priests as interlopers.

Jurors tended to rely upon the Jacobins to shelter them from persecution. The clubs of friends of the constitution, for their part, treated oathtakers like royalty, showering them with commendations and presents, escorting them in pomp through the streets, and looking on with an indulgent eye as parishioners sought their blessing and knelt to kiss the hem of their garments. Only rarely do we hear a sour note. If we accept the authenticity of a letter published in the *Patriote français* on February 23, Montargis wanted more than oaths. When priests embraced heretics and engraved the Rights of Man on the walls of the temples, then, and only then would they be true patriots.

Almost every club experienced some loss of Catholic laymen and priests in early 1791, as the result of defections or purges. But, all in all, the religious schism gave a shot in the arm to the Jacobin movement. Older societies which had limped along in 1790, like Le Mans, Rodez, Angoulême, and Artonne, now began to convene with greater regularity, hold public sessions, and enroll new personnel. Some rival patriotic circles merged in self-defense. And the rate of club foundations shot skyward. The Paris Jacobins contributed to this new sense of mission with a circular of January 9, bidding affiliates to use all means short of violence to thwart ecclesiastics who preached "war in the name of a God of peace." Versailles printed 2,000 copies of this address, and numerous societies responded with publications appealing to citizens to seek "peace and concord in the midst of the torches of fanaticism." Tulle, on January 20, challenged its non-conformist Bishop and chapter to a formal debate on the merits of the Civil Constitution of the Clergy. Societies of "surveillance" materialized in several departments, and numerous clubs adopted "vigilance" as a watchword. Limoux announced that every Sunday thirty of its members would roam the countryside to preach observance of the laws. Rouen and Strasbourg decided to place agents in the parishes of their vicinity to keep a watchful eye on priests who were to be replaced. And patriots in the Vendée created a "société ambulante" to move from town to town combating "fanaticism."

"Surveillance" bred more denunciations. In the opening months of 1791 scarcely a day passed without new indictments of fanaticism. Tours, on one occasion, presented to its city council six incendiary pamphlets which were circulating in the Indre-et-Loire. Brest apprized the *comité des recherches* of the National Assembly that rebel priests of St.-Pol de Leon had threatened to strike the names of non-supportive parishioners from baptismal registers. Nantes reported a clandestine press in a convent. Aigues-Vives railed about some canons who had counseled the people that "juring priests are unworthy of consecration." Amiens lamented the scandalous revolt of its college. Autun disclosed that its vicaires-généraux had started a monetary fund for non-oathtakers. Langres and Bourges chafed over the failure of their district and departmental officials to silence non-jurors. Montfort complained of refractory priests still burning incense. And Clermont-Ferrand deplored monks who wore their habits out of ignorance or contempt of the law.

A recurrent theme in club correspondence of early 1791 was the wicked influence of non-jurors on women. In Strasbourg, a riot of females led the society to demand the closing of a seminary. A mob of mothers and children invaded the Hotel de Ville at Millau to prevent the mayor from implementing the law of November 27. The club of Bourg had to make the most strenuous efforts to quiet the fears of country women. At Ste.-Foy a band of fanatical dames rose up in defense of a curé who refused to read fiats of the National Assembly. Yssengeaux sniffed disdainfully that "beatified ones" of its parts could not write but knew how to babble insults at the constitutional vicar. And Le Mans groaned that "women are sent away from the confessional and threatened with excommunication unless they remove their husbands from that 'school of satan,' that is to say, our society."

In towns where the clergy refused to pledge their loyalty to the Constitution, the clubs worked manfully to see that worship went on uninterrupted. Two jurors in the society of Vire volunteered to staff the city's parish churches until the installation of new ministers. Tours penned an invitation to loyal ecclesiastics of its district to receive confession and administer the sacraments in thirty parishes deprived of priests. But these were stopgap measures. The only permanent and legal solution, as clubbists realized, was to call the electoral colleges into session to name successors. Pressure was applied to district and departmental officials to convoke electors immediately, and howls of protest went up at every delay.

Elections began in late January and ran their course over the next four months. As a royalist pamphleteer observed, the influence of the clubs had "never been so apparent." Balloting for the episcopate took place first. On the eve of voting, the societies became locked in a fierce struggle with ex-prelates and chapters for mastery of departmental electoral colleges. Bourges published an eloquent rebuttal to the Bishop Puységur, who maintained that his seat was not vacant. When La Tour du Pin Montauban asserted that the Church would regard everyone who voted as a heretic, Auch threatened to publish the names of all traitors who were absent from the electoral assembly.

Fearing that money problems might deter electors from making the journey to the departmental seat, Périgueux distributed a list of members who would provide free lodging. Bergerac established a fund to pay for travel expenses and, along with St-Brieuc, petitioned the National Assembly to defray all costs. Legislators might have been wise to approve this request, for attendance figures were disappointingly low. At Bourges, only 198 electors answered the roll calls compared to 325 the previous year. In the Vendée, 173 of 471 eligible voters showed up, and 28 of these abstained. Claude Fauchet was elected Bishop of the Calvados by only 35 percent of the college.

The clubs engaged in a vendetta against absentees, and started a campaign for the wholesale renewal of electors. Ironically, however, the shrunken electoral assemblies enhanced Jacobin influence. The one of the Pas-de-Calais was chaired by the president of the club of Arras and opened with a mass which club members attended in a body. At Bourges, *sociétaires* were elected secretaries and tellers. Coutances, Foix, Gueret, and Nancy deputized members to deliver instructions. And clubs at sites of the electoral colleges held daily public meetings. Electors invited to the society of Castres (March 13–16) were regaled by speakers defending the Civil Constitution of the Clergy. According to newspaper accounts, Caen stuffed 1,200 members and visiting electors into its assembly hall on March 14, the day of the nomination of the new bishop. The *Journal de Meurthe* reported that 200–300 electors hastened to the meetings of the club of Nancy on March 13–14. Strasbourg enrolled 133 electors as members on March 4–5. The *Club Central* of Lyon supposedly had 2,000 citizens at its sessions of February 26 to March 1; many electors had come, we are told, "to collect information which they could use in choosing functionaries." Nantes, Périgueux, and Rodez also lectured eligible voters about traits to be looked for in prospective bishops.

Contemporaries charged that club lobbied for specific candidates, and some evidence exists to support this assertion. Soissons, Cherbourg, and Le Mans, it appears, stumped for Grégoire. Bourges at first campaigned for

Louis Charrier de la Roche; but when he turned down the post, it opted for Pierre Anastase Torné, a cleric whose virtues had been extolled by the Paris Jacobins. When Riom asked affiliates in the Puy-de-Dôme to suggest "some individuals worthy of being elevated to the episcopate," Artonne responded by designating four (none of whom were chosen). The popular societies of Lyon and St.-Etienne prepared lists of acceptable ecclesiastics and claimed credit for the naming of the Abbé Antoine Lamourette as bishop of the Rhône-et-Loire.

About nineteen deputies of the Constituent were rewarded with episcopates. The electors also nominated a number of clubbists. The Drôme opted for a leader of the Society of Friends of the Constitution of Valence. Toulouse furnished bishops for the Haute-Garonne and Gers. The Abbé Volfius, past president and founder of the club of Dijon, was elected in the Côte d'Or. And the Lot-et-Garonne chose a member of the Society of Friends of the Constitution of Bordeaux. The last-minute victory of Fauchet in the Calvados no doubt owed much to an editorial of Carra on his behalf. Other winners had more or less announced their candidacies to the clubs by circulating tracts in defense of the Civil Constitution. Barthe, voted Bishop of the Gers, had won renown in the southwest through his *Conférences théologiques*. Le Verdier, of Choisy-le-Roi, had mailed his discourse to the club of Rouen just days before his election as bishop of the Seine-Inférieure. The curé of La Guiole (named Bishop of the Aveyron) had favored the society of Rodez with a transcript of a *Conférence ecclésiastique*. Charrier de la Roche (Cher and Seine-Inférieure) was the author of the widely read *Questions sur les affaires présens de l'Eglise de France avec des réponses propres à tranquilliser les consciences* [Questions on the Present Affairs of the French Church with Suitable Answers to Calm Consciences]. And the Oratorian priest Luc-François Lalande (Bishop of the Meurthe) had penned a popular *Apologie des décrets de l'Assemblée nationale sur la constitution civile du clergé*, [Defence of the Decrees of the National Assembly on the Civil Constitution of the Clergy].

Whether the bishops owed their positions to Jacobin electioneering or not, they received club backing on assuming office. If the new leaders of the Constitutional Church lived close by, the societies notified them of their good fortune and escorted them in triumph to the cathedral church. To those in Paris or distant departments, letters of congratulation went winging. As the bishops journeyed to their official residences, clubs on route staged elaborate welcoming demonstrations: sending out printed invitations, decorating altars, and installing seats and podiums. Deputations of *sociétaires* greeted the episcopal coach outside the gates, presented tokens of esteem, delivered honeyed speeches, and then marched with the official cortege into the city. After a Te Deum or low mass, the guest of honor invariably visited the society, where the president embraced him and extolled his virtues. Not uncommonly, banquets followed. Finally, with great pomp, the clubbists escorted the prelate part way to the next commune.

Particularly lavish ceremonies took place when the bishops reached their destinations. Albi invited every society in the Tarn to send representatives to the episcopal installation there. Not to be outdone, its municipal rival, Castres, organized a showy demonstration of its own. During solemnities for the Bishop of the Mayenne, 2,000 citizens purportedly swarmed into the club of Laval. Perhaps 2,500 people assembled at the society of Marseille on May 16 for the reception of the Bishop of the Bouches-du-Rhône. The municipality of Bourges, on the request of the club, ordered citizens to illuminate their homes. Sometimes, however, the authorities did not cooperate. Amiens denounced certain administrators who failed to show up at the installation of its bishop. The society of Langres complained that district officials did everything in their power to subvert the celebrations there, even scheduling a public execution on the same day.

The demonstrations of the spring of 1791 were both simple outpourings of joy and calculated efforts at propaganda. In the Calvados, where Fauchet had been threatened with excommunication by the former Bishop, Cheylus, the societies took particular pains to demonstrate popular support. Bayeux prepared for his coming by printing one of his past speeches, and on his arrival treated him "like an angel descended from heaven." At Caen he was granted membership and praised effusively by the president of the society. The "friends of the constitution" of Lisieux led the parade to the principal church and then hosted a feast of thanksgiving. In Honfleur Fauchet blessed a flag and gave an address which the *sociétaires* printed and forwarded to Parisian journalists. Before the society of Vire, he read a much-admired essay on "the social order"; afterward he attended a banquet for more than one hundred people.

Here and there, prelates emerged as leaders of the societies. This was especially true in dioceses where the majority of clergy and people remained faithful to the old order, and the Jacobins represented the only clientele on whom the new bishops could rely. In the Calvados, Fauchet became for a few months a high potentate drafting key addresses for the clubs and issuing instructions in their names. Through the society of Bourges, Torné propagated the Revolution and energized the clergy of the Cher. At Beauvais, the Bishop Massieu likewise acquired a temporary ascendancy. Under his direction, in April the club adopted a motion excluding *refractaires* from a funeral service for Mirabeau.

Massieu's predecessor had anathematized the elections, and in late April Beauvais voted to print 1,200 copies of a response. Sister societies remained busy composing rebuttals to their ex-bishops as well. The most striking new element in the anti-hierarchical tracts of the spring of 1791 was the violence of the language. Blois likened its ex-bishop to a viper spitting venom. In one of Douai's pamphlets, the constitutional bishop of the Nord,

Primat, was compared to the virtuous and wise Fénelon; in contrast, the former bishop of Arras, Conzié was depicted as a libertine whose life had been consecrated to voluptuous pleasures.

Dissident French hierarchs received powerful reinforcement in March 1791 when the Pope chastised Lomenie de Brienne, the Bishop of Sens, for taking the oath. The pontifical letter to Lomenie caused a tremendous stir in the clubs. Sens denounced it to the National Assembly; St.-Marcellin reported in alarm to the Jacobins that bad-intentioned individuals had addressed copies to constitutional priests in its district; and Genon burned two mannequins on its main square, one of the Pope holding the bull and another of the infamous Abbé Maury sitting at his feet. But this was small stuff compared to the emotions aroused when the royalist journalist Royou distributed two Papal *Briefs* throughout France in early May. Dated March 10 and April 13 the *Briefs* in question declared the National Assembly's religious reforms to be a breach of Church doctrine and annulled the episcopal elections. Oathtakers were told to retract in forty days or face suspension.

Reluctant to believe the Pope guilty of such statements, the clubbists of Sezanne, Béthune, and Gray reasoned at first that Royou had fabricated the *Briefs* out of the air. As a whole, however, the societies accepted the encyclicals at face value and condemned Pius VI. Speaking of the Roman pontiffs, the Abbé Viard of Ligny queried: "Is there a single corner of Europe where their caprices, their selfish hatreds, have not caused the blood of thousands of men to flow?" Several societies composed printed responses, and smoke from ceremonial burnings blackened the sky of France. Guingamp received the two *Briefs* on May 17 and immediately began to cast about for means "to bring contempt and ridicule on these dark works fabricated to terrorize timid spirits and to set off a religious war in the Kingdom." Eventually, it decided on the following action: forty-one members, carrying the offending documents, marched solemnly to the central square, where the municipal officers were waiting along with a great concourse of citizens. Such was the fury of the crowd that the encyclicals were ripped and manhandled en route. The mayor was given the lacerated remains of one *Brief*, the other went to the club president; numbers of Royou's *Gazette* were passed around. On signal, all were thrown into the flames.

Elections for the replacement of non-juring priests took place in district assemblies, mainly in March, April, and May. Again, the clubs attempted to encourage attendance, pointing out in print that the naming of priests was the people's right from the earliest days of the Church. Paimboeuf compelled all qualified voters in its ranks to take a solemn vow to be present. Bergerac considered offering free lodging to the electors of its district, and voted to compile lists of absentees. And virtually every society in a district capital held daily public meetings in which scores of electors could be found.

On the last day of the electoral assembly at Sezanne a deputation from the club declared: "How sweet it is to see among the new ecclesiastics, citizens with whom we have formed the most holy alliance." Elsewhere too, many of the replacements turned out to be members or designates of the societies. At Vire, where the club had given electors enumerations of jurors and non-jurors for reference purposes, the new priest and all of his vicars were Jacobins. The curé of Bergerac offered thanks to the *sociétaires* "for all the interest that you have deigned to take in my election." Hearing of a surplus of juring clergy in the Haute-Vienne, La Rochelle asked Limoges to send priests to fill its vacant parishes. St.-Malo wrote to Guingamp requesting lists of good curés who would be willing to move. Tours recommended to Strasbourg two brave ecclesiastics who could speak German and who wanted parishes in Alsace. And Strasbourg referred to Colmar the name of the good curé of Battenheim, whose parish was to be downgraded to a vicarate.

In parishes where elected priests replaced non-jurors, troubles usually occurred. The old curé frequently remained nearby. Parents took their children to him for confirmation and baptism. Relatives of the dying sought him out to administer the last rites. Young people asked him to preside at their weddings. And in private chapels, homes, fields, anyplace which was available, the faithful flocked to hear the *réfractaire* give mass and communion. Pierre de la Gorce described the situation of the constitutional priest thusly:

> In the parish which will be his, no one leads his way. For him, no one rings the bells, no one takes the trouble to dress the altar. The rectory is left empty, like a place despoiled before abandoning it to the enemy.... In the night his erstwhile parishioners devastate the garden of the parsonage, throw straw in the well, deposit refuse outside the door, and put sand in the locks. When the juror leaves, children follow him imitating the crow of the cock in allusion to the treason of St. Peter. On his passage, farmers loose their dogs.

In these circumstances, constitutional priests turned for help to the clubs, and the latter took responsibility for their protection. Representatives of all the societies of the Puy-de-Dôme met in congress at Clermont-Ferrand to consider the problem of popular resistance to the Civil Constitution and possible remedies. It became common practice for clubs to delegate members to attend installation ceremonies for new curés. A Jacobin of Vire volunteered his child to be the first baptized by the elected priest. St.-Brieuc proposed to form an army of volunteers in Brittany to march wherever "good" priests faced persecution. One by one, the constitutional clergy were absorbed into the clubs of their regions. As an added defense against "fanatics," juring priests created parish societies. Eymoutiers was founded on June 19, 1791 by the Abbé Masmoret, constitutional priest. Lemembre, curé of Chavennes, established the society of Châteauneuf-sur-Cher. The soul of the club of Montbron, and founding father, was the cleric Monsieur Raoul. The curé of Isbergue (Pas-de-Calais) instituted a society at Moulinghem. Dozens of other examples could be cited.

With each day's passage, the societies demanded stringent new laws from the National Assembly. St.-Flour and Moissac sought the extension of the oath to all ecclesiastics, whether they were public functionaries or not. Quimper, Lorient, Pont de Vaux, Penne, and Fleurance urged that the pensions of non-jurors be reduced or stopped. Brioude invited the legislators to strip nonconformists of priestly powers. Tulle, Béziers, Arles, St.-Flour, Reims, Sizun, Rodez, and Avranches called for the expulsion of ex-priests from their parishes. Brest and Nantes wanted them to be exiled three or four towns away; Condrieux suggested herding them together in the chief-places of the departments; Strasbourg desired, at the very least, their removal from the frontiers; Blois asked the society of Nantes to provide ships so that all *réfractaires* could be sent to the wilds of Africa or America!

Vire had suggested in September 1790 that the clergy be permitted to marry so that they would "truly become citizens." By the summer of 1791 this sensitive subject was being discussed in a number of clubs. Strasbourg, in August, asked the National Assembly if the Church should retain exclusive control over registers of marriage and baptism. As the audacity of "fanatics" mounted, some societies even became involved in acts of violence. In two separate incidents at Libourne in May, priests were seized, paraded around the city on donkeys, and stoned by the populace. What is more, the Libourne club sent a boastful account to the Paris Jacobins. Although physical assaults and murders remained rare in 1791, the time was approaching when terror would become the accepted practice in dealing with "bad priests."

Bibliography

A. COBBAN, *Aspects of the French Revolution* (1970).
W. DOYLE, *Origins of the French Revolution* (1980).
J. EGRET, *The French Pre-Revolution, 1787–88* (1978).
A. FORREST, *The French Revolution and the Poor* (1981).
J. GODECHOT, *The Counter-Revolution: Doctrine and Action, 1789–1804* (1971).
L. HUNT, *Politics, Culture, and Class in the French Revolution* (1984).
D. JOHNSON, ed., *French Society and the Revolution* (1976).
G. LEFEBVRE, *The Coming of the French Revolution* (1947).
M. LYONS, *France under the Directory* (1975).
R. R. PALMER, *Twelve Who Ruled: The Committee of Public Safety During the Terror* (1941).
A. SOBOUL, *The French Revolution* (trans., 1975).
T. TACKETT, *Religion, Revolution, and Regional Culture in Eighteenth-Century France: The Ecclesiastical Oath of 1791* (1986).
C. TILLY, *The Vendée* (1964).

The Genesis of German Conservatism

KLAUS EPSTEIN

One of the ironies of history is that conservatism, an ideology dedicated to preserving the wisdom of the past, is actually a modern intellectual phenomenon. It could arise only after traditional European religious and political ideas had encountered the sharp challenge and hostile criticism of Enlightenment writers and after some of those critical ideas had been adopted by governments.

Conservatism is usually associated with the reaction to the French Revolution, but many of its key ideas and outlooks developed during the twenty years before 1789 in opposition to the enlightened absolutism of central and eastern European rulers, particularly Frederick the Great of Prussia and Joseph II of Austria. Both monarchs surrounded themselves with persons of enlightened outlook, pursued policies of rational reform and taxation, and were unfriendly to religious institutions in their monarchies. Joseph II confiscated monastic land.

The spokesmen for the then-emerging conservative position claimed that the rationalist ideas of the Enlightenment led to skepticism and immorality. Without traditional religious faith, they argued, most human beings would lead disorderly, undisciplined lives. Reason alone was unable to provide a foundation for everyday morality. The conservatives used these arguments to defend traditional social customs and the ongoing role of religion and the church in social and political life. They particularly denied that human beings could achieve any kind of significant moral progress. All of these arguments were intended to defend the social and political status quo.

The new conservatives used a variety of tactics in the crusade against the Enlightenment. Wherever possible, they persuaded governments to use censorship or to make difficult the publication of critical journals. They attacked all modes of progressive education that seemed intended to demonstrate the possibility of moral improvement

From Klaus Epstein, *The Genesis of German Conservatism*. Copyright © 1966 by Princeton University Press. Excerpt pp. 65–83 reprinted by permission of Princeton University Press.

or the desirability of social mobility. Although they hated the world of journalism, they entered it by founding journals to further their cause. Until the outbreak of revolution in France, these conservatives and their ideas had at best mixed success, but thereafter governments and aristocracies across Europe adopted and propagated their views for well over half a century.

Conservative attitudes have existed throughout recorded history, in the sense that men have felt hostile to changes in their accustomed and cherished world. They are correlative with the fact of change itself, and are basically rooted in the human fear of the unknown and desire for a predictable environment. There have been many changes throughout history which have provoked not only a psychological uneasiness but an articulate expression of Conservative defense. The conspirators who assassinated Caesar believed themselves to be defending the old senatorial constitution against a new type of tyranny. The Saxon Widuking defended the gods of his fathers against the new religion of Charlemagne. The Dominican Inquisition defended Catholic Orthodoxy against the Albigensian heresy, and the Jesuits of the Counter Reformation defended the unity of Christendom against the rebellion of the Protestant Reformers. John Hampden defended, against the new claims of royal prerogative, the ancient right of Englishmen not to be taxed without their consent; at the same time the Prussian nobleman Kalckstein defended the traditional rights of the East Prussian *Stände* [estates] against the encroaching absolutism of the Great Elector.

All these cases—selected at random—are examples of defense of a specific *status quo* at a specific time against specific attack. What is significant in the eighteenth century—in Germany around 1770—is that Conservatism, while remaining in substance a defense of concrete institutions *ad hoc*, developed for the first time the *self-conscious* attitude of a distinctive *Weltanschauung* [world-view].

Brutus, Widuking, Hampden, et al., did not feel that they were defending a social, political, and cultural order *in toto* against a general attack animated by the vision of a wholly new conception of what society should be. They felt, no doubt, that what they defended had an importance going beyond the immediate case, and that defeat might have far-reaching repercussions. From this feeling it was in theory only a small step toward an explicit Conservative *Weltanschauung*—a small though crucial step, and one which was not taken in Germany before Justus Möser. It was taken at that time as an inescapable response to the challenge of the *Aufklärung* [Enlightenment] with its general program of transforming every sector of life. The

Aufklärung forced men with Conservative inclinations to abandon their unreflective Traditionalism—their instinctive and inarticulate acceptance of the *status quo*—in favor of an explicit and self-conscious defense of the *totality* of society. Even more, it forced Conservative men to criticize the practice of *Aufklärung* criticism per se, since the case-by-case reply to specific attacks upon specific institutions never yielded more than temporary defensive victories. It was the fate of Conservatism from its very beginning that, although it condemned criticism and argument, it was unable to avoid either. The emergence of Conservative thought and argument in fact contributed to that perennial battle of ideas which Conservatives find perhaps the most deplorable aspect of modernity.

It must be repeated that the tragic predicament of Conservatism is apparent from the hour of its birth. Conservatives value a society in which everyone accepts the established order without controversy, and where intellectual activity is either at a low level or devoted to the refinement of existing pattern of life rather than to criticism. They abhor and resent the critical habit—systematized during the *Aufklärung*—of questioning everything and never being contented with anything. They are forced, however, by the insuppressible new critical mood to defend traditional institutions—Churches, governments, and social structures—when and as they are attacked. They instinctively feel that the battle is already half lost because of the fact that they are compelled to fight it at all. They must argue, though they hate argument; defend, where unquestioned acceptance alone can give emotional satisfaction; persuade, where persuasion ought to be unnecessary and is unlikely to be effective. The terms of controversy are invariably set by the Party of Movement, and Conservatism is forever doomed to fight an essentially defensive battle. Its argumentative triumphs are at best Pyrrhic victories, for even a successfully defended institution is transformed into something very different from one which was never challenged sufficiently to necessitate defense. A militant virtue is only a poor substitute for the charms of innocence, and innocence once lost can never be regained. This is the fundamental meaning of the saying attributed to Talleyrand that "no one who has not lived before 1789 can ever know how good life can be." The necessity of developing an *explicit* Conservatism is for true Conservatives the infallible symptom that the golden age has vanished forever.

The Critique of the Criticism of the Aufklärung

It was natural for Conservatives to break out of their defensive ramparts and launch a vigorous counterattack against the spirit and methods of the *Aufklärer* [Enlightenment writers]. Their counterattack may be usefully analyzed under two headings: first, the criticism of the results of the

Aufklärung, on the theory that a tree may be judged by its fruits; second, an attack upon the motives of the *Aufklärer*, and their alleged vices.

Conservatives asserted that the *Aufklärung* led, visibly and inevitably, to the triple evils of skepticism, immorality, and the undermining of all constituted authority. The rationalist approach to religion destroyed belief in the basic truths of traditional religion. These truths were not (in the Conservative view) contrary to reason, but they certainly did not rest upon reason alone; and the *Aufklärer* were fundamentally misguided when they declared reason the sole yardstick of credibility. The *Aufklärer* were in fact deeply hostile to miracle, mystery, and authority. The outlook which resulted from their repudiation of these three cardinal elements of historic Christianity might initially be a "natural" religion which retained the essence of Christianity (such as the Creator-God, the moral law, and immortality) while repudiating all of its so-called "historical accidents." This position, however, was neither logically compelling to intellectuals nor practically attractive to the broad mass of the people; it frequently proved a mere halfway house to outright skepticism and materialism.

The Swiss poet and scientist Albrecht von Haller (1708–77) was an early critic of skepticism. His argument is especially significant because it rested upon purely utilitarian grounds instead of appealing to religious dogma. Haller asserted that skepticism inevitably undermined belief in the foundations of morality of encouraging the emergence of a new type of man—one who devoted his life to the pursuit of sensuous pleasures unrestrained by the thought of an avenging God in the world to come. Such a man would recognize no moral restraints at all—an attitude leading to the following results in private life: the replacement of marriage by temporary liaisons; the neglect of children or even their exposure as a nuisance; the murder of elderly parents as their survival became an inconvenience; while friendship, because it usually required some sacrifice, would become virtually unknown. The public results would be equally disastrous: honor in commercial transactions would disappear; servants would cease to be loyal to their masters; oaths would become worthless; the fear of temporal punishment would become the only restraint upon crime, and even this would be diluted by the corruptibility of judges; while no prince could henceforth rely upon his administrative personnel, or even entrust his personal safety to his bodyguard. It was truly a situation where Hobbes' "war of all against all" would be an accurate description of man's condition.

Haller provided the following portrait of the new skeptical man:

> The skeptic who denies an avenging God, and an eternal life to come, restricts our happiness to the brief period of our terrestrial life, in duration, and to the enjoyment of sensual pleasure in substance.... He asserts that every man has a right to happiness and that he must find it where he may; and that a criminal deserves it as much as a saint. The pleasures of love—more especially

the animal side of love—and the most refined tickling of our senses are considered man's highest good; they alone make us happy even if it is a happiness without honor and devoid of approval by our fellow-men. This happiness must never be restrained by that old pedant called VIRTUE. The very concept is a figment of the imagination, a mere invention of human contrivance, indeed an alien plant which does not grow up naturally in our hearts. The torments of an uneasy conscience, or that sense of guilt which relentlessly pursues us, must be dismissed as a mere prejudice incubated in us through parental blows administered during childhood; one must anesthetize conscience or at least so stuff its mouth that it will be forced to shut up. One must never think of God, and it has been proved that there is no Afterlife: there is, therefore, nothing to fear except the single creature that can still mar our happiness: the public hangman. Even philosophers, who otherwise fear nothing either above or below the earth, must watch out for him, but for him alone.

Haller then contrasted the moral anarchy produced by skepticism, and the ensuing "war of all against all," with a picture of the harmonious life of a traditionalist Christian:

Christian faith brings results exactly opposite to those produced by unbelief. Religion unites competing efforts and wills in the single center which is God. His law demands that we love Him above all else and our neighbor as ourselves. What infinite wisdom and what infinite power for good rests in this simple faith! Revelation teaches us that we are not destined for this world alone; that worldly goods should therefore be enjoyed only with reserve and that our hearts should never cling to them. We know that our sojourn in this world is but temporary, and that death will see us passing into a spiritual world from which fleshly pleasures are banished and all ambition loses its meaning. We are, indeed, by nature *lowly* creatures who require transfiguration by the grace of God before being worthy of entering into his presence and that of thousands of creatures with a nature far superior to ours [the angels].

In this present world we are all brothers charged with the obligation of doing unto others whatever we would do toward an infinitely rewarding God if He appeared in our midst in human disguise and required our help: a conception far more compelling than any ethical code promulgated by mere human rhetoric. From these few basic laws flow all civic virtues, and if they were obeyed the happiness of mankind would ensue spontaneously and inevitably.

To balance his earlier portrait of the vices of the skeptic Haller devoted the rest of his essay to the virtues of the Christian. He contrasted the comfort of Christian family life with the disorder produced by temporary sexual liaisons; the Christian education of children with their neglect by parents absorbed in the pursuit of pleasure; the Christian satisfaction with every station in life, and the moral duty to perform the obligations of one's station, with the skeptic's pursuit of ambition and sensual gratification without bounds; the Christian observance of the moral law, enforced by consciousness of an omnipresent God, with the skeptic's license restrained only by fear of police detection; and the Christian conception of government, where obedience to duly constituted authority was a sacred duty, with the "war of all against all" inevitable in a society of skeptics. Haller stated the classic Conservative contention that no civilized society can dispense with religious foundations; he added that these foundations could only be Christian so far as European society was concerned. The total disintegration of European civilization was still prevented by the residual influence exercised by Christianity. European society was depicted as living off the religious capital accumulated during the centuries preceding the *Aufklärung*. There could only be gloomy perspectives about what would happen if the replenishing of Europe's Christian capital were not soon begun.

Other Conservative writers joined Haller in the contention that reason could never provide the basis for a morality adequate to meet society's needs. A prominent Bavarian Conservative, Karl von Eckartshausen (1752–1803), argued emphatically that traditional religion was the foundation of what morality still survived in Europe—and that morality could only be based upon religious custom and tradition, not the rational convictions of individual persons:

"Are you not aware," he asked the *Aufklärer* who never ceased to criticize traditional custom, "that the moral law loses much of its efficacy if it is not drummed into us during childhood—at a period long before our reason is in a position to judge all the misfortunes which vice inevitably brings upon man?" Eckartshausen accused the *Aufklärer* of destroying the sense of shame: "The feeling of shame which we experience when we are justly punished is one of the most precious gifts which nature has bestowed upon us." There was no substitute for the fear of divine punishment in buttressing morality, especially for materialists who tended to view earthly punishment through "the wheel or even more cruel tortures as no different in principle from a heavy attack of gout or colic." These utilitarian reasons made it imperative for Europe to continue to cherish its Christian traditions, even apart from their dogmatic truth. Eckartshausen went so far as to insist that, if Christianity were by chance untrue—though he himself was a fervid believer—it would nonetheless require preservation since it constituted the only possible basis for European morality. He appealed to the *Aufklärer* to heed the example of Socrates, whom they often hailed as an early fellow spirit: Socrates had always carefully observed Athenian religious customs—which he did not pretend to respect upon religious grounds—since he understood that they were the only possible basis for Athenian morality.

A further result of the *Aufklärung* was the destruction of all respect for constituted authority. No institution, however venerable, was immune to criticism; the *Aufklärer* not only turned destructive criticism into a personal habit, but also urged all men, however common or uneducated, to join them in this habit. A Lutheran clergyman of Pomerania named Daniel Joachim Köppen was one of many Conservative authors who defended the need for authority, secular and divine, on general grounds. He wrote in 1789—quite independently of the French Revolution—that no one had yet demonstrated that

> the common people, as they are now constituted or are ever likely to become, are capable of discovering for themselves the True and the Good. It is notorious that the common people—that is, the greater part of mankind: servants, day-laborers, proletarians, common artisans and many others whose formal status may be superior, but whose character is similarly primitive—are incapable of doing so, both on account of their biological stupidity and their external circumstances of life. They obviously require guidance from above. This fact will remain a fact so long as common people remain common people...; so long as men are born brutish and ignorant—and this will remain the case until mankind disappears from the earth—and secure moral education only through instruction and leadership from some outside source...; so long as the content of this education is not an indifferent matter but something which shapes the entire adult character of a people. All these considerations make it indispensable to have some supervision over the religious and moral principles which are imposed upon the common people from outside their ranks. And who is to exercise this necessary supervision? It is obviously the task of constituted authority.

This elitist and authoritarian argument has been used time and again by Conservatives from the eighteenth century until our own age.

Conservatives were not satisfied with pointing out the disastrous consequences wrought by the *Aufklärung* in destroying religion, morality, and authority; they also proceeded to argue *ad hominem* against the personal vices of the *Aufklärer*. It would be unfair to accuse Conservatives of being the first to stoop to personal attack, for Radical publicists chronically denounced their foes as a band of stupid, egotistic, obscurantist, callous, and unimaginative men. The Conservatives replied to this unflattering stereotype by denouncing the *Aufklärer* as a band of fanatical and ruthless zealots dedicated to purely negative criticism because they were unsuited to any constructive profession. They were also attacked as unbalanced personalities who lacked any sense of the importance of emotion, mystery, and tradition in human affairs, and were blind to the claims of national feeling.

Conservatives loved nothing better than to castigate the fanaticism and intolerance of the *Aufklärer*—attitudes all the more offensive because the *Aufklärer* claimed self-righteously that *they* sought to slay intolerance and fanaticism as distinctively *Conservative* vices. Eckartshausen devoted an entire public speech (April 5, 1785) to the *Literary Intolerance of Our Century*, exclaiming:

> O tolerance, tolerance, what a wonderful word! frequently exclaimed but seldom practiced in our "enlightened" century! The false philosophers of the *Aufklärung* shout imperiously: Think as we think! or else we will brand you as obscurantists in our writings and whip and scourge you through half the world. So shout the executioners of literature, and they do not hesitate to nail the honest man to the gallows of their journals.

Eckartshausen went on to brand the superstitious fanaticism of the *Aufklärung* in the following rhetorical appeal to his enemies:

> Tell me, when was superstition as ridiculous as your philosophy? When has it shown such a hot-tempered zeal to win proselytes? When did superstition flood the world with so many ridiculous, contradictory raging pamphlets? When did it seek to prejudice the world against hostile sects with so many falsifications, dictionaries, verses and anecdotes?

The pamphleteers of the *Aufklärung* were notorious in Eckartshausen's eyes for their bad temper, prejudice, vindictiveness, and penchant for character assassination.

There was much Conservative criticism directed against the ruthless methods employed by "enlightened despots"—more especially the Habsburg Emperor Joseph II—as they promoted the cause of *Aufklärung*. To give only one example: the Hannoverian Conservative writer Ernst Brandes wrote a sharp attack against the method of Joseph's ecclesiastical reforms. It should be noted that Brandes, as a Protestant, had no sympathy for monasticism, and fully recognized the fiscal needs of the Austrian state which made some suppression of monasteries inevitable. He protested, however, against the precipitate character of the emperor's actions, the needless cruelty directed against individual monks, the barbarous destruction of priceless art treasures, the utter want of reverence toward foundations often hundreds of years old, and the failure to prepare public opinion gradually for whatever steps were necessary. Brandes attacked the reforming emperor for his characteristic indifference to the feelings of others, so that even his most benevolent actions were resented as tyrannical, especially when they interfered with the customary life of the common people; examples were his suppression of superfluous holidays and his campaign against burial in unsanitary and uneconomical wooden coffins. Joseph was a typical *Aufklärer* in his arrogant belief that he knew best what was good for other people, that traditional society must be reconstructed in accordance with rationalist blueprints; that every opponent of reform was either stupid or vicious, and probably both; and that the whole program of *Aufklärung* must be implemented as quickly as possible regardless of any obstacles which stood in the way.

Conservatives frequently denounced the pamphleteers of the *Aufklärung* as a group of unemployable hacks incapable of holding down respectable jobs. Eckartshausen drew the following unflattering picture of the publicists of the *Aufklärung* in the vigorous language characteristic of the polemics of the age:

> They are men devoid of true philosophy, filled with confused so-called "enlightened" concepts which they have sucked up in a thoroughly fuzzy manner, and regurgitate without prior digestion. They lack all knowledge of human nature, since their life has been confined to the study or at best the coffee-house. They are in fact so-called "men of genius" with holes in their pants (*meistentheils Genies in zerrissenen Hosen*); lackeys or members of secret societies; or self-styled wits (*Witzlinge*) who pour out their gall upon whoever lacks concepts as confused as their own. Their helpers and satellites, scattered through the length and breadth of Germany, include everywhere perennial malcontents and many conceited people who believe that they possess a monopoly of wisdom,—when in fact they are only eager to find a pot where they can place their (intellectual) excrement (*die dann froh sind, wenn sie einen Topf haben, wo sie ihren Unrath ausleeren können*). They believe that they possess the capacity to rule states while in fact they cannot even manage their private affairs and are up to their necks in debts they are unable to pay.

Conservatives asserted that the *Aufklärer* were unbalanced men oblivious to many important sides of human life. Their cocksure rationalism easily led to an atrophy of the emotional faculties (*Gefühl*); on this point the early Conservatives agreed with the poets of the *Sturm und Drang* [storm and stress] and such prophetic-mystical writers as Johann Georg Hamann (1730–1787), the "Magus of the North." They asserted that the *Aufklärer* tended to forget the claims of passion, reverence, and sentiment as they viewed life in a spirit of narrowly philistine utilitarianism. Their rationalism tended, moreover, to make them dangerously "unhistorical" in their view of the world. They cared little for the individuality which characterized historical development; their preoccupation was rather to discover and apply general principles valid everywhere and at all times. The "historicist movement"—what Friedrich Meinecke called "one of the greatest intellectual revolutions achieved by the Western mind"—inevitably became a powerful ally of Conservatism, though many of its founders and early champions, most notably Johann Gottfried Herder (1744–1803), personally sympathized with much of the program of the *Aufklärung*.

Conservatives objected to the a priori faith of the *Aufklärer* that the universe—far from being either mysterious or opaque, as had long been thought—was in fact easily intelligible. Eckartshausen was one of many Conservative writers who not only stated, but positively reveled in, the belief that much of the world was ultimately incomprehensible. Only God could understand the mysterious universe which He had created. How could the finite intelligence of man possibly secure a full understanding of a universe whose infinity was obviously incongruous with it? God in His mercy wisely supplemented the inevitable defects of human understanding through Revelation, but even Revelation contained many mysterious elements. If it were otherwise, argued Eckartshausen, belief would become mere mechanical assent and cease to be a Christian virtue. A mature man must learn to live with mystery and like it; he must avoid the naïve error of the *Aufklärer* of believing that all useful and necessary truth was crystal-clear; for "doctrine may contain much that is unintelligible without on that account ceasing to be necessary and useful truth."

The belief of the thinkers of the *Aufklärung* in human progress was primarily based upon their faith in the beneficial results of scientific knowledge, which included the enhancement of material welfare and human happiness. But what if knowledge in the really essential areas of life —religion, morality, et cetera—was in fact stationary because of the inapplicability of scientific method, and in practice even regressive because of the rise of skepticism? Brandes for one rejected the idea that genuine progress had actually taken place in recent centuries. There had, to be sure, been some advance in the standard of living; but this had only led to an increase in luxury, extravagance, and immorality. There had been some advance in literacy, but this only exposed uncritical minds to the disastrous doctrines of the *Aufklärung* and thereby led them into temptations which it would have been better to avoid. Real progress could only mean individual *moral* progress and a more profound grasp of Christian truth; there was, unhappily, not a shred of evidence that either had taken place. On the contrary, the rise of immorality and skepticism was all too evident. Only shallow philistines could believe that there had been cultural progress since the ancient Greeks. Did the *Aufklärung* produce a greater philosopher than Plato, a greater historian than Thucydides, a greater biographer than Plutarch, or a greater painter than Raphael? The worst aspect of the doctrine of progress was—in Brandes' eyes—that it provided men with a psychological surrogate for belief in personal immortality and thereby helped to undermine a Christian doctrine essential for personal morality and social stability. It also provided men with an utopian vision of the future in which everything appeared possible, and paralyzed Conservatives with an enervating fatalism arising from the belief that they were fighting an ultimately hopeless battle against an irresistible tide.

A final charge delivered against the *Aufklärer* was that they were devoid of German national sentiment. Their ideas were universal in content and Western European in origin; these facts suggested the effectiveness of a nationalist counterattack. Should Germans not cherish German ideas and institutions which were the result of Germany's distinctive historical heritage? This theme played as yet a comparatively small role in the predominantly cosmopolitan eighteenth century; but it anticipated what was to prove the most influential Conservative argument in the nineteenth.

Suffice it to say at this point that German Conservatism could rely not only sociologically upon the main forces of German society—as outlined in the previous section—but intellectually upon many of the most powerful currents of German cultural life. The cult of *Gefühl* [sentiment] of the *Sturm und Drang*, the prophetic mysticism of Hamann, the historicism of Herder, the discontent with civilization expressed by Brandes, and the rising German national sentiment—all these could be used by intellectual Conservatives in their assault upon *Aufklärer* and *Aufklärung*.

Methods of Conservative Defense

The public defense of German society of the 1770's and 1780's consisted primarily of the suppression of voices of Radical criticism—a task made difficult... by the multiplicity of the German state system. There were, however, many attempts at censorship which were invariably justified by the argument that ordinary men were quite incapable of discussing public affairs in a mature manner. Even the Prussian government, generally known for its liberal attitudes, sometimes employed this argument in order to silence editors who had caused offense. To give only one example: some articles in Gökingk's *Journal von und für Deutschland* [*Journal by and for Germany*] had led to complaints by some of Prussia's neighboring states whose princes had been criticized. Two Prussian ministers, Count Finkenstein and Count Hertzberg (the latter, incidentally, known for his *Aufklärung* principles), thereupon sent a stiffly worded reprimand to the *Regierung* [government] of Halberstadt (the district in which the *Journal* was published) on December 13, 1784:

> A private individual does not possess the right to issue public judgments (let alone unfavourable judgments) upon the actions, procedures, laws, proclamations or decrees of sovereigns, their ministers, administrative boards, or courts of justice. This applies, of course, also to the publication and distribution of news privately received about such sovereigns, their courts, et cetera. It is obvious that a private individual, necessarily lacking intimate knowledge of the general context of affairs and the motives of public figures, is quite incapable of rendering a judgment concerning them which is worth hearing....
>
> The nation will neither be intellectually illuminated nor morally improved by being exposed to reckless discussion of its affairs; rather it will be corrupted. The incautious drive for *Aufklärung*, which characterizes the present age, degenerates all too easily into an impertinent license; it tramples upon whatever is sacred and venerable; it makes all established values contemptible in the eyes of the people, confuses its concepts, and promotes sedition, disobedience, license and rebelliousness without either educating or improving the nation.

This general argument was frequently implemented by the call for the suppression of specific journals which had caused offense. Enraged Conservatives did not hesitate to recommend the employment of economic and other pressures upon those princes who refused to silence "seditious" editors. A much-discussed example involved Count August von Limburg-Styrum, the masterful bishop of Speyer, who had issued an exceedingly Conservative political catechism to his subjects. It was ridiculed by Schlözer in the *Staatsanzeigen* [*Political Advertiser*] in a manner most offensive to the bishop. Schlözer wrote as a Hannoverian subject, which made the Hannoverian government responsible—at least in Styrum's view—for the opinions expressed. When a direct complaint to the Hannoverian government yielded no results, the bishop called upon the Regensburg Diet to punish Hannover; when the Diet refused to take any action, he called upon his fellow sovereigns to strike at Hannoverian interests by an organized boycott of Göttingen, Schlözer's university. This farfetched proposal was, however, turned down by his fellow princes; the suggestion shows, however, how far Conservatives were willing to go in opposition to the *Aufklärung*....

Conservatives frequently lamented the rise of *Publizität* [publication] and newspapers per se; they were sometimes not far from the view that the invention of printing, so often hailed by the *Aufklärung* as a milestone and guarantee of human progress, was in fact the main source of mankind's modern troubles. A corollary of this view was to deplore the rise of that popular education which was beginning to make some small encroachments upon mass illiteracy. Did this not merely result in giving common men access to poisonous ideas and thereby making them discontented with their traditional lot in life? The *Popularphilosoph* [popular philosopher] Christian Garve, in a book dealing with agrarian conditions in his native Silesia, reported the view of the landlord class upon this problem in the following paraphrase:

> Our forefathers never had occasion to quarrel with their illiterate serfs: an illiteracy which did not prevent fields from being cultivated at least as well as they are today, and manners being unquestionably purer. Today many peasants can not only read and write, but they also begin to master arithmetic; some even start to read books. Does this make them better men? do their lives become less dissolute? have they become more obedient subjects, or better cultivators of the soil? On the contrary: is it not true that manners have visibly declined? and that lords experience far more difficulty in maintaining authority over their serfs than they did when the latter were still illiterate? If one investigates who have been the village troublemakers [Silesia experienced some minor peasant turbulence], who have been the misleaders of the people: one always finds that they come from the ranks of those who have attended school the longest, who are puffed up by their pretence to wisdom.... It is a general rule today that the most honest peasant is invariably the stupidest and the most ignorant. The officer on the drill ground has exactly the same

experience as the landlord on his estate: the most uncouth and ignorant peasant will invariably make the best soldier. He can be treated as if he were a machine, and when he is so treated one can rely upon him absolutely.

Conservatives attacked with special venom the progressive education introduced by Basedow and his disciples. They asserted that the *Philanthropine* [philanthropists] were corrupters of youth which produced men strong on *Aufklärung* but useless for any kind of constructive work in society. Basedow's ideal of training the *whole* man—instead of encouraging specialization—and of teaching children in a playful spirit only what they wanted to learn when they felt themselves ready for it aroused a mixture of hostility and ridicule. J. G. Schlosser (1739–99), a prominent Badenese official who wrote widely on political, economic, and educational topics, put the case for early specialization in the following terms:

> The vocations of men are in most cases so incompatible with the all-around development of their faculties [advocated by Basedow] that I would almost say that one cannot start early enough to encourage the atrophy of two-thirds of those faculties; for most men are destined for vocations where they cannot use them in later life. Why do you castrate oxen and colts when you prepare them for the yoke and the cart, yet wish to develop the totality of human powers in men similarly condemned to the yoke and the cart? They will jump the furrow if you give them the wrong preparation, or kick against the traces until they die.

The function of education was, in Schlosser's view, *not* the production of versatile "all-around" men, but rather the preparation of men capable of performing useful—however humble—social functions unspoiled by excessive expectations: "It is very simple to idealise the 'highest degree of perfection'; it is very difficult to define the appropriate degree of the good." As an example of the danger of too much well-roundedness Schlosser condemned Basedow's penchant for athletics: what was the point of turning all children into athletes when most of them would be forced to live sedentary lives as adults? The greatest danger of all lay in the playful, joyful, diversified life of the *Philanthropine* (Basedow believed that children should change activities every half hour). This was the worst kind of preparation for real life: "Are the philanthropists not mistaken when they fail to accustom their charges early to steady work, especially continuous, prolonged, and strenuous mental work?" Life required that allotted work be finished before a man started on recreation; Basedow taught his pupils, on the contrary, a hopeless confusion between work and recreation. An example was his teaching of foreign languages as a sort of game, instead of relying upon the traditional method of memorizing words. Schlosser was skeptical about the substantive results of the new method; and he was certain that the traditional method possessed "character building value" in encouraging industry, attention, and patience: "A man who spent his childhood in play must, on the other hand, remain a playing child all his life."

Ernst Brandes criticized the principle of teaching children only what they could understand when and as they were ready for it. This principle ignored the fact that some important things were not a matter of understanding at all, but rather of sentiment and habit—for example, religion, which Basedow treated lightly because its principles obviously exceeded the comprehension of children. Basedow provoked Brandes' anger by his refusal to teach his charges any prayers before they were ten on the grounds that earlier prayers could only be a mumbling of ill-understood words.

Eckartshausen passed the following final judgment upon the practices of the educational reformers à la Basedow:

> They are too impatient to wait for the autumn: they want to have blossoms and fruits at the same time. They claim to see the adult in the child, in fact they turn the adult into a perpetual child. They provide us with forced green plants from their hothouses, plants which carry the hotbed flavor (*Mistbettengeschmack*) for the rest of their life, and offend the gums of every healthy man. They expect our children to learn everything as a game—and produce young men who remain playboys all their lives and look down upon every serious and strenuous activity as mere barbarism.

Although Conservatives often deplored the rise of popular education (especially progressive education), the spread of literacy, and the prevalence of *Publizität*, they reluctantly realized that all of these developments had an irreversible character. There was little to be gained by nostalgic regret for the past and sterile denunciation of the present: the task facing Conservatives was rather one of "getting the Conservative message across" in competition with the writings of *Aufklärung* authors. To this end Conservatives wrote and distributed in quantity a number of popular expositions of Conservative religious and political principles in the 1780's. For example, Jakob Friederich Feddersen, a Lutheran *Domprediger* [cathedral preacher] of Braunschweig, wrote a *Christian Book of Moral Instruction for Townspeople and Peasants*, which was circulated in tens of thousands of copies upon the suggestion of King Christian VII of Denmark. Written in a simple style, it was replete with homely examples drawn from everyday life as it described the duties of a Christian man in marriage, in educating his children, in earning a livelihood, in church attendance, in political loyalty, et cetera. Feddersen urged his lower-class readers to abide by the traditional Christian virtues, and demonstrated that it was equally to their temporal and eternal advantage to do so....

A series of Conservative journals began publication around 1780 in a deliberate attempt to break the power of the *Aufklärung* over the mind of the educated classes of Germany. They were at first exclusively of a religious-theological character. The Giessen theology professor H. Köster, a figure easily ridiculed by the *Aufklärer* because he had written a defense of the Devil's existence which quickly reached a third edition, sought to rally all the Protestant foes of the *Aufklärung* in his *Die neuesten Religionsbegebenheiten* [*Newest Religious Occurrences*] (Giessen, 1777–96). The Mainz Jesuit Hermann Goldhagen (1718–94) attempted the same task for the Catholic part of Germany in his Mainzer *Religionsjournal* [*Journal of Religion*] (1776–94); Goldhagen was an especially virulent foe of Josephinism. He secured powerful support from a group of Augsburg Jesuits under the leadership of Joseph Anton Weissenbach (1734–1801), a prolific writer best known for his two-volume work on *Die Vorbothen des neuen Heidenthums* (*The Harbingers of the New Paganism*). The Augsburg Jesuits published a vigorous review journal, *Kritik über gewisse Kritiker, Rezensenten und Broschürenmacher* [*Critique of Certain Critics, Journalists, and Pamphleteers*] (1787–96), which sought to refute every book and pamphlet produced by the writers of the German *Aufklärung*. The Jesuits also stressed the need to fight pamphlets not just with critical reviews but with counterpamphlets written in a popular style and distributed on a scale similar to that of the propaganda of the *Aufklärung*. They themselves wrote many pamphlets and reprinted numerous others, especially anti-Josephine tracts, in a series launched in 1783.

Conservatives felt rather helpless in the face of the "enlightened absolutism" of men like Joseph II. They could not easily preach rebellion against a legitimate monarch (however misguided his policies), while the Jesuit doctrine of tyrannicide, long an albatross around the neck of the Catholic party and coresponsible for the Papal suppression of the Jesuits in 1773, was obviously obsolete. The sole hope of Conservatives lay in the strength of the public opposition provoked by Joseph's doctrinaire ruthlessness and lack of ordinary human considerations—and Austrian Conservatives naturally did everything in their power to fan this opposition against the Josephine reforms. In countries and provinces where effective *Stände* [Noble Estates] bodies had survived—most notably Hungary and Belgium—Conservatives attempted to mobilize them on behalf of the threatened *status quo*. Where *Stände* bodies no longer existed—or were hopelessly impotent—there was no institutional remedy for the evils of "enlightened despotism"; here Conservatives had no choice but to suffer in resignation until the monarchs abandoned their reform programs under the panic produced by the French Revolution....

Bibliography

P. P. BERNARD, *The Limits of Enlightenment: Joseph II and the Law* (1979).
T. C. W. BLANNEY, *Joseph II and Enlightened Despotism* (1970).
M. BUTLER, ed., *Burke, Paine, Godwin, and the Revolution Controversy* (1984).
D. CAMERON, *The Social Thought of Rousseau and Burke* (1973).
O. CHADWICK, *The Popes and European Revolution* (1981).
J. C. D. CLARK, *English Society, 1688–1832* (1985).
R. COBB, *Reactions to the French Revolution* (1972).
A. COBBAN, *Edmund Burke and the Revolt against the Eighteenth Century*, 2nd ed. (1960).
M. FREEMAN, *Edmund Burke and the Critique of Political Radicalism* (1980).
G. P. GOOCH, *Germany and the French Revolution* (1923).
I. KRAMNICK, *The Rage of Edmund Burke: Portrait of an Ambivalent Conservative* (1977).
F. O'GORMAN, *Edmund Burke: His Political Philosophy* (1973).
R. PAULSON, *Representations of Revolution, 1789–1820* (1983).
J. D. POPKIN, *The Right-Wing Press in France, 1792–1800* (1980).
E. WANGERMANN, *From Joseph II to the Jacobin Trials: Government Policy and Public Opinion in the Hapsburg Dominions in the Period of the French Revolution*, 2nd ed. (1969).

Children and unmarried women, or widows, often tended machinery in early textile mills. *The Mansell Collection*

PART THREE

The Nineteenth Century

The nineteenth century witnessed remarkable changes in European life and society. The industrial power of western Europe led the rest of the world. There was a vast migration of Europeans from the countryside to the city and later in the century from Europe to both North and South America. The forces of nationalism and the armies of Piedmont and Prussia forged the new states of Italy and Germany. The ideals of nationalism and the necessity of building strong states also made the already existing nation-states more conscious of themselves and of their national identities.

European thought in the nineteenth century became more complex in the wake of the quarter-century of French revolutionary and Napoleonic wars. Franklin Baumer's essay explores the manner in which concerns with the irrational came to the fore. He also describes the new awareness of history that would play such an important role in nineteenth-century European nationalism, and examines how the romantic writers began to urge the necessity of organic concepts of society in the face of growing social dislocation.

Industrialism and migration generated new social conditions in Europe. New roles and new modes of employment became possible and necessary for women. Joan Scott and Louise Tilly analyze how young women from the countryside adopted their lives and expectations to work in an urban environment. They emphasize the manner in which these women carried traditional rural customs and expectations into their lives in cities. Anthony Wohl describes in vivid detail the diseases that haunted all urban life and the efforts of both government and the medical profession to deal with the deadly problem.

Nation-states came to be consolidated in a variety of ways in the middle of the century. Wars of unification were only one device. Eugen Weber explores another, little-examined device in nation-building—the new school systems that educated the young in values of secular citizenship and civilization rather than according to religious values. In many respects he demonstrates that the schoolmasters were the great nation-builders. The most powerful new state on the continent was imperial Germany, which had been united by the conservative army and monarchy of Prussia. Gordon Craig analyzes the constitution of that new nation to explain how, even under the constitutional government so long demanded by nineteenth-century liberals, conservative institutions held sway and largely determined the future course of German history.

The Romantic World

FRANKLIN L. BAUMER

Few intellectual movements have caused more controversy among historians than romanticism. There is general agreement that between approximately 1775 and 1830 certain ideas about human nature, knowledge, religion, society, and history came to the fore in Europe and that they were different from those that characterized the mid-eighteenth-century Enlightenment. But historians differ as to whether there was a single romantic movement that encompassed all of these various ideas or whether each major European nation underwent a different romantic experience. Furthermore, because romantic writers often (though not always) criticized the adequacy of reason to interpret the human situation and glorified nonrational features of human nature, there has also been much disagreement as to whether the legacy of romanticism was good or bad for European life and culture.

One method of analysis that tends to clarify many of the issues associated with romanticism is to consider it as a broad, multifaceted reaction against many of the leading ideas of the Enlightenment. Here a number of significant contrasts present themselves. The Enlightenment writers had praised the spread of the light of reason; romantic writers tended to be fascinated by dark subjects and by the world of dreams. The eighteenth-century *philosophes* admired Newton's mechanistic concept of nature; the romantics frequently criticized Newton and portrayed nature in organic terms. The Enlightenment was associated with criticism of religion and with viewing God as far removed from everyday life, whereas romanticism fostered a revival of religion and a concept of God that found divinity present in nature and accessible through subjective human feelings. Eighteenth-century writers admired the ancient world, while the romantics displayed all manner of enthusiasm for the Middle Ages.

Many factors have been used to explain these shifts in taste and thought, but certainly one of the most important was the turmoil associated with the years of the French Revolution and the Napoleonic Wars. Those events cast doubt on the widespread eighteenth-century

Reprinted with permission of Macmillan Publishing Company from *Modern European Thought: Continuity and Change in Ideas, 1600–1950* by Franklin L. Baumer. Copyright © 1977 by Franklin L. Baumer.

conviction that human reason could suffice as the primary guide to human affairs. It was in that climate of confusion, suffering, and radical change that many intellectuals began to reassert the positive value of feeling, religion, social organism, and reverence for the past.

The roots of the Romantic World lay deep in the eighteenth and even the seventeenth century. The Romantic World is commonly represented as a counter-movement to the Enlightenment, just as the Enlightenment is said to have countered the supernatural Christian system. Although there is truth in this view, it should be understood that the Romantic Movement would not have been the same without the Enlightenment, that in part it actually grew out of the Enlightenment, and that in any case it did not constitute a simple return to the world the Enlightenment had left behind.

In truth, the Romantic Movement was as much a revolution as a counter-revolution. It may, indeed, be thought of as the first great protest against the "modern world," that is, the rational-scientific civilization, which had begun to form in the seventeenth century, and which assumed major proportions in the eighteenth century. But it protested in the name of a new modernity. Some of the romantics thought of themselves as "modern" in the sense of Christian, and anticlassical in artistic taste. But they were modern in still another sense. We might say that they were more modern than they knew, especially in their exploration of the night-side of life, of dreams and the unconscious, and in providing the theoretical basis for modern nationalism. In these, among other areas, the romantics obviously set in motion waves of thought that were not to have their full impact until the twentieth century.

There is a special difficulty, however, in trying to define romanticism. This is not only because of the "plurality of romanticisms" to which Arthur Lovejoy called attention. Lovejoy could discover no "one fundamental 'Romantic' idea" in the welter of national movements that others had loosely identified as romantic. Lovejoy also noted a cleavage between "Germany and the West," which became a common topic of discussion during World War I, and continued to be such on through World War II. This cleavage was traced back to the Romantic Movement, which Ernst Troeltsch and others claimed to be peculiarly German, or, at any rate, radically different in Germany than in other countries. Pluralism, however, and a certain amount of nominalism too, is common to all intellectual movements, and one fails to see how it applies more to romanticism than to, say, the Renaissance or Reformation. Mainly, the difficulty in defining romanticism stems rather from the nature of the movement itself. The romantics, of whatever country, had a penchant for the mysterious and put a premium on individual feeling and expression. They also throve on paradoxes. Consequently, it is not always easy to know what the romantics were talking about. What exactly did Friedrich Schleiermacher mean, for instance, by "expansive soaring in the Whole and the Inexhaustible"? Or the philosopher, Friedrich Wilhelm von Schelling, by "real-idealism"? The difficulty is compounded by the word romanticism itself, which was uncommonly vague save among the Germans, not universally acceptable even to the romantics themselves, and variously understood. Moreover, it had little or no institutional organization, no central publishing venture such as the eighteenth-century *Encyclopédie*, no central doctrine, not even so loose an authority as the Bible constituted during the Protestant Reformation....

What, essentially, was romanticism? It is easier to say what it was not, or what European romantics were opposed to. John Stuart Mill, no romantic himself, but a sympathetic and informed observer, put his finger unerringly on what the romantics disliked. Romanticism, he said in an essay on Armand Carrel (1837), represented a reaction "against the narrownesses of the eighteenth century." Although Mill was speaking here primarily of literature, it is clear from what follows, and from other essays, conspicuously the famous one on Coleridge, that Mill thought of romanticism as a revolt against narrowness on many fronts, in philosophy and science, and in historical and political thought, as well as in poetry and the drama. "Fractional," "partial," "insignificant," "poor," were among the adjectives Thomas Carlyle employed in an essay on Diderot (1833); he denounced "Diderot's habitual world" as "a half-world, distorted into looking like a whole." The reference in both cases was, of course, to the European Enlightenment, which by then had become a stereotype, and partly also a caricature. The romantics thought that world too narrow, because of its addiction, as they believed, to geometric thinking and the allied doctrine of neoclassicism, or else to Lockean empiricism. The geometric spirit, though metaphysically bold, tried to subject all life to reason, and thus to mechanize and demean it. Neoclassicism, similarly ambitious in seeking out nature's ideal patterns, imposed universal and iron rules on art and the artist. Empiricism offended for the opposite reason, because it was too skeptical, because it severely limited human knowledge to the sense world of appearances. Newton became an arch-symbol of this narrowness....

In opposition to Newton's world, suffused in light, the romantics offered their own nighttime world. The night, in contrast to day or light, signified that which "dost uplift the heavy wings of soul," and carry it beyond the space-time world into infinite regions. "How paltry and childish seems now the Light to me!" said the German poet-philosopher Novalis (Friedrich von Hardenberg). Novalis preferred, to the flashing stars seen in the sky, "the infinite eyes which the Night has opened to me." This was one of the most positive marks, or predispositions, of the romantic mind: its yearning for the Infinite, which was manifested in a great variety of ways, both secular and religious. Goethe, though he had affinities, not always admitted, for certain features of romanticism, once said: "The highest happiness of man as a thinking man is to have probed what is knowable and quietly to revere what is unknowable." This was a "classical" rather than a romantic maxim, putting limits, as Kant had done, on what the human mind could know and aspire to. Yet Goethe too, through Faust, also reached for the Infinite in his own special way, as did other romantics, whose metaphysical sense was not so highly developed as Novalis....

Romanticism touched off a religious revival. This revival took many forms, not least of which was a new nature mysticism. All the forms were inspired, however, as Carlyle intimates, by a deep sense of metaphysical loss, occasioned by the Enlightenment and its revolutionary aftermath. It was widely believed that the world had lost its metaphysical and religious bearings in the eighteenth century, and that men needed to recover them if there were ever again to be heroes and great works of art. In "the Unbelieving Century" God had become non-existent or peripheral and bound by his own rational laws. Carlyle vividly describes this feeling of loss in his chapter on "The Everlasting No" in *Sartor Resartus* (1833–1834), that great source book for romantic views on God and religion. Carlyle's spokesman, Professor Teufelsdröckh, tells of the spiritual crisis he went through (obviously owing to the corrosive effect of Enlightenment skepticism): how, as "the spirit of Inquiry" took possession of him, he had moved from doubt to disbelief, and consequently was shut out from hope. At best, he thought, there might be "an absentee God," sitting idle since the first Sabbath, and looking at the Universe from the outside in.

But how to recover a living faith? Some romantics never succeeded in doing so, and their failure was doubtless a source of melancholy. Many, on the other hand, went over or back to Roman Catholicism, though they discovered new and romantic reasons for doing so. Others remained Protestant, though they, too, gave their religion a romantic look. Still others, however, and they were not few, renounced "church clothes" altogether, and invented new gods and new mythologies. One of these was William Blake, who, in his epic poem "Jerusalem," served up an exceedingly bizarre mixture of Christian and private mythology. Such perhaps also was Novalis who, though certainly a Christian, preferred to shroud his religion in mystery and fable. "The great mystery has been revealed to all, yet remains eternally unfathomable," says Sophia (Wisdom) in "Klingsor's Fairy Tale." But such, above all, were the natural supernaturalists, those like Carlyle himself, who discovered a new sort of god at work in the world and in nature. Indeed, this god, immanent rather than transcendent, appears in some shape or form in nearly all the varieties of romantic religious experience.

The Vicomte de Chateaubriand, author of *The Genius of Christianity* (1802), called "the Bible of Romanticism," is a good example of the new type of Roman Catholic apologist. In order to resurrect a cult supposed to be in its grave, Chateaubriand proposed, not rational proofs of the existence of God, or a restatement of doctrine, but a direct appeal to the human heart. "The Christian religion," he said, "is itself a species of passion, which has its transports, its ardors, its sighs, its joys, its tears, its love of society and solitude." Chateaubriand showed how poetic Christianity was, how mysterious, how aesthetically satisfying (especially in its churches, which, in contrast to Greek temples, however elegant, excited feelings of awe and infinitude), and how impressive also was its historic achievement. Far from being hostile to civilization, as Gibbon had said (though not consistently), Christianity contributed to it a superior morality, a great art and literature, and every sort of improvement, ranging from agriculture to the most abstract sciences. Were he to rewrite his book, Chateaubriand said later in his *Memoirs*, he would show further how Christianity had laid the basis for true social cohesion, equality, and justice. This was an appeal calculated to win the hearts even of young men, in a time of mental and moral shipwreck (as Chateaubriand represented it).

At almost exactly the same time a young chaplain in Berlin, educated by Moravian Pietists, was trying to revive Protestantism, by appealing, however, more to individual experience than to social usefulness. All the chief notes of romantic Protestantism appear in Friedrich Schleiermacher's "theology of feeling," notably in the early *Addresses on Religion to its Cultural Despisers*, which he wrote in 1799, at the insistence of his romantic friends in the Prussian capital. Schleiermacher advocated turning away from French culture, which had become indifferent to religion, as well as from deism and rational theology in general. After wrestling with Kant since his university days, Schleiermacher rejected the latter's "religion within the limits of reason alone," which made God and immortality depend on man's moral consciousness. Religion was not the same thing as morality, or philosophy. Like so many of his contemporaries, Schleiermacher thirsted for the Infinite, which was something quiet different from trying to reconcile religion with reason, or to reduce it to ethics. "True religion," he said in his famous definition, "is sense and taste for the Infinite." But where was the Infinite to be found?—In man's inmost soul, in "feeling," he said. Despite his resistance to Kant, Schleiermacher had learned from the critical philosopher to distrust rational proofs of God's existence, hence to move religion back to a precognitive state. Feeling, however, was individual, even though it was also a faculty of the human soul and corresponded in some way, not made very clear, to an objective reality. Schleiermacher distrusted the generalizing and universalizing of Enlightenment religion. For a long time, he said, he had been content with the discovery of a "universal reason." But later Schleiermacher saw that man must rise to "the still higher level of individuality." "I was not satisfied to view humanity in rough unshapen masses, inwardly altogether alike." Thus, Schleiermacher individualized, as well as psychologized and emotionalized religion. Each individual was a unique embodiment of the All, and experienced the All in his own unique way. If Schleiermacher's God was not pantheistic, he was certainly immanent, to be found in the world, more particularly in man's soul. As head, later on, of the theological faculty at the new university of Berlin, Schleiermacher was able to influence Protestant theology profoundly in this new and "romantic" direction.

The romantics also characteristically found God in Nature, not all of them, of course, not Alfred de Vigny or Blake, or Lord Byron, but certainly an impressive number. These "natural supernaturalists," revolting against the Newtonian machine, sought to make nature a place in which man could once again live and feel close to God, and thus solve the problem of dualism that had plagued thinking men since the time of Descartes. The impetus to this new way of thinking about nature came from, among others, Rousseau, whom the contemplation of nature sent into mystical ecstasies (as in *Les Rêveries du Promeneur Solitaire*, 1776–1778); Goethe, who is his morphological studies was always trying to discover the original and inner principle of things, the eternal in the finite; "holy Spinoza," revived in Germany in the late eighteenth century, who appeared to teach an immanent God, identical in some fashion with the universe. This new nature mysticism blossomed in Schelling's *Naturphilosophie*, much admired by Samuel Taylor Coleridge as well as the Germans; in Wordsworth's nature poetry; and in landscape painters such as John Constable in England and David Caspar Friedrich in Germany....

Man, as understood by the romantics, was not the measure, as in "classical" thought. They commonly saw man in the context of great cosmic forces that enveloped him in a whole or infinity greater than himself. "Man," said Dr. Carus in his *Nine Letters on Landscape Painting* (1831), "when he contemplates the magnificent unity of a natural landscape, is made conscious of his own insignificance and, feeling that everything is a part of God, he loses himself in the Infinite and renounces his individual existence." This emphasis on a greater whole by no means contradicts an equally strong emphasis on individuality, already noted in Schleiermacher, or on human creativity. It does, however, make clear the essentially metaphysical nature of romantic man. In romantic anthropology, man is not merely "bent toward the earth," as Victor Hugo so graphically put it, but "thrown toward heaven, his fatherland."

This explains why the romantics undertook their own Copernican revolution in epistemology. Man had to be endowed with knowing faculties that were commensurate with his metaphysical needs and ambitions. Lockean epistemology was obviously inadequate to the task, since it made knowledge dependent, very largely, on sense impressions. Even Kant, though he made the mind more active with his famous categories, limited knowledge to appearances in the phenomenal world. Hence, Coleridge, very much anti-Locke, though grateful to "the sage of Koenigsberg" (and perhaps not perfectly understanding him), posited a special faculty of the mind, which he surprisingly called "Reason," to distinguish it from the

"Understanding." This famous distinction, expressed by nearly all the romantics in one form or another, was already familiar in Germany, thanks to the philosopher F. H. Jacobi, and to Kant himself. The "Understanding" (*Verstand*), to be sure, could only know appearances. In Schopenhauer's metaphor, it resembled a man who goes round and round a castle sketching the facade, but never finding an entrance. "Reason" (*Vernunft*; Jacobi called it *Glaube*, or faith), however, could penetrate the walls, that is, get behind appearances to the thing-in-itself, or, in Coleridge's words, take as its field "invisible realities or spiritual objects." It was "the organ of the supersensuous." Coleridge, in this respect typical of the general romantic endeavor, transformed the mind from a mirror (or *tabula rasa*) into a lamp which could throw its beam over "A new Earth and new Heaven,/ Undreamt of by the sensual and the proud."

Coleridge, overflowing with metaphors, also compared the mind to a plant, which assimilates the outer elements, but which by its respiration makes its own contribution to the environment. In other words, the mind was also wonderfully creative, capable not only of penetrating the mysteries but of rendering and vivifying them in works of original genius. By means of Imagination, sister to Reason, and described by Coleridge as an "esemplastic" or shaping power, man could bring new worlds to life, by creation and invention. This was supremely true of the artist, who, indeed, became the ideal man of the Romantic World, displacing the *philosophe*. For Shelley, for instance, the poet was more than human, a visionary participating in the eternal, lifting the veil from "the hidden beauty of the world." Similarly, for Schelling, who developed a full-blown philosophy of art, the artist, alone of men, directly intuited the Absolute, and hence presented in his work "an infinity which no finite understanding can fully unfold."

This romantic doctrine of the genius cannot be fully understood, however, without reference to the unconscious. Indeed, romantic anthropology, in general, assumed the existence of an "irrational," or unconscious, mind. If the romantics did not invent the unconscious, they were the first to talk about it freely and at length. The unconscious was used to explain not only the creative process but also the "night side" of human life, the world of dreams, monsters, and apparitions. It was more a metaphysical than a scientific concept. The artist was commonly pictured as an unconsciously growing plant, or as a vessel through whom the Eternal acted and expressed itself. Some, like the artist-poet William Blake, believed in poetic automatism. "I have written this Poem," Blake said of his *Milton*, "from immediate Dictation ... without Premeditation and even against my Will." Of course, the unconscious expressed itself preeminently in dreams. Here the contrast between romantic and Enlightenment thought is striking. The latter attempted to reduce the dream to a natural phenomenon, originating in sense experience and explicable by mechanical laws. The state of wakefulness was the superior state; in dreams the "soul" lost touch with the real world. Romantic psychologists like Dr. Carus and von Schubert, the latter the author of a seminal book on the *Symbolism of Dreams* (1814), stood this proposition on its head. In dreams, man speaks a superior language, which enables him to look backward and forward, without the usual temporal restraints, hence to be prophetic. In dreams the soul, precisely because it is withdrawn from sense impressions, has contact with divine reality, thus enabling the "hidden poet" in man to emerge. The opening lines of Novalis' novel *Heinrich von Ofterdingen* (1799) make clear the new romantic view. Heinrich and his father are talking about dreams. "Dreams are froth," says the father, who is a skeptic. "The times when heavenly visions were seen in dreams have long passed by." Heinrich objects. Maybe dreams are not sent directly from heaven, but should we not think of them, nonetheless, as "heavenly gifts," which rend the mysterious curtain that hides our inward natures from view, release the chained fancy, and guide us "in our pilgrimage to the holy tomb."

As stated earlier, the unconscious cut two ways. It could lead man to a superior world, but it could also let loose the demonic in him. The romantics were acutely aware of an anxious and troubled human nature, of forces hidden in man that could tear him and his world apart. Von Schubert himself gave lectures on the "night side" of science, warning of the evil as well as good manifestations of the unconscious. Heinrich von Kleist, influenced by von Schubert's theories, peopled his dramas of the same period (1806–1808) with figures like Panthesilea, the Amazon queen, who was swept away by elemental passions, or Kätchen von Heilbronn, in whom love was represented as a primitive, unconscious force. And Coleridge, though he extolled man's Reason and god-like Imagination, nevertheless, in his greatest poem, made his hero commit an essentially irrational (unconscious) crime, the killing of the albatross, for which he must suffer until he became conscious of what he had done....

Arthur Schopenhauer was the philosopher of this night side of romantic anthropology. Schelling, too, detected dark impulses, largely unconscious, in the soul, but was optimistic about man's freedom to overcome and transmute them. Schopenhauer, however, did not believe in freedom, or at least did so only to a limited degree. In *The World as Will and Idea* (1818), Schopenhauer identified the thing-in-itself (that is, reality) as "the will to live," and this will was blind, planless, groundless, riding herd on man, involving him in endless striving, hence suffering and strife. "Eternal becoming, endless flux, characterises the revelation of the inner nature of will." Only by denying his own nature, that is, will, by stilling desire altogether, or turning to aesthetic contemplation, can man achieve any sort of peace. Schopenhauer's will is reminiscent of the Freudian id. Moreover, Schopenhauer keeps saying that men are not what they pretend to be; "they are only masks." Tear off the mask, look into the unconscious (though Schopenhauer does not actually use the word), and what does one see? A boundless egoism and malice, causing misery to self and other selves, caused by the overriding will to live. Schopenhauer wrote in a later essay on human nature:

It is a fact, then, that in the heart of every man there lies a wild beast which only waits for an opportunity to storm and rage, in its desire to inflict pain on others, or, if they stand in his way, to kill them.... In trying to tame and to some extent hold it in check, the intelligence, its appointed keeper, has always enough to do. People may, if they please, call it the radical evil in human nature.... I say, however, that it is the will to live, which, more and more embittered by the constant sufferings of existence, seeks to alleviate its own torment by causing torment in others.

Romantic ideas about social and political organization can be understood only in the light of this anthropology, as well as the general history of the period. Romanticism has been accused of nearly every political sin in the book, of revolution as well as reaction, of protofascism and antinomianism, even of *Weltpflucht*, or lack of concern for social problems. And it is true that over several generations romanticism ran nearly the whole gamut of contemporary political creeds, from conservatism to liberalism and socialism and even anarchism. However, as this statement implies, most romantics did take sides in the political conflicts of the times. It is simply not true that they shied away from politics, or refused to think about it, though not many romantics actually held public office. Indeed, out of the Romantic World came a number of strikingly new and influential ideas concerning the organization of societies.

Of these ideas, one stands out above all the others, namely the social organism. This was not, of course, a new idea. Nevertheless, it now made new sense and was given a new twist. Its contemporary appeal is easy to understand. It reflected the fear of chaos in an age of revolution, the dismay felt by many, not merely the aristocracy, at the toppling of institutions and the dissolving of ancient ties. Yet it also antedated the French Revolution in, for instance, the reflections of Rousseau and Burke (not so opposed to each other in political mood as the latter liked to think) and Herder. Thus, the social organism represented a revulsion not only against the excesses in Paris during the Revolution but also against the entire Enlightenment way of thinking about social problems.

Coleridge hits the keynote in one of his "lay sermons" on politics, *The Statesman's Manual* (1816), in which, among other things, he summarized his views on the causes of the Revolution and France's subsequent "chastisement." He attributed the debacle largely to false ideas, not least of which was

> the general conceit that states and governments might be and ought to be constructed as machines, every movement of which might be foreseen and taken into previous calculations; the consequent multitude of plans and constitutions, of planners and constitution-makers, and the remorseless arrogance with which the authors and proselytes of every new proposal were ready to realize it, be the cost what it might in the established rights, or even in the lives, of men....

To this "machine" conceit Coleridge opposed "the right idea of the State," which he described as a "moral unit" or "organic whole." That is, Coleridge thought of the state—or society—as more like an organism than a machine. The English Constitution, for instance, was not *made* as a machine is made; it *grew* as an organism grows over a period of time. The state further resembled an organism in consisting, not of atomic individuals, each pursuing his own selfish interest, but of organs—the historic organs of king, church, and proprietage—each contributing in different ways to the life of the whole.

This organic theory was neither original with Coleridge nor was it confined to England. It became, indeed, a quite common view among the romantics of all countries, many of whom, like Coleridge, started out as enthusiasts of revolution, and were subsequently disillusioned. Coleridge himself inherited the idea from Edmund Burke, who, years before, had castigated the revolutionaries for treating politics as though it were a "geometrical demonstration," without reference to human nature or history. Burke's influence became pervasive in Germany as well as in England, but the Germans did not need Burke to tell them that the times called for a new emphasis on *Gemeinschaft*. The German romantics attacked a political science based on the abstract model of geometry, and substituted for it a sort of political biology, which stressed "natural" growth as opposed to conscious planning, and community feeling as opposed to mere individual rights. Schleiermacher sounds like Burke when, in a paper read before the Royal Academy of the Sciences in Berlin in 1814, he denounced contemporary political "engineers" for treating states always as "objects upon which man has to exercise his ingenuity," and never as "historical formations of nature." "Never has a state, even the most imperfect one, been made."

For most romantics, especially after the Revolution, the nation or nation-state constituted the highest form of social organism. Thus, the latter was not necessarily a reactionary concept. Romanticism, in fact, contributed more to the rise of nationalism, soon to become one of the great modern myths, than either the Jacobins or Napoleon. This romantic nationalism, it should be understood, did not negate romantic individualism. It is true that the spectacle of the Revolution, and its aftermath of French imperialism, engendered a stronger feeling of identity between the individual and the state, particularly in Germany. Nevertheless, the romantics were careful, even at the height of Germany's War of Liberation, to preserve the dignity of the individual, especially the genius. The new thought was that the individual could best develop his potentialities in the corporate community and with the help of the state, which was now represented as a cultural leader.

The more important point, however, is that romantic thought depicted the nation itself as a great individual, different from, though not necessarily antagonistic to, other nations. That is, romantic individualism expressed itself politically chiefly in the idea of the nation. This idea is another instance of the romantic revolt against the generalizing and universalizing tendencies in eighteenth-century thought. In his *Addresses to the German Nation* (1808), the philosopher Fichte, who had moved from an earlier rationalism to a romantic view of society, speaks of the "individuality of nations."

> Spiritual nature was able to represent the essence of mankind only as highly manifold gradations of individuals, and of individuality, in general, of nations. Only in so far as each one of these nations, left to itself, develops and takes shape in accordance with its own peculiarities, and in so far as each individual in each of these nations also develops and takes shape in accordance with this common peculiarity as well as with his own individual peculiarity, is the phenomenon of divinity reflected in the way it should be....

Herder had developed this idea years before when as a young man he took a sea voyage from Riga to France, observing en route the peculiarities of each country as it passed before his eyes and beginning to form in his mind the idea of a *Volk* and *Volksgeist*.

The national idea, however, underwent considerable change in the hands of successive romantic thinkers. A largely cultural idea at first, it took on a more political cast, particularly in Germany, under the impact of French imperialism. Herder's nationalism, for instance, was purely cultural and humanitarian, whereas Fichte's, hammered out in the shadow of France's humiliation of Prussia, was political as well as cultural. Herder's chief contribution to nationalism was the idea of the *Volk*, which in turn was based on his idea of nature. As will be recalled, what impressed Herder about nature was not its mechanical regularity but its richness and variety. "Nature," he wrote, "has distributed its gifts differently according to climate and culture.... Let us rejoice that Time, the great mother of all things, throws now these and now other gifts from her horn of plenty and slowly builds up mankind in all its different component parts." This variety, he thought, extended to the history of peoples. In the course of history, each *Volk* came to have a unique character, or soul (*Geist*), exhibited preeminently in its religion, language, and literature. The *Volk* was not formed by a contract, or by man's will; it grew, as an organism grows and ultimately becomes a living whole greater than its individual parts. Though Herder championed the cultural rights of all peoples, including the Jews and Slavs, he addressed himself primarily to Germans. He reminded the Germans of their great literary heritage, setting the example by his collection of *Volkslieder*, urging freedom from imitation of classical and French models. Herder emphasized the youth of German culture, and the great future that lay before it. In a word, he called upon the Germans to become conscious of themselves as a unique and creative people, who had a significant contribution to make to civilization.

These social and political ideas provide a natural bridge to romantic ideas about history.... Historicism did not originate with the Romantic

Movement, but the latter provided the favorable climate that it needed to grow and spread. It became, in fact, still another facet of the romantic revolt against the generalizing tendencies of the Enlightenment.

The word "historicism" (a translation of the German *Historismus*) is of late nineteenth-century, not romantic, vintage, and since its appearance it has acquired a number of quite different and even contradictory meanings. Correctly used, however, it means real empathy for the past, along with the twin ideas of temporal individuality and development. In the late eighteenth and early nineteenth centuries these conceptions seemed new by comparison with certain Enlightenment ideas about history.

The romantic empathy for history is implied, of course, in the organic conception of society. It went much deeper than a mere interest in history, or even a conviction that history had something to teach. It really amounted to a piety. The romantics, living in times of rapid change, saw the folly of cutting loose completely from the past, of trusting to naked reason rather than history. They learned to revere their ancestors rather than to deplore them, to see in the historic nation a society with which they could identify even while it continued to grow. Edmund Burke had this piety, and his bias was on the side of "continuity," "old prejudices," "prescription," all favorite words. No greater tribute to history has ever been made than in the following apostrophe in Burke's *Reflections on the Revolution in France* (1790):

> We know that we [modern Englishmen] have made no discoveries; and we think that no discoveries are to be made, in morality; nor many in the great principles of government, nor in the ideas of liberty, which were understood long before we were born.... Instead of casting away all our old prejudices, we cherish them, etc.

Yet not even Burke quite catches the "historic passion" (as the French historian Augustin Thierry called it) that motivated the romantics: their ability not merely to revere history but to feel their way back into past ages, to understand each on its own terms, and to appreciate "local color" (again Thierry), that is, the unique spirit of each.

Herder conceptualized this new historicism in two seminal essays. In the first, written in 1774, he compared history to a tree, which throws out many branches and is forever renewing itself. He was especially concerned just then to puncture the pride of the Enlightenment, which preened itself on its own accomplishments and handed down lofty judgments of praise or blame on past ages. The butt of his criticism was a minor Swiss writer named Isaak Iselin whose *History of Mankind*, published ten years earlier, had celebrated man's progress from savagery to the civilization of the Age of Reason. In opposition to this doctrine of progress, Herder proclaimed an historical relativism. In opposition to the generalizing tendencies of "the philosophers," he upheld the individuality of cultures and peoples. "Each nation, also each epoch," Herder said, "has the center of its happiness in itself, just as each sphere has its center of gravity." That being so, there can be no universal standards of judgment. If you truly wish to understand another country or century, you must plunge deeply into it, and "feel it all inside yourself." Thus, Herder rehabilitated all ages and peoples, the Egyptians and Phoenicians, as well as the Greeks and Romans, also the Middle Ages, which he refused to treat with condescension. The only age that Herder had nothing good to say for was his own, which he thought overrefined, too rational and mechanized in its thinking to be vital. When he wrote this early piece Herder had not yet freed himself completely from Rousseau's historical pessimism.

Of all the past ages of history, the Middle Ages had the greatest appeal for the romantics. Other ages also came in for praise, including ancient Greece, which the poet Hölderlin, for instance, romanticized as a country still in touch with holy nature. But only the Middle Ages, stretched to include the Christian martyrs of the reign of Diocletian at one end and Shakespeare and Milton at the other, could inspire a cultural movement of the magnitude of the Gothic Revival. This movement embraced nearly every field of thought: religious thought (Christian apologetics of Chateaubriand, and the Oxford Movement in England); historiography (impressive studies of the Norman Conquest, the Dukes of Burgundy, the Crusades, and the like by "romantic" historians such as the Thierry brothers, de Barante, and Michaud); the novel (notably novels by Sir Walter Scott, Hugo, and Chateaubriand, which everybody read, including the historians); art and architecture (including the Houses of Parliament, designed by Sir Charles Barry after the fire of 1834, and many neo-Gothic churches by Welby Pugin).... The Gothic Revival also inspired the restoration of medieval buildings, such as Cologne cathedral, and collections of medieval paintings and historical documents. The *Monumenta Germaniae Historica*, pet project of the newly founded (1819) Society for the Early Study of German History, is an example of the latter. Not all romantics, to be sure, discovered the same things in the Middle Ages. It was not so much Christianity that caught Herder's eye as the Germanic Middle Ages, a youth movement spearheaded by the Goths, Angles, Franks, and others, which brought new vitality and energy to a civilization grown feeble. Not unexpectedly, Herder described the Middle Ages in Germany as an age "uniquely itself." Novalis is more typical in his idealization of the Middle Ages as a great Age of Faith, characterized by unity, mystery, and "the sacred sense," which evaporated in the Age of Reason that succeeded it. The Middle Ages were also frequently represented as the golden age of chivalry, now threatened by a ruthless industrialism, as well as a period of craftsmanship and good taste.

Herder's second essay, the longer but unfinished *Ideas for a Philosophy of History* (1784–1791), brings out more the concept of development, as the first essay had struck the new note of individuality ("virtues peculiar to a nation or century") and relativism. In this essay Herder talked about "the education of mankind" and its striving toward *Humanität*. By *Humanität*

(Humanity) Herder meant man's essentially "human essence," his noble constitution for reason and freedom, his finer senses and impulses, including his sympathy for others, which Herder said "is not ready made, but potentially realizable." Herder had finally got Rousseau out of his system. He now compared history to a chain, each link of which is necessary to "God's epic through all centuries, continents, and generations." This was not, however, a doctrine of progress, at least not in the Enlightenment sense. There was enough of Rousseau still left in Herder for him to be skeptical about progress toward some future perfect state. *Humanität* was a value or guiding principle, approximated by each culture in its own peculiar way, and perhaps never fully realizable by any culture on earth. Still, Herder was now thinking more in terms of a goal, and of progress toward that goal. Herder had come to realize more fully the developmental aspect of history, how history changes shape "like an eternal Proteus," how each people carries on its back what had gone before, and yet tries to improve on it, to approximate *Humanität* more nearly, each, to be sure, in its own peculiar way. Already in the first essay Herder had exclaimed, "This indeed is genuine progress, continuous development.... Becoming on a grand scale!" This historicism bore fruit in later writers, as has been said, and conspicuously in Hegel, who despite real and important differences from Herder, nevertheless enshrined it as a doctrine. In the chapter on "The Principle of Development" in the *Lectures on the Philosophy of History*, Hegel contrasted history with nature. Nature could only repeat itself endlessly (Hegel obviously did not have a romantic conception of nature). History, on the other hand, was never static and was characterized by change, by perpetual novelty, and by progress toward perfectibility, the nature of which, however, was still "undetermined." In Hegel, Spirit also embodied itself historically in the particular, that is, in the *Volksgeist*....

Romantic historicism commonly explained history by the operation of "spiritual," as opposed to material forces. "It is the spiritual always that determines the material," Carlyle said, and for Carlyle, as for many romantics, Spirit worked through heroes, and thus shaped the course of history. "The History of the world is but the Biography of great men" who, Carlyle kept saying in his popular lectures *On Heroes and Hero-Worship* (1840), "are sent into the world." Nevertheless, Carlyle's hero was no puppet like Hegel's "World-Historical Individual," who was always more the object than the subject of history, used by "the cunning of reason" to do its will. Carlyle's hero stands out as a creative individual, inspired from above but not determined, whose thoughts and actions make or break history. Carlyle reacted even more strongly against determinism from below. "Man is heaven-born," he insisted, "not the thrall of Circumstances, of Necessity, but the victorious subduer thereof." The romantics would have none of the current environmentalism, popularized by the Enlightenment, which tended to denigrate heroes as the products of "circumstance" or social conditions.

In retrospect, romanticism shapes up as an even more important movement than has been supposed. Despite the evanescence of some of its ideas, romanticism put its permanent stamp on the modern world. Its modernity consisted above all in its awareness of becoming. The romantics were conscious, far more so than the *philosophes*, of living in a world of endless change. "Truth," said Carlyle, quoting Schiller, "*immer wird, nie ist; never is, always is a-being.*" But for Carlyle, as for most romantics, this was, for the most part, an intoxicating rather than a terrifying prospect. In change, Carlyle goes on to say, "there is nothing terrible, nothing supernatural; on the contrary, it lies in the very essence of our lot and life in this world." Change was not yet terrifying, because becoming could still be connected up, though not necessarily in traditional ways, with being. Or perhaps it would be more accurate to say that being was now identified with becoming, which is to say that truth was thought to unfold only in a world perpetually in process.

Bibliography

M. H. ABRAHMS, *The Mirror and the Lamp: Romantic Theory and the Critical Tradition* (1958).
M. H. ABRAHMS, *Natural Supernaturalism: Tradition and Revolution in Romantic Literature* (1971).
J. S. ALLEN, *Popular French Romanticism: Authors, Readers, and Books in the Nineteenth Century* (1981).
I. BERLIN, *Vico and Herder: Two Studies in the History of Ideas* (1976).
K. CLARK, *The Romantic Rebellion* (1973).
J. ENGELL, *The Creative Imagination: Enlightenment to Romanticism* (1981).
H. C. HATFIELD, *Aesthetic Paganism in German Literature from Winckelmann to the Death of Goethe* (1964).
G. G. IGGERS, *The German Conception of History: The National Tradition of Historical Thought from Herder to the Present Day* (1968).
H. M. JONES, *Revolution and Romanticism* (1974).
J. J. MCGANN, *The Romantic Ideology: A Critical Investigation* (1983).
H. PEYRE, *What is Romanticism?* (1976).
P. STANTON, *Pugin* (1971).
J. E. TOEWS, *Hegelianism: The Path toward Dialectical Humanism, 1805–1841* (1980).
W. VAUGHN, *German Romantic Painting* (1982).
A. WALICKI, *Philosophy and Romantic Nationalism: The Case of Poland* (1982).
C. WELCH, *Protestant Thought in the Nineteenth Century* (1972; 1985).
R. WELLEK, *Concepts of Criticism* (1963).

Women's Work and the Family in Nineteenth-Century Europe

JOAN W. SCOTT AND LOUISE A. TILLY

Much confusion has surrounded our understanding of the experience of women in the labor force in the nineteenth century. It has often been assumed that women in the home were engaged in nonproductive activity and that the transfer of women from the home to some kind of formal workplace involved a relatively sharp social change. In point of fact one of the most striking features of the economic and social experience of these women, who were drawn primarily into domestic service, garment making, and textile manufacturing, was the manner in which they carried traditional rural values, practices, and structures into the new urban and industrial setting.

The family economy was the most important structure for women both prior to their migration to the city and thereafter. In rural areas women performed a large number of significant economic functions within the household. As children and young adults they might earn wages to supplement parental income. They might also save some of their wages to provide a dowry for their marriage. Once married, they would often continue to work in their new home, sewing or weaving while attending to their children. The married woman was frequently in charge of both the financial and domestic management of the household.

Women transferred a number of these roles to the city. Most of the women engaged in domestic service, garment making, and textile production were young and single. They were the members of the rural family who could be most easily spared from the farm work. All three modes of employment brought them into a life involving some kind of "household" situation. The young women thus employed would send part of their wages home to supplement their parents' income. They would also save money to prepare the way toward eventual marriage. And the kind of work pursued in domestic service or in cloth and clothes preparation was the kind of work traditionally done by rural

---

Reprinted from Joan W. Scott and Louise A. Tilly, *Comparative Studies in Society and History*, vol. 17 (1975), pp. 38–41, 43–64, by permission of Cambridge University Press. Copyright © Cambridge University Press.

women. When a young woman from the country working in the city eventually married, she would usually leave the labor force but not stop working altogether. While rearing her children, she would often undertake part time work, frequently sewing, that she could pursue in the context of her household as a contribution to the family economy.

By the end of the century the work and economic experience of women had become infused with many individualistic values, but the initial experience of women entering the labor force reflected a remarkable degree of continuity of values and practices drawn from rural life into urban.

The women who worked in great numbers in the nineteenth century were overwhelmingly members of the working and peasant classes. Most held jobs in domestic service, garment making or the textile industry. In England in 1841 and still in 1911 most working women were engaged in domestic or other personal service occupations. In 1911, 35 percent were servants (including laundresses), 19.5 percent were textile workers and 15.6 percent were engaged in the dressmaking trades. In Milan, according to the censuses of 1881, 1901 and 1911, a similar concentration of women in domestic service existed, with garment making ranking second and textiles much less important than in England. Similarly, in France, excluding agriculture, textiles, garment making and domestic service were the chief areas of female employment. In France, 69 percent of working women outside agriculture were employed in these three fields in 1866: domestic service, 28 percent; garment making, 21 percent; textiles, 20 percent. In 1896, the proportions were altered, but the total was 59 percent: domestic service, 19 percent; garment making, 26 percent; textiles, 14 percent.

Despite very different rates of industrialization in England, France and Italy, the evidence strongly suggests that women in all three cases did not participate in factory work (except in textiles) in large numbers. Rather, economic and social changes associated with urban and industrial development seem to have generated employment opportunities in a few traditional sectors in which women worked at jobs similar to household tasks. The economic changes leading to high employment of women included the early industrialization of textiles and the nineteenth-century pattern of urbanization, with cities acting as producers of and markets for consumer goods and as places of employment for domestic servants. The expansion of production of consumer goods involved the growth of a large piece-work garment industry. Production moved from the workshops of craftsmen to the homes of people who sewed together pre-cut garments. This change in the process of production generated employment opportunities for large numbers of women. The subsequent decline of this method of producing ready-made goods and its replacement by factory production, as well as the decline of textiles and the growth of heavy industry, led to lower female participation in the work forces of all three countries we have examined.

The kinds of jobs available to women were not only limited in number and kind; they also were segregated—that is, they were held almost exclusively by women. The women who held these jobs were usually young and single. In Milan, about 75 percent of women aged 15 to 20 worked in 1881 and 1901. In female age groups over 20, employment in textile manufacture and garment making declined sharply, presumably as women stopped work after marriage. The only female occupation with appreciable proportions (50 percent or more) of workers aged over 30 was domestic service, in which celibacy prevailed. In Great Britain, similar age patterns are evident in the scattered available data. Most women operatives in the Lancashire cotton mills in 1833 were between 16 and 21 years old. Only 25 percent of female cotton workers were married in the Lancashire districts in 1841. Hewitt argues for an increase in proportions either married or widowed among cotton operatives peaking sometime in the 1890s and declining thereafter. The highest percentage of married women in this occupation was about one-third. The much less specialized labor force of London in the 1880s was primarily aged between 15 and 25 years.

When census figures finally provide marital status, some big national differences can be noted. In 1911, while 69 percent of all single women in Britain worked, only 9.6 percent of married women did. In France in 1896, 52 percent of all single women were in the labor force, and 38 percent of married women. Although our evidence is impressionistic and scattered, it looks as though as industrialization advanced (at least in the pre-1914 period), fewer married women worked. Thus Britain, the more advanced industrial country in 1911, had the lower proportion of married women workers; on the other hand, in France, in which both agriculture and manufacturing were organized on a smaller scale than in Britain, more married women were in the labor force.

Why did women work in the nineteenth century and why was the female labor force predominantly young and single? To answer these questions we must first examine the relationship of these women to their families of origin (the families into which they were born), not to their families of procreation (the family launched at marriage). We must ask not only how husbands regarded their wives' roles, but what prompted families to send their *daughters* out into the job market as garment workers or domestic servants.

The parents of these young women workers during industrialization were mostly peasants and, to a lesser extent, urban workers. When we examine the geographic and social origins of domestic servants, one of the largest groups of women workers, their rural origins are clear. Two-thirds of all the domestic servants in England in 1851 were daughters of rural laborers. For France, we have no aggregate numbers, but local studies suggest similar patterns. In his study of Melun, for example, Chatelain found that in 1872, 54 percent of female domestic servants were either migrants from rural areas or foreigners. Theresa McBride calculated that in Versailles from 1825 to 1853, 57.7 percent of female domestic servants were daughters of peasants. In Bordeaux, a similar proportion obtained: 52.8 percent. In Milan, at the end of the nineteenth century, servants were less likely to be city-born than any other category of workers.... Let us now attempt to reconstruct the historical experience of women workers during the early stages of industrialization. Since most were of rural origin, we will begin by examining the peasant or family economy whose values and economic needs sent them into the job market.

Commentators on many different areas of Europe offer strikingly similar descriptions of peasant social organization. Anthropologists and social historians seem to agree that regardless of country 'the peasantry is a pre-industrial social entity which carries over into contemporary society specific elements of a different, older, social structure, economy and culture'. The crucial unit of organization is the family 'whose solidarity provides the basic framework for mutual aid, control and socialization'. The family's work is usually directed to the family farm, property considered to belong to the group rather than to a single individual. 'The individual, the family and the farm appear as an indivisible whole'. 'Peasant property is, at least *de facto*, family property. The head of the family appears as the manager rather than the proprietor of family land'.

These descriptions of Eastern European peasants are echoed by Michael Anderson in his comparison of rural Lancashire and rural Ireland early in the nineteenth century. He suggests that in both cases the basis of 'functional family solidarity... was the absolute *interdependence* of family members such that neither fathers nor sons had any scope for alternatives to the family as a source of provision for a number of crucially important needs'. Italian evidence confirms the pattern. Although in late nineteenth-century Lombardy a kind of *frèreche* (brothers and their families living together and working the land together) was a frequent alternative to the nuclear family, the household was the basic unit of production. All members of the family contributed what they could either by work on the farm, or, in the case of women and the young, by work in nearby urban areas or in rural textile mills. Their earnings were turned over to the head of the household; in the case of brothers joined in one household, the elder usually acted as head. He took care of financial matters and contractual relationships in the interests of all. For Normandy in the eighteenth century, Gouesse's recent study has described the gradual evolution of reasons given for marriage when an ecclesiastical dispensation had to be applied for. At the end of that century, reasons such as 'seeking well-being', or 'desire to live happily' became more common. Gouesse considers these differences of expression rather superficial; what all these declarations meant, although few stated this explicitly, was that one had to be married in order to live.

'The married couple was the simple community of work, the elementary unit'. In nineteenth-century Brittany, 'all the inhabitants of the farm formed a working community...linked one to the other like the crew of a ship'.

Despite differences in systems of inheritance and differences in the amount of land available, the theory of the peasant economy developed by Chayanov for nineteenth-century Russia applies elsewhere. The basis of this system is the family, or more precisely the household—in Russia, all those 'having eaten from one pot'. It has a dual role as a unit of production and consumption. The motivations of its members, unlike capitalist aims, involve 'securing the needs of the family rather than...making a profit'. The family's basic problem is organizing the work of its members to meet its annual budget and 'a single wish to save or invest capital if economic conditions allow'.

Members of the family or household have clearly defined duties, based in part on their age and their position in the family and in part on their sex. Sex role differentiation clearly existed in these societies. Men and women not only performed different tasks, but they occupied different space. Most often, although by no means always, men worked the fields while women managed the house, raised and cared for animals, tended a garden and marketed surplus dairy products, poultry and vegetables. There was also seasonal work in the fields at planting and harvest times. Martin Nadaud, a mason from the Creuse, expressed a husband's expectation for his wife this way:

> We know there are countries where women marry with the oft-realized hope of having to work only in the house; in France, there is nothing of the sort, precisely the contrary happens; my wife, like all other women of the country was raised to work in the fields from morning until night and she worked no less...after our marriage...

Of course the wives of masons from the Creuse were in a peculiar position. Their husbands were gone for long periods of time building houses in Lyon or Paris. They had to do all agricultural chores since the division of labor in the Creuse was between women who handled most of the agricultural tasks and men whose primary work was as artisans in the cities. Women's work on the farm was so important there that at one point Nadaud's family tried to arrange a marriage for him with a girl whose mother was widowed. That way, the Nadaud family farm would acquire two female hands instead of one.

Despite the peculiarity of the Creuse, however, Nadaud's expectation that women would work seems typical of peasant economies. Eilert Sundt's reports on the Norwegian peasantry in the mid-nineteenth century show that women were needed as workers, so experienced and often older women were the choice of young men as wives. Sundt wrote, 'the material progress of a family depended as much upon the wife as upon the husband'. And

Frederick Le Play, describing marriage customs of Slavic peasants noted that 'the peasant takes a wife to augment the number of hands in his family'.

Women labored not only on the farm, but at all sorts of other work, depending in part on what was available to them. In most areas their activity was an extension of their household functions of food provision, animal husbandry and clothing making. Documentation of this can be found in almost every family monograph in the six volumes of Le Play's *Les ouvriers européens*. There was the wife of a French vineyard worker, for example, whose principal activity involved the care of a cow. 'She gathers hay for it, cares for it and carries its milk to town to sell.' Another wife worked with her husband during harvest seasons and 'washed laundry and did other work...for farmers and landowners in the neighborhood'. She also wove linen 'for her family and for sale'. Other women sewed gloves or clothing; some took in infants to nurse as well. In the regions surrounding the silk-weaving city of Lyon, the wives and daughters of farmers tended worms and reeled silk. Similarly, in Lombardy, seasonal pre-occupation with the care of the hungry worms filled the time of women and children in the household.

Work of this type was a traditional way of supplementing the family income. Indeed, Le Play insisted on including all activities of family members in his budgets because, he argued, 'the small activities undertaken by the family are a significant supplement to the earning of the principal worker'. In fact, he often noted that not only did women work harder than men, but they contributed more to 'the well-being of the family'. Often women's work meant the difference between subsistence and near starvation. Pinchbeck cites a parish report on rural women who, in a time of economic crisis, could find no work: 'In a kind of general despondency she sits down, unable to contribute anything to the general fund of the family and conscious of rendering no other service to her husband except that of the mere care of his family.'

In non-farming and some urban families a similar situation seems to have prevailed. In fact, Chayanov's description of the peasant economy seems a fitting characterization of pre-industrial working class social arrangements. In *The World We Have Lost* Peter Laslett describes the household as the center of production. The workshop was not separated from the home, and everyone's place was at home. In the weaver's household, for example, children did carding and combing, older daughters and wives spun, while the father wove. In the urban worker's home, a similar division of labor often existed. Among Parisian laundry workers, for example, the entire family was expected to work, although women were uniquely responsible for soaping and ironing. This kind of business, in fact, was as well run by women as by men. And parents willed their shops and their clientele to their daughters as frequently as to their sons. Wives of craftsmen sometimes assisted their husbands at their work of tailoring, shoemaking and baking. Sometimes they kept shop, selling the goods and keeping accounts. The wives of skilled cutlery workers served as intermediaries between their husbands and their masters. They not only picked up materials for their husbands to work on at home and transported finished products back to the employer, but they also negotiated work loads and wages.

When the husband worked away from home, women engaged in enterprises of their own. Like their rural counterparts, urban working-class women contributed to the family economy by tending vegetable gardens and raising animals—usually some pigs and hens—and marketing the surplus. Some women set up cafés in their homes, others sold the food and beverages they had prepared outside. A Sheffield knifemaker's wife prepared a 'fermented drink called "pop", which she bottled and sold in the summer to the inhabitants of the city'. These are early-nineteenth-century examples, but Alice Clark refers to gardening and the garment trades in seventeenth-century England. She cites another expedient of poor women, 'selling perishable articles of food from door to door'. This practice continued in the nineteenth century. Le Play details the work of a German miner's wife who 'transported foodstuffs on her back. Two times a week she goes to [the city] where she buys wheat, potatoes, etc. which she carries [10 kilometers]... Some of this food is for her household, some is delivered to wealthy persons in town, the rest is sold [for a small profit] at the market'. In eighteenth-century Paris and Bordeaux, among the popular classes, 'it was generally accepted that womenfolk had an important part to play in the domestic economy. Most took a job to bring in an additional income'. They worked as domestics, laundresses, seamstresses, innkeepers, and beasts of burden—hauling heavy loads many times a day. They also begged and smuggled if they had to. 'The importance of the mother within the family economy was immense; her death or incapacity could cause a family to cross the narrow but extremely meaningful barrier between poverty and destitution'. The popular culture which valued the work of women existed in France during much of the nineteenth century.

The indispensable role of women was demonstrated, too, by the fact that in many communities, widows could manage a farm alone (with the assistance of a few hired hands) whereas widowers found the task almost impossible. It is also demonstrated vividly in times of financial hardship. Hufton insists that women were the first to feel the physical effects of deprivation, in part, because they denied themselves food in order to feed the rest of the family. Other observers describe a similar situation. The report Anderson cites from Lancashire is representative of conditions in Italy, England and France: 'an observation made by medical men, that the parents have lost their health much more generally than the children and particularly, that the mothers who most of all starve themselves, have got pale and emaciated'.

The role women played in the family economy usually gave them a great deal of power within the family. Scattered historical sources complement the more systematic work of contemporary anthropologists on this point. All indicate that while men assume primacy in public roles, it is women who prevail in the domestic sphere. Hufton even suggests they enjoyed 'social supremacy' within the family. Her suggestion echoes Le Play's first-hand observation. In the course of his extensive study of European working-class urban and rural families (carried out from the 1840s–70s), he was struck by the woman's role. 'Women are treated with deference, they often... exercise a preponderant influence on the affairs of the family (*la communauté*).' He found that they worked harder and in a more sustained fashion than their husbands and concluded that their work, their energy and their intelligence 'makes them more fit... to direct the family'.

The key to the woman's power, limited almost exclusively, of course, to the family arena, lay in her management of the household. In some areas, wives of craftsmen kept business accounts, as did the wives or daughters of farmers. Their familiarity with figures was a function of their role as keeper of the household's accounts, for the woman was usually the chief buyer for the household in the market place and often the chief trader as well. Primitive as was the accounting these women could do, it was a tool for dealing with the outside world. Working-class women also often held the purse strings, making financial decisions, and even determining the weekly allowance their husbands received for wine and tobacco. Le Play's description of the Parisian carpenter's wife was typical not only of France:

> She immediately receives his monthly wage; it is she who each morning gives her husband the money necessary to buy the meals he takes outside the house. To her alone... in conformity with the custom which prevails among French workers, are confined the administration of the interior of the home and the entire disposition of the family resources.

Indeed, this practice was so linked to the wife's role that when factories replaced the home as the location of work for craftsmen, factory owners sometimes paid directly 'to the wives the wages earned by their husbands'. Whether in Lorraine, Brittany or Lancashire, among Northern English miners, peasants or London workers, women seem to have dominated family finances and some areas of family decision making. 'The man struts, presides at the table, gives orders, but important decisions—buying a field, selling a cow, a lawsuit against a neighbor, choice of a future son-in-law —are made by *la patronne*'. Or, as a retired farmer from a French village remarked to a visiting anthropologist: 'The husband is always the *chef d'exploitation*... Well, that's what the law says. What really happens is another matter, but you won't find that registered in the *Code Civil*'.

It is important here to stress that we speak here of married women. Whatever power these women enjoyed was a function of their participation in a mutual endeavor, and of the particular role they played as a function of their sex and marital status. Their influence was confined to the domestic sphere, but that sphere bulked large in the economic and social life of the family. In this situation, women were working partners in the family enterprise.

Daughters were socialized early, in lower-class families, to assume family and work responsibilities. 'Daughters...begin as soon as their strength permits to help their mother in all her work'. Frequently they were sent out of the household to work as agricultural laborers or domestic servants. Others were apprenticed to women who taught them to weave or sew. In areas of rural Switzerland where cottage industry was also practiced, daughters were a most desirable asset. It was they who could be spared to spin and weave while their mothers worked at home; and they gave their earnings 'as a matter of course to the economic unit, the maintenance of whose property had priority over individual happiness'. Whatever her specific job a young girl early learned the meaning of the saying, 'woman's work is never done'. And she was prepared to work hard for most of her life. Many a parent's advice must have echoed these words to a young girl, written in 1743: 'You cannot expect to marry in such a manner as neither of you shall have occasion to work, and only a fool would take a wife whose bread must be earned solely by his own labor, and who will contribute nothing towards it herself.' Women were expected to work, and the family was the unit of social as well as economic relationships: these were the cultural values held by families who sent their daughters out to work in the early stages of industrialization.

Women's work was in the interest of the family economy. Their roles, like those of their husbands, brothers and fathers, could be modified and adjusted to meet difficult times or changing circumstances. Here Chayanov's discussion of the limits of self-exploitation is instructive:

> When our peasant as worker entrepreneur is not in a position to develop an adequate sale of his labor on his own farm and to get for himself what he considers sufficient earnings, he temporarily abandons his undertaking and simply converts himself into a worker who resorts to someone else's undertaking, thus saving himself from unemployment in his own.

This means that traditional families employed a variety of strategies to promote the well-being of the family unit. Sometimes the whole family hired itself out as farm hands, sometimes this was done only by men, at other times by one or more children. Supplemental work in domestic industry was frequently resorted to by mothers of families in time of greater need or economic crises. That is why such work was so often seasonal or undertaken sporadically. The custom of sending children of both sexes out to serve on other farms, or to work in nearby cities was yet another expedient—a way of temporarily extending the family beyond its own limited resources in order to increase those resources and thereby guarantee economic survival.

As major structural changes affected the countries of Europe (in the late eighteenth century in England, much later in France and Italy) these strategies were adapted and new ones were developed (in the face of new pressures and opportunities) to attain the traditional goals of the family economy. In Western Europe in the nineteenth century population growth was causing land-shortage in some areas. In addition, rationalized large-scale agriculture was putting marginally productive lands under great competitive pressure. New forms and methods of industrial production also transformed the location and nature of the work of rural and urban craftsmen. In this situation, it became increasingly necessary for family members, but particularly for children, to work away from home. The development of domestic industry, of rurally located textile mills and the expansion of urban populations (with their increased demand for consumer goods and domestic services) provided opportunities for these people to work.

In Lombardy, for example, the northern Italian province of which Milan is the capital, peasants had long practiced labor intensive farming on small holdings. During the nineteenth century, peasants were increasingly unable to support their growing families on these holdings. They seized options similar to the temporary expedients they had customarily employed. Women and girls, whose work on the farm was less productive than that of men, went to work in nearby rural silk mills. Others went to Milan as domestic servants or garment workers, into what were essentially self-exploitative, low-paying, marginally productive jobs. The point was to make enough money to send home.

In the hinterland of Zürich, described by Rudolf Braun, another sort of strategy developed. Originally among landed peasants all family members worked to make ends meet—as domestics, as soldiers, or as quasi-servants in the households of their siblings who had inherited land. Everyone turned his money over to the family. 'The maintenance of the property had priority over individual happiness...the question of who got married and at what age, was less an individualistic decision than a family agreement'. Demographic and economic pressures made some families landless, others had to supplement their farming with work in rural industry, particularly textiles. In these areas the system of *Rastgeben* arose. This was the practice of children paying their parents a set amount for room and board. If they did not work at home, but spun at another house, the children paid the landlady the *rast*. Once such money or work had been given as a matter of course. The practice became formalized and the size of the contribution specified as work relations among family members changed. Braun tells us that modifications of this sort eventually broke down family solidarity. He is undoubtedly right. The important point of the Zürich example for our argument, however, is that in the process of transformation old values and practices informed strategic adaptations to new conditions.

Similar examples can be drawn from non-farming families as well. The first industrial revolution in England broke the locational unity of home and workshop by transferring first spinning and then weaving into factories. Neil Smelser's study of *Social Change in the Industrial Revolution* shows, however, that in the first British textile factories the family as a work unit was imported into the mills. 'Masters allowed the operative spinners to hire their own assistants... the spinners chose their wives, children, near relatives or relatives of the proprietors. Many children, especially the youngest, entered the mill at the express request of their parents'. This extension of the family economy into factories in early industrialization declined after the 1820's, of course, with the increased differentiation and specialization of work. But the initial adjustment to a changed economic structure involved old values operating in new settings.

This is eminently demonstrable in the case of women workers, the single ones who constituted the bulk of the female labor force and the less numerous married women as well. Long before the nineteenth century, lower-class families had sent their daughters out to work. The continuation of this practice and of the values and assumptions underlying it is evident not only in the fact of large numbers of single women working but also in the age structure of the female labor force, in the kinds of work these women did and in their personal behavior.

The fact that European female labor forces consisted primarily of young, single women—girls, in the language of their contemporaries—is itself an indication of the persistence of familial values. Daughters were expendable in rural and urban households, certainly more expendable than their mothers and, depending on the work of the family, their brothers. When work had to be done away from home and when its duration was uncertain, the family interest was best served by sending forth its daughters. Domestic service, the chief resort of most rural girls, was a traditional area of employment. It was often a secure form of migration since a young girl was assured a place to live, food, and a family. There were risks involved also; servant unemployment and servant exploitation were real. Nevertheless, during the nineteenth century, though many more girls were sent into service and moved farther from home than had traditionally been the case, the move itself was not unprecedented. Domestic service was an acceptable employment partly because it afforded the protection of a family and membership in a household.

This was true not only of domestic service, but of other forms of female employment. In Italy and France, textile factory owners attempted to provide 'family' conditions for their girls. Rules of conduct limited their activity, and nuns supervised the establishments, acting as substitute parents. *In loco parentis* for some factory owners sometimes even meant arranging suitable marriages for their female operatives. These factory practices served the owner's interests too, by keeping his work force under control and limiting its mobility. They also served the interests of the girls' families more than those of the girls as individuals, for the girls' wages sometimes went directly to their parents. We do not wish to argue that the factory dormitory was a beneficent institution. The fact that it used the family as model for work and social relationships, and the fact that the practice did serve the *family* interest to some degree, is, however, important.

In the needle trades, which flourished in urban centers, similar practices developed. The rise of ready-made clothing production involved a two-fold transformation of garment-making. First, piece-work at home replaced workshop organization. Only later (in England by 1850, in France by the 1870s depending on the city and the industry, in Italy, still later) did new machinery permit the reorganization of the garment industry in factories. In the period when piece-work expanded women found ample opportunity for work. Those who already lived in cities customarily took their work home. Migrants, however, needed homes. So, enterprising women with a little capital turned their homes into lodging houses for piece-workers in their employ. While these often provided exploitative and miserable living conditions, they nonetheless offered a household for a young girl—a household in which she could do work similar to what she or her mother had done at home.

Domestic service, garment-making and even textile manufacturing, the three areas in which female labor was overwhelmingly concentrated, were all traditional areas of women's work. The kind of work parents sent their daughters to do, in other words, did not involve a radical departure from the past. Many a wife had spent her girlhood in service at someone else's house. Piece-work and spinning and weaving were also common in traditional households. The *location* of work did change and that change eventually led to a whole series of other differences; but, initially, there must have been some comfort for a family sending a daughter to a far-off city in the fact that they were sending her to do familiar, woman's work.

As parents sent daughters off with traditional expectations, so the daughters attempted to fulfill them. Evidence for the persistence of familial values is found in the continuing contributions made by working daughters to their families. If in some cases factories sent the girls' wages to their parents, in others, girls simply sent most of their money home themselves. In England, it was not until the 1890s that single working girls living at home kept some of their own money. Earlier, on the continent, their counterparts 'normally turned over all their pay to the family fund'. The daughter of a Belgian locksmith first served her family by tailoring. She habitually gave her family all her earnings 'and thus had no savings at the time of her marriage'. Irish migrants sent money back from as far away as London and Boston. And, even when they no longer expected to return home to marry and live in their natal villages, French and Italian servant girls continued to send money back home. The servant girls working for the Flahaut family during the period 1811 to 1877 in rural France sent money home to their parents. There were regular arrangements by which Monsieur Flahaut sent foodstuffs instead of money or paid the rent on the father's farm or sent clothing and coal directly to the parents of his servant girls.

Sometimes, too, younger or unemployed brothers and sisters received these payments which were deducted from the domestic's wages. Hubscher tells us that for certain farmers who rented their lands, their daughters' contributions were 'indispensable, without them it would have been impossible to cultivate the fields they rented'. He adds that the 'financial support' of the daughters for their parents 'seemed absolutely normal to both' parties. It represented a 'strong family solidarity which required a mature and economically independent child to contribute to the support of its relatives'. Mill girls in Lombardy also made contributions to their families and, if they lived close enough, the families sent regular baskets of food. According to one autobiographical report, the employer actually sent a man and wagon around to the girls' villages weekly to pick up their families' food baskets.

In Lancashire 'considerable contact was maintained' between migrants and their families. Money was sent home, members of the family were brought to the city to live by family members who had 'travelled' and sometimes even 'reverse migration' occurred. The children of married daughters working in Norwegian cities as domestics were sent home to be raised by grandparents. In this case, the young husband and wife continued to work separately as domestics to save to set up their own household. Even when whole families migrated to the United States, they carried these traditional practices with them. Willa Cather notes in *My Antonia* that immigrant girls' work as domestics or farm hands 'contributed to the prosperous, mortgage free farms' their parents built in Nebraska.

The cultural values which sent young girls out to work for their families also informed their personal behavior. The increase, noted by historians and demographers, in illegitimate birth rates in many European cities from about 1750 to 1850 can be seen, paradoxically, as yet another demonstration of the persistence of old attitudes in new settings. Alliances with young men may have begun in the city as at home, the girls seeking potential husbands in the hope of establishing a family of their own. The difference, of course, was that social customs that could be enforced at home, could not be in the city.

When a girl was far from home, her family had little control over whom she married, or when. The pressure that kept a Swiss daughter spinning at home until she was forty could not affect the choices of a daughter who had migrated to the city. In fact, her migration implied that she was not needed in the same way at home. The loneliness and isolation of the city was clearly one pressure for marriage. So was the desire to escape domestic service and become her own mistress in her own home as her mother had been. The conditions of domestic service, which usually demanded that servants be unmarried, also contributed to illicit liaisons and led many a domestic to abandon her child. This had long been true; what was different in nineteenth-century Europe was that the great increase in the proportions of women employed in domestic service outstripped increased employment in manufacturing. This meant that more women than ever before, proportionately, were employed in this sector, which was particularly liable to produce illegitimate children.

Yet another motive for marriage was economic. Girls in factories were said to be fairly well-paid, but most girls did not work in factories. Women in the needle trades and other piece-work industries barely made enough to support themselves. (Wages constantly fluctuated in these consumer product trades and declined after the 1830s in both England and France. Women in these trades were also paid half of what men received for comparable work, often because it was assumed that women's wages were part of a family wage, an assumption which did not always correspond with reality.) In the rural households they came from, subsistence depended on multiple contributions. The logical move for a single girl whose circumstances took her far from her family and whose wages were insufficient either to support herself or to enable her to send money home, would be to find a husband; together they might be able to subsist.

It may well be that young girls became 'engaged' to their suitors and then followed what were in many rural areas customary practices: they slept with the men they intended to marry. When they became pregnant, however, the men either disappeared, or continued living with them, but did not marry them. Sometimes the couple married after the child or children were born. The constraint of the traditional necessity to bring a dowry to her marriage sometimes meant that a woman worked while cohabiting with her lover until the requisite trousseau was put aside. The absence of the moral force of family, local community and church prevented the fulfillment of marital expectations. Lack of money and severe economic pressures, as well perhaps as different attitudes and expectations on the part of the men, kept them from fulfilling their promise. The testimony of abandoned women to Henry Mayhew indicates that often (a) there was no money for a proper wedding; (b) the men's jobs demanded that they move on; (c) poverty created a possible emotional stress; and (d) traditional contexts which identified and demanded proper behavior were absent. Young girls, then, pursued mates and behaved with them according to traditional assumptions. The changed context yielded unanticipated (and often unhappy) results.

Even among prostitutes, many of whom were destitute or unemployed servants and piece-workers, a peculiar blend of old and new attitudes was evident. In pre-industrial society, lower-class women developed endless resources for obtaining food for their families. Begging was not unheard of and flirtations and sexual favors were an acknowledged way of obtaining bread or flour in time of scarcity. Similarly, in nineteenth-century London, prostitutes interviewed by Mayhew explained their 'shame' as a way of providing food for their families. One, the mother of an illegitimate boy, explained that to keep herself and her son from starving she was 'forced to resort to prostitution'. Another described the 'glorious dinner' her solicitations had brought....

Not all single working girls were abandoned with illegitimate children, nor, despite the alarm of middle-class observers, did most become prostitutes. Many got married and most left the labor force when they did. Both the predominance of young single girls in the female labor force and the absence of older married women reflect the persistence of traditional familial values. When they married, daughters were no longer expected to contribute their wages to their parents' household. Marriage meant a transfer from one family to another and the assumption of some new roles. Single girls, however, carried the values and practices of their mothers into their own marriages. The traditional role of a married woman, her vital economic function within the family economy, sent her into the labor force when her earnings were needed by the household budget. When the income of her husband and children was sufficient for the family's needs, she left the labor force. Mothers of young children would sometimes leave the labor force *only* after their oldest child went out of work. Over the developmental cycle of the family, this pattern is valid, but in cases of temporary need, such as sickness, or in the case of the death of a money earner, the married woman would go back to work. Even without a money contribution, however, her contribution to the family economy was nevertheless substantial. In the 1890s in London, the wives of the lower classes 'had great responsibility, whether they earned a salary of their own or not, they handled most of the family's money and were responsible not only for food shopping, but for paying the rent, buying clothes, keeping up insurance payments and overseeing school expenses for their children'.

Although increasingly the location of work in factories or shops outside the home made such work more feasible for single women, some married women continued to find jobs. Industrialization only gradually transformed occupational opportunities. Old jobs persisted for many years alongside the new. Women who married industrial workers and who lived in cities imported old styles of behavior into new contexts. Much of the work performed by married women was temporary. Anderson describes varieties of domestic employment for married women in Preston in 1851. Many helped their husbands, others ran 'a little provision shop or beer house'. Well over a third of those who worked, he continues, 'were employed in non-factory occupations. Many others also worked irregularly or part time' and often were not even listed in official records as having an occupation. Indeed, Anderson's formulation for Lancashire that 'patterns of family structure in towns can only be explained as hangovers from rural patterns' has much wider application. Whether in the cities and towns of Europe or in America, the patterns of work of married women resembled older, pre-industrial practices. Immigrant women in New England textile mills, for example, were 'the only large group of regularly employed married women' other than blacks. Smuts explains that they were attracted by the familiar work of spinning and weaving and, more important, by the opportunity of working with their children. 'A mother whose children worked could look after them better if she worked in the same mill'. Depending, of course, on their past experience, immigrant women adapted their skills to American conditions. Thus Italian mothers with their children picked fruit and vegetables around Buffalo, New York, an activity reminiscent of southern Italy. Italian women on New York's lower East Side sewed pants or made paper flowers with their daughters at home. Their husbands, lacking these skills, dug ditches and swept the streets. When these same women followed their work into factories and sweatshops, the husbands sometimes kept house and cared for the children. Married Irish women with only agricultural experience became domestics. But many cleaned New York office buildings at night so they could care for their families during the day.

Whether they worked outside the home or not, married women defined their role within the framework of the family economy. Married working-class women, in fact, seem almost an internal backwater of pre-industrial values within the working-class family. Long after their husbands and children had begun to adopt some of the individualistic values associated with industrialization, these women continued the self-sacrificing, self-exploitative work that so impressed Le Play and that was characteristic of the peasant or household economy. Surely this... is the meaning of the testimony of a woman from York cited by Peter Stearns: 'If there's anything extra to buy such as a pair of boots for one of the children, me and the children goes without dinner—or mebbe only 'as a cop o' tea and a bit o' bread, but Him allers takes 'is dinner to work, and I never tell 'im'. As long as her role is economically functional for her family, familial values make sense for the lower-class woman. And the role of provider and financial manager, of seamstress and occasional wage earner was economically functional for a long time in working class families.

Perhaps most illustrative is this case history which embodies the collective portrait we have just presented. Francesca F. was born in about 1817 in a rural area of Moravia and remained at home until she was 11. She had a typical childhood for a girl of her class. She learned from her mother how to keep house and help on the farm, and she learned at school how to read, write, figure and, most important of all, sew. At eleven, she was sent into domestic service in a neighboring town. She worked successively in several different houses, increasing her earnings as she changed jobs. At one house she acquired a speciality as a seamstress. She saved some money, but sent most of it home, and she returned home (to visit and renew her passport) at least once a year.

Until her eighteenth year, Francesca's experience was not unlike young girls' of earlier generations. Her decision to seek her fortune in Vienna, though, began a new phase of her life. With the good wishes of her parents, she paid her coach passage out of her savings and three days after she arrived she found a job as a maid. She lived with the bourgeois family she worked for for six months. Then she left for a better position which she held until her master died (six months). Yet another job as a domestic lasted a year.

At twenty, attracted by the opportunities for work available in a big city and tired of domestic service, she apprenticed herself to a wool weaver. He went bankrupt after a year and she found yet another job. That one she quit because the work was unsteady and she began sewing gloves for a small manufacturer. Glove-making was a prospering piece-work industry and Francesca had to work 'at home'. Home was a boarding house where she shared her bed with another working girl of 'dubious character'. Unhappy with these arrangements, Francesca fortunately met a young cabinet maker, himself of rural origin with whom she began living. (The practice of sleeping with one's fiancé was not uncommon in rural Moravia according to Le Play.) She soon had a child whom she cared for while she sewed gloves, all the while saving money for her marriage. (Viennese authorities at this time required that workers show they could support a family before they were permitted to marry. The task of accumulating savings usually fell to the future bride.)

Three years after she met the cabinet-maker, they were married. Francesca paid all the expenses of the wedding and provided what was essentially her own dowry—all the linens and household furnishings they needed. The daughter of rural peasants, Francesca was now the mother of an urban working-class family. Although the care of her children and the management of her household consumed much of her time, she still managed to earn wages in 1853, by doing the equivalent of 125 full days of work, making gloves. (Although it amounted in Le Play's calculation to 125 days, Francesca sewed gloves part of the day during most of the year.)

As long as piece-work was available to her, Francesca F. could supplement her husband's wage with her own work. With the decline of such domestic work, however, and the rise of factories, it would become increasingly difficult for the mother of five young children to leave her household responsibilities in order to earn a wage. Economic conditions in Vienna in the 1850s still made it possible for Francesca to fulfill the role expected of a woman of the popular classes.

Traditional values did not persist indefinitely in modern or modernizing contexts. As families adapted customary strategies to deal with new situations they became involved in new experiences which altered relationships within the family and the perceptions of those relationships. As the process of change involved retention of old values and practices, it also transformed them....

The major transformation involved the replacement of familial values with individualistic ones. These stressed the notion that the individual was owner of him- or herself rather than a part of a social or moral whole. They involved what Anderson calls 'an instrumental orientation' of family members to their families 'requiring reciprocation for their contribution in the very short run'. These attitudes developed differently in different places depending in part on specific circumstances. Nonetheless, the evidence indicates an underlying similarity in the process and the final outcome. Sons first, and only later daughters, were permitted to keep some of their earnings. They were granted allowances by their parents in some cases; in others a specified family contribution was set, in still others the child decided what portion of her pay she would send home (and it diminished and became increasingly irregular over time). Anderson points out that in Preston, high factory wages of children reversed normal dependencies and made parents dependent on their children. The tensions created by the different priorities of parents and children led to feuds. And in these situations children often left home voluntarily and gladly and 'became unrestrained masters of their destiny'.

Long distance and permanent migration also ultimately undermined family ties. And the pressures of low wages and permanent urban living, the forced independence of large numbers of young girls, clearly fostered calculating, self-seeking attitudes among them. They began to look upon certain jobs as avenues of social and occupational mobility, rather than as a temporary means to earn some money for the family. Domestic service remained a major occupation for women until the twentieth century in most of Europe. (In fact, in the mid-nineteenth century the number of women employed as domestics increased tremendously.) Nonetheless, as it embodied traditional female employment, a position as a servant also began to mean an opportunity for geographic and occupational mobility. Once the trip to the city and the period of adjustment to urban life had been accomplished under the auspices of service, a young girl could seek better and more remunerative work. Her prospects for marrying someone who made better money in the city also increased immeasurably.

Their new experiences and the difficulties and disillusionment they experienced clearly developed in young women a more individualistic and instrumental orientation. They lived and worked with peers increasingly. They wanted to save their money for clothes and amusements. They learned to look out for their own advantage, to value every penny they earned, to place their own desires and interests above those of their families.

Decreased infant mortality and increased educational opportunity also modified family work strategies. And instead of sending all their children out to work for the family welfare, parents began to invest in their children's futures by keeping them out of the work force and sending them to school. (Clearly this strategy was adopted earlier for sons than daughters—the exact history of the process remains to be described.) The family ethic at once sponsored intergenerational mobility and a new individualistic attitude as well.

A number of factors, then, were involved in the waning of the family economy. They included the location of job opportunities, increased standards of living and higher wages, proximity to economic change, increased exposure to and adherence to bourgeois standards as chances for mobility into the bourgeoisie increased, ethnic variations in work patterns and family organization, and different rates of development in different regions and different countries. All of these factors contributed to the decline of the family as a productive unit and to the modification of the values associated with it. The decline can be dated variously for various places, classes and ethnic groups. It reached the European peasant and working classes only during the nineteenth century, and in some areas, like Southern Italy, rural Ireland and rural France, not until the twentieth century. The usefulness of the family model as a unit of analysis for social relationships and economic decision making, however, has not disappeared.

A great deal more work is needed on the redefinition of family relationships and on the changes in the definition of women's work and women's place that accompanied it. Clearly many things changed. The rising standard of living and increased wages for men, which enabled them to support their families, made it less necessary for married women to work outside the home. (In early industrialization, such work also exacted great costs in terms of infant and child mortality.) Even for single women, economic change reduced traditional work opportunities, while new jobs opened up for those with more education. After World War I, for example, domestic service was much less important as an area of employment for young women. A smaller number of permanent servants who followed that occupation as a profession replaced the steady stream of young women who had constituted the domestic servant population. The rise of factory garment production seems to have limited work available for women in Milan and elsewhere. On the other hand, the growth of new jobs in expanding government services, in support services for business, in commerce, in health services and in teaching provided work opportunities, primarily for single women, especially for those with at least a basic education.

There is evidence also that women's role in the household, whether as wives or as daughters, was modified with time. In Britain, women in working-class families began to lose control over finances early in the twentieth century, but the process was not complete until World War II. Working girls began to receive spending money of their own only at the end of the nineteenth century. After about 1914, more and more single girls kept more and more of their wages, and wives began to receive a household allowance from their husbands, who kept the rest and determined how it was spent. The rhetoric of some working-class organizations also suggests a change in ideas about family roles. Labor unions demanded higher wages for men so that they could support families and keep their wives at home. Some socialist newspapers described the ideal society as one in which 'good socialist wives' would stay at home and care for the health and education of 'good socialist children'.

The changes that affected women's work and women's place in the family late in the nineteenth and in the twentieth centuries are subjects which are virtually unexplored by historians. They cannot be understood, however, apart from the historical context we have presented. It was European peasant and working-class families which experienced at first hand the structural changes of the nineteenth century. These experiences were anything but uniform. They were differentiated geographically, ethnically and temporally and they involved complex patterns of family dynamics and family decision making. The first contacts with structural change in all cases, however, involved adjustments of traditional strategies and were informed by values rooted in the family economy. It is only in these terms that we can begin to understand the work of the vast majority of women during the nineteenth century. We must examine *their* experience in the light of *their* familial values and not our individualistic ones.... Their values cannot be logically or historically tied to the political enfranchisement of women. The confusion about women's work and women's place begins to be resolved when assumptions are tested against historical data. The evolutionary model which assumes a single and similar experience for all women, an experience in which political and economic factors move together, must be discarded in the light of historical evidence.

Bibliography

M. ANDERSON, *Family Structure in Nineteenth Century Lancashire* (1971).

J. A. BANKS, *Victorian Values: Secularism and the Size of Families* (1981).

M. HEWITT, *Wives and Mothers in Victorian Industry* (1958).

J. R. LEHNING, *The Peasants of Marlhes: Economic Development and Family Organization in Nineteenth-Century France* (1980).

A. MCLAREN, *Sexuality and Social Order: The Debate over the Fertility of Women and Workers in France, 1770–1920* (1983).

J. MURRAY, *Strong Minded Women and Other Lost Voices from Nineteenth-Century England* (1982).

I. PINCHBECK, *Women Workers and the Industrial Revolution, 1750–1850* (*1969*).

F. K. PROCHASKA, *Women and Philanthropy in Nineteenth-Century England* (1980).

P. ROBERTSON, *An Experience of Women: Pattern and Change in Nineteenth-Century Europe* (1982).

N. SMELSER, *Social Change in the Industrial Revolution: An Application of Theory to the British Cotton Industry* (1959).

B. G. SMITH, *Ladies of the Leisure Class: The Bourgeoises of Northern France in the Nineteenth Century* (1981).

G. D. SUSSMAN, *Selling Mothers' Milk: The Wetnursing Business in France, 1715–1914* (1982).

M. VICINUS, ed., *Suffer and Be Still: Women in the Victorian Age* (1972).

M. VICINUS, ed., *A Widening Sphere: Changing Roles of Victorian Women* (1980).

J. R. WALKOWITZ, *Prostitution and Victorian Society: Women, Class, and the State* (1980).

Fever! Fever!

ANTHONY S. WOHL

Perhaps no single factor of everyday life in the past so differs from the present day as the presence of widespread deadly infectious diseases of unknown origin. During the nineteenth century these included cholera, a disease wholly new to the European experience, typhus, typhoid, influenza, and diptheria. Most of these diseases took a heavier toll among the poor living in crowded city slums than among the middle class or the aristocracy, yet even the latter were not immune, as seen in the death of Prince Albert, husband of Queen Victoria, from typhoid.

    Several changes occurred in the public attitude toward these deadly diseases during the course of the century. The experience of cholera during the 1830s, which killed persons across the social spectrum and which was previously unknown in Europe although well known in Asia, shocked the English government into taking action. Most of the government's activity related to better sewage and improved water supply. Thereafter, both local and national governments in Britain cautiously but steadily assumed more responsibility for public health. Those efforts could make only limited progress because of the nature of medical knowledge at the time. Not until the third quarter of the century had the germ theory of disease been adequately formulated, but for many years thereafter both physicians and government authorities were hesitant to adopt it over competing theories. Meanwhile, many people, but especially the poor, still used folk medicine. Even when preventatives were known, such as vaccination for smallpox, there arose both moral and local political opposition to government-mandated use of the remedy. Nonetheless, despite the scientific confusion and political rivalries, most of these diseases had been brought under a *reasonable* degree of control by the turn of the twentieth century. The emphasis on the word *reasonable* should perhaps be especially noted because in the second decade of the twentieth century an influenza epidemic swept across Europe and America, leaving millions stricken and dead in its wake.

Reprinted by permission of the author and publishers from *Endangered Lives: Public Health in Victorian Britain* by Anthony S. Wohl (Cambridge, Mass.: Harvard University Press). Copyright © 1983 by Anthony S. Wohl and by J. M. Dent & Sons (Publishers) Ltd.

Cancer, heart attacks, and traffic accidents are part and parcel of our modern society and we tend not to brood on them unless they strike close to home. The fear and threat of untimely death lies submerged in our consciousness. Similarly in the nineteenth century, more time and thought were devoted to the immediacy of the enjoyment or struggle of living than to the possibility of early death. The Victorians ritualized death to help innoculate themselves against its shock: the rich turned funerals into ornate pageants calling for a special kind of etiquette and even decorative arts, the poor turned them into occasions, partly for the same psychological imperatives, to be with family and neighbours, to apply the comforting balm of tradition, to drink, eat, gossip, pray and commiserate. Wakes enabled homage to be paid to the dead and mitigated the feelings of loss and despair experienced by the survivors. The possibility of sudden and often painful death from one or other of the many epidemic diseases of the day simply was one of the inescapable facts of nineteenth-century life.

But to say this is not to suggest that the shock of death to the survivors was slight. When 'fever' struck it might leave its mark on entire neighbourhoods and the sight of parents, siblings, or young children slowly succumbing or suddenly dying could not help but affect surviving family members. The sadness and grief could be softened only partially by the fatalism of the age. Social and medical historians tend to dwell on the cold figures of mortality, but such statistics give little indication of the debilitating weakness of those who survived or of the misery, both pecuniary and psychological, which illness or death brought. To the poor disease could mean dropping into the ranks of pauperism and the stigma of poor relief. To society at large it could mean the disruption of normal life and a sense of stress and urgency which approached that of a community under siege.

During the eighteenth century a series of good harvests and thus improved food supplies had resulted in a decline in major epidemics, a falling death rate and a sustained growth of the population. Even the rapid urbanization of the early stages of the industrial revolution had not altered the pattern of general progress. But all this changed sharply just before Victoria ascended the throne. The alarming return to an age of epidemics was well publicized and placed in a statistical context by the figures released from the annual census data, the newly-formed office of the Registrar-General, and the investigations of the Statistical Society of London. The resulting awareness of high mortality did much to make urban development under the late Georgians, with its relatively high-density, inner-city living, suddenly suspect and encouraged the exodus of the wealthier classes to the suburbs. The rise, once again, of widespread infectious and contagious diseases, and especially of cholera, a disease new to the English experience and the first national epidemic since the seventeenth-century plague, served to remind the Victorians that their society, however progressive, was not immune to the scourges of the past.

The major epidemic diseases, though conveyed in a variety of ways (by contaminated water, foodstuffs, clothes and utensils, by body lice, flies, or droplets from the mouth) and thus calling for a variety of remedies and preventive measures, were all influenced by cleanliness, diet, personal hygiene, public sewerage, or domestic living arrangements. These diseases called for more than the doctor's healing art or the research chemist's endeavours. They called for the state to inspect and ultimately control the excesses of unregulated urban growth and rural neglect: in short, they projected the state into public health and placed it, in the position of guardian, over the environment.

Of the fatal diseases of the period, cholera had an impact out of all proportion to its statistical importance. Following an inexorable progress from Asia across Europe, it first struck in England in 1831–2, again in 1848–9, and, with diminished virulence, in 1853–4 and 1866–7. Roughly 32,000 people died from cholera in 1831–2, 62,000 in the epidemic of 1848–9, another 20,000 in 1853–4 and about 14,000 in 1866–7. But as important as the number dying was the high percentage of fatalities among those contracting the disease—between 40 and 60 per cent—and the speed with which cholera could strike. The victim could be dead within a few hours of the first apparent symptoms. But more generally he died after several days of suffering from violent stomach pains, vomiting, diarrhoea, and total prostration, during which the body turned cold, the pulse became imperceptible, and the skin wizened. During the final stages the afflicted might well be taken for dead, and gruesome stories circulated of premature burial and the poor victim's anguished attempts to claw free of the coffin. The sudden death of apparently healthy people added still further to the fear. As the *Methodist Magazine* wrote in considerable alarm in 1832:

> To see a number of our fellow creatures, in a good state of health, in the full possession of their wonted strength, and in the midst of their years, suddenly seized with the most violent spasms, and in a few hours cast into the tomb, is calculated to shake the firmest nerves, and to inspire dread in the stoutest heart.

Cholera was thus a 'shock disease'.

Reports from the Continent of attacks on the authorities or doctors and hyperbolic accounts such as those in the *Lancet* ('No rank escapes its attack...whole families are exterminated—civilised nations changed to savage hordes...all grades and bonds of social organisation disappear.') added to the general unrest. *The Times* was certainly exaggerating in 1831 when it wrote of 'great panic' and 'complete panic', but the following year thirty riots associated with cholera occurred in London, Liverpool, Manchester, Exeter, Birmingham, Bristol, Leeds, Sheffield, Glasgow, Edinburgh, Greenwick, Cathcart, Paisley, and Dumfries. By contrast, the outbreak of cholera in Hull, Selby and Leeds in the spring of 1832 did not prevent the inhabitants of nearby York attending the mass rallies on the 1832 Reform Bill, nor did it put a damper on Race Week. The majority of the riots were inspired by fears that medical students and doctors were taking advantage of the cholera to obtain bodies for their anatomy classes, and it was rumoured that they were murdering cholera victims. 'Choleraphobia', which could strike miles from the centre of the epidemic —when cholera first appeared in Sunderland in the north, panic almost immediately erupted in Caernarvon, Gloucester, Norwich, and Plymouth —was almost always linked with fears of body-snatching ('Burking'), premature burial, or burial in unconsecrated ground. The wake required that a decent amount of time should pass between death and burial and the authorities' insistence upon expeditious burial of cholera victims cut into the custom of a good 'send off'. The very numbers dying prevented burials being accorded the dignity and ritual which custom demanded. Clergymen said hasty prayers from a safe distance outside the graveyeard and funerals were not well attended, for, as Charlotte Yonge commented, 'the living had to be regarded more than the dying'. The Irish especially were outraged by the improper and hasty burials and they sometimes managed to hold off the authorities when they came to bury the body. In the notorious London slum, Seven Dials, the police refused to go near the body of a cholera victim which the relatives were protecting from a hasty burial. The local magistrate called for special constables to go in and get the body but was told by the beadle 'the parish couldn't git a special constable no how; none of the householders wouldn't serve'. Eventually some watermen volunteered to carry off the body for a payment of 5s each, the large sum (equivalent to some two or three days' work) representing the 'wages of fear'.

With the whole neighbourhood in a frenzy of whitewashing, with the pungent smell of burning pitch, used for fumigation, hanging over them, and with the constant, mournful rumbling of hearses, the impact of cholera was highly visible. Dumfries, where several thousand inhabitants fled the town at the first signs of cholera, took on the character of a ghost town: 'Scarcely an individual was met with in the street', observed Dr Alison, 'the medical men's gigs and the hearse only were heard....' In Bilston, near Wolverhampton, the vicar wrote that 'all kind of business is at a stand; nothing reigns here but want and disease, death and desolation', while in Wolverhampton itself a local doctor described how:

> In all quarters there were the sick, the dying, and the dead.... The general silence of the city, save when broken by the tolling of the funeral bell...was most remarkable; the streets were deserted, the hurried steps of the medical men and their assistants, or of those running to seek their aid, alone were heard, while the one-horse hearse, occasionally passing on its duty, was almost the only carriage to be seen in the usually busy streets.

It is remarkable that there was in fact so little panic. Indeed the first two cholera epidemics, occurring as they did in time of political and social unrest, reveal the inherent stability of English society.

This is all the more remarkable in view of the complete inability of the authorities to contain, let alone prevent or cure the dreadful disease. Cholera was contracted by swallowing water or food which had been infected by the cholera vibrio, a minute bacillus. The vibrio could last up to five days in meat, milk, or cheese, less in green vegetables, and up to sixteen days in apples, and it could dwell up to a fortnight in water. It was most often spread by water contaminated by the excreta of cholera victims, or by flies which hatched in or fed upon the diseased excrement....

Medical opinion was hopelessly divided on the causes of cholera. The fact that between 1845 and 1856 over 700 works on cholera were published in London suggests not only that it was a 'shock' disease but that its causes and prevention were subject to a wide variety of interpretations. The contagionist theory met with great opposition, partly because it implied the need to establish internal quarantine and quarantine meant loss of trade. A *cordon sanitaire*, it was argued, would result only in greater poverty and unemployment for the masses, thereby increasing the risk of spreading cholera. In any case, there was hardly the bureaucracy available for satisfactory inland quarantine; the army raised the spectre of repression and martial law and the local constabulary was woefully ill-prepared for such measures. When in Stratford-upon-Avon the authorities decided to cordon off the town they had to rely upon a posse of old men, a rag-tail element not entirely inappropriate for that Shakespearian town. But, more important, cholera affected some members of a family but not others and so contagionist theory was damaged. The alternative theory, that cholera was spread from miasmas of filth—as Chadwick put it, from 'epidemic atmosphere' or 'deleteriously impregnated air'—at least moved in the right direction of focusing attention upon filthy conditions, especially inadequate sewerage and accumulations of excrement.

Adequate excrement removal was, however, a long-term proposition and the epidemics called for immediate action. A variety of remedies was offered, and most of them suggest that in combating epidemic disease the Victorians were closer to the Middle Ages than to our own time. The *Lancet* in a flurry of optimism, reported in 1831 that a community of East European Jews in Wiesniz had escaped the cholera raging all around them by rubbing themselves with a liniment composed of wine, wine vinegar, camphor powder, mustard, ground pepper, garlic and cantarides (made from crushed dried bodies of beetles, and better known as the aphrodisiac, 'Spanish Fly'). Purveyors of patent medicines had a field day: among the concoctions offered as remedies for cholera were Daffey's Elixir, Moxon's Effervescent Magnesium Aperient, and Morrison the Hygienist's Genuine Vegetable Universal Mixture. Many, no doubt, turned to the more inviting and readily available 'remedy' of twenty drops of laudanum in a wine glass of brandy!

Hardly more effective, but at least offering some spiritual solace, were the prayers and fast-days suggested by churchmen of several denominations. Cholera, it was thundered from a thousand pulpits, was God's punishment for moral and spiritual laxity, drunkenness, failure to observe the sabbath, and other sins, including advocacy of enfranchisement for the Jews and marriage with the deceased wife's sister! The evangelicals especially asked the poor to place their trust in prayer, and the Congregationalists offered 'Moral Preservatives against cholera'—temperance, cleanliness, industry, fortitude, and gospel reading. The Unitarians took a more rational approach: the obvious sin, they argued, was the general 'condition of the lower classes' which was 'an invitation to disease'; prayer 'may heal the wounded spirit but not the maimed body. It may purify the heart but not the atmosphere...'

Much the same attitude was taken by Lord Palmerston when, during the visitation of 1853, he was asked by church groups to declare a national day of fasting. 'The Maker of the Universe', the Home Secretary replied, 'established certain laws of nature for the planet in which we live; and the weal or woe of mankind depends upon the observance or neglect of those laws.' Palmerston suggested it would be far more efficacious to set about the 'purification and improvement' of the working-class districts of all towns in order to destroy the

> sources of contagion which, if allowed to remain, will infallibly breed pestilence, and be fruitful in death, in spite of all the prayers and fastings of a united but inactive nation. When man has done his utmost for his own safety, then it is time to invoke the blessing of Heaven to give effect to his exertions.

Sir John Simon, looking back on events at the end of his long career, took Palmerston's stand to be symbolic and 'characteristic of a new era'. That era, marked by the determination of the central government to guide and direct local communities, had its beginnings in the cholera epidemic of 1832 and the demands it made upon the government to act. While the central government had done nothing about the 'fevers' which were endemic in all large towns and which were, in the long run, responsible for far more deaths than cholera, it was now compelled to take action. A temporary Board of Health was quickly established after hurried consultation between the Privy Council and the Royal College of Physicians. It was composed of the President and four Fellows of the Royal College of Physicians, the Superintendent-General of Quarantine, the Director-General of the Army Medical Department, the Medical Commissioner of the Victualling Office and two non-medical civil servants.

In 1831 and 1832 this temporary Board of Health issued a series of recommendations in the form of Sanitary Regulations. These called upon local governments to establish boards of health and it was suggested that their personnel include one or more magistrates, a clergyman, a certain number of 'substantial householders', and (a recommendation which distinguished these boards from earlier local bodies) one or more medical men. The local boards, it was recommended, should appoint district inspectors—the first such to be suggested on a national scale by the central government—to report on 'the food, clothing and bedding of the poor, the ventilation of their dwellings, space, means of cleanliness, their habits of temperance'. Houses were to be whitewashed and limed, and linens cleaned, and cholera hospitals were to be established; quarantine of the stricken was called for, although in a very half-hearted fashion, and food and flannel clothing were to be distributed to the poor. These recommendations suggest that under the extreme pressure of the cholera crisis the government did realize that domestic cleanliness and adequate clothing and good nutrition were necessary to increase resistance to disease. Over the next two decades, however, the emphasis moved, under Chadwick's influence, to the more public areas of water supply and main drainage.

Most of the Board's recommendations were sensible, but the authorities were in the dark about the causes of cholera, and so together with sound advice about personal and domestic cleanliness it offered a veritable stew of dietary advice:

> take for dinner a moderate quantity of roast beef in preference to boiled, with stale bread and good potatoes, two glasses of wine with water, or an equivalent of good spirits and water, or of sound porter or ale. Eat garden-stuff and fruit sparingly, and avoid fat, luscious meats. In short, whilst under apprehension of cholera, use a dry nutritive diet, sparing rather than abundant, observe great caution as to eating suppers, for cholera most frequently attacks about midnight, or very early in the morning.

The same circular acknowledged frankly that 'no specific preventive against cholera is known to exist' and its recommendations conjure up visions of rather desperate quackery: moderate bleeding (10–12 oz) by leeches, warm baths followed by flannel rubs, a mixture of castor oil and laudanum, and plasters of mustard, peppermint, and hot turpentine. Interestingly the *Lancet* found little to criticize in these remedies, but commented that the Board had not put sufficient emphasis upon the role of doctors.

Across the country local communities were sufficiently frightened to set up temporary boards of health and to wage somewhat haphazard war on filth along the lines suggested by the General Board. Unprecedented amounts were spent on cleansing operations: Edinburgh for example spent £19,000 to combat the epidemic of 1832. But the local boards were temporary and, as devastating as cholera was, once it disappeared it tended to be forgotten, and reforms hastily improvised to meet the challenge were not made the basis for a comprehensive approach to public health problems in general. Looking back on the year, the *Annual Register* for 1832 declared that there had been too much fear: 'everywhere it [cholera] was much less fatal than preconceived notions had anticipated', it wrote, and 'the alarm was infinitely greater than the danger. When the disease gradually disappeared... almost everyone was surprised that so much apprehension had been entertained.' When cholera appeared again a decade and a half later it ruthlessly exposed how little the local authorities had done. Even the 1848 epidemic failed to produce local boards of health across the country and far too many centres of population muddled along with their archaic, hopelessly inefficient, and ignorant commissions of police or of sewers, lighting, or paving.

In 1885 when Dr Ballard undertook a special survey of cholera for the Local Government Board he concluded that 'we can now look forward with less dread than perhaps the population of any other European country to the introduction of epidemic cholera.' It was certainly a rough barometer of the general sanitary improvements... that although cholera appeared in sixty-four communities in 1893 it was confined to just a single attack in forty-two of them. As the MOH [Medical Officer of Health] of the Local Government Board wrote in relief and jubilation, 'such a result, altogether unique in the history of cholera, was, I believe, largely due to the improved sanitary circumstances of England.' By 1896 the government could dismiss cholera as one of the 'exotic diseases'. While the mean annual death rate (per million living) from cholera was 231 in the period 1848–72, it had dropped to an insignificant 0.006 between 1901–10.

Between the first and second cholera epidemics both the contagionist theory of disease and the belief that it was simply a punishment from God were far less widely voiced, but the miasmic theory continued to exert its hold on medical opinion even beyond the path-breaking experiments by Dr William Budd and Dr John Snow in 1849. Budd, who had done extensive research into the causes of typhus and typhoid concluded in 1849 that cholera was 'a living organism of a distinct species, which was taken by the act of swallowing it, which multiplied in the intestine by self-propagation', and Snow gave this new theory wide currency in his *On the Mode of Communication of Cholera* (1849). In 1854 Snow was given the opportunity to prove his theories when he dramatically and conclusively traced cholera deaths to houses supplied by the suspect water of the Southwark and Vauxhall water company. When he managed to persuade the local authorities to lock the handle of a pump in Broad Street in Soho (a compact area where over fifty people a day were dying of cholera) the deaths there came to a sudden halt, and although it was not until 1883 that Koch succeeded in isolating the cholera bacillus, Snow's work marked a triumph for the young science of epidemiology.

Although cholera had a dramatic impact unequalled by any other diseases it was 'fever' which throughout the nineteenth century stimulated the most action from both central and local authorities. Cholera came and went, but, as the Privy Council noted in 1864, 'typhus fever appears never to be wholly absent....' Frequently rising to epidemic proportions, the various fevers were always endemic, always lurking as a threat to the nation's health. Fever drew attention to filth and to poverty and so forced authorities to come to terms with *public* health, that is, with social and environmental conditions, with living standards broadly construed.

Typhus, known also as Irish fever, goal fever, ship fever, putrid fever, and camp fever, was a rickettsial disease, spread mainly by the faeces of the body louse; conditions of overcrowding greatly encouraged the spread of the disease. The mortality rate was high—even quite late in the century about one-third of all notified cases ended in death. The decline of typhus in the 1870s was widespread throughout England. In 1869, when typhus was first differentiated from typhoid, there were 4,281 typhus deaths in England and Wales. During the 1870s typhus deaths averaged almost 1,400 a year. Over the next decade the average was further reduced to under 400. Together with typhoid and continued fever this reduction accounted for almost one-quarter of the total decline in deaths between 1851–60 and 1891–1900. In Liverpool, a port city of poor immigrants, casual labour, and overcrowding, and hence a good indicator of the hold of a filth disease, the annual average death rate for typhus declined from 748 (1856–65) and 652 (1866–75) to 238 (1876–85) and just twenty-five (1896–1905). Between 1906 and 1913 fatalities from the disease dwindled to an insignificant number, under six a year. Significantly, though typhus continued to exist it had obviously been controlled—its presence in a Liverpool court no longer carried the threat of an uncontrollable epidemic.

How are we to account for this remarkable decline? It has recently been argued that 'the dramatic decline of typhus in the 1870s was probably more powerfully determined by the natural history of the disease itself than by any consciously planned modification of the physical environment'—an argument based in part on the chronology of the decline, which, it is claimed, occurred *before* the effects of better sewerage and water supply could have made themselves felt over a wide population. In support of this argument it is suggested that the areas suffering most from epidemic typhus were often the last to receive proper water supplies and it was not until the 1870s, for example, when the disease was already in decline, that running water was laid on in working-class districts of London where typhus had been endemic. This interpretation, with its stress upon 'an exogenous change in the virulence of the infective micro-organism itself' and its de-emphasis of 'consciously planned programmes of urban reform', does not dismiss the latter entirely but only seeks to rearrange 'the hierarchy of causal factors'.

Certainly there is much to support this revisionist thesis, for the decline in typhus deaths was, though far from uniform, widespread from 1870 onwards, while improved sanitation in the 1860s and 1870s was not. Typhus became less virulent and fatal even in those areas untouched by sanitary improvements. And yet one may question whether typhus could have declined as dramatically as it did where it was most prevalent—in the densely-packed courts and alleys of the great cities—if improved excrement removal had not accompanied the weakening of the micro-organism itself.

Typhus declined at a slower rate in those towns (Belfast, Dublin, Sunderland, Liverpool) which were slow in the mid-Victorian period to effect improvements in sanitation and water supply, or where widespread poverty and filth co-existed. If a micro-organism is in decline it needs only the slightest additional factors (dietary improvements, for example) to weaken its impact further, and while it is true that typhus weakened its terrible hold before the introduction of comprehensive sewerage and water schemes throughout Britain, even the smallest improvements made in the 1860s —especially the attack on polluted heaps of exposed excrement..., the introduction of much more sanitary dry conservancy pans and pails, taken together with increased use of cotton (more easily washed than woollen) underclothing and bedding—probably hastened its decline. If nature itself was a major factor in the decline of typhus as a killer, it was nature assisted and encouraged by the efforts of the municipalities.

Throughout the first half of the nineteenth century typhus and typhoid were confused with one another. Whereas typhus was a rickettsial disease spread by the body louse, typhoid was bacterial, and was spread, like cholera, by ingesting contaminated food and drink. The carrier from person to person could often be immune to the disease and this added to the mystery of typhoid. The typhoid patient displayed all the tell-tale signs of 'fever'—he became listless, lost his appetite, developed a high, continuous fever, often accompanied by a rash, and profuse diarrhoea (which never accompanied typhus). It could be water-borne, and unlike typhus, it not only continued as a major disease throughout the nineteenth century, but it also affected all classes. Prince Albert died of it and Edward, Prince of Wales, contracted a severe case in 1871 after staying at the country home of the Countess of Londesborough, near Scarborough. Both his groom and the Earl of Chesterfield, who had also stayed in the house, died of the disease. That the Heir Apparent so narrowly escaped death served as a timely warning to the more comfortable classes to look to their own house drainage. Two years later an outbreak of typhoid hit Caius College, Cambridge, and drew attention to the primitive sanitary conditions of the colleges from which England drew her leaders. Although it could be conveyed in a number of ways, typhoid must also be termed, like other diarrhoeal diseases, a filth disease. Probably the greatest number of typhoid deaths throughout the nineteenth century were caused by water that had become contaminated by diseased human faeces. In Stockport, for example, the incidence of typhoid in houses rated under £5 which were equipped with inefficient privy pits was almost four times higher than in the same class of house equipped with w.cs, and eightfold higher than in houses rated between £5 and £8. When in 1870 the Privy Council sent Dr Buchanan to investigate what it thought to be an outbreak of typhus (it was in fact typhoid), he found conditions that made diarrhoeal disease inevitable: 'arrangements for excrement disposal and water supply such that people must drink their own excrement.'

The provision of sewers, which no doubt helped to reduce the number of fatalities from typhus, may, ironically, have increased the number of typhoid deaths, for all too often the sewers poured contaminated filth into the rivers which were a major source of drinking water.... Whatever the reasons, typhoid continued to be endemic down to the end of the century. Local authorities and the Local Government Board were puzzled by the disease and as soon as they turned to one possible source of transmission another would become suspect—water supplies, milk, foodstuffs like watercress and shellfish, were all at one time or another held responsible for outbreaks of typhoid. The counties of Northumberland, Durham, and Yorkshire struggled against recurring epidemics of typhoid, and Darlington, Stockton, and Middlesborough were among the towns that continued to have epidemic typhoid down to the end of the century—all three towns drew their water from the Tees, a river into which some twenty villages sent their untreated sewage. In general, deaths from typhoid were twice as numerous in towns as in the countryside.

Thus typhoid continued to serve as a barometer of inadequate water supplies and sewerage down to the end of the century. When, in communities like Maidstone, epidemic typhoid appeared, the Local Government Board or the local MOH would seize the occasion to conduct what amounted to a trial of the local water authority. Even where other sources of infection were suspect (such as milk, or the general contamination of the soil by excreta) typhoid was often a prelude to pressure on the local water company to improve the quality of its supply.

Despite all the uncertainty and ignorance surrounding the origins and transmission of typhoid, improvements in water supply and sewerage did succeed in reducing its virulence. The death rate from typhoid in the decade 1891–1900 was almost half that of 1871–80 and by 1904 the death rate was well under one-third the rate that had prevailed throughout the 1870s.

So far we have considered epidemic diseases which are intestinal, but among the major diseases of the nineteenth century there were several which were respiratory or pulmonary. Influenza, for example, was endemic throughout the century and pandemics occurred in 1830–1, 1836–7, 1843, 1847–8, 1855, 1870, and again in 1889–92. In the outbreak of 1847–8 there were 50,000 deaths in London alone from influenza, a figure some five times greater than that for cholera deaths in 1849. Influenza was greatly encouraged by the diet of the poor which lowered their resistance, and by their general social condition, particularly the necessity to walk to and from work, their damp houses, and the high cost of fuel. For most of the century influenza was accepted with resignation; it did not begin to arouse the concern of public health officials until the present century.

Several other diseases became epidemic as a result of the generally low standard of nutrition and therefore lowered resistance, none more so than scarlet fever. Scarlet fever was viewed with dread, for the chances of a child (95 per cent of all cases were of children under ten years of age) who contracted it dying of the disease were very high. As late as the 1880s in Edinburgh about one child died for every fourteen catching the disease, while in the great epidemic of 1880 it carried off almost one child in five who contracted it. Although contaminated milk was suspected, the exact cause of the disease was unknown, and it remained a major killer throughout the century. In 1863, 34,000 died of it and in 1874 over 26,000. In London alone it caused over 1,000 deaths as late as 1891. John Simon, frustrated by the failure of sanitary measures to contain it, called in 1869 for a quarantine system as strict as that applied to diseased animals and for the establishment of quarantine hospitals. Quarantine was obviously impossible to enforce in the crowded dwellings of the poor, and although the need was pressing, local authorities, partly out of ignorance about the transmission of the disease, partly out of parsimony, were very slow to provide isolation wards, either in children's hospitals or in general hospitals. Some thirty years after Simon first made his plea, local authorities were still failing, against the wishes of the local MOH, to isolate scarlet fever cases. Children thus moved freely from homes where scarlet fever (and measles, another highly contagious childhood disease) had struck to school and back again. Where isolation facilities, backed up by immediate notification and stricter control of milk supplies were introduced, the results could be dramatic. In general, between 1861 and 1891 scarlet fever deaths declined by 81 per cent. This was partly due to the decline in the potency of the scarlet fever streptococcus or to the heightened immunity of urban populations. The various factors combined to make scarlet fever's decline responsible for some 19 per cent of the total decline in death rates over the second half of the nineteenth century.

Also dreaded and fatal was diphtheria, called 'croup', 'inflammation of the throat', 'putrid sore throat', 'malignant sore throat', 'disease in the throat' or 'throat fever', names which suggest by their vagueness the ignorance which surrounded the disease. From a sore throat diphtheria could quickly develop into blood poisoning, heart failure, or the growth of a membrane across the tonsils, which required a tracheotomy, often performed, when time was vital, by a pen-knife or hat-pin. Diphtheria was listed with scarlet fever by the Registrar-General until 1860 and it was not until the second half of the century that it began to receive serious scientific attention. In 1883 Edwin Krebs succeeded in isolating the bacterium and in 1894 an anti-toxin was introduced into general use. Just like scarlet fever, the percentage of those contracting diphtheria who died was very high—some 20–25 per cent, and, again like scarlet fever, its cause and transmission continued to puzzle public health officials, who tended (with cause) to blame insanitary milk supplies. The rapid increase in deaths of children under fifteen from diphtheria in the last two decades of the century was particularly frustrating to MOH and, as with measles and scarlet fever, a controversy raged over the impact of the Education Act of 1880 upon the increased morbidity. The 1880 Act put teeth into the 1870 Education Act by compelling local authorities to mark school attendance, and it was argued that it was the increased contact of children with one another which was causing the rise in death rates.

Of all the killers, respiratory or intestinal, tuberculosis was the greatest, perhaps accounting for one-third of all deaths from disease in the Victorian period. It thus remained the 'White Plague', the 'Captain of the Men of Death' so feared by John Bunyan in the seventeenth century. Although it had been long associated with artists and poets, and although it affected all classes, it was intimately connected with nutritional standards, and it hit hardest in those urban working-class districts which were ill-ventilated and overcrowded. It spread most rapidly and was most virulent where there was repeated exposure to a diseased person in confined quarters. The prevalence of consumption among tailors had caught the attention of Dr Guy early in the century, and its incidence among others working in crowded conditions —potters, miners, hosiers—attracted the attention of the Privy Council. It is difficult to chart the course of t.b. with any confidence, for it was often confused with other diseases, including cancer, and it was not a fully notifiable disease until 1912. Nevertheless, it seems that between 1851–60 and 1901–10 t.b. mortality was roughly halved. Encouraging though this decline was, the fact remains that t.b. grew in *relative* importance until at the end of the century it lay second only to heart disease as a major cause of death. It was claimed in 1894 that every single year it accounted for three times as many fatalities as were recorded in total, from action and disease, in the Crimean War. Nevertheless, its decline was significant: it accounted for about half of the *total* decline in the death rate over the second half of the century.

Even more than the other diseases so far mentioned, tuberculosis provides a 'sensitive index of living conditions in a community'. In order to be controlled it required long-term improvements in housing conditions, dietary standards, and the quality of milk.... [T]here were improvements in these last two areas, and if the general stock of housing did not improve significantly and if overcrowding remained a grave problem, at least the very worst slums and back-to-backs (where deaths from t.b. ran some 50 per cent higher than in other types of housing in the same area) were less typical of working-class housing conditions after mid-century.

The efforts of voluntary associations and MOH to improve standards of personal hygiene probably helped in the decline of t.b. Local authorities at the end of the century tried to control the 'promiscuous expectoration which transmitted t.b.' In Oldham the authorities issued and circulated a handbill to every house which stressed that t.b. was highly infectious and could be conveyed by matter spat up by the consumptive person: the handbill forbade spitting in public rooms, railway carriages, and other public places, advised that handkerchiefs and rags used by consumptives should be destroyed immediately after use, and informed the public that the local authority would disinfect houses occupied by t.b. sufferers. Similarly, the Brighton public health authorities issued 'Precautions for Consumptive Persons', in which they urged people not to spit 'except into receptacles the contents of which can be destroyed before they become dry'. The local MOH hoped that England would follow the example of the U.S.A. and prohibit spitting in all public places. Some aspects of preventive medicine cannot be quantified: the admonition to use handkerchiefs and not to spit no doubt played some small part in the decline of air-borne infections. Perhaps health authorities were slow to enforce codes against spitting and to insist upon strict controls on milk because they were so slow to adopt the germ theory of diseases. Some seventeen years after the discovery of the tubercle bacillus in 1882 the President of the State Medicine section of the British Medical Association could declare:

> I say that we can fight phthisis on the old lines, by improving heritage when that is possible, by improving the homes and conditions of life and labour which are always possible and always call loudly for interference. But this insane hunt after the tubercle bacillus, as if it could be bottled up in a twopenny-halfpenny spittoon and got rid of, is the insanest crusade ever instituted on illogical lines.

Correct in his view of what lowered resistance to t.b., he displayed an all-too common unwillingness to accept the basic cause. Meanwhile the fear of t.b. remained and the poor resorted to folk remedies, such as eating live snails and maggots or breathing the air emitted by pigs, cows, or horses, and to quack medicines. To do so was doubtless more comforting than to wait for long-term improvements in living standards.

Of all the major epidemic diseases of the nineteenth century only smallpox was contained and turned back by means of a medical discovery. The decline of smallpox deaths accounted for 5 per cent of the total reduction in mortality from disease in Victoria's reign, and it was accomplished through means—compulsory vaccination—which brought the state into public health in the most direct and, in the opinion of some contemporary critics, most dictatorial fashion. Vaccination, following the process first used by Jenner in 1798, came into general use by the time Victoria ascended the throne. Indeed, state medicine had its first early rumblings when in 1808 a Resolution was passed in Parliament to the effect that 'public benefit would be derived from the establishment of a Central Institute in London for the purposes of rendering Vaccinia Innoculation generally beneficial to his Majesty's subjects.' In 1832 the National Vaccine Establishment (under the direction of the Royal College of Physicans until taken over by the Privy Council in 1860), issued over 100,000 charges of Jenner's lymph, and between 1837 and 1839 another 800,000.

More than anything else it was probably the smallpox vaccination centres which introduced the Victorians to the notion of government intervention in matters of health. *The Graphic* wrote in 1871 that a 'whole nation solemnly baring its left arm and waiting to be scratched—it is a ludicrous image. The very earnestness with which people go about it tends to make it laughable.' But although the *Graphic* found a vehicle for its humour in the 'calm satisfaction' of those vaccinated, the 'gloomy resignation' of those preparing for it, and the 'shrinking terror' of those 'actually under the lancet', the scene, whatever elements it might hold of the human comedy, had some highly significant aspects. It represented and revealed, after all, a willingness on the part of the general public to put its faith sufficiently in medical science to allow itself to be injected with elements of a dreaded disease, and in fact the entire process represented a remarkable breach in the general concept of *laissez-faire* and freedom from government intervention. Not unexpectedly a powerful anti-vaccination movement sprang up to preserve the sanctity of the human body and the integrity of the body politic. On both religious and political grounds it was argued that the rights of the individual had to be defended against this new menace of a doctoring state. Rather like today's opposition to the compulsory wearing of crash helmets for motorcyclists, it was maintained that the individual must be allowed to take his chance on death rather than be coerced into submissive conformity by a busybody, police state. Women like Ann Supple, who received twenty-five summonses for refusing 'to be party to the poisoning of her baby' as she put it, and who faced gaol rather than submit to vaccination, became martyrs to the cause.

The Victorian state did not impose compulsory vaccination on the nation without first going through a trial period of voluntary vaccination. The smallpox epidemic of 1837–40, in which almost 42,000 people died, represented a challenge which had to be met: the response was a *permissive* vaccination act (1840) which enabled anyone to be vaccinated at public expense and which placed upon the already busy poor law authorities the burden of carrying out the vaccinations. It was not until 1853, following a study by the Epidemiological Society of London, that a *compulsory* vaccination act was passed. This made it obligatory for parents to have their infants vaccinated within three months of birth. Although it made the process of vaccination much more common throughout the nation it was still administered in a haphazard fashion and a further smallpox epidemic occurred between 1870 and 1873 (in which some 44,000 people died, almost a quarter of these in London alone). The appearance of this epidemic had coincided with a select committee on smallpox from which another Smallpox Act (1871) had resulted, designed to tighten up the compulsory nature of vaccination by making it obligatory for local boards to appoint vaccination officers, by imposing fines of up to 25s on those who refused to have their children vaccinated, and with imprisonment for non-payment of the fine.

One would have thought that the epidemic of 1870–3 would have been sufficiently frightening to persuade the nation to adopt vaccination on a comprehensive and thorough scale, but in fact the reverse happened, and the anti-vaccination movement gathered momentum and strength in the final quarter of the century, with the result that the percentage of infants receiving vaccination declined from 85 per cent of all births in 1873 to slightly over 70 per cent in 1897. The efficacy of smallpox vaccination was hardly in question: in the epidemic of 1871 the mortality rate in London among those contracting the disease who were vaccinated was only 10.7 per cent: the mortality rate among the non-vaccinated was 45.9 per cent. Obviously the opposition was based on other considerations.

The anti-vaccination movement began in earnest following the appointment, under the 1871 Act, of vaccination officers throughout the country, and the growing practice of the Privy Council of sending out inspectors to check up on local vaccination stations. This 'interference' by the central government, coupled with the obligation now put on local authorities to appoint vaccination officers, and the impossibility of opting for alternative methods, such as the Leicester method of notification and isolation, all smacked of a violation of local liberties. The underlying fear, for so long evident in the country at large, that government interest in public health might lead to dictatorial decrees, had, in the opinion of many, finally been realized. The government, hitherto an agent of information and persuasion, had now emerged in its true colours, as a monster of control. To these arguments were added cries about the dignity of the human body and the 'unnaturalness' of vaccination (to which the *Lancet* responded that it was 'unnatural' to wear clothes or to ride in a train!). Opposition to compulsory vaccination was also based on religious principles, namely that it was sinful to inject impurities into the blood—an argument that eventually won recognition under the 'conscience clause' of the 1898 Smallpox Act, despite the counter-argument that such beliefs amounted to 'omissional infanticide.'

The leading force behind the anti-vaccination movement was Leicester. Despite its generally poor sanitary condition, Leicester, a town of relatively full employment and little overcrowding, had had a good record against smallpox, achieved by the 'Leicester method' of compulsory isolation of smallpox victims, the quarantining of all those who had had any contact with the patient, and a vigorous programme of cleansing, disinfecting, and, where necessary, burning of infected bedding and clothing, and the disinfecting of houses. In 1869 the Leicester Anti-Vaccination League was formed, and together with the London Society for the Abolition of Compulsory Vaccination it carried on an energetic and dedicated campaign against the central government's policies. Between 1869 and 1884 sixty-one imprisonments occurred in Leicester for non-compliance with the smallpox acts, and the movement culminated in a great demonstration in 1885, which drew together anti-vaccination forces from over fifty towns. Although the decline in smallpox was due far more to vaccination than to any sanitary improvements, the Vaccination Act of 1898 introduced the 'conscience clause' which enabled parents to avoid compulsory vaccination of their children. By the end of 1898 the number of certificates granted to conscientious objectors under the Act was 203,143, with Lancashire accounting for over a quarter; Leicester requestd 28,524 certificates. Even though it was often difficult to get life insurance, rent a dwelling, or get a job without proof of vaccination (it was required for all London County Council and London council housing), there were thousands of unvaccinated babies at the end of the century. From a low of only 3.8 per cent of all registered births in England and Wales in 1875 and 5.7 per cent in London in 1881, the percentage of unvaccinated babies rose steadily to 22.3 per cent and 26.6 per cent respectively in 1898. The reduction in the number of vaccinations suggests not only the decrease in its urgency with the decline of the disease (and the number of carriers) itself, but the degree of apathy, or ignorance toward preventive medicine which still prevailed and the strength of feeling about being bullied by a paternalistic state into good health. The struggle over vaccination suggests that improved national health depended on more than vigorous government commitment or even scientific discoveries. Also needed were the co-operation of local government and health officers, the support of the medical profession as a whole, and the willingness of the public at large to accept the judgment and policies of state medicine.

It is clear that different diseases required different government action. Typhus, typhoid, cholera and other diseases spread by micro-organisms in water, milk or food, and affecting the bowels, or spread by fingers and flies, were capable of being contained by a vigorous purification of water supplies, better excrement disposal, and improved personal hygiene. But other infectious diseases were spread by viruses in air-borne droplets of saliva, and if, as one medical authority has recently written, 'probably with every breath we take in a room where there are more than one or two people, some of these flakes from other people's saliva pass into our noses', a process which is greatly accelerated by coughing and sneezing, it is clear that measures other than sanitary engineering were necessary. Several diseases—t.b., measles, smallpox, scarlet fever—could be rendered less dangerous by a system of early notification and isolation. These preventive measures, no less than the attack on filth, required close co-operation between central and local health authorities and between health officers and the general public.

Aggravating the problem of air-borne disease was the enormous amount of overcrowding which prevailed in almost all the major centres of population, the lack of adequate isolation facilities, and the extensive population movements of the nineteenth century, which on the one hand injected new waves of healthier and younger country men and women into the towns, thus raising general health standards, but, on the other, placed in close proximity to one another immigrants who had built up little resistance or immunity to a variety of diseases which flourished in the densely-packed industrial towns. There was perhaps little the government could do about internal migration movements (in any case their impact upon the etiology of disease is certainly most complex); the solution to the problem of overcrowding lay,...in a variety of long-term solutions arrived at painfully through a process of much trial and error; notification and isolation were, however, something that the government could advocate and enforce. Unfortunately they were slow in coming.

As early as the 1860s Simon was calling for an effective system of notification and isolation to combat infectious disease, but his call went unheeded, and in 1874, from his central perspective at the Local Government Board, he attributed the persistently high death rates to two main factors—the omission 'to make due removal of refuse-matters, solid and liquid, from inhabited places', and the license permitted 'to cases of infectious diseases to scatter abroad the seeds of their infection.' Despite Simon's constant urging, the provision of isolation hospitals or isolation wards in already existing hospitals, was a matter of too little too late. In 1883 only thirty-four towns, with an aggregate population of only 2,500,000, had introduced a system of compulsory notification of infectious diseases. The system of notification had been left a matter for local option and had clearly been found wanting. Huddersfield had adopted notification as early as 1879, and a system of notification was in force in Bolton, Burton, Nottingham, Jarrow, Llandudno, Derby, Leicester, Oldham, Preston, Edinburgh, Warrington, Blackburn, Norwich, Rotherham, and Blackpool from 1879, but it was not until the passage of the Infectious Disease (Notification) Act of 1889, almost twenty years after the Association of MOH first began their agitation for it, that the system was adopted throughout England. Interestingly, t.b. was not included in the list of notifiable diseases, partly, it seems, because it was felt that it would impose an economic hardship (through enforced isolation) upon the large number of sufferers. One of the reasons for the slow adoption, on a voluntary basis, of a system of notification was that the medical profession was divided on the issue, for while both the groups saw the necessity for notification, the local MOH wanted the responsibility for notification to fall on the general practitioners and the GPs wanted it to rest squarely on the shoulders of the house-owners. In a rare example of working-class interest and initiative in public health affairs, the Trade Unions Congress of 1883 passed a resolution in favour of compulsory notification, containing the demand, well ahead of its time, that any resulting loss of wages should be compensated for out of the local rates.

The Infectious Disease (Notification) Act of 1889 made notification by doctors to the local authority compulsory in London and optional throughout the rest of the country. It was immediately adopted by seventy-five local authorities and, by 1891, by 555 urban and 372 rural sanitary districts. In that year the Local Government Board estimated that the acts had been adopted (but not necessarily enforced), in areas populated by some 20,000,000 of the 26,000,000 people living in England and Wales. Of the 141 provincial towns with populations of over 25,000, all but thirteen had adopted the Act and by 1893 some 25,000,000 people were, theoretically, living under its protection.

This broad adoption of a permissive act marks a commitment by local authorities to preventive medicine that obviously went well beyond the improvement of drains and sewers, water supplies, and paving, all of which, loosely speaking, could come under the heading of 'town improvements', or 'civic beautification'. In part it represented the growing acceptance at the local level of the germ theory of disease and it may well have been inspired by an awareness, after the compulsory Education Act of 1870, that without notification and isolation infectious diseases caught and conveyed by children might become more widespread. With more children going to school—between 1870 and 1889 the percentage of children between five and fifteen attending school increased from 22.7 to 55 per cent—and mingling with one another in crowded classrooms, diseases such as scarlet fever and measles became more widespread. With both the promotion of teachers and with government grants dependent upon full attendance, there was very little incentive for teachers to report cases of infection.

The adoption of a permissive act was one thing, but the provision of isolation facilities to make it effective was quite another, for that involved the local authority in additional expense and left it wide open to the charge of extravagance from the ever-vigilant rate-payers. There was, in any case, considerable anxiety, often amounting to fear, concerning isolation hospitals, for it was by no means certain that hospital authorities could guarantee that the diseases supposedly bottled up inside would not escape to pollute and threaten the surrounding neighbourhood. Thus in Edinburgh local rate-payers argued that the sewage from the infectious disease ward of the Lauriston Place Infirmary might flow into the main sewers and so infect the whole town. When the Metropolitan Asylums Board first embarked upon the provision of isolation hospitals in 1870 local inhabitants raised a fierce enough opposition to close some and delay the opening of others, and at the end of the century Windsor had to erect its temporary, corrugated-iron smallpox hospital alongside the sewage farm, far away from the residential areas. One manual for healthy living, written in 1885, included 'infectious hospitals' in its lists of 'cemeteries, sewage works, dust yards, and bank holiday neighbourhoods' as things to avoid when considering the site for a new house!

Thus the actual provision of special isolation wards and hospitals was very slow in coming. As late as 1879 only 296, or about one-fifth, of the 1,510 provincial sanitary authorities possessed some means of isolating infectious diseases and even as late as 1891 the total had advanced to only 400 or so. Once again, as in so many other areas of public health, the problem was predominantly one of money, for although government loans were available, the ultimate burden was still on the local rates. In Derbyshire, for example, there were two local health authorities with rateable values of only £4,000 p.a. each, and four or five other districts with rateable values of between £4000 and £8000. 'Such districts', wrote the County MOH for Derbyshire, 'could not possibly afford to put up proper hospitals, nor to maintain them if put up.' There was, consequently, only one authority in Derbyshire, a county with a population of over 426,000, which had erected a permanent isolation hospital by 1895. The Isolation Hospitals Act, 1893, enabled county councils to establish isolation hospitals, but here again the costs involved dampened the enthusiasm of all but the most ardent advocates of preventive medicine. In 1882 the Local Government Board estimated that it cost between £200 and £300 a bed to build a hospital, and this was well beyond the means of most small rural districts as well as many towns. When Liverpool belatedly provided some 300 beds it had to spend over £80,000.

In the 1890s the Local Government Board thus discovered that in most areas of the country facilities for isolation of epidemic infectious diseases were woefully inadequate. In Bishop Auckland, in Durham (population of 10,000 approximately), there was an isolation hospital, but it was a converted dog kennel, with only five beds and no disinfecting apparatus. Carlisle had just thirty-two beds and no disinfecting equipment for a population of some 40,000. Burslem and Burton-on-Trent, both pottery towns with high incidences of infectious lung diseases, had just eighteen and thirty beds apiece for populations, respectively, of 32,000 and 46,000. Llanelli, a town with a population of 24,000 had no isolation hospital at all. Wigan was better served, with sixty beds for a population of 50,000. The bigger towns were not much better provided for. Leeds (population over 367,000) had one 'house of recovery' with sixty-four beds, a smallpox hospital with thirty-six beds, and a small convalescent shelter for children suffering from scarlet fever. Bolton (115,000) had been the first town in England to obtain powers for the compulsory notification of infectious diseases (in 1877), and it imposed a dual obligation on both doctors and householders to report infectious diseases, but it had no effective isolation wards until the Borough Fever Hospital was built in 1882. In 1895 it had thirty-two beds and a few cots. Liverpool, like so many other towns, had relied on the local workhouses to provide accommodation for patients suffering from infectious diseases. In 1885 the Local Government Board sharply rapped the Liverpool Corporation over the knuckles for its failure to provide isolation facilities and suggested that some 750 beds were required. Eventually the town was stirred into action, and by 1892 had provided three isolation hospitals with a total accommodation for 298 patients, out of a total population of almost 518,000. Manchester (505,000) did not provide any municipal hospital, but relied upon subsidies to the Manchester Royal Infirmary, which had 372 beds in isolation wards. Birmingham (478,000) had provided some 400 beds. Preston, a notoriously insanitary town with a population of over 107,000, had provided no isolation facilities whatsoever.

However inadequate these facilities were, they were superior to rural areas, where there was no alternative to the parish workhouse. In London things were much better, for the 1867 Metropolitan Poor Act provided the town with a network of infectious diseases hospitals, organized by the Metropolitan Asylums Board. The Board's first fever hospital, for smallpox and scarlet fever patients, and for paupers only, was erected in 1870, and the Board's work was extended gradually until a range of infectious diseases was provided for, and admission to the Board's hospitals was no longer restricted to paupers only—the removal of the stigma of pauperism had been strenuously urged by the Metropolitan MOH. By 1893 the Metropolitan Asylums Board actually possessed, or was in the process of building, over 5,000 beds in 'fever' hospitals. Whereas in 1873 only about two per cent of all scarlet fever deaths occurred in hospitals in London, and only 11 per cent in 1883, by 1894 that figure had risen to 74 per cent; similarly, for diphtheria, the percentage rose from about four per cent in 1888 to 38 per cent in 1894—an indication not so much of the ineffectiveness of the hospital treatment or the insanitary state of hospitals as of the greater numbers of sufferers from these infectious diseases, many in the advanced stages, being admitted to the municipally-run hospitals. The compulsory Notification of Infectious Disease Act prompted the Metropolitan Asylums Board to step up its work and more people were placed in its hospitals in the year 1893 than during the entire decade, 1881–90.

The compulsory Notification Act of 1889 was passed right after the Local Government Act of 1888 which, among other things, established County MOH. These county officers could sometimes bring pressure to bear on local authorities. Thus the County MOH for the West Riding of Yorkshire concentrated in his early years on infectious diseases and urged local authorities to put the Notification Act into immediate effect and to build adequate isolation facilities. Under his constant urging, the number of local authorities in the West Riding adopting the Act rose from seventeen (at the end of 1889) to ninety-six by 1891, and between 1895 and 1901 the percentage of notified cases of smallpox, diphtheria, scarlet fever and typhoid which were admitted to hospital rose from 14 percent to 30.4 percent.

The provision of hospital accommodation for patients suffering from infectious diseases was never a top priority for local authorities, and it was only after considerable prodding from the Local Government Board and the introduction of comprehensive legislation that isolation hospitals were built. One cannot say that local authorities responded with quite the same vigour to the germ theory of disease as they had, some thirty years earlier, to the pythogenic. Sanitary engineering, however costly, could at least appeal to the Victorian's sense of energy, and his civic pride, to say nothing of his sense of smell. Notification and isolation hardly had the same dramatic appeal; indeed they had connotations of quarantine and incarceration.

Yet if halting and erratic, the Victorian response to the major epidemics was quite remarkable. With the exception of smallpox these diseases had to be contained without the benefits of anti-toxins, yet they *were* contained. In an age of rapid urban and population growth this must surely be seen as a triumph for preventive medicine. It is a testimony also to the resourcefulness and earnestness of the Victorians. Of course they did not bow gracefully to the necessity of following central government directives, nor did they swallow willingly the bitter pill of compulsory legislation. Indeed relations between the central government and local authorities were often strained and bitter—a struggle between two growing bodies, one using the vocabulary of national health and strength, efficiency and progress, the other using the vocabulary of low rates, local option, independence, and freedom....

Bibliography

J. BRAND, *Doctors and the State: The British Medical Profession and Government Action in Public Health, 1870–1912* (1965).
W. COLEMAN, *Death Is a Social Disease: Public Health and Political Economy in Early Industrial France* (1982).
M. DUREY, *The Return of the Plague: British Society and the Cholera, 1831–1832* (1979).
J. EYLER, *Victorian Social Medicine: The Ideas and Methods of William Farr* (1979).
S. E. FINER, *The Life and Times of Sir Edwin Chadwick* (1952).
T. GELFAND, *Professionalizing Modern Medicine: Paris Surgeons and Medical Science and Institutions in the Eighteenth Century* (1980).
R. LAMBERT, *Sir John Simon, 1816–1904, and English Social Administration* (1963).
R. E. MCGREW, *Russia and the Cholera, 1823–1832* (1965).
M. PELLING, *Cholera, Fever, and English Medicine, 1825–1865* (1978).
F. B. SMITH, *Florence Nightengale: Reputation and Power* (1982).
F. B. SMITH, *The People's Health, 1830–1910* (1979).
C. E. WINSLOW, *The Conquest of Epidemic Disease: A Chapter in the History of Ideas* (1943; reprint, 1980).
A. J. YOUNGSON, *The Scientific Revolution in Victorian Medicine* (1979).

Civilizing in Earnest: Schools and Schooling

EUGEN WEBER

Nation-building was a complex process in nineteenth-century Europe. Politicians, diplomats, and soldiers played very important roles. But no less fundamental to the process was the establishment of a sense of belonging to a nation rather than to a local district or province and the replacement of religious and local values with the values of national citizenship and civic culture. The chief institution carrying out that latter process was the school, which both inculcated new values and equipped students with skills that allowed them to participate in the larger national economic and political life.

The task of creating citizens through schooling, as seen here in the case of France, was a very complicated and difficult one, especially among the peasantry of the countryside. It involved the furnishing of new schools as well as more and better-trained teachers, and establishing the perception that education was genuinely useful. Prior to the 1880s French education had been rather haphazard. Peasant children were schooled so they might meet the requirements of taking first communion. Poorly trained, part time teachers staffed the schools and provided few skills relevant to the life of the peasant working the land. Moreover, most peasants were not only illiterate, but in many cases spoke not French but rather some form of patois or local dialect.

In the early 1880s, under the leadership of Jules Ferry, the French government adopted a number of new mandatory education policies. Thereafter, the local school teacher became a kind of missionary of French secular education. The French language was taught along with French history and geography. In this manner secular schooling replaced religious. The teacher also taught polite behavior and personal hygiene. The education provided by the new schools expanded the world of the peasant child, who gradually began to grasp that the skills acquired and the school certificate itself could open the way to new kinds of work less arduous than tilling the land. The child's

---

Reprinted from *Peasants into Frenchmen: The Modernization of Rural France, 1870–1914*, by Eugen Weber, with the permission of the publishers, Stanford University Press. Copyright © 1976 by the Board of Trustees of the Leland Stanford Junior University.

parents also came to see that the skills of reading and accounting taught in the schools had uses in the world of agriculture as national market forces came to bear more directly on their lives. Politically and culturally, the new schools led students to see a world beyond their village and to regard themselves as French citizens and as part of the larger nation.

The school, notably the village school, compulsory and free, has been credited with the ultimate acculturation process that made the French people French—finally civilized them, as many nineteenth-century educators liked to say. The schoolteachers, in their worn, dark suits, appear as the militia of the new age, harbingers of enlightenment and of the Republican message that reconciled the benighted masses with a new world, superior in wellbeing and democracy. Observers have pointed out that there were schools before the 1880's, and have quarreled with implicit assumptions or explicit statements that there was no popular education under the Ancien Régime. But we shall see that the now-classic image of a profound change of pace, tone, and impact under the Third Republic is roughly correct if it is placed in the proper context.

The context matters because schools did in fact exist before Jules Ferry, indeed were numerous; and so, to a large extent, did free education. What made the Republic's laws so effective was not just that they required all children to attend school and granted them the right to do so free. It was the attendant circumstances that made adequate facilities and teachers more accessible; that provided roads on which children could get to school; that, above all, made school meaningful and profitable, once what the school offered made sense in terms of altered values and perceptions.

It is my purpose in this chapter to sketch the development of schooling in this particular context, to suggest how it fits the changes indicated above, and to show that its success was an integral part of a total process. It was only when what the schools taught made sense that they became important to those they had to teach. It was only when what the schools said became relevant to recently created needs and demands that people listened to them; and listening, also heeded the rest of their offerings. People went to school not because school was offered or imposed, but because it was useful. The world had to change before this came about.

The schools that priests or laymen ran for the poorer classes before the last quarter of the nineteenth century tended, in the nature of things, to put first things first. First things were those the masters thought important: the ability to gabble the catechism or a part of the Latin service. The teaching of even elementary reading, writing, and arithmetic was rare before the Revolution, reflected the prefect of Yonne in 1810, and teachers were little interested in "broad public education, I mean the sort concerning the greatest number of people." In any case, a great many teachers taught whatever they taught with limited competence. Until 1816, no title or proof of competence was required from a teacher. And though in the cities and larger towns this could be remedied, popular schooling suffered. It went on suffering on this score for quite some time, under the rod of men like the dominie of the secondary school of Noyers (Yonne), whose schoolroom was so ill-swept and so full of spiders "that one could hardly make out Citizen Colibeau through the spiderwebs, especially when he gave his lesson as he habitually did in nightcap, dressing gown, and sabots."

The schoolroom or schoolhouse tended to be ramshackle. At Moulle (Pas-de-Calais) a whole wall collapsed in 1828 during a friendly scuffle between teacher and pupils. In 1850 the school at Sauvat (Cantal) was an abandoned bakehouse whose roof was separated from the walls, so that the snow got in. Throughout the 1870's we hear of ceilings crumbling, floors collapsing, paneless windows—sometimes no windows at all, the chimney providing the only ventilation. Living and teaching quarters were hard to tell apart; in Eure-et-Loir teachers or their wives did their household chores, prepared meals, and baked bread during class, and some also slept in the classroom on a folding bed. Perhaps just as well, since otherwise the schoolroom might have been even more poorly equipped: quite a few lacked tables; some until the 1880's had neither seats nor stove. Body heat helped, and we find one mayor (in 1837) asserting that the children's breath ensured a reasonable temperature. Dark, humid, crowded, unventilated, unfurnished, unlit, unheated or smelly and smoky when a fire or stove was lit, drafty, unwelcoming, and ugly, such was the great majority of schools right through the end of the 1870's. Most had no yard, let alone a latrine. In 1864 a school inspector, reporting on the lack of cesspools or other sanitary facilities, noted that some schools did provide a fenced-in area in a corner of the backyard. The manure amassed there was removed from time to time and used as fertilizer—"the beginning of progress, ... unknown a dozen years ago."

At Nouvion-en-Thiérache (Aisne) there were "no maps, no blackboards, no tables or desks" in the 1850's. Each pupil had a wooden plank that he placed on his knees for writing; the master sharpened the students' quills, and when he was called away to sing in the church, his sister kept the class in order while she cleaned her salad. This was not unusual, and informality of this sort must have interrupted many a dreary lesson. If the schoolroom was in the village hall, the community's records were likely to be kept in a corner cupboard, with adults filing in at any time to verify a document or to seek the teacher out for other functions; and it was not unknown for a wedding celebration to be held there, even sometimes during class.

The teacher himself was another problem. In the first half of the nineteenth century, he could well have been a retired soldier, a rural constable, the local barber, innkeeper, or grocer, or simply a half-educated peasant's son. Seven of the 15 teachers in Rennes in 1815 were ex-convicts. Balzac's figure of the village teacher, Fourchon, who ended as a poacher, part-cordwainer, part-begger, and fulltime drunk, was evidently an acceptable stereotype under the July Monarchy. In any case, most teachers worked at another job, ranging from farming their own land or someone else's, weaving (in Eure-et-Loir one kept his loom in the schoolroom), mending shoes, and digging graves to serving as the village choirmaster or village registrar. Even in 1872, when teachers had moved up in the world from their low condition of the 1830's, we find what must have been most if not all of the 395 public teachers of Eure-et-Loir doing something else on the side: 359 acted as registrars, 273 as choirmasters or church organists, and 14 as sextons, beadles, or bellringers; two were janitors and sweepers, one a gravedigger, and ten tobacconists; two ran the local telegraph office, and 36 sold insurance....

I have quoted the reports of school inspectors. They came into existence in 1833 as part of a law introduced by Francois Guizot, then Minister of Public Instruction. That law set the foundations of the people's schooling. It required every commune or group of neighboring communes to set up and maintain at least one elementary school; it reaffirmed the standards of competence for teaching that had been set by royal ordinance in 1816, and prohibited the operation of a school without an official certificate that such standards had been met; it decreed that each department should set up, alone or jointly with its neighbors, a normal school to train primary school teachers; and it produced quick results. In 1833 France had 31,420 schools attended by 1.2 million children; by 1847 the number of schools had doubled, and the number of pupils had increased almost threefold. In the same period the number of normal schools increased from 38 to 47. This last had its importance. We must realize that the mass of the teachers in the public elementary schools in the mid-1880's probably came out of these normal schools of the July Monarchy; and that, however slowly, their training and quality improved as a result....

The next great change came in the 1880's. It would have come earlier had the Minister of Education Victor Duruy had the chance to develop the plans he elaborated in 1867. But he did not, and most of his initiatives remained in the project stage. Hence the importance of the reforms introduced by Jules Ferry. In 1881 all fees and tuition charges in public elementary schools were abolished. In 1882 enrollment in a public or private school was made compulsory. In 1883 every village or hamlet with more than 20 school-age children was required to maintain a public elementary school. In 1885 subsidies were allotted for the building and maintenance of schools and for the pay of teachers. In 1886 an elementary teaching program was instituted, along with elaborate provisions for inspection and control....

One reason for the slow progress in eliminating illiteracy, strangely ignored by even the best accounts of education in France, was the fact that so many adults—and consequently children—did not speak French. ...[I]n 1863 by official tally...some 7.5 million people, a fifth of the population, did not know the language. And...even that figure is questionable. The actual number was probably much larger, particularly if one includes those whose notions of the language were extremely vague.

The greatest problem faced by the public schools in the 8,381 non-French-speaking communes, and in a good few of the other 29,129 where French was said to be in general use, was how to teach the language to children who never or hardly ever heard it. The oft-repeated claim that they were learning their mother tongue could hardly have rung true to those whose mothers did not understand a word of it. "The children [of Lauragais] don't have to learn simply how to read and write," commented M. F. Pariset in 1867. "They have to learn how to do so in French, that is, in another language than the one they know." The result was that, for a lot of them, the instruction received in school "leaves no more trace than Latin leaves on most of those who graduate from secondary school. The child... returns to patois when he gets home. French is for him an erudite language, which he forgets quickly, never speaking it." Officially, the problem was faced by denying its existence and forcing even those who could scarcely master a few words to proclaim, as in a catechism, that what *should* be true was true and what they *knew* to be true was not: "(1) We call mother tongue the tongue that is spoken by our parents, and in particular by our mothers; spoken also by our fellow citizens and by the persons who inhabit the same *pays* as us. (2) Our mother tongue is French." So read an army examination manual in 1875. Unofficially, the schools continued to struggle to make the slogan true. Teaching French, "our beautiful and noble mother tongue," asserted Ferdinand Buisson, the leading light of Republican education in the 1880's, "is the chief work of the elementary school—a labor of patriotic character." The labor proved long and hard....

This could not have happened as long as schools remained irrelevant to a great many people; and this they did into the last quarter of the century. Most peasants wanted their children to work and contribute to the family budget. If they sent them to school at all, it was usually for the sole purpose of getting them past their first communion, a crucial rite of passage. Once that was accomplished, the child was withdrawn. Parents send their children to school for a few winter months before their communion, grumbled a Breton teacher in 1861, and that short time was almost exclusively devoted to learning the catechism, an awkward business since the children could not read. For this reason communions were made as early as possible, between the ages of ten and twelve. As a result school enrollments of children past that age diminished sharply, and children soon forgot the little they had learned, mostly by rote, lapsing once again into a "state of complete ignorance."

In any case the country school provided little stimulus to learning for its pupils, not even the challenge of exposure to more motivated students.

Parents in comfortable circumstances who were willing and able to keep their children in school for a time preferred to send them to the bourg or to a boarding school. More important, the offspring of wealthier parents, aware that schooling would play a part in their later activities, assimilated more and retained more of what they learned. The parents took more interest in their work. Thus the children of the poor had access to poorer schools, less time to attend them, and far less reason to make the most of such opportunity than their better-off mates....

Where and when children were registered in school, what matters, after all, is not their enrollment as such, but their attendance. This varied with the region and its ways, but tended generally to be restricted to the winter months. As actual or potential workers, children were free for school only when there was no work. In the Limousin they did not say that a child had been in school for three years but that he had three winters in school. He entered it in December, after the chestnuts had been gathered and the migrants he had helped replace had returned home, and left in late March or early April when the migrants set off again. Similarly, in Côte-d'Or and the Jura, which had more elementary schools for their outlying villages and hamlets than most departments, children usually had to work much of the year, and attended class for only a few months in the winter, forgetting in the interval whatever they had learned. The only ones who benefited from schooling were the sons of those with sufficient means to do without their help. In the Doubs, on the other hand, winter is hard and long. This kept the children in school longer, and they picked up more. Yet even children who did not help their parents left school in March or April. In Lozère children attended school four months a year at most. After Easter, only infants were left; schools were either closed down or turned into day nurseries (1877). In Manche parents were happy to leave children in school during the years when they would only get underfoot around the house, but wanted to withdraw them as soon as they were able-bodied, precisely when they would be at their most teachable (1892). Alain Corbin concludes that child labor disappeared only slowly, between the 1870's and the late 1880's. By the end of the century, at any rate, inspectors could note a greater regularity in school attendance in the winter. Continued complaints of irregularity now referred to the rest of the year. Grumbles were bitter, but standards had been raised.

We have arrived at the fundamental cause of that "indifference" to book learning that Philippe Ariès, like Destutt de Tracy before him, finds indigenous to the countryside. The urban poor had occasion to use the skills picked up in parish schools and to observe the opportunities of improving their position with that learning. In the countryside, such skills brought little profit, their absence small disadvantage, and there were fewer chinks in the armor of misery through which curiosity or enterprise could find escape. The *Statistique* of Vendée, regretting in 1844 that the department's inhabitants "showed little inclination for the study of sciences and polite literature, or for the culture of fine arts," sounds ridiculous until it shows that it understands why this was not surprising: "Far from the sources of inspiration and taste, they were rarely in a position to know their value or [to find] any object of emulation." Objects of emulation were scarce in the countryside, sources of inspiration even scarcer.

School was perceived as useless and what it taught had little relation to local life and needs. The teacher taught the metric system when *toises, cordes,* and *pouces* were in current use; counted money in francs when prices were in *louis* and *écus*. French was of little use when everyone spoke patois and official announcements were made by a public crier in the local speech. Anyway, the school did not teach *French*, but arid rules of grammar. In short, school had no practical application. It was a luxury at best, a form of more or less conspicuous consumption. Corbin has pointed out the significant role that all this played in the lack of interest displayed by parents and children. When Martin Nadaud's father wanted to send him to school, neighbors and relatives argued that for a country child school learning was useless, enabling him merely to make a few letters and carry books at mass. Teachers and school inspectors failed to persuade the peasants that reading and writing had any value in themselves. And parents found their reticence justified by the slight difference in the situation of those who attended school and of those who did not. When Ferdinand Buisson linked poor school attendance to a lack of concern for the moral benefits that children could derive, he was in the great (abstract) tradition. Yet show people a practical benefit that they could understand, and the problem would shrink to manageable proportions. Rural inhabitants, explained a village mayor, were "only very vaguely conscious of an intellectual or moral culture that has no immediate or tangible relation of pecuniary profit." That seemed to make sense. Before a man could want his child to go to school, he would have to abandon "the gross material interests" that were all he understood. Not so. It was when the school mobilized those interests that men began to care....

My point is that it needed personal experience to persuade people of the usefulness of education. Certain migrants had learned this, and we have seen how they and their children recognized at an early date "the value of instruction and the profit one can derive from it in the great centers." Through the second half of the century, school attendance in migrant Creuse was far better than in neighboring Haute-Vienne and Corrèze— higher by 7 percent and 12 percent, respectively, in 1876. Another spur to schooling came from the military law of 1872, not only because it abolished the purchase of substitutes, but also because it provided advantages for men who could read and write and threatened illiterate conscripts with an additional year of service. The school authorities made haste to refer to these facets of the law to persuade parents to send their children to school. In Isère a poster was even displayed in every schoolroom, and teachers were required to read and discuss it at least every two weeks, presumably arguing that the fulfillment of one patriotic duty could help lighten the burden of another.

But another army was growing, as important as the regular one—the body of public and private employees, access to which was opened by the school certificate, the certificate of elementary studies. The little school of Roger Thabault's Mazières put its graduates into the numerous jobs that opened up there (and elsewhere), with economic, social, and political development: the town's 15 civil servants in 1876 had become 25 in 1886, and there were seven railway employees as well. Ambition was encouraged by propaganda. "A good primary education allows one to secure a post in several state services," the student was told in a first-year civics text published in 1880. "The government servant has a secure position. That is why government posts are in great demand." They were. Given the chance, many peasants wanted to stop being peasants, to change to something else. In 1899, 40 former natives of the little village of Soye in Doubs, population 444, worked as functionaries elsewhere, and 14 inhabitants worked as domestics in town. The prefecture of Seine received 50,000 applications for 400 openings in its departments.

Other times had seen the growth of a state bureaucracy that triggered the expansion of education to fill the available posts. Such educational booms, however, had been restricted to relatively high social groups. Under the Third Republic the means for those too humble to have gotten their share of the educational pie were made available just when the ends (i.e., the jobs) emerged to reinforce and justify their use. Around the 1880's even rural laborers began to lend attention to the schools. As the number of jobs expanded and getting one became more than an idle dream, the education that would help secure such prestigious jobs became important. Even more so the certificate to which it led. Scattered encomiums to its practical uses appear in the late 1870's. By 1880 Pécaut could report that the school certificate "is slowly being accepted. Families realize that this small diploma can be of use for several kinds of jobs; hence they consent ever more frequently to leave their children in school for a longer time." Schools were still badly housed, still far from home, but children now were made to attend even when they lived six km away, because "the idea of the utility and the necessity of elementary schooling" had caught on so well.

The recognition of new possibilities and of the school as a key to their exploitation was in full evidence by the 1890's. By 1894 practically every child in a village of Lower Provence that had been almost totally illiterate a generation earlier was attending school, even those who lived one and a half hours' walk away. In the southwest the image of little boys doing their homework of an evening by the light of the dying embers became a reality. Municipal councils voted rewards for teachers whose pupils won the coveted certificate. Families became avid for it; they celebrated when a child got one; too many failures could become issues raised at council meetings. In a natural evolution, the school certificate, significant because of the material advantages it could help secure, became an end in itself. "It is an honor to get it," wrote a little girl (and wrote it very badly: "être ademise s'est un honneur davoir son certificat d'étude"), about what popular parlance dubbed the "Santificat." The passing of the examination became an eminent occasion, competing in importance with the first communion. Men who had taken it in the 1880's remembered the questions that they had to answer, had every detail of their examination day graven in their memories. To take one example among many, here is Charles Moureu, member of the Academy of Medicine and professor at the Collège de France, speaking at the graduation ceremony of his native village in the Pyrenees in 1911: "I could if I wanted to recite by heart the exact details of the problem that turned on the things Peter and Nicholas bought and sold."

There were of course more immediate gains: there would be no more need to go to the nearest town to consult a solicitor or a notary when one wanted to draw up a simple bill or promissory note, make out a receipt, settle an account in arrears, or merely write a letter, explained a thirteen-year-old schoolboy in the Aube. The literate man did not have to reveal his friendships, his secrets, his affairs to some third party. *And* he could better himself—in local politics, or teaching, or the army (whence he returned with a pension and decorations, achieving a position "that places him above the vulgar crowd").

The vulgar crowd was full of the sort of peasants whose stereotyped image filled current literature: they spoke ungrammatically, used characteristic locutions, mishandled the small vocabulary at their command, and "do not look more intelligent than other peasant farmers around them." The only escape from this was education, which taught order, cleanliness, efficiency, success, and *civilization.* Official reports coupled poor education with rude, brutal ways. Where schooling did not take hold, "ways are coarse, characters are violent, excitable, and hotheaded, troubles and brawls are frequent." The school was supposed to improve manners and customs, and sooth the savage breast. The polite forms it inculcated "softened the savagery and harshness natural to peasants." Improved behavior and morality would be attributed to the effects of schooling. Schools set out "to modify the habits of bodily hygiene and cleanliness, social and domestic manners, and the way of looking at things and judging them." Savage children were taught new manners: how to greet strangers, how to knock on doors, how to behave in decent company. "A bourgeois farts when his belly is empty; a Breton [peasant] burps when his belly is full," declared a proverb that seems to confuse urban and rural differences with race. Children were taught that propriety prohibited either manifestation; and also that cleanliness was an essential part of wisdom.

The schools played a crucial role in forcing children to keep clean(er), but the teachers had to struggle mightily to that end. Hair, nails, and ears were subject to regular review; the waterpump was pressed into frequent use; the state of clothes, like the standards of the child's behavior out of school, received critical attention and constant reproof. Study, ran the text of one exercise, "fills the mind, corrects false prejudices, helps us order speech and writing, teaches love of work and improves capacity for business and for jobs." What does study tell us? Among other things: cold baths are dangerous; the observance of festivals is a religious duty; labor abuses the body less than pleasure; justice protects the good and punishes the wicked; tobacco is a poison, a useless expenditure that destroys one's memory, and those who use it to excess live in a sort of dream, their eye dead, incapable of paying attention to anything, indifferent and selfish. And then there was the lesson of Jules and Julie, who are rich and therefore do not work at school; and who, having learned nothing, are embarrassed later by their ignorance, blushing with shame when people laugh at them for the mistakes they make when speaking. Only the schools could "change primitive conditions," declared Ardouin-Dumazet. The primitive conditions themselves were changing, and schools helped their charges to adapt to this.

Of course they did more—or they did it more broadly. If we are prepared to set up categories with well-drawn limits, society educates and school instructs. The school imparts particular kinds of learned knowledge, society inculcates the conclusions of experience assimilated over a span of time. But such a view, applicable to specific skills and subjects, has to be altered when the instruction offered by the school directs itself to realms that are at variance with social education (as in the case of language or measures), or that social education ignores (as in the case of patriotism). In other words, the schools provide a complementary, even a counter-education, because the education of the local society does not coincide with that needed to create a national one. This is where schooling becomes a major agent of acculturation: shaping individuals to fit into societies and cultures broader than their own, and persuading them that these broader realms are their own, as much as the pays they really know and more so.

We come here to the greatest function of the modern school: to teach not so much useful skills as a new patriotism beyond the limits naturally acknowledged by its charges. The revolutionaries of 1789 had replaced old terms like schoolmaster, regent, and rector, with *instituteur*, because the teacher was intended to *institute* the nation. But the desired effect, that elusive unity of spirit, was recognized as lacking in the 1860's and 1870's as it had been four score years before.

School was a great socializing agent, wrote a village teacher from Gard in 1861. It had to teach children national and patriotic sentiments, explain what the state did for them and why it exacted taxes and military service, and show them their true interest in the fatherland. It seems that there was a great deal to do. The theme remained a constant preoccupation of eminent educators. Twenty years after this, student teachers "must above all be told... that their first duty is to make [their charges] love and understand the fatherland." Another ten years, and the high aim is again repeated, that a "national pedagogy" might yet become the soul of popular education. The school is "an instrument of unity," an "answer to dangerous centrifugal tendencies," and of course the "keystone of national defense."

First, the national pedagogy. "The fatherland is not your village, your province, it is all of France. The fatherland is like a great family." This was not learned without some telescoping. "Your fatherland is you," wrote a thirteen-year-old schoolboy dutifully in 1878. "It is your family, it is your people [*les tiens*], in a word it is France, your country." "The fatherland is the *pays* where we are born," wrote another, "where our parents are born and our dearest thoughts lie; it is not only the *pays* we live in, but the region [*contrée*] we inhabit; our fatherland is France." The exercise was a sort of catechism designed to teach the child that it was his duty to defend the fatherland, to shed his blood or die for the commonweal ("When France is threatened, your duty is to take up arms and fly to her rescue"), to obey the government, to perform military service, to work, learn, pay taxes, and so on.

At the very start of school, children were taught that their first duty was to defend their country as soldiers. The army—and this was important, considering the past and enduring hostility to soldiers and soldiering—"is composed of our brothers or parents" or relatives. Commencement speeches recalled this sacred duty in ritual terms—our boys will defend the soil of the fatherland. The whole school program turned on expanding the theme. Gymnastics were meant "to develop in the child the idea of discipline, and prepare him ... to be a good soldier and a good Frenchman." Children sang stirring songs like the "Flag of France," the "Lost Sentry," and "La Marseillaise." Compositions on the theme were ordered up, with title and content provided: "Letter of a Young Soldier to His Parents. He tells them that he has fought against the enemies of the fatherland, has been wounded ... and is proud (as they must be too) that he has shed his blood for the fatherland." And teachers reported with satisfaction how they implanted the love of the fatherland by evoking "those memories that attach our hearts to the fatherland" from history, and then "develop[ed] this sentiment by showing France strong and powerful *when united*."

There were no better instruments of indoctrination and patriotic conditioning than French history and geography, especially history, which "when properly taught [is] the only means of maintaining patriotism in the generations we are bringing up." Could it be that other social forces were doing little to stir or inculcate it? Unfortunately, most teachers knew history badly, geography still worse. When, around the 1870's, they taught French history—or began to teach it—they tended to string out reigns and dates, and seldom seem to have got further than the Middle Ages. History was ignored, and civics absent from the teaching program, complained Félix Pécaut in 1871. It was quite possible "to use French history to form French citizens, make the free fatherland be known and loved; but no elementary attempt of this sort has yet been made." This was not surprising. "Teachers certificated in 1850–1868," more than half those teaching in 1879, "have never studied French history and do not know it," grumbled a school inspector in Vendée. And "teachers begin, it is still new and rare, to present the chief events of French history," reported another in Haute-Saône. The job would be undertaken in textbooks like Lavisse's *First Year of French History*, a book thoroughly bent to show and to justify the rise of French patriotism and unity—refocused from the *petite patrie* to the larger one. Reading it, children were told, "you will learn what you owe your fathers and why your first duty is to love above all else your fatherland—that is, the land of your fathers."

Just as the mother tongue was not the tongue of their mothers, so the fatherland was somewhere more (indeed, something else) than where their fathers rather obviously lived. A vast program of indoctrination was plainly called for to persuade people that the fatherland extended beyond its evident limits to something vast and intangible called France. Adults were too deeply rooted in their backwardness. But it was hard work to persuade even children, for all their malleability, without the panoply of material that became available only in the 1870's. Under the Second Empire, "children know no geography, see no maps, know nothing concerning their department or their fatherland" (Lot-et-Garonne). Children "were completely unaware of the existence of their department or of France" (Dordogne). "Notions of geography have become a general need" (Doubs).

Maps of France began to be supplied soon after the Franco-Prussian War, distributed by the state. First urban schools, then rural ones, were endowed with wall maps. By 1881 few classrooms, however small, appear to have lacked a map. Some, of course, served "only as ornaments." But they inculcated all with the image of the national hexagon, and served as a reminder that the eastern border should lie not on the Vosges but on the Rhine. They were also powerful symbols, not only of the asserted fatherland, but of the abstractions young minds had to get used to. How difficult this latter exercise remained is suggested by a circular of 1899 announcing the distribution of engravings of "views of different French regions that will lend concreteness to the idea of the fatherland."...

Teachers taught or were expected to teach "not just for the love of art or science...but for the love of France"—a France whose creed had to be inculcated in all unbelievers. A Catholic God, particularist and only identified with the fatherland by revisionists after the turn of the century, was replaced by a secular God: the fatherland and its living symbols, the army and the flag. Catechism was replaced by civics lessons. Biblical history, proscribed in secular schools, was replaced by the sainted history of France. French became more than a possession of the educated: it became a patrimony in which all could share, with significant results for national cohesion, as the 1914 war would show.

But the effects of school went further. In the first place, the literary or written language children learned in schools was as alien to the spoken tongue as spoken French itself was to their native dialect. In other words, schools began their work by propagating an artificial language, and this was true even for French-speakers. They did this largely through the discipline of dictations, "the instrument of a learned and universal language" beyond the local ken. As a result, many students learned to express themselves freely and easily in speech, but had difficulty when it came to writing or to expressing thought in an idiom close to that of the written word. We can glimpse this best in the surviving files of gendarmerie reports, which are often drawn up in a stilted administrative style and relate even simple events in an awkward and convoluted manner.

A striking result of this (much worse in areas estranged by dialect) was that "for months or years [the children] give no sign of intelligence, merely imitate what they see done." Just as legislation can create crime by fiat, so education created stupidity by setting up standards of communication that many found difficult to attain. "Our children cannot find, and indeed have no way to find, enough French words to express their thoughts," reported a Cantal teacher. The result was a divorce between school learning, often acquired by rote, and assimilation, which helped slow down the progress of the schools. Memorization saved the trouble of "having to translate one's thoughts into correct French." It also divorced word from reality. Many children "can spell, but syllables have no meaning for them; can read, but fail to understand what they read, or to recognize in writing some words they know but whose orthography is alien," or to identify words learned in French with the objects around them. "You will learn it, this language of well-bred people, and you will speak it some day," promised a prize-giver in Dordogne in 1897. The future tense used in such improbable circumstances suggests a possible reason why, by 1907, the number of illiterate conscripts seems to have been slightly higher than in the immediate past. The absolute banning of the native tongue, which had been helpful in teaching French as a second language, inhibited the learning of idiomatic French and impeded its full assimilation.

This is not to say that French did not make great strides forward. It did. But writing remained a socially privileged form of expression, and the French of the schools and of the dictations was an alienating as well as an integrative force. Prehaps that was what a school inspector meant when, looking back from 1897, he declared: "Ignorance used to precede school; today on the contrary it follows schooling."

Of course there were (from the school's point of view) positive results; and these too went beyond the immediately obvious. The symbolism of images learned at school created a whole new language and provided common points of reference that straddled regional boundaries exactly as national patriotism was meant to do. Where local dialect and locutions insulated and preserved, the lessons of the school, standardized throughout France, taught a unifying idiom. In Ain, the Ardennes, Vendée, all children became familiar with references or identities that could thereafter be used by the authorities, the press, and the politicians to appeal to them as a single body. Lessons emphasizing certain associations bound generations together. The Kings of France were the older sons of the Church, time was the river that carried all in its waters, a poet was a favorite of the muses, Touraine was the garden of France, and Joan of Arc the shepherdess of Lorraine. Local saws and proverbs were replaced by nationally valid ones, regional locutions by others learned in books: castles in Spain rose above local ruins, and golden calves bleated more loudly than the stabled ones. The very mythology of ambition was now illustrated by landscapes that education had suggested, more stirring than the humbler ones at hand and by this time no less familiar. These are only aspects of the wide-ranging process of standardization that helped create and reinforce French unity, while contributing to the disintegration of rival allegiances.

The cultural underpinnings of rural society, already battered by material changes, were further weakened by shifting values. First of all, manual labor was devalued—or better still, the natural aversion to its drudgery was reinforced. The elementary schools, designed to form citizens, neglected producers. The school glorified labor as a moral value, but ignored work as an everyday form of culture. The well-established contrast between the plucky, mettlesome spirit of the *courageux* and the idle *fainéant*—the one hardworking, especially or only with his hands, the other avoiding manual labor—was translated into scholastic terms. Soon, the idle boy was the one likely to be the most pressed into hard physical labor, the plucky boy the one most enterprising with his books. It made good sense, for the rewards of work now came to those not doing what had once been recognized as work. But it opened a crack—one more—in age-old solidarities.

In a great many homes, illiterate adults depended on small children to carry out what were becoming essential tasks—accounting, correspondence, taking notes, reading aloud pertinent documents or newspaper items. And new literacies at whatever level made new ideas accessible, especially to the young, to whom certain profound changes in the political climate of country districts were now attributed. In any case, the relationship between school and social claims was not ignored in their own time: "The Republic has founded schools," sang Montéhus, the revolutionary chansonnier, "so that now the people have learned how to count. The people have had enough of the pauper's mite; they want an accounting, and not charity!" More important, where, as in Brittany, a determined campaign taught new generations French, "children and parents form two worlds apart, so separated in spirit, so estranged by speech, that there is no more community of ideas and feelings, hence no intimacy. Often, as a matter of fact, any kind of relationship becomes impossible." This is both exaggerated and suggestive of a generation gap more easily discerned in modern societies than in traditional ones. But even granting the exaggeration, the corrosive effects of one sort of education on a society based on another kind are undeniable.

Like migration, politics, and economic development, schools brought suggestions of alternative values and hierarchies; and of commitments to other bodies than the local group. They eased individuals out of the latter's grip and shattered the hold of unchallenged cultural and political creeds —but only to train their votaries for another faith.

Bibliography

J. ALBISETTI, *Secondary School Reform in Imperial Germany* (1983).

K. AUSPITZ, *The Radical Bourgeoisie: The Ligue de l'Enseignement and the Origins of the Third Republic 1866–1885* (1982).

D. R. BROWER, *Training the Nihilists: Education and Radicalism in Tsarist Russia* (1975).

J. CHANDOS, *Boys Together: English Public Schools 1800–1864* (1984).

R. GELDER, *Education in Provincial France, 1800–1914: A Study of Three Departments* (1983).

J. S. HURT, *Elementary Schooling and the Working Classes, 1860–1918* (1979).

J. C. MCCLELLAND, *Autocrats and Academics: Education, Culture, and Society in Tsarist Russia* (1979).

J. A. MANGAN, *Athleticism in the Victorian and Edwardian Public School: The Emergence and Consolidation of an Educational Ideology* (1981).

D. G. PAZ, *The Politics of Working-Class Education in Britain, 1830–1850* (1981).

L. S. STRUMINGHER, *What Were Little Girls and Boys Made Of? Primary Education in Rural France 1830–1880* (1983).

G. WEISZ, *The Emergence of Modern Universities in France, 1863–1914* (1983).

The Constitution of the German Empire

GORDON CRAIG

Otto von Bismarck was in more ways than one the founder of the German Empire. His diplomatic ventures involving Prussia in three wars between 1863 and 1870 established a united Germany under Prussian leadership. For over twenty years Bismarck served as Chancellor of that nation. But Bismarck also wrote the constitution of the German Empire. In fact he wrote two constitutions—one for the North German Confederation in 1867 and a second for the German Empire proclaimed in the Hall of Mirrors at Versailles in 1871. This constitution had consequences for Germany and ultimately for Europe that were little less momentous than Bismarck's diplomacy.

Written constitutions had been a traditional goal of nineteenth-century political liberals throughout Europe. But just as Bismarck had achieved the liberal goal of a unified Germany through the conservative institutions of the Prussian army and monarchy, so also did he forge a written constitution that protected conservative interests and allowed traditional conservative institutions to dominate potentially liberal ones. Immense authority was placed in the hands of the Emperor and his Chancellor. The Reichstag, or Parliament, had the power of debate and approval but could not initiate legislation. Important local powers resided with the various states, and that situation also removed possible initiatives from the Reichstag. Perhaps most important, the army remained quite independent. Its budget did require Reichstag approval, but eventually such approval covered a budgetary period of seven years.

Historians and other observers have always been puzzled over why the Reichstag did not seek to expand its powers. Among the explanations are the heritage of Hegelian political philosophy, the memory of the failure of the Prussian parliament to curb the monarchy and the army in the 1860s, and the very real fear that should the Reichstag become too active Bismarck and the Emperor might simply, on their own authority and backed by the army, promulgate a new, even more conservative constitution. In any case virtually all key

Copyright © Oxford University Press 1978. Reprinted from *Germany 1866–1945* by Gordon A. Craig (1978) by permission of Oxford University Press.

decision-making authority resided with the Emperor and his direct appointees, thus establishing a situation that had momentous consequences during the diplomatic crisis of the summer of 1914.

Among the many messages sent to Berlin by friendly governments after the formal proclamation of the new Empire was one from the government of the United States of America. In it President Ulysses S. Grant congratulated the German Government in the name of the American people for having completed the long-desired unification of its territory and for its decision to embark on its new career as a federal union like the United States itself, a decision, the President indicated none too delicately, that showed a desire for speedy progress towards the blessings of democracy.

This engaging exercise in self-satisfaction must have amused its recipient, Prince Bismarck, and he subsequently made a point of assuring American visitors gravely that he had been much influenced by the United States constitution when making his own plans for Germany. It is quite possible that he had gone so far as to read that document, but it would be difficult to demonstrate that he borrowed anything from it. The similarities that President Grant found between the two constitutions were as superficial as his prophecy concerning Germany's future political course was erroneous.

One should not, of course, be too hard on the President. He was not alone in failing to understand the constitution of the German Empire. Indeed, in 1867, when it was being considered in its original form, as the constitution of the North German Confederation, a fair number of German politicians, charged with protecting the interests of their states, had also failed to understand it until after they had accepted it and had learned belatedly that they had misinterpreted clauses that were to affect them very nearly. In its original form and in the somewhat amended one it assumed when it was adapted in 1871 to the needs of the imperial federation, the constitution was a complicated instrument. This was necessarily so, because its author set out deliberately to draft a document that would provide the legal basis for the kind of national union desired by public opinion and by German economic interests, while at the same time preventing the resultant state from entering upon the road that President Grant believed it was destined to travel. The basic purpose of the constitution, in short, was to create the institutions for a national state that would be able to compete effectively with the most powerful of its neighbours, without, however, sacrificing, or even limiting, the aristocratic-monarchical order of the pre-national period. This task invited complication, and it was in fact achieved at the price of ambiguities and contradictions that were always awkward and, as the years passed, invested German parliamentary life, and politics in general, with an increasing amount of friction and frustration.

I

The Empire was a union of eighteen German states of various sizes and forms of government, and one administrative territory, the so-called Reichsland, which comprised the conquered provinces of Alsace and Lorraine and was administered by an imperial governor-general. The federal government consisted of an executive, in the persons of the Emperor and his Chancellor and their staffs, a Federal Council (Bundesrat), composed of delegations from the separate states, and a National Parliament (Reichstag), which was elected by universal manhood suffrage and secret ballot.

The federal executive possessed important powers, particularly in areas that could affect the life and death of citizens. The Emperor exercised control over the whole area of foreign policy, with the right to make treaties and conclude alliances, as well as to declare war and conclude peace. By virtue of the royal power of command (*Kommandogewalt*), a constitutional concept which jurists found it difficult to explain or define, he commanded the forces of all of the German states in time of war and most of them in time of peace (although, when doing so, it was in his capacity as King of Prussia rather than Emperor, a point to which we shall return); and he had appointive and administrative powers of remarkable breadth and importance, such as the right to declare martial law in case of civil disorder and, in emergency, to declare federal execution against dissident member states and to sequester their territory and their rights of sovereignty. In addition, he was empowered to appoint and dismiss the Chancellor and all other officials of the federal government, to summon, prorogue, and close the Reichstag, to publish and supervise the execution of all federal laws. Finally, he possessed the right to interpret the constitution, a privilege whose importance cannot be overestimated. Bismarck sometimes claimed in his last years, when he had become impatient with restrictions on his own authority, that he was the only interpreter of the constitution, for he was its author. But the Chancellor was only the agent of the Emperor, as Bismarck's own case proved, and Laband, an authority on this ambiguous document, claimed that the monarch was 'the guardian of the constitution'.

Acting through the Reichstag and the Bundesrat, the federal government had legislative authority in the field of commercial and tariff policy, matters of transportation and communications, control of the banking system, coinage and international exchange, weights and measures, patents, consular rights, and other matters of importance to Germany's economic well-being.

It had the right to collect tolls and sales taxes on certain articles like sugar, salt, tobacco, beer, and spirits, and received the income of the postal and telegraph systems.

It will be apparent from this that quite considerable powers were left to the individual states. In all matters that affected the citizen's daily life and the safety and well-being of his family, they possessed jurisdiction. Thus such important areas of public life as education, health services, and police were within the purview of the separate states rather than the federal government, and so were civil liberties, for it must be noted in passing, as one more curiosity of the imperial system, that, unlike the constitutions of other nations, and unlike the German constitution of 1849, Bismarck's included no bill of rights or declaration of fundamental liberties. In addition, the execution of most of the laws that were passed by the federal government was left to the governments of the individual states, the federal government merely reserving the right of supervising the administrative arrangements made for this purpose. Tolls and postage due to the federal government were collected by local authorities and then transferred, a system that subtly underlined the states' disinclination to tolerate federal intervention in local matters. In another respect, the states had financial prerogatives denied to the central government, for they alone had the right to collect direct taxes, a privilege that the federal government tried vainly to have modified as financial difficulties mounted in the Wilhelmine period.

In the rights they enjoyed the member states were not equal, the larger ones having exacted certain privileges from Bismarck as their price for joining the union. All of the states of southern Germany which had not been members of the North German Confederation were exempted from the taxes upon beer and spirits, which gave them a preferred position in the national tax structure. The kingdoms of Bavaria and Württemberg were allowed to retain their own railway, postal, and telegraph systems, and were permitted military privileges not extended to other states. Württemberg administered the affairs of its own army and appointed most of its officers, despite the fact that its contingent became a part of the Prussian army. Bavaria retained full command of its armed forces in peacetime, and continued to have a separate War Ministry and General Staff, although their activities were closely supervised by the Prussian military. As a matter of prestige, the Bavarian Government insisted also on the retention of certain rights of diplomatic representation, and to satisfy its desire for an influence on policy-formulation a foreign affairs committee was established within the Bundesrat under Bavarian presidency and with two other permanent members (Saxony and Württemberg) and two elected ones. This gratification was all but meaningless, since Bismarck was no believer in foreign policy by committee and consulted the committee only once in the course of his twenty years as Imperial Chancellor.

All of the individual states sent delegations to the Bundesrat, and it was theoretically possible for them to use that body as a means of changing the constitution in their interest whenever they cared to do so. But the most striking feature of the Federal Council was the strong position occupied by Prussia, which, by virtue of its size and influence in Germany as a whole, possessed 17 of the 58 votes cast in that body. This was more than enough to enable it to block constitutional amendments that were not to its own interest, and Bismarck at the outset was always confident that in basic matters Prussia would stand on the side of the federal government and would veto any proposed constitutional change that would subvert the Reich it had founded.

Nevertheless, the states retained very extensive powers, a fact that caused much agonizing on the part of advocates of a high degree of centralization. The historian Heinrich von Treitschke, an ardent battler for the concept of a Prussian-controlled unitary state, was appalled by the reserve clauses in the treaties between the North German Confederation and the south German governments and felt that this would mean that the Empire would be hobbled from the beginning by those forces of particularism which had, for so long, stood in the way of effective unification. As a practical politician, Bismarck knew that the concessions he had made, while offensive to some, were the most effective way of breaking down the resistance of the southern governments ('The maiden is ugly,' as someone said at the time, 'but she has got to be married'), and he could take comfort in the fact that, apart from the financial exemptions, the privileges would not amount to much. One distinguished Bavarian politician agreed with him. Prince Hohenlohe-Schillingsfürst said that it would have been wiser of his government to have been concerned less with the retention, for sentimental reasons, of specific Bavarian institutions and more with enhancing Bavarian influence in all federal matters that would affect the kingdom.

Apart from his concern over the practical problems that had to be dealt with promptly in the last months of 1870, Bismarck had other reasons for the attitude he adopted towards states' rights. The south German states were not the only ones that viewed the elaboration of federal institutions with distrust and had a jealous regard for their own privileges and traditional ways. In a sense, the Prussians were as particularistic as the Bavarians, and they had no more desire to merge with the Reich (*in das Reich aufzugehen*) than they had shown in 1849. Bismarck agreed with this attitude, although for reasons of his own. The continued existence within the Reich of an enlarged Prussian state with a virtual monopoly of military power, with a position in the Bundesrat superior to that of the other states, and with a parliamentary system of its own, based on a form of suffrage which was not democratic but favoured the propertied classes, was the best possible assurance against any possibility of the federal government succumbing to the forces of liberalism and democracy. In Bismarck's constitutional system, the federal government was given enough influence (particularly with Prussian backing) to keep the particularism of the south within safe bounds, while Prussia was allowed to retain sufficient power to protect the aristocratic-monarchical system by discouraging dangerous experiments on the part of the federal government. The provisions of the constitution, and the omissions from the constitution, that favoured states' rights were inspired by Bismarck's attitude towards the theory of checks and balances, although the elaborateness of his application of that theory might have bewildered its author Montesquieu. In Bismarck's system, as Otto Pflanze has written, every pressure was neutralized by a counter-pressure—the principle of centralization by that of states' rights, the separate states by the federal government, the federal government by Prussia, the nation by the dynasties, and the Reichstag by various legal and psychological factors built into the imperial system.

II

One could, without insuperable difficulty, compose a reasonably plausible argument to the effect that the German Empire of 1871 was the creation of the German people, or, at least, that the Reich would never have come into being if it had not been for the persistent and growing popular desire for unification. Certainly, the German people had a better claim to authorship than the German princes, whose selfishness and narrowness of view had been notorious over the centuries and whose lack of national sense had been demonstrated by their perpetual internecine quarrels and their not infrequent alliances with foreign Powers. Yet Bismarck was little interested in their actual historical role in the process of unification when he stage-managed the proclamation of the Reich at Versailles. He not only gave the princes the privilege of offering the imperial crown to William I of Prussia (who showed little gratitude for this generosity but, at least, unlike his brother in 1849, did not refuse the gift) but also built upon this contrived gesture a constitutional theory that held that the Reich was the creation of Germany's dynastic houses.

There was, in short, to be no nonsense about popular sovereignty in the new Empire. The German people were not to be allowed to claim the dangerous powers that the American people, for example, could demand on the basis of their Declaration of Independence and the preamble of their constitution. On the contrary, it was to be clear from the outset that the Reich was a gift that had been presented to them and that, if it were not properly appreciated, it might be withdrawn. The unspoken corollary to Bismarck's constitutional theory—which was to obsess him during his last year in office—was that, if the situation warranted it, if the German people did not in fact show the loyalty and gratitude that their leaders had a right to expect, then the princes could unmake their own creation and refashion it in any way they saw fit.

In the years of constitution-making, Bismarck was still reasonably confident with respect to the loyalty of the broad masses of the German people, and, while setting his face against theories of popular sovereignty, he did not hesitate to give them the weapon that has always been the principal instrument of such sovereignty, namely the ballot. When he had first announced his support of the idea of giving the vote to the people, it had been during the last stages of the political duel with Austria, and he had been principally interested in taking a position in national affairs that would embarrass his antagonist and bring public opinion to the support of the Prussian cause. But when the necessity of outmanoeuvring the Austrians had passed, he did not change his mind, presumably because he believed that the common people could be counted upon to respond instinctively to appeals to their loyalty. He wrote in 1866:

> At the moment of decision the masses will stand on the side of kingship, regardless of whether the latter happens to follow a liberal or a conservative tendency.... May I indeed express it as a conviction based on long experience that the artificial system of indirect and class elections is much more dangerous than that of direct and general suffrage, because it prevents contact between the highest authority and the healthy elements that constitute the core and the mass of the people. In a country with monarchical traditions and loyal sentiments the general suffrage, by eliminating the influences of the liberal bourgeois classes, will also lead to monarchical elections.

Because he felt this way, he saw to it that both the constitution of the North German Confederation and that of the Reich that succeeded it provided that elections to Parliament should be by vote of all male citizens who had reached the age of twenty-five and that this vote should be held by secret ballot.

This was less revolutionary than William I had thought when Bismarck first proposed it to him. Bismarck had no intention of allowing the National Parliament to be filled with genuine members of the lower classes, who might be too conscious of the condition of their fellows and too intent upon correcting it. He prevented this possibility by the simple expedient of stipulating that Reichstag members would receive no salaries. He also seriously restricted parliamentary power. The Reichstag's assent was required for all legislation, but it had few powers of initiative and for the most part merely acted upon matters brought before it by the Chancellor and the Federal Council. Draft legislation that it disliked it might amend or delay or even defeat, although in the last case, if the matter was considered important by the government, it could do so only at the cost of a dissolution of the Reichstag, followed by new elections, a prospect which parliamentarians did not ordinarily relish. It had no legal control over the Chancellor, for although the constitution declared that official to be the 'responsible' minister, this did not mean that he was responsible to the Reichstag or that a defeat of his policies would necessarily lead to his retirement, as it would in English constitutional practice. Nor did the Reichstag possess the kind of right of interpellation that would have forced the Chancellor to explain and defend policies in which its members had an interest at a time of their own choosing. Indeed, some important areas of policy were virtually closed to them. While Bismarck was Chancellor, he encouraged the Reichstag to interest itself in all aspects of the nation's economic policy, but he set his face firmly against debates about the extension of parliamentary powers or excursions by the Reichstag into the fields of foreign affairs and military policy, which he regarded as lying within the competence of the Chancellor's Office and the Crown. In the case of the military, indeed, even the Reichstag's power of the purse was meaningless during most of the Bismarck period.

Despite the limitations that he placed upon it, there is no doubt that Bismarck regarded the Reichstag as an important part of his constitutional system. At a time when the forces of particularism had not been fully subdued, it was a living symbol of the nation's hard-won unity and, as such, a control over divisive forces. In the management of Germany's foreign relations, it was a convenient and effective sounding-board, by means of which German attitudes and objectives could be given resonant expression. Bismarck had already demonstrated, at the height of the dispute over the Grand Duchy of Luxemburg in 1867, the way in which a parliamentary debate could be used to impress foreign opinion, and on frequent occasions during his chancellorship he was to resort to the same technique. Finally, as long as he could manage the Reichstag better than anyone else and secure its backing for government policy, the Reichstag provided Bismarck with a means of demonstrating to the Emperor, upon whose continued favour his own retention of office depended, that he was indispensable. For Bismarck, a well-behaved and cooperative Reichstag was a kind of insurance policy, and this was no less true in the case of his successors in office.

This being so, it is necessary to ask why the parliamentarians did not realize that the Chancellor was more dependent upon them than it might appear from the text of the constitution, and why they did not use the tactic of stubborn resistance, if not obstreperousness, to increase the Reichstag's influence in the state. The rights of debate and assent were, after all, not negligible powers, and they were protected by the legal stipulation that the Reichstag could not be prorogued indefinitely and that new elections must follow promptly upon dissolution.

That there was no more resort to obstructionism and that it was ineffective when tried is to be explained in large part by the nature of the Reichstag's membership and its attitude toward the role of the Parliament in the state. German parliamentarians as a group never acquired the self-confidence and sense of collegial solidarity that were enjoyed by members of Parliament in England or congressmen in the United States or that was common, in Germany, to bureaucrats and army officers. Although many gifted men sat on its benches, they were exceptions among a membership of mediocre minds. The Reichstag did not attract the best in the nation, and those who came to it did not seem to grow in its service. In its early days the percentage of notables and wealthy amateurs among its ranks was high; later these were replaced by an increasing number of full-time professional politicians, often serving particular economic interests. Except for a progressive narrowing of view, the change was not particularly significant. Common to both the Reichstags of Bismarck's years and those of the period before the First World War was a notable lack of enthusiasm about the prospect of challenging the political establishment—that is, the Crown and its agencies—in matters of political importance. This reluctance to seek and fight for widened influence is perhaps understandable in the Reichstag of the 1870s, for the memory of the Prussian constitutional conflict of the 1860s was still green, and few of the deputies who had been a part of that relished the thought of its repetition. This, as much as anything, explains the cave-in of the National Liberals in 1874 over the question (in itself a memory of the 1860s) of the military budget. But it is striking that in the subsequent period there was no diminution of the Reichstag's reluctance to demand a role in determining the requirements of national interest, and it is clear that many parliamentarians were uncertain about the legitimacy of such a demand. Because of this the Reichstag remained a body that reacted more than it acted, a legislative body which, because its members had no faith in their own ability to assume responsibility, contributed to the general lack of direction that characterized German politics after Bismarck's strong hand was removed.

It is tempting ... to attribute the excessive modesty with which members of the Reichstag regarded their role to the success that [Hegel] had had in persuading Germans that the institutions and forms of civilian life had no essential importance except in their relation to the State. This Hegel defined in a highly involved argument in his *Grundlinien der Philosophie des Rechts* (1821) [*Philosophy of Right*] as the highest form of freedom, which was attainable by the individual only when he had realized and transcended the limitations of the family on the one hand and civil society on the other. In Hegel's formulation, the State has at times an almost comically abstract quality, as when he describes it, in terms that tickled the fancy of the young Lassalle, as 'the reality of the substantial will which it has in its generalized self-awareness, the reasonable in and for itself'. But this description is followed by a passage that is, politically, both suggestive and ominous, as Hegel distinguishes between the State and civil society as such.

> If the State is confused with civil society, and is defined by security, the protection of property, and personal liberty, the interest of individuals as such becomes the ultimate purpose for which they are united, and it would follow that it is something arbitrary to be a member of the State. But the State has a very different relation to the individual; the State is objective spirit itself, and the individual has objectivity, truth, and morality only insofar as he is a member of it. The union as such is true substance and purpose, and what defines individuals is the fact that they lead a general life; their further specific satisfaction, activity, mode of behaviour has this substance and general validity as its starting-point and result.

Ralf Dahrendorf has pointed out that the decisive implication of these lines is that civil society—because it is constructed out of many individuals with contrary interests and passions and numerous parties and groupings that are competing for advantage—is incapable of bringing about a satisfactory constitution of human society. For this something else is needed—something that rises above the structures of civil society entirely—and that something is the State.

There can be no doubt that the long-delayed attainment of German unity was bound to give new weight to this theory, and ... Gustav Rumelin in 1870 could claim that Hegel's theory of history had now been confirmed. In these circumstances it was easy to identify the State with the Prussian Crown and its instrumentalities, the bureaucracy and the army above all, and to regard all agencies that sought to dispute their authority as mere manifestations of that divisiveness that characterized Hegel's civil society and had characterized Germany in its pre-national stage. No one was more effective in giving wide currency to the political implications of this identification than Heinrich von Treitschke, whose *German History*, an elaborate and eloquent tribute to the Prussian Crown, was perhaps the work that was most representative of the new national spirit, and whose enormously popular lectures on politics at the University of Berlin had deep and continuing influence on the generation that was to come to political responsibility after 1890. Although Treitschke distanced himself from the philosophical premises of Hegel's argument, he repeated its substance in his own rejection of the pluralistic society. Thus, in his lectures, he had no hesitation in declaring:

> Law and peace and order cannot come to the multiplicity of eternally struggling interests from inside themselves but only from that power that stands above society, armed with a force that is capable of taming wild social passion. Here one begins to get a clear conception of what can be called the moral sanctity of the State. It is the State that brings justice and reciprocal tolerance into the world of social conflict.

Here Hegel's abstraction has been transformed into the ultimate reality and, as Dahrendorf rightly says, the logical constitutional consequences were inescapable. To the neo-Hegelians and to Treitschke's auditors the Imperial Reichstag symbolized the conflict of interests and the mutual antagonism of parties that were destructive of true unity and that had to be resolved by the only authority that was in its essence non-partisan, the Crown. Whatever claims jurists like Paul Laband might make for its competence, the authority of the Reichstag was fatally compromised from the outset in the minds of those who, for emotional or intellectual reasons, accepted the new national conservatism that Treitschke preached. Unfortunately, until after the turn of the century, when the authority of the Crown was diminished by the behaviour of William II, the great majority of Germany's parliamentarians, if we leave the Socialists apart, did accept that philosophy.

III

In the proceedings in the Galerie des Glaces [Hall of Mirrors] in Versailles on 18 January 1871, the delegation of deputies from the Bundestag of the North German Confederation played, as has already been indicated, a negligible role. They were, however, although somewhat grudgingly, allowed to observe what went on, and some of them were appalled by what they saw. They had reason to be, for the ceremony resembled nothing more or less than a military review, a kind of *Großer Zapfenstreich* [great retreat], with Psalms 66 and 21 intoned by a soldiers' chorus, prayers at command..., the liturgy according to the *Militär-Kirchenbuch* [*Military Churchbook*], and, after the Emperor's proclamation, a thunderous playing of 'Heil Dir im Siegerkranz' [Hail to You in Victor's Garlands] and Frederick the Great's 'Hohenfriedburg' March by a military band. Except for the parliamentarians, nearly everyone was in uniform, with side-arms and decorations. Bismarck was no exception. Although he was at this time involved in a bitter dispute with Helmuth von Moltke, the Chief of the General Staff, in which the principle of civil supremacy was at stake, he did not allow this to affect his sartorial taste. He wore the blue coat of the Magdeburger Kürassiere with the insignia of a lieutenant-general, the orange ribbon of the Order of the Black Eagle, and high riding-boots, and carried a pointed helmet in his hand.

All in all, it was a brave show, but one need only look at Anton von Werner's painting of it to understand the better remark of the Catholic politician Ludwig Windthorst, who said, 'Versailles is the birthplace of a military absolutism like that brought to bloom by Louis XIV.' How were these arrogant warriors, whom Werner shows clustered around the warlord, to be kept under restraint?

Anyone who studied the constitution with this question in mind would have received little reassurance. Apart from the articles which placed the command of all federal forces in the hands of the Emperor, the most important provisions were to be found in Articles 60 and 63. The second of these stipulated that 'the Emperor determines the peacetime strength, the structure, and the distribution (*Einteilung*) of the army', and it was doubtless intended by its author to avoid the kind of parliamentary disputes about army organization that had produced the constitutional crisis of the 1860s. As it stood, it seemed to give the Emperor a kind of blank cheque for anything he might wish to do with his army. On the other hand, he was bound by the provisions of Article 60 of the constitution, which declared that the size of the armed establishment in peacetime must be determined by law; and there was no doubt that this gave the Reichstag an opportunity to exercise considerable control over the armed forces, particularly if its members insisted that the law determining the strength of the armed forces and its accompanying budget be periodically reviewed.

Such implementation of Article 60 the government was determined to prevent. In the debates of the constituent assembly of the North German Confederation in the spring of 1867 Bismarck had worked strenuously to establish the principle that the strength of the army and the funds provided should be automatically calculated on the basis of the size of the population, a system which, if accepted, would have effectively removed military affairs once and for all from the competence of the Reichstag. The liberal deputies had fought back so strenuously that Bismarck, not wishing to jeopardize the constitution as a whole, had agreed to a compromise, the so-called 'iron budget', which stipulated that the size of the army would, until 31 December 1871, be set at 1 per cent of the population and that the government, for its support, should be granted 225 talers for each man under arms. In 1871 this law was prolonged for another three years, but this was not enough for the army chiefs, who had set their hearts on financial security and complete freedom from parliamentary interference, and, in 1874, with the full support of the Emperor, they sought to settle the issue once and for all. At their urging, the government submitted to the Reichstag a draft law setting the size of the army at 401,659 men, a figure that was to be considered permanent in peacetime until such time as the government should announce a modification. This law was introduced by Moltke, doubtless in the hope that deputies would be too impressed by the victor of Königgrätz and Sedan to oppose his desires.

This tactic did not work, strong resistance to a permanent law manifesting itself in all parties except that of the conservatives, and a situation arose that resembled in some particulars the conflict between Crown and Parliament that had reached its height in 1862. It proved easier to solve, however. Bismarck, in ill health at this time and distracted by foreign affairs, had had, if we can believe what he told the British ambassador, no part in drafting the law, which had been largely the work of Roon, the War Minister, and the Emperor himself. Nor was he much enamoured of it. He had, during the constitutional crises, been the doughtiest defender of the army against parliamentary pretensions, but he was not enthusiastic over the prospect of an expansion of the army's role in the state. In both 1866 and 1870 he had had serious disputes with Moltke, whom he accused of poaching in his own preserve, and he suspected Edwin von Manteuffel, formerly Chief of the Military Cabinet and now one of the strongest supporters of the draft law, of intriguing against him in the hope of succeeding him as Chancellor. Leaving these personal factors aside, Bismarck did not enjoy the thought of having a law enacted that would not only free the army from parliamentary restraints but would make it independent of the civilian authority, which resided in his own person. So he rather relished the discomfiture of the soldiers when their plans went awry, and he resolved to use their difficulties to demonstrate how much they needed him.

He accomplished this by playing upon that essential weakness of the Reichstag members that has been commented on above: their dislike of finding themselves in opposition to the authority of the state. In a series of conversations with key parliamentarians, Bismarck said that it was becoming clear that, in a time of national insecurity, the Reichstag was resolved to render the country powerless. This was being done, moreover, by men who had been elected by patriotic electoral districts after they had posed as supporters of his own policies. If they thought that they could with impunity abandon the duty of supporting the best interests of the Reich, a dissolution of the Reichstag and new elections would prove them wrong. This hint was enough to throw the opponents of the draft law into disarray; they were soon accusing each other of having, by doctrinaire politics, caused what the distinguished Heidelberg jurist Bluntschli called a 'childish conflict between the Reichstag and the Emperor'; and before long there was a manifest desire for a compromise. Bismarck provided it. The strength of the army was established at the figure called for in the original draft law, but it was to stand for only seven years, after which time it had to be renewed.

The Septennial Law did not please the leaders of the army, and the Emperor himself seems initially to have resented Bismarck's willingness to compromise with people whom the monarch had, in a speech delivered after his bill had run into trouble, described as 'internal enemies' who were attempting to shackle 'the leadership of their imperial war-lord'. Upon reflection, however, William came to a more philosophical view. After all, he wrote to the War Minister, 'really in our time seven years are almost half a century when one thinks of the seven years from 1863 to 1870! In this way, we have the army organization intact for seven years and, after seven years, we will perhaps find ourselves *before*, or even *after*, another war; if not, then the population will have grown and we will have to increase the recruits...'

The military chiefs had, in fact, every reason to be satisfied. They had secured themselves against tight budget control, and they were protected against other forms of parliamentary interference by Article 63 of the constitution and by certain special circumstances arising from the curious relationship between the army and the Empire. The salient fact was that, in the strictest legal sense, there was no imperial army; the national force was an army made up of contingents from the separate states, under Prussian command. This being so, there was no imperial War Minister, unless Bismarck was to be regarded as such. The Chancellor did bear ultimate responsibility for military affairs before the Reichstag, but this did not mean a great deal, since he had no control over the internal affairs of the army. They lay within the competence of the Prussian War Minister, whose authority extended to all of the armed forces of the Empire and who supervised the General Staff, the Academy of War and other military schools, and the logistics, supply, and personnel departments. In the Reichstag, it was this official, rather than the Chancellor, who generally answered questions that might be raised by deputies curious about military developments; but trying to elicit information from him was always a frustrating experience, since he was empowered to answer points raised about imperial forces, if he wished, but not about the Prussian army, and was permitted to discuss administrative matters, but nothing that related to the command of the army (which the Emperor regarded as nobody's business but his own).

The military chiefs were not, however, content with the advantages that this situation gave them. In their eyes, the army was a church that needed worshippers and expected them to bring gifts but had no intention of giving them vestry privileges. To the high priests in the Military Cabinet and the General Staff, the War Minister's parliamentary function was a potential threat to the inviolability of their office, and they sought, therefore, if not to eliminate it, then to render it innocuous. In 1883, ... they succeeded, with Bismarck's assistance; and from that success can be dated the growing irresponsibility of the military establishment, which was to bear such tragic fruit in 1914.

IV

It will have become apparent from what has been said so far that the constitutional structure of the new German Empire was so clumsy and so full of contradictions and ambiguities that it would not be easy to run the Reich efficiently. Bismarck's system of checks and balances was so elaborate that even its author was uncertain at the outset about how it was to be managed. With his jealous regard for his own authority, he intended as far as possible to keep power in his own hands, but how was that to be done, and from what office? In the days when he was drafting the constitution of the North German Confederation, Bismarck apparently intended the office of Chancellor to be a relatively modest one; the Chancellor was to be little more than the presiding officer of the Bundesrat and would, like the other Prussian delegates to that body, receive his instructions from the Prussian Foreign Minister, that is from Bismarck himself. When the Reich was founded in 1871, Bismarck had long since given up that view and, indeed, the rather excessive emphasis upon Prussian supremacy implied by it. Indeed, he apparently intended to shift the balance the other way, for he assumed the position of Federal Chancellor and began to build up a strong Chancellor's Office (Reichskanzlei) under Rudolf Delbrück, while giving up the position of Minister President of Prussia (although not that of Foreign Minister). This did not work, and there was so much friction between the Prussian and federal governments that, after five months, Bismarck resumed the Prussian premiership. Without his roots in Prussian soil, he said, he was incapable of directing imperial affairs. 'If you make me only a minister of the Reich,' he said later, 'then I am sure that I will be just as bereft of influence as any other minister.'

Yet even with the three key positions in his strong hand, Bismarck found it difficult to run the affairs of the Empire without constantly having to deal with conflicts of competence between its component parts and to wrestle with problems that were the result of compromises written into the charter. He was never free of the irritation caused by indifferent execution of federal laws by local agencies or of the fear that privileges accorded to the Crown and the army might by misused by irresponsible advisers or ambitious brass-hats. At the same time, the constitutional system provided so many opportunities for obstructionism and even for defiance of federal authority that the most expeditious way of solving crises often seemed to be to threaten to resort to constitutional revision, or, in plainer words, to the correction of the situation by force rather than existing law. Between 1867 and 1871 various state governments had been bullied into co-operation by these means, and on frequent later occasions the fear of a *coup d'état* persuaded other groups to be co-operative. Early in his official life Bismarck had explained the technique to his friend Roon. 'Once there has been some rattling about with references to proclamations and the making of *coups*, my old reputation of being given to the frivolous application of force stands me in good stead, for people say, *"Nanu, geht's los!"* [There now, he's going off again]. Then all the people in the middle and all the half-hearted moderates are ready to negotiate.' He never abandoned his belief in the efficacy of the method and he was not alone in believing in its legitimacy. In a sense, as Michael Stürmer has written, the threat of destroying the constitution was a constitutional factor of major importance in Imperial Germany.

Bibliography

H. BOEHME, *The Foundation of the German Empire: Select Documents* (1971).
L. L. FARRAR, JR., *Arrogance and Anxiety: The Ambivalence of German Power, 1848–1914* (1981).
T. S. HAMEROW, *The Social Foundations of German Unification, 1858–1871* (1972).
I. V. HULL, *The Entourage of Kaiser Wilhelm II, 1888–1918* (1982).
K. H. JARAUSCH, *Students, Society, and Politics in Imperial Germany: The Rise of Academic Illiberalism* (1982).
A. J. MAYER, *The Persistence of the Old Regime: Europe to the Great War* (1918).
O. PFLANZE, *Bismarck and the Development of Germany, The Period of Unification, 1815–1871* (1963).
J. J. SHEEHAN, *German Liberalism in the Nineteenth Century* (1978).
J. J. SHEEHAN, ed., *Imperial Germany* (1976).
F. STERN, *Gold and Iron: Bismarck, Bleichroder, and the Building of the German Empire* (1977).
F. STERN, *The Failure of Liberalism: Essays on the Political Culture of Modern Germany* (1972).
H. WEHLER, *The German Empire, 1871–1918* (1985).

One of the last British soldiers killed on the Western Front in November 1918.
Library of Congress

PART FOUR

Imperialism, War, and Revolution

The central event of twentieth-century European history was World War I. Political, social, and economic life as well as intellectual sensibilities have never been quite the same after the outbreak of that conflict. From Ireland to Russia the political map of Europe was redrawn. The war effort and the vast number of deaths in combat brought new pressures on the social structure. The resentments arising from the peace treaty and the postwar economic dislocation sowed the seeds for many of the interwar years' authoritarian political movements.

The first inklings of that conflict occurred in the late nineteenth-century great-power rivalry for overseas empire. By the closing decades of the century the industrial economy, made even stronger by the inventions of the second industrial revolution, ensured that the European nations were the most powerful on earth. Daniel Headrick demonstrates the remarkable extent to which Europe's world domination was based on its technological prowess at the time and the military advantage its technology gave it over other nations. That military power would, of course, only too soon be turned by Europeans against each other.

In 1914 virtually no one had expected a long war. Michael Howard discusses the pre–World War 1 expectations of the officers and general staffs as to the character of future war and suggests why the cult of the offensive, which sent tens of thousands of men to their deaths, held sway for so long. As the war continued with previously unimaginable losses, domestic political discontent began to surface. Nowhere was that discontent more important than in Russia. Tsuyoshi Hasegawa explains the manner in which the war effort changed the economic structure of Petrograd and how pressures of wartime production led to worker unrest that various radical political parties would use to their own revolutionary ends.

In the wake of the hundreds of thousands of wartime casualties and the destruction of so many values and shared social expectations, various writers attempted to suggest what Europe would have been like had the war not occurred and so many talented persons not died. Robert Wohl discusses how the myth of a generation of gifted Englishmen lost in the war came to explain for many people why England so faltered during the twenties and thirties. In that regard he demonstrates that a myth about the past really furnished a myth for the present.

The Tools of Imperialism: Technology and the Expansion of European Colonial Empires in the Nineteenth Century

DANIEL R. HEADRICK

By the close of the nineteenth century, the European powers, most especially Great Britain, France, and Germany, directly or indirectly governed and sought to exploit vast areas of the non-European world. Europeans had partitioned virtually all of Africa. Britain directly ruled the Indian subcontinent and exercised broad informal influence over much of Latin America as well as over areas of English settlement in Canada, Australia, and New Zealand. France governed Indo-China, and all of the powers enjoyed special trade relations with China that had been imposed by force. With the Spanish-American War of 1898, the United States appeared on the world scene as an imperial power.

This "new" imperialism—a name that distinguishes the phenomenon from the conquests of the sixteenth century—has stirred a vast and still largely unresolved debate among historians over the motives of the imperial powers. Factors relating to drives for economic profit, considerations of naval strategy, advantages for the domestic policy of imperial statesmen, and the need for Europeans to impose order over foreign situations that had become unstable have been brought to the fore as explanations.

Questions other than those of motives may also be raised about the "new" imperialism. Many of these are no less important, and some are more easily solved. One such question is how Europeans could so flagrantly and effectively impose their wills on other peoples. The key factor in that exercise of power would appear to be the technology of transport and weaponry that Europeans brought to the effort. This technology included the steamboat, which permitted the penetration of inland rivers and strategically important shallow coastal water,

Reprinted with the permission of the author and University of Chicago Press from "The Tools of Imperialism: Technology and the Expansion of European Colonial Empires in the Nineteenth Century," by Daniel R. Headrick, in *Journal of Modern History*, vol. 51 (1979), pp 234–262. Copyright © 1979 by The University of Chicago.

advances in medical technology, especially the discovery of quinine, which permitted Europeans to survive the diseases in areas where their boats could penetrate, and finally, the sheer capacity for firepower made available through breechloading rifles, smokeless powder, and machine guns, which gave very small European armies or even small groups of Europeans deadly technological superiority over the peoples they sought to conquer. The significance of this technology is particularly demonstrated on those rare occasions, as in Ethiopia in 1896, when Europeans met defeat at the hands of non-European peoples armed with advanced weapons.

For a wave of imperialism to come about requires one of three possible scenarios: Adequate means are at hand and an increase in the motives triggers the event; sufficient motives exist and new means come into play which bring about the event; or, finally, both the motives and the means change, and both lead to the event. The first scenario—which [Rondo] Cameron sums up with the words "Western superiority... was a fact of long standing"—has formed the basis of the debate until now. It is the purpose of this paper to challenge the view by arguing that technological changes were indispensable to the expansion of Europe in the nineteenth century and profoundly affected its timing and location. Thus the third scenario becomes historically the more accurate one.

A model of causality in which the technical means are as indispensable as the motives does not imply that the two are unrelated. On the contrary, the appearance of a new technology can reinforce or trigger a motive by making the desired end possible or acceptably cheap. Conversely, a motive can provoke a search for appropriate means. So we must steer between two dangerous determinisms: the technological ("what can be done will be done") and the psychological ("where there's a will there's a way"). What this paper proposes, then, is not to combat any of the positions already taken in the great debate over the causes of the new imperialism but to add a new dimension to it.

Of the many devices and processes that Europeans used to penetrate and conquer their Asian and African empires in the nineteenth century, the earliest to appear was the steamboat. From the days of Vasco da Gama until the Russo-Japanese War, the Europeans possessed control of the seas, but their power only extended as far as the shore line. The great sailing men-of-war off the coasts of China, Japan, or Africa may have insulted or annoyed the inhabitants but could not conquer their lands. In the harbors and on the rivers that led to inland cities, European warships were difficult to maneuver, subject to grounding, and vulnerable to coastal cannon fire.

The limits of naval power determined the relations between Britain and China before the Opium War. While English ships could fire upon the Chinese forts at the mouth of the Pearl River—and did so as early as 1637—they could not threaten Canton nor any other important city. It was therefore easy for the Chinese to consider the English "barbarians from the sea" and refuse to take seriously the entreaties of such distinguished ambassadors as Lord Macartney in 1793 or Lord Amherst in 1816.

It was steam that opened up the rivers and shallow waters of the world to the Europeans. Early attempts to propel a boat by steam power—that of the Marquis de Jouffroy d'Abans on the Rhone in 1783, of John Fitch on the Delaware in 1786, of William Symington and Patrick Miller on the Clyde in 1788—had all failed for lack of an engine both small and powerful enough. In the first decade of the nineteenth century improvements in the steam engine removed this handicap. In 1807 Robert Fulton's *Clermont* proved that a steamboat could be a commercial success. This demonstration quickened the pace of development. In the second decade of the century steamboats of various kinds were built in America, Britain, and France, culminating in the establishment of regular steamer service between England and Ireland in 1816 and in the first transatlantic crossing by the *Savannah* under steam and sail in 1819.

Soon thereafter steamers appeared in Asian waters. The first was the little *Diana*, built at Kidderpore near Calcutta in 1823. Another craft, the steam dredge *Pluto*, was launched a year earlier but its engine was not attached to paddlewheels until 1824. The next year, the first steamer to reach Asia from Europe, the *Enterprize*, arrived after a voyage of 103 days, sixty-three of which were under steam.

These three craft soon became pioneers in imperialism. For in 1824 the Honorable East India Company had launched the first large-scale river war in modern history, against the Kingdom of Burma. The three steamers were requisitioned for war duties. The *Enterprize* served as a transport, ferrying troops and supplies from Calcutta to Burma. The *Pluto*, equipped with two cannon and four carronades, served as a floating battery during the attack on the Arakan coast. The *Diana* became the star of the war. She reconnoitered the Irrawaddy, chased and captured Burmese war boats, ferried troops, towed sailing ships, bombarded enemy positions with her Congreve rockets, and steamed up the river to Amarapura, 500 miles from the sea. The Burmese called her the "Fire Devil." The East India Company would have won the war without her, but she hastened the victory. With her help, Britain acquired Arakan, Pegu, and Tenasserim. The age of gunboat imperialism had begun.

Despite these successes, the early steamers were beset with problems. Their hulls suffered not only the usual indignities of all wooden vessels —dry rot, vermin, water seepage—but they also had problems which sailing ships avoided. The pounding of the machinery was hard on their wooden structure. The engines and fuel stole precious space from the crew, the stores, and the magazine. There was danger in a wooden ship with roaring fires on board and sparks flying out the chimney. Finally, due to the weakness of wood, a wooden ship large enough to carry engines and guns could not be made both shallow enough for river travel and strong enough to withstand the longitudinal stresses of ocean waves.

The solution was to build boats of iron. As early as 1787 the great iron founder and gunmaker John Wilkinson had experimented with an iron barge on the Severn. Further experimentation, however, was delayed three decades by the conservative mentality of British shipbuilders. Since iron does not float, they said, wouldn't an iron ship sink? Wouldn't it rust away, or attract lightning, or shatter on the high seas, or become burning hot in the sun? As a result of these compunctions, no sea-worthy iron boat was built until 1815, and not until 1820 did an iron steamboat, the *Aaron Manby*, prove it could steam across the Channel and up the Seine. For an iron boat not only floated, it was actually lighter and of greater capacity than a wooden one of equal displacement, since a two-and-a-half-inch iron beam could do the work of an oak girder two feet thick. Iron also proved to be more resilient than wood, less easily damaged by grounding, and easier to repair. An iron boat could be built with watertight bulkheads, greatly diminishing the dangers of shipwreck. And best of all, iron boats could be built in new shapes and dimensions difficult to achieve in wood: large but shallow-draft river boats or huge ocean liners. It is to iron that later ships owed their incredible diversity and specialization.

The idea of an iron steamer was not persuasive in itself but required visionary innovators. In one direction it led to the ocean liner, culminating in Isambard Kingdom Brunel's gigantic *Great Eastern*. In another, less grandiose but just as consequential, were the river steamers. In this field the pioneers were the Lairds of Birkenhead. In 1829 William Laird and his son John founded the firm of William Laird and Son and built their first iron boat, a sixty-ton lighter for use on Irish lakes. Two years later, news arrived that Richard Lander had traced the course of the River Niger by canoe from the Bussa Rapids to the Delta, thus completing the journey begun by Mungo Park three decades before. Macgregor Laird, William's younger son and the adventurous one in the family, decided to steam up the Niger from the sea and open up the interior of Africa to British trade and influence. His self-proclaimed motives were the mixture of philanthropy, Christianity, and profit hunger one often finds in explorers' narratives of the time: "... to create new and extensive markets for our manufactured goods, and fresh sources whence to draw our supplies; ... to raise their fellow creatures from their present degraded, denationalized and demoralized state nearer to Him in whose image they were created."

Yet this son of a shipbuilder was as much an enthusiast for technical progress as for business and religion:

> We have the power in our hands, moral, physical and mechanical; the first, based on the Bible; the second, upon the wonderful adaptation of the

Anglo-Saxon race to all climates, situations, and circumstances... the third, bequeathed to us by the immortal Watt. By his invention every river is laid open to us, time and distance are shortened. If his spirit is allowed to witness the success of his invention here on earth, I can conceive no application of it that would receive his approbation more than seeing the mighty streams of the Mississippi and the Amazon, the Niger and the Nile, the Indus and the Ganges, stemmed by hundreds of steam-vessels, carrying the glad tidings of "peace and good will toward men" into the dark places of the earth which are now filled with cruelty.

With other Liverpool businessmen Laird founded the African Inland Commercial Company "for the commercial development of the recent discoveries of the brothers Lander on the River Niger." They had two boats built. One, the *Quorra*, was a wooden steamer of 145 tons, 112 feet long and eight deep, with a forty horsepower engine. The other, the 55-ton *Alburkah*, measured seventy feet long by six-and-a-half feet deep, had a sixteen horsepower engine, and was built of iron. Both ships were heavily armed: In addition to handguns, the *Quorra* carried a four-pound swivel gun, an eighteen-pound carronade, and eight four-pound carriage guns; the *Alburkah* carried a nine-pound and six one-pound swivel guns.

In 1832 Macgregor Laird, Richard Lander, and their two steamers, accompanied by a sailing ship with supplies, headed for the Niger delta. The little *Alburkah* was the first iron steamer ever to venture out onto an ocean. The fleet arrived safely at the Bight of Benin, and from there the steamers successfully navigated through the delta and up the Niger as far as its confluence with the Benue. As a demonstration of the power of steam to penetrate Africa, the expedition was a great success. As a venture in commerce and religion, however, it failed completely. Technological advances, in overcoming one obstacle of nature, often bring to light another. In this case it was malaria: Of the forty-nine whites on the expedition, forty died, and Laird himself returned home in 1834, having lost his fortune and his health in Africa. The motives were all there, but the means were not. The European penetration of Africa had to wait another twenty years.

Though tropical Africa was still closed to European penetration, the Lairds had proven the value of iron steamers. The firm began to build a great number of them for distant destinations. Their *John Randolph*, sent to Savannah in 1834, was the first iron steamer to operate in American waters. In 1836 Francis Rawdon Cherney explored the Euphrates River on the Laird-built iron steamer *Euphrates*. And in 1837 Mehemet Ali purchased the *Egyptien* to navigate the Nile. But their greatest success was to be in the Far East, where their boats contributed a great deal to the growth of British power.

The first steamship to reach China was the *Forbes*, which arrived there from Calcutta in 1829 or 1830. The English merchant colony in China quickly recognized the potential value of steam for river transportation. In

1835 they petitioned their Chinese counterparts for permission to send the little steamer *Jardine* up the Pearl River from Macao to Canton.

Anglo-Chinese relations were tense. Several British diplomatic missions had failed to persuade the Chinese government to permit more trade. Meanwhile the English thirst for tea and the Chinese craving for opium were growing apace. When in 1834 the East India Company lost its monopoly on the Chinese trade, merchant adventurers began crowding in, sensing huge profits in the tea and opium business. What the British traders called free enterprise was smuggling and piracy to the Chinese officials, and what was law enforcement to them the traders saw as unjustified and whimsical interference.

So the Chinese were not pleased at the thought of a "fire ship" steaming up to Canton. The acting governor ordered it to stay away: "... if [the captain] presumes obstinately to disobey, I, the acting governor, have already issued orders to all the forts that when the steamship arrives they are to open a thundering fire and attack her. On the whole, since he has arrived within the boundaries of the Celestial Dynasty, it is right that he should obey the laws of the Celestial Dynasty. I order the said foreigner to ponder this well and act in trembling obedience thereto." But the foreigners were not reduced to trembling obedience by threats of thundering fire from the forts along the river. As William Jardine, one of the richest of the traders, said in 1834: "Nor indeed should our valuable commerce and revenue both in India and Great Britain be permitted to remain subject to a caprice, which a few gunboats alongside this city would overrule by the discharge of a few mortars."

These tensions finally led to the Opium War. Behind the British willingness to attack one of their best trading partners lay the knowledge that they now had the "few gunboats" they needed to make a mockery of the "thundering fire" of the Chinese forts. In 1836 John Laird had offered to build an iron frigate for the Royal Navy, but the Admiralty rejected his idea. The East India Company, fortified by its experience in Burma, was not nearly so conservative. In 1839 the Secret Committee of the Court of Directors of the Company commissioned him to build a most unusual ship, to be called the *Nemesis*. She was the biggest iron ship to be built up to that time: 184 feet long, displacing 630 tons, and propelled by two steam engines of sixty horsepower each. She was armed with two pivot-mounted thirty-two-pound guns, five six-pounders, ten small swivel guns, and a rocket launcher, and she could carry a crew of up to ninety men. Despite her size, she only drew six feet of water fully loaded, less when ready for battle. This was not just another steamboat but a weapon of imperialist warfare, "peculiarly adapted for that particular service," said her captain, William Hall.

On March 28, 1840 the *Nemesis* left England bound for Odessa, "much to the astonishment of everyone; but those who gave themselves time to reflect, hardly believe it possible that such could be her real destination."

Once at sea, Captain Hall announced to the crew that she was headed for Ceylon instead; she was thus the first iron steamer to pass the Cape of Good Hope. In Ceylon, Hall received orders to proceed to Malacca, and there he was finally told his real destination: China. He arrived off Macao on November 25, 1840.

The *Nemesis* was not the only steamer to see action in the Opium War. A number of wooden steamers from the Bay of Bengal—the *Atalanta*, the *Madagascar*, the *Queen*, even the old *Enterprize*—came to lend their support. A year later the new frigate *Sesostris* arrived, and so did the *Phlegethon*, another Laird-built iron river steamboat. By the end of the war, eighteen steamers saw action in China, of which fifteen belonged to the East India Company. With the arrival of the steamers, especially the *Nemesis*, Sino-European relations acquired a whole new character. No longer was it the classic futile confrontation of the whale and the elephant. The steamers brought modern warfare into the heart of China.

China was well equipped for seventeenth-century warfare. Against Western attack her main defense was a line of forts on the Bogue below Canton, at Taku on the approaches to Peking, and at several other points along the coast. These forts were heavily armed, but their cannon, some of which were two centuries old, were charged with weak and unreliable powder and embedded in the masonry so they could not be aimed. In 1840 the forts of the Bogue were easily silenced by broadsides from the British ships of the line, then taken by marines. On water the Chinese were similarly out-gunned, for their war junks were large unwieldy affairs armed with two to six pieces of artillery lashed to blocks of wood and impossible to aim. Their crews carried swords, spears, and gingals. Attempts to remedy this situation proved futile. Before the war began, Commissioner Lin had bought the British warship *Cambridge*, but he lacked both the guns to arm her and sailors skilled in handling a European ship. Against the ordnance of the British ships, the coasts of China were almost defenseless. And to the problem that navies had always faced against coastal defenses, the British now had a solution: steamers.

In some instances—as in the attack on the Bogue forts or on the city of Tinghai—steamers were used as tugboats to pull the big ships of the line into position to fire their broadsides at the enemy. At other times they pulled boats full of marines to the site of amphibious attacks; shallow-draft steamers like the *Nemesis* were especially suited to such operations. With their quick maneuvers and Congreve rockets, river steamers could sink the best Chinese war junks with no trouble. They were also very effective against another favorite Chinese river tactic: fireboats filled with oily cotton set ablaze and cast adrift to smash against the British men-of-war. The steamers simply grappled them with hooks and pulled them out of reach of the warships.

Perhaps the most spectacular feat of the *Nemesis* was the attack on Canton from the rear in February 1842. While the sailing fleet slowly worked its way up the Pearl River, the *Nemesis* made her way through narrow inland channels which no warship had ever dared enter, destroying junks, bombarding forts, and terrorizing the population.

That the war did not end sooner only shows how long it took the Chinese government to realize what it was faced with. The loss of Canton was a defeat, but not yet a disaster. A year later, however, the British launched a major offensive up the Yangtze: eight ships of the line, ten steamers, and a host of lesser craft took part in it. The Chinese countered with paddle-wheel gunboats of their own, but without steam-engines to move them, they were an easy prey to the British steamers. At Chinkiang the fleet seized the junction of the Yangtze River with the Grand Canal. At this point the Chinese government realized that the British could cut Peking off from its rice supplies, and so it capitulated. Britain had found the means to impose her will on China.

The Opium War is no doubt the most striking case of the use of steamers in an imperialist venture, but it was far from the last. When in 1852 the British again attacked Burma, steamers were quite common in Indian waters, both as riverboats and as oceangoing ships. The East India Company had steam service on the major rivers of India, and the Peninsular and Oriental Steam Navigation Company was serving the Far East on a regular schedule. It was a simple matter to requisition a few of both kinds of steamers, in addition to the specialized gunboats *Rattler*, *Sesostris*, and *Phlegethon*, to make the success of this attack a forgone conclusion.

The story of Commodore Perry's visit to Japan in 1853–54 is too well known to warrant repeating here. It is worth pointing out, however, that this event does not belong only in histories of Japan and America but in the history of technology as well. At the very time that Perry was steaming into Tokyo Bay, a Russian fleet under Admiral Putiakin, which also included steamers, had appeared off the coasts of Japan. It was steam, not any individual or nation, which broke down the walls of Tokugawa Japan.

Other imperialist wars in Asia at that time followed much the same pattern. The Second Opium War (1856–60) was a repetition of the first, in weapons as in other ways. The Royal Navy used over twenty-five gunboats and other small steamers in its attack on Canton, on the Chinese fleet, and on the Taku forts near Peking. Gunboats also figured prominently in the French conquest of Tonkin in 1873–74 and of Annam in 1883, and in the Third Anglo-Burmese War of 1885. By the end of the century, the steamship and the river gunboat had become not just the instruments but the very symbols of European power in Far Eastern nations that had coastlines and navigable rivers. One of the protagonists of the colonial conquests of that time, Colonel W. F. B. Laurie, put it succinctly. Steamers, he pointed out, were "a 'political persuader,' with fearful instruments of speech, in an age of progress!"

In Africa, as Macgregor Laird discovered in 1832, the steamboat was not sufficient to carry the European presence into the interior. Here the obstacle was malaria, and only after it had been overcome could other technological advances become effective. There have been a number of scholarly studies by Philip Curtin, Michael Gelfand, and others on the influence of malaria on European-African relations. A brief summary of their findings will, therefore, suffice.

Although malaria was prevalent in many parts of the world, the variety caused by the *Plasmodium falciparum*, found only in Africa, was by far the deadliest. The death rates for newcomers to West Africa reflect this fact. In the 1790s among first-year European military personnel stationed in West Africa, the death rates ranged from 46 to 72 percent; for those who survived their first year, the death rate in subsequent years fell to about 10 percent. One study for the years 1817–36 found the death rates per annum of British soldiers in Britain to be 1.53 percent; in Sierra Leone it was 48.3 percent; and in the Gold Coast, 66.83 percent. While yellow fever, dysentery, and other ills played a part in these deaths, malaria was certainly the principal culprit. For good reason the British government withdrew almost all white military personnel from West Africa, replacing them with African or West Indian soldiers, whose death rates were lower.

Malaria was also the cause of disasters that befell countless expeditions into the interior of Africa. Early Portuguese missions up the Congo (1485) and into the interior of Mozambique (1569) suffered great losses. British explorers of the late eighteenth and early nineteenth centuries fared no better. William Bolt's expedition at Delagoa Bay in 1777–79 lost 132 out of 152 European members; Mungo Park's into the upper Niger in 1805 lost all Europeans; Captain James Tuckey's up the Congo in 1816 lost nineteen out of fifty-four; and the Lander-Laird expedition up the Niger in 1832–34 lost forty out of forty-nine, including Lander. In 1841–42 the British government sent a major expedition under Captain Trotter up the Niger on board three iron-hulled steamers, the *Albert, Wilberforce,* and *Soudan*; again tragedy struck as fifty-five out of 152 Europeans succumbed, much to the embarrassment of the government.

Despite these failures, the lure of Africa continued unabated. Part of this pressure was economic and philanthropic, but a large part was due to the ever enthusiastic Macgregor Laird. In 1852 he and some fellow businessmen set up the African Steamship Company, the first shipping line to offer a regular monthly service between England and Africa. This shipping line was to engage in the usual trade with the coastal middlemen. Laird knew, however, that even greater profits would await those who could overcome the disease barrier of the African interior and thus bypass the middlemen, and so he persisted in urging more expeditions.

The solution to malaria was a triumph not of science but of experimental technology. The plasmodium of malaria was not isolated until 1880, and the role of the anopheles mosquito as its vector was only discovered in 1898. By then a practical preventive, quinine prophylaxis, had been in use for many decades. Europeans had been familiar with the antimalarial properties of cinchona bark since the seventeenth century. Unfortunately its effectiveness was hampered by a number of drawbacks: It had to be imported from South America and was subject to deterioration, adulteration and price gouging; its use ebbed and flowed with medical fashions; it was used as a remedy rather than a preventive; and worst of all, it tasted awful. After a period of popularity in the eighteenth century, British doctors lost faith in the bark, for it did little to cure falciparum malaria and had no effect at all against yellow fever and all the other fevers which were then confused. Instead they prescribed bloodletting, blisters, mercury to cause salivation, and calomel for purgation. These treatments only served to kill a few more who might have survived without them.

Then in 1820 two French chemists, Joseph Bienaimé Caventou and Pierre Joseph Pelletier, isolated the quinine alkaloid of cinchona. Beginning about 1826 many experiments were carried out, mainly by British naval physicians stationed on the West African coast who were most concerned with tropical diseases. Their evidence began to show that quinine could be an effective prophylactic against malaria. By the 1830s quinine was being produced at a price low enough for general use. The practice of bleeding was falling into disfavor, and in the 1840s mercury and calomel treatments also began to decline. By 1848 Europeans along the Gold Coast started keeping quinine pills by their bedside, ready to be taken at the least sign of fever. Authoritative works appeared on the subject, including Dr. T. R. H. Thomson's "On the Value of Quinine in African Remittent Fever" and Dr. Alexander Bryson's *Report on the Climate and Principal Diseases of the African Station* and "On the Prophylactic Influence of Quinine."

In 1854 came the conclusive demonstration. Macgregor Laird received a contract from the Admiralty to build yet another steamer at his brother John's shipyard: the *Pleiad*. This was an iron-hulled schooner of 260 tons, with a steam engine of sixty horsepower turning a screw propeller. The captain, Dr. William Balfour Baikie, was a physician who saw to it that all Europeans on board religiously took their daily quinine. The ship sailed up the Niger and back, and no one died.

The discovery of quinine prophylaxis opened the gates to the European invasion of Africa. The *Pleiad* was quickly followed by other steamers that began regular journeys up and down the Niger, bypassing the delta middlemen and bringing British trade and eventually British domination into the Nigerian hinterland. Explorers like Richard Burton, John Speke, Gustav Rohlfs, Verney Cameron, and Henry Stanley carried with them supplies of quinine; all came down with malaria, but recovered and continued their travels. David Livingstone had his own "Livingstone pills" composed of quinine, calomel, rhubard, and resin of julep, which he gave to the whites who accompanied him; many suffered from malaria, but few died. When his drugs were stolen during his last expedition, he wrote in his journal: "I felt as if I had received the sentence of death," and not long after he died.

Explorers like Livingstone and Stanley and conquerors like de Brazza on the Congo, Dodds in Dahomey, and Gentil in Chad also made use of steamboats whenever they could. Given the difficult topography and flora of much of Africa, it is doubtful that Europeans could have penetrated the continent so fast or dominated it so thoroughly if they had had to do so on foot. And it is certain that they could never have done so without an antimalarial drug. Such was the demand for quinine that the cinchona forests of Peru could not keep up with it. In 1854, the year of the *Pleiad* expedition, the Dutch started cinchona plantations in Java with seeds smuggled out of Bolivia; six years later they were followed by British plantations near Madras. By the early twentieth century almost all the world's quinine came from these two areas. Thus European colonialism in Asia furnished the *sine qua non* of the scramble for Africa.

Both steamers and quinine prophylaxis represent the kind of technology that overcomes the obstacles of nature. But in venturing into new places Europeans also encountered the resistance of the inhabitants, a resistance which called forth the power of weapons and tactics. The history of imperialism is intertwined with developments in the art of war.

European superiority in land warfare was of long standing. Yet in distant parts of the world where indigenous peoples had the advantages of numbers and knowledge of the land, imperialism required not simply a one-to-one advantage but a crushing superiority, a disparity in power so great that small military units, even on occasion private exploring and trading parties, could overcome native resistance. This degree of superiority did not appear until the mid-nineteenth century and was the result of the revolution in firearms.

No period in history produced so dramatic a development of infantry weapons as the nineteenth century. In terms of effective firepower the distance between the rifle of World War I and the Napoleonic musket was greater than between the latter and the bow and arrow. Unlike quinine prophylaxis and river steamers, the modern gun was developed almost entirely for use among Europeans and Americans, and its application to colonial warfare was a fortuitous side effect. Yet ironically this new technology changed the balance of power in the non-Western world far more than it did in the West itself.

The development of the modern gun was the result of a complex series of minor advances from many different sources, some of them centuries old. Among them we can distinguish two stages. In the first stage percussion caps, rifling, cylindro-conoidal bullets, and paper cartridges brought the muzzle-loader to its peak of perfection. The second stage began with the breechloading Prussian needle gun and culminated in the Maxim gun. The shift from muzzle-loaders to breechloaders in the 1860s was no ordinary technical improvement. It dramatically widened the power gap between Europeans and non-Western peoples and led directly to the outburst of imperialism at the end of the century. To understand this momentous change, we must consider European and non-Western weapons and tactics and the resulting disparity of power, both before and after the 1860s.

At the beginning of the nineteenth century the standard weapon of the European infantryman was the muzzle-loading smoothbore musket with a bayonet. The Brown Bess, which British soldiers used up to 1852, was much the same weapon their forefathers had used at Blenheim in 1704. This gun had an official range of 200 yards, but even at half that distance it was so inaccurate that soldiers were advised to withhold their fire until they saw the whites of their enemies' eyes. Even so, said the gunmaker W. W. Greener, they commonly shot away their weight in lead for every enemy they killed. Since muzzle-loaders took a minute or more to reload, they were more useful as pikes than as guns.

The earliest change introduced into infantry guns was rifling. This caused the bullet to spin on its axis and fly straighter. The idea had long been used in experimental and sporting guns. In the War of Independence some American soldiers used hunting rifles with an effective range of 200 yards, roughly twice that of the Brown Bess. Likewise some French soldiers of the Revolution were armed with rifles, as were a few elite rifle corps in the British army. Yet the rifles of the early nineteenth century had drawbacks which made them unsuited to mass warfare. Bullets large enough to spin properly were difficult to ram home, and the barrels fouled very fast, making them even harder to load. Sportsmen could afford the care and attention that rifles required, but ordinary soldiers could not be expected to show such skills in the heat of battle. That is why the mass armies that fought in the Napoleonic Wars eschewed rifles. Nonetheless experiments with rifling continued, and special units such as the British Rifle Brigade or the Chasseurs d'Orléans, who went off to Algeria in 1830, were armed with rifles.

Another important advance was the percussion cap. Until the early nineteenth century, gunpowder had been ignited with a flintlock, a method which worked only in dry weather. In 1807 Alexander Forsyth introduced the use of fulminates as priming powders, and in 1816 Thomas Shaw patented the copper percussion cap. In tests by the Woolwich Board of the British army the new Brunswick percussion-cap rifle misfired only 4.5 times per thousand rounds, as compared with 411 times per thousand for flintlocks. As a result of these tests a few select British units were equipped in 1836 with Brunswick rifles. The impact of these guns can be judged from this account of a battle near Canton in 1841: "A company of sepoys, armed with flintlock muskets, which would not go off in a heavy rain, were surrounded by some thousand Chinese, and were in eminent peril when two companies of marines, armed with percussion-cap muskets, were ordered up, and soon dispersed the enemy with great loss."

The third important advance was the cylindro-conoidal bullet, developed to overcome the inaccuracy of the muzzle-loader. Ideally a bullet should be small enough to slip down the barrel easily, yet large enough to grip the rifling on the way out. Early efforts concentrated on making the bullet swell at the moment of firing. Of these, the most successful was that of Minié, whose bullet was long and pointed, with a plug at the back to make it expand. Not only did the Minié bullet take the rifling and spin well, but its streamlined shape helped give it a flat trajectory. The results were amazing. At 100 yards the Minié rifle hit the target 94.5 percent of the time, compared to 74.5 percent for the Brunswick; at 400 yards the figures were 52.5 and 4.5 percent, respectively. In 1849 Minié rifles were issued to units of the French army and two years later to some British troops. Since Europe was then at peace, the new weapons had to be tried out elsewhere. The French sent their Chasseurs d'Afrique (formerly Chasseurs d'Orléans) to fight the Algerians with new long-bullet rifles, while the British tested their Minié rifles against Africans in the Kaffir War of 1852. This stage in the evolution of the gun reached its peak in 1852–53 when the British army replaced the Brown Bess with the Enfield rifle which fired the new bullets. This was the first European military gun to be made on the "American system" of interchangeable parts. Its great advantage, like that of the French Minié, was its accuracy; it had an official range of 1200 yards and an effective one of 500 yards, five or six times greater than the Brown Bess....

Despite their astonishing range, these new rifles were slow and awkward to use. Soldiers needed a minute to reload, standing up in full view of the enemy. The guns emitted tell-tale puffs of smoke. They fouled badly. Their paper cartridges were delicate and vulnerable to moisture. And they could not be fired and reloaded on the run or on horseback. In their impact on Europe's imperial ventures, they were soon overshadowed by their successors, the breechloaders.

In Africa the gun revolution completed what quinine prophylaxis had begun. Its impact has been well documented in the *Journal of African History* and in Michael Crowder's *West African Resistance.* Guns were no novelty to most of Africa. North Africans had possessed firearms since the Renaissance. Before 1830 the people of Algeria made their own guns, sometimes with European barrels and locks; the cheaper, more common weapons were entirely homemade. South of the Sahara firearms had been introduced by the Portuguese and the Arabs. Here Africans seldom manufactured their own guns; lacking waterwheels to drive bellows, they could not achieve temperatures high enough to make good barrels. Yet those who lived near the coasts had no trouble obtaining guns and ammunition from European traders. These "Dane guns" were cheap, poorly made, and apt to burst. Yet they were most suited to the prevailing technology, since village blacksmiths could easily repair them if they broke, and since African gunpowder, being uncorned, was just weak enough for them. Bad as these weapons were, they were better than those of the Chinese who fought in the Opium War with matchlocks, spears, bows and arrows, and gingals.

Since Africans imported all their firearms, guns were progressively rarer as one got further from the coast. From a military point of view the interior of Africa was then divided into two zones. In the states of the savanna region, there was little sleeping sickness to kill off horses. There the mainstay of armies was the cavalry dressed in quilted cloth or leather and armed with shields, swords, and spears. Infantry troops carried bows and arrows, battle-axes, clubs, and javelins. Cities were protected by walls and moats. Firearms were few and costly, and ammunition and powder were too precious to be used in target practice. Some rulers dared not entrust their soldiers with guns until the day of battle. Despite a centuries-long acquaintance with firearms, the Sudanese states were just entering the age of guns when the Europeans interrupted them.

In the forest regions and in eastern and southern Africa, cavalry was rare and states were more loosely organized. Here large areas existed where the only firearms belonged to occasional Arab or European travelers and traders. Among the Africans the spear, the bow, poisoned arrow, and the assegai or throwing-spear were the favored weapons.

Before the 1860s the regions of Africa with the most backward weaponry were protected from European invasion by disease and remoteness. Only in a few places did Europeans venture beyond the coasts. In the Ashanti War of 1826, as in the First Anglo-Burmese War or the Opium War, British victories were the result of artillery and Congreve rockets and were heavily dependent on water transportation. The history of South Africa in the early nineteenth century is that of a long stalemate between a small number of whites armed with muskets and a larger number of Africans with assegais, axes, and a few guns. This stalemate was not broken until the whites obtained breechloading rifles and field artillery after the mid-century.

When the French attacked Algeria in 1830, they found the Algerian and Turkish troops armed with muskets and rifles equal to their own and often more accurate at long ranges. Soon the people of the hinterland arose under the direction of the brilliant guerrilla chief Abd el-Kader. To conquer Algeria, France poured in more and more troops. By 1846 there were 108,000 French soldiers, or one-third the French army, fighting an enemy of half that number. While these soldiers were equipped with the latest in guns, so were those of Abd el-Kader; at one point his army had 8,000 rifles of which 2,000 were English guns smuggled in through Morocco. It took France two decades of bitter and pitiless warfare to impose her rule on that recalcitrant colony. The conquest of Algeria may well serve as an example of imperialism without the benefits of technological superiority. The motivation was there, as was the willingness to sacrifice treasure and manpower.

What was lacking was the advantage which technological innovation gave the Europeans in their later imperial conquests.

That innovation was breechloading. The idea was simple: If a gun could be opened at the breech then it could be reloaded quickly and from a prone position. Furthermore a tighter and harder bullet could be used, making the rifling much more effective and increasing the range and accuracy. Breechloading is another of those inventions that recurred over many centuries until finally it worked. It, in turn, opened the door to other, more complex developments.

The earliest military breechloaders were the Sharp carbine used in the Mexican-American War of 1848 and the Dreyse needle-gun adopted by the Prussian army in the forties and fifties. Other nations still considered these weapons curiosities, as the British choice of the muzzle-loading Enfield in 1853 testifies. But in the war with Denmark in 1864 and again in the war with Austria in 1866, the needle-gun gave the Prussians two great advantages: Not only could Prussian soldiers fire three times faster than their enemies, but they could do so lying down or kneeling. No sooner had breechloading proven itself in battle than the French proceeded to rearm with the Chassepot, an even better weapon than the needle-gun. The British, somewhat more conservative, converted their Enfields to breechloading by fitting them with the Snider breech mechanism. After a final demonstration in the Franco-Prussian War, every European army switched to breechloaders.

Early military breechloaders fouled quickly and leaked hot gases out the breech; and the more they fouled the more they leaked, until soldiers had to hold them at arm's length to fire. This practice greatly impaired their effectiveness. The Royal Laboratory at Woolwich, which conducted extensive tests on breechloaders, realized that their weakness was the paper cartridge. A metal cartridge would solve these problems. In 1866–67 Colonel Boxer of the laboratory developed a brass cartridge that held the bullet, powder, and cap together, that was sturdy and waterproof and, best of all, sealed the breech during the explosion, allowing accurate aim. The Snider-Enfield of 1867 was the first military rifle of this new generation. Its range was extraordinary: While the needle-gun was accurate at 350 yards and the Chassepot at 650, the Snider-Enfield had a range of 1,000 yards. All major European armies scrambled to develop new weapons that could use the new metal cartridges. In the 1870s British soldiers were armed with the Martini-Henry, the French with the Gras, and the Germans with the Mauser.

In the eighties two more developments completed the gun revolution. One was the invention of smokeless explosives in 1885. These powders, based on nitrocellulose or nitroglycerine, were nonfouling, impervious to dampness, and more powerful than gunpowder. They propelled smaller bullets faster, hence further in a flat trajectory. Soldiers could now fire undetected and unhindered by clouds of smoke. Between 1886 and 1891 all

European armies abandoned the old gunpowder. The British even developed a specially stable explosive, Cordite, for use in the more extreme climates of the colonies.

The second invention was the magazine and the repeating mechanism. Repeating rifles existed at the time of the American Civil War, but were prone to explode when one bullet touched another. In 1877 the Scottish watchmaker James Lee patented a safe box-magazine. It was quickly adopted by every major army. In 1880 the French converted their Gras to Gras-Kropatchek repeaters, and in 1886 they replaced them with the newer Lebel; both weapons were tested in the Sudan. In 1884 the German army converted its Mausers to magazine loading, while the British did the same to a variety of rifles: Lee-Enfields, Lee-Burtons, Lee-Metfords. By the nineties military single-shot rifles were obsolete everywhere in Europe.

The repeating rifle carried to its logical extreme became the machine gun. The first machine gun, the Gatling, appeared in the American Civil War. Just before the Franco-Prussian War the French developed the Montigny mitrailleuse. Both of these weapons were multibarreled and hand cranked, and as unwieldly as field artillery without anywhere near the range. Furthermore they frequently jammed in the midst of battle. The British bought a dozen Gatlings in 1869 and by the eighties were using Gatlings on small boats and in the colonies. Then in 1884 Hiram Maxim developed the first truly automatic repeating rifle. It was light enough for infantry soldiers to carry, it could be set up inconspicuously, and it spat out eleven bullets per second. The next year Lord Wolseley, conqueror of the Ashanti, paid Maxim a visit and "exhibited the most lively interest in the gun and its innovator; and, thinking of the practical purposes to which the gun might be put, especially in colonial warfare, made several suggestions to Mr. Maxim." The Maxim gun was to prove as decisive in the colonial wars of the turn of the century as the rapid-fire rifle had been in the seventies and eighties.

The last bit of "progress" in the evolution of the gun arose in response to the special needs of empire. In the words of the historians of guns, Ommundsen and Robinson; "... savage tribes, with whom we were always conducting wars, refused to be sufficiently impressed by the Mark II bullet; in fact, they often ignored it altogether, and, having been hit in four or five places, came on to unpleasantly close quarters." The solution to this unpleasantness was patented in 1897 by one Captain Bertie-Clay of the Indian ammunition works at Dum-Dum: the mushrooming or "dum-dum" bullet. This particular invention was so vicious, for it tore great holes in the flesh, that Europeans thought it too cruel to inflict upon one another, and used it only against Asians and Africans.

By the 1890s the gun revolution was complete. Most European infantrymen could now fire fifteen rounds of ammunition in as many seconds, lying down undetected, in any weather, with an effective range of up to half a mile. Machine gunners had even more power. Though the generals were not to realize it for many decades, the age of raw courage and cold steel had ended, and the era of arms races and industrial slaughter had begun.

The gun revolution, like any other technological change, could not be confined to its creators. But the spread of the new guns and tactics was a most difficult and uneven process and may thus serve as a case study of technological diffusion under pressure. In China the defeat in two wars against European powers and the difficult struggle against the Taiping revolutionaries led many to reconsider the myth of Chinese superiority, at least in technical and military matters. In the sixties and after, a "self-strengthening movement" persuaded the government to purchase Western guns and warships and set up shipyards and arsenals. Yet these efforts were hampered by low budgets. In 1885, upon witnessing a demonstration of the Maxim gun, the Chinese emissary to London, Li Huang Chang, declared that China could not afford a gun that used up five British pounds worth of cartridges a minute. At that time, half the Chinese soldiers carried matchlocks, one quarter had percussion flintlocks, and only a quarter were armed with breechloaders; auxiliary troops had no firearms at all but carried spears and bows and arrows. As late as the Boxer Rebellion of 1900 a Russian force was able to assault Peking with two machine guns and four cannon, against thousands of Chinese soldiers armed with muskets. In the end, the failure of the self-strengthening movement was a result of the decay of Manchu leadership and the conservative nature of Chinese society.

The gun revolution penetrated Africa in a number of ways. As the Europeans rearmed with breechloaders in the sixties and seventies, and with repeating rifles in the eighties, they discarded vast quantities of surplus weapons. Many of these found their way to Africa by the coastal or trans-Saharan trade. In regions where Europeans needed African laborers, as in South Africa from the 1850s on, they often could only purchase these services for guns. And wherever white settlers had modern weapons, their black neighbors found ways to obtain them also. Yet the whites, whether settlers, military men, or missionaries, had reason to fear the acquisition of guns by Africans and tried to restrict their sale. Like many regulations of the time, the Brussels Act of 1892 made a clear connection between European interests and the gun revolution: It restricted the sale of flintlocks to Africans living between the twentieth parallel north and the twentieth south and prohibited the sale of breechloaders completely. Yet these restrictions were more symbolic than real. What mattered in the end was the more advanced technology and purchasing power of the Europeans.

The new weapons of the sixties and after were so powerful that those who owned them often got their way by demonstration alone. Among the European explorers of Africa, some, like Heinrich Barth, David Livingstone, and René Caillé, made their way unarmed by befriending the people they visited. Others, however, mounted quasi-military expeditions: Samuel White Baker searched for the source of the Nile with 1,000 men and enough arms and ammunition to last him years; Stanley explored the Congo with hundreds of men and did not hesitate to fire elephant guns and explosive bullets at Africans who had never seen firearms before. Between these extremes, most explorers carried a few guns, both to hunt game and to impress their hosts. Malamine, a Senegalese associate of Savorgnan de Brazza, became the sole representative of France on the Congo thanks to a repeating Winchester with which he made himself the most successful and popular hunter in the region. Gustav Rohlfs, traveling through Bornu, occasionally intimidated the local inhabitants with his rifles. And Hauptmann Kling explored central Ghana with a machine gun to knock down walls and inspire awe. At no time in history was the distinction between tourists and conquerors been so blurred as it was in late nineteenth-century Africa.

Colonial battles in Africa became increasingly lopsided as the century drew to a close, both because the weapons of the Europeans were constantly improved and because the last African areas to be conquered were often the furthest from the coasts, hence had the most difficulty obtaining those very weapons. In the wars of the sixties, as between the British and the Ethiopians or between the Orange Free State and the Sotho, the Europeans had breechloaders and field artillery, while the Africans had muskets and spears. The Europeans won the battles, but not decisively enough to take over the land. In the seventies and eighties the statesmen of Europe, in a display of arrogant certainty unprecedented in the annals of conquerors, drew lines on the map of Africa to indicate where their future conquests would lie. They were only reflecting their faith in the absolute power of European weapons to overcome any native resistance. In the Ashanti War of 1873–74 and in the Zulu War of 1879 the victories of small European or European-led units over African armies of tens of thousands showed just how powerful Gatlings and breechloaders were. In 1887 a French army of 1,400 men armed with Gras-Kropatchek repeating rifles defeated Mahmadou Lamine. Gardner and Nordenfeldt machine guns (improved versions of the Gatling) figured in the British takeover of Egypt in 1882–84.

In the nineties the high commands, which stoutly resisted the introduction of Maxim guns into their European armies, consented to send a few to the colonies. These guns, along with field artillery and repeating rifles, turned battles into one-sided massacres. In 1891 near Porto Novo a French unit of 300 men defeated the entire Fon army in a two-and-a-half hour battle by firing 25,000 rounds of ammunition. In 1897 the Royal Niger Company conquered the Caliphate of Sokoto with a force of thirty-one Europeans and 507 African troops armed with seven small cannon and six Maxims. In Chad in 1899 a French force of 320 mostly Sudanese soldiers defeated Rabah's 12,000 warriors with their 2,500 guns.

Probably the best known of these colonial wars was Lord Kitchener's conquest of the Sudan in 1898. He brought with him six heavily armed steamers and four other boats. His army had forty-four pieces of artillery and twenty Maxims. On September 2, 1898 the expedition encountered the main Dervish army of 40,000 men at Omdurman. Winston Churchill left this description of the battle:

> The infantry fired steadily and stolidly, without hurry or excitement, for the enemy were far away and the officers careful. Besides, the soldiers were interested in the work and took great pains. But presently the mere physical act became tedious.... And all the time out on the plain on the other side bullets were shearing through flesh, smashing and splintering bone; blood spouted from terrible wounds; valiant men were struggling on through a hell of whistling metal, exploding shells, and spurting dust—suffering, despairing, dying.

The battle was over within a few hours; 11,000 Dervishes and forty-eight British soldiers lay dead. Churchill commented; "Thus ended the battle of Omdurman—the most signal triumph ever gained by the arms of science over barbarians. Within the space of five hours the strongest and best-armed savage army yet arrayed against a modern European Power had been destroyed and dispersed, with hardly any difficulty, comparatively small risk, and insignificant loss to the victors." As Churchill noted, the significant, indeed the indispensable factor was "the arms of science" which produced the great disparity in firepower between Europeans and Africans.

The strategy and tactics of the new imperialism deserve a special mention because of what they reveal about the culture of war. Colonial armies seldom encountered guerrilla tactics. Instead they were time and again attacked in frontal assaults by great masses of warriors on open battlefields. This was true of the Chinese, the Zulu, the Ndebele, the Dervishes, the Fon, and so many others. These troops often displayed the highest discipline and courage, and the tactics most suited to the kind of warfare to which they were accustomed. But against European guns these tactics were obsolete. Firing on the run, reloading standing up, or running to get close enough to hurl a javelin were, under the circumstances, suicidal.

Against the open assault of masses of warriors, the imperialist forces resurrected the square of Napoleonic times, a human fortress surrounded by an impenetrable wall of bullets. It was a near-invincible defense against attacking forces armed with inferior weapons, no matter how numerous. A battle of this kind took place in October 1893 near Zimbabwe in Southern Africa. A column of fifty British South African Police had encountered the 5,000 Ndebele warriors of King Lobengula. The Ndebele carried assegais and shields. The whites had four Maxims, a Nordenfeldt, and a Gardner. Lt. Col. Graham Hutchison, a British writer of the purple-prose school of imperial history, described the confrontation:

> Fierce tribesmen, inflamed with racial fanaticism, armed with the assegais, formed their impis, and in great force went forth to battle; while a thousand

war-drums, in wild crescendo, beat their primitive tatoo of vengeance amid the scattered kraals. The B.S.A.P., though hurriedly reinforced by volunteer Rhodesians, were from the outset greatly outnumbered.... They stood on the defensive, forming a wagon laager, within which had been concentrated women, children and provisions, and provoked the Matabele to charge. Maxim guns were placed at the angles of the laager: and it is recorded how again and again hordes of Matabele bit the dust far beyond the thrust of the deadly assegai.

Not everywhere did the Europeans encounter peoples with such obsolete armaments and tactics, for some Africans and Asians had learned that to fight an enemy armed with modern weapons one needed either equally modern weapons, or guerrilla tactics, or both. There were many such cases, from the Japanese to the Afghans and from the Sotho to the Riffi. Two examples will suffice.

In the Western Sudan the French encountered Samori Touré, an upstart state builder, religious leader, and military innovator. Starting with 500 soldiers and thirty-six repeating rifles in 1887, his army accumulated 4,000 repeaters by 1898. With skillful guerrilla tactics he held the French at bay for a decade, but was finally doomed when his supplies of fresh weapons and cartridges were cut off by an Anglo-French agreement.

Emperor Menelik of Ethiopia was luckier. Starting with a larger base and more of the latest weapons, he confronted a weaker enemy. The battle of Adua in 1896, in which he defeated the Italians, was both a proof of Ethiopian valor and an omen of a time to come in which non-Western peoples would command the deadly firepower of the Europeans and close the power gap.

The European imperial forces of the late nineteenth century, engaged in the largest strategic offensive since the days of Genghis Khan, won most of their battles by such defensive tactics as the square and the wagon laager. Col. Charles Callwell, author of *Small Wars*, the classic study of colonial warfare, recognized this curious juxtaposition of offensive strategy and defensive tactics but did not pursue its implications. He took the weapons superiority for granted, hardly commenting on it. Instead, throughout his book he stressed the superiority of European and European-trained soldiers over peoples he called hordes, fanatics, barbarians, savages, or, at best, semicivilized. He attributed the victories of the Western forces to zeal, resolution, daring, courage, initiative, vigor, boldness, and other such moral virtues.

If Callwell's interpretation is typical of his caste and time—and I believe it is—then it helps to explain what happened in World War I. For over forty years European armies had fought only colonial wars, and mostly with great success. Their colonial conquests reinforced the Napoleonic theory that a bold offensive strategy coupled with overwhelming firepower would surely lead to victory. What they overlooked was that the new guns were defensive weapons, and that it was defensive tactics that had won them their empires. The soldier in the trench in Flanders with his machine gun or his rifle was as invulnerable as his counterpart in the square at Omdurman or the wagon laager in Ndebeleland. The string of racist epithets that the Callwells of the turn of the century applied to non-Western peoples hid from them a most unpalatable fact: Against the hail of steel from the new weapons, vigor and *élan vital* were of no use, for the European soldier going over the top on the Western Front was as helpless and vulnerable as any Dervish or Ndebele. Hence the effect of modern guns on the battlefields of Europe was the exact opposite of what it had been in the colonies. Instead of bringing the quick and cheap success that everyone expected, they made victory impossible.

Bibliography

W. BAUMGART, *Imperialism: The Idea and Reality of British and French Colonial Expansion, 1880–1914* (1982).

W. BRUNSCHWIG, *French Colonialism, 1871–1914: Myths and Realities* (1966).

B. COHEN, *The Question of Imperialism: The Political Economy of Dominance and Dependence* (1973).

W. B. COHEN, *The French Encounter with Africans: White Response to Blacks, 1530–1880* (1980).

P. CURTIN, *The Image of Africa: British Ideas and Actions 1780–1850* (1964).

C. C. ELDRIDGE, *England's Mission: The Imperial Idea in the Age of Gladstone and Disraeli, 1868–1880* (1974).

D. K. FIELDHOUSE, *The Colonial Experience: A Comparative Study from the Eighteenth Century* (1966).

D. K. FIELDHOUSE, *Economics and Empire, 1830–1914* (1973).

D. R. HEADRICK, *The Tools of Empire: Technology and European Imperialism in the Nineteenth Century* (1981).

R. KOEBNER, and H. D. SMITH, *Imperialism: The Story and Significance of a Political Word, 1840–1960* (1964).

W. H. MCNEIL, *The Pursuit of Power: Technology, Armed Force, and Society since A.D. 1000* (1982).

C. REYNOLDS, *Modes of Imperialism* (1981).

R. ROBINSON and J. GALLAGHER, *Africa and the Victorians* (1961).

W. H. SCHNEIDER, *An Empire for the Masses: The French Popular Image of Africa, 1870–1900* (1982).

W. D. SMITH, *The German Colonial Empire* (1978).

Men against Fire: Expectations of War in 1914

MICHAEL HOWARD

World War I saw the slaughter of an unprecedented number of soldiers on the part of all European combatants. Hundreds of thousands of men were killed or wounded in remarkably short intervals. Why did commanding officers repeatedly send their troops into frontal assaults against enemy troops who could not be seen and who were armed with machine guns or rapid repeating rifles? What were the ideas and historical experiences that persuaded military commanders to follow these tactics?

Near the turn of the century military opinion on such matters had been quite divided. Changes in military technology and weaponry had seemed to render traditional infantry charges relatively ineffective in both the Franco-Prussian War of 1870 and the Boer War of 1898. There had also arisen much debate over whether cavalry should be armed with rifles or with the traditional sabre. Behind the debates over both the cavalry and the infantry charge lay the whole question of the value of shock tactics on troops in the midst of battle.

Then in 1905 Japan defeated Russia in the Russo–Japanese War. The Japanese commanders had ordered infantry charges. The defeated Russian Army had employed rifle-armed cavalry. The Russo–Japanese War received careful study throughout European military circles, and from the experience of that conflict European military theorists reasserted the fundamental importance of the military offensive and the infantry charge. It was into such deadly and futile charges that they ordered hundreds of thousands of troops during the course of World War I.

Reprinted from *International Security*, vol. 9, no. 1, "Men against Fire: Expectations of War in 1914," by Michael Howard, by permission of The MIT Press, Cambridge, Massachusetts. Copyright © 1984 by the President and Fellows of Harvard College and the Massachusetts Institute of Technology.

In 1898 there was published in Paris a six-volume work entitled *La Guerre Future; aux points de vue technique, economique et politique* [*The Future War from the Technical, Economic, and Political Viewpoints*]. This was a translation of a series of articles which had been appearing in Russia, the fruit of collective research but masterminded and written by one of the leading figures in the world of Russian finance and industry, Ivan (or Jean de) Bloch (1836–1902). Sometimes described as "a Polish banker," Bloch was in fact an entrepreneur almost on the scale of the Rothschilds in Western Europe or Carnegie in the United States. He had made his money in railroad promotion, and then turned to investment on a large scale, promoting and sharing in the great boom in the Russian economy of the 1890s. He had written prolifically about the economic problems of the Russian Empire, and was increasingly alarmed by the degree to which they were complicated, then as now, by the military need to keep abreast, in an age of rapidly developing technology, with the wealthier and more advanced states of the West. Having been responsible for organizing the railway supply for the Russian armies in their war with the Ottoman Empire in 1877–78, Bloch had an unusual grasp of military logistics. And he brought to the study of war an entirely new sort of mind, one in which the analytical skills of the engineer, the economist, and the sociologist were all combined. His book was in fact the first work of modern operational analysis, and nothing written since has equalled it for its combination of rigor and scope.

Only the last of the six volumes was translated into English, under the title *Is War Now Impossible?* This volume conveniently summarizes the argument of the entire work, and it was itself summarized by the author in an interview with the English journalist W. T. Stead which is printed as an introduction to the book. Bloch began by stating his conclusions: war between great states was now impossible—or, rather, suicidal. "The dimensions of modern armaments and the organisation of society have rendered its prosecution an economic impossibility." This could be almost mathematically demonstrated. The range, accuracy, and rate of fire of modern firearms—rifles lethal at 2000 meters, artillery at 6000—made the "decisive battles" which had hitherto determined the outcome of wars now impossible. Neither the infantry could charge with the bayonet nor cavalry with the saber. To protect themselves against the lethal storm of fire which would be unleashed on the modern battlefield, armies would have to dig themselves in: "the spade will be as indispensable to the soldier as his rifle.... That is one reason why it will be impossible for the battle of the future to be fought out rapidly.... Battles will last for days, and at the end it is very doubtful whether any decisive victory can be gained."

Thus far Bloch was not breaking new ground. He was only setting out a problem which intelligent officers in all European armies had been studying ever since the experience of the Franco–Prussian War in 1870 and the Russo–Turkish War in 1877–78 had shown (quite as clearly as, and rather more immediately than, those of the American Civil War) the effect of modern firearms on the battlefield. The introduction of "smokeless powder" in the 1880s, increasing the range and accuracy of all firearms and making possible the near invisibility of their users, would, it was generally agreed, complicate the difficulties of the attack yet further. But even these, it was widely assumed, would not change the fundamental nature of the problem.

The answer, it was believed, lay in the development of the firepower of the assailant, especially of his artillery. The assaulting infantry had to approach closely enough, making all use of cover, to be able to deploy a hail of rifle fire on the defenders' positions. Artillery must cooperate closely, keeping the defenders' heads down with shrapnel and digging them out of their trenches with high explosives. As for machine-guns, these, with their mobility and concentrated firepower, were seen as likely to enhance the power of the attack rather than the defense. "Fire is the supreme argument," declared Colonel Ferdinand Foch in his lectures at the École de Guerre in 1900. "The superiority of fire...becomes the most important element of an infantry's fighting value." But the moment would always come when the advance could get no further: "Before it is a zone almost impassable; there remain no covered approaches; a hail of lead beats the ground...to flee or to charge is all that remains." Foch, and the majority of French thinkers of his time, believed that the charge was still possible and could succeed by sheer dint of numbers: "To charge, but to charge in numbers, therein lies safety.... With more guns we can reduce his to silence, and the same is true of rifles and bayonets, if we know how to make use of them all." Others were less sure. The Germans, who still after thirty years had vivid memories of the slaughter of their infantry at Gravelotte, preferred if possible to pin the enemy down by fire from the front but attack from a flank. Nobody was under any illusion, even in 1900, that frontal attack would be anything but very difficult and that success could be purchased with anything short of very heavy casualties. There would probably indeed have been a wide measure of agreement with Bloch's calculation, that a superiority at the assaulting point of 8 to 1 would be necessary to ensure success.

Bloch's War of the Future: Society versus Society

It was in the further conclusions which Bloch deduced from his study of the modern battlefield that he outpaced his contemporaries—not so much because they disagreed with him, but because they had given the problems which he examined virtually no thought at all.

What, asked Bloch, would be the eventual result of the operational deadlock that was likely to develop on the battlefield? "At first there will be increased slaughter—increased slaughter on so terrible a scale as to render it impossible to push the battle to a decisive issue.... Then, instead of a war fought out to the bitter end in a series of decisive battles, we shall have to substitute a long period of continually increasing strain upon the resources of the combattants." This, would involve "entire dislocation of all industry and severing of all the sources of supply by which alone the community is enabled to bear the crushing burden.... That is the future of war—not fighting, but famine, not the slaying of men but the bankruptcy of nations and the break-up of the whole social organisation." In these circumstances the decisive factors would be "the quality of toughness and capacity for endurance, of patience under privation, of stubborness under reverse or disappointment. That element in the civil population will be, more than anything else, the deciding factor in modern war.... Your soldiers," concluded Bloch grimly, "may fight as they please; the ultimate decision is in the hands of *famine*." And famine would strike first as those proletarian elements which, in advanced industrial societies, were most prone to revolution.

It is important to recognize that Bloch got a great deal wrong. He assumed that the prolonged feeding and administration of the vast armies which rail transport made possible would be far beyond the capacity of the military authorities, and that armies in the field would quickly degenerate into starving and mutinous mobs. He predicted that the care of the sick and wounded would also assume unmanageable proportions, and that on the battlefield the dead and dying would have to be heaped up into macabre barriers to protect the living from enemy fire. As did many professional soldiers, Bloch doubted the capacity of reservists fresh from civil life to stand up to the strain of the battlefield: "it is impossible to rely upon modern armies submitting to sacrifice and deprivation to such an extent as is desired by military theorists who lose sight of the tendencies which obtain in Western society." In fact the efficiency with which armies numbering millions were to be maintained in the field, the success with which the medical services were, with certain grisly exceptions, to rise to the enormous task that confronted them and the stoical endurance displayed by the troops of all belligerent powers in face of hardships worse than Bloch could ever have conceived were perhaps the most remarkable and admirable aspects of the First World War. Bloch, like so many pessimistic prophets (including those of air power a generation later), underestimated the capacity of human societies to adjust themselves to adverse circumstances.

But Bloch also had astonishing insights. The scale of military losses, he pointed out, would depend on the skill of the commanders, and "it must not be forgotten that a considerable number of the higher officers in modern armies have never been under fire"; while among junior officers the rate of casualties would, if they did their job as leaders, be inordinately high. Finally, there was the problem of managing the wartime economy; what were the long-term effects of that likely to be? "If we suppose," Bloch surmised, "that governments will be forced to interfere in the regulation of prices and to support the population, will it be easy after the war to abandon this practise and re-establish the old order?" Win or lose, therefore, if war came "the old order" was doomed—by transformation from above if not by revolution from below.

This remarkably accurate blueprint for the war which was to break out in Europe in 1914, last for four and a half years, and end only with the social disintegration of the defeated belligerents and the economic exhaustion of all was the result, not of second-sight, but of meticulous analysis of weapons capabilities, of military organization and doctrine, and of financial and economic data—five fat volumes which still provide a superb source book for any student of the military, technological, and economic condition of Europe at the end of the nineteenth century. Nobody took Bloch's economic arguments and attempted to disprove them. They were just ignored. Why, it may be asked, was so little account taken of them by statesmen and military leaders? Why did they continue on a course which led ineluctably to the destruction of the old order which Bloch so unerringly predicted? The question is one uncomfortably relevant to our own times.

The answer is of course that societies, and the pattern of international relationships, cannot be transformed overnight on the basis of a single prophetic insight, however persuasively it may be argued. Bloch's thinking and influence were indeed two elements in persuading Czar Nicholas II to convoke the first International Peace Conference which met at the Hague in May 1899, and were even more significant in mobilizing public support throughout Europe for that conference's objectives. But the conference was no more than a ripple in the current of international politics. A more immediate problem, as Bloch himself repeatedly pointed out, was that there existed nowhere in Europe bodies charged with the task of thinking about the problems of warfare in any kind of comprehensive fashion, rather than about the narrowly professional questions that concerned the military. As for the military specialists, they were not likely to admit that the problems which faced them were insoluble, and that they would be incapable in the future of conducting wars so effectively and decisively as they had in the past.

Lessons of the Boer War

The force of Bloch's arguments, however, was powerfully driven home when, within a few months of the publication of *La Guerre Future*, there broke out in South Africa a war in which for the first time both sides were fully equipped with the new technology—magazine-loading small-bore rifles, quick-firing artillery, machine guns—and things turned out on the battlefield exactly as he had predicted. The British army, moving in close formations and firing by volleys, were unable to get anywhere near an enemy whom they could not even see. At Spion Kop, at Colenso, at the

Modder Rover, and at Magersfontein, their frontal attacks were driven back by the Boers with horrifying losses. As the leading British military theorist, Colonel G. F. R. Henderson, who accompanied the army in South Africa, wrote shortly afterwards:

> There was a constant endeavor to make battle conform to the parade ground... to depend for success on courage and subordination and to relegate intelligence and individuality to the background... the fallacy that a thick firing line in open country can protect itself, outside decisive range, by its own fire, had not yet been exposed. It was not yet realised that the defender, occupying ingeniously constructed trenches and using smokeless powder, is practically invulnerable to both gun and rifle.

Unsympathetic continental observers tended to play down the significance of the South African experience on the grounds that the British army and its commanders were unsuitably trained for confronting a "civilized" adversary, having been spoiled by the easy victories in Egypt and the Sudan. Further, they suggested that the differences in terrain made the lessons to be learned from that war, as they had made those from the American Civil War, irrelevant in the European theater. The British themselves, while unable to deny the unsuitability of their traditional tactics and training to the transformed conditions of warfare, could nonetheless point out that, once they had mastered the necessary techniques, they had been able successfully to go over to the offensive, and had then rapidly won the war. This they had done by pinning down the Boers in their positions by firepower and maneuvering round their flanks with cavalry—cavalry used not in its traditional role for shock on the battlefield, but to develop the kind of strategic mobility which was essential if the problems created by the new power of the defensive were to be overcome. When in 1901 Bloch described to an audience at the British Royal United Services Institution how the experience of the British army in South Africa, repeated as it would be in Europe on an enormous scale, precisely illustrated his arguments, his audience was able to point out that in fact Lord Roberts had shown how to combine the tactical advantages of firepower with the strategic advantages of horse-borne mobility to secure precisely those decisive results which Bloch had maintained would, in future, be impossible.

A study of the voluminuous military literature of the period shows that between 1900 and 1905 a consensus developed among European strategic thinkers over two points. The first was the strategic importance of cavalry as mobile firepower. If the firepower of the defense made it now impossible for cavalry to assault unshaken infantry—a view which had been reluctantly accepted ever since the disasters of the Franco–Prussian War of 1870 —cavalry would now develop their own firepower, enhanced by mobile quick-firing artillery and machine guns, and exploit opportunities on a scale undreamed of since the days of the American Civil War. The South African experience indeed sent back intelligent cavalrymen, especially in England, to studying the Civil War, often for the first time. In the British army, it was laid down that the carbine or rifle would henceforth be "the principal weapon" for cavalry. But for most cavalrymen this was going altogether too far. In no country in Europe was this proudest, most exclusive, most anachronistic of arms prepared to be, as they saw it, downgraded to the role of mounted infantry. That kind of thing could be left to colonial roughriders. Writing as late as 1912, the German general Friedrich von Bernhardi bitterly observed that "The cavalry looks now... upon a charge in battle as its paramount duty; it has almost deliberately closed its eyes against the far-reaching changes in warfare. By this it has *itself* barred the way that leads to greater successes." Within the cavalry in every European army therefore a controversy raged which was settled only by the kind of compromise expressed by the British Cavalry Manual of 1907:

> The essence of the cavalry spirit lies in holding the balance correctly between fire power and shock action... it must be accepted as a principle that the rifle, effective as it is, cannot replace the effect produced by the speed of the horse, the magnetism of the charge, and the terror of cold steel.

The mood of the cavalryman on the eve of the First World War is perhaps best captured in an analysis of British military doctrine published in 1914:

> Technically the great decisive cavalry charge on the main battlefield is a thing of the past, yet training in shock tactics is claimed by all cavalry authorities to be still essential to the strategic use of the arm, and even on the battlefield shock tactics may, under special conditions, conceivably still be possible, while brilliant opportunities will almost certainly be offered for the employment in perhaps a decisive manner of the power conferred by the combination of mobility with fire action.... For whatever tactics are adopted, the desire to take the offensive will always remain the breath of life for cavalry, and where shock action is impossible, the cavalryman must be prepared to expend, rifle in hand, the last man in an advance on foot, if the victory can thus only be achieved.

So training in shock action continued; for even the reformers had to admit that cavalry would have to meet and defeat the enemy's cavalry, presumably in a gigantic mêlée, before it could fulfil its strategic task. "The opening of future wars," wrote von Bernhardi in 1912, "will, therefore, in all likelihood be characterised by great cavalry combats."

So the cavalry continued to practice sword drill; and the infantry continued, for the same reason, to practice bayonet drill. The German writer Wilhelm Balck saw no reason to alter, in the 1911 edition of his huge study of *Tactics*, the doctrine preached in the first edition of 1896:

The soldier should be taught not to shrink from the bayonet attack, but to seek it. If the infantry is deprived of the arme blanche, if the impossibility of bayonet fighting is preached... an infantry will be developed which is unsuitable for attack and which moreover lacks a most essential quality, viz. the moral power to reach the enemy's position... [And he went on to quote from the Russian General Dragomirov, a well-known fanatic on the subject:] "The bayonet cannot be abolished for the reason, if for no other, that it is the sole and exclusive embodiment of that will-power which alone, both in war and in everyday life attains its object, whereas reason only facilitates the achievement of the object."

The British General Staff manuals expressed the same idea slightly differently: "The moral effect of the bayonet is out of all proportion to its material effect, and not the least important of virtues claimed for it is that the desire to use it draws the attacking side on." To deprive the infantry of their bayonets would be like depriving the cavalry of their swords; it "would be to some extent to take away their desire to close."

That brings us to the second point over which a rather more troubled consensus developed among European military thinkers as a consequence of the South African War: the unprecedented difficulty of carrying through frontal attacks, even with substantial artillery support, would now make necessary more extended formations in the attack. On this point also there had been a continuing controversy ever since 1870. The normal formation for the infantry attack, inherited from the Napoleonic era, consisted of three lines. First came the skirmishers in open formation, making maximum use of cover so as to reach positions from which they could bring a concentrated fire on the enemy in order, in cooperation with the artillery, to "win the fire fight." Behind them came the main assault line, normally in close formation under the immediate control of their officers, to assault with the bayonet. Finally came the supports, the immediate tactical reserve.

The German army, remembering the massacres of their infantry in the assault at the battles of Wörth and St. Privat in August 1870, had always inclined to the view that once the attacking infantry came under fire, close formations in the old style would be impossible. The main assault line would itself now have to scatter and edge its way forward to thicken up the skirmishers or extend their line, feeling for an exposed flank. Effectively it was now the skirmishers who bore the brunt of the attack, and success could be achieved only by the dominance of their fire. The bayonet, if used at all, would only gather up the harvest already reaped by the rifle and the gun.

This was the doctrine against which Dragomirov and his disciples everywhere set their faces. It must be admitted that it did present real problems. Once the assaulting troops were scattered and left to themselves, out of range of the officers whose task it was to inspire them and the non-coms whose job it was to frighten them, what incentive would there be for them to go forward in face of enemy fire? Once they went to ground behind cover, would they ever get up again? There were several notorious instances in 1870 when substantial proportions of German assaulting formulations had unaccountably "got lost." Colonel Ardent du Picq, who had been killed in that war and whose posthumously published *Etudes sur le Combat* contain some of the shrewdest observations on troop morale that have ever been written, had described the terrifying isolation of the soldier on a modern battlefield (even before the days of smokeless powder) once he was deprived of the solid support of comrades on either side which had enabled men to face death ever since the days of the Roman legions. "The soldier is unknown even to his comrades; he loses them in the disorientating confusion of battle, where he fights as a lonely individual; solidarity is no longer guaranteed by mutual surveillance." All now depended on the morale and reliability of the smallest units; "by force of circumstances all battles nowadays tend more than ever to become soldiers' battles." How could these lonely frightened men, deprived of the intoxication of drums and trumpets, the support of their comrades, the inspiration of their leaders, find within themselves the courage to die?

The French army, its traditions of martial leadership and close formations for the attack antedating even the Napoleonic era, was particularly reluctant to accept the logic of the new firepower. For a decade after 1870 its leaders had attempted to impose the open tactical formations on their units, but they never really succeeded. By 1884 regulations were again prescribing "the principle of the decisive attack, head held high, unconcerned about casualties." The notorious regulations of 1894 laid it down that attacking units should advance elbow to elbow, not breaking formation to take advantage of cover, but assaulting *en masses* "to the sound of bugles and drums." Stirring stuff, and the French were not alone in preferring it that way. So did the Russians, in spite of their chastening experiences before Plevna in 1877; and so did the British. They also, after a decade of uncertainty inspired by the events of 1870, returned to their old traditions. In the regulations of 1888, wrote Colonel Henderson:

> The bayonet has once more reasserted itself. To the second line, relying on cold steel only, as in the days of the Peninsula, is entrusted the duty of bringing the battle to a speedy conclusion.... The confusion of the Prussian battles was in a large degree due to their neglect of the immutable principles of tactics and ... they are a bad model for us to follow. The sagacity of our own people is a surer guide and if, after 1870, we wanted a model, the tactics of the last great war waged by English-speaking soldiers would have served us better.

The Americans on both sides had always launched frontal attacks in close formations, having found that "to prevent the battle degenerating into a protracted struggle between two strongly entrenched armies, and to attain a speedy and decisive result, mere development of fire was insufficient." The lesson was clear: "close order whenever it is possible, extended order only when it is unavoidable."

By 1900 Henderson was a sadder and a wiser man. Events in South Africa had once again shown the world that under fire close order was *not* possible; and the argument that it was good for morale was seen to be ludicrous. "When the preponderant mass suffers enormous losses; when they feel, as others will feel, that other and less costly means of achieving the same end might have been adopted, what will become of their morale?... The most brilliant offensive victories," went on Henderson, "are not those which were mere 'bludgeon work' and cost the most blood, but those which were won by surprise, by adroit manoeuvre, by mystifying and misleading the enemy, by turning the ground to the best account, and where the butchers' bill was small." A generation later Henderson's countryman Liddell Hart was to elaborate this insight into an entire philosophy of war, but long before 1914 the British army was to discard this subversive suggestion that discretion might be the better part of valor.

Over the matter of close *versus* open formations for the attack, however, the South African experience was generally seen to be decisive. Even the French high command, while attributing the catastrophes which had overtaken the British entirely to Anglo-Saxon ineptitude, rewrote its regulations in 1904, abandoning the *coude à coude* [elbow to elbow] formations of 1894 and prescribing advance by small groups of covering each other by fire—the kind of infantry tactics that were to become general in the Second World War. It is doubtful however whether these eminently sensible guidelines made any impression on an army which had been thrown, in the aftermath of the Dreyfus case, into a state of administrative confusion verging on anarchy. Certainly the performance of the French infantry in 1914 shows no evidence of it. In any case, such tactics demanded of the ordinary soldier a degree of skill and self-reliance such as neither the French nor any other European army (with the possible exception of the Germans) had hitherto expected, or done anything to inculcate, either in their junior officers or in their other ranks.

And there remained unsolved the nagging, fundamental problem of *morale*—a problem all the greater since a large part of all armies would now be made up of reservists whose moral fiber, it was feared, would have been sapped by the enervating influences of civil life. Concern about the morale of the army was thus generalized, among European military thinkers, into concern about the morale of their nations as a whole; not so much whether they would stand up to the economic attrition which Bloch was almost unique in foreseeing, but whether they could inculcate into their young men that stoical contempt for death which alone would enable them to face, and overcome, the horrors of the assault.

The Russo–Japanese War and the Superiority of the Offensive

It was while this concern was at its height that war broke out between Japan and Russia in the Far East. In February 1904 the Japanese navy launched a surprise attack on the Russian fleet at Port Arthur and, with local command of the sea thus secured, effected amphibious landings on the Korean and Manchurian coasts. It took the Japanese army a year to establish themselves in the disputed province of Manchuria, capturing Port Arthur by land assault and fighting its way north along the railway to capture the main Russian forward base at Mukden in a two-week battle involving altogether over half a million men. It was a war fought on both sides with the latest products of modern technology: not only magazine rifles and quick-firing field artillery but mobile heavy guns, machine guns, mines, barbed wire, searchlights, telephonic communications and, above all, *trenches*. The Russo–Japanese War proved beyond any doubt that the infantryman's most useful weapon, second only to his rifle, was a spade. Though the war inevitably had unique characteristics — both sides fought at the end of long supply lines, in sparsely inhabited country, which sharply limited the scale of force they could employ — it could not be dismissed, as so many conservative thinkers on the Continent dismissed the Boer War, as a colonial irrelevance. The Russian army was one of the greatest — certainly one of the largest — in Europe. The Japanese had had their armed forces equipped and trained by Europeans, mainly Germans, to the finest European standards. European — and American — military and naval observers with the fighting forces sent back expert reports on the operations, which were digested and mulled over by their general staffs. The British, the French, and the German armies all thought it worth their while to produce multi-volume histories of the Russo–Japanese War, and for the next ten years, until interest was eclipsed by events nearer home, its lessons were analyzed in the most precise detail by pundits writing in military periodicals. It was neither the Boer War nor the American Civil War nor even the Franco–Prussian War that European military specialists had in mind when their armies deployed in 1914: it was the fighting in Manchuria of 1904–5.

As usual, the experts tended to read into the experiences of the war very much what they wanted to find. Conservative cavalrymen observed the failure of the Russian cavalry, trained as it was to the use of the rifle, to achieve anything very much either on the battlefield or off it; absence of "the offensive spirit" making both its raids and its reconnaissance remarkably ineffectual. Reformers noted, on the contrary, how effectively the Japanese had deployed their cavalry in the role of mobile firepower, and the important part it had played at the battle of Mukden. Everyone agreed that artillery, with its accuracy, range, and rate of fire, was now of supreme importance; that it must almost always employ indirect fire; that shrapnel rather than high explosive was its most effective projectile; and that the consumption of ammunition would be enormous. Valuable lessons were learned about supply and communication problems and the need for inconspicuous uniforms; every European army quickly reclothed its armies in various shades of brown or grey, and it was political rather than military conservatism that fatally delayed this reform on the part of the French. But most important of all was the general consensus that infantry assaults with the bayonet, in spite of the South African experience, were still not only possible but necessary. The Japanese had carried them out time and again, and usually with ultimate success.

The Japanese bayonet assaults came, it was true, only at the end of a long and careful advance. They approached whenever possible by night, digging in before dawn, lying up by day, and repeating the process until they could get no further. Then, breaking completely with the European tradition of advancing in extended lines, they dashed forward in small groups of one or two dozen men, each with its own objective, moving rapidly from cover to cover until they were sufficiently close to assault. A French observer described one such scene:

> The whole Japanese line is now lit up with the glitter of steel flashing from the scabbard.... Once again the officers quit shelter with ringing shouts of "Banzai!" wildly echoed by all the rank and file. Slowly, but not to be denied, they make headway, in spite of the barbed wire, mines and pitfalls, and the merciless hail of bullets. Whole units are destroyed—others take their places; the advancing wave pauses for a moment, but sweeps ever onward. Already they are within a few yards of the trenches. Then, on the Russian side, the long grey line of Siberian Fusiliers forms up in turn, and delivers one last volley before scurrying down the far side of the hill at the double.

The Japanese losses in these assaults were heavy, but they succeeded; and, so argued the European theorists, such tactics would succeed again. "The Manchurian experience," as one British military writer put it, "showed over and over again that the bayonet was in no sense an obsolete weapon.... The assault is even of more importance than the attainment of fire mastery which antecedes it. It is the supreme moment of the fight.... Upon it the final issue depends.... From these glorious examples it may be deduced that no duty, however difficult, should be regarded as impossible by well-trained infantry of good morale and discipline."

It was this "morale and discipline" of the Japanese armed forces that all observers stressed, and they were equally unanimous in stressing that these qualities characterized not only the armed forces but the entire Japanese nation. General Kuropatkin, the commander of the Russian forces, noted ruefully in his memoirs:

> In the late war... our moral strength was less than that of the Japanese; and it was this inferiority, rather than mistakes in generalship, that caused our

defeats.... The lack of martial spirit, of moral exaltation, and of heroic impulse, affected particularly our stubbornness in battle. In many cases we did not have sufficient resolution to conquer such antagonists as the Japanese.

The same quality gave a representative of Japan's British ally, General Sir Ian Hamilton, almost equal concern:

It is not so much the idea that we have put our money on the wrong horse that now troubles me.... But it should cause European statesmen some anxiety when their people seem to forget that there are millions outside the charmed circle of Western Civilisation who are ready to pluck the sceptre from nerveless hands so soon as the old spirit is allowed to degenerate.... Providentially Japan is our ally.... England has time, therefore—time to put her military affairs in order; time to implant and cherish the military ideal in the hearts of her children; time to prepare for a disturbed and an anxious twentieth century.... From the nursery and its toys to the Sunday school and its cadet company, every influence of affection, loyalty, tradition and education should be brought to bear on the next generation of British boys and girls, so as deeply to impress upon their young minds a feeling of reverence and admiration for the patriotic spirit of their ancestors.

Such expressions of admiration for the creed of Bushido are to be found widely scattered in the military and militarist literature of the day. Particularly important for our purposes, however, was the general recognition that the Japanese performance had proved, up to the hilt, the moral and military superiority of *the offensive*. The passive immobility of the Russians, in spite of all the advantages they should have enjoyed from the defense, had in the long run ensured their defeat. It was a conclusion which the military everywhere, after the miasmic doubts engendered by the Boer War, embraced with heartfelt relief. "The defensive is never an acceptable role to the Briton, and he makes little or no study of it," wrote Major General Sir W. G. Knox flatly in 1914. "It was not by dwelling on the idea of passive defense," wrote the Secretary of State for War R. B. Haldane in 1911, "that our fore-fathers made our country what it is today." In Germany General von Schlieffen, on retiring as Chief of the General Staff in 1905, held up to his successors the model of the German armies in 1870: "Attacks, and more attacks, ruthless attacks brought it unparalleled losses but also victory and, it is probably true to say, the decision of the campaign." And his successor, the younger von Moltke, acknowledged the heritage: "We have learned the object that you seek to achieve: not to obtain limited successes but to strike great, destructive blows.... Your object is the annihilation of the enemy, and all efforts must be directed towards this end."

Nowhere was the lesson more gratefully received, however, than in France. Marshal Joffre, whose offensive operations from 1914 through 1916 are now generally considered to have been a succession of unmitigated disasters, described the French reaction to the Russo–Japanese War in his Memoirs with quite unrepentant frankness. After the Boer War, he wrote,

> a whole series of false doctrines... began to undermine even such feeble offensive sentiment as had made its appearance in our war doctrines... an incomplete study of the events of a single war had led the intellectual elite of our Army to believe that the improvement in firearms and the power of fire action had so increased the strength of the defensive that an offensive opposed to it had lost all virtue.

After the Russo–Japanese War, however,

> our young intellectual elite finally shook off the malady of this phraseology which had upset the military world and returned to a more healthy conception of the general conditions prevailing in war.

Joffre admitted that the new passion for the offensive did take on a "somewhat unreasoning character," citing Colonel de Grandmaison's famous lectures of 1911 as an example. "Unreasoning" is the right word. One must always, declared de Grandmaison to his audience,

> succeed in combat in doing things which would be *impossible* in cold blood. For instance... advancing under fire.... We must prepare ourselves for it, and prepare others by cultivating, passionately, everything which bears the mark of the offensive spirit. To take this to excess would probably still not be far enough.

There was nothing in this to indicate the careful use of ground and of mutual fire support which had characterized the actual Japanese tactics — tactics in fact remarkably close to those prescribed in the despised French infantry regulation of 1904. But de Grandmaison was not so much setting out a military doctrine as echoing a national mood — a generalized sense of chauvinistic assertiveness which dominated the French "establishment," civil and military alike, in 1911–12. It was a mood which did much to restore the morale of an army battered and confused after the excesses of the Dreyfus affair, but it could not of itself create the battlefield skills which had also characterized the Japanese army, and without which "the spirit of the offensive" was not so much an assertion of national morale as a generalized death wish. It was in this mood that French officers led the attacks in August–September 1914 which within six weeks produced 385,000 casualties, of which 100,000 were dead.

Bloch died in 1902, but he could have taken much comfort from the experiences of the Russo–Japanese War. Its battles were prolonged, costly, and indecisive. Victory came through attrition; and defeat, for Russia, brought revolution. But Bloch's critics could equally well argue that his major thesis had been disproved. War had been shown to be neither impossible, nor suicidal. It was still a highly effective instrument of policy for a nation which had the courage to face its dangers and the endurance to bear its costs—especially its inevitable and predictable costs in human lives. Those nations which were not prepared to put their destinies to this test, they urged, could expect no mercy in the grim battle for survival which had always characterized human history and which seemed likely, in the coming century, to be waged with ever greater ferocity. It was in this mood, and with these hopes, that the nations of Europe went to war in 1914.

Bibliography

L. ALBERTINI, *The Origins of the War of 1914*, 3 vols. (1952, 1957).
T. ASHWORTH, *Trench Warfare, 1914–1918: The Live and Let Live System* (1980).
V. R. BERGHAN, *Germany and the Approach of War in 1914* (1973).
W. Y. CARMAN, *A History of Firearms from the Earliest Times to 1914* (1955).
F. FISCHER, *Germany's War Aims in the First World War* (1967).
O. J. HALE, *The Great Illusion 1900–1914* (1971).
P. KENNEDY, *The Rise of the Anglo-German Antagonism, 1860–1914* (1980).
P. KENNEDY, *The War Plans of the Great Powers 1880–1914* (1978).
M. KRANZBERG, and C. W. PURSELL, JR., eds., *Technology and Western Civilization*, 2 vols. (1967).
L. LAFORE, *The Long Fuse* (1965).
S. E. MILLER, *Military Strategy and the Origins of the First World War* (1985).
J. H. MORROW, JR., *German Air Power in World War I* (1982).
D. PORCH, *The March to the Marne: The French Army 1871–1914* (1981).
K. ROBBINS, *The First World War* (1984).
Z. STEINER, *Britain and the Origins of the First World War* (1977).
L. C. F. TURNER, *Origins of the First World War* (1970).

Petrograd Worker Unrest in World War I

TSUYOSHI HASEGAWA

Revolution broke out in Russia in February, 1917. By November the Bolsheviks had achieved control of the revolution. Although long-standing injustices, inefficiencies, and social grievances associated with the tzarist government provided the long-term causes for political unrest in Russia, it was the experience of World War I that precipitated events more rapidly than almost anyone might have imagined before 1914. The Russian war effort incurred a series of devastating military defeats on the front and harsh conditions of domestic production that roused the ongoing labor discontent that had already been stirring before the conflict.

Petrograd (formerly St. Petersburg and at present Leningrad) was the key center of worker unrest. The city had the largest concentration of workers in war-related industries, and this workforce had expanded during the conflict. At the same time, with a few exceptions, real wages fell sharply as working hours were extended and as food shortages developed. The government response to labor discontent was armed repression. Nonetheless, Petrograd workers sought to protect their interests through the few legal means at their disposal, such as the insurance movement, trade unions, workers' cooperatives, and reading and cultural clubs. All of these institutions became forums for political activity and for political rivalry among the several working class political parties.

The major vehicle for worker protest in Petrograd, however, was the strike. Strikes were organized both by workers and by professional revolutionaries. Although the strikes occurred against the backdrop of military defeat and tzarist pressures against liberal members of the Duma, the causes and goals of the strikes related more directly to concerns of the workers themselves, including wages, food, and police repression. Between 1915 and 1916 the number of workers involved in strikes rose dramatically. Furthermore, workers from a variety of industries gradually became involved. The wave of strikes that

Reprinted with the permission of the University of Washington Press from *The February Revolution: Petrograd, 1917* by Tsuyoshi Hasegawa. Copyright © 1981 by University of Washington Press.

commenced in February, 1917, was so militant and widespread that the turmoil led to the breakdown of the tzarist government and to revolution. Of the various revolutionary groups seeking to undermine the tzarist regime, the Bolsheviks succeeded most skillfully in meshing their own political goals with the social and economic protest of the Petrograd labor force.

Nothing was more dangerous to the tzarist regime than the political and social isolation of the working class, which was outside the existing social order—never integrated into privileged society. The heavy concentration of workers in a few large cities, the preponderance of large plants, and the peculiar mixture of advanced technology with the backwardness of Russian industrial development all contributed to the explosive, destructive nature of the working class. If the workers welcomed the outbreak of the war, their patriotic enthusiasm soon gave way, with the military defeat and the government's corruption, to disillusionment and then to anger as the cost of living increased sharply. The government's repressive policy, which eliminated practically all legal avenues of protest, drove them to radical action. By the end of 1916, the workers, who had been silenced by the onset of the war, began to listen to the revolutionary agitators calling for an overthrow of the tzarist regime. It is important, therefore, to examine the source of the rapid radicalization of the workers in Petrograd.

Petrograd was the largest industrial center in Russia. At the beginning of 1917, it had 8.3 percent of the nation's factories within its boundaries, producing 22 percent of the total industrial output. Also the greatest number of workers were concentrated in Petrograd. At the beginning of 1914 they numbered 242,600, or 9.1 percent of the total work force in Russia. In three years of war this number rose to 392,800, an increase of 62 percent. An additional 24,200 worked in neighboring regions outside the capital, where such large plants as Izhora, Sestroretsk Weapons, and Schlüsselburg Gunpowder Factories were located. Altogether, Petrograd and its neighboring regions had 417,000 workers or 11.9 percent of all the workers in Russia.

Such a rapid expansion of Petrograd industry was closely connected with the war. By August 1916, 94 percent of the workers and 61 percent of the factories in Petrograd were engaged in military production. The war drastically changed the composition of the workers by trade. The number of metalworkers doubled to 237,400 or 60 percent of the total work force in Petrograd. Although their proportion declined during the war, textile workers were the second largest group (44,100 or 11.2 percent). Third were chemical workers, who had increased by 85 percent, numbering 40,100 or

10.2 percent. Another important effect of the war was the increased number of large plants. The average number of workers per factory rose from 536 in 1913 to 974 in 1917. At the beginning of 1917, 132 factories alone, comprising only 13 percent of all factories, employed 317,328 workers or 80.7 percent of the total work force in Petrograd. The average number of workers per factory in this category was 2,404. The largest was the Putilov Factory, which employed more than 24,000, followed by the Petrograd Pipe Factory (19,046), Treugol'nik (15,338), Obukhov (10,600), Okhta Explosives (10,200), and the Petrograd Cartridge Factory (8,292). All were involved in war production and, with the exception of Treugol'nik, all were owned by the government.

It should be noted that at the background of the revival of the workers' movement during the war, there was a tremendous expansion of Russian industry, particularly of those sectors connected with war production. This expansion created an acute labor shortage, especially of skilled metalworkers, and it was these metalworkers who participated most actively in the strike movement. They enjoyed relative security—in a labor market where they were in great demand, they could present their demands more forcefully than their comrades in other industries that did not share the prosperity created by the war boom. Shortly after the beginning of the war, the government discontinued the practice of drafting skilled workers into the army, and those who had been already drafted gradually came back to the factories.

It was not the privileged workers in the largest plants, where wages and fringe benefits were much better than those in lesser factories and where the government paid much closer attention both in "carrot" and "stick," that stood at the vanguard of the radical workers' movement. The most active participants in the strike movement during the war came from those metal manufactories in the Vyborg District that employed between 1,000 and 8,000 workers—New Lessner (6,500), Parviainen (7,300), Aivaz (4,000), Promet (3,000), Phoenix (1,940), Erikson (2,200), and Nobel (1,600). Although more definitive conclusions have to await further research, it appears that in the government-owned large munition factories the workers tended to be older and had worked in the same plant for many years, while the workers in these Vyborg factories tended to be younger and the turnover rate was higher. If this hypothesis is correct, it appears that the major impetus of the radicalization of the Petrograd workers came from these highly skilled, confident, young metalworkers whose economic benefits were much better than those in other sectors in industry but not as good as the older, skilled workers in the large government plants. Also the size of these factories, not so big as to preclude rapid communication among the workers nor so small as to be suppressed easily by the factory administration and police, contributed to the rapid mobilization of the workers....

The first factor that contributed to the revival of the workers' movement during the war was the deterioration of wages. Although the nominal wages of Petrograd workers were one and one-half times higher than the national average, the difference was eaten up by inflation. The real wages of Petrograd workers in 1916 were 90 to 95 percent of the 1913 level, and by February 1917, they had dropped an additional 15 to 20 percent. These figures, however, do not reveal the wide fluctuation among various industries as well as between skilled and unskilled workers. Only in two industrial sectors, the metal and chemical industries, did the real wages increase, by 20 and 13 percent, respectively. In the food and textile industries, where women and children were predominant, the wages were less than half those of metalworkers. The phenomenal increase in the cost of living was directly responsible for the decline in real wages. In October 1916 when prices were compared with those of 1913, rye and wheat flour went up by 243 percent and 269 percent, buckwheat by 320 percent, wheat by 308 percent, salt by 500 percent, butter by 845 percent, meat by 230 percent, sugar by 457 percent, and shoes and clothes by 400 to 500 percent. It is no wonder that the most important economic demand of the workers during the war was for an increase in wages.

Leiberov and Shkaratan argue that there emerged during the war labor aristocrats who constituted the social basis for the moderate Socialists. The data of wage distribution of New Lessner indicate the following: 27 percent of all the workers received less than 60 rubles; 25 percent between 60 and 100 rubles; 20 percent between 100 and 140 rubles; 19 percent between 140 and 200 rubles; 5 percent between 200 and 240 rubles; and 4 percent more than 240 rubles a month. Leiberov and Shkaratan estimate that about 5 to 7 percent of Petrograd workers belonged to labor aristocrats who earned more than 250 rubles a month. It is not likely, however, that amount of income inversely corresponded to the degree of participation in the strike movement. Young, skilled metalworkers who constituted the core of the strike movement may not have been the highest wage earners but they earned more than the average worker. Nevertheless, more precise conclusions must await a further statistical study.

Also contributing to the rise of the strike movement were the long working hours. The average work day in the metal industry was eleven to twelve hours, and some of the textile and leather workers frequently worked more than twelve to thirteen hours a day. This intensification of labor resulted in an increase of accidents and sickness to almost one and one-half to twice the 1913 level. In 1915 factory inspectors found 1,372 violations of health and security regulations, but ten factory owners only were fined a total of 385 rubles. In the same year there were 321,898 labor fines imposed on workers, exacting a total of 109,633 rubles. The neglect of security measures often led to tragic accidents. On April 16, 1915, an explosion in the Okhta Gunpowder Factory destroyed two workshops and eight neighboring residential buildings, killing 110 persons and wounding 220 more. On November 15, 1915, poor ventilation of a workshop in Treugol'nik led to the poisoning of 39 women workers, along with symptoms of hysteria

—shouting, crying, and laughter. Five days later another 11 workers were affected by poisonous gas in the same workshop. In October 1915, 50 anonymous workers of Langenzippen sent a petition to factory inspectors requesting intervention on their behalf to have two ventilation pipes installed in the workshop, since "every worker complains of a headache" resulting from "smoke and the smell of oil." The factory management had refused their request, replying, "You don't need such pipes. You will get cold, since heat will escape and the air is harmful to you anyway."

Factory workers endured a long work day under hazardous conditions, and they had little at home to provide ease or comfort. The crowded conditions in the workers' districts have already been mentioned. Because of the tremendous influx of new labor in Petrograd, the shortage of housing was acute—a situation that led the managements of large plants to build dormitories in the factory compounds. Rent skyrocketed—by the end of 1916 the average monthly rent had increased to twelve rubles, compared with three to four rubles before the war. Many tenants unable to pay the rent were literally thrown out into the streets.

But the most important question for the workers in Petrograd after the summer of 1915 was that of the food supply. The amount of flour transported to Petrograd Province dropped from 65 million poods [1 pood = 36.113 pounds] in 1914 to 57 million in 1916, and to 28.6 million in 1917, or 44 percent below the 1913 level. In the fall of 1915, wheat flour, meat, sugar, and butter disappeared from the market, and it became difficult to buy matches, soap, candles, and kerosene. Workers had to stand in long queues after work to buy a loaf of bread, and often by the time they got off work the bread had all been sold.

The government had no solution for the problems of the workers, but relied almost exclusively on oppression to keep them in hand. Trade unions were driven underground immediately after the outbreak of war. Workers' publications were closed down and their editors arrested. With the arrest of activists, the workers' sick-fund organizations were decimated, and the workers' group of the city-wide Insurance Council ceased to exist after the arrest of all but two members. An Okhrana [secret police] agent proudly reported: "Until now in Petrograd there has been no work by trade unions, and the association of pharmacists is the only trade union functioning at the time of war." Strikes were outlawed and strikers were punished with hard labor of four months to four years. The Moscow *gradonachal'nik*, Klimovich, stated: "All strikes ... which inevitably result in a slowdown of supply to the army, are a clear aid to our enemy, and cannot be other than a sinister betrayal of our brave soldiers and treason to the fatherland." On September 2, 1915, General Frolov, commander of the Petrograd Military District, issued a warning to workers that any participation in strikes would lead to a trial before a military tribunal and result in an indefinite period of exile.

Repressive as these measures were, they did not stop the workers' strikes, which remained the only effective means to express grievances.

When in the summer of 1915 the strike movement showed signs of revitalization, the government discussed the possibility of militarizing labor. On August 2, 1915, the minister of trade and industry presented a proposal to the Council of Ministers to place all industries engaged in war production under the jurisdiction of the War and Naval Ministries and to regulate workers by military discipline. Under this proposal the workers "should be deprived of the right to leave or stop work or service." The Council of Ministers, however, decided not to adopt this measure for fear that such militarization of labor would provoke widespread protest. In the fall of 1915 the strike movement gained impetus and at the beginning of 1916, the Council of Ministers returned to the question of militarization of labor. It decided to punish the strikers instead by sending them to the front. Leiberov and Shkaratan cite the following figures: 30 workers of New Lessner, Erikson, Neva Shipyard and others in July 1915; 80 workers of Lebedev in August 1915; 800 workers of Phoenix and Parviainen in February 1916; 172 workers of Neva Shipyard in April 1916; 130 workers of Petrograd Metal in May 1916; and 1,750 workers of major factories in October 1916; altogether 6,000 strike leaders were mobilized into the army during the period between July 1915 and December 1916. From these figures it appears certain that the government systematically used this punitive measure to discourage strikes, not realizing that it was contributing to the spread of revolutionary sentiments in the army units.

Factory owners continued to use a system of "blacklisting"—the circulation of a list of political undesirables among the members of the Petrograd Association of Factory Owners as well as among military authorities. Although the factory owners pledged not to hire anyone on the list, the acute shortage of skilled workers and the ease with which the activists could conceal their identities rendered blacklisting ineffective.

Despite police repression, Petrograd workers managed to maintain their legal and illegal networks of activities. During the war four types of legal organizations attempted to protect the workers' interests: insurance organizations, trade unions, workers' cooperatives, and cultural and educational clubs and circles.

The Insurance Law of 1912 gave the workers the right to establish a sick-fund office in factories, which in turn sent representatives to the provincial and city Insurance Councils. Although the Insurance Councils were made up mostly of representatives of the factory owners and were placed under the strict supervision of the minister of trade and industry, the workers were given a legal outlet through which they could protect their collective interests. From 1912 to 1914 the workers waged an insurance campaign, creating the workers' sick funds in factories, electing a workers' group in the Insurance Councils, and establishing a journal, *Voprosy strakhovaniia*. The campaign was organized under the influence of the Bolsheviks, and *Voprosy strakhovaniia* became the Bolsheviks' legal journal. After the outbreak of the war, the government closed down *Voprosy strakhovaniia* and arrested leading activists of the insurance movement, which, however, did not completely eliminate all the insurance organizations. Although the workers' group in the Insurance Councils ceased to function, the sick funds at the factory level continued and provided the workers with their only viable legal organization. Early in 1915 the activists in the sick-fund organizations began to reestablish contact with each other and by February the workers' insurance group began functioning and *Voprosy stakhovaniia* reappeared. This campaign was, as in the prewar period, organized by the Bolsheviks, who again controlled the insurance journal and who used it to spread their influence among the Petrograd workers. Professional Bolshevik revolutionaries such as A. A. Andreev, S. Roshal', V. V. Kuibyshev, and M. I. Kalinin worked in the sick-fund organizations in various factories as "experts" in insurance matters. To fill the eleven positions vacated by the arrested representatives in the fifteen-member workers' group of the Insurance Council, the activists launched an election campagin from December 1915 through January 1916. The result was an overwhelming victory for the Bolsheviks, who elected ten, conceding only one to the Mensheviks. The Okhrana, with good reason, regarded the insurance organizations as "Social Democratic reserve battalions," and relentlessly persecuted the activists. From August 1914 to December 1916 the government conducted seventy-seven "search and destroy" operations in the sick-fund organizations. Since by the fall of 1916 four of the workers' representatives had been arrested and only two remained, another election was held in October 1916. The Bolsheviks took four of the five new seats.

The workers' insurance movement provided workers with their legal organizational base and activists in the sick funds strove to achieve maximum protection for the workers, as provided by the Law of 1912. Although shackled by the government's censorship, they managed to publish a legal journal, which addressed itself, in between the censored blank pages, to the workers' economic issues. The Bolsheviks, who led the insurance campaign during the war, took advantage of every opportunity to spread their political slogans through insurance activities. By the end of 1916 there existed in Petrograd eighty sick-fund organizations, which recruited more than 176,000 members about 45 percent of the total number of Petrograd workers.

Another organization the workers attempted to restore during the war was the trade union. The workers repeatedly petitioned the government for permission to re-form legal unions. Fifteen different trades presented such petitions between December 1914 and February 1917, but only five were permitted, and after August 1916 no new trade unions were allowed. During the war until February 1917, there existed in Petrograd eleven underground workers' trade unions and three legal nonproletarian trade unions (clerks in printing plants, pharmacists, and doormen). Even the largest, the Union of Metalworkers, had only 4,000 members out of a total of 237,400 metalworkers, and its functioning was constantly hampered by factional struggles between Bolsheviks and Mensheviks for control. The rest of the trade unions organized a few hundred workers at most and, in general, their illegal existence made them almost meaningless. The activists therefore preferred to spend their energy in other legal outlets.

The never-ending inflation forced the development of another type of legal organization: the workers' cooperative. The first was established in November 1915, through the joint efforts of the factory owners (Old Lessner, Erikson, Nobel, and Phoenix) in the Vyborg District and the Menshevik leaders (Gvozdev, Breido, and Abrasimov). The main task of the cooperatives was to purchase food and other essential items and distribute them at low prices to the consumers. In less than a year eleven workers' cooperatives sprang up in various parts of the city and succeeded in recruiting 11,000 members and by February 1917 there were twenty-three cooperatives with 50,000 members. If the insurance movement developed under the influence of the Bolsheviks, the cooperative movement was led by the moderate Mensheviks, who controlled *Trud*, the legal journal devoted to the cooperative movement. In April 1916 the Petrograd Union of Consumers' Associations was formed as a coordinating center of all the workers' cooperatives in Petrograd. The cooperative movement, however, did not remain merely an economic organization. The Mensheviks used the cooperatives as a point of contact between the workers' movement and the liberal opposition, as well as a basis to expand their influence among the wide masses of workers. In the beginning of 1916, an Okhrana agent reported: "The revolutionary-minded elements are attempting to use the cooperatives... exclusively as a form of legal possibility."

Another network for the workers' movement comprised the cultural clubs and circles in factories and evening classes organized by liberal philanthropic activists at the People's Houses. In many large factories there were semilegal cultural clubs and reading circles. The reading materials and discussions in these clubs were avowedly political and designed to inculcate class consciousness among the masses of workers. They served also as centers for underground activists to recruit fellow travelers and were often used illegally as gathering places for strike organizers to plan strategy. It is not known how many such clubs and circles existed or how many workers participated, but their role in providing activists with a meeting place was not insignificant.

Nevertheless, the workers' greatest weapon remained the strike, although that movement quickly subsided immediately after the outbreak of war. On July 19, responding to the mobilization, the hard core of the workers' movement, around 27,000 in number from the large metal manufactories in the Vyborg District, staged a demonstration against the war, but they were quickly chased away by mounted police. Another contingent of about fifty demonstrators boldly marched on the Nevskii Prospekt only to be attacked by angry patriotic crowds. These two demonstrations were the last resonance of the strike movement that had climaxed in the general strike two weeks before the war. After that, the strike movement was moribund until the summer of 1915. While 110,000 workers had struck on January 9, 1914, the anniversary of Bloody Sunday, only 2,600 workers celebrated the traditional day of protest in 1915. When the Bolshevik Duma deputies were arrested in November 1914, no strikes occurred; and when they were brought to trial in February 1916, strikes were organized only in six factories, involving 340 workers. The war had two psychological effects on the workers. First, patriotic fervor had seized a small segment of workers in Petrograd. To the consternation of the veteran underground revolutionaries, these workers marched at the head of the patriotic demonstrations singing, "God Save the Tsar." "Our class struggle," lamented one of the Bolshevik activists, "went down the drain." In some factories workers demanded the firing of engineers and foremen with German names. Second, there was a pervasive fear among the workers that they might be drafted into the army. "The workers clung to the lathe, as a drowning man grabs a straw, in order to stay in the factory."

The defeat of the Russian army in the spring and summer of 1915, however, drastically changed the workers' mood. On July 4, 1915, more than 1,500 workers of New Lessner went on strike for higher wages, thus signaling a new wave in the strike movement. Henceforward, the New Lessner workers stood at the forefront of every major wartime strike in Petrograd. Within a week the strike spread to other factories, including the Putilov Shipyard, Neva Shipyard, and Erikson. In the last two factories, illegal strike committees were formed by the underground revolutionary activists, including the Bolsheviks and the Mensheviks. The sudden increase in strikes alarmed the authorities. The commander of the Petrograd Military District, General Frolov, warned that participation in strikes would be punished. On July 12, all the members of the strike committee of Neva Shipyard and 103 strikers of Erikson who refused to return to work were arrested by the police.

In June, a strike in a large textile factory in Kostroma—a province northwest of Moscow—resulted in a police shooting that killed twelve workers and wounded forty-five. It did not immediately arouse a strong protest among Petrograd workers. But on August 10, the police, overreacting to a demonstration of textile workers in Ivanovo-Voznesensk, fired on them, killing thirty and wounding fifty-three. On August 17, when the news reached Petrograd, the workers at Aivaz Factory struck. In the following two days the strike spread to large factories in the Vyborg, Narva, and Peterhof districts, involving 22,500 workers in twenty-three factories, all in protest of the Ivanovo massacre. The political strikes in August coincided with the rise of economic strikes. For the first time since July 19, 1914, the strikers clashed with the police, and some cases of vandalism of food stores were reported. In Mozhaiskaia Street near the barracks of the Semenovskii

Regiment, a crowd of women, joined by the newly recruited soldiers of the Eger Regiment, attacked the police and wounded twenty policemen. Military police had to be brought in to restore order.

The authorities reacted to the strike movement in August swiftly. From August 29 to September 2 the police arrested underground revolutionaries and activists in the insurance movement. In the Putilov Factory alone thirty workers were arrested, including twenty-three Bolsheviks (five of whom were members of the Bolshevik Petersburg Committee), six Socialist Revolutionaries, and one Menshevik. The mass arrest provoked a city-wide general strike. On September 2, more than 6,000 workers in the Putilov Factory struck. Workers from seven different Putilov workshops assembled in the factory courtyard and passed a resolution that included a number of demands: recall of Bolshevik deputies from exile; release of the arrested Putilov workers; establishment of a responsible ministry; drafting of policemen into the army; and a 15 percent increase in wages. They also protested the threatened prorogation of the Duma. The contents of the resolution had strong Menshevik overtones. In response to the Putilov strike, an All-City Strike Committee was hastily created by the activists of various underground party organizations. It appealed to workers of other factories to support the Putilov strike and to create a soviet of workers' deputies. The Petrograd workers responded with a four-day strike, which involved 25,800 workers at four factories on September 2; 56,900 workers at thirty-seven factories on September 3; 71,700 workers at sixty factories on September 4; and 32,200 workers at sixteen factories on September 5. The four-day strike involved a total of 82,700 workers from seventy factories.

It is interesting to note that the All-City Strike Committee endorsed the idea of the creation of a soviet of workers' deputies, which had played a dominant role in leading the workers' strike movement in St. Petersburg in the 1905 Revolution. Where the initiative to create a soviet originated during the September strike is not clear, but the Bolshevik Petersburg Committee as well as the Mensheviks supported the idea. In the absence of a viable workers' organization that could coordinate the strike and assume effective leadership over the workers' movement in the entire city, it was not surprising to see the revival of the notion of the soviet among activists, some of whom must have participated in the struggle during the 1905 Revolution. It was reported that workers in the Putilov Factory began electing their deputies to the soviet on September 2, and that on the following day an election was held in a number of Vyborg factories.

The general strike, however, revealed wide differences among leaders of the workers' movement. The Socialist deputies in the Duma were afraid that a workers' movement beyond their control would frighten the fragile coalescence that was the Progressive Bloc away from active political struggle against the government.... On the evening of September 5, the enlarged meeting of the All-City Strike Committee discussed whether to continue the strike. All groups but the Bolsheviks advocated calling it off. The September general strike was ended.

The sudden revival of the workers' strike movement in Petrograd coincided with the defeat of the Russian army and the political crisis involving the government's relationship with the Duma. To what extent did these events influence the strike movement? Were the workers' strikes a protest against the defeat of the Russian army? Were they staged in response to the government's repression of the Duma liberals and in sympathy with the liberal opposition? The three-day strikes from August 17 through 19 took place in direct response to the Ivanovo massacre. There is no evidence to indicate that the workers were concerned with the fate of the Russian army in the battlefield or that they had demonstrated their sympathy with the Progressive Bloc that was being formed. The proletarian solidarity and their utter indifference to the conflict between the government and the liberal opposition were indicative of the course that the labor movement was to take in the future. Also important to the strike movement in the summer of 1915 were the workers' economic grievances. If the defeat of the Russian army influenced the workers' movement, it created a crack in the "sacred unity," a slight show of weakness of which the workers took advantage to air their grievances.

The second wave of the strike movement from the end of August to the beginning of September coincided with the prorogation of the Duma. But the government's repressive measure against the liberals was not a major factor—the movement was initiated as a protest against the arrest of the Putilov workers. Although the resolution adopted by the Putilov workers contains a protest against the prorogation of the Duma and a demand for formation of a responsible ministry, that seems to be an exception. Okhrana reports describing in detail the four-day strike contain no other mention of the Duma. It appears, therefore, that just as the three-day strike in August was in reaction to the Ivanovo massacre, the four-day strike in September was in reaction to the police arrest of the Putilov strikers. The workers' strike movement during the war had a distinct class nature. It developed independently of the liberal opposition and its struggle with the government. There was nothing in common between the liberals and the workers' movement, and Miliukov, Maklakov, and other moderate liberals who feared the workers' strike movement more than the government's repression had a good reason for doing so.

Although political strikes sharply declined after the September strike, economic strikes sustained the new level achieved in July 1915. Economic strikes never surpassed ten a month between July 1914, and June 1915, but they fluctuated between thirteen and twenty-nine from July through December 1915. The workers not only demanded higher wages but also reinstitution of factory elders, the rehiring of fired workers, better working conditions (ranging from installation of a new ventilation system to repair of the roof and soap in the toilets), and polite treatment of workers by the management. It is significant also that many textile factories that had not been involved in political strikes participated in economic strikes in the latter half of 1915. Also in the fall of 1915, Petrograd workers were involved in lively discussions concerning the election of the workers' representatives to the War Industries Committee.

The change in mood of the workers that had developed within a year was vividly manifested in the traditional January 9 strikes in 1915 and 1916: only 2,600 workers at fourteen factories struck on the anniversary of Bloody Sunday in 1915, but more than 61,000 at sixty-eight factories joined the strike in 1916. These figures are all the more remarkable if one considers that the moderate Mensheviks and the workers' group of the War Industries Committee opposed the strike on the grounds that the workers were not sufficiently united to strike decisively. On this day the workers displayed greater militancy than earlier in confronting the police. Unlike the year before, there was a small demonstration in the Vyborg District. As the demonstrators met on the Sampsonievskii Prospekt with the police, a military truck transporting soldiers drove into the mounted police who were attacking the demonstrators. The crowd cheered the incident.

The strike movement peaked again in February and March 1916. On February 4, 230 workers of the electrical workshop of the Putilov Factory struck, demanding an increase in wages of 70 percent. Their economic strike was immediately exploited by underground activists—the Bolshevik collectives, which numbered 80 to 100 in the Putilov Factory, in cooperation with the Mezhraiontsy and the radical wing of the Mensheviks, decided to expand the strike to the entire factory. A mass rally was held in the factory courtyard, where the Bolshevik orators, Egorov (member of the Petersburg Committee), Efremov, and I. I. Bogdanov (Mezhraionets), made fiery speeches appealing to the workers to support the electrical workers. The strike expanded to three other workshops, involving more than 5,800 workers. On February 6, the factory administration shut down the factory and announced that workers who did not return to work would be immediately fired. The strike leaders met at the sick-fund office and decided to appeal to the other workers to support the Putilov strike. Egorov was dispatched to the Vyborg District to coordinate the workers' offensive between the Putilov strike and the Vyborg District. The rank-and-file workers in the Putilov Factory, however, were disturbed by the takeover of the strike movement by professional revolutionaries. Frightened by the possibility of losing their jobs, and induced by the administration's partial concessions to their demands, the workers returned to work on February 10. The general strike that the Bolshevik activists hoped to generate did not materialize.

But the management's concession—a 3 to 28 percent wage increase for those who earned less than 100 rubles a month—did not satisfy the Putilov workers. On February 18, employees in the new-shell workshop struck with the demand for a wage increase of 70 percent. The strike quickly spread to other workshops. On February 22, the administration resorted to a lockout for the second time and fired the strikers. More than 2,000 Putilov strikers were ordered to report to military service. On February 29, the Special Council for Defense decided to sequester the Putilov Factory into the government's artillary administration. This drastic measure provoked an immediate reaction from the Vyborg workers and on February 29 the workers of New Lessner, Baranovskii, Nobel, and Parviainen staged a sympathy strike. On the next three days, March 1 to 3, the major factories in Petrograd went on strike, involving 73,000 workers at forty-nine factories.

The New Lessner workers consistently led the strike movement in Petrograd in 1915 and 1916. Here among 6,000 workers was the strongest Bolshevik collective, numbering thirty to forty members, of whom four members in the Petersburg Committee—V. V. Schmidt, N. P. Komarov, P. R. Boiarshinov, and T. K. Kondratiev—led underground party activities. On March 17, 650 workers of the instrument and small-shell workshops of New Lessner went on strike and demanded a wage increase of 10 to 60 percent. On the following two days 1,950 workers from other workshops joined the strike, demanding a wage increase, polite treatment, and better sanitary conditions. A five-member strike committee was established under the leadership of a Bolshevik, N. V. Kopylov, and on March 21 the entire factory was struck. The administration resorted to a lockout, and fired all the strikers, of which about six hundred were drafted into the army. The defeat of the New Lessner strike was costly, since most political workers, including all the Bolsheviks, were driven out of the factory. With its defeat, the strike movement quickly abated.

The workers' strike movement had reached a new stage. According to Leiberov's study, during the thirteen months from July 1914 to July 1915, political and economic strikes had involved a total of 76,362 workers at 147 factories; but during the next thirteen months—from August 1915 to August 1916—the figures rose to 541,858 workers at 633 factories. The monthly average rose from 11.3 factories and 5,874 strikers in the first thirteen months to 48.7 factories and 41,681 strikers in the next thirteen months. In the following six months from September 1916 to February 1917, just prior to the February Revolution, the monthly average further rose to 88.3 factories and 98,225 strikers.

The worsening food supply situation and the general "Crisis of power" undoubtedly contributed to the revival of the strike movement in the fall of 1916. The workers' anger with inflation and the food shortage reached such a point that usually moderate leaders of the workers' group in the Central War Industries Committee admitted that "one provocation would be sufficient to ignite a disorder in the capital which might result in sacrifices in the thousands and tens of thousands." If the workers' group concluded from this that the leaders of the workers' movement should exercise restraint, the Bolsheviks attempted to exploit the food crisis for the general struggle against the tsarist regime. At the beginning of October, the Petersburg Committee instructed the party workers to "demonstrate to the masses that the problem of the cost of living increase is closely related to the struggle for a democratic republic and the end of the war." In various factories, such as Phoenix, New Lessner, and Erikson, groups of workers had held meetings since October 13 to discuss the problems of inflation and the food shortage. Some of the workers attempted to stage a demonstration in the main streets only to be chased away by the police. This tremor led to a sudden eruption on October 17, when even to the surprise of the radical activists, the workers of Parviainen, Russian Renault, and New Lessner went on strike, and staged a demonstration along the Sampsonievskii Prospekt. When the demonstrators approached the barracks of the 181st Infantry Regiment where a crowd of soldiers sympathetically watched the workers' demonstration through the barracks fences, the police attacked the demonstrators. This angered the soldiers, who threw rocks and bricks at the police. Shouting, "Beat the police," the soldiers jumped over and crawled under the barrack fences and joined the demonstrators. The demonstrators, now outnumbering the police, surrounded them and took away their sabers and revolvers. It was only after the Cossacks and the training detachment of the Moscow Regiment arrived at the scene that order was restored. According to one of the soldiers who took part in the demonstration, A. Ivanov, former Bolshevik worker in the Putilov Factory, there were in the 181st Infantry Regiment many former strike participants, like himself, who continued political agitation in the military units. The military authorities later arrested 130 soldiers, and the 181st Infantry Regiment was removed from Petrograd. By the end of the day, 27,300 workers from ten factories had participated in the strike in the Vyborg District. On the following day, October 18, the strike spread to 46,300 workers at thirty-four factories in the Vyborg, Petrograd, Vasilievskii, and Moscow districts, and on October 19 to 75,400 workers at sixty-three factories in all parts of the city.

The three-day strike was followed by another wave of strikes at the end of October. The second was purely political, and it was called by the Bolsheviks. The Petersburg Committee decided to appeal to the workers to stage a political strike against the trial of the Bolshevik sailors in the Baltic Fleet who had been arrested because of their revolutionary activities, and against the arrest of the soldiers of the 181st Infantry Regiment. On October 26, the opening day of the trial, 25,800 workers at thirteen factories participated in the strike; it spread to 52,500 workers at forty-seven factories on October 27, and on the third day to 79,100 workers at seventy-seven factories. If one remembers that the Petersburg Committee's strike call for the trial of the arrested Bolshevik Duma deputies attracted only 340 workers at six factories in February 1915, the strike figures in the second half of October clearly demonstrate the increased radicalization of the Petrograd workers and the growing influence of the Bolsheviks. This in turn contributed to the radicalization of the workers' group, which, aware of their slipping influence, tried to recover the lost ground.

After October, the strike movement subsided. Such was the inevitable aftermath of every explosion of labor unrest. The leaders had been arrested, the networks of communications and organizations were broken, and the workers needed time to recover from the emotional strain. Those who had been fired needed to find other jobs, often by disguising their identities. Nevertheless, the ebb of the workers' movement in November and December 1916 did not mean that the workers became apathetic and inactive. Strikes subsided, but sporadic attacks on food stores became rampant. When the strike movement picked up momentum again in January 1917, after two months' lull, it was to engulf a wider segment of the Petrograd workers, and eventually to develop into a revolution.

Petrograd workers can be divided into four groups according to their participation in wartime strikes. The vanguard of the strike movement were the metalworkers of Aivaz (4,100), Baranovskii (1,300), Vulkan (1,100), Dinamo (2,100), Nobel (1,600), Promet (3,000), Parviainen (7,300), Old Lessner (1,100), New Lessner (6,500), Phoenix (1,900), Diuflon (820), and Erikson (2,200). These workers, approximately 33,000, were the backbone of every major strike during the war. Particularly important were the two factories, Parviainen and New Lessner. Of these twelve factories all but Dinamo (Narva District), Vulkan (Petrograd District), and Diuflon (Petrograd District) were located in the Vyborg District. All were privately owned factories. They were by no means the largest plants in Petrograd, but those employing between 1,000 and 8,000 workers (with the exception of Dinamo). With the exceptions of Diuflon and Erikson all were engaged in weapon and munitions production. Diuflon was producing electrical machines and instruments. Erikson specialized in the production of telephones, but during the war it had also expanded its production to weapon manufacturing.

The second group consisted of workers whose participation was primarily limited to economic strikes, although some of them sporadically joined the political strikes. Three distinctly different workers belonged to this group. First were the workers of the state-owned largest munition factories: Neva Shipyard (6,100), Obukhov (10,600), Petrograd Metal (6,700), Putilov (24,400), Franco-Russian (6,700), Baltic Shipyard (7,600), and Putilov Shipyard (4,200). But other munitions factories such as Arsenal (4,000), Petrograd Cartridge (8,300), Orudinskii (3,500), Cable (2,300), Admiralty Shipyard (4,500), Okhta Explosives (10,200), and Okhta Gunpowder (5,700) were involved in no strikes during the war. Second were workers of metal factories engaged in weapon production: Rosenkrantz (3,800), Langenzippen (2,500), Ekval' (300), Russian Renault (1,700), Semenov (700), Armaturnyi (1,000), Siemens-Schückert Electrical (2,000), Koppel (600), Petrograd Wagon (2,000), Puzyrev (200), Russian-Baltic Motor (400), Lebedev Aeronautics (1,100), Russian-Baltic Aeronautics (500), Sliusarenko (200), and Stetinin (2,000). Third were textile workers: Voronin, Liutsh, Chesher, Nikol'skaia Manufacture (1,500), Lebedev Jute (1,000), Leontiev (600), Nevka (2,700), Neva Cotton (2,000), Okhta Cotton

(900), Pal' (1,800), Petrovskaia (1,700), Sampsonievskaia (1,600), and Northern Weaving (1,000). Altogether 100,000 workers of this group persistently fought for economic gains, but they were not always active supporters of political strikes. In particular, textileworkers did not join political strikes until the beginning of 1917.

The third category comprised workers of factories who struck once or twice during the war, but on the whole remained inactive. This group include 16,300 metalworkers, 9,300 textileworkers, 2,200 in paper manufacturing, 1,100 wood processors, 17,900 in leather and shoe manufacturing, 4,700 food and tobacco processors, 1,800 chemical workers, and 1,000 others—altogether 54,300 workers. The total of these three categories was 187,400. Since these figures represent all the workers of the struck factories and therefore have an obvious upward bias, the actual participants in strikes are presumed to be much smaller. Even this inflated figure is only 47.7 percent of the total workers in Petrograd in January 1917. Thus more than half of the Petrograd workers remained in the fourth category, those who never struck during the war.

There is no reason to believe, however, that the silent majority of these workers accepted their misery meekly. The general trend of the strike movement clearly indicates that the movement led by the vanguard of the metalworkers was gradually drawing the often cautious workers of the largest plants as well as less organized sector of the working class. The political and economic strikes that had developed differently throughout 1915 and in the beginning of 1916 had shown a trend to merge into one in late 1916.

The workers in Petrograd were the fundamental source of instability in Russian politics during the war. The patriotism at the outbreak of the war was quickly dissipated as wartime reality hit. Excluded from the established order of society and deprived of legal organizations to air their grievances, yet asked to continue their sacrifices for "national honor and pride," the workers became receptive to the agitators' call for radical action.

Bibliography

J. H. BATES, *St. Petersburg: Industrialization and Change* (1976).
W. H. CHAMBERLIN, *The Russian Revolution, 1917–1923*, 3 vols. (1950–1953).
J. L. H. KEEP, *The Russian Revolution: A Study in Mass Mobilization* (1976).
L. H. HARMSON, ed., *The Politics of Rural Russia, 1905–1914* (1979).
N. M. NAIMARK, *Terrorists and Social Democrats: The Russian Revolutionary Movement under Alexander III* (1983).
R. PEARSON, *The Russian Moderates and the Crisis of Tsarism, 1914–1917* (1977).
A. RABINOWITCH, *Prelude to Revolution: The Petrograd Bolsheviks and the July 1917 Uprising* (1968).
A. RABINOWITCH, *The Bolsheviks Come to Power* (1976).

S. Schwarz, *The Russian Revolution of 1915: The Workers' Movement and the Formation of Bolshevism and Menshevism* (1967).
T. H. Von Laue, *Why Lenin? Why Stalin?* (1964).
A. Ulam, *The Bolsheviks: The Intellectual and Political History of the Triumph of Communism in Russia* (1965).
A. K. Wildman, *The End of the Russian Imperial Army: The Old Army and the Soldiers' Revolt (March–April 1917)* (1980).

Lost Legions of English Youth

ROBERT WOHL

World War I had been so vast in its extent, the suffering so staggering, the social and political change so stunning, and the peace settlement so disillusioning that writers pondered and repondered the experience. Throughout western Europe a literature of war poetry, novels, autobiographies, and memoirs appeared by the end of the 1920s. These works not only retold the story of the Great War but also provided larger interpretations of the meaning of the event.

In England these writings established the legend that the Great War had sacrificed the best men of the youthful generation that was approaching adulthood in 1914. As a result of this irreparable loss of talent and energy, the character of British life and the position of the British Empire experienced major decline. This thesis is subject to much doubt, and the facts of the situation do not measure up to the demands of the legend; but in the decades after World War I the alleged absence of that golden generation became a common explanation used to account for the loss of British prestige and power.

There is a legend about the history of twentieth-century England. Like all legends, it exists in many variants and was the product of many minds. Though it is nowhere written down in its entirety, fragments of it are to be found in many books and it lives on in the national memory and the oral tradition. It goes something like this.

Once upon a time, before the Great War, there lived a generation of young men of unusual abilities. Strong, brave, and beautiful, they combined great athletic prowess with deep classical learning. Poets at heart, they loved the things of the mind for their own sake and were scornfully detached from the common struggle. Although stemming from all parts of England,

N.B. Note that the dates in parentheses after certain names indicate the year of birth of those persons who were part of the generation of 1914.

Reprinted by permission of the author and publishers from *The Generation of 1914* by Robert Wohl (Cambridge, Mass.: Harvard University Press). Copyright © 1979 by the President and Fellows of Harvard College and by George Weidenfeld and Nicolson Ltd.

they were to be found above all at Oxford and Cambridge, and in the case of the younger men, at the better public schools. When the war broke out, they volunteered for service in the fighting forces and did whatever they could to hasten their training and secure their transfer to the field of battle. Their main fear was that the war would end before they arrived at the front. Brought up to revere England and to do their duty, they embraced their country's cause and accepted lightheartedly the likelihood of early death. Most of them were killed on the battlefields of Gallipoli, Ypres, Loos, the Somme, Passchendaele, and Cambrai. Those who were not killed were mutilated in mind and body. They limped home in 1919 to find that their sacrifice had been in vain. The hard-faced, hard-hearted old men had come back and seized the levers of power. Youth had been defeated by age. Civilization had been dealt a fatal blow. Few in number, tired and shell-shocked, disillusioned by what they found at home, they sat by helplessly during the interwar years and watched the old politicians flounder in incompetence and squander their victory. The peace was lost; English hegemony in the world was lost; the empire was lost; even traditional English values were lost, as the English submitted to the tyranny of foreign models. Eventually a second war came to seal the disaster of the first, and England slipped pusillanimously into the category of second-rate powers. All might have been different if only the splendid young men of 1914 had not given up their lives on the fields of Flanders and the beaches of Gallipoli....

The war poets had provided the theme: doomed youth led blindly to the slaughter by cruel age. But a decade passed before this theme was developed in prose in a systematic or sustained fashion. Then came a rash of books about the generation of 1914 and their war experiences, many of which became runaway best-sellers. These books were pessimistic, cynical, and some times very bitter and brutal. All seemed like an extended gloss on the epigraph from Barbusse's *Under Fire* that [Siegfried] Sassoon had placed at the beginning of his 1918 collection of poems, wherein Barbusse asserted that war brought in its wake everything that was basest in man: "wickedness to the point of sadism, egoism to the point of ferocity, the need for pleasure to the point of madness." Most of these books were by people born in the 1890s, who had been just out of school when the war began. Though sometimes cleverly written, they did not come easily to their authors, many of whom had tried to write about their experiences soon after the war ended, had failed or been too discouraged to continue, and had resumed the effort only when the public again appeared ready to hear about the war. Then manuscripts were fetched from trunks and the presses began to groan with dozens and eventually hundreds of war books, until the critics cried out for mercy and respite. While focused on the period of the war, most of these books tried to encompass the prewar and postwar periods as well, thus putting back together, at least in memory, worlds and compartments of life that the war had torn asunder. Some were written as novels; more often they abandoned all claim to fiction and were called memoirs, autobiography, or testaments; all were meant to provide a record of personal experience that would throw light on the collective experience and fate of an entire age-group.

First, in 1928, came Edmund Blunden's *Undertones of War* and Sassoon's *Memoirs of a Fox-Hunting Man*. Blunden (1896) anticipated and helped to shape the approach of later war books by abandoning any attempt to describe the general context of warfare within which his personal experience took place. He chose to concentrate on "the little things" that filled the foreground of life at the front, and he was at his best when evoking, in prose that was often heavily literary and self-consciously mannered, "the bitterness of waste" that developed in 1917 among the survivors of the Somme attacks. "The uselessness of the offensive, the contrast in the quality of ourselves with the quality of the year before, the conviction that the civilian population realized nothing of our state, the rarity of thought, the growing intensity and sweep of destructive forces—these views brought on a mood of selfishness. We shall all die, presumably, round Ypres." Sassoon's memoir, lightly fictionalized and at first published anonymously in a small edition, was notable chiefly for the understated and patrician irony with which the now famous poet contrasted the world in which he had grown up—a world of Elysian air, "green hedgerows that had been drenched by early morning sunlight," untroubled downs, gentle horses, loving aunts, deferential servants, and "merry" hop-pickers from the slums of London—with the dim, grey, ugly world of the Western Front. His protagonist George Sherston is plunged in 1916 into a world of warfare and ugliness that his prior life has not prepared him to understand. As the book ends on Easter Sunday 1916, Sherston's groom has died at the front from pneumonia and his friend Dick Tiltwood, "a shining epitome of his embittered generation," has been killed mending wire. Sherston realizes with regret that the war is going to destroy his past; and standing in a "dismal ditch," he can "find no consolation in the thought that Christ has risen."

The big year for war books in England was 1929. Some twenty-nine were published, as compared with twenty-one in 1928 and only six in 1926. Of these the most important were the translation of Erich Maria Remarque's *All Quiet on the Western Front*, Robert Graves's *Good-bye to All That*, and Richard Aldington's *Death of a Hero*. These books bore the same relationship to Blunden and Sassoon's genteel memoirs that a soldier's conversation bore to a Brooke sonnet. *All Quiet on the Western Front*, which enjoyed an immense success in England, selling more than 250,000 copies in its first year after being serialized in the Sunday papers, was an inspired exercise in neogothic Grand Guignol. Remarque's soldiers die like flies, splattered across the wall of the trench so that "you could scrape them off... with a spoon and bury them in a mess-tin." Before they die, they desert, refuse to attack out of cowardice, steal the watches of their wounded comrades, haggle over the boots of a dying friend, and show concern for no cause larger than their basest bodily needs. At the heart of his book, Remarque later explained in a letter to General Sir Ian Hamilton, commander of the Dardenelles expedition, was "the intention of presenting the fate of a generation of young men who, at the critical age when they were just beginning to feel the pulse of life, were set face to face with death."

Good-bye to All That was more distanced, less bitter, more in the stiff-upper-lipped tradition of the British public school. As such, it was more to the taste of the London critics who found it a "gay book and a gallant one" because of its "attempt to be detached and to maintain a saving sense of humour." But Graves's book too made nonsense of civilian ideas of patriotically inspired courage among the troops by pointing out that an infantry officer's effectiveness in the line was largely a function of how long he had been there. "The unfortunates were officers who had endured two years or more of continuous trench service. In many cases they became dipsomaniacs." This apparently innocent remark will shock no one today; it did shock in 1929 when the pretense was still maintained that drink was a malady of the lower orders and not a source of courage for officers and gentlemen. Graves's soldiers fight not for king, country, or God, but for their regiment's honor, or for their friends, or sometimes because they enjoy it. They are not especially gallant. Indeed, they show a deplorable insensitivity to their comrades' fate and do not always remember to take prisoners. It was true that Graves's anecdotes were meant to shock and that the book occasionally struck a note that came close to sounding comic. But if the text left any doubt about the author's attitude toward the war, he clarified it by writing a typically irreverent letter to the editor of the *Times Literary Supplement* in which he explained that "the average British soldier of 1914–18, unlike his predecessors, the scum of the gaols who sacked Badajoz, had to be duped into the toughness and immorality that made a successful civilized fighter, by lying propaganda and a campaign of organized blood lust. This was the peculiar dirtiness of the Great War." There was nothing comic about this.

Aldington's *Death of a Hero* was by far the shrillest of these books. Critics generally do not recommend it today, but anyone trying to understand the attitudes of English survivors of the war would be well advised to read it. Written in the form of a novel, it was an angry indictment of the generation of late Victorians who had lightheartedly sent their sons to die on the battlefields of France and Flanders. Aldington (1892) attempted to establish a connection between the sexual hypocrisy of the Victorians and the jingoistic mood that prevailed in England between 1914 and 1918. "It was the regime of Cant *before* the War," he cried, "which made the Cant *during* the War so damnably possible and easy. On our coming of age the Victorians generously handed us a charming little check for fifty guineas —fifty-one months of hell, and the results." Aldington's protagonist George Winterbourne goes "heroically" to his death in November 1918, "a wrecked man, swept along in the swirling cataracts of the War." His wife and his mother will not miss him, for they have already found consolation in lovers; and his father will justify it all in the name of the mysterious ways of God. No other war book drew such a stinging contrast between those who stayed at home or safely behind the lines—especially the women—and those at the front who inured themselves to hardship without becoming cruel and who fought and died for a cause in which they no longer believed. The reviewer of the *Times Literary Supplement*, himself an ex-combatant, wrote admiringly of Aldington: "We do not wish him in this 'Death of a Hero' other than he is—a man appalled by the inhumanities suddenly concentrated upon those who were in their hopeful youth at the outbreak of the War, and assailing with inspired intensity those who seem responsible for and apathetic towards the sacrifice."

More war books followed in 1930, chief among them Sassoon's *Memoirs of an Infantry Officer*, Frederick Manning's *Her Privates We*, and Henry Williamson's *The Patriot's Progress*. This last book narrated in a blunt, tough, machine-gun prose the adventures of private John Bullock, a London clerk who volunteers for service in August 1914 and who is invalided home in 1917 after being stripped of every illusion about a war that at one point he perceives as "slavery." In a text of fewer than two hundred pages, profusely illustrated with line drawings, Williamson (1895) presents a gallery of inglorious episodes meant to expose the iniquity and degradation of war as it was lived by the men in the ranks. The reader is told in quick succession about a soldier who blows his brains out because he cannot bear the pressure of life at the front; a mutiny of British troops, which is sternly repressed; an attack in which six hundred out of seven hundred men failed to return; an attempt by the hero to induce fever by chewing cordite in order to stay out of the line; a visit to a prostitute followed by drunkenness and a failure to report for parade; two weeks of field punishment imposed by an unfeeling colonel; and the third battle of Ypres, where John Bullock loses his best friend and his leg. By 1917 "John Bullock took no heed of the dead men, nor of the wounded on the stretchers. He was just kept going by one hope: the hope of getting a wound which would put him out of the war ... Every time the brutal droning of shells increased into the deep, savage, sudden buzzing which told they were going to burst near, he crouched and sweated and cringed." Shaking with fear, John Bullock attacks when ordered, only to be blown into a shell crater. He returns home without ever having seen a German, to the disgust and disbelief of his father, who hoped that his son would bag at least one Hun. As the book ends with the one-legged John Bullock taking the air in a London park on Armistice Day, it is clear that "the patriot" is now a superfluous man whose sacrifice will soon be forgotten."

Efforts were made to counter this view of the war and the reaction of the war generation to it. Douglas Jerrold (1893) wrote an indignant pamphlet exposing "the lie about the War" and arguing that the war books of

1929–1930 were statistically false in representing as frequent what in fact was rare and historically inaccurate in claiming that the men who fought the war lost all faith in what they were doing. Jerrold insisted that "no honest, dispassionate, and *really* frank retrospect of war, no crystallisation in words of its full store of memories and ultimate meaning by decently humble and conscientious men, will reflect anything but a mixture of good and bad, intensified above the *tempo* of peace but in proportions fundamentally the same." Jerrold also pointed out shrewdly that the new war books achieved their literary effect by focusing on the sufferings of the individual soldier and separating him from the larger units of which he was a part. They obscured the fact that the war was a collective struggle and that important collective issues were at stake. In his book *A Subaltern's War*, published in 1929 and reissued in 1930, Charles Carrington (1897) also claimed that the legend of disenchantment was false. "Disillusion," he submitted, "came in with peace, not with war; peace at first was the futile state." Still another ex-combatant felt after reading this literature that the war had not been as the new books described it.

> One was not always attacking or under fire. And one's friends were not always being killed. One had friends in those days, and one has hardly any now. And friendship was good in brief rests in some French village behind the line where it was sometimes spring, and there were still fruit trees to bloom, and young cornfields, and birds singing. And even after the first great disillusionment, that followed the Somme, reached England through men coming home, young subalterns still went out from school full of enthusiasm. One wanted to get there oneself and see what it was like, even though one knew.

These lonely and uninfluential voices failed, however, to dissuade the majority of the English literary establishment from what had now become an *idée fixe*. They continued to assert, with Sassoon, that the war had been a dirty trick played by the older generation on the younger, that it had been a "crime against humanity," and that it was responsible for most, if not everything, that was wrong with England. In retrospect, it is easy enough to understand why they did so. By the end of the 1920s most English intellectuals believed that the war had been a general and unmitigated disaster, that England's victory was in reality a defeat, and hence that the men who had caused England to enter the war and to fight it through to the bloody end were either mercenary blackguards or blundering old fools. Such ideas could rally radicals as well as reactionaries.

From a conservative point of view, it seemed evident that the war had demolished the old world beyond all hope of restoration. Upper-class people found their actions increasingly limited by the state, their inherited rights threatened by the Labour party and the unions, and their economic superiority undermined by a diminished and fluctuating pound. Some members of the landed aristocracy had been forced by death duties to subdivide their estates and sell them off to profiteers, who had made their money (or added substantially to it) while the sons of the former owners had been dying in the field. It was also true that English might and prestige in the world had slipped, to the point that no one could delude himself into thinking that Britannia ruled the waves or that England was *primus inter pares* in the club of global powers. Who would have dared to write in 1929, as a well-known journalist had done so confidently just a decade before, that "the British Empire is sure of at least as long a lease of life as the Roman *Imperium*"? In short, the England of Victoria and Edward was dead and gone forever.

Viewed from the Left, things looked little better. The war had not made possible a breakthrough into some new and more dynamic future. The old elites, led by Stanley Baldwin, had proved themselves incapable of putting the country back on its feet. But neither were they willing to give up the reins of power. They plodded along, tediously, from concession to concession, a tired and defeated army making an agonizingly slow retreat. The Labour party appeared briefly to carry the standard of the future. But by 1931 Labour had disappointed most of its intellectual supporters. Voted into power by a large majority in 1929, Labour's leaders quickly pledged their allegiance to the doctrine of fiscal conservatism and demonstrated an appalling dearth of new ideas. The Socialist Ramsay MacDonald emerged as the Baldwin of the Left. Nor had the war brought Europe peace. The persistence of tension among the continental countries and the mounting tide of German nationalism were additional reminders that the "war to end all wars" had been fought in vain. What was more natural than to blame this dreadful situation on the Victorians and the hard-hearted old men who lacked courage, compassion, and imagination. Thus intellectuals old enough to remember the prewar world but young enough to equate it with innocence and untested youth bemoaned the fate of their "depleted" generation and reflected on the absence of really "first-rate" men. They predicted that England, like Europe, was heading for a terrible disaster, though few were willing to go as far as Sir Oswald Mosley (1896), who bolted the Labour party in 1930 and declared war against the old men "who muddled my generation into the crisis of 1914, who muddled us into the crisis of 1931—the old men who have laid waste to the power and glory of the land."

Mosley slipped toward Fascism. Henry Williamson and a handful of intellectuals followed him. Mosley described the British Union of Fascists, which he founded in October 1932, as an alliance of the war generation and English youth directed against an aging and incompetent establishment. Yet in England, unlike in Germany, the generational idea was even more popular among intellectuals of the Left than it was among intellectuals of the Right. The classic example of English lost generation literature, Vera Brittain's *Testament of Youth*, was written by a woman of strong socialist and feminist convictions. A student at Oxford when the war broke out, Brittain (1895) volunteered for overseas service as a nurse after her fiancé was killed in action in France. Before the war ended, she had lost her brother and two close male friends to whom she was devoted. Brittain decided in 1925 to write a novel based on her experiences. Not until November 1929, however, did she begin to draft the book. In the meantime, seeing the hit play *Journey's End* and reading the war books of 1928–1929 had convinced her that her story was worth telling and that she should cast it in the form of a generational memoir. "After reading these books, I began to ask: 'Why should these young men have the war to themselves? Didn't women have their war as well?'... With scientific precision I studied the memoirs of Blunden, Sassoon, and Graves. Surely, I thought, my story is as interesting as theirs? Besides, I see things other than they have seen, and some of the things they perceive I see differently."

Testament of Youth was too self-indulgent, too self-pitying, and too lacking in self-irony to be good literature. But it sold well and gained its author considerable notoriety when it was published in 1933. It owed this success to the fact that it made explicit, as no other war book had, the narrative sequence within which many English survivors of the war had come to perceive their past. This form was an adaptation of the medieval romance. First came a phase of innocence identified with the years before 1914. As Vera Brittain's talented young heroes graduate from their public school in July 1914, they have no premonition of "the threatening woe" that their "adventurous feet" will "starkly meet." Then followed the ordeal of war service in France. Full of enthusiasm when they volunteer, they lose their heroic illusions before dying in a war that they have come to regard as evil and futile. The third stage in the narrative was the return to England. Battered by "storm winds," a few survivors make their way home, only to discover that they are "ghosts of a time no future can restore." They are condemned by their fate to "desolately roam for evermore an empty shore." The final disillusionment was the survivors' discovery that the sacrifice of the dead had been in vain. The so-called victory had in fact been a setback for civilization; war would come again; another idealistic generation would be destroyed.

It was on this doom-filled note that *Testament of Youth* ended. The war generation had failed in its mission. The survivors had been too few in numbers and too dispirited by their experience to remove the old men from power. "Perhaps, after all, the best that we who were left could do was to refuse to forget, and to teach our successors what we remembered in the hope that they, when their day came, would have more power to change the state of the world than this bankrupt, shattered generation." Vera Brittain's lament seems to have touched some deep emotions in the English reading public; within six years, *Testament of Youth* sold 120,000 copies. It was reissued in 1978.

By the outbreak of the Second World War in 1939 the idea of a lost generation had installed itself securely in English minds and was on the verge of hardening into a generally accepted interpretation of recent English history. To be sure, it appeared most frequently on the pens of journalists and memoir writers, in obituaries, and in conversations among academics at high table; but it sometimes crept obliquely into the books and articles of serious historians. Meanwhile, an interesting shift in usage had begun to occur. "Lost" generation was increasingly being equated with "missing" generation; the idea of disorientation and discontinuity was being subordinated to the suggestion of physical absence, so much so that the term was sometimes used as if there had been no survivors worth mentioning at all.

This strange idea made its way like a rumor passed on and further distorted in each retelling. Already in 1930 a leading English magazine, *The Nation*, had published an article whose author had asserted, without contradiction from the editors, that "if you look you will not find in England in politics, in business, in the professions any young men of that generation occupying the higher and better paid posts." The lost generation had few survivors, he added parenthetically, and the few there were had been "hustled out of England in the years immediately after the War as if their survival had indeed been a mistake and they were something to be hidden so that the War might be done with and forgotten." In 1942 the historian E. L. Woodward expressed bitter disappointment with the treatment meted out to the war generation by their elders and remarked hyperbolically that "The men who came back from the war have counted for less, perhaps, in the political life of their country than any generation during the last two or three centuries." Assessing this interpretation of recent English history in 1964, Reginald Pound, a well-known biographer and himself a volunteer in 1914, concluded in a book entitled *The Lost Generation* that the real losses in the Great War were losses of cultural potential and of character. "There was no estimating the extent to which creative thought was depleted, or the cost to learning, literature and science of the destruction of so many strong and cultivated intelligences." Pound wondered if those missing would have "resisted the Satanic forces that have invaded the arts? Could they have seen to it that their second-rate would not become our first-rate, or have arrested the decline of moral indignation into unheroic tolerance?" In Pound's view, British national life presented "as never before the embarrassing spectacle of men of minor powers wrestling with major responsibilities. There is impoverishment at all levels." The publishers of this volume were so impressed by these reflections that they placed them on the flyleaf of the book and repeated them in a short description of the book's contents placed just inside the cover. The legend is so hallowed that even an historian determined to be revisionist can fall prey to it. Recently, Robert Skidelsky asked if Mosley might not have pulled off his revolt against the established parties in 1930 if only so many men of his age-group had not been killed in the war. On reflection, Skidelsky believed that there were not enough young Tories, Liberals, and Labourites to rally to Mosley's cause when he embarked upon the creation of the New party. "But for the 'missing generation' there may have been many more of them, and the history of England might have been very different."

An historian determined to rewrite British history from the point of view of the subordinate classes would have little trouble demolishing the myth of the missing generation. British losses were proportionately less than those of the other major European countries that went to war in 1914. With an approximately equal population, France had twice as many dead: and if Britain's losses had been at the same rate as Germany's in relation to population, they would have totaled 1,200,000 instead of 700,000. True, the number of males aged twenty to forty, per thousand of the population, dropped between 1911 and 1921—but only from 155 to 141, hardly a devastating or radical change so long as one remains on the level of statistics. Three years after the war ended, the population included more than five million men born between 1882 and 1901. These age-groups had borne the brunt of front-line war service. Losses among them had been terrible. But not sufficient to destroy a generation—if one defines a generation in mass terms as a group of people of roughly similar age bound together by a common historical experience and a common fate.

Yet figures like those just cited do not get at the kernel of the lost generation myth. For the myth holds that the best men died. Supposedly, the purest and noblest, the strongest and most cultivated had fallen; the weakest and least courageous had survived. This process of reverse selection had meant "failure and calamity in every department of human life" and was held responsible by some for the decline of England and the coming of the Second World War.

One is inclined to dismiss this idea as elitist nonsense. First of all, one of the main characteristics of trench warfare during the First World War was its impersonality and the fact that death was meted out at random to brave and cowardly alike. The chances were far greater that one would be killed by an unseen machine gun, a bomb projected blindly from an enemy trench, or an accidental artillery hit than by a soldier's rifle or a bayonet in anything resembling direct combat. Many soldiers died without ever glimpsing the enemy. Survival had little to do with purity or nobility, though one could argue that stronger and better-nourished men from the more affluent sectors of society had a greater chance of withstanding the rigors of the climate, the danger of infection, and the fatigue brought on by hard physical labor and irregular sleep. Many were killed because they were too tired to take cover or too wet and miserable to care whether they lived or died. Intelligence also helped in staying alive: Some soldiers stubbornly refused to wear gas masks or neglected to inform themselves about snipers when entering new sectors. Robert Graves may have had these facts in mind when he shocked the local rector and his parishioners at a memorial service held soon after the war had ended by telling them that "the men who had fallen, destroyed as it were by the fall of the Tower of Siloam, were not particularly virtuous or particularly wicked, but just average soldiers." His advice to the survivors was that they "should thank God that they were alive, and do their best to avoid wars in the future."

There is no reason, therefore, to believe that the age-groups who fought the war were too reduced in numbers to play a role in postwar England, or to think that the survivors were any worse—or better—than the men who died. Why then did the notion of a missing generation take such deep root in England? Primarily, no doubt, because of the small and well-defined nature of the English elite and its unprecedented involvement in the actual fighting of the war. It is easy to forget that Britain differed from other continental powers in that before 1914 military service was not a sacred obligation incumbent upon all able-bodied male citizens, but a profession practiced by a privileged few—generally the less talented sons of the upper classes—and a refuge and dead end for members of the lower orders who had been unable or unwilling to make their way in civilian life. Between 1914 and 1918 this changed. The army became a fate that the majority of men born between 1880 and 1899 shared. This fate embraced men of all social categories. In the records left for posterity and in the annals of the higher culture, however, it was associated almost exclusively with members of the middle and upper classes.

In retrospect, it is clear enough how and why this happened. Though men of all social backgrounds rushed to volunteer during the early stages of the war, those from the upper and middle classes were healthier, larger, and more easily spared from their peacetime occupations (if they had one); thus they were more likely to be passed for active service and sent to France or Flanders where five of every nine who fought were killed, wounded, or missing. Losses among university and public school graduates were especially high, because they were preferred as junior officers. Junior officers suffered heavier losses than the men who served under them. It was the job of junior officers to lead attacks, conduct raids, and see to it that the wire in front of their trenches was mended. They risked their lives when asked to, knowing that it was their function to set an example to their men. The younger the junior officer and the more privileged his education, the more likely he was to be killed.

Heavy and unprecedented losses within the younger age-groups of the upper and middle classes created a collective trauma that intensified with every year of the conflict. One way that those at home coped with these losses was by directing their rage against the German enemy and denouncing presumed spies and slackers who were not doing their bit; another was by celebrating the dead and pretending that their death was glorious and lucky. Obituaries were published in the *Times*; memoirs by parents, friends, and teachers were written and circulated; plaques, busts, and memorials were installed in schools and universities. In many cases, the fallen officer's poems and correspondence were collected and published. Everything was done to keep the memory of *these* dead—that is, the dead of the elite—alive. Later when the war had ended and its fruits appeared so meager, these losses became a popular way of explaining British decline.

There was nothing mythical about these losses—only about the uses to which they were later put. The "firstborn" of England's sons fell in dismaying numbers during the Great War. Figures to illustrate this can be taken almost at random. Of the 5,588 Etonians who served in the war, 1,159 were killed and 1,469 were wounded. Robert Nichols calculated that among the 136 members of his college at Oxford from the classes of 1911, 1912, and 1913 who served, 31 were killed in action or died of wounds. Two hundred and twenty-eight members of Guy Chapman's Oxford college, Christ Church, died in the war, a number that represented three years' intake of students in that college. Several eminent families lost their eldest sons; some lost two or three sons in the space of a year.

Still, the fact remains that most men who served, even from within the elite, came back. Two—Anthony Eden and Harold Macmillan—became prime ministers of England. Countless others served in Parliament and occupied less exalted but still important positions in public life. They ran ministries, political parties, and publishing companies; they wrote newspapers, books, and book reviews; they administered businesses and universities; they directed scientific institutes and laboratories; they represented their nation abroad; and they shaped the mentality of their countrymen in many and varied ways. Their momoirs would now stock several library shelves, and few of them fail to pay homage in those books to the better and more brilliant men from their age-group who died. This raises a perplexing question, more elusive than the one concerning origins with which we have just dealt: Why did survivors of the Great War perpetuate the myth? What stake could they have had in keeping alive the idea of a lost or missing generation?

The answer is that the myth of the missing generation provided an important self-image for the survivors from within the educated elite and a psychologically satisfying and perhaps even necessary explanation of what happened to them after they returned from the war. The cult of the dead became a means of accounting for the disappointments of the present. To be sure, this cult had its origins in the war experience itself. It reflected the natural guilt of the survivors who knew they had no right to live when those around them had died, as well as their angry feeling, stronger in England than anywhere else, that they had been the victims of a dirty trick played by History incarnated in the evil form of the Older Generation. Owen's war poetry had already sounded most of the essential themes: the grandeur of the fighting forces; the betrayal of Youth by Age; and the tragic nature of his generation's fate. But the sentiments his poetry expressed might have faded with time and renewed activity, if it were not for the fact that the return to England and the experience of life during the twenties and early thirties confirmed them. What the survivors found upon returning was not a home fit for heroes, but a "long weekend" in which life was experienced as being "downhill all the way" and a "contrary experience." In this atmosphere of decline, nostalgia for the past, and persistently postponed crisis that was England between the wars, the myth of the lost generation with all its references and meanings performed an important function for the survivors. It evoked the childhood world they had lost; the friends and acquaintances who had perished in the war; the disorientation and estrangement they had experienced upon returning home; the battles they had fought and lost during the two decades that followed 1918. And at the same time, it explained their inability to achieve the greatness that they had been brought up to believe would be theirs and that many of them felt they had achieved, even if only fleetingly, on the fields and in the trenches of the Great War. By focusing on the extraordinary virtues of those who fell, by pointing to the gaps in their ranks, and by blaming their defeats on the resistance of the older generation, the survivors from within the privileged classes accounted for the depressing disparity between their dreams and their accomplishments.

Among the more famous and articulate English war survivors, T. E. Lawrence was alone to understand and to denounce the dangerous uses of the myth of the lost generation. This is all the more surprising because Lawrence himself, by his actions and writings, had contributed to the articulation and credibility of the myth during the immediate postwar period. Like Rupert Brooke, Lawrence had already created a legend around himself before the war began. But in Lawrence's case, there was a good deal more substance to the legend and more authentic mystery surrounding the circumstances of his life. His father, Thomas Chapman, an Irish nobleman of Protestant background, had abandoned a wife, four daughters, and a position of eminence and financial solidity to run off with the family's Scottish governess. The couple changed their name to Lawrence and had five sons, the second of whom, Thomas Edward, was born in 1888. Eventually, the family settled in Oxford, where they lived modestly and to themselves on an income of £300 a year. Such economy precluded the style of life that Thomas Chapman had known in Ireland and forced the Lawrences to tighten ranks and to substitute spiritual for financial resources. Everything indicates that these spiritual resources were great. Sarah Lawrence was a Calvinist of strict observance and deep belief who sought to compensate for the terrible sin of carrying off another woman's husband by living an otherwise pure, blameless, and abstemious life. A woman of iron will and unflagging determination, she successfully imposed her values on her husband and her sons. Of the five, one became a missionary, only one married, and all took away from their mother the conviction that the spirit must stand stern guard over the vile and ever-present appetites of the body. Sarah also taught her boys that they must settle for nothing less than high achievement. In T. E.'s case, this feeling took the form of a yearning for adventure, an ambition he fired and kept alive, both as a boy and as an adult, by the reading of medieval romances.

Looking at the early photographs of Lawrence, one finds it hard to reconcile the image with the legend. Yet those who knew Lawrence when he was young remembered him as an extraordinary boy in a band of extraordinary brothers—"a nest of young eagles," the Oxford don Ernest Barker called them, with T. E. the fastest and most free-flying of them all. From early youth, he demonstrated a knack for learning languages, a capacity for physical endurance, and a memory for archaeological detail. He was especially fascinated by the military architecture of the Middle Ages, and by the age of eighteen he had acquired an expert's knowledge of the field. He was also a great traveler—and, unlike Brooke, an authentic adventurer. Between 1906 and 1909 he explored French castles and churches on bicycle, sometimes doing as many as 250 kilometers in a single day and living on milk, bread, cheese, and fruit when he could find and afford them. These trips, however, were a mere preparation for the real adventures of the next few years. In 1909 Lawrence went to the Middle East for the first time on a walking tour of Syria to gather information for his Oxford thesis on Crusaders' castles. Despite the illness, adversity, and harassment he encountered on his journey, he was so captivated by the country and its inhabitants that he returned in December 1910 to undertake excavations at Carchemish, an ancient Mesopotamian site on the Euphrates River. While at Carchemish Lawrence worked on his Arabic and showed himself adept at winning the respect and confidence of the local population. Although he could have looked forward to a career as an archaeologist, he preferred to think of himself during this period as "an artist of sorts and a wanderer after sensations." He had just returned to Oxford for a brief vacation when the war began.

Three Lawrence brothers—T. E., Frank, and Will—volunteered for service and were commissioned. By September 1915 two of them had died in France. T. E.'s war was luckier and much more glamorous. After a year and a half of relatively undangerous service with military intelligence in Cairo, he got himself transferred to the newly constituted Arab Bureau and, despite his young age, low rank, and lack of seniority, became a central figure in the planning and execution of the Arab revolt against Turkey. In October 1916 he made his first trip to Arabia to establish contact with Abdullah and Faisal, the sons of King Hussein, Sheriff of Mecca; and in 1917–1918 he became the effective commander and strategist of Faisal's forces, with whom he entered Damascus triumphantly in October 1918. The story of Lawrence's campaigns in the desert—what he did, what he failed to do, what he claimed to have done—is still in dispute and probably always will be. What matters from the point of view of our theme is that Lawrence was able to act out in the real world the romantic dreams that so many young men entertained when they went off to war in 1914. He blew up bridges, scouted behind the Turkish lines, engaged in guerrilla raids, and never knew the immobility and impersonality of trench warfare that so afflicted Sassoon, Graves, Owen, and others. He became a full-fledged hero and was acknowledged by the world as such.

Yet in the end Lawrence too was transformed by his war experience: The patriotic and stiff-upper-lipped volunteer of 1914–1915 became an unhappy, self-doubting Hamlet who symbolized better than anyone else the postwar disorientation of the men who had fought the war. Lawrence himself has given bountiful clues as to how and why this change came about. Eighteen months of continual exertion and deprivation, he said, weakened his body. A brief episode in Turkish captivity, which culminated in a savage beating and perhaps in Lawrence's rape, degraded his spirit and his image of himself. This image of purity was further undermined when he discovered within himself the capacity for bloodlust and reprisal that he had formerly associated with primitive and non-European peoples. Any of these experiences could have triggered the change that took place in Lawrence's personality; but the chances are that the real origin of his psychic wound lay elsewhere. An extraordinarily complex man, Lawrence could not bear the burden of his own success. The illegitimate son of Thomas Chapman could never shake the feeling that he was a hypocrite and a trickster. Deep within himself he felt unworthy. He suffered from the realization that he was playing out his childhood ambitions and fantasies at the expense of individuals who were dying and peoples whose destinies were being trifled with in the pursuit of aims that had little to do with their desires or well-being. He was unable to reconcile his double role as an agent of British national interests in the Middle East and the liberator of the Arabs from foreign domination, for he knew, or suspected, that the one was not compatible with the other. The growing awareness that he could not make good on his promises to the Arabs merged with the pain deriving from his soiled image of himself to create a tremendous wave of disgust and self-hate. By July 1918 Lawrence had concluded that his job was "too big" for him. Everything had begun to feel unreal. It was as if he were a daydreamer, a player on a foreign stage, "in fancy dress, in a strange language, with the price of failure on one's head if the part is not well filled." "Achievement, if it comes, will be a great disillusionment, but not great enough to wake one up."

Achievement came, but not easily. Back in London and then in Paris during the Versailles Peace Conference, Lawrence fought for the interests of Faisal and the Arabs. A lieutenant-colonel covered with decorations, the interpreter and advisor of Prince Faisal, and thanks to the efforts of Lowell Thomas a world-famous figure, he was able to move, for a brief moment, at the pinnacle of world politics. He had the ear and admiration of Lloyd George, Clemenceau, Wilson, and Colonel House. He was one of the few ex-combatants to see the peace conference from the inside. What he saw did not please him. He watched in misery and growing frustration as the possibilities for change opened up by the victory were thrown away. In the case of the Middle East, the cause of the Arabs was sacrificed to the fears and ambitions of the French. The Syrian Kingdom, for which Faisal had fought and which the British had pledged to attain for him, was entrusted to France in the form of a protectorate. Lawrence's dream of three Arab kingdoms freely associated with Great Britain vanished in the smoke of unfulfilled promises. Lawrence expressed his feeling of betrayal and defeat in a strange and beautiful preface to an early version of *Seven Pillars of Wisdom*, his history of the Arab revolt. Though full of special references to the Arabian campaigns and understandably more positive in its presentation of the war experience itself, it falls exactly into the narrative pattern that characterizes the English prose works of the late 1920s and early 1930s: innocence, followed by betrayal and defeat at the hands of the older generation.

> We were fond together, and there are here memories of the sweep of the open places, the taste of wild winds, the sunlight, and the hopes in which we worked. It felt like morning, and the freshness of the world-to-be intoxicated us. We were wrought up with ideas inexpressible and vaporous, but to be fought for. We lived many lives in those whirling campaigns, never sparing ourselves any good or evil; yet when we achieved and the new world dawned, the old men came out again and took from us our victory, and remade it in the likeness of the former world they knew. Youth could win, but had not learned how to keep, and was pitiably weak against age. We stammered that we had worked for a new heaven and a new earth, and they thanked us kindly and made their peace. When we are their age no doubt we shall serve our children so.

Lawrence sought to make his own peace. He fled from the glare of his fame; but his reputation followed him as inexorably as his shadow. Briefly drawn back into politics in 1921–1922 by Churchill when the Middle Eastern settlement devised at Versailles collapsed, he helped to install Faisal on the throne of Iraq, secured the kingdom of Trans-Jordan for Faisal's brother Abdullah, then seized the first available opportunity to withdraw from public life. To the surprise and consternation of his friends, who by then included a sampling of the leading minds and statesmen of England, he gave up a fellowship at All Souls College, Oxford, changed his name to Ross, and joined the Royal Air Force as a simple enlisted man. This decision was not as irrational as it seemed to his friends at the time. Lawrence loved engines and fast vehicles and felt strongly that conquering "the air . . . [is] the only first-class thing that our generation has to do." Sick of leading other men and being invested by them with qualities he did not believe he possessed, he wanted to experience the air force from the ranks. Most of all, he longed to escape from his self and his past, which had become intolerable to him. Perhaps he hoped that the R. A. F. would restore to him the sense of purpose, close comradeship, and self-discipline that he had missed ever since leaving the army.

Meanwhile, Lawrence completed his history of the Arab revolt, which he hoped would be a masterpiece of the magnitude of *The Brothers Karamazov*, *Zarathustra*, and *Moby Dick*, his favorite classics. He had begun to feel that his future might lie in writing, and he set out, with his usual thoroughness, to learn the trade. Again he was disappointed. Though his writer friends were full of admiration and generous with their praise when they read it, *Seven Pillars of Wisdom* was seriously flawed, and Lawrence knew it. The book was too personal and too limited to the perceptions and experiences of the author to be a satisfactory account of the war against the Turks; and at the same time, it hid too much and was too cryptic to be a truly great psychological portrait of the man who led the Arab revolt. It was neither history nor fiction, but a strange combination of the two that left out all the links that would have been necessary for a real understanding of the story. Lawrence himself came to feel that his vision of the war had been distorted by the mood of disillusionment in which he had written his account. If the book had been written later, he told Frederick Manning, it might have been happier—and more objective.

Lawrence's dissatisfaction with his own war book led him to approach with skepticism the war writings of his contemporaries. In 1929, when the war-book boom was getting underway and self-pity among the survivors had become a respectable and financially profitable attitude, Lawrence warned his friends against blaming all their current problems on the war. The war, he noted, seemed more horrible in retrospect than it had seemed when they were in it. It was a change in the survivors and their situation, he thought, that had produced this blurring of perspective. When the translation of *All Quiet on the Western Front* appeared in England, Lawrence dismissed it as "postwar nostalgia shoved into the war period" and "the screaming of a feeble man." "The worst thing about the war generation of introspects," he complained to Henry Williamson, "is that they can't keep off their blooming selves." The war, he repeated again and again, was something that had to be overcome, for it had been an "overwrought time, in which we had lost our normal footing." Lawrence seems to have feared that the legend of a lost generation was becoming an excuse for inaction and self-indulgence on the part of many men like himself who had fought and distinguished themselves during the war. It was not true, he protested, that no first-rate men were left among the war survivors. "What an uncertain, disappointed, barbarous generation we war-timers have been," he wrote to the painter William Rothenstein in 1928. "They said the best ones were killed. There's far too much talent still alive."

Today we can distance ourselves from the myth in a way that even Lawrence could not, and sort out fact from fiction. Like most myths, the English myth of a lost generation did correspond to a reality. It referred simultaneously to the severe losses suffered within a small and clearly defined ruling class and to the difficulties that survivors from this class (and others below it) had in adjusting to the political and social realities of postwar England. Families from all social strata suffered; but elder sons from the dominant political and cultural elites died in disproportionate numbers, and their loss was publicized in what now appears to have been a disproportionate (if understandable) way. The term "missing generation" in England meant "missing elite." Missing elite" meant the decimation, partial destruction, and psychological disorientation of the graduates of public schools and universities who had ruled England during the previous half-century. Reading the literature on the lost generation, one seldom has reason to remember that of the 700,000 British combatants who died during the war, only 37,452 were officers—and yet it is these 37,000 and not the troops they commanded who are enshrined in the myth.

Many sons of the elite, certainly, were missing from the postwar scene. Even if they had survived, however, they would have discovered, as Siegfried Sassoon did, that their world had died, for the war accelerated already firmly entrenched and irreversible tendencies toward the broadening of access to political power, the growth of government bureaucracy and the welfare state, the emergence of organized business and labor as a challenge to the rule of the gentlemen-scholars and the landed gentry, and the decline of British power throughout the world. They had been brought up to rule a country and an empire; in midlife they discovered that they were going to have to preside over the transformation of the country, the phasing out of their values, and the dissolution of the empire. Small wonder, then, that they felt "fallen in a gap wide between two worlds."

What was missing in England during the interwar period, therefore, was not merely men of ability and character who had fallen in the war. It was the conditions necessary for the realization of the dreams of the "firstborn" among those who survived—fantasies of power and greatness with which the privileged members of the generation of 1914 had been brought into the world. These dreams, as Lawrence came to understand, had to be abandoned and replaced by others, more suited to the circumstances in which the English and other Europeans now found themselves. This was a demanding and unpleasant task, which most members of this generation were unable or unwilling to undertake and carry through to its conclusion, as Lawrence did in giving up his own fantasy of power and joining the Royal Air Force as a simple airman. The English generation of 1914 blamed the loss of their world on the war; but the truth was that Ithaca had begun to change long before they had embarked for Troy.

Bibliography

B. BERGONZI, *Heroes' Twilight: A Study of the Literature of the Great War*, 2nd ed. (1980).

M. CADOGAN, *Women and Children First: The Fiction of Two World Wars* (1978).

F. FIELD, *Three French Writers and the Great War: Studies in the Rise of Communism and Fascism* (1975).

P. FUSSELL, *The Great War and Modern Memory* (1975).

H. KLEIN, ed., *The First World War in Fiction: A Collection of Critical Essays* (1976).

A. MARWICK, *The Deluge: British Society and the First World War* (1965).

R. N. STROMBERG, *Redemption by War: The Intellectuals and 1914* (1982).

A. J. P. TAYLOR, *English History, 1914–1945* (1965).

M. P. A. TRAVERS, *German Novels on the First World War and Their Ideological Implications, 1918–1933* (1976).

Adolf Hitler (1889-1945) at a Nazi party rally in Nuremburg in 1934. *National Archives*

PART FIVE

Authoritarianism and Diplomatic Confrontation in the Mid-Twentieth Century

The harsh character of the Peace of Paris, the social dislocation caused by the war, and the victory of the Bolsheviks in the Russian revolution established a new postwar political and diplomatic landscape.

In Germany, the recently established Weimar Republic had to contend with those provisions of the Versailles treaty that mandated the payment of reparations to the victorious powers. However, Sally Marks suggests that the controversial reparations may have been less disruptive to economies than politicians at the time and most historians since have usually claimed. She also notes the manner in which the Weimar government resisted making the required payments.

Nonetheless, during the decade of the twenties reparations remained for many Germans a symbol of defeat. The state of mind, and the social disruption caused by the war and the inflation of the early twenties, aided the rise of extremist political parties. Richard Hamilton describes the recruitment of the early members of the Nazi party and their transition from defeated and often unemployed German soldiers to loyal and fervent party members.

While the Weimar Republic struggled for domestic stability and international respect, the revolutionary Bolshevik government set about reorganizing Russia into the Soviet Union. During its isolation from the rest of the world during the twenties, a long power and policy struggle took place within the governing Communist party. Robert Tucker analyzes Stalin's establishment of himself as the sole ruler in both the nation and the Soviet Communist party in the face of strong internal party competition.

The Nazi achievement of power in 1933 brought on a determined German effort to revise the peace settlement. The German flouting of the Versailles treaty and other aggression was met by a policy of appeasement that culminated in October, 1938, with the Munich Pact. Ronald Smelser looks at German foreign policy aims from the standpoint of the Nazi party leadership in an attempt to understand whether appeasement ever had any chance of success. Then Williamson Murray examines the military resources of the powers in 1938 and raises the question of whether it would have been more advantageous to have gone to war with Germany in 1938 rather than in 1939.

The Second World War brought an end to European hegemony in the world. After 1945 the continent lay between two vast superpowers, the United States and the Soviet Union. In 1949, as a result of the postwar expansion of Soviet influence in eastern Europe and the Berlin blockade, the United States and the nations of western Europe formed the North Atlantic Treaty Organization (NATO), which remains the key alliance in the diplomacy of both the U.S. and western Europe. Michael Mandelbaum traces the formation of the alliance and its fortunes in the nuclear age.

The Myths of Reparations

SALLY MARKS

The Paris peace settlement of 1919 left a number of legacies that haunted international relations during the interwar years. These included the fate of the successor states in eastern Europe, an uncertain and ultimately powerless League of Nations, and the failure of the United States to ratify the treaty and join the League. But the two most troubling issues that complicated European diplomatic and economic relations and that fueled German domestic political unrest were the imposition of reparations on Germany and the question of alleged German "war guilt" associated with them.

Reparations were transfer payments of cash, materials such as timber and coal, and state properties from Germany to the victorious powers, as mandated in principle by the Versailles treaty and set forth in detail by a postwar allied commission. Considerable division of opinion arose between the allied powers, especially between France and Britain, in regard to German capacity to pay and the proper means to enforce payment. The sharpest disagreement occurred in 1923, when France invaded the Ruhr over the issue of late payments. German leaders of all political persuasions were determined to resist and to stall transfers. Their tactics included allowing the value of the mark to fall, passive resistance after the French invasion of the Ruhr, and a series of ongoing renegotiations, such as the Dawes Plan of 1924 and the Young Plan of 1929. Although traditionally Germany has been viewed as a relatively helpless victim of allied greed, these tactics succeeded to a remarkable extent; the Germans paid a relatively small proportion of the vast amount demanded. In point of fact, German resistance to reparations transferred many costs, such as war pensions, that had been intended to be financed by German payments to the budgets of the allies.

At its heart the issue of reparations was more political than economic. France had expected ongoing reparation payments to function as a continual reassertion of the German defeat in 1918. German resistance to reparation payments was one of several modes of rejecting the finality of defeat and of asserting an active German role in

---

Reprinted with the permission of the author and the editors of *Central European History* from "The Myths of Reparations" by Sally Marks, in *Central European History*, vol. 11 (1978). Copyright © *Central European History*.

postwar international relations. That foreign policy goal had been pursued under the Weimar Republic well before the Nazi seizure of power.

N. B. The reader should note that in this essay the rate of exchange is approximately four German marks to the dollar and that the term *billion* is used in the American sense of 1000 millions.

Reparations after World War I can be divided into two categories: non-German reparations, which remain largely *terra incognita* to the historian, and German reparations, an excruciatingly tangled thicket into which only a few intrepid explorers have ventured. Understandably, most students of twentieth-century history have preferred to sidestep the perils of travel on territory of extreme financial complexity and, as a consequence, a number of misconceptions about the history of German reparations remain in circulation. This brief summary is not addressed to those few brave trailblazers, whose work it indeed salutes, but rather to those many who have assiduously avoided the subject and to the myths about reparations which still adorn studies of the Weimar Republic and interwar history.

The myths about German reparations begin with the Versailles Treaty. The much-criticized "war guilt clause," Article 231, which was designed to lay a legal basis for reparations, in fact makes no mention of war guilt. It does specify "the responsibility of Germany and her Allies for causing all the loss and damage to which the Allied and Associated Governments and their nationals have been subjected as a consequence of the war imposed upon them by the aggression of Germany and her allies." That Germany committed an act of aggression against Belgium is beyond dispute. Further, upon the theory of collective responsibility, the victors incorporated the same clause, *mutatis mutandis*, in the treaties with Austria and Hungary, neither of whom interpreted it as a declaration of war guilt. In later years, however, German politicians and propagandists fulminated endlessly about "unilateral war guilt," convincing many who had not read the treaties of their injustice on this point.

While Article 231 of the Versailles Treaty established an unlimited theoretical liability, Article 232 in fact narrowed German responsibility to civilian damages as defined in an annex. Much ink has been wasted on the fact that civilian damages were stretched to cover war widows' pensions and allowances for military dependents. In reality, since the German reparations bill was established in 1921 on the basis of an Allied assessment of German capacity to pay, not on the basis of Allied claims, these items did not affect German liability but merely altered distribution of the receipts. In brief, inclusion of pensions and allowances increased the British share of the pie but did not enlarge the pie. The chief effects of the expanded British claim were to increase vastly the difficulties of inter-Allied agreement on a reparations settlement and to heighten German resentment as German opinion reacted to the misleading appearance of enlarged liability. In this matter, as in so many other aspects of reparations, appearance and reality diverged, giving rise to one of the many myths of reparations.

Much has also been made of the fact that the treaty did not specify the total German reparations liability. While some financial uncertainty was thus engendered in both Germany and the victor states, and Germany was able to propagandize effectively about the iniquity of having to sign a "blank check," delay was actually in Germany's interest. Because of inflated popular expectations in the victor countries, the reparations totals discussed at the peace conference were astronomic, ranging to sixteen times the amount finally set. The British experts, Lords Sumner and Cunliffe, were so unrealistic that they were nicknamed "the heavenly twins." As time passed, the proposed figures were progressively reduced and by 1921 a substantial degree of realism had set in.

Finally, the Versailles Treaty specified that Germany make an interim payment of 20 billion gold marks before May 1, 1921, by which time the Reparation Commission was to set the total liability. In fact, 20 billion marks is approximately what Germany paid during the entire history of reparations. During the interim period, she paid less than 8 billion marks, mostly as credit for transferred state properties. Technically, none of this was considered reparations, as it was fully consumed by prior charges, notably occupation costs and the expense of provisioning Germany. In time, however, there developed a certain tacit recognition of the 8 billion as reparations.

Reparations were to be paid in several categories. There were to be periodic cash payments and deliveries in kind, that is, continuing shipments of certain commodities. For Germany, "kind" meant coal, timber, chemical dyes, and pharmaceutical drugs. The gold value of the shipments was to be credited as payment against Germany's total reparations bill. With two exceptions, reparations credit was also given for state properties in territories transferred to the victors, such as the Saar coal mines and German state railways in districts awarded to Poland. Except in the case of Alsace-Lorraine, countries receiving German territory assumed part of the German imperial and state debts as of August 1, 1914. Finally, reparations included certain one-time requirements. Return of art treasures did not receive reparations credit but materials to replace the destroyed Library of Louvain did. Similarly, supplies of livestock, agricultural implements, factory machinery, and construction materials in compensation for wholesale removals during the German retreat were credited to the reparations account.

The reparations provisions of the treaties with Austria and Hungary were similar in broad outline to those imposed upon Germany. Again, the total figure was left unspecified, and the costs of carrying out the peace treaties were to be prior charges against payments made, not credited to reparations accounts. However, credit was to be given for payment in cash, deliveries in kind, and transfer of state properties, while the successor states also were to assume substantial portions of the prewar Austro-Hungarian state debt. The Bulgarian treaty set a fixed sum, which was soon revised downward. In the unratified Treaty of Sèvres, Turkish reparation liability was sharply limited in view of the magnitude of Turkish territorial losses, and in the Treaty of Lausanne it was eliminated altogether. Austria became so impoverished that she paid no reparations beyond credits for transferred property, while Hungary paid little. As it became clear that Germany was the only defeated power able to pay appreciably, the battle was joined over German reparations.

Some controversy arose over credits for transferred state properties and one-time restitution shipments, but there was constant dispute over all varieties of continuing German payments in cash and kind. While shipments of dyes occasioned much difficulty, most of the problems were not of Germany's making. In this connection, it should be noted that, contrary to common belief, the United States had claims upon Germany amounting to almost $1½ billion (or nearly 6 billion gold marks) and that the United States received regular shipments of dyes until late in 1922, when she renounced her right to reparations dyes. Counting mixed claims of private individuals, Rhineland occupation costs, and governmental reparations claims, the United States eventually received over 400 million gold marks.

Dyes were a peripheral issue, however, and the United States government was a peripheral power in the reparations question. Attention focused upon cash, coal, and timber, while the actively concerned Allied powers were France, Britain, Italy, and Belgium, who were to receive the lion's share. Coal shipments were below quotas almost from the outset. At the Spa Conference in July 1920, the victors agreed to pay Germany a five-mark premium for each ton of coal, officially to provide better nourishment for the miners, and advanced Germany sizeable loans to facilitate coal shipments. Still the quotas were not met. An Allied occupation of the Ruhr to force Germany to meet her obligations was first discussed at the London Conference of March 1920, and was seriously considered at Spa. Thereafter the question arose frequently, as defaults continued under the permanent plan which replaced the interim scheme in 1921.

As required by the Versailles Treaty, the Reparation Commission announced on April 27, 1921, a total German liability of 132 billion gold marks. This figure was a Belgian compromise between higher French and Italian totals and a lower British figure. It represented an assessment of the lowest amount that public opinion in continental receiver states would tolerate. The British pressure for a lower total and the continuing British effort thereafter to reduce German reparations derived from an assumption that restoration of British economic prosperity depended upon a rapid return to prewar patterns of trade which in turn required an immediate German economic revival. As British leaders assumed that sizeable German reparations payments would delay this sequence of events or overstimulate German exports to the detriment of British producers, they opposed enforcement of substantial reparations requirements upon Germany.

Historians have focused upon the figure of 132 billion without examining the nature of its implementation. The London Schedule of Payments of May 5, 1921, both enshrined this sum and demolished it. The full liability of all the Central Powers combined, not just Germany alone, was set at 132 billion gold marks, subject to certain arithmetic adjustments. The German debt, however, was to be organized in three series of bonds, labeled A, B, and C. Of these, the C Bonds, which contained the bulk of the German obligation, were deliberately designed to be chimerical. They were entirely unreal, and their primary function was to mislead public opinion in the receiver countries into believing that the 132-billion-mark figure was being maintained. Allied experts knew that Germany could not pay 132 billion marks and that the other Central Powers could pay little. Thus the A and B Bonds, which were genuine, represented the actual Allied assessment of German capacity to pay. The A Bonds, amounting to 12 billion gold marks, constituted the unpaid balance of the interim 20 billion, while the B Bonds amounted to 38 billion. Therefore the A and B Bonds represented the total German reparations liability to face (or nominal) value of 50 billion gold marks or $12½ billion, an amount smaller than what Germany had recently offered to pay. The London Schedule also established modalities of payment toward redemption of the A and B Bonds, including two schedules of quarterly deadlines for fixed and variable annuities.

In the summer of 1921, Germany met her first cash payment of one billion gold marks in full. She did so because west German customs posts and an area around Düsseldorf were under Allied occupation. These measures had been taken in March 1921, primarily in an effort to induce a satisfactory German offer, and were continued to force German acceptance of the London Schedule. After the 1921 cash payment, the Allies relinquished the customs posts but remained at Düsseldorf. Thereafter, Germany paid a tiny portion of the variable annuity due in November 1921 and small amounts on annuities due in early 1922, but made no further payments in cash until after the Dawes Plan went into effect late in 1924. Through 1922, payments in kind continued, although never in full, while a variety of expedients papered over the absence of cash payments. However, these stopgap measures would expire at the end of 1922 when either a new reparations plan had to be imposed or the London Schedule would revert to full force.

By the summer of 1922, it was clearly impossible to restore the London Schedule, which was in virtual abeyance, but there was no agreement on what to do. By this time, Germany's currency depreciation had become acute. This depreciation had begun during World War I and had continued at an erratic pace. A conjunction had developed between reparations deadlines and dramatic inflationary lurches of the mark. Germans argued that reparations were destroying their currency while British and French experts agreed that Germany was deliberately ruining the mark, partly to avoid budgetary and currency reform, but primarily to escape reparations. In this, the Entente experts were correct. Those historians who have accepted the German claim that reparations were the cause of the inflation have overlooked the fact that the inflation long predated reparations. They have similarly overlooked the fact that the inflation mushroomed in the period from the summer of 1921 to the end of 1922 when Germany was actually paying very little in reparations. They have also failed to explain why the period of least inflation coincided with the period of largest reparations payments in the late 1920s or why Germans claimed after 1930 that reparations were causing deflation. There is no doubt that British and French suspicions late in 1922 were sound. The Reich Chancellery archives indicate that in 1922 and 1923 German leaders chose to postpone tax reform and currency stabilization measures in hopes of obtaining substantial reductions in reparations.

However, the Entente agreement on the facts yielded no solutions, as Britain and France drew opposite policy conclusions from the same assessment. The British maintained that, since Germany had succeeded in destroying her currency, she should be granted a full four-year moratorium on all reparations payments to facilitate financial reconstruction, while the French objected to awarding a long moratorium as a bad conduct prize and insisted upon Allied seizure of something—mines, state forests, customs post, or whatever—as a revenue-yielding guarantee that payment would eventually resume. The British opposed the seizure of "productive guarantees," arguing that any compulsion would damage German recovery, while the French maintained that a moratorium without them would mean the end of reparations. Through the latter part of 1922, neither the Reparation Commission nor Allied conferences achieved any compromise.

The tension heightened on December 26 1922, when the Reparation Commission by a three to one vote, with Britain dissenting, formally declared Germany in default on timber deliveries. There was no disagreement about the fact of the default nor its size. Contrary to historical myth, the timber default was massive even though 1922 timber quotas had been based upon (and in most categories revised downward from) a German offer. Nor was there any Allied dispute about the causes of the default, which implied German governmental bad faith. But Britain opposed declaring the default for fear that declaration would lead to action. The only feasible Entente action of consequence was an occupation of the Ruhr Basin, which Britain opposed with mounting vigor as the prospect came closer. While no action was taken on the timber default, its declaration raised the spectre of a formal declaration of coal default in January, as French patience was exhausted and French leaders became determined to use the technicality of repeated coal defaults to force execution of the Versailles Treaty in general. Coal quotas were monthly; Germany had fulfilled them in January and October of 1920, but otherwise had defaulted regularly in varying amounts, despite several downward quota revisions, especially after Germany lost the Silesian coal fields. Thus in January 1923 there occurred the thirty-fourth coal default in thirty-six months.

On January 2, 1923, the Entente powers and Germany met at Paris. Each country except Belgium brought a plan and published it at once, thus inflaming public opinion everywhere. The German plan, offering a Rhineland pact and thus foreshadowing Locarno, was an unsuccessful attempt at distraction from reparations default. The French and Italian plans called for limited economic sanctions and Entente unity, although France declared that, in the absence of full unity, she would take more drastic steps. The British brushed both plans aside and insisted that theirs was the only basis for discussion. The new British prime minister, Andrew Bonar Law, ailing, inexperienced in reparations, and distracted by domestic politics and the Turkish crisis, had accepted the plan of Sir John Bradbury, British delegate to the Reparation Commission. This scheme was merely a variation of one already rejected by France, and it had been termed "impossible of execution" by Germany. It was so excruciatingly complex that Carl Bergmann, the leading German expert, grumbled that he would rather pay reparations than master the Bradbury Plan. Amongst its other unpalatable features, the British scheme would have destroyed all Belgian benefits from reparations, granted Germany a four-year moratorium (twice what she had requested in December) on payments in cash and kind without any productive guarantees, required open cancellation of the C Bonds (a politically difficult act), reduced and reconstructed the Reparation Commission to end French preponderance therein, provided a British veto on any punitive measures against future defaults, and accorded Britain full dictation of Entente policy on non-German reparations. As this plan would have meant the practical end of reparations, no continental politician could accept it and expect to remain in office. None did, and the conference failed.

On January 9, 1923, the Reparation Commission declared the coal default by a vote of three to one and, by the same vote, decided to occupy the Ruhr. On January 11, French, Belgian, and Italian engineers entered the Ruhr to procure the coal, accompanied by small contingents of French and Belgian troops. Britain stood aloof, denouncing the occupation as immoral and illegal, but rendered it feasible by permitting France to mount it on British-controlled railways in the Rhineland. While the question of morality perhaps depends upon viewpoint, the British legal opinion was based more upon what British leaders wished the Versailles Treaty had said than upon what it actually did say. Although no definitive ruling was ever made, since a unanimous opinion of the Reparation Commission was impossible, a close reading of the text of the Versailles Treaty indicates that the majority view had much legal substance.

As German passive resistance escalated the Ruhr occupation into a major military operation, Britain refused to take sides and thus both prolonged and exacerbated the crisis. Bonar Law dreaded breach with France and refused to recognize that it had arrived. As he wished above all to keep the breach from becoming irreparable, he took no decisive action in either direction. He also failed to understand the French premier, Raymond Poincaré. In the weeks before the occupation, Bonar Law ignored evidence that Poincaré was seeking to avoid such a drastic step, and he never realized that, in combination with the French right, notably Alexandre Millerand, he had forced Poincaré into the Ruhr by rejecting more moderate options. Once the step had been taken, Poincaré recognized that France had played her last trump and must win on this card or go down to permanent defeat. She was inherently weaker than Germany and had already failed to enforce delivery of alleged war criminals, to obtain German compliance with the military clauses of the treaty, or to gain any effective German participation in the costly French reconstruction of the devastated provinces. If Germany did not pay reparations and remove some of the burden from France, her innate economic superiority, together with further progressive crumbling of the peace treaty, would soon tip the balance altogether. In applying the ultimate sanction of the Ruhr occupation, Poincaré was above all making a final effort to force Germany to acknowledge her defeat in World War I and to accept the Versailles Treaty. He well knew that the fundamental issues were not coal and timber but rather survival of the treaty and of France's victory in the war. The British never realized that they were watching an extension of World War I and, comprehending neither the basic issues nor France's genuine need for coal and money, could not understand why Poincaré hung grimly on when Italy and Belgium lost heart.

The British, who clearly won the propaganda battle, also claimed that the Ruhr occupation was unprofitable. Misleadingly, they compared the Ruhr receipts to the London Schedule of Payments, ignoring the fact that the London Schedule was dead beyond recall and that the choice, at their own insistence, had been between the Ruhr receipts and nothing. In fact, the Ruhr occupation was profitable, modestly so at first and then very considerably after the end of passive resistance. After all expenses and Rhineland occupation costs, the net Ruhr receipts to the three powers involved and ultimately to the United States amounted to nearly 900 million gold marks.

Others benefited as well. As the German government financed passive resistance from an empty exchequer, the mark reached utter ruination. The astronomic inflation which ensued was a result of German policy, not of the occupation itself. The inflation enabled the German government to pay off its domestic debts, including the war debt, and those of the state enterprises in worthless marks. Certain industrialists close to the German cabinet profited greatly as well. The ailing British economy also benefited considerably from the disruption of German exports, but British officials would never acknowledge this fact, even to themselves. Convinced that their economic data bore no relation to the evil event, they never ceased to urge resolution of the crisis.

Their urgings became more imperative after a new German government under Gustav Stresemann abandoned passive resistance in September 1923 and quickly terminated the inflation. A new reparations plan was necessary, along with German financial reconstruction and a scheme to extract France and Belgium from the Ruhr. Other powers quickly combined to minimize the damage to Germany, and France found herself increasingly isolated. A decline of the franc further weakened her diplomatic position. When President Calvin Coolidge indicated that American experts could participate as private citizens in drawing up a new reparations plan, thus facilitating the essential involvement of American bankers, a certain degree of inevitability set in. Poincaré could and did delay, but he could not prevent altogether. Thus the Dawes Committee began work in January 1924. Its labors signified that while Poincaré had won the war, he had lost the peace.

The Dawes Plan of April 9, 1924, operated at two levels. Its precise technical details owed much to the Belgian *Études* of June 11, 1923, concerning potential sources of reparations revenues, while the deliberately ambiguous political settlement was chiefly the work of the American expert, Owen D. Young. Although the Dawes Committee indicated that the problem of the Ruhr occupation was outside its frame of reference, it tacitly assumed an immediate end to the economic occupation and reduction of the military occupation to a skeleton force (to save French face). The plan called for complete reorganization of German finances with foreign supervision, a large international loan to Germany, and an Agent-General for Reparations in Berlin to oversee a complex supervisory structure. To raise revenues toward reparations, the plan demanded mortgages on German industry and the state railways, reassumption of domestic indebtedness by the German government, and sweeping tax reform to end the anomaly (and Versailles Treaty violation) of much lower tax rates in Germany than in the victor powers. While some accounts indicate otherwise, in fact the incorporation of occupation costs, commission costs, and all other previously prior charges into the global amount of annual German reparations payments effectively reduced the total reparations bill, although the size of the reduction was unclear, as the duration of the plan was not specified. Germany would pay one billion marks the first year, chiefly out of the international loan, increasing amounts for three years, and $2\frac{1}{2}$ billion gold marks for one year. Thereafter she would pay $2\frac{1}{2}$ billion marks plus a percentage based upon a complex index of German prosperity.

The call for commensurate taxation in the Dawes Plan was political window-dressing on the order of the C Bonds of the London Schedule. Tax rates equivalent to those in the victor powers were not imposed because the leading British expert, Sir Josiah Stamp, estimated that such rates would yield a surplus applicable to reparations of 4½ billion marks a year, far more, he thought, than could be transferred. The transfer problem (that is, the difficulties involved in transferring real resources from one country to another or, in effect, in converting German wealth into foreign currencies for reparation payments without depreciating the mark) plagued the history of reparations and provided a convenient impediment to payment. Those who for political reasons stressed the impediments to transferring reparations generally remained silent about that vast investment of foreign capital into Germany before and after the Ruhr débâcle, which constituted transfers of real wealth lost to the foreign investors through hyperinflation or debt repudiation and which provided Germany with foreign exchange for reparations payments. As to the German payments themselves, such transfer difficulties as arose with payment of the first billion in 1921, which constituted the only payment of substance before the Dawes Plan went into effect, were largely induced by Germany in an effort to escape reparations. In the later history of reparations, with the reduced payments of the Young Plan, transfers caused no problem. Under the Dawes Plan itself, protection against potential transfer difficulties was provided by specifying that Germany pay reparations into the new German *Reichsbank* and empowering an Allied Transfer Committee under the American Agent-General for Reparations to decide when transfers could safely be made.

When the Dawes Plan was issued in April 1924, the countries concerned were uniformly unenthusiastic for widely varying reasons, but each accepted it for lack of an alternative. There remained the mechanics of its implementation, reconstruction of the Reparation Commission, and arrangements to remove France from the Ruhr. These were devised at the London Conference of July and August 1924, which was a personal triumph for the British prime minister, Ramsay MacDonald. He deserves considerable credit for jollying his reluctant colleagues toward compromise, although the inexperience of the new French premier, Édouard Herriot, eased his task. Behind the scenes, however, decisive pressure was exerted by representatives of J. P. Morgan and Company, whose imprimatur was essential to raise the large loan to Germany upon which the Dawes Plan depended. Further, the French franc had continued to decline, and France urgently needed loans from American bankers, again dependent upon Morgan approval. Thus France had to accept the final scheme, even though Morgan agents required provisions making future sanctions against default virtually impossible, since the American loans would extend for twenty-five years, whatever happened to reparations. Financial crisis and diplomatic isolation equally obliged France to swallow other unattractive terms. As a perceptive British observer remarked, "The London Conference was for the French 'man in the street' one long Calvary... as he saw M. Herriot abandoning one by one the cherished possessions of French preponderance on the Reparation Commission, the right of sanctions in the event of German default, the economic occupation of the Ruhr, the French-Belgian railway Régie, and finally, the military occupation of the Ruhr within a year...."

Under the Dawes Plan, Germany always met her obligations almost in full, thanks largely to a flood of foreign loans which at least equaled the amount paid in reparations. Each year there was a slight default, probably as a point of honor, but never enough to cause a stir. However, as the French knew, Germany had always considered the plan a temporary expedient and counted upon revision before payments became onerous. After the Agent-General for Reparations called for a more permanent scheme late in 1927, Germany took up the call in 1928 as the Dawes standard year of 2½ billion marks approached. Further, early in 1928 Stresemann openly sought immediate unconditional evacuation of the Rhineland. French leaders, badly scarred by the severe financial crisis which France had suffered in 1926 and aware that the bargaining value of an early Rhineland evacuation was declining as the treaty date for withdrawal drew closer, decided to trade early evacuation for French military and financial security. Thus the Geneva communiqué of September 16, 1928, issued by the Entente powers and Germany, called for a new, permanent, and final reparations plan, an early Rhineland evacuation, and a commission of verification to engage in permanent inspection of the demilitarized zone.

As the reparations plan was the most complicated part of the package, it was dealt with first. Thus, in an effort to achieve "final liquidation of the war" and of the postwar, a committee under Owen D. Young devised a New Plan in the spring of 1929. It specified that Germany pay annuities in varying amounts, all below the Dawes standard-year figure of 2½ billion, for fifty-nine years, the duration of Allied debt payments to America. These annuities would cover all charges, including service of the Dawes Loan, but only 660 million marks (generally about one-third) of each annuity was unconditionally payable, the remainder being postponable under certain conditions of economic or monetary distress. This device papered over the gap between Entente expectations and German views of her capacity to pay, although the French demand for financial security was partially met by awarding her five-sixths of the unconditional annuities. Futher, Germany succeeded in keeping annuities for all of the first ten years below two billion marks and expected either the end of reparations or another reduction within that period. Finally, in an effort to put reparations on a purely commercial basis, transfer protection was substantially reduced, while both the Reparation Commission and the entire Dawes supervisory structure were abolished. In their stead, a Bank for International Settlements was established in Basel to receive and disburse reparations payments and to provide a much-needed agency for cooperation among central banks. In its second function, the Bank still survives as the sole legacy of reparations.

The first Hague Conference to implement the Young Plan in August 1929 was largely consumed by Entente dispute over allocation of the receipts and by the related political questions. Stresemann, whose goal was to make an "unconditional Rhineland evacuation" conditional upon another reduction of reparations payments, was considerably abetted in his maneuvers by the new British Labour government, which successfully demanded a greater share in the Young conditional annuities, declared that it would withdraw British forces from the Rhineland before Christmas, and showed little interest in French security. Thus France had to abandon the commission of verification and advance the evacuation date in order to gain the reduced but supposedly permanent reparations settlement. While the essential decisions were taken in August, a second Hague Conference was necessary in January 1930 to formalize matters and to provide a comprehensive settlement of non-German reparations. By then, hostility to the Young Plan in Germany had already become acute, expressing itself in a plebiscite in December 1929 in which Adolf Hitler gained significant national attention and valuable right-wing financing. Further, 5.8 million voters registered opposition to the Young Plan. While this raised questions about future German good faith, the sole guarantee of fulfillment, it did not overturn German ratification. As the plan had been designed to go into effect on September 1, 1929, it was made retroactive to that date, and Germany was paying less than half what she would have owed under the Dawes Plan. Her reward for accepting this reduction was evacuation of the Rhineland on June 30, 1930.

When Germany slid into acute financial crisis on the heels of the September 1930 election, German leaders began to seek reparations relief, although the initial credit crisis itself was caused primarily by a dramatic flight of capital in response to Hitler's electoral success, not by reparations. Since the French countered with political conditions, notably in regard to the Austro-German customs union proposal, an impasse developed. It was broken by President Herbert Hoover's sudden proposal for a one-year moratorium commencing July 1, 1931, on all intergovernmental debts. This represented the reaction of American investors to the deteriorating situation in Germany and was designed to insure the safety of private investments, which were specifically exempted from the moratorium. In brief, for creditor nations, including America, private investments would be put ahead of public accounts.

France, which would suffer a net loss under the scheme, recognized that, once halted, reparations would never resume. In addition, she hoped to obtain a political moratorium on treaty revision, German naval rearmament, and the customs union in return for a reparations moratorium. Predictably, France protested the Hoover proposal, noting that Germany's problem was credit, not reparations, and that even with reparations the German budget was virtually balanced, unlike those of most European countries. Surely she could pay the unconditional annuities. Germany had indeed expected to pay that much; the British Treasury conceded that she had this capacity, but insisted that nothing short of a full moratorium would satisfy panicky private investors. To save French face and to maintain a precarious fiction of continuing payment, a paper device decreed that Germany would pay reparations to herself, and the moratorium went into effect.

During the Hoover moratorium year, the worldwide depression deepened. As Hoover found it politically impossible to renew the moratorium in a presidential election year, Britain and France belatedly called the Entente powers and Germany together at Lausanne in June 1932 to effect "a lasting settlement." What they arranged was a fiction. Germany was to make a final lump sum payment of three billion gold marks after the convention was ratified. But it was never ratified, since the four principal recipients signed an agreement not to do so until war debt relief was obtained from America, which was known to be impossible. Thus the Lausanne Convention was a dead better. Thereafter reparations were overtaken by events, as the futility of inviting Hitler to discuss payment became evident to all. Reparations were never formally canceled, but fell into limbo as they became increasingly unrealistic.

After the Lausanne Convention, reparations per se met their de facto death, but in actuality the problems they were designed to resolve still remained. The ultimate effect of German failure to pay reparations in substantial quantity was transfer of the burden to the victors. Reconstruction of the devastated regions still had to be paid for. Pensions for disabled veterans and war widows still remained. So did Allied war debts. In the end, the victors paid the bills. It is evident that the net effect of World War I and the peace settlement was the effective enhancement of Germany's relative strength in Europe, particularly in regard to her immediate neighbors. As Gerhard Weinberg has remarked, "The shifting of the burden of reparations from her shoulders to those of her enemies served to accentuate this disparity."

In addition to reinforcing German economic superiority, the history of reparations generated a vast bureaucracy, a mountain of arcane documents, much bitterness, endless propaganda, more than its share of historical myths, and just over 20 billion gold marks or $5 billion, which was predominantly financed by foreign loans, many of which were eventually repudiated by Hitler. It is evident that Germany could have paid a good deal more if she had chosen to do so, particularly since she paid little out of her own considerable resources. But Germany saw no reason to pay and from start to finish deemed reparations a gratuitous insult. Whether it was wise to seek reparations from Germany is arguable, although the consequences of not seeking them would have been far-reaching, as the failure to obtain them proved in time to be. Certainly it was unwise to inflict the insult without rigorous enforcement. In the last analysis, however, despite the fact that reparations claims were intended to transfer real economic wealth from Germany to the battered victors and despite the financial complexity of the problem, the reparations question was at heart a political issue, a struggle for dominance of the European continent and to maintain or reverse the military verdict of 1918.

Historians, distracted by the intricacies of the reparations question, have either avoided the problem altogether or have tended to focus upon German capacity to pay, often on the basis of dubious assumptions, instead of addressing the more relevant question of German will to pay or, to be precise, determination not to pay. German leaders clearly recognized the political implications of the reparations issue and, from beginning to end, devoted their inexhaustible energies to avoiding or reducing payments. As the international climate became increasingly hostile to the use of force during the twenties, Germany had her way in the end at great cost to herself and to others. Since Germany would not pay and the other Central Powers could not, reparations dwindled and died. The tangled history of reparations remains to confound the historian and also to demonstrate the futility of imposing large payments on nations which are either destitute or resentful and sufficiently powerful to translate that resentment into effective resistance.

Bibliography

D. H. ALDCROFT, *From Versailles to Wall Street: The International Economy in the 1920's* (1976).
E. W. BENNETT, *Germany and the Diplomacy of the Financial Crisis, 1931* (1962).
R. E. BUNSELMEYER, *The Cost of the War, 1914–1919: British Economic War Aims and the Origins of Reparations* (1975).
M. L. DOCKRILL and D. GOOLD, *Peace without Promise: Britain and the Peace Conferences 1919–1923* (1981).
C. KINDLEBERGER, *A Financial History of Western Europe* (1984).
C. S. MAIER, *Recasting Bourgeois Europe: Stabilization in France, Germany, and Italy in the Decade after World War I* (1975).
K. L. NELSON, *Victors Divided: America and the Allies in Germany, 1918–1923* (1976).
D. P. SILVERMAN, *Reconstructing Europe after the Great War* (1982).
S. A. SCHUKER, *The End of French Predominance in Europe: The Financial Crisis of 1924 and the Adoption of the Dawes Plan* (1976).
M. TRACTENBERG, *Reparations in World Politics: France and European Economic Diplomacy, 1916–1923* (1980).

The Recruitment and Training of Early Nazi Militants

RICHARD F. HAMILTON

Where did the National Socialist Party (NSDAP) draw its militant members during the 1920s? The question is a difficult one because in the early years of the decade the Nazis seemed to be just one more radical political group in the turbulent Weimar Republic. Drawing upon a number of recent studies which are listed in the bibliography, Richard F. Hamilton presents a composite picture of the kinds of people who joined the party and worked for its success. The pattern which emerges is that of men who having fought in the World War then passed in to the *Freicorps* and finally after the disbandment of the *Freicorps* drifted into the NSDAP. They were people who encountered immense difficulty in adjusting to civilian life in the Weimar Republic and who often encountered difficulty finding employment. Their own experience as part of the defeated German army and as participants in the paramilitary groups used to establish order in the early years of the Weimar Republic made them especially resentful of the peace settlement and the ongoing humiliation they believed Germany endured. Their personal grievances meshed with what they understood to be national grievances.

By the middle of the twenties and later strong student interest in National Socialism began to emerge. The engaged students often belonged to *volkisch* or patriotic clubs. These students who had been children during the war and adolescents during the most disruptive years of the Weimar Republic often felt the Republic failed to realize Germany's national destiny. As with the disgruntled veterans, the students came to believe that the Nazis provided an organizational basis from which personal and national discontent could be addressed.

The National Socialist Party also served to meet significant economic and psychological needs. It provided a social framework and some employment for its members who frequently could not fit into the civilian workforce. After 1925 when it adopted at Hitler's insistence a policy of legal pursuit of power, the party organized speakers schools and other party activity which provided work with modest income that

From Richard F. Hamilton, *Who Voted for Hitler?* Copyright © 1982 by Princeton University Press. Excerpts reprinted with permission of Princeton University Press.

might supplement other wages. By the close of the decade when the pressures of the depression led to further disintegration of German society and further national turmoil, the party constituted a social organization to which members could feel loyalty and within which they could find purpose.

The NSDAP Cadres

It is clear that the party had large numbers of militants and, moreover, that it had very capable ones. One must consider why that was the case. Or, put somewhat differently, one must ask how they were able to assemble this army of militants. Because the thesis of this chapter is complex, it is useful to consider it first in brief outline.

Everything begins with the war. All the individual and organizational developments, in one way or another, stem from the 1914–1918 experience. By itself, the war would provide only the necessary conditions for the later development, since other countries, England and France, for example, were also major participants in the war and yet did not see the equivalent quantitative development of fascist movements. But, as we shall see, there were some peculiar organizational developments within the German military, elements of which were carried over into the postwar period. Germany was unique too, among the combatant nations, in its widespread and fervent belief that the end result was unjust. Then, too, for Germany the war did not end in November 1918. For many, it was continued in struggles on the borders of the Reich, both east and west, and in the nation's cities. The most important organization here, of course, was the Freikorps. As a consequence, the most enthusiastic fighters were provided with continuous military experience; for some, it lasted to 1923.

At that point, with the ending of the inflation and the arrival of the American loans, neither government nor business was interested in supporting these freewheeling armies. To obtain the loans, it was necessary to provide at least the appearance of order and stability. The official Freikorps units were disbanded, not without considerable difficulty..., and the operations of the unofficial ones were severely checked. This control was possible because a degree of centralization had occurred during the inflation. With official sources of support withdrawn, only the major industrialists were still in a position to support these free-enterprise armies. The "uncontrollables" lost out because they could simply be denied funds.

There were signs of a major strain within the ranks at this time. The devoted fighters wished to continue the relentless struggle. But the major fighting organizations available to them now restricted their activity. This was a period of search and movement as the old fighters shifted from one paramilitary organization to the next. Some authors have argued that the bases for both left and right extremism dried up during this flourishing middle period of the republic. But this is doubtful since the membership of the Stahlhelm, and later of the Sturmabteilung, showed steady and continuous growth during those years. Some Freikorps fighters felt a professional disdain for the National Socialists, seeing the Munich *Putsch* as a miserable amateurish performance. To march through a narrow street without weapons and with no cover, to march directly in the face of enemy guns was, in their expert opinion, idiotic. But in the good years of Weimar, the uncontrolled National Socialists proved to be the most relentless of the available organizations, and they, accordingly, drew the fighters into their ranks. It was the *failure* to receive major industry support that left them free to take the radical position. And that freedom was the condition that allowed them to gain the numbers and talents enabling them to move in the early 1930s.

The positive side of the argument..., then, is that the National Socialists' core cadres consisted of men who had followed this peculiar career, first in the war, then in the five years of intermittent postwar combat, then in various paramilitary organizations of the middle period, eventually, in ever-increasing numbers, coming over to the National Socialists, to the party, and to the Sturmabteilung. Drawn from all over Germany, these cadres were highly mobile (in the military sense of that term). Young, tough, and resourceful, they were also, because of their wide-ranging experience, adept in the tactics of small-unit struggle. They also served as heroic models for later generations of German youth, particularly for the more nationalistic segments of the middle classes. These cadres carried the National Socialist message first to the cities, and then, most importantly, to the towns and countryside. There, they were responsible for the party's decisive electoral victories.... There is a further implication of this argument: were it not for these cadres, the conditions alone (whether historical, social, cultural, or economic), would not have been sufficient to generate those victories....

The Freikorps

Individual grievances, even those that are widespread and deeply felt, do not ordinarily affect events. Only when those holding the grievances come together, when their grievances take an organizational form, is an impact possible. In this case, the organization in question, the Freikorps, was created by the revolutionary government and, for a while at least, received support and approval not only from the government but also from some major business interests, from the landed aristocracy, from the official SPD press, and, up to the time of the Kapp *Putsch,* from the liberal press, most notably, the *Vossische Zeitung* and the *Berliner Tageblatt.*

The German revolution of 1918 was a most peculiar instance of the species. As many writers point out, it did not involve the overthrowing of a government; more accurately, it was the withdrawal of a government. Prince Max of Baden, the last chancellor of the old regime, simply turned the powers of government over to the leader of the majority Social Democrats. "Herr Ebert," he said, "I commit the German Empire to your keeping." Ebert, the leader of the revolutionary government, somewhat reluctant to accept this grant, asked his predecessor to stay on as an administrator, but the prince refused.

The new government found itself in a difficult position. The municipal police forces were not strong enough to deal with the assorted revolutionary forces present on the streets of Germany. The army units, many of them, dissolved as soon as they arrived in their home communities, and many of the others were of questionable reliability. There were, in short, few loyal forces available to back up the new government. Any small group of semiorganized hoodlums could, however, impose its will on the government. An instance of this sort appeared just before Christmas when a battalion of revolutionary sailors, in Berlin ostensibly to protect the government, instead at one point captured the government to back up its wage demands. Faced with such problems, the government felt it necessary to rely on more "dependable" military forces.

One must consider the processes of recruitment into the Freikorps; again our discussion is based on the important work of Robert Waite. The key figures in the Korps were young officers, mostly lieutenants and captains. The organizer of one of the earliest of these groups had at first used older officers, following the principles of the old imperial army, but he soon changed his mind. "I learned," he said, "that my earlier theory was completely wrong. I have observed many very young officers in difficult situations in which they conducted themselves admirably.... Youth has the advantage of carelessness, or enterprising spirit, and above all, of patriotic fervor on its side—qualities that are not to be despised."

The forces were exclusively volunteer units. And careful selection was made among those offering their services. There is little evidence available on the details of these processes, but it is clear that urban manual workers did not volunteer in any significant numbers and that the young ex-officers, most of whom would originally have been from nonmanual backgrounds, did respond. There are some suggestions that workers, particularly those with left orientations, were discouraged from joining. Selection, it seems, followed the lines of personal contacts, the leaders of the new units seeking out members of their former companies who were proven fighters. Where the mass conscript army would contain a wide range of outlooks, extending from enthusiasts to haters of war, the highly personal volunteering and selection processes used here resulted in battalions composed almost exclusively of military enthusiasts, or, if one will, of war lovers.

Waite notes the ample material advantages to be gained by enlistment. There was the base pay of thirty to fifty marks a day (in 1919). Soldiers were guaranteed food, pension contributions, family allotments, demobilization payments when they ended their service, and uniforms. In the Baltic campaign, it was widely believed that they would receive land grants on the occasion of their ultimate success. In addition to the material perquisites, there were also the psychic benefits. The soldiers who could not fit into *bürgerliche* (civilian or bourgeois) society could in these units continue the work they had done for the last four years. As for their outlooks, the future supreme SA *Führer* for western Germany put it this way: "People told us that the War was over. That made us laugh. We ourselves are the War. Its flame burns strongly in us. It envelops our whole being and fascinates us with the enticing urge to destroy. We obeyed ... and marched onto the battle fields of the postwar world just as we had gone into battle on the Western Front: singing, reckless and filled with the joy of adventure as we marched to the attack; silent, deadly, remorseless in battle."

And the future National Socialist minister president of Saxony claimed that "the pure *Landsknechte* [freebooter, a favorite expression of the Freikorps members] didn't much care why or for whom they fought. The main thing for them was that they *were* fighting.... War had become their career. They had no desire to look for another.... War made them happy—what more can you ask?"

The numbers involved in the Freikorps have been variously estimated. Ernst von Salomon, the leading chronicler of Freikorps activities, gives figures between 50,000 and 150,000. Gustav Noske, the minister of defense, estimated the numbers at 400,000, and the Independent Socialist Hugo Haase put their numbers at over a million. Part of the difficulty stems from the fact that they were irregular troops and that their numbers fluctuated considerably. Another problem stems from the variety of the units classified under the heading Freikorps. Apart from the basic units, there were also emergency volunteers (Zeitfreiwilligen), civil guards (Einwohnerwehr or citizens' defense), security police (Sicherheitspolizei), and armed student formations (in Münster there was the Akademische Wehr). The "real" Freikorps units were the highly mobile, self-sufficient fighting forces, the other units serving more specialized functions. The civil guards performed garrison duty, "maintaining order" in the community after the Freikorps' "liberation." Waite estimates the number of men directly involved in the "real" Freikorps units as "somewhere between 200,000 and 400,000."

A major source of recruits, as already indicated, was the younger officers. Again Waite supplies some important details. The war had created numerous opportunities for social mobility. Roughly half of the 22,112 active officers in the army at the beginning of the war were killed. By the end of the war most of those surviving had been removed to the rear echelons so as to preserve them for further duty. The losses among the 29,230 reserve officers were also extremely high. This being a mass war, "opportunities" were also created by the enormous expansion in the size of the military operation, the army having 270,000 officers at the end of the war. The overwhelming majority of the newly promoted officers would have assumed positions of power and responsibility for the first time in their lives. Many would also have recognized that equivalent positions were not likely to be available for them in civilian life. Since the Versailles-imposed limit allowed only 4,000 officers for the 100,000-man army and since these were to be drawn almost exclusively from the surviving members of the active officer corps, this meant that over a quarter of a million young battle-trained officers faced civilian careers. For many of them, particularly for the war lovers, it was not a happy thought. As they put it, once "peace broke out," they faced a very unpleasant prospect, that being the "soul-destroying" life of a civilian. Going to work as a salesman, or as the representative of an insurance company, or even, if lucky, rising to the rank of office manager, were possibilities they viewed with little enthusiasm.

For them the Freikorps provided an outlet for their interests and talents; it gave them a second chance. A study of Bavarian officers, one of the few studies of occupational mobility available for this period, showed that 22.6 percent of the second lieutenants and 27.6 percent of the first lieutenants continued their military careers in the Freikorps. Waite notes that the percentages among the higher officers were definitely lower. Von Salomon (as quoted by Waite) says that "senior officers showed surprisingly little inclination to enter Free Corps service" and that "majors were received by the troops themselves as an unwelcome burden." ...

Next to the veterans, Waite reports, students formed the largest group in the Free Corps. He described them as young idealists, brought up to believe "in the moral righteousness of Germany's cause" and at the same time as persons "stunned by the magnitude and the suddenness of the collapse." Many of them, he says, felt cheated of their right to fight for the fatherland by the Armistice; now, in the Freikorps, they were getting a second chance.

There was a back and forth movement between the military and academic settings. Demobilized soldiers came into the universities. Some of them left later on to join the Freikorps. Members of the more irregular of these units would drift back into the universities again between campaigns. Thus some of the war-created outlooks were brought into the universities. These fighters provided role models for many of the younger students, particularly for those of nationalist persuasions. And here, too, the highly selective volunteering and recruitment processes were continued, thus replenishing and adding to the ranks of the older fighters. This linkage allowed the units to bridge the generations, bringing in even younger cohorts. This is a point to which we will return later in this chapter.

What did the Freikorps do? An answer to this question has been provided at various points throughout this work; therefore only a brief overview is required here. As official government-sponsored units, they made their first appearance in Berlin, toward the end of the week-long uprising in January of 1919. They played a decisive role in defeating the KPD's March undertaking of 1919, displaying their lethal capacities for the first time. In addition to "cleaning up" some smaller cities, Bremen Leipzig,

Halle, Gotha, and Brunswick among others, their most renowned action of this early period was the "liberation" of Munich in the first days of May.

Some complex border struggles then occupied them, the most important of these being the Baltic venture of 1919. With British approval, these German units operated in the Baltic, at first fighting against the invading Red Army. Nominally under the authority of a newly created indigenous government, they proceeded to overthrow this sponsorship thus making the British position untenable. Many of these fighters wished to salvage the war through the creation of a satellite state under the leadership of the ethnic-German barons whose families had settled there in previous centuries. Having been promised land (a promise that had no justification, incidentally) they saw themselves as the vanguard of a new German settlement in the east. But their victories (including the overthrow) undid them. As one of them put it, in typically pungent prose, "Wir haben uns totgesiegt" (roughly, "We have killed ourselves with victory"). The German government ordered them home. After refusals, mutinies, and assorted acts of rebellion, they did finally return to Germany....

The next major event in the Freikorps' history was an attempt to overthrow the Weimar government. Various units, the most notable of which was the Ehrhardt Brigade, marched on Berlin forcing the government to flee, this being the initial event in the Kapp *Putsch* of March 1920. The collapse of this five-day government was recounted in the previous chapter, the principal weapon of the government, it will be remembered, being the use of the general strike. In the discussions following its collapse, the Freikorps fighters placed the blame squarely on the generals and politicians. The politician Kapp was clearly incompetent. And their commanding general, Walther von Lüttwitz had also demonstrated incompetence in the organization of the *Putsch*. In the face of the general strike, moreover, he had reacted with what to the average Kämpfer (fighter) was a distressing and incomprehensible restraint. "Everything would still have been all right," one of them said, "if we had just shot more people." Another agreed; as he put it, "Blood is the cement of revolution."

In addition to further discrediting politicians and higher-level officers, this failure meant, as von Salomon expressed it, "that for the first time the road was now completely open to the young men's own political thinking." Hitler's bid for power in November 1923, he says, was "not conceivable without this development in their political thinking." Hitler's movement, for them, had a very striking advantage; it was a movement of front soldiers, of fighters, not of "higher ups."

The last action of the Freikorps prior to the official dissolution, was the effort against the Communists in the Ruhr. The latter... had taken over cities from Düsseldorf to Dortmund as their contribution to the general strike effort. Freikorps units, including that of the putschist Hermann Ehrhardt, were ordered into the Ruhr for one last government-sponsored operation.

At this point, the government, under increasing pressure from the Allies, moved to dissolve its own creation. Understandably, the members of these organizations were very much opposed to this prospect. A hasty search for guises or fronts occurred, to provide the cover under which the formations could be maintained. Some settled on estates in Silesia and elsewhere in the east; there they continued their activity as "farm laborers." Some groups reappeared as patriotic veterans' organizations. One famous Freikorps leader, Gerhart Rossbach, organized a part of his force into a "detective bureau" and another part into a "savings society." The latter was outlawed by the Prussian minister of interior. Rossbach then changed it into a Union for Agricultural Instruction, declaring that he could "organize new outfits faster than [the authorities] can dissolve them." Some joined the already existing veterans' organizations, many going into the Stahlhelm, but most Freikorps veterans found it "too stuffy and conservative." The great favorite of the ex-Freikorps fighters, Waite says, was the fiercely anti-Semitic Deutschvölkischer Schutz-und-Trutzbund. Most of the men who joined these groups also had to seek some kind of civilian employment, the veterans' organizations being an after-work affair.

The various local units of the Einwohnerwehr were coordinated and brought under common leadership in the Organisation Escherich (Orgesch for short) before going underground. The Bavarian government refused to disband these units, thus providing the occasion for the 1923 test of strength with the Berlin government. Some ex-Freikorps people joined this outfit.

One underground organization of considerable importance was the Organisation Consul (O.C. for short). Its task was to dispense vigilante justice. This included murdering officials in the republican government, especially those identified with the collapse in 1918 and with the fulfillment of the Versailles *Diktats*, and those said to have exposed underground military operations or to have acted in the service of the nation's enemies, as for example, the Palatinate separatists. One of the leaders of this organization later testified in court that it had killed some 200 persons in Silesia alone. Among its victims were Matthias Erzberger, a leader of the Zentrum, who, among other things, had signed the Armistice (thus saving Hindenburg the embarrassment), and Walther Rathenau, the nation's foreign minister and architect of the policy of fulfillment.

There was one last occasion on which units of the Freikorps went into battle. Continuous controversy had existed over the Polish border. In the spring of 1921, a group of Polish irregulars crossed over the frontier with the intention of capturing Upper Silesia for Poland. Ex-Freikorpsmen left their jobs and got on the trains crossing Germany, reformed their ranks, and won a decisive victory. Two days after this event, after the storming of the Annaberg, the government order came through declaring the final dissolution of all Freikorps units. Once again the old fighters saw themselves stabbed in the back. While they were giving their lives for Germany, the November criminals, their term for the republic's leaders, did them in....

The Shift to the NSDAP

It was these experienced fighters who, after the dissolution of their units, eventually found their way to the NSDAP and its fighting arm, the Sturmabteilung. Some made the shift early, some after first trying one or more other rightist organizations. As of 1932, the ex-Freikorps men would have formed only a small part of the total membership, as more and more younger persons joined. The argument here is not that they were at all times the numerically dominant force in the party, only that their efforts and abilities were crucial to its early formation, setting the direction for much of the later development. Without this core of Freikorps fighters, the party could not have developed as it did. They provided the local organizing talents and the high level of tactical ability. They also provided the ruthlessness that overwhelmed all opponents. In addition, they played an important role in training the younger generations who later joined their ranks.

The available data do not allow anything even approaching precise statistical support for these claims. Some sense of the flows, may, however, be gained from NSDAP memoirs, from the autobiographies generated by Theodore Abel and further analyzed by Peter Merkl, and from Robert Waite's research.

One of the heroic memoirs, typical of the many that came out of the NSDAP's central publishing house in Munich during the thirties, opens with a gathering of three men in February 1925. They were planning the reconstitution of the NSDAP group in Starnberg, a lovely resort town southwest of Munich.... The three are the author, described as a minor civil servant, Max, the paperhanger, and Gustl, the bricklayer. The introduction continues with a brief review of their military and organizational history—"front soldiers, all three, Freikorps fighters"—none older than 27, all three in the SA, and all three marchers on the ninth of November, 1923.

These three, the author claims, for all practical purposes created the local organization and made it what it was. Others joined in, of course, and worked hard at it, but it was these three who provided the bridge between the old, the pre-1923 party, and the new one, the second try. There is a recurring theme in these recruitment efforts, which the author stresses at one point: "Behind him [the new member] lay the steep, old path: front soldier, Free Corps, Hitler." At another point they pick up another old fighter, and again one hears the same stress: front fighter, Freikorpsman, SA man. The author adds that "in his veins flows purest soldier blood. Golden middle courses, weakness, flexibility, he hates like the plague."

Given the character of Abel's sample of pre-1933 party members, one cannot, of course, have any assurance as to its representativeness. It is likely that the sample would be better educated and have higher class backgrounds than party members generally. Nevertheless, because it is one of the few samples of any kind bearing on the subject, it is worth closer examination.

Some 18 percent of Abel's respondents had "participated in some form of post-war military activities, such as the fights against the Spartacists, the Kapp Putsch, the guerilla warfare in Upper Silesia, or the skirmishes during the Ruhr occupation in 1923." Three out of five of those engaged in the postwar struggles were young men, between 17 and 30 in 1914. In 1930, these men would have been in their thirties or early forties. Contrasting the core group with the entire sample of members (as of 1934), one finds a small segment that was older than the core group and a much larger younger segment, the latter constituting roughly half of the total. The party, then, was an amalgam containing some older members, frequently persons with some traditional military connections and old-school nationalist outlooks, the core of old fighters, and finally, the large group of younger persons attracted to the party in the republic's last years. The key to the NSDAP's later organizational success was to be found in the core group's ability to attract and mobilize this younger cohort.

Merkl handles Abel's qualitative materials somewhat differently, paying more attention to these different generations, to the patterns of flow and recruitment, and to the motivations of each segment. Where Abel indicated that just under one-fifth of his respondents were involved in the postwar struggles, Merkl shows that the war and its aftermath touched and moved a much larger portion. "The vitae of the Abel collection," he says, "largely present the war, the defeat, or the 'revolution' of 1918 as the formative experience of many respondents' lives. If we consider the central experience or influence of each autobiographical statement, we find nearly one-half under the spell of war, revolution, or foreign occupation."

Merkl also reports that the respondents touched by the war mention the enthusiasms of the *Fronterlebnis* [warfront experience], the shattering experience of the collapse, and the hostile reactions to those groups blamed for the defeat. These sentiments he discovers to be most pronounced among the volunteers (as opposed to the professional soldiers and reservists). He also finds that "sustained war enthusiasm and performance actually seem to grow with the length of service." He, too, reports the flow from the military into the Freikorps (and into related paramilitary organizations). The National Socialists old enough to have participated in the early postwar organizations were divided in their choices. The veterans, particularly the volunteers, went into the paramilitary organizations. Those without military experience tended instead to join noncombatant rightist organizations, that is, the *völkische* or conservative opposition groups. They still, however, expressed strong sympathy for the Freikorps and strong hatred for the domestic insurgents.

There were, of course, two distinct periods in the party's history prior to 1933. In the first, ending with the 1923 *Putsch*, its membership obviously came from the prewar and wartime generations. The membership in this period consisted of those affected by the war, those dissatisfied with the outcome and wishing to continue the struggle after 1918. This group continued working for the party in the second period, beginning with its refounding in 1925, their ranks being enlarged, in the later upsurge, by youthful recruits. The segment of the party not directly touched by the war, Merkl says, was moved by "youthful comradeship, schooling, or unemployment."

In the course of this transformation, there appears to have been a shift in the class base of the membership. Abel noted that two-thirds of those involved in the immediate postwar struggles were middle class. Merkl notes that the "economically secure and freewheeling" were first to join the very early party and that "even during the crisis of 1923, and in the following quieter years, the 'haves' continue to be more heavily represented in the brown movement." Only in 1930, he reports, "do the 'have-nots' catch up."

The line of continuity between Freikorps and NSDAP is attested to in the brief biographies contained in an appendix to Waite's book. Friedrich Alpers, a member of the Maercker Freikorps appears as an SA *Sturmführer* in 1930. Willy Andreeson, a veteran of the Baltic campaign and a participant in the Kapp *Putsch*, is later active as an NSDAP *Gau* [local party district] speaker and in 1929 is the director of a *Gau* leadership school. Some joined earlier, such as Karl Busch, active with the Freikorps in Berlin, the Baltic, Upper Silesia, and East Prussia; he joined the party in 1923. Kurt Daluege was a section leader of the Rossbach Freikorps. After a brief period as leader of a "gymnastic society," he joined the NSDAP in 1922, later founding and organizing the Berlin SA. Among those contained in Waite's review is Martin Bormann, who was a section leader in the Rossbach Freikorps and later active in the Organisation Consul. One also finds such leading National Socialists as Hans Frank, Rudolph Hess, Reinhard Heydrich, Erich Koch, and Ernst Röhm. Still another National Socialist who followed this distinctive career was Rudolf Höss, later the commandant at Auschwitz.

The path to National Socialism, then, involved a complicated series of moves—from the war into units of the Freikorps, then into civilian life and into various patriotic, veterans', and paramilitary organizations, eventually reaching the NSDAP.

The Recruitment of Younger Cohorts

A second aspect of the party's growth involved the recruitment and assimilation of younger populations into its ranks. This too appears to have been a product of interpersonal efforts by the early activists, or, if one will, of small-group dynamics. To see how this process worked, we turn once again to Noakes's account, an unfailing source for details on the organizational history. This discussion also points up a source of strain that was to cause the party difficulties right up to 1933.

The first unit of the NSDAP in Lower Saxony was formed in the city of Hanover in the summer of 1921. It had a slow and troubled beginning, but, showing characteristic energy, the founders moved ahead, even disregarding a cautionary warning from Hitler, and extended their activities into the surrounding countryside. The appearance of outside speakers, among them Hermann Esser from the party's Munich headquarters, brought in large audiences and gave the unit both funds and members.

This effort, however, was soon to be eclipsed. Despite its base in the provincial capital, which was also the province's largest city, the party did not find this setting a fertile one. Having escaped the twin plagues of leftist insurgency and Freikorps counterinsurgency..., the city did not have the same heritage of fear, hate, and ideological commitment found elsewhere. After 1920, the fortunes of city and province were directed by *Oberpräsident* Gustav Noske who, Noakes reports, "suppressed extremism from whatever quarter it came." There were, moreover, inadequacies within the local NSDAP leadership; hard-fought factional struggles dissipated the party's efforts for some years.

The "most effective group in Lower Saxony" eventually appeared in Göttingen, that is to say, in the famous university town, the initiative there being taken by a medical student, one Ludolf Haase. Before the war, he had been active in anti-Semitic agitation, an interest he continued after the war before joining "a volunteer battalion, part of the Free Corps." He later came to Göttingen to begin his studies and there, as an extracurricular activity, joined a *völkische* organization. With two other students, he overthrew its leadership and, shortly thereafter, was himself elected chairman. Unhappy with its rather ineffectual membership, he turned to another nationalist and anti-Semitic group. Then, still searching for the adequate vehicle, he traveled to Munich to acquaint himself with a "completely new type of organization" he had heard about, one "which was really aggressive." Finding what he wanted, he joined the NSDAP. In February 1922 he founded the Göttingen branch of the party with twelve members. Because "of a dislike of students among the workers, a caretaker was elected chairman, while Haase controlled the branch from the background." Intellectuals, moreover, were "temporarily banned from joining." And thus, apart from the medical student and a sculptress, the group had a very pronounced lower-middle-class character.

The Göttingen branch soon extended its efforts into the surrounding countryside. Of the units it founded, the most successful one in fact was that of neighboring Northeim, better known to us as Thalburg in William Allen's work. The two founders of Northeim's NSDAP, both eminently lower middle class, had been members of a nationalist paramilitary organization, the Jungdeutscher Orden, when they were picked up by an NSDAP contact man who encouraged them to attend a demonstration in Göttingen that was to be addressed by Haase. Dissatisfied with the vagueness of the Jungdeutschen and moved by the passion of Haase's speech, they joined at once. They were especially impressed by the demand for fellow fighters (*Mitkämpfer*) as opposed to fellow travelers (*Mitläufer*).

Haase's resourcefulness was shown in November 1922 at a point when the NSDAP had been banned. He had scheduled a mass meeting, the unit's first, for November 18, but it was forthwith banned by the local police. Undaunted, Haase raised support from the local paramilitary organizations and, together with "a large number of student associations," marched through Göttingen in a protest demonstration that lasted several hours. The branch doubled its membership as a result, going from twenty-five to fifty, even picking up a chemistry professor in the process. The professor began canvassing, with some success, among his university colleagues. They also formed an SA unit of forty-five members, "largely ex-soldiers and Free Corps."

In the following month Haase organized a front organization to take the place of the banned party. At the first meeting it acquired seventy new members, "mostly students." Success in this transparent effort was aided by the police, many of whom apparently looked the other way when members were placarding the town. The unit also had the support of the leading bourgeois newspaper in the town, the *Göttinger Tageblatt*. Its proprietor, a "racialist since before the war," printed material for the branch free of charge.

In a key paragraph, Noakes makes some important observations about the membership characteristics of this pivotal branch, also telling us something about the grounds for attraction to the NSDAP. Under Haase, we are told, "the Göttingen branch was dominated by a group of student activists." Some of them, we learn, were "to reach important positions within the NSDAP at *Gau* and even at Reich levels." The category "students," it should be noted, especially at that time, meant something quite other than lower middle class.

These student members, many of them obviously younger men, preferred the NSDAP to other *völkische* organizations because of its radical stance and also because the "form of organization" had great appeal. Specifically, the "*Führerprinzip* and the SA, both of which were unique to the NSDAP among the political parties, gave [it] features similar to the organizations of which they had experience and in which they had been moulded—the army and the Free Corps."

In the years following Hitler's *Putsch* attempt and the refounding of the party in 1925, an issue arose that gave rise to considerable controversy within the party, this being the question of electoral activity. Given the limitations placed on the party's activities and given the possibility of a complete ban of the party, Hitler declared legality to be *the* line to be followed. Many of the party's fighters rejected such a tepid course, Ludolf Haase being one of them. The leadership in both Hanover and Göttingen refused to participate in local elections in November 1925. In 1926, however, Hanover decided to go along, accepting the justifications Hitler gave at the national meeting in Weimar that year. But Göttingen continued to reject completely any participation in elections. Early in 1927, the neighboring Brunswick unit sent a complaint to Hitler, arguing that "the failure of *Gau* Göttingen to follow the party line... might create difficulties ... in the coming *Landtag* elections." The incident illustrates Hitler's leadership style. Rather than intervening immediately and giving a direct order, he "continued to humour the extreme anti-parliamentary attitudes of the Göttingen leaders for another year."

It is not clear from Noakes's account what eventually transpired. A decline of activity in the area in 1926 caused some concern in the higher echelons of the party. Noakes thinks that Haase may have returned to his studies. At the end of 1926, the effective leadership of the *Gau* (Hanover-South) was exercised by an ex-agricultural student, and Haase disappears from the later pages of Noakes's work. The organization at this point was no longer dependent upon the abilities of a single individual. When it did finally take up electoral activity, in 1929, in a period when the effects of the economic crisis were already being felt, the NSDAP in Göttingen "succeeded in winning its largest representation in any Council in Germany with the exception of Coburg, where it had a majority." This concentration of NSDAP strength in Coburg, a cultural center and spa, noted as a retirement place for former officers, and in Göttingen, a university city, should have given some pause to those who so uncritically advanced the lower-middle-class hypothesis. At minimum, it should have stimulated some recognition of the complexities of the new development.

Noakes summarizes the relationship of the National Socialists and university students very simply—the student population, he says, "proved peculiarly vulnerable to the appeal of Nazism." This was attested to by the results of student council elections in which the lists of the National Socialist German Students' League showed astonishing successes throughout the nation. One remarkable feature of this development is that it *preceded* the breakthrough of the party in the nation as a whole, a dozen institutions of higher learning already showing percentages of 18 or more in the academic year 1929–1930, that is, well before the NSDAP gained 18 percent of the vote in the September 1930 Reichstag election.

The liberal *Vossische Zeitung* undertook an analysis of these elections in July of 1930 and, drawing on a combination of mass-society and threatened-middle-class themes concluded that it was the "free" students (those not in fraternities) who were most vulnerable. But Noakes indicates that the shift at Göttingen involved a simple exchange—the fraternities lost four seats in the 1929–1930 election and the National Socialists gained four, the free students retaining their single seat.

In terms of ideology and beliefs, the linkage between the student associations and National Socialism was very close. The student associations formed what was probably the leading center of anti-Semitism in the entire nation, the *völkisch* influence there being very strong. At a national meeting of their representatives in Eisenach in 1920, a ban on Jewish members was adopted, and individual units were encouraged to educate their members to believe that "marriage with a Jewish or coloured woman is unthinkable." Demonstrations against Jewish or "politically suspect professors" were organized by these groups in the 1920s. Two hundred students at the Technical University (TH) in Hanover broke up a lecture there in 1925. The university disciplined 11 of the offenders whereupon 1,200 of the university's 1,500 students transferred to the TH in neighboring Brunswick.

The attraction of students to Hitler and his movement, moreover, was not something that began only in the late twenties. A meeting was held at the University of Munich on November 12, 1923, three days after the *Putsch* attempt; attended by two rectors and some eminent professors, it was apparently aimed at conciliation. The police report says that the faculty tried to calm the radical mood, while at the same time, "recognizing the valid national goals of Hitler and his followers, and in part also condemning the government." They were, nevertheless, unable to prevent "a stormy demonstration in support of Hitler."

Harold Gordon presents data on the occupations of pre-*Putsch* members of the party in Bavaria. Out of 1,126 persons for whom such information was available 20 "were professionally trained teachers at the university (technical university) and university preparatory secondary school level, with the bulk being Gymnasium professors." There were 104 university level students, a scattering of other students, and 27 grammar school teachers. One does not need comparative census figures to recognize that the students were well overrepresented in comparison to their presence in the general population. The Munich students were reported as recruiting for the party there and in their home communities in the Bavarian provinces. Even the timing of Hitler's *Putsch* was affected, at least in a minor way, by the student involvement. Gordon notes that the return of the students to the university for the winter semester "had swollen the ranks of the SA noticeably." "These young men," he says, "were full of enthusiasm for the cause and anxious for action. Not only would they chafe at delay, but the pressures of the semester's work might soon reduce the political activity of many of them." Support was also noted elsewhere. In Mannheim, Gordon reports, the fraternities of the Handelshochschule "marched as a unit to join the Putschists."

Those were the students of the early Weimar period, the students who were involved in or otherwise touched by the war. The motives of later student cohorts were somewhat different. Fraternity students, Noakes argues, remained insulated from National Socialism by virtue of their traditional upper-middle-class apolitical outlooks. They were nationalists; they celebrated traditional holidays, wore colorful regalia, drank a lot, and sang patriotic songs, but, he says, this was still a long way from the street marches and beer hall fights of the National Socialists. Eventually, however, especially with the onset of the depression, the party touched on some themes that moved many of these hitherto apolitical idealists: "a movement in which action had priority over thought and which played on the guilt feelings of upper middle-class youth for their social isolation and appealed to their idealism by its claim to a socialist policy and a close relationship with the workers as opposed to what increasingly appeared to be the anti-social exclusiveness of the Corporations. The Nazis offered middle class students the opportunity to indulge their social concern, while remaining true to their nationalist and *völkisch* values which the alternative idealism of the Left repudiated."

Part of the NSDAP's "energy, efficiency and virtuosity" may be explained as the result of this unique selection process, one that recruited tough and capable fighters, men with strong motivating hostilities directed against the republic and its representatives. The party was, moreover, able to replenish and enlarge its ranks by drawing on nationalist student populations, among others, for new recruits among the younger generations.

The Training of Party Members

The party's selection processes provided it with its cadres, with its militants, giving it persons with unique talents and rather unusual degrees of commitment. Those talents were then refined and improved through a series of special training programs, these making still another contribution to the party's efficiency and virtuosity. The people it recruited, especially those drawn from the Freikorps and its affiliates, were specialists in the organization and management of small-scale combat. But Hitler's directive made on the refounding of the party demanded the use of legal means; party activists were now required to engage in everyday routine electoral activities. Such a demand went against the first principles of many old fighters and, as we have seen, this provided a major source of internal dissent. Some old fighters, however, made the transition with ease and soon took obvious delight in defeating the enemy with his own weapons. But for some, the transition, for purely technical reasons, was not easy. They could quickly shout out appropriate orders in hand-to-hand combat, but the making of an election speech was something else; their virtuosity did not lie in that area.

But the virtuosity *of the party* is to be seen once again in its handling of this problem. It created "schools" to provide the necessary training. Since public speaking was so central to its entire operation, it is useful to examine this effort in some detail. Again, it will be seen that the party's efforts stand in sharp contrast to those of its competitors.

The speakers' school, essentially a correspondence school, began as a local initiative in *Gau* Upper Bavaria. Its value was quickly recognized, and it became the official National Socialist Speakers' School in June of 1929.

The aim, according to Himmler's memorandum, was to "impregnate each speaker with lasting and incontestable material so that with the certainty of his knowledge he does not from the outset suffer from stage-fright, as he knows that this material is irrefutable even for his sharpest opponent." Essentially what the school did was to take untrained natural talents and, by drilling them in a basic routine, give them a level of confidence that would carry them through their public speaking efforts and, at the same time, give the audience an appearance of superb competence. The basic technique went as follows:

> After some theoretical instruction, the student in effect memorized a simple speech... and did some mirror-practice with it. At the same time, he wrote a speech on his own and sent it [in] for corrections. Along with the corrected version, [the school] sent questions to prepare the student for the next month's topic. (For example: "A Factory worker complains about low wages. What would you answer?") Thus the training institute had very limited objectives. It offered no political education in any broad sense, but it did provide a large number of speakers with some knowledge of the rudiments of public-speaking techniques, a store of set speeches, and some memorized answers for typical questions from the audience.

At the end of four months of such training, the candidate made his first speech, this in the presence of his *Gau* leader who sent in a report to the school. If the performance was considered suitable, the remaining eight months of training involved actual practice, the student making as many as thirty public speeches before being declared an "official party speaker." Orlow describes the arrangement as "primitive, single-minded, but highly effective."

The *Gau* leaders were expected to nominate two candidates from each of their districts. The students were obliged to pay for their education (two marks per month) once again showing that wherever possible the operations of the party were to be self-financing. As of May 1930, 2,300 party members "had taken part in the course," and the school is said to have trained 6,000 party speakers by January 1933.

To aid local organizations in planning their programs, the party circulated lists of party speakers. The speakers, obviously, varied considerably in their abilities. Some were to be used for large urban gatherings; others were destined for smaller rural audiences (where a bungled performance would have fewer ramifications). Given the limitations of many such speakers, the "party did not expect them to persuade any large number of disengaged Germans to vote for or join the NSDAP, but, hopefully, they would demonstrate the party's interest in the village audience and stir at least some of the hearers to undertake a... journey to a nearby town to hear a rhetorically far more effective Gau or Reich speaker." The speakers also worked out a degree of specialization by subject. The Upper Bavarian *Gau*, for example, not only had speakers on standard NSDAP themes (such as Jewry, Marxism, race, the peasantry, and history), but one whose specialty was attacks on the Bavarian People's party.

The above paragraphs describe what the party offered to its local units. Some sense of the operation as seen from the units themselves and from the perspective of the speakers may be gained from Noakes's account. Why, for example, would one become a speaker? Why would members of the party take the time for a year-long course and pay the required fees in addition to their regular membership dues and frequent assessments? For many, Noakes reports, a financial incentive was involved; speakers were paid seven marks per speech and received free board and lodging while away from home in addition to being reimbursed for travel costs. The sum was not enormous, but, as the employment situation worsened, it became "increasingly important since for many members their income from public speaking became their only means of support."

That fact provides some explanation for the dynamism of the party; it had a strong incentive for continuing political activity after the end of an election campaign. In May 1932, for example, after the two rounds of the presidential election and the Prussian election, the party justified its continued effort because of the need "to employ those *Gau* speakers who, because of their activity for the party have lost their jobs.... We must keep them going so that they are ready for the next election." At that point, in *Gau* Hanover-South-Brunswick alone, there were thirty-two such speakers. It was not only for the speakers, however, that the effort was continued. "The fact that an entrance fee was charged was also an incentive for branch leaders to ensure that their meetings were organized efficiently and with adequate advance propaganda."

Thus, through the simple device of an admission fee, NSDAP meetings were turned into profitable ventures. A *Gau* speaker would be paid his seven-mark fee out of the evening's receipts. He could be fed at the home of a member and, if necessary, also be housed with one of the members. Even if a speaker had to eat on the road and spend the night in a *Gasthaus*, the costs would not be exorbitant. All money then remaining was available for the organizational and propaganda efforts required for the next events. A speaker with a national reputation or a member of the Reichstag would cost more, and because of heavier demands, their services were not as easily obtained. But then, because of their greater prestige, a local group could anticipate a larger audience and a greater return.

The situation of the NSDAP's competitors at this point, especially within the bourgeois parties, was disastrous. Since they did not charge admission, their meetings were pure cost factors, bringing in no return whatsoever. They did not have large cadres to plan ahead and organize meetings. They typically had no forces to defend their meetings from attacks or takeover attempts. They lacked a trained core of specialized speakers. Most of their speakers, moreover, would have had some full-time employment and hence would not have been able to give the same time for this effort as was possible for the NSDAP's speakers. And finally, the depression caused very serious damage to their position. Membership declined bringing a reduction in dues payments and voluntary contributions. Their ability to hold meetings (or to place newspaper advertising) thus declined sharply just as the NSDAP was experiencing its phenomenal takeoff.

It seems likely that these divergent experiences would have had sharply contrasting impacts on party morale. The local NSDAP activists would know that theirs was a winning effort, and that knowledge would make it easy for them to continue, to set things up for the next round. The opposite effect had already occurred at a DVP meeting in a village in Brunswick in April 1928. Despite the "distribution of 200 invitations," only twelve people turned up, and all of them were members of the NSDAP. The speaker found it "the most unedifying meeting" he had "ever experienced... every time I began to speak someone interrupted me. There wasn't a single person there from our lot—they are scared of the national socialist methods."

The National Socialists' first major election victory, in September 1930, brought 107 members into the Reichstag. But the notion of their "coming into" the Reichstag is misleading since much of their activity was conducted elsewhere. The point was expressed by Hitler as early as 1926 when he declared that "for us the deputy's [railroad] ticket is the main thing. This makes it possible for us to send round agitators thereby serving the interests of the Party. The men who represent us in the parliaments do not travel to Berlin to cast their votes but travel around uninterrupted with their tickets in the service of our movement. It was largely through this that we were able to hold over 2,370 mass meetings in the past year." Goebbels made the same point after his election to the Reichstag in 1928: "I am not a MdR [member of the Reichstag]—I am a PI and a PRP: a Possessor of Immunity and a Possessor of a Railway Pass." The railway passes, in short, gave the party a core of public speakers who could make appearances in local communities at a relatively small cost. The Reichstag members were not ordinarily engaged in parliamentary work; it will be remembered that the party staged a demonstrative exodus from the Reichstag in February of 1931, leaving the delegates free for this wide-ranging propaganda effort.

"Political technique" was also developed as a byproduct of the annual mass meeting. Most accounts focus on the massed formations at Nuremberg and the Hitler address, usually laying emphasis on the irrationality of the entire performance. The view from the grass roots, however, was somewhat different. The assembled members lived in tent communities during their stay and had some time for informal socializing, either before the big events or in the late evening after those events. One NSDAP memoir writer says the meeting gave him a sense of the size of the movement, a sense of being part of a large and growing movement. It was an occasion too, he reports, at which one could learn and trade experience. Another of his observations focuses on the diversity of the struggle. As he puts it: "Everywhere the struggle is different. Here they squabble with senile philistines. There with fat-headed farmers. The South Germans defend themselves against the blacks [Catholics] who want to mix church and politics. The East Prussians run up against reaction. In the large cities they have the commune on their necks. The East Hanoverians have to fight with the Guelphs. Everywhere it's different, but everywhere there is struggle." There is a recognition here of the need for different kinds of appeals and tactics, a recognition that is frequently absent from both popular and scholarly works on the subject.

Bibliography

T. ABEL, *The Nazi Movement: Why Hitler Came to Power* (1938).
W. S. ALLEN, *The Nazi Seizure of Power: The Experience of a Single German Town, 1930–1935* (1965).
R. BESSEL, *Political Violence and the Rise of Nazism: The Storm Troopers in Eastern Germany, 1925–1934* (1984).
A. BULLOCK, *Hitler: A Study in Tyranny*, rev. ed. (1964).
T. CHILDERS, *The Nazi Voter: The Social Foundations of Fascism in Germany, 1919–1933* (1983).
H. J. GORDON, JR., *Hitler and the Beer Hall Putsch* (1970).
E. C. HELMREICH, *The German Churches under Hitler: Background, Struggle, and Epilogue* (1979).
M. H. KATER, *The Nazi Party: A Social Profile of Members and Leaders, 1919–1945* (1983).
P. H. MERKLE, *Political Violence under the Swastika* (1975).
J. NOAKES, *The Nazi Party in Lower Saxony, 1921–1933* (1971).
D. ORLOW, *The History of the Nazi Party: 1919–1933* (1969).
D. SCHOENBAUM, *Hitler's Social Revolution: Class and Status in Nazi Germany* (1966).
M. STEINBERG, *Sabers and Brownshirts: The German Students' Path to National Socialism, 1918–1935* (1977).
J. STEPHENSON, *The Nazi Organization of Women* (1981).
R. G. L. WAITE, *Vanguard of Nazism: The Free Corps Movement in Postwar Germany, 1918–1923* (1962).

The Rise of Stalin's Personality Cult

ROBERT C. TUCKER

All of the interwar dictatorships involved cults of personality. That is to say, the person who was the acknowledged leader not only received vast amounts of public attention and personal veneration, but also came to exert extraordinary direct influence on the policies and ideology of both the party and the state. Virtually superhuman powers of political and economic ability and insight were ascribed to the leader, who became in almost every respect larger than life. Such was the case, for example, with Mussolini and Hitler. Beyond doubt, however, the most effective and long-lasting of these cults of personality was that surrounding Stalin in the Soviet Union. Its establishment was neither the inevitable result of Communist ideology nor the legacy of the Bolshevik Revolution. Indeed, it ran counter to both. Rather, Stalin's cult of personality was to a remarkable extent the creation of Stalin himself.

Stalin's personality cult began to emerge as a serious phenomenon in approximately 1930. By that date he had firmly, if not yet absolutely, established his predominance within the Soviet Communist party. In particular for purposes of understanding the polemics of the situation, Stalin had driven Trotsky from the party and established Trotsky's ideas as the single most dangerous deviation from correct (i.e., Stalinist) understanding of Communist ideology. At the same time, Stalin presented himself as the long-time, ever-faithful, confidant and natural successor to Lenin. For that reason, opponents of Stalin who might not be accused of sympathy for Trotsky were rather sometimes accused of Menshevism or the holding of views of the Russian socialists who had opposed Lenin's Bolshevism. The meanings of all these terms and ideologies were changed and redefined by Stalin to meet the occasion at hand.

During 1929 and 1930, Stalin took two decisive steps in establishing a cult around himself. He took upon himself the authority of being the leading living theoretician of Marxism, and his name

Reprinted with the permission of the author from "The Rise of Stalin's Personality Cult" by Robert C. Tucker, in *American Historical Review*, vol. 84 (1979), pp. 347–366. Copyright © Robert C. Tucker.

came to be included with those of Marx, Engels, and Lenin. Second, he set forth his own version of the history of the Bolshevik party, according to which he played a far more important role in its early years than in fact he had. His claims as chief theoretician and historian required a very considerable rewriting and falsification of the past. With the vast power at Stalin's command, however, he had little trouble in finding authors to carry out those tasks. Thereafter, the dual cult of the dead Lenin and the living Stalin became part and parcel of Soviet life, until Krushchev's secret denunciation of Stalin at the Party Congress in 1956.

The cult of Lenin, which Lenin himself opposed and managed to keep in check until incapacitated by a stroke in March 1923, subsequently became a pervasive part of Soviet public life. No single cause explains its rise. Undoubtedly, the Bolsheviks genuinely venerated their *vozhd'* as the man whose personal leadership had been critically important for the movement from its origin to its assumption of power and for the creation and consolidation of the Soviet regime in the ensuing years. But it is also true that after Lenin's death that regime had a pragmatic need for a prestigious unifying symbol. The Lenin cult, whose obvious religious overtones were at variance with the Communist Party's professed secularism, is likewise an example of how Soviet culture came to incorporate certain elements of the Russian past, in this case the ruler cult. For centuries the Russian people, overwhelmingly composed of peasants, had been monarchist in outlook. The Revolution had opened the door for many peasant sons to have careers in the new society. Industrialization and collectivization resulted in the recruitment of millions of people of peasant stock into the working class. They brought with them, along with their Soviet schooling and experience, residues of the traditional peasant mentality, including respect for personal authority, whether it emanated from the immediate boss or from the head of the party and state. The social condition of Russia at the time of the "great turn" (1929–33) was, therefore, receptive to the cult of a deceased leader—or a living one.

Lenin refused to tolerate public adulation—save, with extreme reluctance, on his fiftieth birthday in 1920—and even then he showed dry disapproval of the eulogizing to which his comrades subjected him. Thus, as the public adulation of a living leader, the Stalin cult deviated from previous Bolshevik practice. How and why, then, did the Stalin cult arise?

Realpolitik fused with psychological needs. Politically, a Stalin cult alongside of and integrated into the Lenin cult promised to make Stalin's position more impregnable than it was at the start of the 1930s. Although he had won considerable support and even popularity inside party circles during the early post-Lenin years, Stalin never enjoyed a prestige even remotely comparable to Lenin's. His popularity, moreover, plummeted in the early 1930s as a result of forced collectivization and the concomitant famine of 1932–33. No evidence suggests that he was then in danger of being overthrown; still, his power was not yet absolute, the argumentative-critical tradition lived on (at least in higher party circles), and he had no guarantee against the rise of new opposition in response to new tribulation. So Stalin was undoubtedly concerned to forestall future trouble by making his political supremacy more unassailable. He was shrewd enough to realize that his elevation to a Lenin-like eminence in the regime's publicity would be useful for this purpose. But, important as it was, the political motive does not provide a sufficient explanation. Not only did the cult continue to grow after Stalin's power became increasingly absolute later in the 1930s, but both direct and indirect evidence indicates that it was a prop for his psyche as well as for his power. Boundlessly ambitious, yet inwardly insecure, he had an imperative need for the hero worship that Lenin found repugnant.

That the name "Stalin" symbolized a lofty idealized self to its seemingly earthy bearer was not widely known in Russia. In part, this reflected Stalin's studied effort to emulate in public Lenin's example of modestly unassuming deportment. In private, moreover, Stalin repeatedly affected disdain for adulation. For example, he concluded a letter to an Old Bolshevik, Ia. M. Shatunovskii, in August 1930 by saying, "You speak of your 'devotion' to me. Perhaps that phrase slipped out accidentally. Perhaps. But if it isn't an accidental phrase, I'd advise you to thrust aside the 'principle' of devotion to persons. It isn't the Bolshevik way. Have devotion to the working class, its party, its state. That's needed and good. But don't mix it with devotion to persons, that empty and needless bauble of intellectuals."

But the man behind the mask of modesty was hungry for the devotion he professed to scorn. He showed it by his own actions and by those of functionaries representing him—and by his acceptance of the officially inspired adulation as it rose in intensity during the 1930s. Indeed, in the very month in which he wrote the letter to Shatunovskii, Stalin, also in private, gave lie to that same advice. In June-July 1930 the Sixteenth Party Congress witnessed an out-pouring of public tributes to him. Louis Fischer, who covered that event for *The Nation*, concluded his post-Congress dispatch by saying,

> A good friend might also advise Stalin to put a stop to the orgy of personal glorification of Stalin which has been permitted to sweep the country.... Daily, hundreds of telegrams pour in on him brimming over with Oriental super-compliments: "Thou art the greatest leader..., the most devoted

disciple of Lenin," and the like. Three cities, innumerable villages, collectives, schools, factories, and institutions have been named after him, and now somebody has started a movement to christen the Turksib the "Stalin Railway." I have gone back over the newspapers from 1919 to 1922: Lenin never permitted such antics and he was more popular than Stalin can ever hope to be. It exposes a weak side of Stalin's character which his enemies, who are numerous, are sure to exploit, for it is as un-Bolshevik as it is politically unwise. If Stalin is not responsible for this performance he at least tolerates it. He could stop it by pressing a button.

A press section officer of the Foreign Commissariat, whose duties included the briefing of Stalin on foreign press coverage of Soviet affairs, later confided to Fischer that, when he translated the passage just quoted, Stalin responded with an expletive: "the bastard!" (*svoloch'!*). Evidently, he was stung by the truth of Fischer's observation that he himself bore responsibility for the emerging Stalin cult.

Precisely when this cult took on a life and momentum of its own is not easy to pinpoint. If the official celebration of Stalin's fiftieth birthday in 1929 is taken as the opening episode, there is no immediate sequel. The marking of Lenin's fiftieth birthday had been a one-time affair, and many in high positions may have assumed that Stalin's fiftieth would be similarly observed. Six months later came the acclaim at the Sixteenth Congress. But again the wave subsided. Although his name appeared often in the Soviet press, no steady stream of Stalin idolatry appeared in Soviet publicity in 1930 and most of 1931. Shortly afterwards, however, the cult began to grow. And Stalin himself took certain steps to make it happen.

One such step was in philosophy, one of the numerous fields in which different schools of thought contended for primacy in the relatively pluralistic atmosphere of the period of the New Economic Policy (NEP). In the mid-1920s the so-called mechanistic materialists lost their previously influential position, and a school of devotees of Hegelian dialectics, led by A. M. Deborin, won dominance. Theirs was a positive response to Lenin's invitation to Soviet philosophers in 1922 to constitute themselves a society of "materialist friends of Hegelian dialectics."

Although Lenin had some philosophical writings to his credit, it was not uncommon in the 1920s to place him below Georgii Plekhanov as a Marxist philosopher. Deborin's disciples, moreover, tended to rate Deborin as the Engels of his own time in the field of philosophy.[1] Stalin, by contrast, was widely regarded in Communist Party circles as a *praktik*, save for his theoretical work on the nationalities problem and his codification of Leninist doctrine in *The Foundations of Leninism*; thus, his standing in Marxist philosophy was virtually nil. Interesting evidence on this point exists in the

---

[1] David Joravsky, *Soviet Marxism and Natural Science, 1917–1932* (New York, 1961), p. 170.

form of a list, published in 1929, of writings with which students entering graduate work in the Communist Academy's Institute of Philosophy were supposed to be familiar in advance. Thirty-three works were listed under dialectical and historical materialism—that is, philosophy. Six works by Marx and Engels came first, followed by six works by Lenin, then four by Plekhanov, and then seven by Deborin. Then came entry number 23, Stalin's *Problems of Leninism*, which even at that low ranking was very probably included for diplomatic reasons. The list ended (Western philosophers will be interested to note) with Descartes, Hobbes, Hume, and Berkeley.

For both political and personal reasons, Stalin could not be content with this situation. As the party's *vozhd'* in succession to Lenin, he was duty-bound, in terms of Bolshevik culture, to be a creative Marxist theoretical mind of the first rank—in the political if not in the technical philosophical sense. But beyond those political expectations imposed by the *vozhd'*-role, Stalin had a personal craving for renown as a Marxist theoretician. Nikolai Bukharin, who knew him well, saw this and stressed it in his clandestine conversation with Lev Kamenev in 1928. For many years Stalin had harbored pretensions in Marxist philosophy. He had set forth what he saw as the fundamentals of dialectical materialism in his treatise of 1906–07, *Anarchism or Socialism?* In correspondence in 1908 that vexed Lenin, Stalin had characterized Lenin's philosophical polemics with the Bogdanov group over Machism as a "tempest in a teacup" and commended A. A. Bogdanov for pointing out some *"individual* faults of Ilyich."

Stalin quietly continued, in the midst of intense political activities of later years, to try to enhance his command of Marxism as philosophy. He called upon Jan Sten, a leading philosopher of the Deborin school, to guide him in the study of Hegelian dialectics. Sten's teaching method, the one then used in the Institute of Red Professors, involved the parallel study of Marx's *Capital* and Hegel's *The Phenomenology of the Mind*. Stalin continued to have twice-weekly sessions with Sten from 1925 until some time in 1928, after which Stalin called a halt. Sten reportedly was depressed by the difficulty Stalin had in mastering Hegelian dialectics.[2]

Stalin sounded the characteristic note of the future Stalin school when he told a conference of agrarian Marxists on December 27, 1929 that Marxist theory always needed to keep in step with current practice. Not long afterwards, two young, clever, opportunist-minded philosophers from the Institute of Red Professors, Pavel F. Iudin and Mark B. Mitin, took up the same theme. Along with a third professor, V. Ral'tsevich, they published in *Pravda* on June 7, 1930 a long article that championed the notion that philosophy should apply itself in a new way to the theoretical problems of

---

[2] Roy A. Medvedev, *Let History Judge: The Origins and Consequences of Stalinism*, Colleen Taylor, tr. (New York, 1971), p. 224. The information on the Stalin-Sten sessions came to Roy Medvedev from Sten's friend E. P. Frolov.

practice in building socialism. They lauded Stalin for showing an example of "deepened understanding of Marxist–Leninist dialectics" in his theoretical formulation of the idea of a struggle on two fronts—that is, against deviations of both Left and Right—and called for a corresponding philosophical struggle on two fronts. Although the authors did not openly attack Deborin, the article pointed to his school as the enemy on the philosophical second front. The authors came forward, in effect, as the nucleus of a new, Stalin school in Soviet philosophy. Stalin's approbation—if not inspiration as well—was reflected in the unusual note, published along with the article, that claimed that "the editors associate[d] themselves with the main proposition of the present article."

Soon Stalin personally intervened on the philosophical front. On December 9, 1930 he spoke out on philosophical matters in an interview with a group of philosophers from the Institute of Red Professors. Mitin later quoted him as saying that it was necessary to "rake and dig up all of the manure that has accumulated in questions of philosophy and natural science." In particular, it was necessary to "rake up everything written by the Deborinite group—all that is erroneous on the philosophical sector." Deborin's school was a philosophical form of revisionism that according to Stalin, who had a special talent for coining caustic neologisms, could be called "Menshevizing idealism." It was necessary, he continued, to expose a number of erroneous philosophical positions of Plekhanov, who had always looked down upon Lenin. Stalin kept emphasizing in the interview that Lenin had raised dialectical materialism to a new plane. Before Lenin, he said, materialism had been atomistic. On the basis of new scientific advances, Lenin produced a Marxist analysis of the electronic theory of matter. But, although he created much that was new in all spheres of Marxism, Lenin was very modest and did not like to talk about his contributions. It was incumbent upon his disciples, however, to clarify all aspects of his innovative role.

Stalin was assuming the role of the premier living Marxist philosopher. Albeit coarsely, he spoke as one philosopher, and the authoritative one, to other philosophers. He was clearing the way for self-elevation by mobilizing the subservient, young, would-be disciples to dethrone Deborin and Plekhanov from their positions of eminence in the minds of Soviet Marxist philosophers. "Deborinism" along with "Menshevizing idealism" now became polemical by-words for philosophical heresy in the philosophical journal, *Under the Banner of Marxism*, and other publications. Future lists of mandatory advance reading for graduate students in philosophy no longer put Stalin in twenty-third place, and Deborin's learned treatises did not figure in them at all.

In the interview Stalin did not directly refer to his own philosophical credentials, although he implied them by his pronouncements. But he employed an indirect strategy of cult-building by the way in which he dealt with Lenin. Since he did not actually harbor much enthusiasm for Lenin's philosophical merits, why did he studiously praise Lenin as a philosopher and warn the audience not to be put off by Lenin's modest forbearance to speak about his contributions in this field? For one thing, there was the subtle Aesopian message, which could not have escaped the minds of the alert Iudin and Mitin, that *they* should not be put off by Stalin's own modesty on the same count. But, more importantly, Stalin was promoting Lenin's primacy in philosophy as a vehicle for his own claim to similar primacy. The party's erstwhile politico-ideological chief was presented as its philosophical chief as well—in place of Plekhanov, the acknowledged father of Russian Marxism, who had later become a Menshevik. By thus putting supreme philosophical authority into Lenin's *vozhd'*-role, Stalin helped the philosophers to grasp this broadened conception of that role as applicable to Lenin's successor.

They were quick to do so. In 1931 the organ of the Central Committee, *Bolshevik*, carried a bitter criticism of "Menshevizing idealism" as found in the *Great Soviet Encyclopedia*. Deborin's *Encyclopedia* article on Hegel was the first object of attack. In castigating Deborin and others of his school as carriers of Menshevizing idealism, the *Bolshevik* author stated, "Materialist dialectics really must be elaborated. But this elaboration must be carried out on the basis of the works of Marx, Engels, Lenin, and Stalin...." Here appeared the holy quartet—Marx, Engels, Lenin, Stalin—who together became the symbolic centerpiece of Stalinist thought and culture, replete with the four huge, equal-sized portraits on the facade of Moscow's Bolshoi Theater for May Day, November 7, and other special occasions.

The cult of Stalin as Communism's first philosopher in succession to Marx, Engels, and Lenin had now been founded. But this was not all. Embryonic in this development was the monolithism that became a hallmark of Stalinist intellectual culture in all fields and that distinguished it from pre-Stalinist Bolshevism. To treat, for example, Lenin's philosophical writings, much less Stalin's, as sacrosanct dogma had never before been mandatory. Stalin himself became not only the first philosopher but also the authority figure in some other fields, and in still others a Stalin-surrogate—Andrei Vyshinskii, for example, in jurisprudence—was, so to speak, subenthroned as the authority figure. Part of the role of such Stalin-surrogates was to glorify Stalin's thought in the process of hunting for heresy and establishing Stalinist truth for their own disciplines. Consequently, those chosen as Stalin-surrogates were scholars who combined intellectual acumen, in most cases, with absolutely reliable servility. Anyone with any independence of mind, no matter how zealous a servitor of Communism, was unacceptable.

If Marxist philosophy was the first area Stalin selected for building the stately edifice of the Stalin cult, party history was the second. Here he moved into a field of great political sensitivity, for the annals of the Bolshevik past were the movement's inner sanctum. But he also trod on ground of intense personal concern, namely his own revolutionary biography. Nothing was of more importance to a man who felt driven to view himself as Bolshevism's second Lenin, in the past as well as the present. He made his move in the familiar manner that so many have chosen in their effort to set the record straight: he wrote a letter to the editors.

At the outset of the 1930s, research on the history of the Marxist movement was still pursued with a certain freedom, contentious issues were seriously debated, and work of genuine scholarly character was still produced in Soviet Russia. One set of questions, those concerning the German Social Democratic Party (SPD) and the pre-1914 Second International, was deemed of sufficient interest that in 1929 the Communist Academy's Institute of History established a special group to study them; the group's academic secretary was A. G. Slutskii. Various articles by members of the group were published, one of which appeared in the journal *Proletarian Revolution* in 1930. Slutskii's main topic was Lenin's position in connection with the internal divisions in the pre-1914 SPD. The revisionist wing of that party, led by Eduard Bernstein, was opposed by a dominant centrist group, whose leaders were Karl Kautsky and August Bebel and whose viewpoint was taken by many—Lenin included—to be genuine revolutionary Marxism. On the extreme Left was a group of radicals led by Rosa Luxemburg. Slutskii claimed that as early as 1911 she had grasped and openly discussed the basically "opportunist" nature of Kautskyan centrism, whereas Lenin, though he had shown a certain critical caution toward the Kautsky–Bebel leadership ever since 1907, had continued to base his hopes on it. Lenin himself admitted in a letter of October 1914 that "Rosa Luxemburg was right"; he had not seen through Kautsky's pseudorevolutionism as early as had the German left radicals. Slutskii concluded that Lenin had displayed "a certain underestimation of the centrist danger in the German party before the war."

The publication of this article demonstrates that, although a Soviet Lenin cult existed in the early 1930, it was still possible to publish an article that did not treat Lenin as an icon—infallible, preternaturally foresightful, beyond human limitations. True, the editors of *Proletarian Revolution*—the Old Bolsheviks M. Saveliev, V. V. Adoratskii, M. S. Ol'minskii, D. Baevskii, and P. Gorin—seemed to sense the potential danger, for they inserted an introductory footnote disclaiming any agreement with Slutskii's interpretation of Lenin and announcing the printing of his essay "for purposes of discussion" only. But they clearly were unprepared for the thunderbolt that its appearance provoked from on high. Stalin was infuriated. He wrote a letter of article length, entitled "On Some Questions of the History of Bolshevism," which was simultaneously printed in *Proletarian Revolution* and *Bolshevik* at the end of October 1931.

First, Stalin mauled Slutskii's position beyond recognition, contending that to accuse Lenin of underestimating the danger of "veiled opportunism" was to accuse him of not having been a "real Bolshevik" before 1914: a real Bolshevik could never underestimate the danger of veiled opportunism. It was simply axiomatic that Bolshevism arose and grew strong in its ruthless struggle against all shades of centrism. Thus, the editors should never have accepted Slutskii's "balderdash" and "crooked pettifogging" even as a piece for discussion; the genuineness of Lenin's Bolshevism was not discussable. Second, Stalin protested Slutskii's favorable treatment of Rosa Luxemburg and the left radicals in the pre-1914 SPD. He was profoundly irked by the very idea that Lenin might have had something to learn from these people.

The strong Russian-nationalist tinge of Stalin's Bolshevism was also evident in his letter. He presented a Russocentric view of the history of the European Marxist movement: "Russian Bolsheviks" had a right to treat their own positions as the test of the Marxist revolutionary validity of those of left Social Democrats abroad. Lenin's forecast of 1902 in *What Is To Be Done?*—that the Russian proletariat might yet become "the vanguard of the international revolutionary proletariat"—had been brilliantly confirmed by subsequent events. "But does it not follow from this that the Russian Revolution was (and remains) the key point of the world revolution, that the fundamental questions of the Russian Revolution were at the same time (as they are now) the fundamental questions of the world revolution? Is it not clear that only on these basic questions could one really test the revolutionism of the left Social Democrats in the West?" Neither before nor after the war were Western Marxists to give lessons to their Russian brethren, but vice versa.

To say or imply otherwise, as Slutskii did, was "Trotskyist contraband." To give weight to this ugly charge, Stalin asserted that Slutskii's thesis about Lenin's pre-1914 underestimation of centrism was a cunning way of suggesting to the "unsophisticated reader" that Lenin had only become a real revolutionary after the war started and after he had "re-armed" himself with the help of Trotsky's theory that bourgeois-democratic revolutions grow into socialist ones (the theory of permanent revolution); Lenin himself, Stalin recalled, had written in 1905 that "we stand for uninterrupted revolution" and "we will not stop half way." But "contrabandists" like Slutskii were not interested in such facts, which were verifiable from Lenin's writings. Slutskii, Stalin noted elsewhere in the letter, had spoken in his article of the unavailability of some Lenin documents pertaining to the period in question. "But who except hopeless bureaucrats can rely on paper documents alone? Who but archive rats fail to realize that parties and leaders must be tested by their *deeds* primarily and not simply by their declarations?"

Toward the end of the letter, Stalin's language shifted from the rude to the sinister. In giving Slutskii a forum for his contraband, the editors were guilty of that "rotten liberalism" toward Trotskyist tendencies that was current among a segment of Bolsheviks who failed to understand that Trotskyism had long since ceased to be a faction of Communism but had turned into a forward detachment of the counterrevolutionary bourgeoisie, making war on Communism, the Soviet regime, and the building of socialism in the USSR. Such, for example, was the purpose of the Trotskyist theses on the impossibility of building socialism in Russia and the inevitability of Bolshevism's degeneration.

Here Stalin repeated in public the argument of a memorandum he had written in 1929. Its purport had been to transfer Trotskyist affiliation or sympathies from the category of political error to that of crime against the Soviet state and, hence, to justify repressive action against persons accused of being Trotskyist. As Stalin now spelled out the conclusion to his argument, "Liberalism toward Trotskyism, even though defeated and masked, is thus a form of bungling that borders on crime, treason to the working class." Hence, the editors' task, Stalin continued (mixing his metaphors), was "to put the study of party history onto scientific Bolshevik rails and to sharpen vigilance against Trotskyist and all other falsifiers of the history of our party, systematically ripping off their masks." This task was all the more necessary in that certain genuinely Bolshevik party historians were themselves guilty of errors that poured water on the mills of the Slutskiis. Unfortunately, said Stalin at the end, one such person was Comrade Emelian Iaroslavskii (the dean of Bolshevik party historians as well as the secretary of the Central Party Control Commission), whose books on party history, in spite of their merits, contained a number of errors in principle and of historical character.

Considering what Stalin had said earlier about centrism, it is easy to see why he was outraged by Slutskii's argument that Lenin had underestimated the centrist danger in the German Social Democratic Party. To fight against deviations of the Left and Right was not to be a centrist, Stalin had contended in 1928, any more than it had been centrist of Lenin to combat both Menshevism on the Right and the sectarianism condemned in *Left-Wing Communism* on the Left. Centrism meant "adaptation" and on that account was "alien and repulsive to Leninism." How then—no matter what documents the archive rats might turn up—could a real revolutionary (that is, a Bolshevik), ever, even briefly, underestimate the centrist danger? To a mind that so reasoned, people like Slutskii fully deserved the merciless bawling out that the letter gave them and severe punishment as well. Slutskii was arrested in the later Stalin terror and spent many years in a concentration camp.[3]

But Stalin's letter, in addition to expressing his rage, pursued a tripartite purpose in cult-building. Though it did not mention his own name (how could it?), the letter solicited a Stalin cult in party history just because Stalin wrote it and by the tone and content. First, in writing it (or, conceivably, having it written to his specifications and issued in his name), he arrogated to himself the position of premier party historian and arbiter of contentious issues in that sensitive area. For this the letter did not have to mention Stalin's name, but only to be the thoroughly dogmatic document that it was

---

[3] I am indebted to Roy A. Medvedev and Stephen F. Cohen for the information on Slutskii's subsequent arrest and imprisonment.

and to bear his signature. Merely by publishing the letter Stalin asserted his place as the supreme authority on the very subject that formed the core of the personality cult as it mushroomed in the 1930s: Bolshevism's past and the parts that he and others had played in it.

Second, in the letter just as in the earlier interview with the Mitin–Iudin group of philosophers, Stalin followed the strategy of cult-building via the assertion of Lenin's infallibility. By making the party's previous *vozhd'* an iconographic figure, beyond limitation and beyond criticism, Stalin's letter implicitly nominated the successor-*vozhd'* for similar treatment. Since Stalin was the man whom the party had saluted in 1929 as its acknowledged chief in succession to Lenin, it behooved party historians to be as careful not to find lapses or blemishes in his political past as the letter in effect ordered scholars to be where Lenin's past was concerned. People as experienced in reading delphic utterances as were Bolshevik party intellectuals were bound to draw this inference as they pondered or discussed with one another the implications of the letter. Stalin even gave them a broad hint with a phrase used twice in the letter: "Lenin (the Bolsheviks)." Lenin, by Stalin's fiat, stood for true Bolshevik revolutionism as distinct from any and all false varieties—left, right, or center. The words in parentheses pluralized his revolutionary rectitude; they made it more inclusive without giving names. But anyone with intelligence enough to be a party historian could guess whose name ought to come next on the list of "Bolsheviks" in Stalin's normative sense of the term.

Third, the letter demanded quite explicitly that the party pasts of real revolutionaries be evaluated not on the basis of documents that archive rats might turn up or fail to uncover but on the basis of their "deeds." Naturally, such deeds would have to be documented insofar as possible. Stalin was to become the arch-archive rat of the Soviet Union or, more precisely, the leader of a whole pack, although he often hungered as much for the destruction or concealment of documents as for their discovery or publication. To those capable of discerning his letter's implications, they were that a party historian should not be guided, as had Slutskii, by what he could document, but by what he knew *a priori* must be true—that Lenin, being a "real Bolshevik," could never have underestimated centrism or that Stalin, also a "real Bolshevik," could never have taken an un-Bolshevik position at any juncture. The function of documentary materials, or of their concealment, was to help establish such higher truths. To use them otherwise was to slander and to falsify. Consequently, the message of Stalin's tirade against falsifiers was that scholars had to be ready to falsify (in the normal meaning of the word) whenever *a priori* party-historical truth—as revealed by word from Stalin or his spokesmen—should so dictate.

The cult-building purport of Stalin's letter may be shown further by reference to one work—namely that of Iaroslavskii—that it criticized. Stalin did not clearly specify the nature of the errors to which he was alluding, and Iaroslavskii himself seems to have been somewhat baffled. He wrote Stalin several letters requesting clarification but received no answer. In various party discussions prior to the appearance of Stalin's letter, Iaroslavskii had defended every Leninist's right to voice his view on "any controversial question" without fear of being branded a "revisionist."[4] From Stalin's standpoint, such a position was certainly "rotten liberalism" and, hence, an error in principle. As for historical errors, a quick glance through volume four of the party history, covering the period 1917 to 1921 and published under Iaroslavskii's editorship, could have indicated to Iaroslavskii at least one area of difficulty: while poisonously anti-Trotsky in its account, for instance, of Trotsky's position in the Soviet trade-union controversy of 1920, the book treated Trotskyism as the (wrongheaded) faction of Communism that Stalin now said it had "long since" ceased to be; the book did not show Trotskyism to be, even incipiently, the forward detachment of the counterrevolutionary bourgeoisie that Stalin declared it had become. Even the reprinted photographs seemed ill chosen in some cases. Here, for example, was Lenin's original fifteen-man Council of People's Commissars; Trotsky appeared to the left of Lenin (and Alexei Rykov, appropriately, flanked Lenin on the right), while Stalin appeared in the bottom row, next to the Kremlin wall. And here, too, on another page, was an old photograph of the Soviet delegation to the Brest talks, with Trotsky, its leader, looking handsome and impressive in the top row. What Iaroslavskii may have been a little slow in grasping was that affirmation of Stalin necessitated the retrospective denigration of many others who had played more prominent roles in the Revolution than had Stalin.

Further, this volume of the party history made brief reference to the well-known fact, acknowledged by Stalin himself in a speech in 1924, that in March 1917, prior to Lenin's return to Russia and the issuance of his "April Theses," Stalin had shared with Kamenev and M. K. Muranov "an erroneous position" on policy toward the Provisional Government (they had advocated that the party merely put pressure on the government to leave the war). This easily documentable truth of party history as written before 1929 was one of the Iaroslavskii "mistakes" to which Stalin's letter alluded. It became an "unfact" in party history as rewritten in the 1930s by Iaroslavskii and others. The system of falsification extended to retrospective censorship by or for Stalin of his own earlier writings—the deletion, for example, from later printings of *Problems of Leninism* of Stalin's reference in 1924 to the position he took in March 1917. Subservient writers falsified actual party history in conformity with an idealized image of the "real Bolshevik" for whom straying from the path of revolutionary rectitude was clearly impossible—an image representing Stalin's self-concept. The logical groundwork of this system of falsification was laid in Stalin's letter to *Proletarian Revolution*.

---

[4] Paul H. Aron, "M. N. Pokrovskii and the Impact of the First Five-Year Plan," in John Shelton Curtiss, ed., *Essays in Russian and Soviet History in Honor of Geroid Tanquary Robinson* (New York, 1962), p. 301.

Hell broke loose on the party history and theory fronts as soon as Stalin's letter appeared. The Communist Academy's institutes hastily called meetings to discuss the document's implications for their work. Many editors and scholars were dismissed from their jobs and expelled from the party. *Proletarian Revolution*, after putting out the issue containing the letter, suspended publication in 1932. On reappearing in early 1933, it had a wholly new editorial board, one of whose members was Ivan Tovstukha, Stalin's one-time personal secretary.

Soviet archival sources reveal that all of the Soviet historical journals received instructions to print the text of Stalin's letter and to carry appropriate editorials on its meaning for their respective areas. In a confidential letter of November 26, 1931 to the editorial board of one such journal, *The Class Struggle*, Stalin's erstwhile personal assistant—by then secretary of *Pravda*'s editorial board—L. Z. Mekhlis said that materials in preparation should be written through the prism of Stalin's propositions. The Communist Academy's presidium met on November 31 to review its affiliates' responses to the Stalin letter. K. G. Lur'e, academic secretary of the Society of Marxist Historians, reported that all of the society's sections had been instructed to review the whole literature on the party's history critically in the light of Stalin's "article." Trotskyist contraband had already been brought to light in numerous works. Many writers, for example, had failed to show the earlier leading role of the Russian Bolsheviks on the international Marxist arena. And Lur'e combined the unmasking of contrabandists with criticism of three well-known party figures—Iaroslavskii, Karl Radek, and I. I. Mints.

Proceedings and reports from other academic groups show that not only historians and their histories but all members and sectors of the theoretical front were being brought into line with higher-level, authoritative interpretation of Stalin's letter. A representative of literary criticism denounced the "Menshevik-Trotskyist view" of Maxim Gorky's writings, without indicating what that view was, and said that Stalin's letter necessitated criticism of the literary policy—also not identified—of the Second International. A writer named Butaev reported that the Institute of Economics had set up a special brigade to re-examine economic theory in light of Stalin's letter and to "bring to light Trotskyist contraband in the literature on economics." Examples of such contraband were the still-prevalent petty-bourgeois and Trotskyist ideas that equated socialism with equal remuneration and the view, voiced in a book published in 1931, that Henry Ford's factories and assembly lines were a model for Soviet rationalization of labor processes. The legal theorist E. B. Pashukanis, speaking for the Institute of Soviet Construction and Law, criticized a textbook by two authors (one of them Butaev) that contained no account of what Stalin had said in 1927 about the proletarian state. K. V. Ostrovitianov, an economist, objected to the hitherto-accepted notion that the writings of Lenin and Stalin belonged to "politics" as distinct from "economics," whereas in fact they presented the basic laws of socialism's construction and Soviet economic life. Not surprisingly, Ostrovitianov in later years became the Stalin-surrogate for economics.

A speaker from the Institute of Technology assailed the "narrow technicism" that he said was characteristic of Trotskyism, condemned the "technological policy of social-fascism," and asserted that a review of "literally the entire technological literature" was now needed. A representative of the Institute of Philosophy, in addition to discussing its new tasks, remarked that the Institute of Technology should produce in short order "a work systematizing all of the basic theses of Marx, Engels, Lenin, and Stalin on technology." The representative of the Association of Natural Science wondered why the basic methodological postulates about physics provided by Lenin in *Materialism and Empirio-Criticism* were not being taken as a guide in an attempt "to create a conception of physics, to produce our Marxist-Leninist conception of the structure of matter." Nadezhda Mandelstam, then working in the editorial offices of the journal *For a Communist Education*, recalled later how "all of the manuscripts were rechecked in great panic and we went through huge piles of them, cutting mercilessly. This was called 'reorganization in the light of Comrade Stalin's remarks.'"[5]

The pell-mell rush to ferret out "Trotskyist contraband" and "rotten liberalism" was deeply troubling to many in responsible posts, in part, no doubt—but only in part—because of the pressure and embarrassment they themselves were in some cases experiencing. Stalin was not yet an absolute dictator; some in high places failed to realize that he was on the way to becoming one or to understand what was driving him to it. Several prominent Old Bolsheviks—including Ol'minskii, Iaroslavskii, V. Knorin, and N. Lukin—sought to restrain those "glorifiers" (as Iaroslavskii called them in a handwritten note found decades later in the party archives) who were taking Stalin's letter as a new gospel. Knorin suggested to a meeting of the party group of the Society of Marxist Historians on November 11, 1931 that the letter should simply be seen as a restatement of some basic Leninist tenets. Lur'e, on the other hand, said that party history had lacked all methodology before Stalin's letter appeared and that historians did not grasp the relation between theory and practice. I. I. Mints, who was present at the meeting, wrote a letter to Iaroslavskii, who was out of town, saying that Lur'e, in her "nasty and unsound" speech, had put things less charitably: "Before Stalin's letter there was nothing, and only now does she understand the relation between theory and practice." Yet three weeks later Lur'e reported to the Communist Academy's presidium on the situation in the Society of Marxist Historians. At about the same time, Iaroslavskii warned against certain unprincipled people who wanted "to make capital on this question" of the Stalin letter. But this statement, along with his

---

[5] Nadezhda Mandelstam, *Hope against Hope: A Memoir*, trans. Max Hayward (New York, 1970), p. 259. Although she spoke of it as a letter of 1930 in *Bolshevik*, it is clear from the context that Mandelstam was referring to the 1931 letter to *Proletarian Revolution*, also printed in *Bolshevik*.

handwritten note recalling "how the glorifiers 'worked me over' in 1931," did not see publication until 1966.

One month after Stalin's letter appeared, his headquarters began to take action against those who pleaded for restraint. Lazar Kaganovich gave a long speech at the Institute of Red Professors on December 1, 1931 — the occasion of its tenth anniversary. When the text appeared in *Pravda* some days later, it became clear that the address was meant to reach the whole Soviet intelligentsia. But "address" is a misnomer. The document is best described as a several-thousand-word, peremptory command by drill sergeant Kaganovich ordering the army of the intelligentsia to snap to attention in the light of General Stalin's letter.

Kaganovich introduced his discussion of the letter by stressing the great importance of Marxist-Leninist indoctrination at a time when individuals who had only been members of the party for three to five years comprised one and a half to two million out of a total of two and a half million party members and when the Komsomol numbered five and a half million Young Communists. No one in the party would have disputed the statistics and their general implications, but Kaganovich quickly made it clear that what was at issue was the specific content of party indoctrination. The millions of new members must learn that, if the country once thought the most backward in the world was now the land of socialism, "We owe this to the selfless struggle waged for decades by the best people, headed by Lenin, against the *narodniki*, legal Marxists, economists, Mensheviks, Trotskyists, rightists, and conciliatory elements in the party." Clearly, Stalin was the best of "the best people." Kaganovich then spoke of the "criminality" of slanderer-falsifiers like Slutskii. Radek, Kaganovich continued, had acknowledged his own errors to the party group of the Society of Marxist Historians: he had recognized, furthermore, that Rosa Luxemburg did not always take "a correct Bolshevik position" but had argued that Rosa was a "bridge" to Bolshevism for the best Social Democratic workers. In fact, Kaganovich charged, Radek himself had been a bridge between Rosa Luxemburg and Trotsky.

The importance of Stalin's letter, Kaganovich said, did not lie in its attack on the insignificant ex-Menshevik Slutskii, whom Stalin had pulverized in passing, but in exposing the rotten liberalism shown by the editors of *Proletarian Revolution* toward deviations from Bolshevism and distortions of party history. And this journal was not the only weak spot. A still weaker one was Comrade Iaroslavskii's four-volume history, criticism of the errors of which would "undoubtedly develop further." Among his illustrations of the history's grave errors, Kaganovich mentioned its "erroneous and harmful assessment of the role of the Bolsheviks in the first period of 1917, [its] foul slander of the Bolsheviks." Kaganovich delivered this veiled rebuke to Iaroslavskii for his reference to Stalin's "erroneous position" in March 1917. Then came a methodological pointer: the key to a comprehensive party history was the "flexibility of Lenin's tactics," not passages in which Lenin said, in so many words, "Kautsky is a bastard." What, in short, a "real Bolshevik" said or failed to say at a particular time was not the touchstone of party-historical truth; the documents must be interpreted according to the canons of the real-Bolshevik-revolutionary-can-do-no-wrong school.

Kaganovich ended with an implicit call for an intensification of the ongoing hunt for heresy. Difficulties were rife, the fight was not over, the class struggle was continuing. "Opportunism is now trying to creep into our ranks, covering itself up, embellishing itself, crawling on its belly, trying to penetrate into crannies, and trying, in particular, to crawl through the gates of the history of our party." In his recent speech Radek was wrong to describe the Comintern as a channel through which many different currents and brooklets flowed into the Bolshevik party. The party was no meeting place of turbid brooklets but a "monolithic stream" capable of smashing all obstacles in its path. The meaning was as clear as the metaphor was mixed: fall in line or be destroyed.

The pleaders for restraint—and others—fell into line. Within the twelve days following Kaganovich's speech of December 1, *Pravda* carried letters of recantation from Radek, Iaroslavskii, and the party historian Konstantin Popov. Radek pleaded guilty to all of Kaganovich's charges and joined the attack on "Luxemburgianism." Iaroslavskii acknowledged a whole series of "the grossest mistakes" in the four-volume history, including "an objective, essentially Trotskyist treatment of the Bolsheviks' position in the February-March period of the Revolution of 1917" (Trotskyist, presumably, because Trotsky was one of those who had called attention to the generally known facts about Stalin's position at that time). He also disavowed the view, reportedly expressed by Mints in a recent speech, that the authors of the four-volume history had erred in their objectivity and that what was now being asked of party historians was "not so much objectivity as political expediency." No, lied Iaroslavskii, the party had not and could not demand that historians surrender their objectivity; the problem was that the authors of the four-volume work had sinned against objectivity. Resigning himself to the situation, Iaroslavskii started work on the glorifying biography of Stalin that was published in 1939.

Plainly, to confess to heresy was not enough; the heretic had to join the inquisition. Only by entering the ranks of the accusers could he expect to have his recantation taken seriously. To denounce Trotskyist contraband on the part of others demonstrated the genuineness of one's own "real" Bolshevism—that is, Stalinism. Recantation followed by denunciation was becoming a ritual of Soviet political culture. Iaroslavskii's public disavowal of his friend Mints was but one of many examples.

Still, Stalin did not yet wield absolute power. Those higher in the hierarchy of power than Iaroslavskii could suggest the need for restraint. Among them was P. P. Postyshev, then a full member of the party Central

Committee, a member of its Orgburo, and one of four Central Committee secretaries serving under General Secretary Stalin. As a secretary, Postyshev was in charge of the Central Committee's Organizational Department and its Department of Agitation and Propaganda, whose functions included oversight of the press. In a speech at a district party conference in Moscow, he stressed the great significance of Stalin's letter and then took various party cells to task for their failure to distinguish between an individual's particular mistakes and a "system of views." Of course, there were concealed Trotskyists in the party's ranks, who must be exposed and expelled. But there were also comrades who had simply erred. Instead of denouncing them as deviationists and kicking them out of the party—as did some who had been asleep but now wanted to "show themselves" (and then go back to sleep)—errant comrades should be criticized in a comradely way. Postyshev's fate after trying to curb the excesses of the heresy hunt was instructive: arrested in 1938, he was killed in 1940 in one of Stalin's concentration camps.

The master-builder of the Stalin cult was the cult-object himself. But many others, ranging from men in Stalin's entourage like Kaganovich and Mekhlis to obscure ideological workers like Lur'e, assisted. Who, we may now ask, were the glorifiers? Some, without doubt, were persons devoted to Stalin or to the man they idealistically perceived him to be; others were simply careerists who may have lacked strong qualification in intellectual work but who were shrewd or, perhaps, cynical enough to grasp the opportunities for self-advancement inherent in the Stalin-glorifying enterprise. One climber who made his way to the top by this route was the head of the Georgian secret police, Lavrentii Beria, who with Stalin's backing became party chief of the Transcaucasus in 1932. The one indispensable quality shared by all of the glorifiers, high and low, was pliability. In very many ways the aggrandizement of Stalin required the twisting of truth and the falsification of historical fact. As Iaroslavskii himself expressed it, the glorifiers had to be "unprincipled," pliable enough to ignore their scruples and still their consciences insofar as the cult-building enterprise required.

The letter to *Proletarian Revolution* was a turning point in the cult's evolution. From the time of its appearance forward, idolatry of Stalin became one of Russia's major growth industries. No field of Soviet culture was exempted from finding inspiration for its activities in Stalin's letter. The journal *For Proletarian Music*, for example, devoted its editorial in January 1932 to "Our Tasks on the Musical Front" in light of the letter, and the corresponding editorial in the February 1932 issue of *For a Socialist Accounting* bore the title, "For Bolshevik Vigilance on the Book-Keeping Theory Front." But revolutionary history and Stalin's place in it remained the central concern. A small example, typical of many, was an article published in *Pravda* shortly after Stalin's letter appeared. It denounced a book on Comintern history on the grounds that Stalin's name was only mentioned twice and said, "Without showing Comrade Stalin's leading role in the history of the Comintern, there can be no Bolshevik textbook on the history of the Comintern."

Having asserted himself as premier party historian, Stalin delivered another lecture in reply to two party members, Olekhnovich and Aristov, who had written separately to him in response to the letter; and his answers, dated January 15 and 25, 1932, were published in *Bolshevik* (and then in other publications) the following August. Olekhnovich, apparently, had tried to show himself more Stalinist than Stalin and suggested that "Trotskyism *never was* a faction of Communism" but "was *all the time* a faction of Menshevism," although for a certain period of time the Communist Party had wrongly *regarded* Trotsky and the Trotskyists as real Bolsheviks. In knocking this construction down, Stalin showed the hair-splitting quality of his mind. Undeniably, he said, Trotskyism was once a faction of Communism but oscillated continually between Bolshevism and Menshevism; even when the Trotskyists did belong to the Bolshevik party, they "were not *real* Bolsheviks." Thus, "in actual fact, Trotskyism was a faction of Menshevism before the Trotskyists joined our party, temporarily became a faction of Communism after the Trotskyists entered our party, and again became a faction of Menshevism after the Trotskyists were banished from our party. 'The dog went back to its puke.'"

These further pronouncements only confirmed to professionals that they should look to Stalin's writings and sayings as scripture. As if to meet their need, party publications in 1932 started printing early Staliniana, such as Stalin's virtually unknown letter of 1910 to Lenin from Sol'vychegodsk exile and his little-known "Letters from the Caucasus" of that same year. Meanwhile, the glorifiers set about rewriting history in accordance with Stalin's canons and in a manner calculated to accentuate his role and merits in the party's revolutionary past, while discrediting those of his enemies. The skewed Stalinist version of Bolshevism's biography began to emerge. Grosser falsification still lay ahead.

The rise of the Stalin cult did not bring the eclipse of the Lenin cult, only its far-reaching modification. Instead of two cults in juxtaposition, there emerged a hyphenate cult of an infallible Lenin–Stalin. In some respects, Lenin now "grew" in stature: he became the original "real Bolshevik" who could not have erred. But by being tied like a Siamese twin to his successor, he was inescapably diminished in certain ways. Only those facets of his life and work that could be connected with Stalin's were available for full-scale idealization, and whatever did not in some way include Stalin had to be kept in the background. In effect, some parts of Lenin's life had to be de-emphasized and others rearranged, modified, or touched up to put Stalin in the idealized picture.

Thus, Stalin was now portrayed as sharing in Lenin's exploits, was declared to be from an early time Lenin's right-hand man, on whom the leader leaned for counsel and support at key points in the development of the Revolution and after. The marking on May 5, 1932 of the twentieth anniversary of *Pravda*'s founding may be taken as an illustration. At the beginning, said *Pravda*'s anniversary editorial, Lenin "wrote articles for the paper nearly every day—with the closest participation and guidance of Comrade *Stalin*, particularly when Lenin was hiding underground." So in the dual cult the younger figure emerged as Lenin's alter ego, who naturally took over when Lenin himself was away from the immediate scene of action. Symptomatically, the article was accompanied by a large portrait not of Lenin but of Stalin and contained a lengthy quotation from Stalin's recollection of 1922 on the paper's early days.

By now Iaroslavskii had not simply fallen in line but had joined the vanguard of the glorifiers. Invited to contribute an article in commemoration of the twentieth anniversary of the Prague Conference of January 1912, he found a shrewd way of enthroning Stalin in retrospect practically as a founder of the Bolshevik party. As Lenin had testified, Bolshevism had existed as a political current from 1903, when the Bolshevik–Menshevik schism occurred at the Russian Marxist party's Second Congress. But the Bolshevik Party's formal existence dated only from the all-Bolshevik Prague Conference of 1912, at which Lenin converted what had been a faction into a separate party no longer organizationally tied to the Mensheviks. In the aftermath of the Prague Conference Stalin was elevated (by co-optation, not election) for the first time to membership in the party's Central Committee. Iaroslavskii obscured the embarrassing fact of Stalin's co-optation by saying, "At the conference a Bolshevik Central Committee was elected in the persons of Lenin, Stalin, Zinoviev, Ordzhonikidze, Belostotskii, Shvartsman, Goloshchekin, Spandarian, and Ia. M. Sverdlov (some of these comrades were co-opted into the Central Committee subsequently)." And by writing with heavy emphasis—"The Prague Conference was a *turning point in the history of the Bolshevik Party*"—he contrived to portray Stalin by indirection as having been present at the party's creation.

Even clever party theorists were in some cases slow in comprehending the transformed personality cult and in applying its special canons. One person who illustrates the early confusion was S. E. Sef, a zealous glorifier, who was managing secretary of the journal *Marxist Historian*. He gave the provisional title "Marx, Engels, Stalin" to the lead article of a planned special issue commemorating the upcoming fiftieth anniversary, in March 1933, of the death of Marx. His omission of Lenin was corrected before the issue appeared. Sef had failed to grasp that Lenin *qua* co-leader remained a cult-object. In the dual cult, however, the figure of the successor in some ways now began to tower over that of the predecessor. For example, a foreign correspondent's count of "political icons" (portraits and busts of leaders) in display windows along several blocks of Moscow's Gorky Street on November 7, 1933 showed Stalin leading Lenin by 103 to 58.[6]

---

[6] Eugene Lyons, *Moscow Carrousel* (New York, 1935), pp. 140–141.

Stalin was now being sung, especially by poets from the Orient, where versified flattery of rulers is a centuries-old art. "To the *Vozhd'*, to Comrade Stalin" was the title of a long poem by A. A. Lakhuti, translated from Persian into Russian. A typical stanza reads,

> Wise master, Marxist gardener!
> Thou art tending the vine of communism.
> Thou art cultivating it to perfection.
> After Lenin, *vozhd'* of Leninists.

Meanwhile, scholars in Oriental studies were enjoined to apply the works of Stalin as well as those of Lenin to problems of the national-colonial revolution in the East. A pamphlet on the history of the Georgian Communist Party was attacked for treating the period from 1917 to 1927 in a spirit of "national deviationism" (that is, Georgian nationalism) contrary to Stalin's orientation; and among those who were later reported from Tbilisi to have condemned the offensive pamphlet was Lavrentii Beria. Stalin's early revolutionary years in Transcaucasi now began to attract reverent attention. A pamphlet published in Georgia portrayed the young Stalin as a heroic leader directing underground revolutionary activities in Batum in 1901–02.

The cult kept growing in official publicity during 1933. *Pravda* marked the fiftieth anniversary of Marx's death on March 14 by lauding Stalin's theoretical contributions to materialist dialectics and concluded, "Stalin's name ranks with the great names of the theoreticians and leaders of the world proletariat—Marx, Engels, and Lenin." The phrase "classical works of Marx, Engels, Lenin, and Stalin" was now commonplace. Partizdat, the party publishing house, was savagely criticized for its failure to eliminate a series of minor misprints in the latest printing of the fastest selling of the classics, Stalin's *Problems of Leninism*. "As if 'minor' misprints are allowable in a book by Comrade Stalin!" the critic parenthetically exclaimed. Overall figures released in early 1934 show that the classics had been published in 1932–33 in the following numbers: seven million copies of the works of Marx and Engels, fourteen million of those of Lenin, and sixteen and a half million of those of Stalin, including two million copies of *Problems of Leninism*. That collection of Stalin's articles and speeches was by then well on the way to becoming probably the world's best seller of the second quarter of the twentieth century.

From that time forward, to the end of Stalin's life, his aggrandizement through the personality cult continued incessantly.

Bibliography

K. E. BAILES, *Technology and Society under Lenin and Stalin: Origins of the Soviet Technical Intelligentsia, 1917–1941* (1978).

J. BARBER, *Soviet Historians in Crisis 1928–1932* (1981).

S. F. COHEN, *Bukharin and the Bolshevik Revolution: A Political Biography, 1888–1938* (1973).
R. V. DANIELS, ed., *The Stalin Revolution: Fulfillment or Betrayal of Communism* (1965).
I. DEUTSCHER, *The Prophet Armed* (1954).
I. DEUTSCHER, *The Prophet Unarmed* (1959).
I. DEUTSCHER, *The Prophet Outcast* (1963).
G. M. ENTEEN, *The Soviet Scholar-Bureaucrat: M. N. Pokrovskii and the Society of Marxist Historians* (1978).
L. R. GRAHAM, *The Soviet Academy of Sciences and the Communist Party, 1927–1932* (1967).
D. JORAVSKY, *Soviet Marxism and Natural Science, 1917–1932* (1961).
R. MEDVEDEV, *Let History Judge: The Origins and Consequences of Stalinism* (1971).
R. C. TUCKER, *Stalin as Revolutionary, 1879–1929: A Study in History and Personality* (1973).
R. C. TUCKER, *Stalinism: Essays in Historical Interpretation* (1977).
N. TUMARKIN, *Lenin Lives! The Lenin Cult in Soviet Russia* (1983).
A. B. ULAM, *The Bolsheviks: The Intellectual and Political History of the Triumph of Communism in Russia* (1965).

Nazi Dynamics, German Foreign Policy and Appeasement

RONALD M. SMELSER

The Munich Agreement of 1938 remains the most controversial and, in the opinion of many, the most notorious international agreement in modern European history. The two following selections consider the Munich Pact from two generally neglected viewpoints—that of the goals of German foreign policy and that of the military situation at the time.

The British policy of appeasement was based on the conviction that the terms of the Paris settlement had established unacceptably harsh conditions for Germany, that certain adjustments in postwar borders were rationally and even morally acceptable, and that by means of these limited modifications the aggressive tendencies of Hitler's Germany could be halted. These views assumed that a peaceful international order could be achieved by rationally addressing what amounted to a justifiable grievance of a major European power.

The question that arises is whether the Nazi Germans in charge of foreign policy viewed the matter in the same manner. There seems to be little question that by 1938 they did not. There was intense competition and confusion within the Nazi regime over the making of foreign policy. By the late 1930s, persons with radical foreign policy goals had come into control of the decision-making apparatus. Readjustment of the postwar borders was not their goal. Rather they entertained visions of a vast reshaping of world power and of a major German advance throughout eastern Europe. The formulators of this policy were often middle- or lower-middle-class Germans who, despite the domestic success of National Socialism, could not achieve the social status and acceptance they desired within German society. They believed that an empire in eastern Europe would give them an arena for realizing both their national imperial goals and their personal social ambitions. Persons of this outlook came to dominate German

Reprinted with the permission of George Allen & Unwin (Publishers) Ltd. from *Fascist Challenge and the Policy of Appeasement*, W. J. Mommsen and L. Kettenacker, eds. Copyright © 1983 by George Allen & Unwin Ltd.

foreign policy circles at the very time that Hitler himself had decided Britain would never be his ally and would in all probability be a military enemy.

In consequence, when Britain decided to undertake a policy of active appeasement based on reasonable limited adjustment of grievances, its diplomats confronted German counterparts seeking a virtually unlimited empire in eastern Europe and doubting whether a peaceful future with Britain was possible.

One of the crucial questions in assessing the policy of appeasement during the late 1930s is whether that policy ever had a reasonable chance of success under the prevailing circumstances. To address that question one must develop as complete an understanding as possible of the nature of the threat posed to the international system at the time, an understanding which entails centrally a grasp of Germany's foreign policy during these years, for Germany, although not the only, was the most dangerous of the challengers to the international *status quo*.

Here a whole cluster of issues appear from the outset to complicate the problem: to what extent did Hitler's foreign policy represent elements of continuity and discontinuity? What was the relationship, if any, between foreign and domestic policy in Nazi Germany? How crucial was Hitler's role, including his plans and decision-making process, *vis-à-vis* other factors in determining foreign policy? These and other questions must be addressed—and indeed have been in a number of recent publications on German foreign policy. But the work so far has been of necessity tentative and exploratory; many questions still await an answer, many trains of events their interpretive framework. The whole issue of appeasement gives us the opportunity to continue to address the complex question of the threat posed by Nazi Germany.

In this paper I will assert a close connection between domestic and foreign policy. I propose that the Nazi regime, arising as it did out of a society in disintegration, posed by its very nature, apart from any concrete goals in the mind of the dictator, a revolutionary threat to the stability of the international order during the 1930s. Moreover, I would suggest that this threat did not represent a challenge to Hitler as chief foreign policy formulator, but rather dovetailed closely with his own long-range goals, gave impetus to his own eagerness to radically alter the face of Europe and, in fact, provided a momentum on all fronts that his own day-to-day style of leadership failed to do. Finally, I would suggest that what amounted then to a dual threat to the system—Hitler himself and, in a nearly autonomous way, the regime over which he presided—operated in such a way as to very nearly preclude success on the part of the appeasement policy especially as it was timed and practised.

By now it has been firmly established and generally accepted by most scholars that the Nazi regime was hardly the efficient monolith its propagandists made it out to be. Rather, it was a competitive bureaucratic jungle, characterised by confused and overlapping jurisdictions, personalised power, duplication of function and administrative chaos. This bureaucratic 'state of nature', this war of all against all, unarguably redounded to Hitler's benefit, for it enhanced his power by putting him in the position of ultimate arbiter. And perhaps for that very reason he encouraged the rivalries and exacerbated the confusion in his decisions—or lack of them. But the chaotic Führer-State was far more than simply a function of Hitler's erratic leadership techniques: it was a reflection of and a response to what had happened to German society in the years preceding the Nazi *Machtergreifung* [seizure of power] and was a phenomenon which was not only revolutionising German society, but which also had ominous implications for the international *status quo*, for it provided the dynamic which propelled the Nazi revolution far beyond the borders of the German Reich.

The well-known and often observed dynamic of the Nazi system derived in large measure from the general disintegration of German society which took place during the 1920s and 1930s in the wake of national defeat and economic catastrophe. That societal disintegration produced in turn a radical disjuncture among the variables of class, status and wealth and destroyed any national consensus which might have existed. Politically, this was reflected in the total breakdown of the Weimar Republic and its liberal parliamentary form of government.

National Socialism arose as a concrete response to this situation of political fragmentation and social disintegration and achieved much of its success by promising (1) to restore national consensus, in part by redefining what the nation was, who belonged to it and who did not, and (2) to create a world of equal opportunity to all in the process of creating a utopian society freed of caste and class strife. One of the ways in which the Nazis tried to realise these rather nebulous if noble sounding goals once they were in power was, paradoxically, to desociologise politics (that is, to pretend that the class struggle had been terminated) and simultaneously to politicise society. This second step was particularly important, because it enabled the Nazi leaders to direct Germans towards what already during the Weimar period had been the most open path of upward mobility—politics.

Indeed, it has been observed that the Nazis had no parallel in Germany in introducing a sense of public spiritedness on a widespread grass roots level among people who traditionally had been 'apolitical'. By creating, then, through the party a mechanism by which to involve ordinary people in an expanded arena of politics the Nazis could address simultaneously their dual problem of restoring national consensus and opening opportunity, by creating in the minds of Germans a close link between the fate of the nation and their own career advancement. If one could aid in building the *Volksgemeinschaft* and build a career at the same time, so much the better. In this context, of course, it was desirable to make the world of politics as broad as possible, hence the emergence of what Fraenkel has called the 'dual state', one in which, as he says, 'the "political" sphere is not one sphere of the state separated from the others by law; it is an omnicompetent sphere independent of all legal regulation'. It is this combination of factors—the confluence of career opportunity, a sense of redefining the nation and an expanded realm of politics—that created the arena for dynamic political entrepreneurship which characterised Nazi Germany from the outset. It was a world which seemed to offer no limitations beyond the parameters set by the often vaguely expressed will of the Führer: no limitation on the accumulation of power, for it was almost a caricature of the open-ended liberalism of the nineteenth century; no limits on jurisdiction, for the individual was not just filling an office or a post, he was creating a totally new society. Hence, the multiplicity of plans in the minds of Nazi big-wigs which betrayed their own sense of omnicompetence: the SA-State of Roehm, the Labour-State of Ley, the Stahlhelm-State of Hierl, the HJ-State of Schirach, and ultimately the most successful in its multi-jurisdictional reach—the SS-State of Himmler.

This world of political free enterprise was made even more competitive by the additional factor of chaos. The striking thing about the Nazi political structure was its lack of rules. This absence of norms, of course, redounded to the benefit of Hitler himself, for it made him the ultimate and only arbiter, and so he encouraged it. But the chaos existed for other reasons as well, reflecting again the fragmentation of German society. In all modern societies, there is a tendency to replace traditional organic associations (kinship, village, guild) with functional ones (trade and manufacturing associations, unions, and so on). Indeed, this development seems to be an accompanying phenomenon of modernisation. In liberal societies, that is, those which have a broad societal consensus, this process goes on within a generally accepted political and constitutional framework which provides a set of impersonal rules by which these functional associations may be created and interrelate with one another. In the absence of a broad societal consensus, however, no normative framework exists, and chaos is liable to result from the process. This is precisely what happened in Germany. Even before the Nazis came to power, German society, basically illiberal in its development, socially only part way into modernisation, lacked the social consensus which would have supported the orderly change from organic to functional association. After the Nazis came to power the situation became worse. Faking the existence of a social consensus, the Nazis proceeded quite consciously to enormously accelerate the process by destroying wholesale traditional, organic, autonomous organisations and replacing them with their own politicised 'functional' ones within the sphere of the regime. For them it was a necessary task and an integral part of the *Gleichschaltung* policy by which they established their control over the German people. But the very lack of consensus which lay behind the lie of *Volksgemeinschaft*, the same lack of social consensus which had been a hallmark of German society before the *Machtergreifung*, continued to prohibit the formulation of any set of rules by which the new associations would function or relate to each other. The result was that the new 'functional' associations, that is, the personal bureaucratic empires of Nazi big-wigs like Ley, Goebbels and Himmler, would be operating, not in a normative structure, but in a competitive jungle.

No wonder then that from the outset these Nazi competitive structures spilled over the normally prescribed boundaries by which functional groups operate and relate to one another in modern society. This was true with respect to the means by which they operated, which came to include treachery, intrigue and even murder, and in terms of their range of activities, which exhibited the pronounced tendency to collect a series of otherwise unrelated jurisdictions as part of a bureaucratic empire. In what 'liberal' country, for example, could a Hermann Goering have managed to be head of the air force, economic tsar, chief forester, foreign policy meddler and much else besides? Important to our considerations here, however, is that the lack of rules also enabled the Nazi functional organisations to spill over the boundary which separated domestic politics from foreign policy.

This already existing tendency to allow a dynamic progression from the arena of domestic policy to that of foreign policy was exacerbated by yet another feature of German society at the time—the continued existence of the former ruling classes and the necessity to reach an accommodation with them. It is well known that Hitler frustrated the desires on the part of millions of his middle- and lower-middle-class followers to create a new society in their image in that he came to terms with the traditional forces he needed to make Germany powerful and to realise his dreams of conquest —the army, the civil service and big business. Because this accommodation was necessary, the regime, whether consciously or not, took the sting out of its failure to completely restructure the country by recreating society in a parallel Nazi world. The component parts of this Nazi world...were the 'functional' associations to which I have alluded. The hallmark of this parallel society was that one could rise faster and have a better chance to realise one's utopian dreams in it than in the real society. It was, after all, easier to become an SS general than a regular army general, to run an SS office than to be a *Staatssekretär*, because in the parallel society the roadblocks posed by the old society were absent. The criteria of birth, established wealth, status and membership in an 'old boy' network were replaced by the more accessible ones of political loyalty and racial purity. The problem was—as the continued presence of titled conservatives and wealthy *Generaldirektoren* gave witness—that both societies continued to exist side by side, and any ambitious Nazi had to go on living in both.

Therefore, every political aspirant lived in a kind of force field of tension created by the fact that the status and rewards of the one society did not often translate into the currency of the other. Indeed, despite the fact that many upwardly mobile Nazis hated the older class society and those who stood at its apex, at the same time they often could not escape its symbols, rewards and sanctions. It was as if they realised the bogus nature of the shadow Nazi world and tried to square the circle either by trying to become part of the other world, or to translate the successes in the Nazi world into its own rewards, or—most ominously—when these devices did not succeed, to lash out beyond the old society in a manner which would ultimately destroy it. We have much evidence for this perceived tension at virtually every level of the Nazi system. Within the context of the appeasement issue, for example, it is interesting to note that Ribbentrop's first attempt to venture into the world of foreign policy was to submit an essay in application for the post of *Staatssekretär* in the Auswärtiges Amt in 1933. And while, of course, creating his own functional organisation in the shadow world, the *Büro Ribbentrop*, never ceased trying to translate his activities into the coinage of the traditional realm. Twice more, in 1935, he requested that Hitler make him *Staatssekretär*. Ultimately, of course, he was appointed Foreign Minister and, characteristically, largely abandoned his 'functional' *Büro* in the shadow world.

It is this very tension, and the inability to overcome it, that will help cause the dynamic of the Nazi system, not only with respect to the tendency of Nazi formations to spill beyond the realm of traditional jurisdictions, but more importantly, for them all as a group to overreach the borders of German society itself—into the social *tabula rasa* of Eastern Europe. For only there could Nazi dreamers and power-seekers create a world in which only their symbols, sanctions, power and status would have exclusive validity. This obviously has enormous consequences for German foreign policy, for it means that the very mechanism by which Nazi political society functioned practically predisposed that system to challenge the international social and political order, completely apart from any concrete plans that Hitler might have formulated. As we shall see, it was the misapprehension of this fact that allowed the appeasers to go on as long as they did in pursuing a policy which, given the nature of the Nazi system, was probably futile from the start. As far as the dictator himself was concerned, this interpretation of the dynamics of Nazi society and the tendency for the organisations that made up the regime to spill over into a foreign policy of expansion suggests that there was no real tension between Hitler and the system. Rather it is more likely that the two, Hitler, with his *Stufenplan* for achieving German hegemony over Europe and then the status of a world power, and the dynamic, if frustrated, group of Nazi political entrepreneurs, were operating in tandem. Hitler was well aware of the dynamic which propelled his regime. He was animated by some of the same drives which characterised his followers. His task was to formulate, more carefully, the *Endziele* and alternately to restrain, or unleash, the dynamic as thought useful. In light of this fact one would suggest that views of German foreign policy which are too Hitler-centric miss one important source of the pressure behind the expansionist policy of Nazi Germany.

It is necessary at this point to demonstrate that the Hobbesian state of nature that characterised the Nazi system domestically also obtained, if to a more limited extent, in the foreign policy area as well. Contemporary observers certainly noted the fact. Already in July of 1933 Mussolini complained:

> There seemed to be six if not seven members of the German government who acted from time to time as foreign minister. Hitler...Neurath...Goering... Papen, Goebbels and Rosenberg, not to mention General Blomberg who was brought into all discussions of foreign affairs. This rendered dealing with the German government a matter of considerable difficulty.

Over four years later, the Italians were still complaining. Mussolini's son-in-law, Italian Foreign Minister Count Ciano, said on the occasion of Lord Halifax's visit to Berlin in November 1937:

> Zuviel Hähne im Hühnerstall. Es gibt mindestens vier Aussenpolitiken: die von Hitler, die von Goering, die von Neurath, die von Ribbentrop. Von den kleineren ganz abgesehen. Es ist schwierig, vollkommen auf dem laufenden zu bleiben.[1]

Not only Germany's friends noticed this tendency; representatives of her potential enemies did so as well. French Ambassador André François-Poncet observed with respect to foreign policy:

> There is not merely one minister, nor is there only one foreign office. There are a half-dozen. When it is a question of Austria, Habicht is heard. When it is a question of Hungary or Rumania, one perceives that Rosenberg and his office still retain a particle of authority. When it is necessary to take up the Saar, or the Vatican, or France, one addresses Papen. When there is a reason to send a message to Mussolini, it is Goering who leaps into his airplane. Even the influence of the whimsical Dr Hanfstaengl comes into play when America is under discussion.

Even the man ostensibly in charge of carrying out German foreign policy, Neurath, told a visitor in the summer of 1937: 'Don't take Goering too

---

[1] ["There are too many roosters in the chicken coop. There are at least four foreign policies—Hitler's, Goering's, Neurath's, and von Ribbentrop's apart from the smaller ones. It is difficult to remain completely current."]

seriously. In Germany, everyone concerns himself with foreign policy.' What contemporary observers noted has been largely confirmed by scholarship during the past decade or so. I do not propose here to discuss in detail the various organisations involved in the formulation of Nazi foreign policy, but rather to make several generalisations about them germane to the theme of appeasement.

(1) Competing Nazis ventured into the foreign policy arena for a variety of reasons, most of which arose from that same combination of utopian vision, careerist opportunism and inadvertent spill-over produced by the very dynamic of the system as we have described it. Ernst Bohle, founder of the *Auslandsorganisation* of the party, dreamed of harnessing ethnic Germans all over the world as tools for National Socialism. His goal was to help bring Germany into the first rank of world powers. 'I was absolutely fascinated and dominated by the conception of a German Reich which, in spite of a completely different structure, would, in every respect, enjoy absolute equality with England in the concert of world powers.' Himmler dreamed of a great racial empire to the East, where he could realise his visions of resettlement. Rosenberg cherished visions of a break-up of the Great Russian state and an accompanying *nordisch-deutsch* racial renewal. None of these men thought small. On the contrary, their vision is to a great extent millennial, reflecting perhaps a combination of frustration and aspiration.

Occasionally, forays into foreign policy would be a result of simple expansion of a domestic power structure: as when Propaganda Minister, Goebbels, tried to get control of Nazi propaganda abroad; or when the SS extended its intelligence activities beyond Germany's borders in search of exiles and ideological enemies. Sometimes foreign policy involvement would arise from a dilettantism with a particular geographic predisposition: Goering's fascination for Italian or Polish relations, Rosenberg's interests in Hungary and Romania, Ribbentrop's mercurial relationship with the English, to name only the most important. But more often than not, in any given case, a multiplicity of motives was involved. The best example for this was the SS, whose involvement in foreign policy was a gradual affair arising from intelligence activities, ideological dreaming, solid business interest, police work and its own troubles generally in defining a mission for itself.

In all cases, though, the ultimate effect of this activity was aimed in one way or another at changing the *status quo* in Europe and the world. What all these dreams and ambitions have in common was a disruption, a radical one, even a millennial one, of the international system.

(2) The same tensions and conflicts created by the existence of two parallel societies in the domestic arena were reproduced as well in the foreign policy sphere. Indeed they are, if anything, more clearly delineated here, because the two conservative strongholds which were vital in Germany's foreign relations—the army and the Foreign Office—were involved. It was here that the Nazi rulers had to make the most far-reaching

accommodations in terms of personnel, and here where conservatives seemed to preserve their traditional power and perquisites. No wonder, then, that the field of foreign policy became one of the main fields of struggle between radical Nazis and conservative traditionalists.

We know now that conservative strength was not what it seemed at the time. But optically it must have seemed so. After all, Hitler's short-range policies dovetailed neatly with the long-range goals of the conservatives, so that there appeared a community of interest which did not really exist. Moreover, Hitler found it necessary to rein in the more competitive foreign policy aspirants from time to time, which made him look perhaps more moderate than we know him to have been. And, finally, even with respect to personnel, aspiring Nazis may be forgiven for having thought that German society had not changed as much as they had hoped it would with the coming of the Nazi regime. Everywhere they looked, the old masters still seemed to be around. The diplomatic corps had a higher percentage of titled aristocrats than during the Weimar period and even the SS itself had a disproportionate number of nobles in its upper ranks. All this was fuel for the fierce fire of jurisdictional conflict.

(3) This rivalry in the foreign policy arena did not represent a steady state, a static situation where each side held its own. Rather it was a dynamic conflict in which over the years between 1933 and 1937 the radicals gradually got the upper hand. Though Neurath and the Foreign Service were more powerful and effective initially than hitherto supposed, as Heineman's new biography of Neurath suggests, it is nevertheless true that by 1936 the conservatives had their backs to the wall through personnel attrition, fierce competition from a variety of Nazis, and Hitler's increasing use of foreign policy agencies other than the traditional apparatus. By the end of 1937 the battle had been won, with serious consequences for the policy of appeasement.

(4) The transfer of the competitive structure of the Nazi state to the arena of foreign policy worked almost entirely to the benefit of Hitler as he began the pursuit of his long-range vision. It allowed him to explore options and probe weaknesses without bearing any of the consequences as head of state. This was most dramatically demonstrated in the case of Austria in July 1934. It gave a set of ideas and tools which helped to counterbalance his own lack of previous experience in foreign affairs. It created situations which he could exploit when he believed the situation to be ripe. This represented a real advantage to the dictator who hated day-to-day governance and preferred to let situations drift until they became critical. Other statesmen did not have his advantage. And finally, of course, the endless rivalry and competition grew out of a dynamic which Hitler knew full well, whatever the varieties of dreams and aspirations might have been, would coincide with his own desire to radically restructure Europe. In this sense, he could be sure that the long-term evolution of Nazi society would coincide with his long-term goals.

Having said this, it is necessary to note that despite the enormous centrifugal force that the dynamic Nazi system generated, there were practical limits in its day-to-day functioning in foreign policy, even though its long-term prospects promised international upheaval. Hitler, careful not to upset the international system before German strength was commensurate with the task, imposed sharper restrictions on the competition in foreign policy than he did with domestic affairs. Here it is very important in the assessment of German foreign policy to strike a proper balance between Hitler's own initiative and control and the spontaneous activities of his underlings.

(5) Finally, it is of great importance to our theme here to note that the culmination of the struggle in foreign policy between radicals and traditionalists in victory for the radicals coincided almost exactly with an increase in German economic and military strength to a point where Hitler believed that he could proceed beyond his short-term goals (and the long-range ones of the conservatives) towards his long-range ones (which coincided with the dreams of many radicals). It is a tragedy that the conjuncture for these two developments coincides in turn with a third — the evolution of British policy from passive to active appeasement. And it is to that problem and its relationship to the structure and formulation of German foreign policy that we must now turn.

It is one of the more tragic conjunctures of the period, that the transition from a policy of passive appeasement to one of active appeasement occurred simultaneously with two other developments which boded ill for the success of that strategy: the gradual realisation on Hitler's part that Britain would not be an ally of Germany, but more likely an enemy; and the victory of the radicals in Germany over the traditionalists.

If we can establish the inauguration of active appeasement with the visit of Lord Halifax to Berlin on 18 November 1937, then this conjuncture becomes clear. Halifax in his discussions with Hitler, Goering and other German leaders himself opened the question of concessions to Germany in Central Europe; that is, he practically established an agenda by means of which the Austrian and Czechoslovak problems could be addressed on an international level. Under more normal, traditional circumstances this would have been a completely rational step: to address problems concerning the powers so that they could be settled peacefully before they reached a stage of crisis where lack of resolution might threaten the peace. But Halifax and the other British statesmen were not operating under traditional circumstances. In Germany, they were dealing with a power whose leader had radical goals far beyond those tolerable within any framework the British envisioned; and whose political system possessed a dynamic which also posed a direct threat to the *status quo*. A succession of events just before and shortly after Halifax's visit dramatically illustrate the point. On 5 November, just two weeks before Halifax's arrival, Hitler, in his secret speech to Neurath and the army commanders, had already put Austria and

Czechoslovakia on an agenda—not one of negotiation but rather of military conquest. Moreover, it also emerged in the speech that he anticipated Britain no longer as an ally, but rather as one potential enemy.

It was also during these last several months in 1937 that the fierce struggle on several fronts within Germany between radical Nazis and more traditional conservatives was approaching an end with the general collapse of the conservatives and victory by the radicals. The resignation of Schacht on 26 November, just one week after Halifax's visit to Berlin, represented more than simply the loss of one prominent conservative. It reflected the break-up of a political united front on the part of big business, and, as one scholar suggests, a further stage in the general disintegration of German society. The result was to give still more impetus, opportunity and *Spielraum* to the competitive Nazi formations. The subsequent scandals surrounding War Minister von Blomberg and Commander-in-Chief of the army, von Fritsch, resulting in Hitler's direct take-over of the military as well as his replacement of Neurath with Ribbentrop as Foreign Minister, represented the collapse of the conservative position in two other former bastions—the army and the Foreign Office. Accompanying these dénouements, virtually unnoticed at the time, but no less ominous, was the victory of the SS in the area of the *Volkstum* struggle, with the dismissal of Hans Steinacher as head of the VDA and the establishment of the *Volksdeutsche Mittelstelle* as a command post for manipulation of German communities abroad. In fact, the capitulation of Konrad Henlein, leader of the Sudeten Germans, to Hitler's will *on the same day* as Halifax's arrival, signalled that even as the British were giving the dictator a legitimate excuse to raise the question of Czechoslovakia's future in the international forum, the leader of the German minority in that country was giving him the tool to deal with Czechoslovakia in a manner not envisioned in British councils. The British knew of most of these developments—at least the changes in personnel, but either underestimated their impact or misunderstood them entirely. Henderson wrote to the king from Berlin that these changes 'left the German army with a say in Foreign affairs' and 'had strengthened the hand of the peace party in Germany'.

Thus, the policy of active appeasement, of taking the initiative in raising issues germane to the peace of Europe instead of passively awaiting moves on the part of the dictator, a policy which might have weighed measurably in the scales if undertaken earlier in the year, was begun under the most inauspicious circumstances towards the end of 1937, and at the beginning of 1938, at a time when Hitler's views of what he might venture without disproportionate risk had expanded to the point where he was willing to see Britain as the enemy, and when the dynamic of the Nazi revolution had cleared the decks for action by eliminating any restraining competition.

Beyond this unfortunate conjuncture of developments, there was another factor which cast a grave shadow over the possibilities offered by the policy of appeasement as it emerged in late 1937. If we look at the goals being pursued by the British government, at the language in which these goals were formulated and at the framework in which the British leadership viewed international relations, it becomes clear that Chamberlain and his associates were operating on a very different plane from that of the Nazi leadership. This fact may be so glaringly obvious that it scarcely needs to be asserted, but I do feel it is important to explore it briefly in one of its aspects, for the extremely divergent views of the world which separated the German from the British leadership themselves are evidence of a disintegration of the international system and suggest, in retrospect, a gloomy prognosis for the policy of appeasement. Where the two groups differed perhaps most greatly was on the subject of empire-building.

The radical differences in goals, language, spirit and concepts which separated the British leadership from the Nazi German in terms of imperial expansion have their origins partly in the very different stages of development in which the two countries found themselves. By the 1930s, Great Britain had reached a stage of development where she was a mature, satiated imperial power. Her leaders for the most part had recognised the aspirations to which both the Wilsonian and Lenin revolutions had given expression and, though the British government was moving at a glacial pace in direction of devolution, it at least had progressed beyond the nineteenth century in its attitudes towards imperialism and empire-building. This is not to deny that there were plenty of Englishmen who still nostalgically harboured Kiplingesque dreams of empire, but the point is that public opinion and that of most responsible leaders had passed them by. Illustrative in this context is the book *The Lost Dominion*, published in 1942 by B. C. H. Calcraft-Kennedy, a high-ranking official in the Indian administration, under the alias Al. Carthill. The book is a passionate plea for Britain's right to rule India and in the traditional manner. But although the author thought that the Raj could continue to control India, by 'administrative massacre' if necessary, he also realised and admitted that it was utopian to try to do so, for public sentiment, shaped by the left-wingers and humanitarians whom the author loathed so much, would never permit such a thing.

Germany, by contrast, having come late to nationhood and only briefly enjoyed the fruits of colonial empire, had not evolved as far as Britain with respect to imperial attitudes. Even Germany's respectable leaders still talked during the 1920s very much in terms of retrieving lost colonies abroad. It was the Nazi political entrepreneurs, though, who really represented a kind of nineteenth-century anachronism in their imperial attitudes. There were several reasons for this. First, Nazi ideology had borrowed heavily on the racial thought of the late nineteenth century and made the racial imperative the core of their dreams of empire. Secondly, the enormous tensions and compulsions which lay at the heart of the competitive Nazi political system generated aspirations and dreams on a Cecil Rhodesian scale. This factor, in turn, was exacerbated by the social backgrounds of many of the Nazi dreamers. A goodly number of them had their origins in the middle and lower-middle class. Only now, with the advent of the Nazi equal opportunity revolution, itself a product of a social upheaval which Engish society had escaped, could they aspire to imperial careers which a generation or two earlier had been reserved for their social betters. They represented then, as far as foreign policy was concerned, 'petit bourgeois Bismarckians'. But the tardy arrival of their chance for empire could still not disguise the fact that in the fourth decade of the twentieth century they were historical anachronisms. A Carl Peters might say with equanimity in the 1880s that he 'was fed up with being counted among the pariahs and wanted to belong to a master race,' and not attract undue attention, because there were plenty of Frenchmen and Englishmen who shared his racial view of empire. That kind of language used nearly half a century later, however, failed to recognise all the changes that had occurred in the interim. It is ironic in this context to realise that Joseph Chamberlain might have understood the Nazis far better than his son, Neville. For this ardent imperialist, ambitious, vain, combative, inexperienced in foreign affairs yet with an eye for power, a man described variously as 'a Sicilian bandit' and 'almost the greatest jingo' in the Cabinet, would have been much more in tune with the Faustian scope of the Nazi thrust forward and vision of empire. What neither Chamberlain would have understood, however—and this was the second factor which put the British and Nazi German leaders during the 1930s on two different planes—was the 'leap' by which the Nazis transferred their imperial vision from the classically recognised field for empire of Africa and Asia to the vast reaches of Eastern Europe. It was Russia and not Tanganyika which was to provide the experimentation ground for Himmler's resettlement schemes, the political battleground for the establishment of Rosenberg's 'Nordische Schicksalsgemeinschaft', the apocalyptic battleground for the destruction of the 'Drahtzieher des Judentums' projected by Goebbels and the geopolitical foundation for Hitler's dreams of Germany's coming role as *Weltmacht*.

There was to be sure a certain terrible logic in this turning to the east for empire. The 'leap' from seeing foreign continents as areas for imperial expansion to seeing the eastern regions of Europe in the same fashion came easy to a people who traditionally over the centuries had expanded in that direction rather than overseas; and the leap must have been all the easier when the rationale of racial superiority came into play. The Nazi goal was a second *Drang nach Osten* with racial and apocalyptic overtones. And indeed the Nazis were not the first Germans to see Eastern Europe in this fashion. Already at the turn of the century Ernst Hasse, head of the Pan-German League, proposed treating certain nationalities such as Poles, Czechs, Jews and others 'in the same way as overseas imperialism treated natives in non-European continents'. The attitude of the generals during the period of military dictatorship which followed Bethmann's dismissal was not much different. And even far more respectable figures than Hasse or the generals had developed from time to time grandiose schemes for the reconstitution of

Eastern Europe. Moreover, given Germany's geographic position, constricted as she was in the heart of Central Europe, an eastward move was the only way in which Germany could gain the requisite continental hinterland to join Britain, with her overseas realm, and America, with its continental base, as world powers. Finally, and perhaps most importantly, the very dynamics of the chaotic Führer-State itself dictated eastward expansion, for only here could the aspiring Nazi imperialist find the social *tabula rasa* which would enable them to escape the tensions which they experienced living in the dual society of Germany. In this sense, the Nazi entrepreneurs may have sensed the same thing that many nineteenth-century statesmen, concerned about the impact of overseas adventure on the established national state at home, had instinctively been aware of—that a new expansion movement 'could only destroy the body politic of the nation state'. For many a National Socialist visionary, steeped in the millenarian vision of a racial empire and disgusted with the flaws in traditional German national life, the image of destruction might well have been an attractive one.

But whatever the compulsions of logic might have been, they represented Nazi logic, not that of the British leaders. Hitler might draw all the admiring parallels he wanted between the British Empire in India and the coming German Empire in Russia, the British would never have been ready (even had they been aware of the exact nature of Hitler's vision) to accept the 'leap' which the Germans had taken. On the contrary, British leaders, with very few exceptions, insisted on placing German aspirations within the strictures both of the traditional European continental balance of power system, and within the system of national self-determination for all peoples established by Wilson in 1918 (although eventually the British by and large backed down on the second, as the Munich Agreement attests).

There was, thus, a stability to British society and in the backgrounds of her leaders over the decades which permitted an evolutionary change in viewing the international relations that was by and large lacking in the much more unstable German society, where a new political élite emerged, armed with apocalyptic visions, animated by a sense of radical mobility and equipped with a set of nineteenth-century imperial ideas.

The disintegration of German society produced a dynamic and radical movement which spilled over into foreign expansion and threatened to overturn established international relationships. The Nazis were abetted in their challenge to the *status quo* by the fact that the traditional international Great Power system itself was in disintegration. The British statesmen, who were confronting the Nazi challenge, were hindered in doing so by the fact that they had one foot in the old system (that of European balance of power and imperial preservation) and one in the new (national self-determination and collective security). As a result, they fell between the stools. Neither approach worked in dealing with the Nazis, because their challenge was too radical to be kept within either system. When the British tried to deal in postwar terms, calling, for example, for the integrity of Austria and

Czechoslovakia, they encountered refusal by Nazis who were thinking at the very least of German domination of Central Europe. When they tried to deal in prewar terms, resorting to the Congress system, as they did at Munich, then their success was only temporary, for Nazi ambitions were great enough to make the balance of power concept itself anachronistic. Indeed, the very fact that the Munich Conference, probably the last example of the European Congress system at work, appears to us today as such a shabby betrayal and disgraceful interlude indicates the extent to which both the ideas of Wilson and Lenin as well as the challenge of Nazism had made it outmoded in 1938.

Bibliography

See the listing following the next essay.

Munich, 1938: The Military Confrontation

WILLIAMSON MURRAY

When British Prime Minister Neville Chamberlain returned from the Munich Conference, he claimed that he and the agreement he had made with Hitler had preserved European peace. In less than a year the German invasion of Poland shattered that peace and opened a general European war. This situation raises the question as to whether the eleven-month period of peace bought by the Munich agreement worked to the later military benefit of the Allied or the Axis side. In other words, from a military standpoint who might or might not have been better off with the commencement of war in October, 1938?

It is always difficult, and some would say impossible, to write the history of what might have been. Nevertheless, analysis of relative military strength, deployment of forces, access to vital supplies and natural resources, and likely international alignments and reactions is possible. Taking those factors into account, it seems likely that Germany would have gone to war on a weaker and more vulnerable footing in 1938 than in 1939. The problems of conquering Czechoslovakia, although by no means insurmountable, would have been different from those encountered when invading Poland, and the international reaction might also have proved more disconcerting for Germany. In other words, Hitler might very well have found himself much less in control of military events in October, 1938, than he did the next autumn after Prague had been invaded, Mussolini had drawn closer to the German side, and the Russian-German Pact had been concluded.

The question of what would have happened had war broken out at the end of September 1938 has concerned many historians, particularly those interested in either condemning or justifying Neville Chamberlain's foreign

Reprinted by permission from Volume 2 (1979), pp. 282–297 of the *Journal of Strategic Studies*, published by Frank Cass and Company Limited, 11 Gainsborough Road, London Ell, England. Copyright Frank Cass & Co. Ltd.

policy. Unfortunately, most students of Munich have regarded the military situation at that time as a peripheral issue. Few historians have studied the strategic situation objectively; most have been content to look for factors supporting their point of view while overlooking those which contradict their position. As a result, arguments over the military situation in 1938 have revolved around two central issues. Those who condemn Munich as a strategic disaster point to Germany's lack of ground strength, her weakness in the West, and her considerable economic difficulties. They suggest that any war in 1938 would have been a relatively quick affair leading to the swift collapse of Nazi Germany. On the other hand, there are those who argue that Britain's air defence in 1938 was desperately weak and that, had war broken out over Czechoslovakia, Great Britain would have collapsed before the onslaught of the *Luftwaffe*. The problem is, however, a far more complex one than either view suggests.

In an article of this length one does not have the space to examine all of the factors which contributed to the European balance of power in 1938. Nevertheless, a general examination of the most important elements in the strategic situation of 1938 suggests that the balance of power inclined much more heavily against Germany in that year than it was to do in 1939. First of all, the *Luftwaffe* was in no position to launch or sustain serious bombing strikes, much less a strategic bombing offensive, against the British Isles in 1938. Those who defend Chamberlain's policies for having saved Britain from the *Luftwaffe* in 1938 have done so on the basis of British air defence deficiencies and on the basis of a *presumed* German capability, which, to be frank, simply did not exist. On the other hand it is just as large a misrepresentation of the situation to tote up the number of divisions on the opposing sides and argue, for example, that with their overwhelming numerical superiority in the West the French army would have surged across the frontier into the Rhineland and on into the Ruhr in October, 1938. That would not have occurred, because in spite of their overwhelming superiority, despite the fact that hardly any of the *Westwall* had been completed, Gamelin and the French High Command had no intention of mounting anything more than the wretched effort they were to mount in September 1939.

Thus, to arrive at a fair evaluation of the question as to what would have occurred in a general European war over Czechoslovakia one must consider not only the actual military situation, but the misconceptions and the inhibitions of the military and political leaders who would have been charged with the conduct of the war. That is the purpose of this article. I will attempt to do so by moving from the specific to the general, from a discussion of the immediate prospects which a German invasion of Czechoslovakia would have enjoyed to the general strategic situation in Eastern and Western Europe, and finally to Germany's overall strategic, economic and diplomatic situation.

MUNICH, 1938: THE MILITARY CONFRONTATION

Only by scraping the bottom of the barrel were the Germans in a position to consider a military invasion of the Czech Republic. In September, 1938, the German Army consisted of forty-eight regular divisions, of which only three were armoured, four were light reconnaissance, and four were motorized infantry divisions. It lacked important items of equipment such as heavy artillery, and possessed almost no reserves except for the overage veterans of the First World War. Moreover, the *Wehrmacht* had inherited five of these divisions from the Austrian Army and the quality of many Austrian units was substantially lower than that of German units. In fact, General Ritter von Leeb was to note that the difference between German and Austrian troops was the difference between night and day.

The three armoured divisions possessed light tanks (Mark Is and IIs) which even by the standards of the time bordered on obsolescence, while a few prototype medium tanks (Mark IIIs and IVs) were available only for combat testing. Without the hitting power and armoured protection of heavier tanks, these armoured divisions would have had a difficult time in gaining and maintaining the freedom necessary for mobile operations.

The great bulk of the German Army consisted of infantry divisions, which to all intents and purposes were organized and equipped almost exactly like German infantry divisions at the end of the First World War. These thirty-seven divisions were no more modern than contemporary infantry divisions in the French Army with their horse drawn artillery and transport. Unlike 1914, there were few trained reserves, a factor which would have hindered even the mobilization of regular army units. The best that the Germans could squeeze out of the existing manpower and material pool were preparations to mobilize eight reserve and twenty-one *Landwehr* divisions, consisting almost entirely of World War I veterans and lacking nearly all equipment and specialists. Even without their equipment, most of these formations would not have been ready for the simplest military tasks. Finally, German industry was not yet capable of supporting active fighting while at the same time producing equipment for the formation of a large number of new divisions.

On the other hand, most of those who have argued strongly against Chamberlain's policy of appeasement have tended to overestimate the capabilities of the Czech Army. While the Czechs mobilized somewhere near thirty divisions to face the threat of thirty-seven German divisions in September, 1938, only nineteen were regular divisions and two of those had been established in late spring, 1938. As with most of the European armies of this period, the Czech Army did not have adequate modern equipment for its reserve units. Nevertheless, the equipment of its regular forces was on a par with western (including German) armies. The Germans were to admit after Munich that most Czech first line divisions possessed excellent weapons. Moreover, the Czechs had succeeded in building considerable fortifications along certain sections of their frontiers, but had begun a concerted effort rather late in the game. The Czechs were particularly prepared to meet a German thrust from Silesia towards Austria.

There were, of course, major weaknesses. The Czech Army High Command seems to have been selected on the basis of participation in the Czech Legion in 1917 and 1918 rather than on the basis of military competence. The Germans did consider Czech regimental and company grade leadership to be quite good, but NCOs were not up to German standards. Overall, German reports on the Czech military acknowledged that the Czechs could have put up strong resistance behind fortifications, but doubted whether Czech troops could have matched German soldiers in open warfare.

German planning for the proposed invasion went through several distinct changes. The initial German plan, drawn up by General Franz Halder and the general staff, emphasized the military aspects of the problem of invading Czechoslovakia, but ignored the diplomatic and political problems such an attack would engender. Their plan called for two major attacks: an army based in Silesia would strike to the south to be met by another army striking north from Austria. This would serve to cut Czechoslovakia at her narrowest point, and trap the bulk of the Czech armies in Bohemia and Moravia. Yet, this first plan failed to take into account the political necessity of gaining a quick victory which would deter the major European powers from intervention. In a stormy conference on 3 September, 1938, Hitler was quick to point this out. He demanded that plans be altered radically to include a massive stroke at Prague from Bavaria. This offensive would include all of Germany's armoured and motorized forces. The capture of Prague, Hitler felt, would prevent the German attack on Czechoslovakia from escalating into a major European conflagration. Hitler then left for the party rally at Nürnberg. Interestingly, Hitler's control over his military chiefs was still less than complete, for Halder and Brauchitsch seem to have made no significant changes in the plans. On 9 September, the military leaders again met with Hitler, and the resulting blowup was characterized by Hitler's military adjutant as a disaster. Hitler again underlined the importance of the drive on Prague, but at this meeting compromised to allow major supporting drives from Silesia and Austria to cut Czechoslovakia in half.

As with most compromises, the final German plan was weaker than either initial conception. In political as well as in psychological terms, Hitler's plan was better. It was certainly more daring, because it would have launched the German motorized forces across difficult terrain, but this attack, as with the Ardennes thrust of 1940, would have been unexpected. Moreover, all of the German armoured and motorized forces would have been concentrated. The final plan, however, distributed the three armoured divisions and three light divisions between three different armies. The drive against Prague would have eventually fought its way into the city, but only after heavy protracted fighting; it did not have the strength to win through in a smashing *fait accompli* to give Hitler the victory he needed to deter other powers from intervention.

Czech dispositions to meet the German threat seem to have been more sensible than Polish dispositions were to be the following year. While the Czechs frittered away much of their strength to defend insignificant border districts, they did establish two substantial groupings of reserves which would have helped them to counter the major German thrusts. The first grouping of reserves lay in the vicinity of Prague and consisted of two mobile divisions, one infantry division, and four reserve infantry divisions, while the second, near the frontier between Slovakia and Moravia, consisted of two mobile divisions, one motorized division, and five reserve divisions. Both of these forces would have been in a position to counter the major German thrusts and to prevent the Germans from gaining the quick, initial breakthroughs which they were to exploit with such ruthlessness in the period from 1939 through 1941.

There is one other major factor which must be addressed in evaluating the course of a German/Czech conflict in the first weeks of October 1938: the weather. For the most part it would have favoured the Czechs, because it was atrocious. Considering the lack of an all-weather capability in the *Luftwaffe*, and the general problems in maintaining its aircraft which the *Luftwaffe* faced in 1938, air support would have been spotty at best. The difficulty in flying close air support missions in bad weather would have resulted in high losses and would have affected German capabilities to support other military operations after the conquest of Czechoslovakia.

In the final analysis, Czech resistance, unsupported by the active intervention of other powers, would probably have lasted as long as Polish resistance was to last in 1939. However, because of the nature of Czech terrain, a better equipped Czech military, and the general weaknesses of the German Army in 1938 (especially the weaknesses of the German tank forces) the Germans would have suffered considerably heavier casualties in men and material. Such a campaign with heavy losses would not have provided the boost which the victory over Poland was to give the *Wehrmacht* in 1939. Moreover, the armoured force would not have been able to prove its strategical potential against the Czechs as it was to do in the Polish campaign. A failure to achieve a dramatic success with the armoured forces would have provided conservatives within the German Army with arguments to use against the innovators like Guderian. Finally, a campaign against Czechoslovakia would have destroyed most of the Czech war material, and might well have caused considerable damage to Czech armament factories. The Czech arms dumps and armament works would prove of great use to the German war machine when they fell, undamaged, into German hands in March, 1939.

The basic strategic problem for Germany, however, was that the attack on Czechoslovakia would not have been confined to a Czech/German conflict, but would have involved the other major and many of the minor powers. Even in Eastern Europe the Germans faced a dangerous situation. The Poles were in a position to intervene with perhaps decisive impact, a Polish thrust across the northern portion of Silesia towards Breslau could have trapped Rundstedt's entire Silesian army. The Poles were, however, playing a waiting game. A Czech politician quite correctly catagorized Polish policy during the crisis as planning to move against Czechoslovakia if France and England remained neutral, to maintain neutrality and wait upon events if only France intervened, but to join the war against Germany if Britain came in. In fact the Poles were to make clear to the British government in the middle of September that their actions in the crisis would depend on what Great Britain did.

Poland's attitude was further complicated by an implacable hostility towards the Soviet Union. With Russia one enters murky waters, because so little documentary evidence is available on the policies of that regime. What is clear, however, is that the possible *military* role which the Soviet Union might have played in the Czech crisis has been exaggerated excessively. To begin with the Soviet Union had no frontier with either Germany or Czechoslovakia. In view of the hostility of both Rumania and Poland towards Russia, it is difficult to see how the Russians could have either attacked German territory or sent substantial military aid to the Czechs. Moreover, and this is a crucial point, Stalin was still in the process of destroying the Red Army by massive purges. The shoddy performances which characterized the Russian armies in the occupation of Eastern Poland, in the war against Finland, and in the first months of 'Barbarossa' indicates that the Soviet Union can hardly be considered a serious factor in the 1938 military situation. There are indications that Stalin was planning to use a major military confrontation between the Western Powers and Nazi Germany as an excuse to settle accounts with the Poles. The bitter exchanges between the Poles and the Russians at the end of September 1938 seem to indicate that both these powers were more interested in renewing their war of 1920 than in meeting the threat that Germany posed.

Nevertheless, the overall struggle situation in Eastern Europe and in the Balkans was considerably less favourable to the Germans in 1938 than it was to be in 1939/1940. To begin with, no matter what the capabilities of the Soviet Union might have been for military action, she would not have been allied to Nazi Germany nor would she have been in a position to aid the German war economy with massive amounts of raw materials, which was to happen with the Non-Aggression Treaty of August 1939. Moreover, Germany had not yet in 1938 succeeded in overawing the smaller nations of Eastern Europe. Yugoslavia and Rumania indicated at least tacit support for Czechoslovakia, and the Rumanians went so far as to warn the Germans that from 3 October, 1939 they could no longer expect deliveries of Rumanian oil. Even the Hungarians, who had every reason to dislike the Czechs, refused to commit themselves to a military venture against Czechoslovakia in spite of considerable German pressure.

What really alarmed the German military, however, was not the situation in Eastern Europe, but the strategic situation in the west. The so-called *Westwall* was a complete sham. Major construction on this fortification line had only begun in the early summer of 1938 and in spite of frantic efforts and a massive commitment of resources only 517 of the planned strong points had been completed. The figure in 1939 would stand at somewhere over 10,000 bunkers completed. Even of those bunkers completed, many were still militarily useless because the concrete had not yet set.

Nevertheless, the unprepared state of these fortifications was not the most serious problem the Germans faced in defending their western frontier. Because fortification work was incomplete, large ground forces would have been needed to defend the west against any major French offensive, and such forces were not available. General Adam, commander-in-chief of the western front, possessed only five regular divisions for the defense of the entire frontier with France and Belgium. In an August conference, Hitler promised Adam that he would receive twenty reserve divisions on the outbreak of war, but he was immediately contradicted by Brauchitsch who warned the Führer that only eight of those twenty could possibly be ready within three weeks of mobilization. This wishful thinking was to become typical of Hitler's performance in the later years of the war, when he let his fingers drift across situation maps, decreeing fortresses where neither men, equipment, bunkers, trenches, nor block houses existed. Similarly, throughout September 1938, Hitler dismissed with a wave of the hand the preponderate strength of the French Army, the unpreparedness of the *Westwall*, and the lack of reserves.

Hitler did hit nail on the head, however, with his realization, which was perhaps intuitive, that the French would be unwilling to seek a military confrontation in the West. Given the disparity between the French and German forces, had they possessed even moderately aggressive leadership, the French were in a position to wage their own *Blumenkrieg* in the Rhineland. As in 1939, such military leadership would not have been available. At the height of the Munich crisis de Gaulle sarcastically commented to Blum about what the army would do if war were to break out: 'it's quite simple... Depending on actual circumstances we will recall the 'disponibles' or mobilize the reserve. Then, looking through the loopholes of our fortifications, we will passively witness the enslavement of Europe.' De Gaulle was correct. Gamelin and the French High Command had no intention of undertaking active military operations against Germany. Gamelin indicated this in his visit and conference with British military and political leaders at the end of September, 1938. He began the discussions by cataloguing French might—a mobilization strength of 5,500,000, 100 divisions, and the Maginot Line—and by pointing out that there were only eight German divisions in the west. But when it came to describing what the French would do if war were to break out, Gamelin waffled. He commented that while immediate military action might be to France's advantage, perhaps one had better wait until Paris had been evacuated. Moreover, he made it clear that the French Army would retreat behind the shelter of the Maginot Line after the Germans had completed the conquest of Czechoslovakia and had begun to transfer troops to the west. The French Army 'would retreat (from German territory) in the manner of Hindenburg in 1917 to their fortifications in the Maginot Line, devastating their territory as they went.' From this account it is apparent that Gamelin, in spite of an admitted seven to one superiority (fifty-six French divisions against an estimated eight German divisions in the west) did not feel that the French Army could gain a significant military victory such as seizing the west bank of the Rhine. Later in the meeting Gamelin again returned to this point and anticipated that after an initial French offensive, his army would have to retreat to the Maginot Line during the course of the winter. There it would await the arrival of a substantial British Army.

Other high ranking French officers were even less optimistic about French prospects in a European war. In a conversation with the British military attaché at the end of September, 1938, General Dentz warned that if war were to come, the *Luftwaffe* would destroy France's defenceless cities. He left the British military attaché with the impression that the French regarded a German annexation of Czechoslovakia as inevitable. On the same day, Colonel Gauche, the head of French military intelligence, commented that 'of course there will not be a European war since we are not going to fight.'

The British military did nothing to encourage the French to take a strong stand. As early as 12 September, the Chief of Air Staff warned that the French might attack the 'greatly' (*sic*) strengthened German fortifications in the west. He suggested that the Chiefs of Staff be authorized to initiate staff conversations to persuade the French of the folly of such action. Thus, it is not surprising that the Chiefs of Staff were to inform a meeting of British ministers at the end of September that they feared that France might start some offensive action against Germany which would not be likely to achieve any effective result. Moreover, in the meeting with Gamelin, Lord Gort, Chief of the Imperial General Staff, and Sir Cyril Newall, the Chief of Air Staff, refused with evident embarrassment to define the military aid which Britain either could or would provide were war to break out in the immediate future.

If, as the evidence indicates, the French were unwilling to undertake serious military operations against western Germany, the key question in analyzing the military situation in the fall of 1938 then becomes the question of what options were open to Hitler for further military operations after the conquest of Czechoslovakia. In 1938/39 German options in the West would have been much more limited than they were to be in 1939/40. This would have been the result of a variety of factors: military, economic, and naval. The most obvious are the military and naval.

After a campaign against Czechoslovakia, the German Army would probably have suffered heavier casualties than it was to suffer in the Polish campaign; it would have possessed fewer armoured divisions than it was to possess by May, 1940, and these would probably have achieved fewer successes than German armour would achieve in Poland; and the army would have been considerably smaller in size. Moreover, it would have been impossible to equip new formations at anything more than a snail's pace, both because Czech arms dumps would have been destroyed in the conquest of Czechoslovakia, and because of economic factors which I shall discuss later in the article. It is hard to see how the Germans could have launched anything more than a hopeless stab against the west, similar in strategic possibilities to the Ardennes thrust of 1944. Certainly the military forces available could not have launched the powerful push through Belgium combined with an armoured thrust through the Ardennes which the Germans were able to launch in May of 1940.

Almost as damaging to Germany's strategic position was the fact that Germany's naval situation was even weaker in 1938 than it was to be in 1939. Neither the *Scharnhorst* nor the *Gneisenau* were ready for action, while the *Bismarck*-class battleships were two years or more from their completion dates. The three largest ships in service, the so-called pocket battleships, were glorified commerce raiders. There were no heavy cruisers, no aircraft carriers, only six light cruisers and seven destroyers. Even more depressing to German naval strategists was the fact that in February 1938 the German Navy could only muster twelve submarines suitable for service in the Atlantic (a further twenty-four sardine cans—*'kleine Unterseeboote'*—were available for use in coastal waters around the British Isles). While the German Navy was able to mount the successful operations against Norway and Denmark in the spring of 1940 on a shoe string (and in the process lose nearly all of its surface units for a protracted period of time), the German Navy had no such capability in 1938 or early 1939. Moreover, the German Naval High Command (*OKM*) seemed doubtful whether it possessed the forces to protect the key trade routes to Swedish iron ore even within the Baltic. In July 1938, the Baltic Fleet Command reported its doubts whether it could protect ore ships from Lulea from Russian interference. The only possibility was to block the Gulf of Finland at the beginning of war with mines, submarines, and surface units, thus keeping the Russians bottled up. Such a strategy was well beyond German capabilities. To guard against Russian submarines the Germans possessed fishing boats which they had requisitioned in August 1938. In an after-action report on the Munich crisis, German naval commanders in the east warned that if the Russians had become involved in a war over Czechoslovakia, the Baltic Fleet could not have performed its missions without substantial reinforcements. Such was the state of German mine layers and supplies of mines, that the *OKM* admitted that it could not have established a partial minefield in the southern portion of the Baltic, which would have hindered but not have prevented Soviet naval operations against trade routes with southern Sweden. The security of the ore route to Lulea could not be guaranteed with or without minefields. Such was the state of the German Navy.

The crux of the matter is the fact that Germany's precarious supply lines to Scandinavian ore (Lulea and Narvik) were a symptom of the dangerous, if not desperate, economic situation in which the Third Reich found herself at the time of the Munich crisis. The British blockade's success in the First World War had underlined the vulnerability of the German economy to economic pressure of any kind. The only natural resource required for the running of a war economy which Germany possessed in sufficient abundance to cover her needs was coal. Yet even with Germany's coal production, there were significant problems in 1938. The western coalfields, particularly those in the Saar, lay close to France and were under the threat of French military operations. Moreover, the demands of the German economy for coal were staggering. The iron and steel industries were the biggest users, but the transport network, synthetic industries, and electric power industries were all heavily dependent on coal. Finally coal was an important source of foreign exchange. German coal exports to Southeastern Europe would be of decisive importance in ensuring the continuance of imports from the Balkan states in the first year of the war. Italy would also be dependent on German coal if she were to come into the war, and because deliveries to her would have to go through Switzerland, deliveries would have to continue to the Swiss.

If German coal supplies would be strained in time of war, the situation with regard to other raw materials was desperate. The shortfall between the demands of the economy and military requirements on one hand, and the production of petroleum products within the Third Reich on the other was tremendous. Due to shortages of foreign exchange in 1938 the Germans possessed almost no petroleum stocks. Despite the immense efforts which the Germans had made in the 1930s to build up their synthetic fuel industry, by the end of 1937 they were importing more fuel than they had at the beginning of the decade. In June 1938 petroleum stockpiles were sufficient only to cover twenty-five per cent of mobilization requirements—on the average, four months of full wartime needs. Supplies of aviation lubricants were as low as six per cent of mobilization requirements. And unlike 1939, it seems dubious whether the Germans would have been able to draw oil supplies from the Soviet Union, while even supplies from Rumania were doubtful.

The German rubber industry was in a similar position. In the 1930, as with the petroleum industry, the Germans put considerable resources into constructing synthetic rubber plants, but the investment did not bear fruit until 1941-42. Only then were the Germans in a position to cover their economic and military requirements from domestic production. Stockpiles, captured war booty, and imports across the Trans-Siberian railroad covered the gap between demand and production in the first two years of the Second World War. In mid 1938 synthetic rubber production covered less than one-sixteenth of German needs. The German situation with other key raw materials such as iron, copper, nickel, etc. was scarcely better.

The capacity of the Germans munitions industry in 1938 gave scant cause for comfort. Production capabilities for gun powder production was less than forty per cent of maximum production in the First World War, while the capacity of the explosives industry was less than thirty per cent of the World War I maximum. This situation so frightened the Germans that a major effort was made to rectify this situation during 1938 and 1939. By August 1939 they had managed to increase capacity for powder production sixty-five per cent and explosive capacity by eighty-five per cent over the 1938 capabilities. While the 1939 figures were still short of what the Germans felt they needed for a major European war, they were high enough to meet the demands of military operations in the first year of the war with the help of stockpiles. In 1938 the Germans would have had considerably greater difficulty in doing this.

Besides the problems of importing sufficient raw materials in time of war or of producing enough material from domestic sources to meet wartime demands, the German economy had been strained to the breaking point in 1938. At this time there was no longer a large body of unemployed from which to draw, while mobilization for the *Anschluss* and the Czech crisis added to the shortages of skilled and unskilled workers. The economy had reached the point where there were worker shortages in almost every segment, particularly in the coal, munitions and aircraft industries. In December, 1938, the *Reichsarbeitsminister* estimated that the economy was short one million workers. Construction on the *Westwall* only served to sharpen these problems. In all, construction on the *Westwall* in 1938 would swallow five per cent of the steel, eight per cent of the wood, and twenty per cent of the concrete used by the German economy in 1938. This led to significant delays in the program to expand munitions and synthetics production, while it also drained labour from other segments of the economy.

In fact the economic strain was so bad in October, 1938, that the Reich's Defence Committee reported:

> On October 8 in consequence of *Wehrmacht* demands (occupation of the Sudetenland) and limited construction on the *Westwall* so tense a situation in the economic sector occurred (coal, supplies for industries, harvest of potatoes and turnips, food supplies) that continuation of the tension past October 10 would have made a catastrophe inevitable.

At a sitting of the Reich's Defence Committee in November, 1938, Göring admitted that the strained economic situation had reached the point where no more workers were available, factories were at full capacity, foreign exchange was completely exhausted, and Germany's financial situation was desperate. Continuing economic difficulties in January 1939 would force the Germans to reduce *Wehrmacht* allocations of steel thirty per cent, copper twenty per cent, aluminium forty-seven per cent, rubber fourteen per cent, and cement twenty-five to forty-five per cent.

Problems in the transportation network were a further reflection of the troubles which beset the German economy in 1938. In mid October *Staatssekretär* Kleinmann warned that railroad difficulties were such that only a fraction of vegetables could be transported, coal supplies for the population were endangered, and export steamers and fishing trawlers could not leave port because of coal shortages. Only 20,000 railroad cars were available to transport coal, although 43,000 were needed to meet fall demands.

In view of the economic situation described above, it is questionable whether the German economy in 1938 possessed the strength to support a breakout from Germany's constrained economic base. Not only was production of synthetics and munitions substantially lower than in 1939, but no help could be expected from Russia and little from the Balkan states. In reality the problem was not so much with the shortage of workers, because great numbers of German workers were engaged in, and would continue up until 1942 to be engaged in, tasks which were peripheral to the German war economy. Rather, in 1938 the German economy simply did not have access to the sources of raw materials which it needed to increase radically armament production. In 1942 the Germans would have the resources of most of the European continent at their disposal; in 1938 they had only the meagre prospects of German territory and what few areas the German army could conquer on which to draw.

Most probably the German economy would not have suffered a cataclysmic collapse had war broken out in the fall of 1938. Instead, the situation would have resembled the slow steady disintegration which took place in the Italian economy in the years 1940–42. The Germans would have had to resort to a series of expedients to meet present demands at the expense of future requirements. As production decreased and as raw materials became in shorter and shorter supply, the *Wehrmacht's* fighting capability would have suffered a corresponding decline. Once this vicious cycle had begun, there would have been little chance that Germany could have escaped the inevitable consequence: military defeat.

The last important factor in weighing the strategic situation in 1938 is the military and diplomatic support which Germany would or would not have enjoyed had war broken out. As I have made clear earlier, it is unlikely that the Germans would have enjoyed anywhere near the economic support they were able to extract from the Balkan region or for that matter from the Soviet Union in the course of the first year of the Second World War. The Rumanian government went so far as to warn the Germans that from the beginning of October they could no longer expect deliveries of petroleum products. On the other hand, it does seem likely that the reaction of the Italian government to the Czech crisis would have been substantially different than it was to be in September 1939. Count Ciano, the Italian Foreign Minister, made it clear on a number of occasions in September that 'if, however, Great Britain came in, then Italy would be compelled to do the same.' On September 28, he went so far as to declare to the British ambassador 'that Italy's interests, honour and pledged word required that she should actively and fully side with Germany.' While the Italians could have ignored such diplomatic statements made in confidence had war broken out, Mussolini placed his government in an impossible situation in the last days of September by emphasizing in public speeches what Ciano was saying in private. In a series of speeches beginning at Trieste on 18 September and continuing through to the 28th, Mussolini publicly and irrevocably committed his government to stand at Germany's side in the case of a military conflict.

The entrance of the Italians into the war would have proffered several important advantages to the Western Powers, which they were to be denied with Italian neutrality when war broke out in 1939. First and foremost, Italian participation against the West would have tightened up the blockade of Germany, while the burden of supplying raw materials to the Italian war economy would have added to the already enormous economic difficulties of the Third Reich. Both the Italian economy and the German economy would have been in conflict for the scarce resources of the Balkans. Considering the Anglo-French naval superiority in the Mediterranean, the Western Powers would have been able to cut the supply lines to Libya and carry out extensive bombardments of the Italian coastal regions.

The Italian military were none too sanguine over the possibility that they might have to participate in a general European war at Germany's side. One highly ranked general warned the German military staff in Rome that there was no prospect for a quick German victory against Czechoslovakia. As a result, he commented, there was a serious possibility of a world war for which the Axis was neither politically nor militarily prepared. Everything was against the Axis if the Czech crisis resulted in a war. Thus, the Italians represented no greater threat to Britain in 1938, than they did in 1936 or 1940, and would have drained German military as well as economic resources. All in all they would have proven to be, as they would in 1940 at the height of German power, a liability of the most serious proportions.

The Japanese attitude throughout the mounting European crisis in 1938 was more ambivalent. While the Japanese were not sorry to see troubles in Europe which would divert the major powers away from the Far East, they had their hands full with the war in China. The Japanese were involved in a major effort to seize Hankow, and were not in any position to add to their list of enemies. Reports from the British embassy in Tokyo indicated that the Japanese had no desire to get involved in another major conflict and to extend their commitments. In August the Japanese ambassador in Paris remarked that the armistice with Russia on the Manchurian frontier resulted from the desire of the Japanese government to avoid having a second war on their hands, as China was already providing sufficient difficulties. The American ambassador in Tokyo supported British doubts that Japan would allow herself to become involved in a European conflict. On 6 October he reported: 'Nor is there any warrant whatever for assuming that the army has any intention of becoming embroiled in troubles in Europe under anything short of the most compelling reasons.' Such reasons were not present in 1938.

Conclusions

The striking feature of the 1938 military situation was the relative unpreparedness of *all* the European nations to fight even a limited, much less a major, war. All were acutely conscious of their weaknesses. For the Germans the problem was compounded not only by their military unpreparedness, but by their economic vulnerability. Thus, German strategy, as in 1939, would have had to have been predicated on winning a war quickly, or at least, if that were not possible, on the conquest of an economic and strategic base from which a long war could be prosecuted. For the Germans, the central question was not whether the German Army could conquer Czechoslovakia. There was no doubt about that and in retrospect it seems likely that it would not have taken the Germans more than a month to complete the task. Such a campaign, however, because of the nature of the terrain, the equipment of the Czech Army, Czech fortifications, and the general state of unpreparedness of the German armoured forces, would have involved significantly higher casualties than the campaign against Poland in 1939. Moreover, such a campaign would have destroyed most of the Czech stocks of armaments which the Germans were to find so useful the following spring, and might well have led to the destruction of the Czech armament industry.

But the conquest of Czechoslovakia would have had only a small impact on the strategic situation of a Germany involved in a world war. The inclusion of Czechoslovakia within the German economic orbit would have done little to alleviate shortages of critical war materials. The central problem for the Nazi regime after the conquest of Czechoslovakia would have been, what next? Germany would have embarked on a world war with an unprepared military and an almost desperate economic situation. She might well have had the Italians as allies, which would have added to her economic and military burdens without bringing any corresponding advantages. The Axis economic area would have been limited to Germany, Italy, Hungary, a damaged Czechoslovakia, and the vulnerable ore trade with Sweden. Military operations against Rumania to conquer vital oil would probably have met a Soviet response and could have led to the destruction of the wells and refineries as had occurred in the First World War.

Earlier I pointed out that France possessed overwhelming superiority on Germany's western frontier, but that the French appeared unwilling and unable to take advantage of the situation if war broke out. Nevertheless, even if the French were unwilling to attack Germany's western frontier, the Germans were in no position to win a strategic victory in the west. This does not mean that after the conquest of Czechoslovakia they would not have tried. As in 1940 the Germans would have had no other choice but to attack through Belgium and Holland in order to acquire the resources necessary for the further prosecution of the war. But it is hard to see how the Germans could have gained the stunning strategic victories of 1940. There were few paratroops for missions such as seizing Belgian and Dutch forts and bridges. The armoured force certainly could not have undertaken the offensive which the Germans launched so successfully through the Ardennes in 1940. Moreover, in view of the shortage of fuel and munitions as well as its internal weaknesses, the *Luftwaffe* could not have intervened as decisively in a land campaign as it was to in 1940. The Germans might also have gained peripheral victories, such as the conquest of Denmark, in order to stave off economic collapse, but each military operation the Germans could launch during this period would have the counter productive result of using up scarce resources without supplying compensatory long range gains for the war economy.

As a result the war would have turned, as had the First World War, and as would the Second, on the economic strength and staying power of the opposing sides. In terms of numbers of divisions, economic resources, industrial capacity, and naval forces the Germans would have faced overwhelming Allied superiority in 1938 whether they faced only Britain and France or an enlarged coalition which included Russia and perhaps Poland. Nevertheless, the war against Germany would not have been easy, nor would it have been quickly won. But the results would have been inevitable and would have led to the eventual collapse of the Nazi regime at considerably less cost than the war which was to break out the following September would involve.

Bibliography

A. ADAMTHWAITE, *France and the Coming of the Second World War, 1936–1939* (1977).
U. BIALER, *The Shadow of the Bomber: The Fear of Air Attack and British Politics, 1932–1939* (1980).
B. BOND, *British Military Policy between Two World Wars* (1980).
H. GATZKE, ed., *European Diplomacy between Two Wars, 1919–1939* (1972).
M. GILBERT and R. GOTT, *The Appeasers* (1963).
M. KNOX, *Mussolini Unleashed, 1939–1941: Politics and Strategy in Fascist Italy's Last War* (1982).
W. N. MEDLICOTT, *British Foreign Policy since Versailles* (1968).
W. MURRAY, *The Change in the European Balance of Power, 1938–1939: The Path to Ruin* (1984).
G. C. PEDEN, *British Rearmament and the Treasury, 1932–1939* (1977).

R. J. Sontag, *A Broken World 1919–1939* (1971).
A. J. P. Taylor, *The Origins of the Second World War* (1966).
T. Taylor, *Munich: The Price of Peace* (1980).
N. Thompson, *The Anti-Appeasers* (1971).
C. Thorne, *The Approach of War, 1938–1939* (1967).
A. Ulam, *Expansion and Coexistence: The History of Soviet Foreign Policy, 1917–1967* (1971).
G. Weinberg, *The Foreign Policy of Hitler's Germany, 1933–1936* (1970).
G. Weinbert, *The Foreign Policy of Hitler's Germany, Starting World War II, 1937–1939* (1980).
R. J. Young, *In Command of France: French Foreign Policy and Military Planning, 1933–1940* (1978).

NATO: The Nuclear Alliance

MICHAEL MANDELBAUM

The Second World War concluded in Europe in April, 1945. Tens of thousands of soldiers and civilians were dead. Many of the cities, roads, bridges, and farmlands on the continent lay in ruins. Also destroyed was the capacity of the major states of Europe to direct their own political future. Europe's destiny now stood lodged largely between the actions and decisions of the two superpowers, the United States and the Soviet Union. Europe had thus entered a new political age.

The dropping of the first atomic bomb by the United States on Hiroshima in August, 1945, demonstrated that the entire world had entered a new military age. From that point onward it was clear that future military conflict might entail a level of destruction previously unimagined.

The formation of the North Atlantic Treaty Organization in 1949 followed four years of Soviet pressure in eastern Europe that had culminated with the Berlin Blockade of 1948. The alliance represented an admission on the part of the western European nations that they were weak and required the support of the United States. On the part of the latter, the alliance represented a guarantee that the United States would not again regard itself as isolated from Europe.

Throughout the life of the alliance, there has existed an ongoing interplay between mutual fear of Soviet aggression and tensions among the allies. The issues surrounding nuclear weapons have played a major role in both situations.

At the heart of the alliance's guarantee in its early years was the sole possession by the United States of atomic weapons. By the late 1950s the Soviet Union had developed both nuclear weapons and the intercontinental missiles to deliver them. That situation raised doubt in the minds of Europeans whether the United States would actually protect them and risk Soviet attack on itself. The major result of that doubt was the decision by France to develop its own independent atomic arsenal. In various ways, including the stationing

---

Reprinted from *The Nuclear Revolution: International Politics before and after Hiroshima* by Michael Mandelbaum, by permission of the author and Cambridge University Press. Copyright © 1981 by Cambridge University, Press.

of a large number of American troops in Europe, the United States attempted to quiet such doubts.

More recently, the positioning of short-range missiles in the European NATO countries has raised new questions and debate. Yet throughout the years of tensions and doubts there has remained the basic need of western Europe for American protection, and that need and the inherent European military weakness have made the alliance enduring if also controversial.

The Atlantic Alliance

Anarchy breeds insecurity, which fosters the impulse for self-protection. This is the logical chain that connects the structure of the international system with the behavior of states, from antiquity to the present. Members of the system can and do draw upon their own resources for protection. When rival states fortify themselves in explicitly competitive fashion, the result is an arms race. States reach out to others, as well, when they feel threatened, seeking to strengthen themselves through alliances, which are as familiar in international politics as arms races.

In Thucydides's account of the Peloponnesian War both Athens and Sparta do both. As they prepared for war, in addition to arming themselves, both "planned to send embassies to the King of Persia and to any other foreign Power from whom they hoped to obtain support, and they tried to ally themselves with other Hellenic states who were not yet committed to either side." Questions of who would ally with whom take up much of the first part of the account. Alliance politics is a theme that runs throughout the story. Alliances are not only common, they are commonly marriages of convenience. In arms races, interests of particular groups may influence the types and numbers of weapons with which states equip themselves; the necessary condition for any arms race, however, is the rivalry that springs from the structure of the international system. Similarly, alliances may unite states with political or cultural affinities, which can reinforce their mutual commitments. The *basis* for those commitments, however, is the need for protection, which arises from the anarchical character of international politics. Without friendship between allies an alliance will be more fragile than when there are affinities between them; without a common enemy there will be no alliance at all. The two coalitions that fought for control of Sicily, Thucydides records, "stood together not because of any moral principle or racial connection; it was rather because of the various circumstances of interest or compulsion in each particular case."

How have nuclear weapons affected alliances? At first glance, the period of international history beginning with the end of the Second World War appears to be a great age of alliances. There are as many sovereign states as at any time in the past, and almost all participate in a broad range of diplomatic activities—exchanges of cordial visits by heads of state, declarations of friendship, and formal documents pledging the signatories to various kinds of cooperation. Of course, only 2 of the more than 150 sovereign states have been major nuclear powers. But these 2, the United States and the Soviet Union, each stand at the hub of a network of ties to other countries, many of which are security commitments. Of these many ties, however, only two truly qualify as nuclear alliances: the American connection with Japan, which is embodied in the Security Treaty of 1950 between the two countries, and the North Atlantic Treaty Organization, which binds together the United States and the states of Western and Southern Europe.

Other American international ties have proven flimsier than these two. During the 1950s, the United States signed treaties of friendship with nations in South and Southeast Asia and in the Middle East as well. Neither the Southeast Asia Treaty Organization (SEATO) nor the Central Powers Treaty Organization [CENTO] committed the United States to the defense of the other signatories as emphatically as was the case with NATO and the Japanese Security Treaty. These less binding treaties were not so much promises to fight side by side as attempts by the United States to win influence by extending assistance, usually military assistance, somewhat as Britain had sent money, but not soldiers, to warring continental powers in the eighteenth century. American military assistance did not always serve its intended purpose. Tanks and planes went to Pakistan, a member of SEATO, to counterbalance the military power of the People's Republic of China. The Pakistanis used them against India, a country whose favor the United States was simultaneously courting and that itself received a generous supply of American armaments.

As for the Warsaw Pact, the joint military organization of the Soviet Union and the Communist-governed states of Eastern Europe, it is not truly an alliance in the sense of a voluntary association. Membership is not voluntary. Soviet troops are stationed in Eastern Europe not only, perhaps not even mainly, to protect these countries from the West but to make certain that the ruling Communist parties remain in power. The relationship between the Soviet Union and the other signatories to the Warsaw Pact is arguably less an alliance like those that the Greek city-states formed just before the Peloponnesian War than a system of indirect rule, of the kind with which Britain dominated parts of Asia and Africa in the late nineteenth and early twentieth centuries. The indigenous rulers retained the trappings of sovereignty and some genuine sovereign prerogatives. Ultimate power, however, rested with the British, who could always force the local chieftains to follow their wishes.

In what sense, then, is NATO a nuclear alliance? How have nuclear weapons made it different from alliances before 1945? It is a defensive peacetime alliance that has endured for three decades, longer than most alliances of the past. In the eighteenth century, for example, states allied for the purpose of fighting, not preventing, wars. Alliances were transitory, forming on the eve of war and usually dissolving soon after the fighting stopped. They were often established secretly.

The main reason for the differences between alliances before the French Revolution and after Hiroshima is the changing nature of war. Two hundred years ago, war was a normal and familiar part of international politics, a continuation of politics by different—but not dramatically different—means. Since 1945, war has come to be regarded as abnormal, horrible, even unthinkable.

This sea change in the character of war stems, of course, from the dramatic expansion of the military force available to states since the eighteenth century. As armed combat has become more destructive, states have become more interested in preventing wars and less interested in fighting them. The goal of avoiding war lends itself more readily to formal peacetime alliances than to the *ad hoc* secret arrangements of the eighteenth century. For a state that aims simply to defend itself, not to attack others, or not to have to fight at all, it is as useful to *look* powerful before the outbreak of war as to *be* powerful afterward.

Disposable force for military purposes has been expanding for almost two centuries. The harnessing of nuclear energy for warfare marked an upturn in that long-term expansion sharp enough to qualify as a military revolution. But it was the third, not the first, military revolution of modern times. Logically, the previous revolutions, the Napoleonic and the mechanical, should have shifted the purposes of alliances away from fighting and toward deterring war. Historically, this was so.

The alliances among the great powers of Europe in the nineteenth century were more enduring, and geared more to stability, than had been the case before 1789. (Of course, the Concert of Europe was as much a system of international management as a series of bilateral security commitments, and its purpose was not just the prevention of war but the enforcement of domestic stability on the continent.) The Triple Entente and the Triple Alliance, the military coalitions that went to war in 1914, were more firmly tied together than previous alliances, although neither was as closely integrated or as patently defensive as NATO. After 1918, the British and French joined together explicitly to try to enforce the settlement. Their purpose was the same as NATO's—deterrence—of Germany rather than the Soviet Union. Nuclear weapons have made NATO a defensive peacetime alliance. In so doing, however, they have helped to continue a trend that has been underway since the French Revolution, and to which the other revolutionary advances in military might have also contributed.

NATO has been a contentious alliance, frequently consumed by intramural crisis and controversy. Dissension among the allies is a feature of all alliances. This is because alliances are limited partnerships. The partners ordinarily agree on one important thing—who their most dangerous enemy is—but not on everything. So there is always tugging and pulling, or, to use the language of politics, threatening and negotiating between and among allies (as between and among adversaries), just as there is, for example, in a coalition government drawn from more than one political party in a parliamentary political system. The cohesiveness of alliances has varied according to the perceived seriousness of the threat being faced, the domestic similarities among the allies, and the range of their common interests. In none, however, has disagreement been wholly eliminated. Every alliance has to some extent been, in Winston Churchill's words, "an exercise in mutual recrimination."

Allies may quarrel about anything. The most serious, most basic, and most common source of friction, however, is what is after all the heart of any alliance: a state's commitment to fight for its ally. That commitment poses two dangers; every member of an alliance has, potentially, two fears. One is that the alliance will not work, that he will be abandoned in his hour of need. The other is that the alliance will work too well, that he will be entrapped in a war he does not wish to fight.

Thucydides records both fears. When Corcyra seeks an alliance with Athens, the Corinthians, the enemies of Corcyra, warn the Athenians that accepting the Corcyrians as allies will lead to entrapment: "You will force us to hold you equally responsible with them, although you took no part in their misdeed." This is exactly what happens. The Athenians try to limit their commitment to Corcyra, but find themselves drawn into battle with Corinth. Later, in the debate over the wisdom of invading Sicily, the Athenian general Nicias argues against the same danger: "Let the Egestaeans, in particular, be told that, just as they started their war with the Selinuntines without consulting Athens so they must themselves be responsible for making peace; and in the future," he adds, "we are not making allies, as we have done in the past, of the kind of people who have to be helped by us in their misfortunes, but who can do nothing for us when we need help from them." The outbreak of World War I offers a more recent illustration of the danger of entrapment. Britain, Germany, Russia, and France were drawn into war by the quarrels of their lesser allies.

If entrapment is one of the painful lessons of the first great war of the twentieth century, abandonment is part of the history of the beginning of the second. Britain and France left their erstwhile ally Czechoslovakia to be partitioned, and then swallowed entirely, by Germany. Similarly, in fifth-century B.C. Greece, Thucydides records, the Corinthians pleaded with the Spartans to fulfill their obligation to stand with them against Athens. "Your inactivity has done harm enough. Give your allies, and especially Potidaea, the help you promised, and invade Attica at once. Do not let your friends and kinsmen fall into the hands of the bitter enemies."

The perennial fears of abandonment and entrapment have lain at the heart of NATO politics, especially during the 1960s. The fact that NATO has been a nuclear alliance, both deploying and facing nuclear weapons, has given particular urgency to these fears. The costs of nuclear war are so high that abandonment becomes powerfully attractive if it means avoiding them: Entrapment is extraordinarily dangerous when it means being swept into a nuclear conflict. Besides aggravating them the nuclear character of the alliance has affected these perennial fears in two other ways. The first is that they have been bound up with, and expressed in, debates about nuclear weapons doctrine, deployment, and control. The second arises from the distribution of nuclear firepower within the alliance. In theory, each ally must fear both abandonment and entrapment. Because NATO's nuclear arsenal rests almost entirely in American hands, however, each of the two fears has been marked on one side of the Atlantic and not the other. It has been the Europeans who have worried about abandonment; entrapment has been largely an American concern.

Another effect of nuclear weapons on alliances, therefore, can be seen in the politics of the Western alliance in the 1960s. The disputes over nuclear strategy stemmed from European fears that at the moment of truth the military and political arrangements on which they relied for their safety would not work, and from American anxieties that the alliance *would* work—not wisely, but too well.

The Fragile Alliance

NATO began life in 1949 as a guarantee pact. The United States guaranteed the safety of Western Europe by pledging to come to its defense if necessary. This was a natural arrangement. America was powerful; Europe, recovering from the devastation of war, was weak; and the Soviet Union seemed menacing, espcially in the wake of the Berlin blockade of 1948. The United States had come to the rescue of Britain and France twice in the twentieth century. Both world wars had begun, however, with the Americans standing aloof. Three years were required in the first instance, and two in the second, for American help to arrive. In a third war the Europeans would not have the luxury of being able to wait. NATO was, in effect, a promise that they would not have to do so, a promise that would not have to be honored if the Soviet Union believed it and refrained from aggressive behavior accordingly.

Then, in 1950, came the Korean War. The mere promise of American assistance seemed inadequate to protect Europe from militant communism. From a simple pledge of help in time of war, NATO turned into a full-fledged peacetime military organization. The United States dispatched troops to Europe. Each NATO nation fielded its own army, but allied military planning was unusually closely integrated, and a supreme commander, invariably an American, presided over all forces.

In the early 1950s the allies made plans for a large land army, comprising ninety or more divisions. They did not come close to reaching this goal. Instead, they continued to rely on the promise of full-scale

American assistance to deter the Soviets. What made the guarantee credible was the American nuclear arsenal. If the Soviet Union attacked Western Europe the United States could visit nuclear destruction on the Soviets in response. The prospect was thought both grim enough and likely enough in Soviet eyes to keep the Soviet army at bay.

Still, the Europeans worried about whether the United States was a truly reliable protector. They fretted that for all the solemn pledges that came from the other side of the Atlantic, the Americans would abandon them in their hour of need. In the early years of the alliance the Europeans also felt some anxiety about entrapment, which probably reached its zenith during the Korean War, when the British in particular feared that the conflict would become nuclear. This did not happen, and when the United States sent several hundred thousand troops to fight in the ongoing civil war in Indochina, few Europeans believed that they themselves would be dragged into it. General nuclear war, whose consequences the Europeans could scarcely hope to avoid, seemed likely to begin not in Korea or Vietnam but in Europe, over an issue like Berlin. The Europeans, then, worried not about being entrapped in Asia but about being abandoned in Berlin. The United States, after all, had a history of isolation from European affairs, which the American political tradition, beginning with George Washington's Farewell Address, had elevated to a principle of state-craft. The Atlantic Ocean was a formidable barrier between protector and protected, even in the jet age.

The history of NATO from its beginning, therefore, was a history of American efforts to reassure Europeans troubled by the prospect of abandonment. One way to reassure them that the United States would defend them was to say so. This high officials of the American government did, and repeatedly. John Kennedy's 1960 declaration "Ich bin ein Berliner" is probably the best-known American proclamation of dedication to the terms of the alliance, but it is far from the only one. Another sign of reassurance was the garrison of American troops in Europe. Their value was thought to lie not so much in their fighting efficiency as in the symbolic expression of American intentions that they represented. They served as hostages to the Americans' willingness to honor their commitments. If the Soviets attacked in Europe, the United States, with all its wealth and power, would have to come to the rescue of its soldiers, and hence of the Europeans. Or at least, in the European view, the presence of American troops improved the chances that the United States would step in to repulse a Soviet attack. The American troops, and indeed NATO as a whole, came to be seen by the Europeans as a "trip wire," set in place to serve as a trigger for the alliance's truly effective military force—the American nuclear arsenal.

None of these expressions of good faith, however, sufficed to allay the fears of abandonment that a development in the second decade of the nuclear age produced. This development was the attainment by the Soviet

Union of the means to launch nuclear attacks against the continental United States.

The credibility of NATO's military arrangements for deterrence for the first decade of the alliance's existence rested on an asymmetry between the United States and the Soviet Union. From bases in Western Europe the United States could launch nuclear attacks against Soviet cities and military installations. The Soviet Union had no way to reach the United States. By the end of the decade this had changed, and the change called the reliability of the American commitment to protect Europe into question. Although immune from Soviet reprisal, the United States risked relatively little by threatening to attack the Soviet Union, even with nuclear weapons. When the Soviets could threaten to bomb American cities in return, however, the American threat seemed to become hollow. In the event of a Soviet assault on Western Europe, would the American leaders really authorize the use of nuclear force against the Soviet Union, knowing that this could bring on terrible devastation to the United States? Would the Americans truly put their own cities at risk to protect Europe's? It was not easy to believe that they would. Americans and Europeans wondered whether the Soviets would believe it.

The development of a Soviet intercontinental nuclear striking force seemed to create a barrier that, although psychological in nature, was even more formidable than the Atlantic Ocean between North America and Western Europe. It seemed to close off the possibility of an American rescue of a beleaguered Europe just as emphatically as the German remilitarization of the Rhineland in 1936 had blocked the path between France and its Eastern European allies, the members of the "Little Entente." The nonnuclear forces of the Soviet Union and the other communist states of Eastern Europe were widely believed to be far superior to NATO's. So a Soviet thrust along the central front in Europe would confront NATO, and especially the United States, with a choice between humiliation and holocaust: either to accept a nonnuclear defeat or to bring nuclear weapons into use, with the risk of incurring fearful retaliatory damage as a result.

The development of a Soviet intercontinental nuclear striking force coincided with the removal from Europe of the main part of the American nuclear arsenal, and this further undermined European confidence in the sturdiness of deterrence. In the 1950s, only American airplanes and medium-range missiles stationed within the borders of the European members of NATO could reach Soviet cities. But the 1960s saw the advent of two new weapons that could be based outside the continent. The Minuteman missile could reach targets from Minsk to Vladivostok within minutes of its launch from the middle of the United States. The nuclear weapon-bearing Polaris submarine was on station at sea; most of the time it needed no land base at all. The Americans promised that an attack on Europe would bring these weapons into play if they were needed. But

Minuteman and Polaris would be far from Europe when a Soviet attack came, and their distance from the scene of battle reinforced European skepticism that they could be counted on to arrive at all.

A Soviet capacity to visit nuclear destruction on the United States was predictable well before it came into being. By the end of 1957, that capacity seemed to exist. The Soviet Union tested an intercontinental ballistic missile (ICBM) in August of that year and then, in October, launched the first earth-orbiting satellite, Sputnik. Suddenly the Soviet appeared to be the masters of space, from whence they would be able to bombard the United States. There was, however, a lag between the moment when the vulnerability of the United States to Soviet attack became obvious and the launching of serious efforts to adjust NATO's military arrangements to compensate for this vulnerability. It fell to the Kennedy administration, which took office in 1961, to try to protect NATO from the consequences of the extended reach of Soviet striking power.

The solution to this problem that the Kennedy administration proposed was to turn NATO from a trip wire into an effective fighting force, by building up its nonnuclear forces to the point at which they themselves could repulse a Soviet attack. The alliance could avoid the choice between humiliation and holocaust by being strong enough to avoid humiliation in nonnuclear combat. The idea was not new in 1961. It simply revived the still unmet expectation that some Americans had held for NATO at its founding. The failure to have strong nonnuclear forces cost little in the early 1950s because an alternative to nonnuclear forces equal to those of the Soviet Union was readily available—the American nuclear arsenal. By 1961, however, the Soviet and American striking forces canceled each other out, and a decisive advantage seemed available to the side that was better equipped to fight a nonnuclear war. The idea of preparing to engage the Soviet Union and the Warsaw Pact at levels of violence below the nuclear threshold came to be known as the policy of "flexible response."

The Europeans opposed it. Their objections arose in part from domestic political considerations. They did not wish to raise taxes or increase conscription into their armed forces. Their chief objection, however, had to do with the logic of the policy itself. Flexible response involved being ready to fight a nonnuclear war in Europe. The Europeans did not want to fight a war of any kind there. World War II had been enough for them. After 1945, moreover, the expansion of nonnuclear force continued apace. The nuclear revolution tended to obscure it, but the extension of the mechanical revolution in warfare after the Second World War placed much greater military power in the hands of governments than they had had before, apart from the development of fusion and fission explosives. When Hitler's army invaded the Soviet Union, it relied heavily on the same mode of transport that had carried Napoleon to Moscow—the horse. There are no horses on the central front in Europe today. If the spread of the nuclear revolution in warfare to the Soviet Union made flexible response seem necessary to the United States, the continuation of the mechanical revolution on the continent made it appear dangerous to the Europeans.

No doubt they would have armed themselves more resolutely if no other form of protection had been available. But there was an alternative to making ready to fight a nonnuclear war as a means of protecting Europe: threatening to fight a nuclear war. The Europeans feared that a policy of flexible response would undercut that threat. Flexible response was designed to give NATO the means to fight a war in Europe that would not immediately become nuclear. The Europeans wished to cultivate the impression that rapid escalation to the nuclear level *would* follow a Soviet attack, because they believed that this impression was what deterred the Soviet Union. Flexible response, the Europeans feared, would give them the worst of all possible worlds: Without a firmly nuclear American guarantee deterrence might be weakened to the point that the Soviets would be tempted to attack. Such a war, even if free of nuclear exchanges, even if the United States stood shoulder to shoulder with the Europeans, was bound to be brutally destructive.

What they feared in the early 1960s was not precisely abandonment. The United States was prepared to contribute to the improvement of NATO's nonnuclear forces. They feared, rather, that the American nuclear arsenal would not be seen automatically as ready to defend Western Europe. The term that came to express this fear was "decoupling." It connoted separation—of nuclear from conventional weapons—for the purpose, the Europeans suspected, of separating North America from Europe as a theater of war.

If the Europeans feared that flexible response would undercut deterrence, the Americans believed that only flexible response could make it credible. Only by being prepared to fight a war of a particular type, they argued, could NATO deter it. If the Soviets knew they could not win a nonnuclear war they would not launch one. If they were confident of their chances at the nonnuclear level, however, they might gamble that NATO would not dare try to save its position by nuclear means.

Their distaste for flexible response did not mean that the Europeans favored reducing the nonnuclear NATO forces that were already in place in 1961. That, they reckoned, might signal a diminution of American determination to keep its commitments to Europe. They therefore favored deploying precisely the level of forces that NATO currently had, no more and no less.

The disagreement about flexible response had the makings of an impasse. The growth of Soviet nuclear power appeared to subvert the arrangements for protecting Europe by deterring a Soviet attack, arrangements that had been put in place in the early 1950s. What the Americans proposed for buttressing deterrence was unacceptable to the Europeans. One European, however, offered a different solution to the problem.

The Entangling Alliance

The European in question was Charles de Gaulle. His response to the growth of Soviet long-range nuclear striking power and the impact that this was widely believed to have had on the effectiveness of NATO's policy of deterrence in the 1960s was the creation of national nuclear arsenals by the alliance's European members.

In the drama of NATO politics in the 1960s the Americans cast de Gaulle as the villain. They came to see him as arrogant and misguided, bent on sacrificing alliance unity for a dream of French grandeur that had, understandably, arisen from the humiliation of World War II, but that that war, and its aftermath, had put forever beyond France's reach. The French President was scarcely a warm, friendly character. He harbored a deep personal distrust of the "Anglo-Saxons"—the Americans and the British. His troubles with the United States did not, however, stem from personal incompatibilities between himself and his opposite numbers on the other side of the Atlantic. Nor did they arise from misunderstandings about the aspirations of the two countries or the workings of the two political systems, although misunderstandings there certainly were. On the contrary, de Gaulle was a thorn in the side of the American government above all because he shared American assumptions about the shakiness of deterrence in Europe, from which, however, he drew different conclusions. He was, above all, the expositor of the nuclear logic of the European members of NATO, and that logic made the Americans as uncomfortable as flexible response had made the Europeans.

De Gaulle accepted the reasoning that underlay flexible response. He agreed that the credibility of the threat upon which Western Europe's safety rested needed to be reinforced. His skepticism went further. He doubted the worth of *all* formal alliances. Abandonment, in his view, was normal. Because alliances were marriages of convenience, he believed, when they ceased to be convenient no ally could be depended upon to fulfill its obligations, no matter how solemnly it had undertaken them. States, according to de Gaulle, pursue their own interests and only these. If it suits the interest of state A to come to the aid of state B then A will come, whether or not a formal promise has been given. If not, the tug of alliance ties will not be powerful enough to overcome the pull of self-interest in the other direction.

This would certainly be the case, in de Gaulle's judgment, for NATO. In the wake of the vulnerability of North America to Soviet nuclear attack, the question arose as to whether American leaders would put New York at risk to protect Paris. De Gaulle had no doubt that they would not. Nor could the Soviet Union be depended upon to believe that they would. But if the United States would not use nuclear weapons in defense of Europe, the Europeans themselves would certainly use them, and the Soviets would certainly believe that the Europeans would use them. So, national nuclear arsenals were necessary for deterrence.

Whereas the United States wanted one center of authority with several military options, de Gaulle proposed several centers of authority each with the same single nuclear option. Accordingly, de Gaulle presided over the beginnings of an independent French nuclear arsenal, whose formal origin dates from 1960, when the first French nuclear test took place.

Even short of protection in a moment of ultimate danger, nuclear weapons had their uses, and de Gaulle appreciated these. They conferred prestige upon their owners. They ensured, in the British phrase, a "seat at the top table" of diplomacy, which de Gaulle coveted for France. An independent nuclear arsenal, even a modest one, seemed both a symbol of and a means to a whole range of prerogatives. Here ornamental and instrumental purposes merged. The most basic prerogative for any state is mastery of its own destiny, and for Europeans, in the nuclear age, as de Gaulle saw it, only the possession of nuclear weapons could secure this prerogative.

De Gaulle was the most obstinate and outspoken proponent of the logic of independent national nuclear forces. This was far from being his private obsession, however. Other Frenchmen shared it. France's nuclear weapons program both preceded and survived his presidency. In time, political parties from all points on the French political spectrum came to endorse the independent *force de frappe*.

The British were not entirely unsympathetic to de Gaulle's views. They whispered their doubts about American reliability, whereas the French President trumpeted his. They preferred to conciliate the Americans, whereas it suited de Gaulle to quarrel with them. Despite these differences of style, however, the British had their own small independent nuclear striking force, and their motives for acquiring it were similar to de Gaulle's.

There were reasons why the American government might have endorsed de Gaulle's thinking, and his nuclear policy. The acquisition of independent nuclear forces by the Europeans offered several advantages. It promised to increase NATO's military strength—the basic purpose, after all, of any alliance. It could ease the burden, both psychological and military, of protecting Europe. The Americans were constantly urging the Europeans to contribute more to the alliance's defenses. And it had the potential to contribute to European unity, which had long been a professed American goal; the Europeans might be expected to pool their nuclear resources, which could, in turn, lead to other forms of political integration.

Quite to the contrary, however, the American government adamantly opposed the development of independent European nuclear forces. In fact, the word the Americans used to describe the spread of nuclear weapons, a word of Latin origin that sounded like a disease (which was the way the

United States saw the matter), perfectly expressed this position: "proliferation." The Americans pressed their opposition despite the potential advantages of national nuclear arsenals, even when it became obvious that to do so was to widen a crack in the alliance. American disapproval of proliferation aggravated a feud with France, to which the United States refused nuclear assistance even when de Gaulle made it clear that he would proceed with his weapons program unaided. The American position ruffled relations with the British as well, which reached their nadir when the Kennedy administration abruptly decided to cancel production of the Skybolt missile, which the British had been counting on to prolong the useful life of their nuclear-equipped bomber aircraft. The ostensible reason for the cancellation was economic. But the fact that the missile was to contribute to the maintenance of another national nuclear arsenal made it easier to put considerations of economy over the claims of alliance solidarity.

The American government argued that independent European nuclear forces were unnecessary; the American striking force was adequate for NATO's purposes. The Americans charged in addition, that separate European forces were bound to be inadequate. They would not be able to meet the standard of assured destruction that, in American eyes, was the measure of strategic usefulness. A force of hundreds of hardened, dispersed intercontinental missiles and dozens of nuclear-equipped submarines such as the United States was assembling was beyond the means of any single European country.

An independent European nuclear arsenal was, in the American view, not only unnecessary and inadequate, but liable to be dangerously provocative. Its owner would be more, not less, vulnerable to the Soviet Union, because in the event of war a small nuclear force would be first on the Soviet list of targets.

The Europeans could, and the French did, reply that independent nuclear forces were not as self-evidently useless, and worse, as American objections to them claimed. True, the technical definition of strategic adequacy—assured destruction—was not easy to achieve, especially for a country without the resources of the United States or the Soviet Union. But neither was a "survivable" striking force wholly beyond the reach of the Europeans. Over time they might hope to build enough missiles—perhaps making these mobile or concealing them or putting them on submarines in order to avoid a preemptive blow—to be confident of being able to reply in kind to a Soviet nuclear attack.

Even a small nuclear arsenal not absolutely certain of surviving a knockout blow, the Europeans could argue, might look dangerous enough to spare its owner a Soviet attack in case of war. If the European country could not be sure of being able to strike Moscow after a Soviet assault, the Soviets, for their part, would not be certain that this would not happen. And even a few hydrogen bombs, even one, could do more damage to the Soviet capital than Napoleon or Hitler had managed. Moreover, insofar as the effectiveness of a deterrent depended partly upon the perceived will of its owner to use it, national nuclear forces were highly effective, because France would undoubtedly be more willing to respond in nuclear terms to an attack on France than the United States would be.

Whatever its shortcomings, a national nuclear arsenal certainly seemed better than nothing for a European member of NATO. And de Gaulle, at least, professed to believe that the alternative to an independent striking force, no matter how vulnerable, was nothing. For providing protection, a nuclear arsenal owned and operated by a Western European nation might stand in relation to the American stock of missiles as a fig leaf to a coat of armor. But in case of a battle, the armor would not, in de Gaulle's view, and might not, in the view of other Europeans, be available. A fig leaf was better than being altogether naked.

At the heart of American opposition to nuclear proliferation within NATO was the fear of entrapment. The Americans did not voice this fear in so many words. To do so would have been undiplomatic, and risky. It would have suggested that the NATO allies might behave recklessly. It could have been construed as implying what the Europeans most feared: that there were wars they would wish to fight that the United States might prefer to avoid. So, American officials referred to the dangers of proliferation in euphemisms: It could lead, they said, to "instability"; it would "complicate" international politics by introducing an unwanted measure of "uncertainty" into national calculations.

There were general reasons why proliferation called up the specter of entrapment for the United States. Small national nuclear arsenals might be tempting targets for preemptive Soviet attacks. In a crisis the Soviet Union might strike at European nuclear arsenals out of confidence of being able to eliminate them; by contrast, if only the far larger, less vulnerable American force were involved the Soviets might behave more cautiously. It was not any particular scenario that troubled the American government in the early 1960s, however, so much as the fact that nuclear weapons were so powerful, national and international experience with them was so limited, and the task of coming to terms with one other major nuclear weapon state had been so trying, that any change in the nuclear status quo was worrisome. The spread of nuclear weapons seemed dangerous because the consequences were not readily predictable. The price of nuclear war was likely to be so high that nothing that might bring it closer was worth risking. In a nuclear environment control seemed all-important, and the diffusion of nuclear capability would make it easier for other nations to act independently and therefore weaken American control. In its most general but also most basic form, American aversion to proliferation came down to a bet like that of Pascal, who reasoned that he had nothing to lose and everything to gain by believing in God: Perhaps no harm would come of an increase in the number of states possessing nuclear weapons; but the harm, if it did come, was potentially so vast that strenuous efforts to keep the number constant were fully justified.

The threat of nuclear proliferation came to be called, in the United States, the "nth country problem." The term suggested that numbers alone made a difference where the national possession of nuclear weapons was concerned. More were worse, no matter which the new nuclear states happened to be. One state in particular, however, especially worried Americans—the Federal Republic of Germany. As the largest nonnuclear NATO member and the one most directly exposed to the Soviet Union, Germany was the logical candidate to follow Britain's and France's nuclear examples. A nuclear-armed Germany was a particularly unhappy prospect. Memories of the Third Reich were still fresh. The Federal Republic had not yet fully established itself as a responsible, sober, peaceful, democratic member of the international community.

A nuclear-armed Germany, especially one torn loose from its NATO moorings, was worrisome to contemplate. Not the least worrisome thing about it was its potential effect on the Soviet Union. Ever since the division of the country, and of Europe, had become a fact of international life, the Soviets had made the denial of nuclear armaments to West Germany a cardinal principle of their foreign policy. Two terrible German invasions in the twentieth century had made the Soviets extraordinarily sensitive to German military power. The United States refused to assist the French nuclear weapons program in no small part out of the fear that the Germans would demand comparable treatment. A German nuclear arsenal in particular, and nuclear proliferation in Europe in general, were as unacceptable to the United States as ways of reinforcing deterrence as flexible response was to the Europeans. So although both sides agreed on the problem, neither would countenance the other's preferred solution.

The Enduring Alliance

Nuclear politics in NATO in the 1960s resembles, in retrospect, a play without a third act. A crisis arose: The development of a Soviet capacity to strike the United States raised fears of abandonment and called into question the credibility of deterrence in Europe. Various solutions were brought forward. None, however, was put fully into practice. Neither flexible response nor proliferation won complete acceptance on both sides of the Atlantic. The Europeans regarded the first as an invitation to abandonment of a particular kind—decoupling; the Americans worried that the consequence of the second would be entrapment.

The Europeans did in fact accept flexible response in 1967, but in a way that seemed to undercut the American purpose in proposing it in the first place. They agreed in principle that the alliance should adopt the policy, but argued that the existing nonnuclear forces in Europe sufficed to carry it out. Rather than putting more troops, tanks, and airplanes into the field, they were content to change the name of the mission of those that were already there.

The European solution to the problem that Soviet strategic power created for NATO—national nuclear forces—had a complicated history, but it, too, was never fully implemented. The United States proposed a scheme known as the Multilateral Force (MLF) for sharing control of some nuclear weapons. This received serious attention beginning in 1963. The idea was for Polaris submarines to be manned by multinational crews. It was, for the Americans, a decidedly second-best solution to NATO's problems. They were not anxious to surrender any degree of control over any nuclear weapons. They feared, however, that the certain consequence of their refusal to do so would be political upheaval in the alliance and perhaps an independent German nuclear arsenal. On the delicate, crucial question of whose finger would actually rest on the submarines' nuclear triggers, the American designers of the MLF were deliberately vague. Finally, in late 1964, President Johnson effectively rejected the scheme.

The problems that Soviet nuclear power created were not only not clearly solved in the 1960s, they reappeared, in different guise, in the 1970s. Concern arose within the alliance over a perceived Soviet advantage in long-range theater nuclear forces, which consisted of Western European-based nuclear weapons capable of striking targets within the Soviet Union and Soviet weapons aimed at Western Europe, and whose relative capacities came to be known as the "Eurostrategic balance." The Western debate about this issue echoed the controversy about flexible response during the Kennedy years. Although the forces in question differed, the basic issue was the same—the requirements of deterrence. The United States had the same fear that the perceived imbalance in nonnuclear forces had stirred during the previous decade—namely, that the Soviet Union would win an engagement at that level, compelling NATO either to accept defeat or to escalate the conflict to the level of intercontinental nuclear war, which would expose North America to nuclear bombardment. The preferred American response was to deploy long-range theater forces comparable to those of the Soviet Union, and in December 1979, NATO voted to do so.

As with flexible response in the 1960s, however, this called up European fears of decoupling, of the separation this time not of nuclear from nonnuclear weapons but of theater-range from strategic armaments. Like the first, the second suggested the separation of the United States from Europe as a theater of war, and this, the Europeans feared, could weaken deterrence by calling into question the willingness of the United States to put all of its military might into the defense of Europe. The French Foreign Minister put it plainly: "The approach based on the concept of a Eurostrategic balance implies that there can be a separate balance of nuclear capabilities assigned to the European theater, isolated from other elements of deterrence. It leads to a 'decoupling' which is precisely what we are trying to avoid. In other words, it would be tantamount to recognizing that the United States' central strategic forces do not cover Western Europe."

The years that followed the demise of the MLF in 1964 were far from harmonious ones for NATO. Apart from the question of how to respond to the Soviet nuclear threat to the United States, disputes over a wide range of issues cropped up. Economics took its place beside security as a source of conflict. The Atlantic partners quarreled about trade, monetary, and balance of payments policies. At one juncture the United States hinted that the continuation of the American nuclear guarantee of Europe would depend upon economic concessions from the Europeans. Political disputes strained relations as well. The American war in Vietnam aroused little enthusiasm in Europe. The 1973 Middle East War imposed an even more serious strain. The alliance partners found themselves, in effect, on opposite sides. The Europeans, fearing for their oil supplies from the Arab states of the Persian Gulf, issued statements sympathetic to the Arabs and largely refused to help the United States resupply Israel while the fighting was in progress.

In 1980 the alliance found itself once again divided, this time over how to respond to the seizure of American diplomatic personnel held as hostages in Iran and to the Soviet invasion of Afghanistan. The United States favored a strong response to both. The Europeans worried about alienating the governments in Tehran and Moscow. The difference stemmed in part from a divergence of interests, from which all alliances suffer. The Europeans' economic stake in Iran, and the political benefits they drew from the relaxation of tensions with the Soviet Union, were both greater than the Americans', so they had more to lose from poor relations with each. The most serious falling-out within the alliance in the years following the demise of the controversies over the MLF and flexible response occurred not between the United States and the Europeans but between two European members, Greece and Turkey, over the governance of the island of Cyprus. A Cypriot political crisis in 1974 prompted Turkish occupation of the island and triggered Greek withdrawal from active participation in NATO affairs.

Still, despite the fact that old problems were not conclusively resolved and new ones arose, NATO remained intact through the 1970s, in more or less its original form, something that had seemed extremely unlikely at the beginning of the 1960s. Then the status quo in the alliance, resting as it did upon the American nuclear guarantee, appeared untenable. Change seemed inevitable. Because Soviet aggression seemed the certain alternative to them, flexible response and national nuclear arsenals seemed essential, to the Americans in the first instance, to the French in the second. They proved to be unnecessary. Why was this so?

It is arguable that, appearances to the contrary notwithstanding, the proposed solutions for the problem that the Soviet capacity to attack the

United States posed for NATO *were* put into practice, perhaps not as fully as the proponents had hoped, but fully enough to keep the Soviet Union at bay. The European agreement in principle to the policy of flexible response was, arguably, more than a semantic maneuver. The nonnuclear forces of NATO and the Warsaw Pact were seen to be more evenly balanced in 1967 than they had been in 1961. This was not because the Americans and the Western Europeans had fielded more troops, however, but because estimates of the number of troops opposing them had become increasingly precise, and the more precise they became the smaller they were. It appeared in retrospect that throughout the 1950s the West had consistently overestimated them. The Europeans' 1967 conclusion that, in effect, NATO had been practicing flexible response all along was not wholly self-serving. It was, at least to some degree, accurate.

As for the preferred European solution to the problem, national nuclear forces, the French could claim to have put it into practice. They did proceed to equip themselves with a nuclear striking force. By 1979 it consisted of four submarines with sixteen missiles each and eighteen intermediate-range missiles. By American and Soviet standards this force was small. The French, however, could argue that, by their standard of deterrence, it was adequate. The French force, despite the protection that submarines provided, might not be absolutely certain of inflicting the level of damage on the Soviet Union in case of a Soviet attack that the Americans had defined as necessary for deterrence. It was very likely, however, to do considerable damage if used. If not kill him outright, the French could plausibly threaten to "tear an arm off the bear" in retaliation for a Soviet attack.

The Germans got no nuclear weapons, and not even the partial control over part of the American arsenal that the MLF envisioned, which remained under the command of the American President. They may not, however, have wanted to have a German finger resting on a nuclear trigger. They may simply have wished to be certain that they would not be relegated to the role of spectators in the alliance, with no say at all in its policies. "Control" in the English sense of the term, one student of NATO politics noted, implies physical possession; *contrôle* in the French usage connotes planning and political direction. The Germans may have wanted the second, not the first. The alliance's Nuclear Planning Group, which came into being on the initiative of the United States after the abandonment of the idea of nuclear sharing, provided it.

None of these explanations for the persistence of NATO in its original form is entirely satisfactory, however, given the widely shared alarm of the early 1960s. If NATO forces seemed a better match for those of the Soviet Union and Eastern Europe after the middle of the decade, the American government never felt able to declare them an even match, or better. Nor was there any reason for the Germans to feel confident that the French nuclear arsenal, however powerful it was, protected them. If the United States would not risk New York to save Paris, after all, why would the

French risk Paris to save Hamburg? The logic of the French view of deterrence led to a German national nuclear arsenal.

There is another possible explanation for NATO's durability. Political relations between East and West improved. The leaders of the American and Soviet governments met periodically. The two countries reached modest agreements limiting nuclear weapons: the Limited Test Ban Treaty of 1963, the Nonproliferation Treaty of 1968, and the Strategic Arms Limitation treaties of 1972 and 1979. A host of scientific and cultural exchanges began. In Europe the status of Germany was put on a firmer footing by a series of accords signed in 1969 and by the Conference on Security and Cooperation in Europe, which convened in Helsinki in 1975 and produced what amounted to a belated European peace treaty, thirty years after the end of World War II.

A state's security is the result of both its own capabilities and others' intentions, of its military power and its diplomatic achievements. NATO, it might be argued, concentrated on the second rather than the first. This explanation is not entirely satisfactory either, however. It reverses the proper order of things. Detente, the improvement of political relations between NATO and the Warsaw Pact, was less a cause than a consequence of military stability. Because they felt secure, the Germans, the Europeans, and the Americans could seek limited reconciliation with the Communist countries.

Peace may have reigned in Europe because the Soviet Union never intended to disturb it. Soviet intentions during the Cold War cannot be known in the absence of firsthand evidence. It is certainly true that in the immediate postwar years the Soviet government had its hands full with reconstructing its own country and tightening its grip on Eastern Europe. It is also true that, once conquered, Western Europe would have been difficult for the Soviet bloc to digest. Still, without some military disincentive it is hard to imagine that the Soviets would not have found *some* way to exert influence, if not control, over the European members of NATO. This, after all, is a familiar feature of international politics. It is the way that great powers have ordinarily behaved. It is almost a law of international relations that large countries abhor a vacuum of power. This is not to say that the Soviet Union has ever been seriously inclined to invade, or even to hold in political thrall—to "Finlandize"—Western Europe. It is to say that in the absence of some form of deterrence, such an inclination very likely would have appeared.

A telling reason why the structure of the Atlantic alliance remained intact, despite the conviction that this could not happen, is that alternatives to it loomed as grossly unattractive. The Europeans refused to support, if not the principle of flexible response, at least the policy of making substantial additions to the alliance's nonnuclear forces; the Americans opposed national nuclear forces. Sharper departures from the founding alliance arrangements were even less feasible. The Europeans had no inclination to switch from the American to the Soviet bloc, and they could not have expected to float between the two and remain free from Soviet influence without substantial military forces of their own. These they could have had. A multinational European military force could have drawn on a larger pool of capital and technology than that of either the United States or the Soviet Union. Such a force, however, especially insofar as it was nuclear, would have presented the same problem that the MLF raised, the problem of deciding whose finger was to rest on the trigger. Eliminating the United States made this problem no easier to solve. A Europe-wide force would have had to be underpinned, and thus preceded, by some measure of political unity. Since 1945 European unity has been a perpetual dream and a recurring hope, but not a reality. The Europeans clung to the United States, "in good logic and bad, in bad times and good," therefore, partly because they had no attractive alternative.

There is an analogy here to the international monetary system. The dollar was as central, and as crucial, to the system that the Bretton Woods conference of 1944 produced as the United States nuclear arsenal was to NATO at its inception. The growth of other national economies and American economic distress eroded the power of the dollar relative to other currencies, giving rise to a felt need for a substitute bulwark of the system. All possible substitutes, however—gold, Special Drawing Rights issued by the International Monetary Fund, and a joint European currency—proved to have drawbacks that rendered them unacceptable. So the dollar, in weakened form, has remained at the center of the system, as the principal form of international reserve and the most popular medium of international exchange.

The absence of an attractive alternative, however, once again is not a wholly satisfactory explanation for NATO's persistence. World War II did not extinguish the will to national independence in Western Europe. Had their safety and political integrity depended on it, the Europeans would have paid the price of a single Europe-wide or several separate national nuclear arsenals, or of building up the alliance's nonnuclear strength. They did not have to pay it. Why did the status quo in Europe *not* change? There is plainly no single answer, but one important reason is that NATO's initial arrangements for the deterrence of the Soviet Union continued to work throughout the 1960s and 1970s.

The Berlin and Cuban crises of 1961 and 1962, respectively, seem in retrospect to bear out NATO's sturdiness. When they occurred they heightened Western Europe's sense of vulnerability. American nuclear power did not prevent a Soviet challenge at the heart of Europe, or ninety miles from the coast of the United States. In both cases, however, the Soviet challenge was turned back. West Berlin remained a free city in the midst of the Soviet sphere of influence; intermediate-range missiles capable of carrying nuclear warheads to targets within the United States were removed from Cuba. In both cases the United States issued an explicit nuclear threat. In both cases the crises were resolved in favor of the status quo, which the United States was trying to preserve. No further crises of comparable magnitude followed.

Even de Gaulle's foreign policy provides support for the proposition that NATO's capacity for deterrence remained robust. In truth, considerations of nuclear deterrence were secondary matters in his foreign policy; what was primary was to assert French independence and to magnify French influence in the world. De Gaulle could afford to regard nuclear politics as secondary because he could be confident that the alliance's nuclear arrangements *would* deter the Soviet Union, despite his professed skepticism as justification for France's nuclear weapons program. He could formally withdraw from the alliance because he knew that he would still enjoy its protection.

Insofar as NATO did keep at bay a Soviet Union able to mount nuclear strikes against the continental United States, both the Europeans and the Americans were proven partly right and partly wrong about the requirements of deterrence. The United States was right that nuclear weapons under exclusively American control sufficed but wrong in insisting that a more diversified defense force was necessary. The Europeans were right that nuclear weapons alone would deter the Soviets but wrong in believing that these had to be in European, as well as American, custody.

This was so, arguably, because the extraordinary power of nuclear weapons stifled any temptation to attack, which uncertainty about an American response might have encouraged. The Europeans could not be certain that the Americans would risk New York to protect Paris, but the Soviets could not be sure that they would *not* do so. The nuclear revolution made uncertainty an argument for restraint. As Raymond Aron put it, "when no one was able to gauge the precise ratio of strength ahead of time, an adventure seemed tempting by virtue of its very unpredictability; now that this unpredictability involves fatalities on the order of tens of millions, even the most adventuresome of leaders might conceivably be inclined to caution." The result has been that, as one student of postwar European politics put it, "successive doctrines may have lacked the rational precision that experts thought necessary, and force levels and capabilities have usually fallen short of those required by doctrine, but the Russians have shown themselves to be most prudent in probing the alliance's self-advertised military deficiencies." Soviet behavior in this sense represented the triumph of common sense over logic. Former British Defense Minister Denis Healey once suggested that one chance in a hundred of a nuclear response to aggression will deter an enemy, although it may not reassure a friend. The observation explains a great deal of the history of the Atlantic alliance.

This leads to a final effect of nuclear weapons on alliances. Because American nuclear weapons did deter the Soviet Union, they made it possible for NATO's original framework to remain in place, and this suppressed normal national impulses for independence. Transatlantic relations would not, in all likelihood, have differed drastically from the shape they took had there been no nuclear weapons. The United States and the Soviet Union would still have been far stronger than any single European state. The Soviets would not have permitted an independent united Germany, and perhaps would not have been willing to countenance a united Germany of any political stripe. The United States, for its part, would not have wanted a Soviet-dominated Germany. The Cold War alignment appears, in retrospect, all but inevitable. With such an alignment Western Europe would certainly have sought a security connection with the United States, with or without a nuclear arsenal. The Europeans would have had to rely upon the United States for protection, especially in the early postwar period. But they would likely not have remained as dependent as has been the case.

The international monetary system again offers a suggestive analogy. At the end of World War II, the European economies were in ruins, and not only was the dollar supreme but American economic policy determined that of Western Europe. As the Europeans recovered, and grew prosperous, they gained a measure of economic independence. None is the equal of the United States in economic terms. There is no substitute for the dollar. The United States remains by far the most powerful single nation in the politics of international economics. But the Europeans and the Japanese do have some independent influence. The balance of influence and initiative between Europe and America in economic matters has shifted markedly in thirty years; where security is concerned, nuclear weapons have perpetuated a balance that was as lopsided in 1980 as it was in 1949.

That it remains lopsided amounts to a curious reversal. The distribution of nuclear force within NATO was at its founding a consequence, and is now a cause of European weakness. At first the Europeans could not, and now they will not, and because of the sturdiness of nuclear deterrence they need not, assemble a nuclear arsenal themselves. In 1949 the United States issued a nuclear guarantee because the Europeans were weak. Now the Europeans are weak because they have, after all, the American nuclear guarantee.

Bibliography

C. D. BLACK and G. DUFFY, eds., *International Arms Control Issues and Agreements* (1985).
E. BOTTOME, *The Balance of Terror: Nuclear Weapons and the Illusion of Security, 1945–1985* (1986).
G. BREWER and M. SHUBIK, *The War Game: A Critique of Military Problem Solving* (1979).
L. T. CALDWELL and W. DIEBOLD, JR., *Soviet American Relations in the 1980's: Superpower Politics and East-West Trade* (1980).
A. W. DEPORTE, *Europe between the Superpowers: The Enduring Balance* (1979).

D. HOLLOWAY, *The Soviet Union and the Arms Race* (1985).
W. W. KULSKI, *DeGaulle and the World: The Foreign Policy of the Fifth French Republic* (1968).
M. MANDELBAUM, *The Nuclear Future* (1983).
L. MARTIN, ed., *Strategic Thought in the Nuclear Age* (1979).
S. E. MILLER, *Strategy and Nuclear Deterrence* (1984).